I0024612

D. V. ALFORD

B.Sc., Ph.D.

BUMBLEBEES

All rights reserved. No part of this publication may be reproduced, stored in a retrieval system, transmitted in any form or by any means electronic, mechanical, including photocopying, recording or otherwise without prior consent of the copyright holders.

ISBN 978-1-904846-80-2

This facsimile of the 1975 edition.
Published by Northern Bee Books (2011)
Scout Bottom Farm,
Mytholmroyd,
Hebden Bridge HX7 5JS (UK)

Bumblebees © D V Alford

Due to the quality of the original colour and black and white plates, this 2011 facsimile has been produced without them. Readers are advised to consult other recent texts for identification purposes.

Current publications include:

Field Guide to the Bumblebees of Great Britain & Ireland -
Mike Edwards & Martin Jenner (2009) ISBN 978-095497-13-11

The Humble-Bee -
F.W.L.Sladen (fine 1989 facsimile of 1912 edition) ISBN 0-951024-23-X

Identification chart taken from Bumblebees -
O.E.Prŷs-Jones & S.A.Corbet (1991)

all of which can be obtained from Northern Bee Books, Scout Bottom Farm, Mytholmroyd, Hebden Bridge HX7 5JS (UK) or on line at www.groovycart.co.uk/beebooks

Design and Artwork, D&P Design and Print
Printed by Lightning Source (UK)

To INGE, INGARET
KERSTIN *and*
MICHAEL

CONTENTS

DISTRIBUTION MAPS

DISTRIBUTION LISTS

Preface

A FOUNDATION stone for any biological study of bumblebees is undoubtedly F. W. L. Sladen's monograph *The Humble-bee*, published in 1912, and throughout the pages of the present book frequent reference is made to this monumental work. Since Sladen's time there have been considerable advances in our knowledge of bumblebee behaviour, biology and taxonomy, and important contributions to these subjects have been made by many workers in several parts of the world. The purpose of the present work, although concentrating on the British fauna, is to give an up-to-date picture of our knowledge of the natural history of bumblebees, which it is hoped will be of interest to both serious students of bees and to naturalists in general.

In the introductory chapter I have attempted to cover briefly the various features of bumblebee anatomy and physiology to which reference is later made in the biological and taxonomic sections, but it has not been my purpose to consider either of these topics in any detail.

Part I, the main section of the book, deals with the biology of bumblebees, and although an emphasis on the British fauna is deliberately maintained, information on foreign species is also included in order to provide a more comprehensive and complete picture of the subject. A general classification of all animal species mentioned is given in Appendix III. Plant common and Latin names are given together throughout the text, but without regard to systematic order or reference to authorities. However, details and a classification of all species mentioned are given in Appendix II. In most cases the plant names employed here are taken from *The Pocket Guide to Wild Flowers* by McClintock & Fitter (1956) as this work is widely used as a field guide by British naturalists.

In Part II the British species of bumblebee are considered at length, the term 'British' being applied in a geographical sense to embrace the fauna of Great Britain and the whole of Ireland; for completeness information from the Channel Islands is also included. In compiling the descriptions of the individual species (Chapter 9) I have been guided very largely by Sladen's original treatment of the subject, and much of the information contained in Chapter 10 has already appeared in my series of papers recently published in the *Entomologist's Gazette*.

Throughout the preparation of this book I have been encouraged by the considerable interest that the subject of bumblebees has aroused among fellow entomologists, general naturalists and students, and it is hoped that the techniques outlined in the final section (Part III) will be of use to those who wish to pursue their interest in a more practical sense.

1

PREFACE

My wife's help and encouragement during many hours of laboratory and field work has made it possible for me to obtain photographs of live examples of all the species of bumblebee presently known to survive in Britain, and to collect representatives of most, if not all, of the more important parasites and nest commensals. Most of the drawings and photographs have been made from material or specimens in my own collection, but I have also had the opportunity to borrow and refer to bumblebees in the collections of the British Museum (Natural History), London, and the Insect Room of the Museum of Zoology, Department of Zoology, University of Cambridge. This help is gratefully acknowledged. Similarly, the facilities of the Balfour Library, Department of Zoology, University of Cambridge, and the library and abstracting services of the Bee Research Association have proved invaluable. It is a pleasure to acknowledge the considerable help received from co-workers both at home and abroad, several of whom have made details of their unpublished work available to me. I am also grateful to Mr. K. G. V. Smith for examining several specimens of Diptera, and Mr. D. Macfarlane for his continued patience in dealing with my numerous enquiries regarding mites. Dr. I. H. H. Yarrow has been a most willing and invaluable source of information on various aspects of the British bumblebee fauna; I am particularly grateful for the benefit of his advice and experience. My thanks are also due to the Biological Records Centre for their help in preparing the Distribution Maps 2 to 27 and to the many participants in the Bumblebee Distribution Maps Scheme who have contributed towards our knowledge of the distribution of the British species. Finally, I wish to thank my wife for translating many German papers and for helping to check the manuscript and proofs.

D. V. ALFORD
Cambridge

CHAPTER 1

Introduction

BUMBLEBEES are familiar insects, and because of their large size, handsome appearance and inquisitive behaviour, they often attract the attention of man. Although most abundant in temperate parts of Europe, North America and Asia, bumblebees also occur within the Arctic Circle, along the northern fringe of Africa, and in South America. They are, however, virtually absent from the tropics, although a few species are found in Brazil. There are no indigenous bumblebees in Australasia, but a few species from Britain were introduced successfully into New Zealand in 1885.

Some insects, including termites, certain wasps, ants, honey bees and bumblebees, are social in behaviour and live in colonies, but the great majority lead a solitary existence and any co-operation between individuals is limited to brief and temporary associations for the purpose of reproduction. In Britain there are well over 200 different species of bee, but no more than ten per cent of these can be regarded as social. Some species of 'solitary' bee, notably *Halictus malacharus*, exhibit a certain degree of sociality, but it is only in the case of bumblebees (*Bombus*) and honey bees (*Apis mellifera*) that an elaborate social system is developed. A social insect is concisely defined by Imms (1947) as 'one in which parent and offspring live in mutual co-operation in a common shelter or nest'.

In the inquiline, so-called 'parasitic', bumblebees of the genus *Psithyrus* (Chapter 7), females are of one type. However, in truly social bumblebees (genus *Bombus*), as in honey bees, the female sex is differentiated into castes. The perfect female is known as the queen, while the typically smaller, usually non-reproductive, females are the workers. Some authorities treat male bumblebees (and male or drone honey bees) as representing a third caste. However, there seems little justification in this since essentially the sexes of social bees differ in just the same way as do those of non-social species which do not have a caste system. Furthermore, 'caste differentiation' or 'caste determination' in social bees usually means features involved in distinguishing between, or factors involved in producing, queens and workers. If males are also regarded as representing a caste then by definition these terms should also include phenomena more conveniently covered by 'sex differentiation' and 'sex determination'. In bees, caste and sex are better considered as separate subjects, and in the present work, therefore, the term 'caste' is applied only to the female.

Although structurally much modified and specialized, a bumblebee is unmistakably an insect, there being a distinct head, thorax and abdomen, a pair of sensory feelers or antennae, three pairs of jointed walking legs, and two pairs of wings (Fig. 1). The integument or body wall is extremely important, acting not only as the

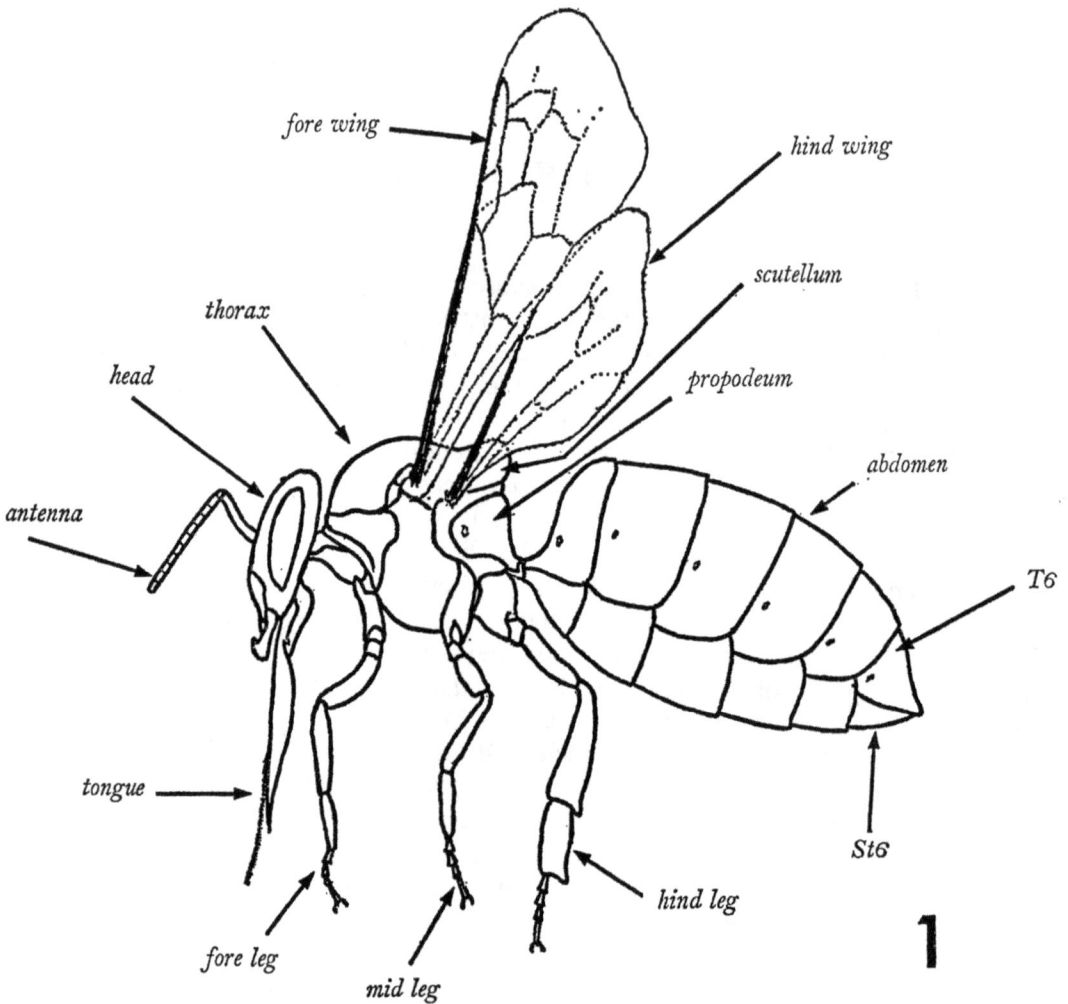

Fig. 1. Generalized structure of bumblebee female.

outer protective 'skin' but also as the skeleton and support for the internal body musculature. It is composed of a single layer of epidermal cells, and these secrete the outer covering called the cuticle. This may become hardened and darkened, following the addition of a chemical called sclerotin or cuticulin, to form the exoskeleton. Ingrowths of this hardened cuticular layer make up variously shaped ridges and projections (the apodemes) which function as attachments for muscles, while outgrowths may become body spines, spurs, and so on. Where little or no sclerotin is present the cuticle remains flexible and more or less colourless. The cuticular layer covers the eyes and body hairs, and also lines internal structures of ectodermal origin, including the fore gut, the hind gut, and the tracheae.

The tough exoskeleton of an adult bumblebee is variably sculptured and extensively pitted or punctured. It may appear shiny where punctation is slight or
sculpturing shallow, but dull where punctation is extensive or sculpturing deep.
These features are of considerable taxonomic importance and will be mentioned
later when discussing the identification of species. In the case of bumblebees, most
of the exoskeleton is more or less black, the often vivid colours associated with
these insects being due to pigmentation of the body hairs forming the so-called
coat or pile and not (unlike, for instance, wasps and certain colourful beetles) to
differences in the colour or properties of the body cuticle. These unicellular hairs
which, to a greater or lesser extent, cover most of the body, may. be more or less

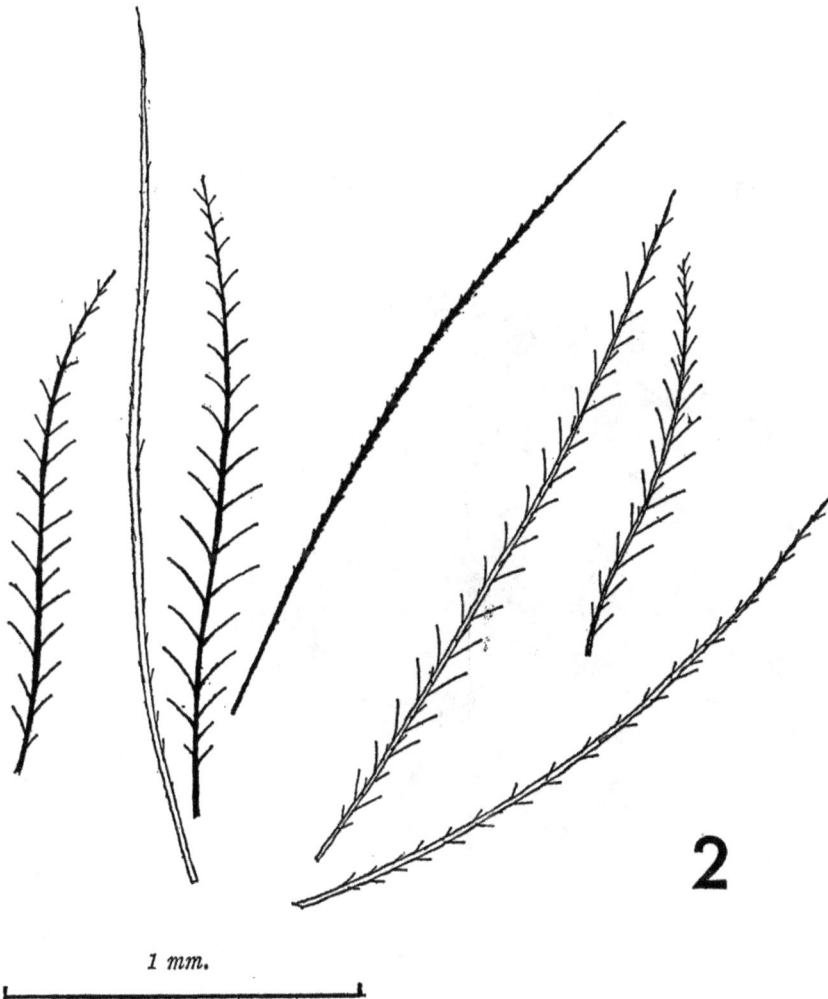

1 mm.

Fig. 2. Body hairs from thorax of *Bombus terrestris* female.

5

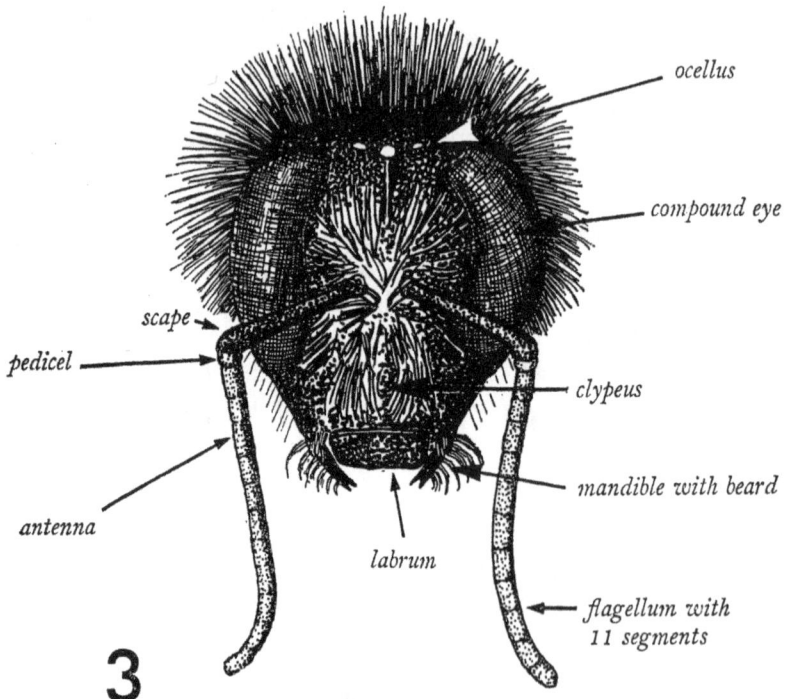

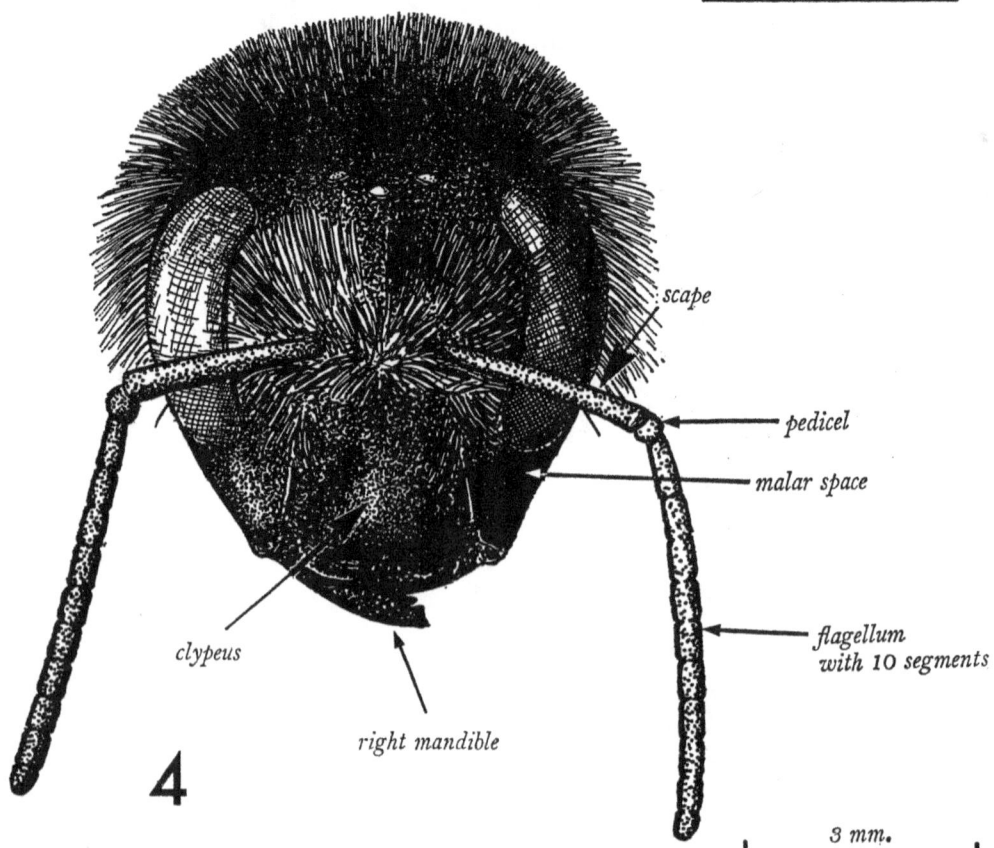

Figs. 3–4. Head of bumblebee. 3, *Bombus ruderarius* male; 4, *Bombus terrestris* female.

simple in form, but are often much branched (Fig. 2). Branched or feathery body hairs are found on both social and solitary bees, but not on social or solitary wasps. This distinction is, no doubt, associated with differences in feeding habits. Bees (unlike wasps)[1] are dependent upon flowering plants for food; they collect both nectar and pollen, the latter adhering readily to their furry coats (e.g. Free & Williams, 1972; Kendall & Solomon, 1973).

The head of a bumblebee contains the brain, various salivary glands, and the anterior part of the alimentary canal and bears a large pair of compound eyes, three simple eyes or ocelli, a pair of antennae, and the mouthparts. The compound eyes are concerned with perceiving or distinguishing colour, shape and movement; they are also able to register the plane of polarized light, thereby aiding navigation. The ocelli probably function as light intensity perceptors. The antennae bear important organs concerned with the senses of smell or touch. Each antenna is divided into a long basal scape, a short pedicel, and a long flagellum which is further subdivided into several so-called 'segments', ten in females and eleven in males. (Strictly speaking the subdivisions of the flagellum are not true segments as they lack muscles and are not articulated upon one another.) The basal flagellar segment (that adjoining the pedicel) is usually taken as the third segment of the antenna; the total number of antennal segments of a bumblebee is, then, twelve in females and thirteen in males (Figs. 3 and 4). The relative lengths of antennae, and of certain of the flagellar segments, are of importance in distinguishing between certain species, particularly in the case of males. Other characteristics of the head are also of taxonomic significance (see Chapters 9 and 10). These include details of the clypeus, which lies between the bases of the antennae and the labrum or upper lip, and features of the genae or 'cheeks', which occur on either side of the head, below the compound eyes and above the articulating point of each mandible. At least in bumblebees, the genal region is most frequently termed the malar space; its relative length, and indeed that of the whole 'face' of the bee, may vary considerably from species to species. Some bumblebees are traditionally known as 'short-faced species' and others 'long-faced species'. A species with a long face will also possess a long 'tongue'. Differences in the form of the mandibles are also important for distinguishing between certain species (Figs. 122 to 124).

The mouthparts of a bumblebee are adapted for biting, lapping and licking (Fig. 5). The long tongue or proboscis is usually folded and retracted below the head, but may be extended when feeding. The mandibles are also used in feeding, as well as for manipulating wax and nest material, for carrying and removing dead larvae from the colony, and for biting in attack or defence; some species of *Bombus* are renowned for biting holes in flowers to 'rob' them of nectar (Chapter 6). Associated with the mouthparts are various salivary glands – the labial glands (postcerebral and prothoracic glands), the hypopharyngeal glands, and the mandibular glands (Figs. 6 to 9). Saliva is used for diluting food, and for softening

---

[1] Wasps will collect nectar from flowers which have readily accessible nectaries, examples are figwort (*Scrophularia*) and ivy (*Hedera helix*), but unlike bees they do not forage for pollen.

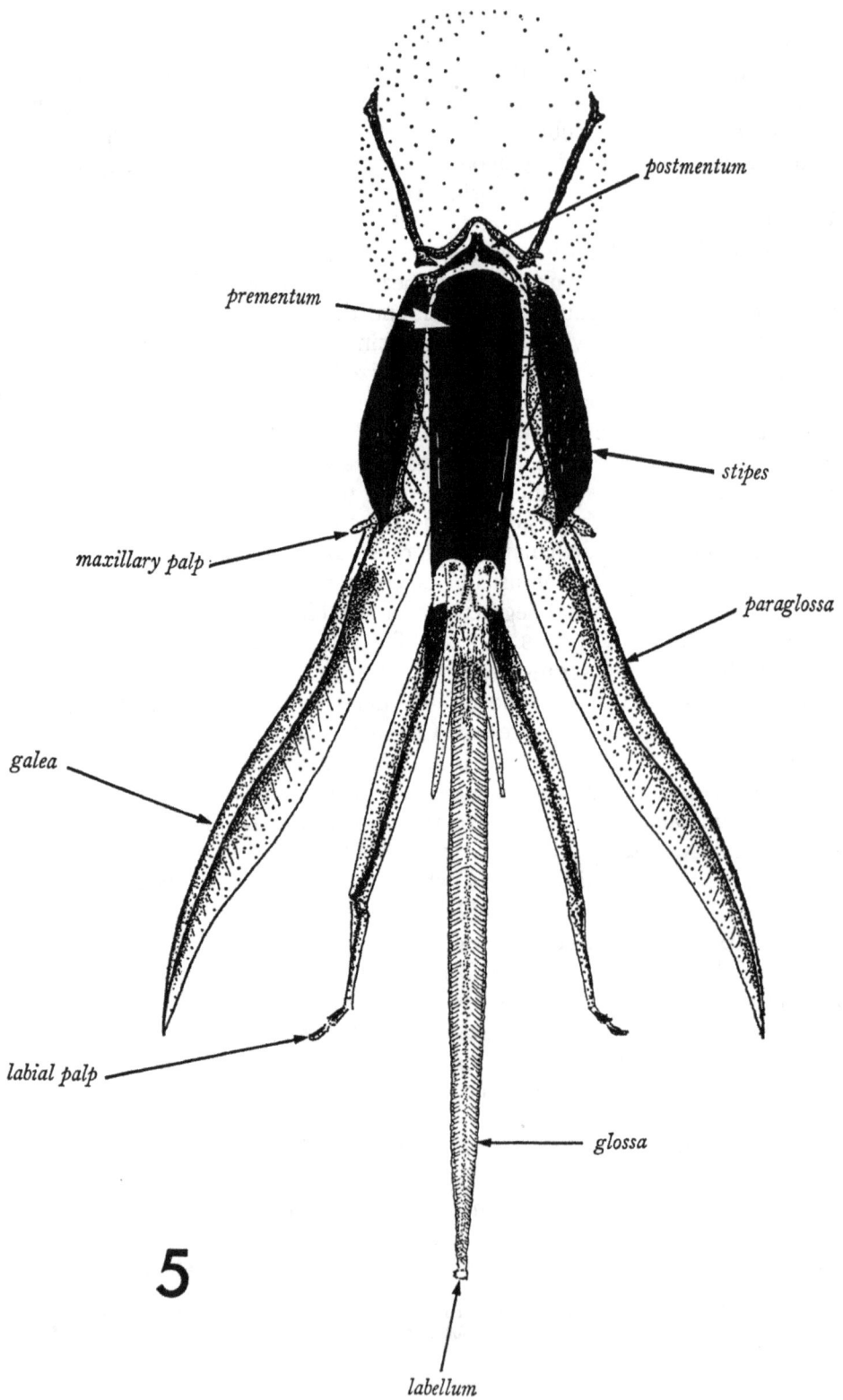

Fig. 5. Proboscis or tongue of bumblebee.

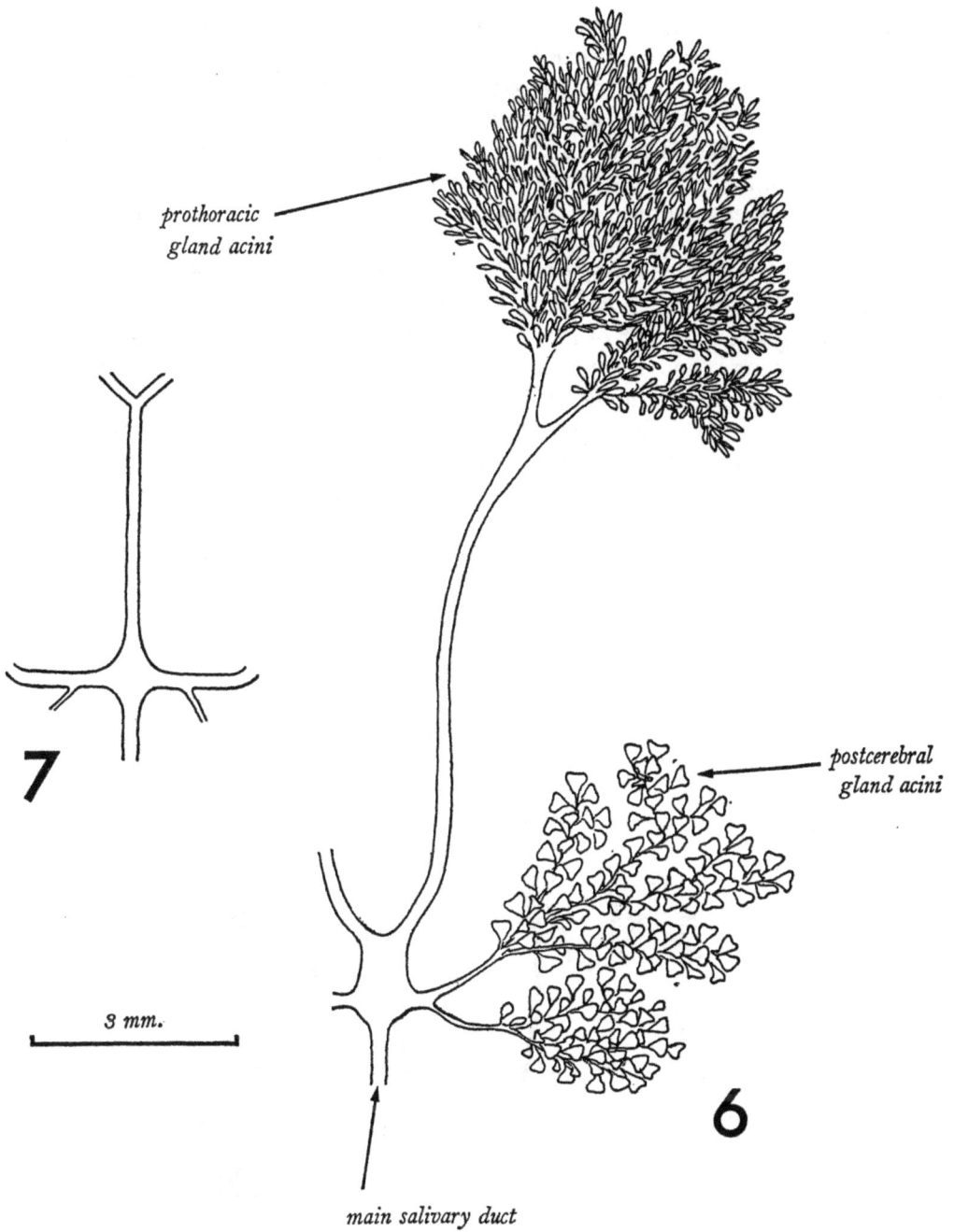

prothoracic gland acini

postcerebral gland acini

7

3 mm.

6

main salivary duct

Figs. 6–7. Labial glands. 6, *Bombus* female; 7, duct junctions of *Psithyrus* female.

cocoons or materials such as wax. The secretions may contain digestive enzymes, for example, amylase (for converting starch to sugar) and invertase (for converting sucrose to the simpler sugars fructose and glucose, both of which can be digested without hydrolysis). These two enzymes are present in saliva produced by the hypopharyngeal glands, but (in contrast with the hypopharyngeal glands of worker honey bees) these glands do not secrete a special brood food ('royal jelly'), although the secretion is, nevertheless, rich in protein (Palm, 1949). The mandibular glands of male bumblebees produce an important, volatile, marking secretion concerned with mating behaviour (Chapter 5).

The thorax is the locomotory centre of the insect, containing the flight (wing) muscles and also the leg muscles. It consists of three thoracic segments, the pro-thorax bearing the first pair of legs, the mesothorax from which arise the mid legs and the fore wings, and the metathorax which bears the hind legs and the hind wings. The bulk of the thorax is formed by the mesothoracic segment, and this terminates posteriorly on its upper surface in a pillow-like bulge called the scutellum. The hindmost part of the thorax, immediately in front of the narrow 'waist' or pedicel, is in reality formed by the first true segment of the abdomen and is termed the propodeum (Fig. 1).

Each leg is composed of a basal coxa, a trochanter, a femur, a tibia, a tarsus

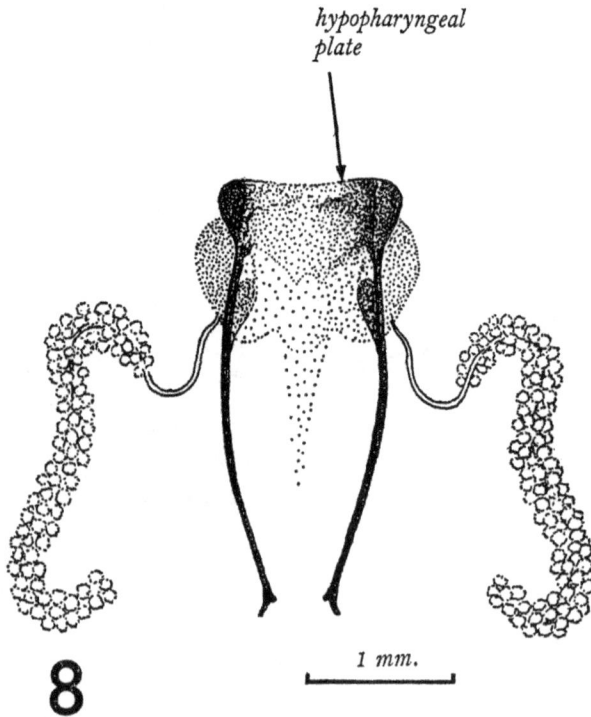

Fig. 8. Hypopharyngeal glands of *Bombus* female.

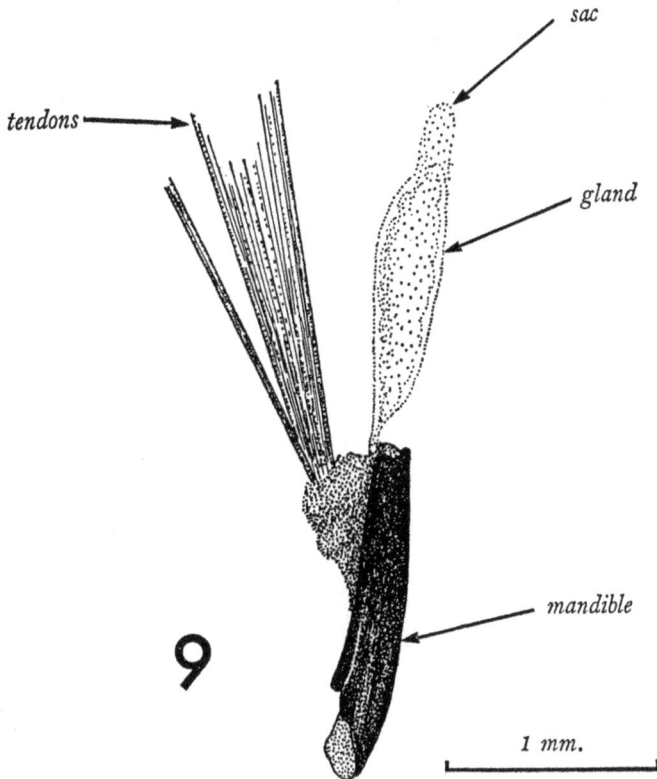

Fig. 9. Mandibular gland of *Bombus* female.

(which is divided into a large basal metatarsus or basitarsus and four smaller tarsal subsegments) and an apical pretarsus which bears a pair of lateral claws and a terminal adhesive pad, the arolium, which enables a bee to gain a foothold on a surface too slippery for the claws to grasp (Fig. 10).

The fore legs each possess an antenna cleaner (Fig. 11) through which the antennae may be drawn to remove any pollen grains or dirt particles that are adhering to them.

The hind legs of *Bombus* females are modified for collecting and carrying pollen. Each hind tibia is more or less flattened and hairless on its outer surface while the surrounding (corbicular) hairs are long and curved, forming the so-called pollen-basket or corbiculum (Fig. 12). The tibiotarsal region (Fig. 13) is modified into a pollen press capable of forcing pollen into the base of the corbiculum from a series of pollen-collecting brushes located on the inner surface of the hind basitarsus. A bee unloads pollen from the corbicula by passing the mid basitarsi over the outer surface of the hind legs in a downward, slicing movement.

The wings of a bumblebee are membranous, more or less transparent, and their supporting venation is relatively simple. In flight each fore wing is linked to the smaller hind wing by a series of hooks. These are located on the leading edge of

11

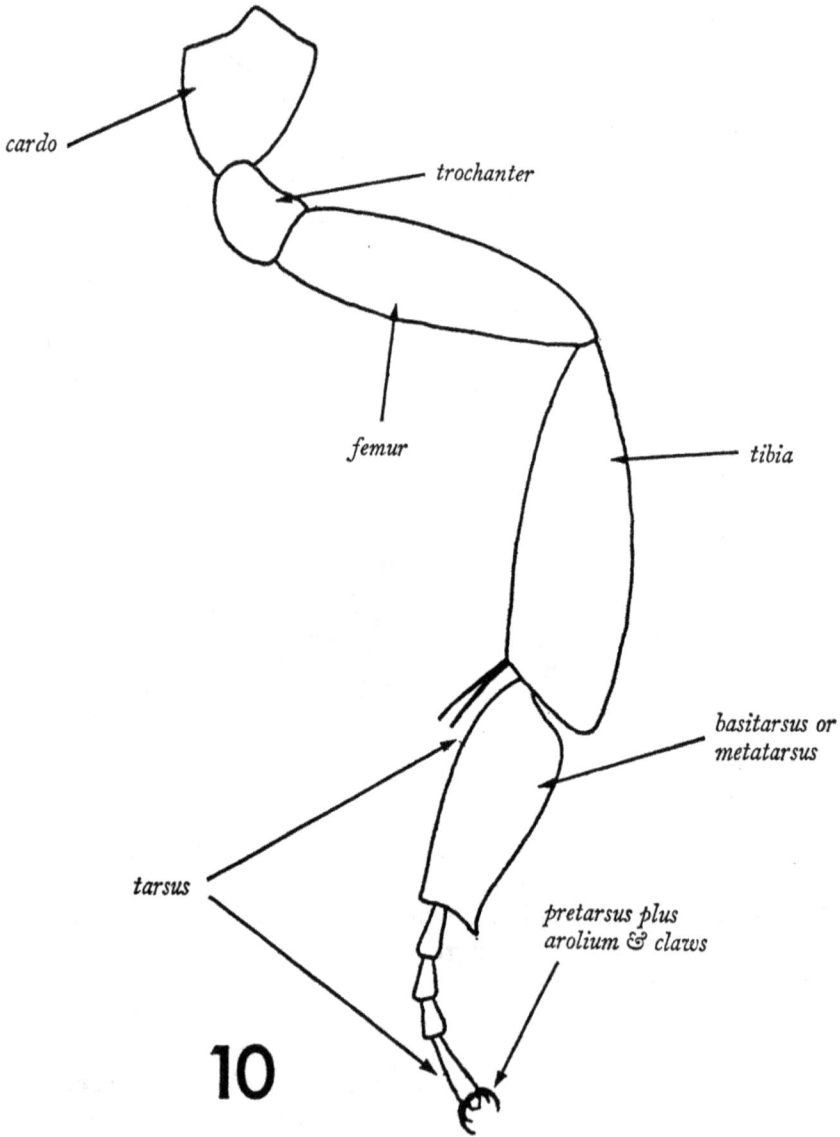

cardo

trochanter

femur

tibia

basitarsus or metatarsus

tarsus

pretarsus plus arolium & claws

10

Fig. 10. Generalized structure of leg of bumblebee.

the hind wing and engage in a fold running along the trailing edge of the fore wing. The number of hooks varies according to the body size of the bee (see Richards, 1949). At rest the fore and hind wings are separated from one another and usually lie flat over the back. At the base of the wings are chitinized plates, the tegulae, which overlie the wing articulating mechanism.

The abdomen is composed of several overlapping, and segmentally arranged, plates. Those on the upper (dorsal) surface of the body are known as tergites, and

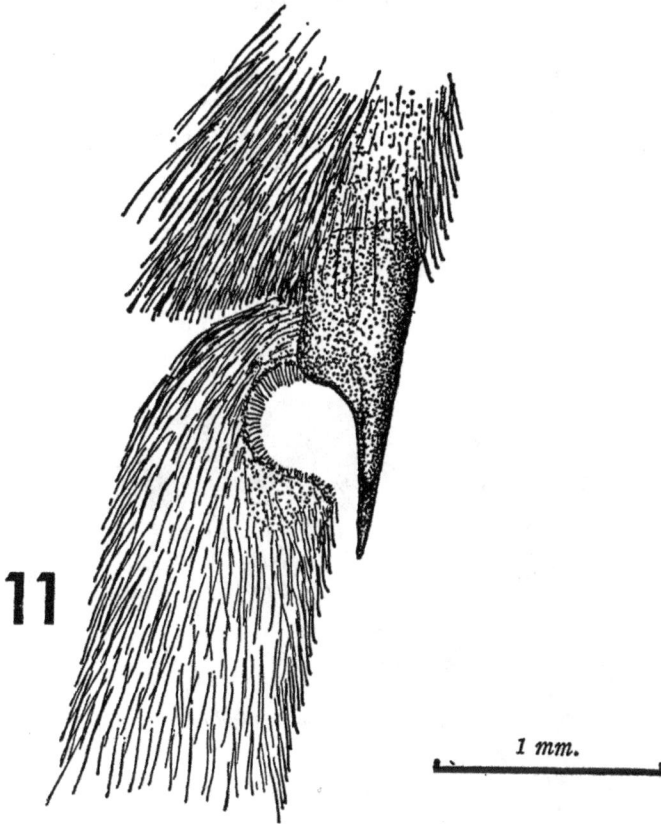

Fig. 11. Antenna cleaner on fore leg of *Bombus* female.

those on the lower (ventral) surface are the sternites. The plates are connected by the abdominal musculature and by intersegmental membranes which permit abdominal expansion, contraction and flexion. The abdomen of a female bumblebee is composed of six visible segments and three hidden, terminal segments, the latter modified in association with the sting (Fig. 14) and concealed within the sting chamber. In males the terminal abdominal segments are also concealed, but there are seven visible dorsal plates (tergites). For convenience in this work, and to reduce confusion, the visible abdominal tergites and sternites are designated T1 to 6 (T1 to 7 in males) and St1 to 6 respectively, the propodeal segment (which forms the posterior part of the thorax) being ignored.

In *Bombus* females, wax-producing cells (the wax glands) are present on T3 to 6 and St3 to 6. Wax is used for constructing brood cells, food storage vessels (for example, honey pots) and comb.[1] The wax is produced by epithelial cells lying immediately below the cuticle, and issues on to the exposed surface of the

[1] Bumblebee wax has a melting point of approximately 35°C. to 45°C., which is about 25°C. lower than that of honey bee wax (beeswax); bumblebee wax and beeswax are very different from each other in both composition and physical properties (see Tulloch, 1970).

13

abdomen, giving the body a somewhat greasy appearance. Wax-producing cells occur below most, if not all, of the exposed surface of T6, but on T5, and more especially on T4 and T3, these cells are completely absent mid-dorsally; the limits of their distribution vary according to the species (Röseler, 1967a). The wax is scraped off the body surface with the hind pair of legs, and injury to a leg may result in wax accumulating on that side of the body. Scent glands are also present in the anterior (apical) part of T6 (Landim, 1963), but their function in bumblebees is obscure.

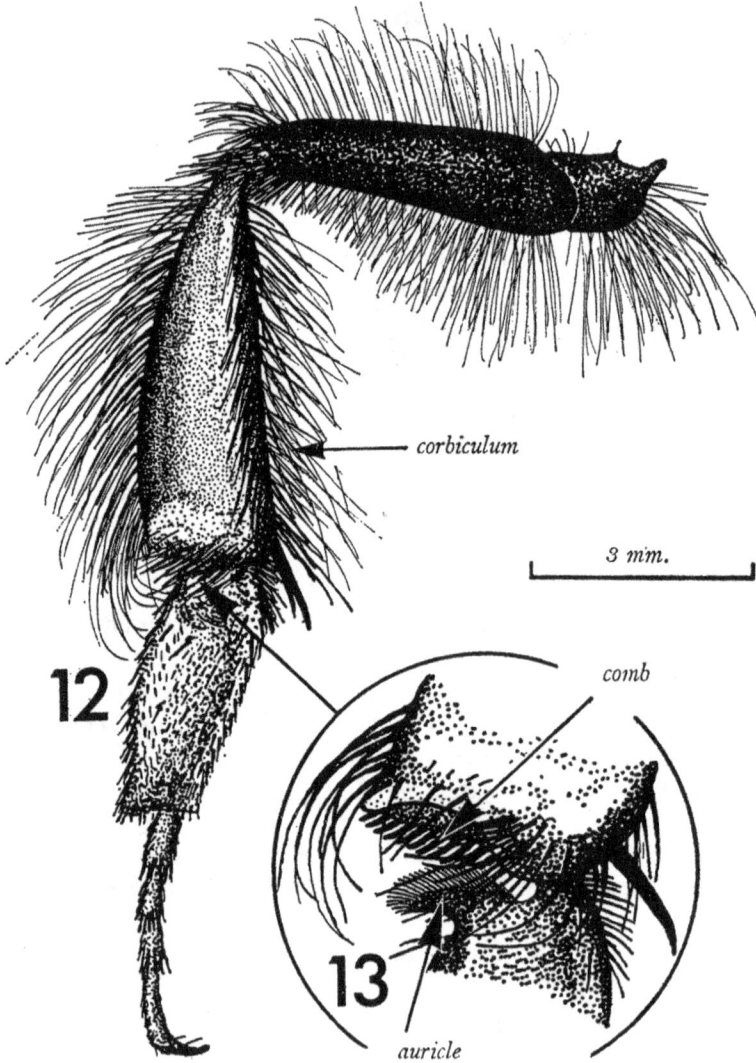

Figs. 12–13. *Bombus terrestris* female. 12, right hind leg; 13, pollen press at articulation of hind tibia and basitarsus.

The internal body cavity (the haemocoel) of an insect is filled with a clear, more or less colourless or yellowish fluid, the so-called blood or haemolymph, which flows throughout the whole body, including the appendages, and bathes all the body organs and tissues. The haemolymph of a bumblebee is circulated by way of a mid-dorsally located muscular, tube-like vessel (the heart, see Plate XXXV) which extends almost the whole length of the body. Haemolymph enters this vessel in the abdomen through small, lateral holes (ostia) and is then pumped forwards by rhythmic, muscular contractions of the vessel walls, eventually to be discharged in

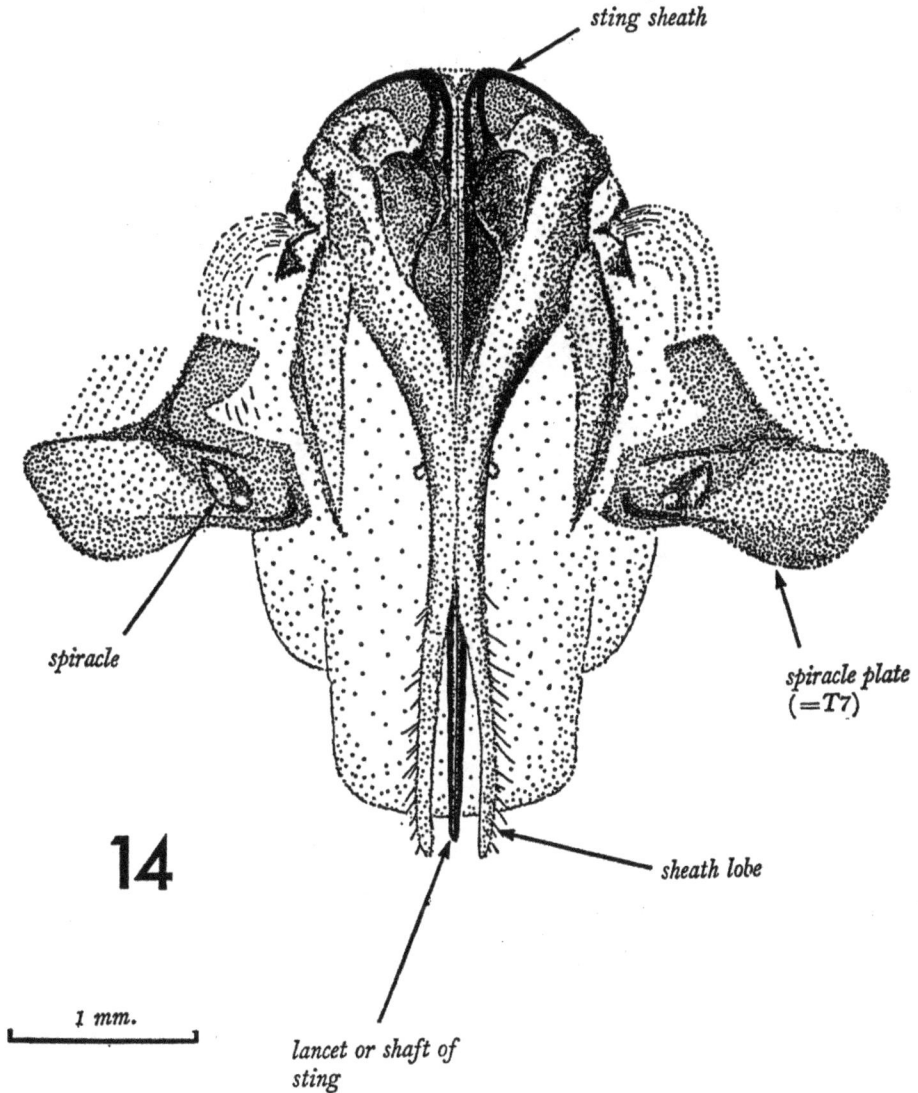

Fig. 14. Ventral aspect of sting of *Bombus* female.

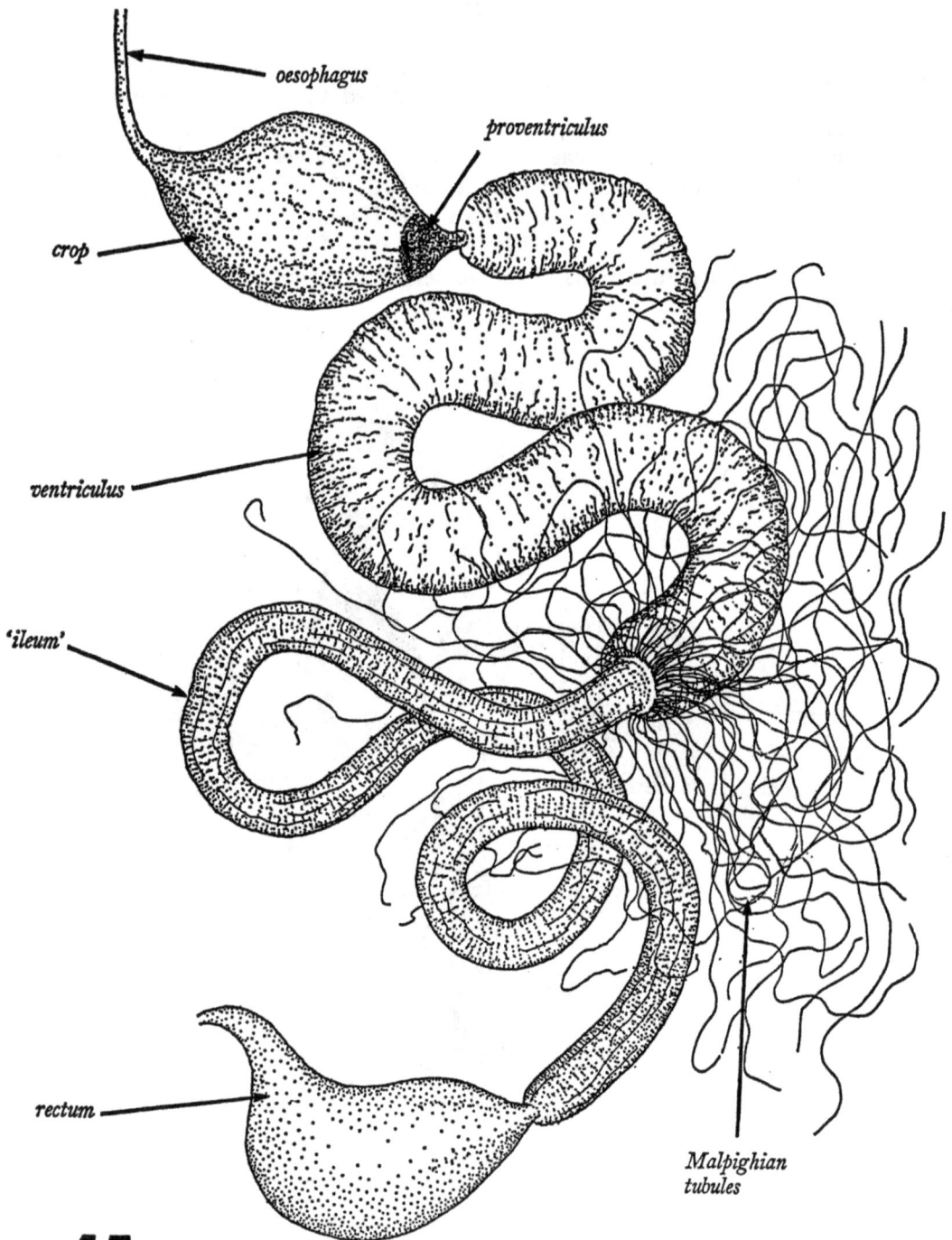

15

Fig. 15. Alimentary canal of *Bombus* female.

16

the head, just below the brain. It then filters backwards through the body cavity, between the various organs, the flow being assisted by pulsating organs or membranes, and particularly by a muscular ventral and a muscular dorsal diaphragm, the latter being attached to the heart. The main function of the haemolymph is to transport nutriment material, derived from the food, to various parts of the body.

The alimentary tract (Fig. 15) is a much modified, convoluted tube extending from the mouth to the anus. The mouth opens into the pharynx, and from this a narrow oesophagus passes through the neck, thorax and petiole into the abdomen where it opens into the crop or honey-sac. The crop terminates in a short, valve-like proventriculus which marks the end of the fore gut or stomodeum. This section serves for the intake, and also for the carriage, storage and regurgitation of food. The mid gut (mesenteron) is composed of a wide tube, the ventriculus, in which digestion and absorption take place. This leads into the hind gut (proctodeum) which is differentiated into a long, relatively thin, anterior 'ileum' and a posterior, sac-like, rectum. Here water and salts are absorbed; the rectum also serves to store waste matter before this can be discharged through the anus. Arising from the extreme anterior end of the hind gut, at its junction with the ventriculus, is a large number of fine, convoluted tubes, the Malpighian tubules. These are intertwined about themselves and are coiled around the various body organs; their function is to accumulate excretory products that are discharged eventually into the gut.

Much of the inner wall of the abdomen is lined with a layer of fat cells. This fat body tissue is relatively sparse in workers and males, particularly in small individuals, but in *Bombus* queens and *Psithyrus* females the fat body is usually well developed, forming sheets of tissue several cells thick. Although the fat body is mainly concentrated in the abdomen, fat cells also occur in the head and thorax. The fat body of an adult bumblebee consists of two types of cell, the actual fat cells or trophocytes, and the oenocytes (Fig. 16). The trophocytes are large or very large, spherical to oval cells and form the bulk of the tissue. The oenocytes are smaller, more or less rounded cells, scattered throughout the fat body, but apparently only in the abdomen. In very young adults remains of urate cells, persisting from the larval stage, may be visible as white concretions dispersed here and there among the trophocytes. The waste matter they have accumulated, however, is soon eliminated from the body via the Malpighian tubules, and the urate cells then disappear.

The colour of the fat body depends upon the amount of pigment contained in the oenocytes. Thus, the tissue appears hyaline or whitish when no pigment is present, and yellowish to golden or dark brown when, as in older bees, pigments have been accumulated. The accumulation of pigments by insect oenocytes is widespread and presumably indicates that the cells perform a regulatory or excretory function. Oenocytes are especially well developed (enlarged) in bumblebees with functioning ovaries and their size is also related to the development of a bee's wax glands (see Alford, 1969a). The most obvious function of the fat body is to store reserves of fat (glycogen reserves are also present), but the insect fat body is in addition a

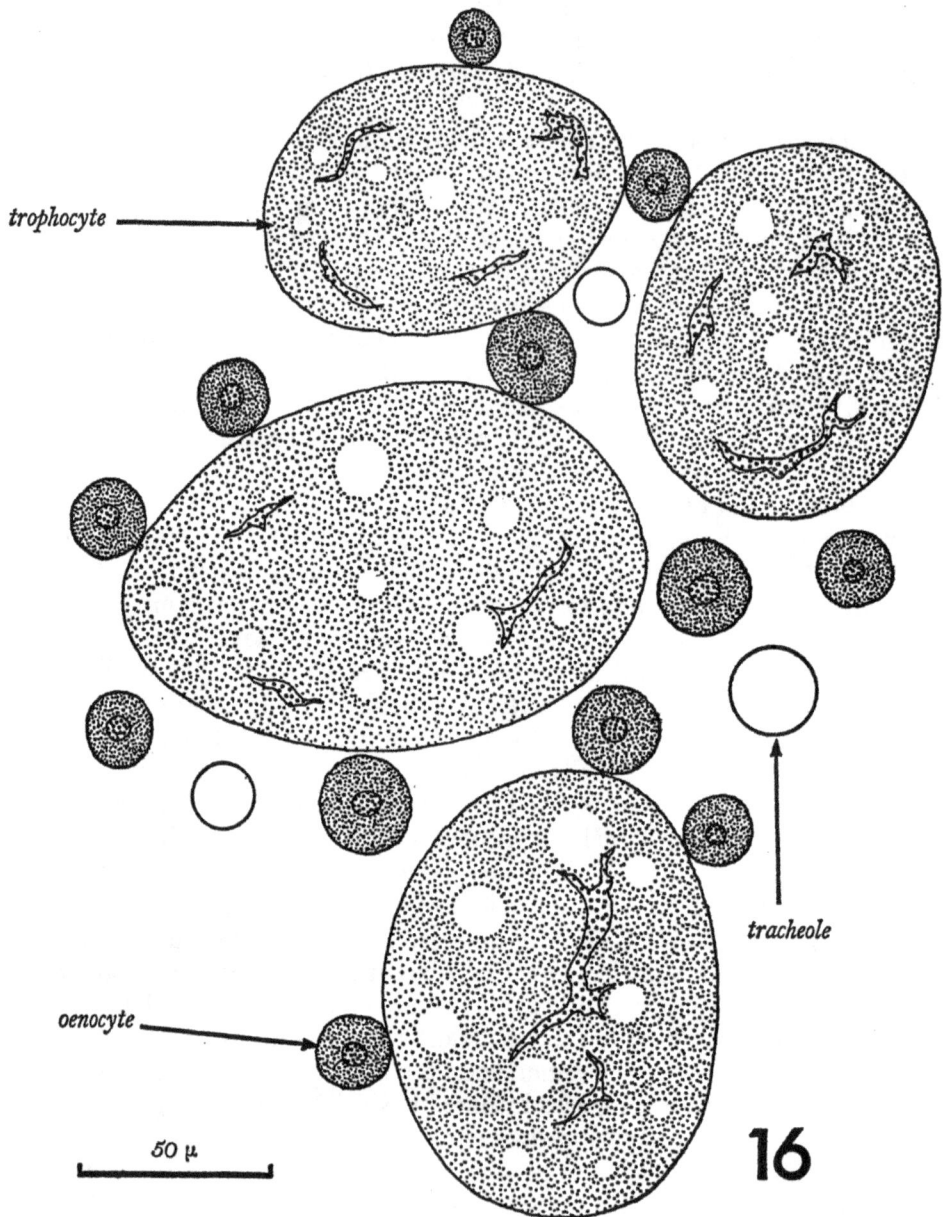

Fig. 16. Section of fat body of overwintered *Bombus* queen.

centre of intermediary metabolism, performing many functions in larvae, during metamorphosis, and in adults (Kilby, 1963; Wigglesworth, 1942, 1972).

The brain of a bumblebee is large, creamish-white in colour, and is composed of four pairs of cerebral lobes (Fig. 17). Below, and immediately behind the brain lies the suboesophageal ganglion; from this arises the central nerve cord which extends ventrally back through the thorax and abdomen. The nerve cord is swollen at intervals along its length to form two large thoracic, and five smaller abdominal, nerve ganglia or nerve centres, from which issue a series of lateral nerves. The brain acts as a perception centre for the senses, and is intimately linked with the antennae (via the deutocerebral lobes), the ocelli (via the protocerebral lobes) and the compound eyes (via the optic lobes). The brain is also the co-ordinating centre of the body. However, many nervous functions of the insect are carried out independently of the brain by the various nerve ganglia – for example, the mouthparts are controlled by the suboesophageal ganglion, locomotion by the thoracic ganglia.

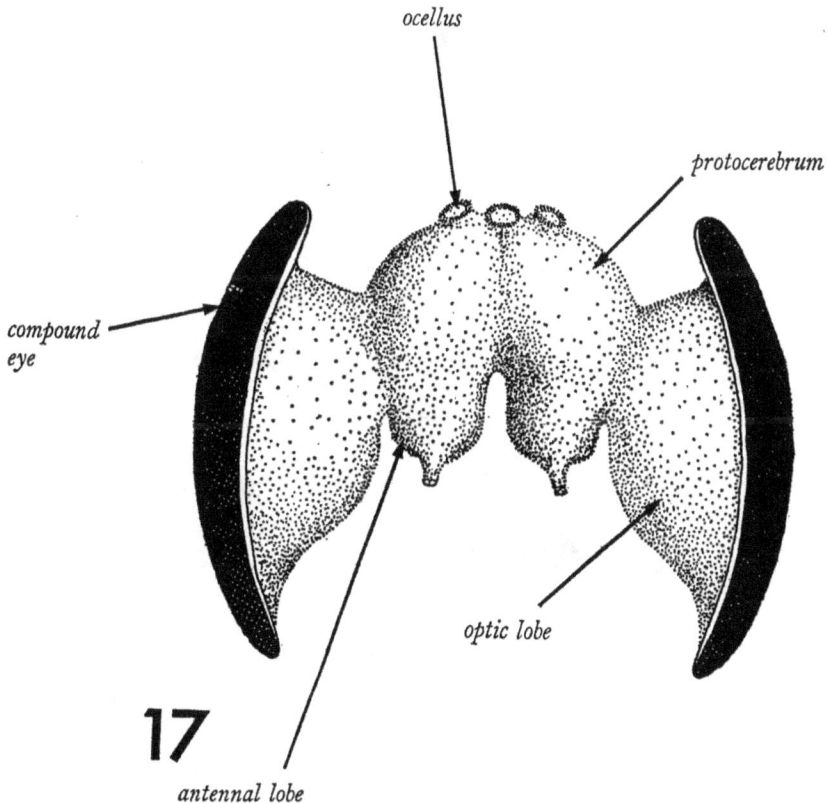

Fig. 17. Anterior aspect of brain of *Bombus* female.

The general physiology, metabolism, development and growth of insects are controlled by hormones secreted by various endocrine organs. In adult bumblebees hormones produced by special neurosecretory cells in the brain may affect, for example, development of the ovaries. Hormones from these neurosecretory cells are stored in two pear-shaped bodies, the corpora cardiaca, lying close behind the brain, immediately astride the oesophagus. These bodies may themselves be secretory, and hormones pass from them into the haemolymph (see Thomsen, 1954). Associated with the corpora cardiaca is a pair of important, rounded secretory bodies, the corpora allata (Fig. 18). Secretions from these bodies significantly affect bumblebee behaviour, although their rôle is poorly understood. The corpora allata are especially well developed in overwintered bumblebees with developing ovaries (Palm, 1948).

The male reproductive system consists of two testes, each situated at the end of a duct, the vas deferens. Part of each vas deferens is swollen and tightly coiled to form an accessory testis in which mature sperms are stored. The vasa deferentia

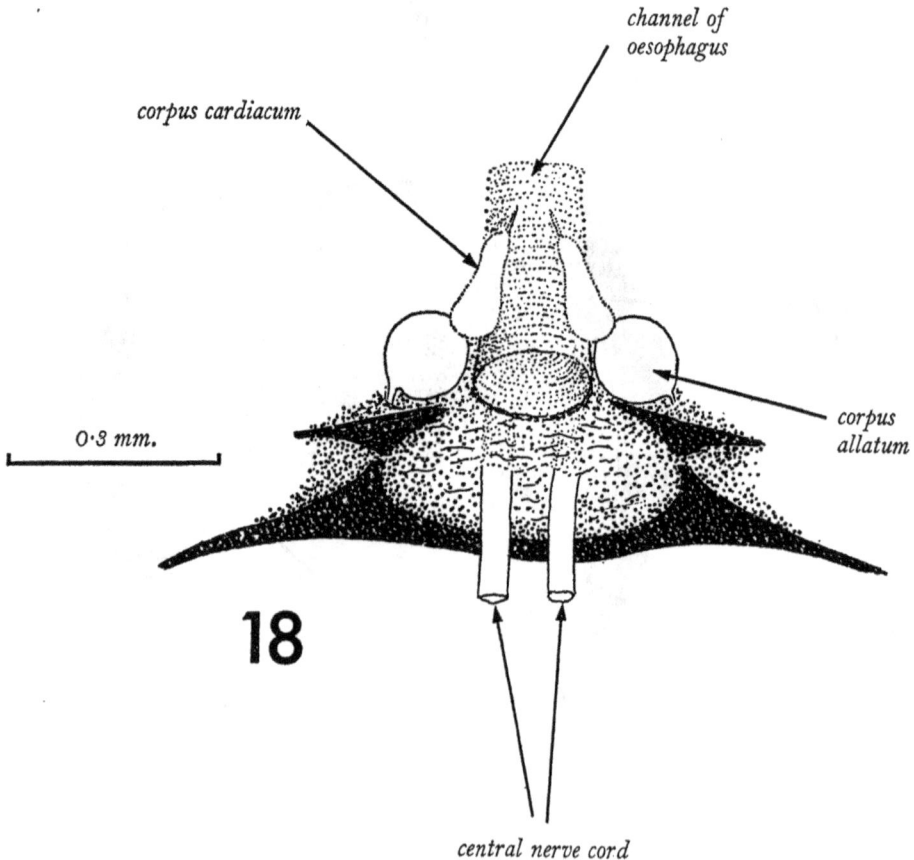

Fig. 18. Dorsal aspect of corpora allata and corpora cardiaca of *Bombus* female.

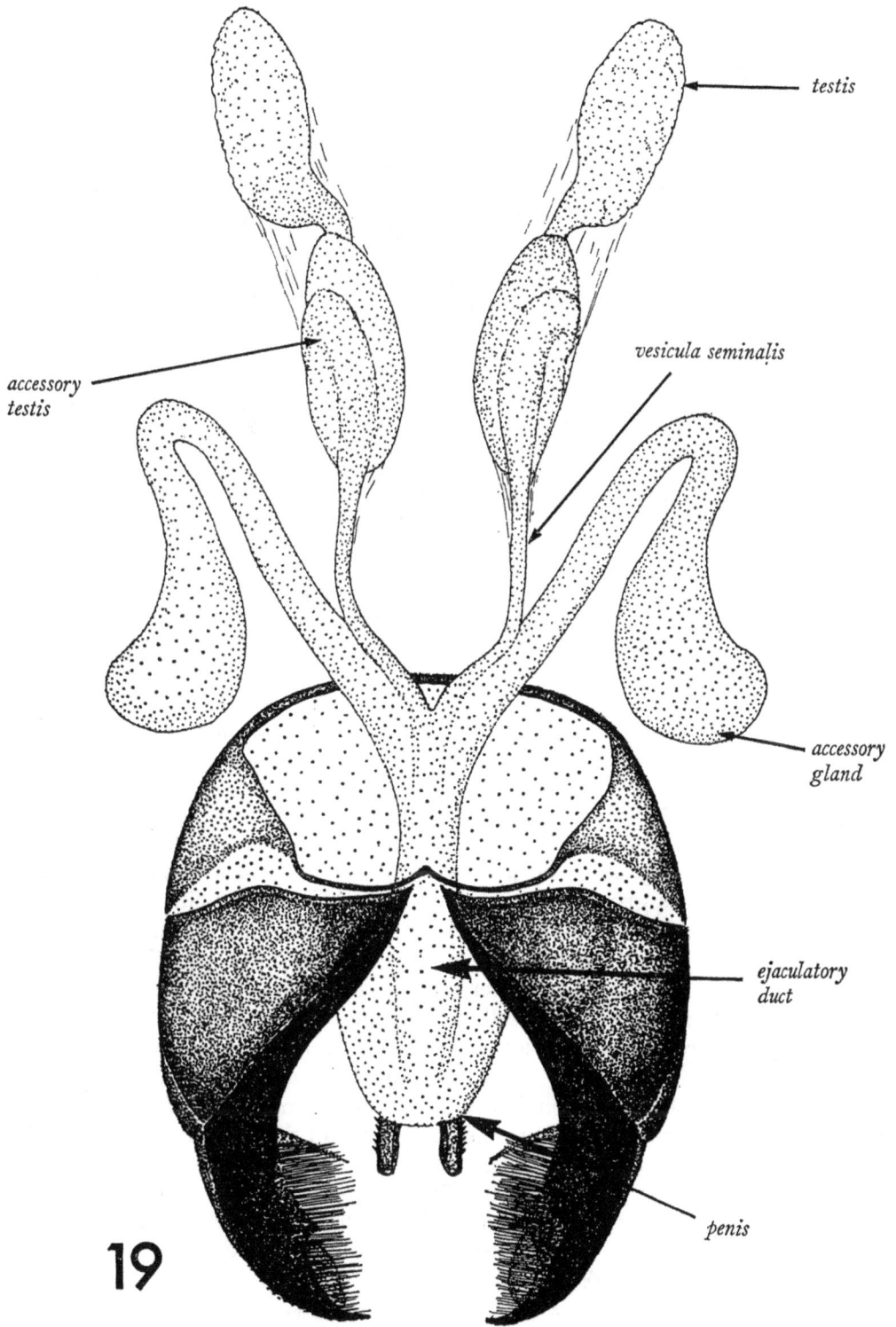

testis

vesicula seminalis

accessory
testis

accessory
gland

ejaculatory
duct

penis

19

B Fig. 19. Reproductive system of *Bombus* male.

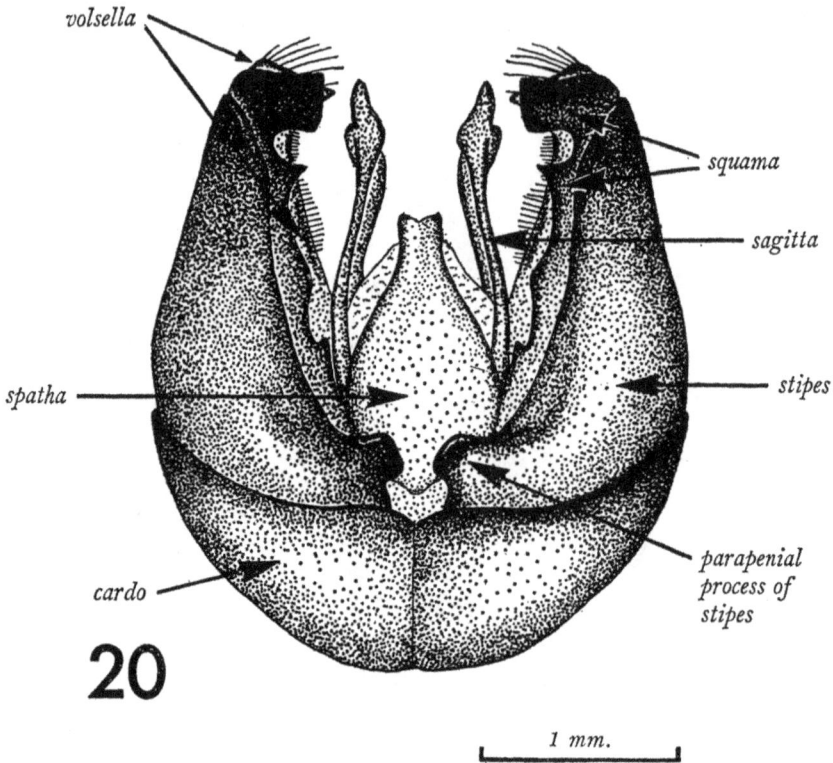

volsella

squama

sagitta

spatha

stipes

cardo

parapenial process of stipes

20

1 *mm.*

Fig. 20. Dorsal aspect of genital capsule (genitalia) of *Bombus lucorum* male.

unite posteriorly to form a median ejaculatory duct which passes through the penis. A pair of accessory glands are also present (Fig. 19). The genitalia form a heavily sclerotized capsule (Fig. 20), the precise features of which are characteristic for each species or species group. At the base of the genitalia is a chitinized ring, the cardo. In the centre lies the penis, which is sclerotized on three faces to form a dorsal spatha and a pair of lateral sagittae. The remainder of the genitalia comprise the so-called 'forceps', formed on either side by the basal stipes, the apical squama and, ventral to the squama, the volsella or lacinia.

In the female there are two ovaries, each divided into four egg-producing tubules, the ovarioles.[1] The ovaries pass into a single median vagina, by way of the paired oviducts. A small, spherical spermatheca, in which sperm received from the male is stored, is connected by a thin duct to the dorsal wall of the vagina (Fig. 21). When sperm is present there is an obvious opaque sphere in the middle of the spermatheca (Fig. 22). In bees, as in other aculeate Hymenoptera, there is no ovipositor, this ancestral structure having become modified to form the sting which is used as a weapon of defence. Eggs of bees, therefore, are deposited directly from the vaginal opening at the base of the sting.

[1] There are more ovarioles in a *Psithyrus* female, frequently as many as ten to fifteen per ovary.

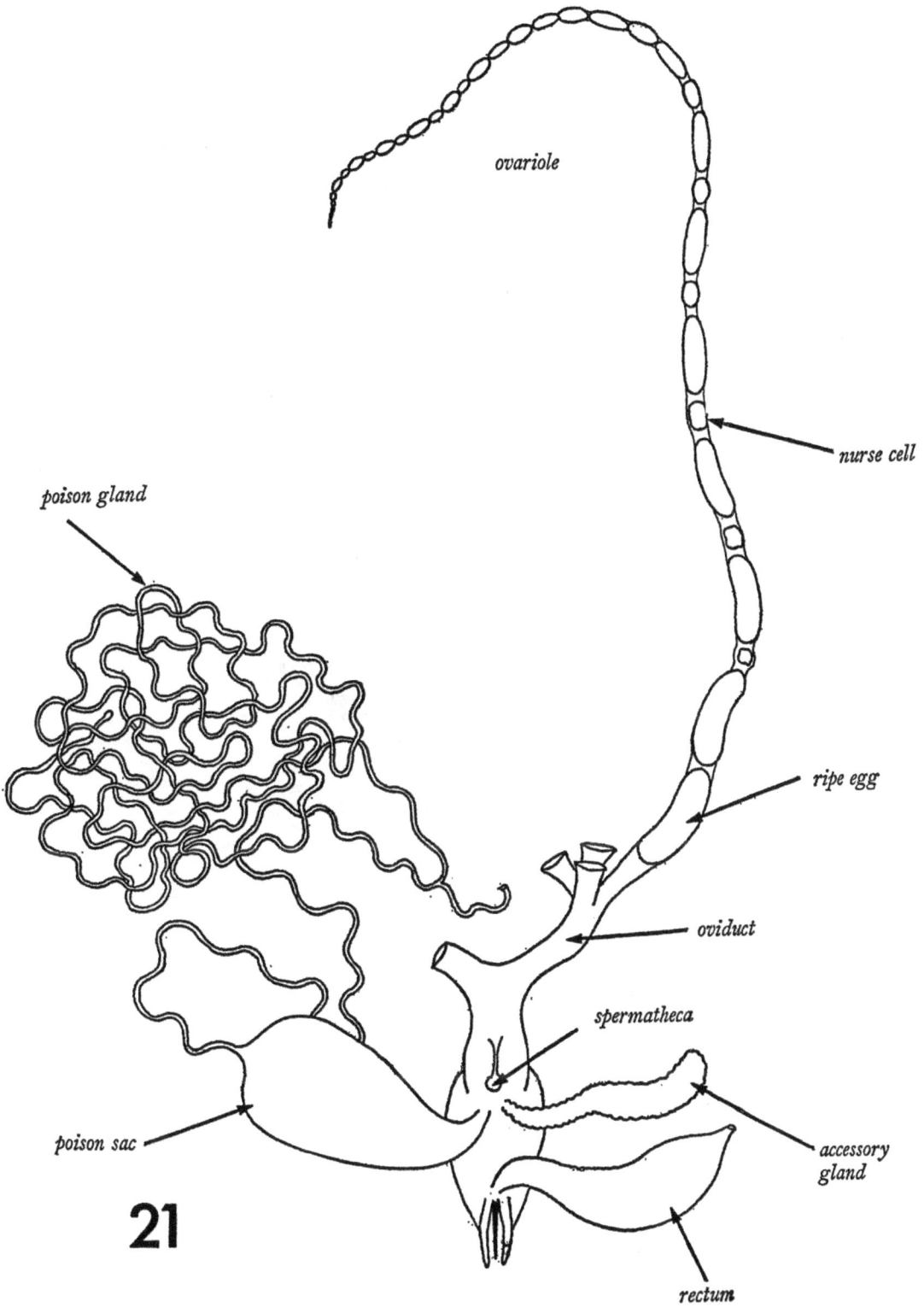

Fig. 21. Reproductive system of *Bombus* female.

The sting mechanism of a bee consists of a complex arrangement of muscles, membranes and plates (see Snodgrass, 1956). Associated with the sting is a large poison sac with its long, thin, convoluted pair of poison glands, and a smaller, sac-like, accessory gland (Fig. 21). Bumblebee venom, which is stored in the poison sac, contains both nucleic acids and proteins, and in detail has been shown to be chemically different to that of honey bees (Mello, 1970). The sting itself terminates in a sharp piercing shaft (for example, Fig. 130) made of three elongate elements with a central canal along which poison may be discharged. Unlike that of a honey bee the sting of a bumblebee is unbarbed, enabling it to be withdrawn following the act of penetration. Structural features of the stings of *Bombus* females, particularly of queens, are important in distinguishing species and will be considered later in more detail.

The ovaries of *Bombus* workers usually remain thin and thread-like, but they are, under certain circumstances, capable of developing. However, as workers do not normally mate, their eggs are never fertilized and only give rise to males. Mated

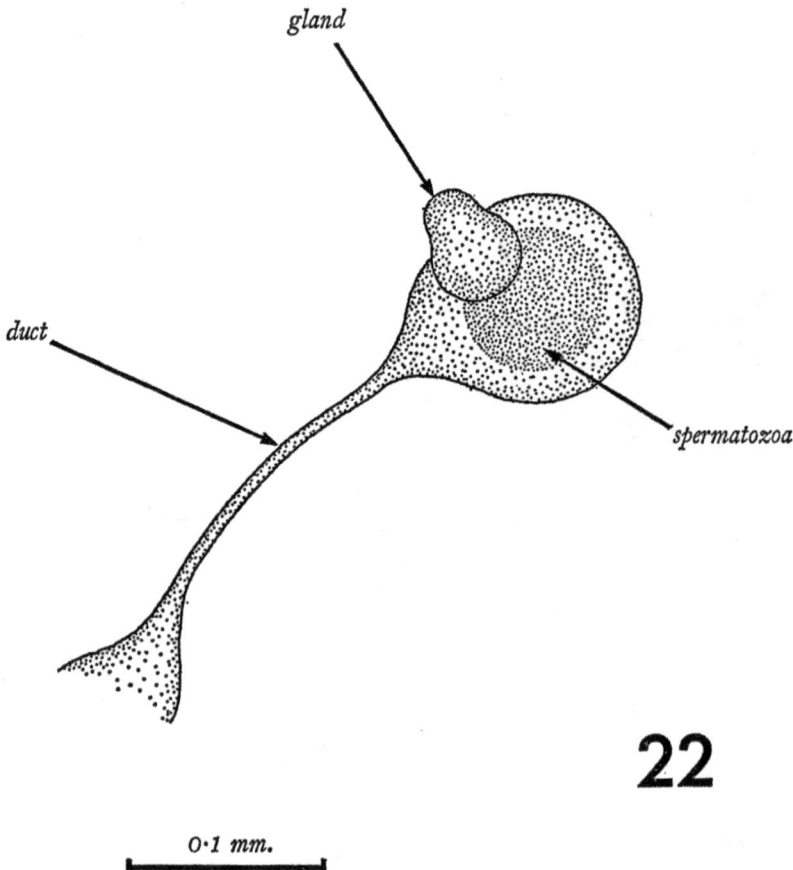

gland

duct

spermatozoa

22

0·1 mm.

Fig. 22. Left lateral aspect of spermatheca of fertilized *Bombus* queen.

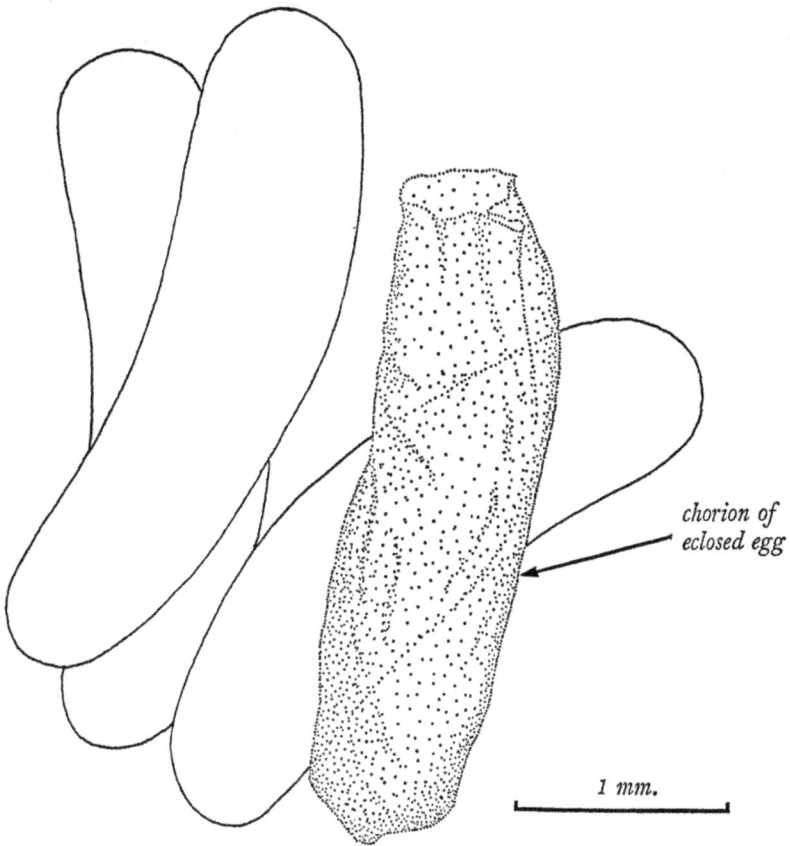

*chorion of
eclosed egg*

1 mm.

Fig. 23. Eggs of *Bombus hortorum*.

Bombus queens or *Psithyrus* females, however, can lay unfertilized (male-producing) or fertilized (female-producing) eggs.[1]

The respiratory system is composed of a complex arrangement of branching tubules, the tracheae, which terminate (in contact with the various body organs and tissues) in a fine ramifying series of microscopic capillaries, the tracheoles. In adults, the tracheae arise from large air sacs which occur in the head, thorax and abdomen; these connect to the outside by way of lateral spiracles, three pairs in the thorax (this includes the pair of propodeal spiracles of the first true abdominal segment) and seven pairs in the abdomen. In female bumblebees the last abdominal spiracle is hidden from view, being present on T7 which is located within the sting chamber (Fig. 14). The air sacs are especially well developed on either side of the

[1] Freak adults of *Bombus* that are partly male and partly female – known as gynandromorphs – have occasionally been found and described (see Röseler, 1962), and Milliron (1960) has reported a case of gynandromorphism in *Psithyrus*.

abdominal cavity, particularly anteriorly, and probably their prime function is to provide buoyancy for flight. Respiratory movements of the abdomen of an inactive bee cause air to be drawn in and out of the first thoracic (mesothoracic) spiracles, but in an active bee producing high levels of carbon dioxide, inhalation also occurs through the abdominal spiracles while exhalation takes place through the propodeal spiracles (see Bailey, 1954). The familiar buzzing of a flying bee is largely due to the passage of air through the thoracic spiracles.

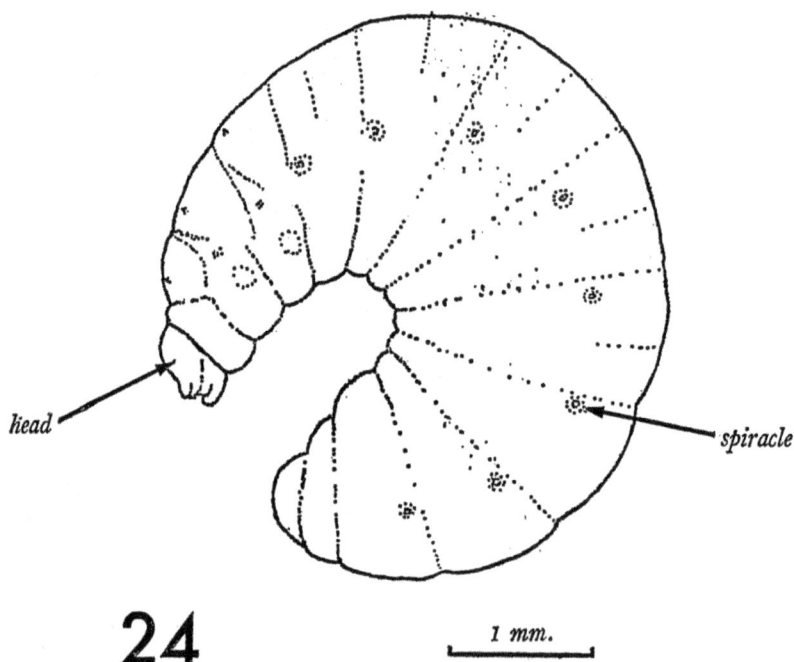

Fig. 24. Lateral aspect of *Bombus* larva.

Before becoming an adult, a bumblebee passes through egg, larval, prepupal and pupal stages, the whole developmental process lasting approximately four to five weeks, depending upon brood-nest temperatures. A bumblebee egg is pearly white in colour and more or less sausage-shaped (Fig. 23). It is covered by a transparent membrane, the chorion, within which the embryo develops. Eventually, a small whitish and sluggish larva emerges, breaking through the chorion at the wider, head end of the egg. The larva has a distinct head and thirteen body segments, three thoracic and ten abdominal (Fig. 24). There are no eyes, legs or wings; the larva is also hairless and is covered by a smooth, transparent, colourless and flexible cuticle. A pair of spiracles is present on both the second and third thoracic segments and on each of the first eight abdominal segments. Although a tracheal system is developed, there are no air sacs.

The mouthparts are mostly soft, fleshy lobes or papillae (Fig. 25) but, and

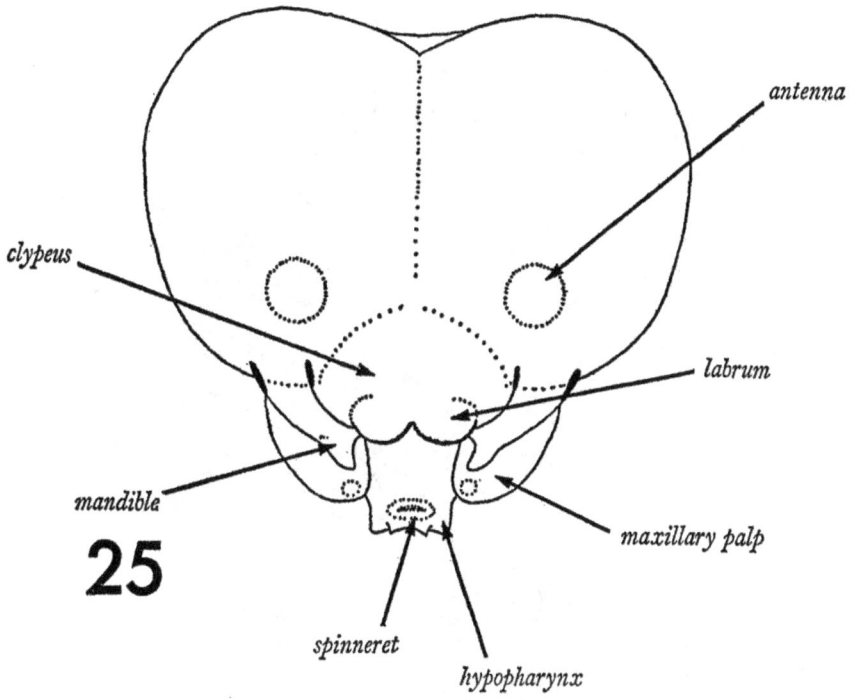

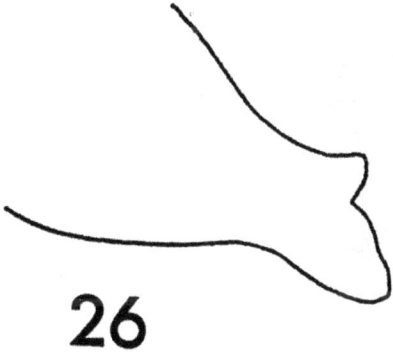

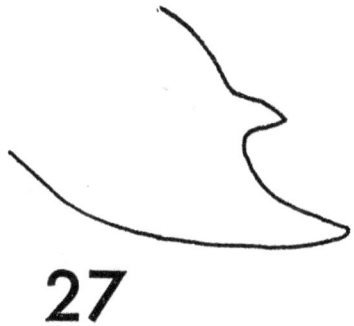

Figs. 25–27. 25, Head of *Bombus* larva; 26, right mandible of *Bombus* larva; 27, right mandible of *Psithyrus* larva.

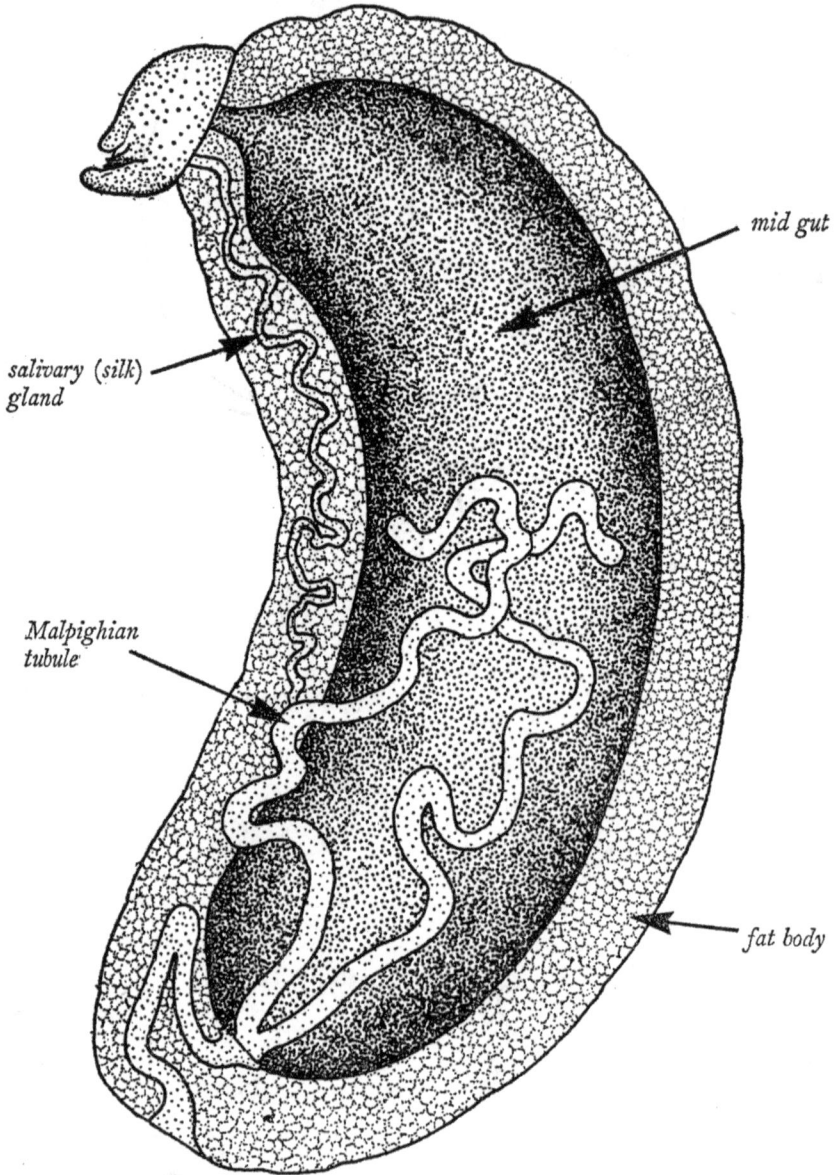

mid gut

salivary (silk) gland

Malpighian tubule

fat body

28

Fig. 28. Alimentary canal of *Bombus* larva.

particularly in the later instars, the mandibles are visible as brownish, sclerotized structures. The larva feeds on pollen and honey supplied by the foundress (mother) queen or nurse (sister) bees in the colony. The contents of the gut may give the larva a yellowish or pinkish tinge. As the larva grows it becomes too large for its cuticle or 'skin' and periodically this must be shed and replaced by a larger one. A larva passes through four instars, and at the later stages of development differences between sexes and castes become evident (Cumber, 1949b). Ritcher (1933) was able to distinguish between fourth-instar larvae of *Bombus* and *Psithyrus* by examining the mandibles, those of *Bombus* being mitten-shaped (Fig. 26) and those of

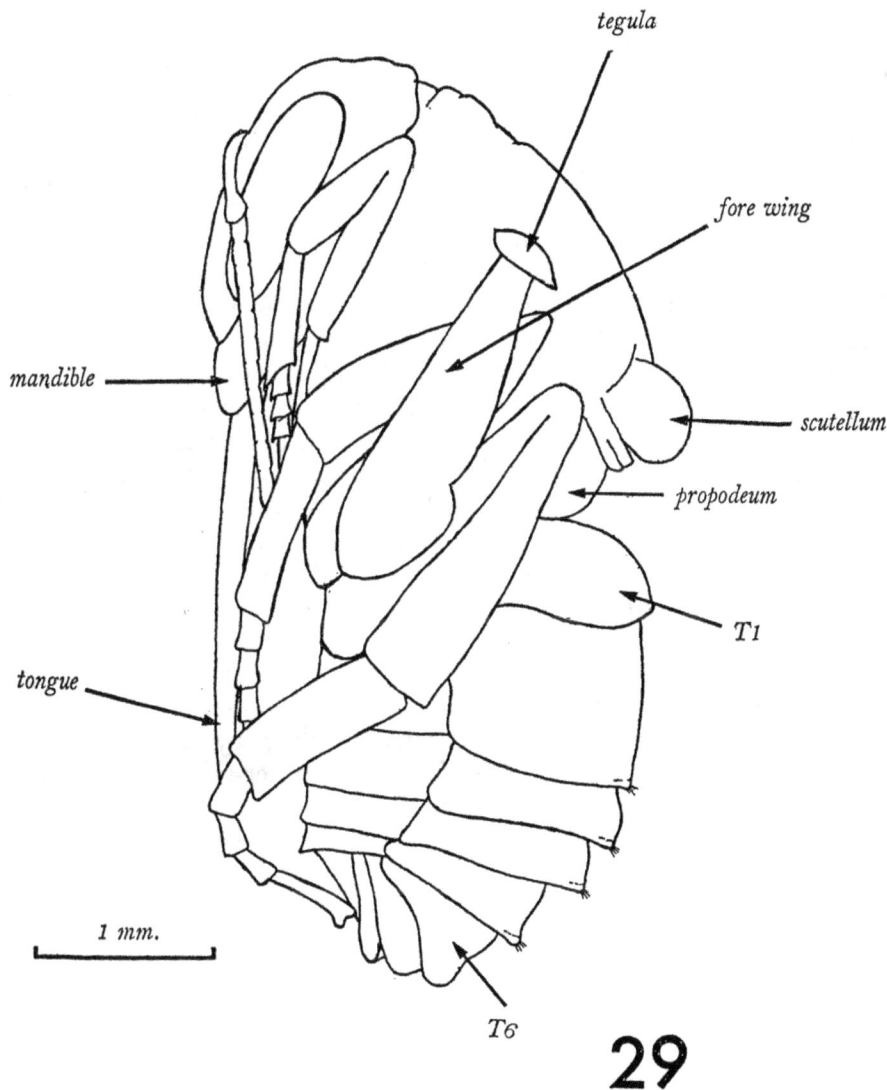

Fig. 29. Lateral aspect of *Bombus* pupa.

Psithyrus falcate (Fig. 27). The precise shape of the mandibles also seems to vary from one *Bombus* group to another, and according to Cumber there are noticeable specific differences in the extent of branching of the atrial spines that arise from the first pair of thoracic spiracles.

In the larva, salivary glands are represented by a single pair of silk-producing glands which extend backwards below the alimentary tract. The silk is discharged anteriorly on the lobe formed by the lower lip (labium) and hypopharynx (Fig. 25). The silk is used by the larva for spinning its cocoon (see Chapter 3).

The gut of the larva is relatively simple (Fig. 28), and the mid gut is a blind-ending sac which only opens into the hind gut in the final larval instar. Waste matter is accumulated, therefore, during most of the larval stage and only voided shortly before pupation takes place.

As in adults, the fat body is an important organ, and large reserves of fat and glycogen are present in the trophocytes. Protein reserves are also accumulated and these are utilized in the formation of the adult tissues during metamorphosis. The hormonal system of the larva is of vital importance. The corpora allata, for example, secrete the well-known 'juvenile-hormone' which suppresses adult characteristics and controls moulting and metamorphosis.

When full-grown the larva enters a transient prepupal stage which has some characteristics intermediate between those of the larva and the pupa. It is here that the first true abdominal segment (the propodeum) becomes incorporated into the thorax. Eventually the larval skin is cast off and the prepupa becomes a pupa.

The newly-formed pupa is soft and whitish in colour. It is unmistakably adult-like in form, although the wings are merely unexpanded pads (Fig. 29). During the ·pupal stage the larval tissues are transformed into those of the adult, the pupa gradually darkening as development proceeds. At the end of the pupal stage the wings expand, the pupal skin is ruptured, and an adult bee emerges.

The size of an adult bumblebee is considerably influenced by the amount of food received during the larval stage; and whether a female *Bombus* larva develops into a queen or worker is also partly governed by the amount of food supplied and consumed. As a general rule queens are larger than workers of the same species and it is usually possible to distinguish between them by size alone. However, exceptions occur and intermediate-sized females, 'worker-sized queens' or 'queen-sized workers', can all occur; caste is, therefore, best considered and defined in terms of an individual's physiological make-up (see Chapter 5).

PART
I

BIOLOGY

CHAPTER 2

Hibernation

IN temperate parts of the world such as the British Isles, bumblebee colonies are annual, since only the young queens are able to survive the winter, while the old, foundress queens, workers and males all die. The young, fertilized .queens produced during the summer enter hibernation, and it is these bumblebees which reappear in the following spring and later form colonies of their own. In the British Isles bumblebees may hibernate for anything from six to eight or even nine months, depending on the species and to some extent on spring temperatures. Hibernation, therefore, occupies the greater part of the life of a normal bumblebee queen, and is a vital and important aspect of bumblebee biology. To refer, however, to the whole period of inactivity as 'hibernation' is strictly incorrect, since many queens enter their winter quarters at the height of summer. The term 'diapause' is therefore more accurate, but since the period of quiescence is continuous and has evolved as a means of maintaining the species through the winter months, the term 'hibernation' is here retained and used to refer to the whole length of the diapause, and not just to that part of it which coincides with the winter.

Several earlier writers on the hibernation of bumblebees (Huber, 1802; Hoffer, 1882–3; Sladen, 1900; Wagner, 1907) were of the opinion that queens overwintered in the ground at considerable depths from the surface. No doubt this assumption, which is now known to be incorrect, was based on the belief that bumblebees would be unable to tolerate temperatures below freezing and would therefore need to burrow deeply (below the frost line) in order to survive the winter. In fact, bumblebees often hibernate at depths considerably less than 10 cm., but this aspect of hibernation will be considered more fully later.

Bumblebees normally hibernate individually in small, spherical or oval cavities which they excavate in the soil (Sladen, 1912; Bols, 1937, 1939; Alford, 1969c) (Fig. 30).

Banks and lightly wooded slopes with a north or north-west exposure are favourite sites for hibernating bumblebees. Sladen has pointed out that such situations will tend not to be warmed by the winter sunshine and thus the bumblebees will remain undisturbed until the warm days of spring. Bumblebees frequently hibernate in the soil beneath trees or under herbage, and have also been recorded overwintering in cavities in stone walls (Skovgaard, 1936), in rotten tree stumps (Frison, 1926; Tkalcu, 1960, 1961; Haeseler, 1972) (in Europe, notably queens of *Bombus hypnorum*), under moss, leaves and piles of rubbish (Verrill, cited by Putnam, 1864; Sladen, 1912; and others), as well as in a wide range of miscellaneous places. I once found two *Bombus lucorum* queens hibernating in the folds of a curtain in an unheated, north-facing first floor bedroom!

The situations in which bumblebees hibernate are typically well-drained. However, very dry soil which, for example, often occurs next to the boles of very large trees, is avoided, possibly because of the dangers of desiccation, but probably also since it is unlikely that a suitable hibernaculum could be hollowed out where the soil is too dry and loose. Pouvreau (1970) found that under experimental conditions

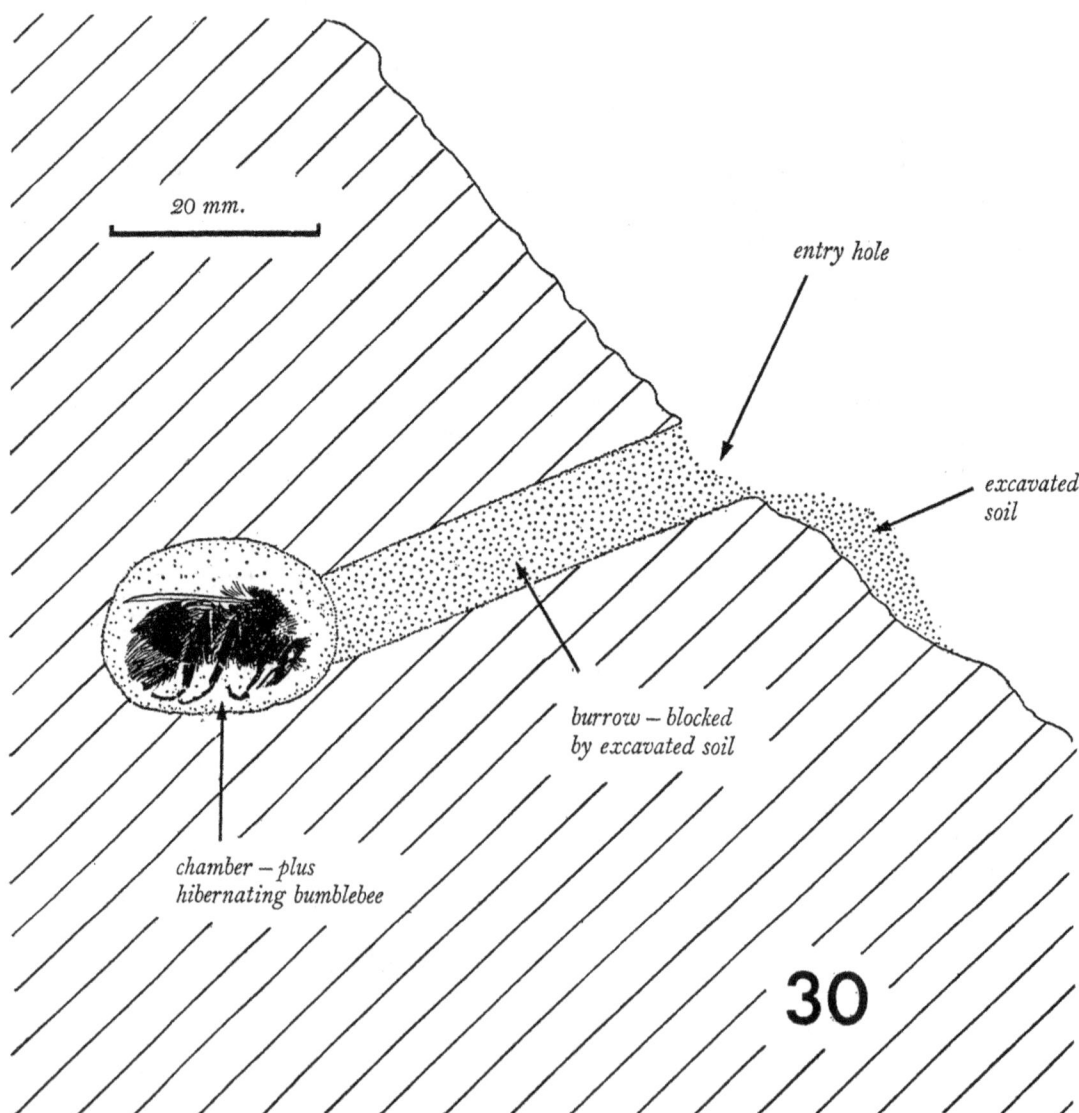

20 mm.

entry hole

excavated soil

burrow – blocked by excavated soil

chamber – plus hibernating bumblebee

30

Fig. 30. Section through hibernaculum of *Bombus hortorum*.

bumblebees showed a definite preference for places where soil humidity was above fifty per cent.

Some species of bumblebee, especially *Bombus lucorum*, are adaptable in their choice of a hibernation site, but most (including *B. lucorum*) tend, in detail, to show definite site preferences. *Bombus lucorum*, *B. terrestris* and *B. pratorum*, for example, most frequently hibernate in the soil at the base of trees. I have also found *B. hortorum*, *B. lapidarius* and *Psithyrus campestris* overwintering close to trees, but only where the ground was particularly steep. Trees growing on north or north-west slopes, where there is a distinct layer of leaf litter around the trunks, are especially favoured. In such situations bumblebees usually form their hibernation chambers immediately below the soil-litter interface, and the depth of the chamber from the surface is thus determined by the thickness of the litter

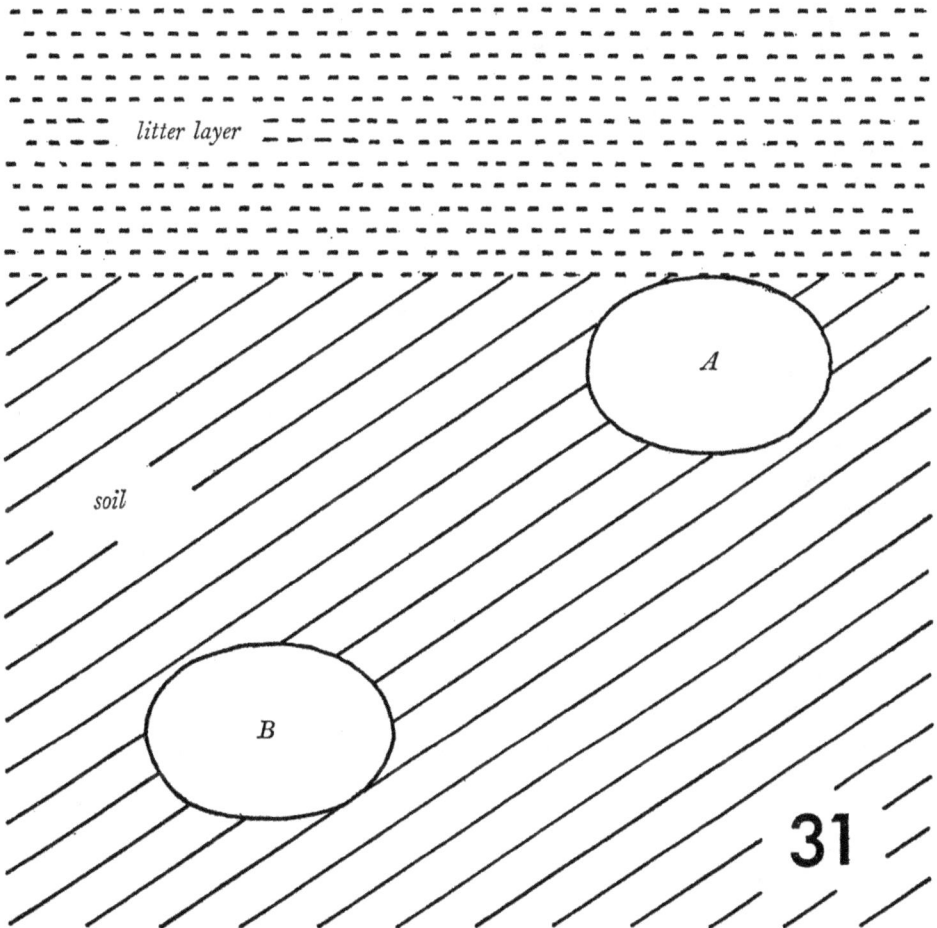

Fig. 31. Position of hibernation chambers in relation to soil-litter interface. A, typical of *Bombus lucorum*, *B. terrestris* and *B. pratorum*; B, typical of *Bombus lapidarius* and *B. hortorum*.

layer. Bumblebees are most frequently present on the downward side of the trees, and although the hibernaculum may be constructed actually against the bole of the tree, they usually occur about 15 cm. from the trunk (Alford, 1969c). Where species of *Psithyrus*, *B. hortorum* or *B. lapidarius* hibernate below a layer of litter (in contrast with the behaviour of queens of *B. lucorum*, *B. terrestris* and *B. pratorum*) they normally burrow down into the soil so that the hibernation chamber lies a short distance below the soil-litter interface; such species will thus tend to hibernate at greater depths than those remaining just below the litter layer (Fig. 31).

Hibernating bumblebees of several species are especially common in some northwest facing banks or slopes. In many parts of the British Isles *B. lapidarius* is common in such sites. This species will hibernate in soil forming small undulations at the sides of woodland tracks, and in the shaded walls of ditches, as well as in banks or slopes many metres high. According to Sladen, *B. lapidarius* tends to select the upper parts of banks or slopes when seeking hibernation quarters. Isolated mounds of soil, such as those thrown up by fallen trees, are also suitable places for hibernating bumblebees, as long as they are shaded. All six British species of *Psithyrus* are known to hibernate in banks or similar sites, as are the following additional *Bombus* species: *B. hortorum*, *B. ruderatus* and *B. subterraneus*. *B. hortorum*, possibly in common with some other species, tends to select the steeper sites. *B. terrestris* and *B. lucorum* also overwinter in banks, but as mentioned above, and also by Sladen (1912), they most frequently occur under trees. Although I have never found hibernating bumblebees in open country, I have observed several species, including *B. jonellus*, *B. magnus*, *B. ruderarius* and *P. rupestris*, searching for suitable hibernation quarters in drystone walls.

Species of the subgenus *Thoracobombus*,[1] including *Bombus pascuorum* (syn. *B. agrorum*), *B. ruderarius* and *B. sylvarum*, rarely if ever hibernate under trees or in banks, and indeed are conspicuous by their absence from such situations. Little is known of the hibernation habits of these species, but it is possible that they overwinter in the soil under miscellaneous herbage. Of these species I have only ever found hibernating queens of *B. pascuorum*, two in the soil under grass and one under bracken litter. Other investigators seem to have been equally unsuccessful in locating hibernating queens of *Thoracobombus* species.

Bumblebees hibernating in banks or slopes either burrow directly into the soil or may pass through a covering of moss. In summer and early autumn bumblebees are readily located in suitable sites since there are often clear signs on the surface which indicate their presence. Typically, a small pile of excavated soil is visible, displaced to a greater or lesser extent down the slope of the ground and surmounted by the blocked up entrance to the hibernaculum. These tell-tale signs are eventually washed away by rain, or in time become otherwise disturbed, and then the presence of a hibernating bumblebee is no longer apparent.

As already mentioned, the depth at which a hibernation chamber is formed may vary from species to species, and this can apply whether the bees hibernate below a

[1] Details of subgenera, etc. are given in Chapter 9.

surface layer of litter or herbage or elsewhere. The depth of a hibernaculum is also determined by soil conditions. *B. lapidarius*, for example, is known to hibernate at greater depths in a light sandy soil than in a heavier, chalky one (Alford, 1969c). Some hibernating bumblebees may be found only 2 or 3 cm. from the surface, although depths of 5 to 15 cm. are more usual. Less often, bumblebees are found at greater depths. Pouvreau (1970) considers the depth at which bumblebees hibernate to be a correlation between the microclimate of the site and the ecological require-ments of the species, and Hobbs (1965a) has suggested that *B. nevadensis* survives on the Canadian prairie whereas *B. rufocinctus* does not, because the former hibernates at greater depths and is thus better protected from the severe winter weather.

The dimensions of a hibernaculum will vary according to the size of the individual bumblebee. In the case of *B. lapidarius*, for example, the burrow is usually about 11 mm. in diameter and the chamber has a maximum width of 26 to 30 mm.

When searching for suitable hibernation quarters, lowered light intensity may be the initial factor guiding bumblebees to a more critical examination of particular topographical features. Once in a potentially suitable area a bumblebee flies slowly over the ground, tacking from side to side, just above the surface, settling at inter-vals and sometimes scratching at the soil or ground covering. When a likely spot is located, and as previously noted humidity will be a limiting factor, the bumblebee commences to dig. Bumblebees use their mandibles and legs when burrowing, and occasionally back out of the ground to force loosened soil out of the way. This soil forms the mound at the entrance, while soil from the lower parts of the hiber-naculum serves to block up the tunnel. The speed of hibernaculum construction will obviously vary according to the depth at which the chamber is formed and the ease of digging; on average, it takes a queen about half an hour before she disappears below the surface. Completion of the hibernaculum, therefore, probably takes between one and two hours. On sloping ground bumblebees face up the slope when digging and continue to face in this direction during the period of excavation of the burrow. This allows the soil thrown up from below to fall clear of the burrow without obstructing the digging operation. In his description of burrowing by a *P. vestalis* female, Bols (1937) stated that the bumblebee frequently turned round whilst burrowing so that soil was thrown out on all sides of the hole. Possibly this method is adopted where the slope of the ground is gentle, but it is not typical of either *Bombus* or *Psithyrus* digging in banks or moderate slopes. If a known hiber-nation site is examined in late summer or early autumn, several unoccupied burrows (uncompleted hibernacula) may sometimes be found. Sladen attributed these to bumblebees having been disturbed during their digging, although in my experience, at least with *B. lapidarius*, I have found that queens are often so engrossed with their labours that they may be covered with a tube or collecting box, and even touched, without being disturbed. If a deserted burrow is examined it is usual to find that it abuts a root, stone, or some other obstruction, at a super-ficial depth. I once watched a *B. lapidarius* queen attempt to burrow into a shallow, chalky soil in a beech wood. After three abortive attempts within a short distance of each other she flew away, and subsequent examination showed that each abandoned burrow ran up against a flint or solid piece of chalk a short distance from the surface. I have never known a queen try to bypass such an obstruction.

During hibernation bumblebees remain in their hibernacula, lying on their backs or in a crouched position with the wings in repose (Fig. 30). If disturbed in the late summer or autumn, bumblebees immediately become active and vibrate their wings, and produce a clearly audible low-pitched buzz. The vibration of their wing muscles rapidly raises their body temperature – body heat may also be generated by chemical means (see Newsholme, *et al.*, 1972) – and the bumblebees are soon able to fly. In mid-winter bumblebees are torpid but (as described by Plath) they will nevertheless become active if warmed in the palm of the hand.

Hibernating bumblebees are sometimes found with their limbs, and occasionally their mandibles, caked with grains of soil. Presumably these have adhered to their bodies during the excavation of the hibernaculum. In the spring overwintered bumblebees frequently retain this dried mud on their bodies; possibly soil could also become attached to bumblebees in the spring as they escape from their hibernacula. Considerable quantities of soil may adhere to bumblebees; Smith (1876) found a specimen in the spring with so much attached to her legs that at first she could not fly. It is historically interesting that Kirby (1802) wrote of a *Psithyrus* female (not knowing of the inquilinous mode of life of the *Psithyri*): 'The posterior tibiae, of one specimen in my cabinet, is covered from one end to the other with a thin coat of pale earth, mixed with particles of sand; they probably use this in constructing their nests or cells.' Similarly, Shuckard (1866) mentioned the presence of soil (clay) on the legs of a large *B. terrestris* female (presumably an overwintered queen). He suggested that the soil was 'required doubtless at home for some domestic repairs'.

Plath (1927b, 1934), Frison (1929) and Townsend (1951) have all reported the finding of many hibernating bumblebees in very close proximity to one another. It was presumed in all these cases, which refer solely to the New World species *B. impatiens*, that the queens were hibernating about the entrance to their maternal nest. Plath, on the evidence of his observations on *B. impatiens*, dismissed Sladen's findings that hibernating queens of *B. lapidarius* sometimes occur in considerable numbers in specifically selected overwintering sites, and suggested that Sladen was also observing queens hibernating next to their nests. Plath's criticisms, however, have since been invalidated (Bols, 1937, 1939; Alford, 1969c). Hibernation and nest site requirements are not identical and normally bumblebees do not hibernate close to their maternal nest, unless by chance the colony happens to be in a suitable hibernation site. It must be conceded, however, that *B. impatiens* (subgenus *Pyrobombus*) may be an exception, although this is not known to be true of British members of this subgenus. Bols (1939) recorded migrations of bumblebees of many species to a suitable hibernation site measuring only 50 by 10 metres, and also recorded mass dispersal from the same area by overwintered bumblebees in the spring. *Polistes* wasps are also known to migrate to and from hibernation quarters

(Rau, 1930). It should perhaps be added that bumblebees do not normally hibernate in their nests, as was once claimed by Hoffer and other early students of bees, although in the tropics males and young queens have been reported by von Ihring (1903) to spend the unfavourable dry season in their maternal nests.

Wagner (1907) assumed that bumblebees of the various species entered hibernation at about the same time of year, in response to the onset of autumn weather. In this connexion he thought that queens reared in sheltered nests took up their winter quarters later than those from more exposed nests. More recently, Stein (1957) suggested that young queens were stimulated to enter hibernation, instead of initiating colonies, by the effects of the wide range in day and night temperatures which occur in the late summer and autumn. Stein neglected to consider, however, that many queens enter hibernation in mid-summer, and also that in the spring when colony initiation does take place, there are also wide differences between night and day temperatures. Furthermore, since bumblebees do not at this time have nests in which to shelter, they may be even more subjected to temperature extremes than would autumn queens.

That the time of entry into hibernation of both European and American bumblebees depends upon the species and not nest situation or ambient temperatures is correctly stated by Plath (1934). Initiation of hibernation in social wasps is also independent of temperature (Roubaud, 1929; Duncan, 1939). In the British Isles queens of *B. pratorum* are among the first to take up overwintering quarters. Colonies of this species are frequently at an end by mid-July or even earlier (but see p. 61), and this is often long before species such as *B. pascuorum* normally produce queens. Queens of *B. terrestris* and *B. lapidarius*, for example, frequently enter hibernation from July onwards, although their colonies continue in existence much later, showing that the motivation is not triggered by the onset of autumn weather. Details of the stimuli which are responsible for initiating a bumblebee's entry into hibernation are unknown. In some insects it has been shown that there may be an association between the inactivity of the corpus allatum and hibernation (de Wilde, 1953; Lees, 1955). This could also be true of bumblebees, since their corpora allata are known to be inactive until the final stages of hibernation (Palm, 1948). This view is substantiated by observations made on overwintered bumblebees parasitized by the nematode *Sphaerularia bombi*; such bumblebees, unlike healthy individuals, have inactive corpora allata and they do not initiate colonies, behaving instead like young queens in that they frequent hibernation sites. Their characteristic behaviour, and its significance, is considered in greater detail later (Chapter 8).

Bumblebees entering hibernation have considerable reserves of fat in their fat bodies, and are normally fertilized. However, Cumber (1953) found some unfertilized queens surviving among bumblebees he was overwintering under artificial conditions, and Milliron (1967) has reported the natural occurrence of unfertilized, overwintered queens. The virtual absence of unfertilized queens both in and following hibernation may be explained in several ways. Either unmated bumblebees are usually unable to survive the winter or do not normally enter hibernation, or the chances of a female mating are very high so that few, if any, remain unfertilized. The development of fat bodies in queens is not dependent upon previous fertilization and as shown by Alford (1969a) the reserves mainly accumulate in the first few days of adult life, that is, before the normal time of mating. This strongly suggests that there is no reason why unmated bumblebees should not survive the winter. It is certainly possible that an unmated queen is reluctant to enter hibernation and, as pointed out by Free & Butler (1959), the sex ratio – that is of *Bombus* queens (*Psithyrus* females) to males – is probably so adjusted that the greatest possible number of females becomes fertilized. Sladen (1912) has estimated that twice as many *Bombus* males as queens are usually produced and a preponderance of males in *Psithyrus* has been noted by Frison (1926) and others. If, as seems likely from the evidence of dissections, most young queens do become fertilized, then this is sufficient to explain the virtual absence of unfertilized queens in and following hibernation.

Before leaving the maternal colony in order to enter hibernation, a queen fills her crop with honey (Sladen, 1912). At the start of hibernation the crop of a large bumblebee may contain more than 200 mg. of honey. Sladen considered that this food was especially needed 'during September, when the ground is often very dry and warm'. At this time a queen's metabolic rate will be somewhat higher than it is for much for the hibernation period, and most of the honey is, in fact, used up during the autumn, as suspected by Sladen (Alford, 1969c). However, it is unlikely that the water content of the honey (approximately 20 per cent) is of importance in offsetting desiccation, since sufficient metabolic water is made available from the breakdown of the fat reserves stored in the fat body. Honey remaining in the crop during the winter is of importance at the end of hibernation, bridging the period of increased metabolic activity from the end of diapause until the bumblebee can emerge and supplement her food reserves by feeding at flowers.

As in other hibernating insects, fat is an important food reserve and large amounts (often more than 100 mg.) are stored in the fat cells or trophocytes. Glycogen is also present. These energy reserves are substantially reduced during the hibernation period (Fig. 32). El-Hariri (1966) found that glycogen, rather than fat, was consumed by hibernating coccinellid beetles during periods of very low temperature; this probably also applies to bumblebees, since the glycogen in their fat cells, unlike the fat, is mainly utilized during mid-winter (Alford, 1969c).

Hibernating bumblebees, when subjected to low temperatures, become cold-hardened by producing glycerol. This acts as an antifreeze and lowers the temperature at which ice crystals will form in the body tissues. Hobbs (1965a) found that the average supercooling points for queens stored at 0·5°C. and 5°C. were −19°C. and −14°C. respectively, the more cold-hardened specimens having manufactured 5 to 6 times as much glycerol as the others. High humidity reduces cold-hardiness in insects (Salt, 1956) and winter survival of bumblebees will be adversely affected if hibernating conditions are too moist. Pouvreau (1970) found that excess moisture also increased the risk of infection by micro-organisms.

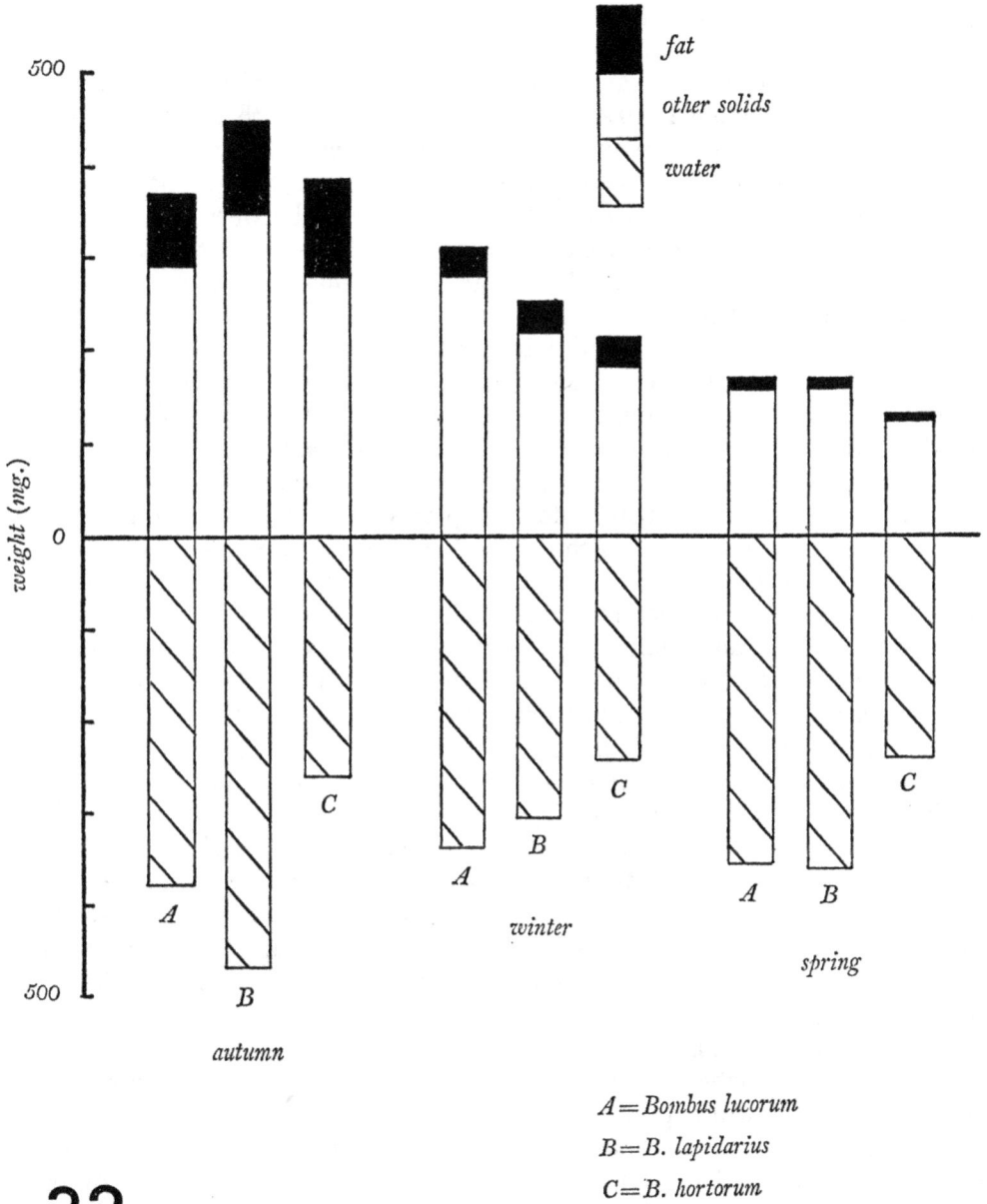

Fig. 32. Utilization of food reserves by overwintering bumblebee queens.

32

A = Bombus lucorum
B = B. lapidarius
C = B. hortorum

It is well-known that some species emerge from hibernation earlier in the spring than others. In the British Isles *B. jonellus*, *B. pratorum*, *B. lucorum* and *B. terrestris* are among the first species to make their appearance, and they are frequently seen in early March or even in late February. The emergence of bumblebees from hibernation is governed by temperature, so that in a late spring their arousal will be delayed. Both Siivonen (1942) and Stein (1956a) agree that from the time that the air temperature rises above freezing point, twenty-five to thirty days elapse before the emergence of *B. terrestris* queens. Stein found that ground temperatures (at a depth of 20 cm., but other details not given) were between 5° and 6°C. when *B. terrestris* queens emerged from hibernation, but 9°C. when the later-emerging species *B. lapidarius* appeared. Holm (1965) also investigated the emergence of *B. terrestris* and *B. lapidarius* queens, and found that in general the latter species started to appear about one month later than the former. Holm also observed that most queens emerged between mid-morning and mid- to late afternoon, when soil temperatures were at their highest. Most queens appeared when soil temperatures at a depth of 4 to 12 cm. were between 10° and 16°C. Holm's results, however, led him to conclude that temperature was not the only factor involved.

It is frequently stated that different species of bumblebee require different temperatures to arouse them in the spring. However, the varying ecological conditions under which bumblebees hibernate, and any effect these might have on the influence of spring temperatures, are usually ignored. Results from temperature measurements in natural hibernation sites (Alford, 1969c) have indicated that, in early spring, hibernation chambers immediately below the soil-litter interface, close to trees, are subjected to higher daily maximum temperatures than are those formed directly in banks or slopes. It would appear to be of significance that early-emerging species such as *B. lucorum*, *B. terrestris* and *B. pratorum* overwinter in the former situations, which warm up more rapidly in spring, while certain later-emerging species, including *B. lapidarius*, *B. hortorum* and *Psithyrus* females, tend to occur in places which warm up more slowly. There is also evidence to indicate that later-emerging species tend to hibernate at greater depths than early-emerging species overwintering in similar sites. Ecological factors are obviously important, but this is not to say that specific differences in threshold temperatures for arousal can or should be ruled out.

It is unlikely that minimum or mean daily temperatures influence the time of emergence of bumblebees, since, as long as their hibernation quarters warm up sufficiently, queens will appear on warm days whether nights are cold or not. Also, even in mid-winter, queens may become active if warmed artificially. In support of this Soulié (1957) has shown that the hibernation of certain ants may be disrupted by frequently repeated temperature maxima and that neither mean nor minimum temperatures are involved.

Although the order of emergence of the various species of bumblebee tends to follow a given pattern, queens of normally late-appearing species sometimes become active very early in the spring and, conversely, individuals of early-appearing species may be considerably delayed in their emergence. By way of example, in his greenhouse-based studies Holm (1965) found in one season that *B. terrestris* queens emerged from 14 February to 8 June, and *B. lapidarius* queens from 22 March to 3 June. Variation within a species may be due to several factors. Queens hibernating in light, sandy, and hence warmer soil, for example, will probably tend to be aroused earlier than those hibernating under similar situations but in damper, heavier and cooler soil. However, as bumblebees seem to hibernate at greater depths in a light, as opposed to a heavy soil, this will inevitably reduce the potential effect of different soil conditions on spring emergence. Nevertheless, the relative exposure of hibernacula, coupled with the effects of local topographical features on spring ambient temperatures, must greatly influence spring emergence. Bols (1939) found that many queens arriving at hibernation sites late in the autumn could only dig shallow hibernacula; such individuals, if they can survive the winter, are likely to emerge well ahead of individuals overwintering at more normal depths.

Observations by Latter (cited by Fox Wilson, 1946) have suggested that light penetrating into the hibernaculum may be effective in arousing hibernating wasps. Most bumblebees, however, hibernate in the dark and will not be affected by light, although it has been suggested that in the case of bumblebees the number of hours of sunshine has some influence (Holm, 1960; Holm & Haas, 1961). A temperature-aroused bumblebee in a natural hibernaculum in the soil will be subjected to the influence of light and other factors, including rain, just prior to its final emergence from the ground, but whether bumblebees remain *in situ* under warm, but otherwise inclement, conditions is not known.

CHAPTER 3

Colony Initiation

THE first appearance of bumblebees in spring, like that of many solitary bees (Dylewska, 1962), tends to coincide with the flowering of willows (*Salix*). In Britain, catkins of several species, including pussy willow (*Salix caprea*) and common sallow (*Salix atrocinerea*), are important sources of nectar (male catkins are also excellent producers of pollen), and large numbers of overwintered queens may be attracted to them. Scarcity of spring forage has a deleterious effect on the survival of overwintered queens (Bohart & Knowelton, 1953), for it is essential that they are able to obtain adequate supplies of both nectar and pollen. Fye & Medler (1954a) considered that the most attractive areas for maintaining bumblebee populations were those with a good succession of spring flowers.

From the time of their emergence from hibernation to the formation of their nests, queens pass nights, or periods of inclement weather, beneath vegetation in the vicinity of their food plants (Cumber, 1953). Queens seek sheltered situations, especially to avoid the dangers of a night frost, but they do not normally burrow into the soil; nor do they attempt to find, or habitually return to, special sites each night, so that once a queen has flown from her overwintering site she does not usually return to it. This is not necessarily true, however, of individuals parasitized by the nematode *Sphaerularia bombi*. The important post-hibernation changes in host behaviour, brought about by the presence of this parasite, will be described and discussed in detail later (Chapter 8).

In a healthy queen (one not parasitized by *Sphaerularia bombi*) the corpora allata become active during the winter period, and secretion of gonadotrophic hormones is then stimulated (Palm, 1948). However, at the time of emergence from hibernation the ovaries are still small and thread-like, but with post-emergence feeding (activity may also be important) they enlarge rapidly. In spring, queens consume considerable quantities of pollen, and without this essential source of protein their ovaries would fail to develop.

Whilst their ovaries are still small, overwintered queens spend much of their time actively flying or foraging; they may also be seen sunning themselves on vegetation, rocks, and other objects. However, once the ovarioles contain conspicuous eggs and nurse cells (Fig. 21) (Cumber, 1954; Miyamoto, 1960) the queens begin to search for nesting sites. In their quest for a suitable nesting place queens diligently explore likely-looking clumps of vegetation or holes in the ground, and they may often be seen busily examining banks, hedgerows, dykes and tracts of rough ground. Details of the searching behaviour of bumblebees vary from species to species (Jordan, 1936a). Surface-nesting species, when in likely-looking terrain (such as rough and tussocky grassland) will repeatedly drop to the ground and fly up again, landing at frequent intervals and then forcing their way into the herbage in search of a suitable place to establish a nest. Underground-nesting species tend to have a faster, more looping flight pattern. They frequently hover over holes in the ground, tacking back and forth, before landing and investigating more thoroughly. Queens may disappear into the ground for several minutes before reappearing and, if unsuccessful, continuing their search elsewhere. As well as examining obvious holes and cracks in banks, walls, and other places, queens of underground-nesting species will also crawl beneath herbage in search of possible entrances to subterranean cavities where nest establishment might be possible. It may take a queen anything from a few days to several weeks to find a suitable site.

A bumblebee nest site must give adequate protection against inclement weather and there must be an available supply of fine material, such as grass, hair, leaves and moss, which the overwintered queen can form into a nest. The vast majority of bumblebee colonies are established in disused nests of small mammals like mice, voles and shrews. Less frequently, birds' nests are utilized and also, on occasions, squirrels' dreys, hedgehogs' nests, and so on. Unlike certain wasps and bees, bumblebees do not forage for nesting material;[1] nor do they burrow into the soil to excavate nest chambers. Occasionally, however, if there is a sufficient and conveniently placed supply of moss, loose grass, or other suitable material, on the surface of the ground, queens of some species (for example, *Bombus pratorum*, *B. muscorum*, and *B. pascuorum*) will form this into a nest. Surface-nesting species often establish their colonies on grassy or mossy banks, and in vegetation at the base of walls; also, their nests are often common in undisturbed open ground where grass forms dense tussocks and where there is a readily available supply of disused mouse or vole nests. Underground-nesting species often rely upon finding abandoned, subterranean nests of small mammals. These are usually located by way of existing underground cracks, crevices or tunnels, a few centimetres to a metre or more in length. Bumblebee nests (unlike their hibernation quarters) are often established in sunny places; wet ground is usually unsuitable, although some species (*B. muscorum* and *B. ruderarius*, for example) seem to be more tolerant of damp conditions than others.

Having selected a suitable nesting place the queen busies herself with manipulating the available nest material. At its centre she forms a tighter-knit mass about the size of a tennis ball which encloses a snug cavity, about 25 to 30 mm. across and 18 mm. high (Fig. 33). This chamber is lined with the finest of the nest material. A small entrance tunnel, leading into the central chamber, is formed, through which the queen is able to pass when entering or leaving. Should the nest material be damp (this is frequently the case with surface nests) it will soon be dried out by the warmth given off by the queen's body.

When a queen leaves her nest site for the first time she carefully orientates to

[1] But see pp. 69 and 167.

its position, rising slowly into the air and flying in ever increasing circles, whilst facing towards the position of the nest, or tunnel, entrance. This procedure is repeated on subsequent occasions, but to a lesser extent, until, finally, she is sufficiently aware of its position that further orientation flights are unnecessary.

The queen soon brings back a supply of nectar in her crop, and some of this may then be daubed on to the innermost strands of nest material. If this nectar is not used as food it dries and helps bind the nest material more firmly together. This probably also improves the insulating properties of the nest material. As a consequence of physiological changes, and of the considerable quantities of nectar consumed, a queen's wax glands develop and wax is secreted, most noticeably

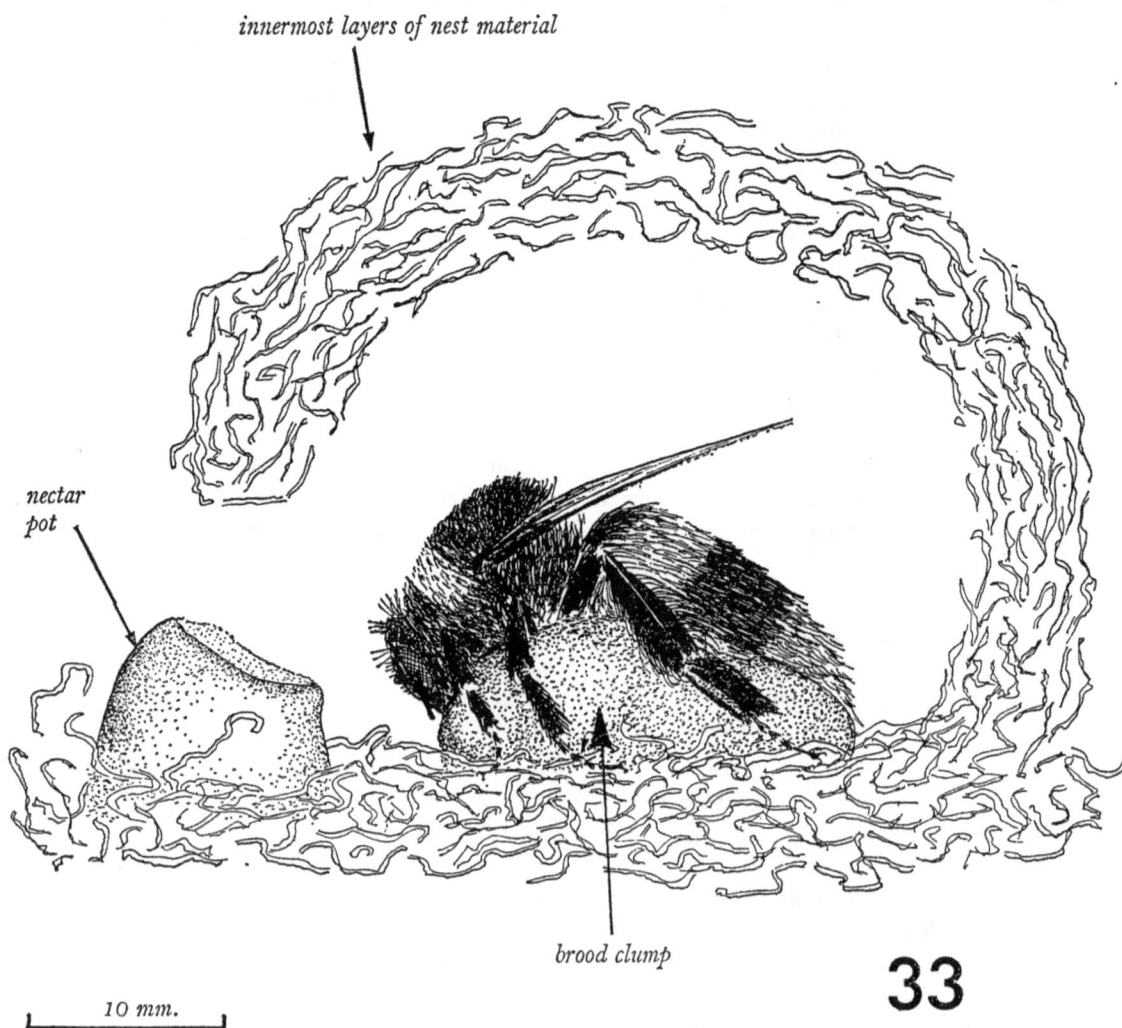

innermost layers of nest material

nectar pot

brood clump

33

10 mm.

Fig. 33. Section through nest showing *Bombus terrestris* queen incubating her incipient brood clump.

from the dorsal half of the abdomen. Röseler (1967a) found that pollen in the diet was also necessary for wax gland development.

Once the nest is prepared, the foundress queen forages and collects some pollen. This is carried back to the nest in the corbicula ('pollen-baskets') on the hind legs and deposited on the floor at the centre of the inner chamber. The queen then moulds the pollen lump with her mandibles. A queen may make several foraging excursions before sufficient pollen is collected, but egg-laying usually begins before the pollen lump is completed. Many species form a cushion of pollen within which they make several cavities or pockets. Eggs are deposited, more or less vertically, within the pollen lump, one per cavity. Some bumblebees, however, including species of the subgenus *Thoracobombus* (and, according to Hobbs [1964a,

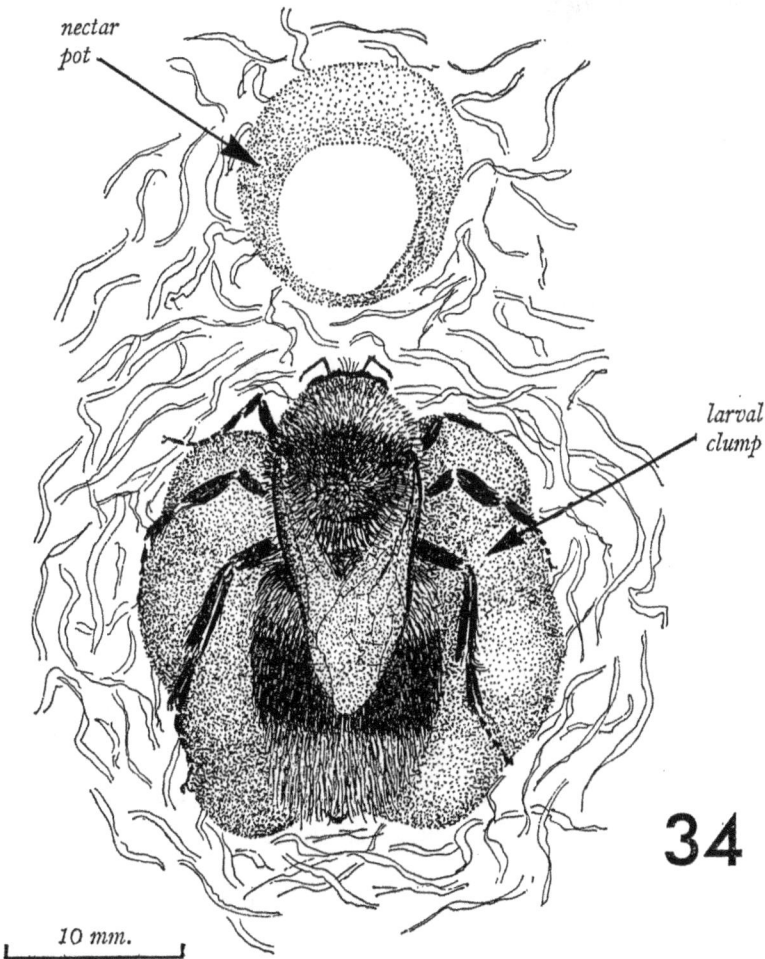

nectar pot

larval clump

34

10 mm.

Fig. 34. *Bombus terrestris* queen incubating her incipient brood clump.

1964b], the Canadian species *B. balteatus* [*Alpinobombus*]) place their eggs, vertically, around the outside of the pollen lump which forms a four-sided pyramid (Alford, 1970a). When eggs are laid within the pollen lump the queen immediately covers them over with additional pollen, which she packs tightly around them on all sides; Rau (1941) found that eggs of *B. americanorum* were so firmly embedded in the pollen that a needle was required to extricate them. The outside of the egg clump is covered with a wax-pollen canopy; the appearance of the pollen and wax-pollen layer is frequently very similar, and care is needed to distinguish one from the other. The colour of an initial egg clump depends upon that of the pollen and wax forming the outer canopy. Most egg clumps are light or dark brown, but some may be reddish or orange-brown. Although clumps generally have a matt texture, some can be very shiny.

The number of eggs deposited in the initial egg clump varies from species to species and also, to some extent, from one individual queen to another. Less prolific species, including *B. humilis*, *B. pascuorum* and *B. ruderarius*, usually lay eight eggs (presumably one from each ovariole); up to sixteen (two from each ovariole) are laid by *B. terrestris* queens and by other prolific species.

The size and shape of a completed egg clump is partly governed by the number of eggs laid, but there are also important specific differences. Those of *B. pascuorum*, and other, similar species are usually cushion-shaped and measure about 6·5 by 6·0 mm. and are 3 mm. high, while those of *B. hortorum*, for example, are wedge-shaped and may reach 10 by 8 mm. with a maximum height of 10 mm. Even larger clumps are formed by some species. Completion of the initial egg clump, including egg-laying, may take the queen several days. It should be emphasized that under normal circumstances eggs of the first brood batch (unlike those of all subsequent batches) are not laid in pre-formed cells of wax; also, they are typically deposited more or less vertically, instead of horizontally, whether on the outside or within the pollen lump (see Hobbs, 1964b, 1965a, 1965b, 1966a, 1966b, 1967b, 1968; Alford, 1970a, 1971). Exceptions do, however, occur, especially in nest-boxes where queens are fed artificially (Plath, 1934; Alford, 1970a).

The arrangement of eggs in the incipient brood batch is frequently symmetrical. For example, where eight eggs are present (as in the case of *B. humilis*, *B. pascuorum* and *B. ruderarius*) they are typically arranged in three rows, a centre row of two eggs and two lateral rows of three eggs each. According to Hobbs this is also true of several Canadian species. This spatial arrangement of individuals is usually maintained during the subsequent development of the incipient brood batch (Figs. 35 to 38). One British species, *B. subterraneus*, is known to add further eggs to the initial batch (Sladen, 1912), but this behaviour is exceptional; the result, in the case of *B. subterraneus*, is a large, untidy brood clump. Observations on related species (Hobbs, 1966b) suggest that this is a common feature among members of the primitive subgenus *Subterraneobombus*.

In addition to forming a brood clump, the queen also constructs a thin-walled,

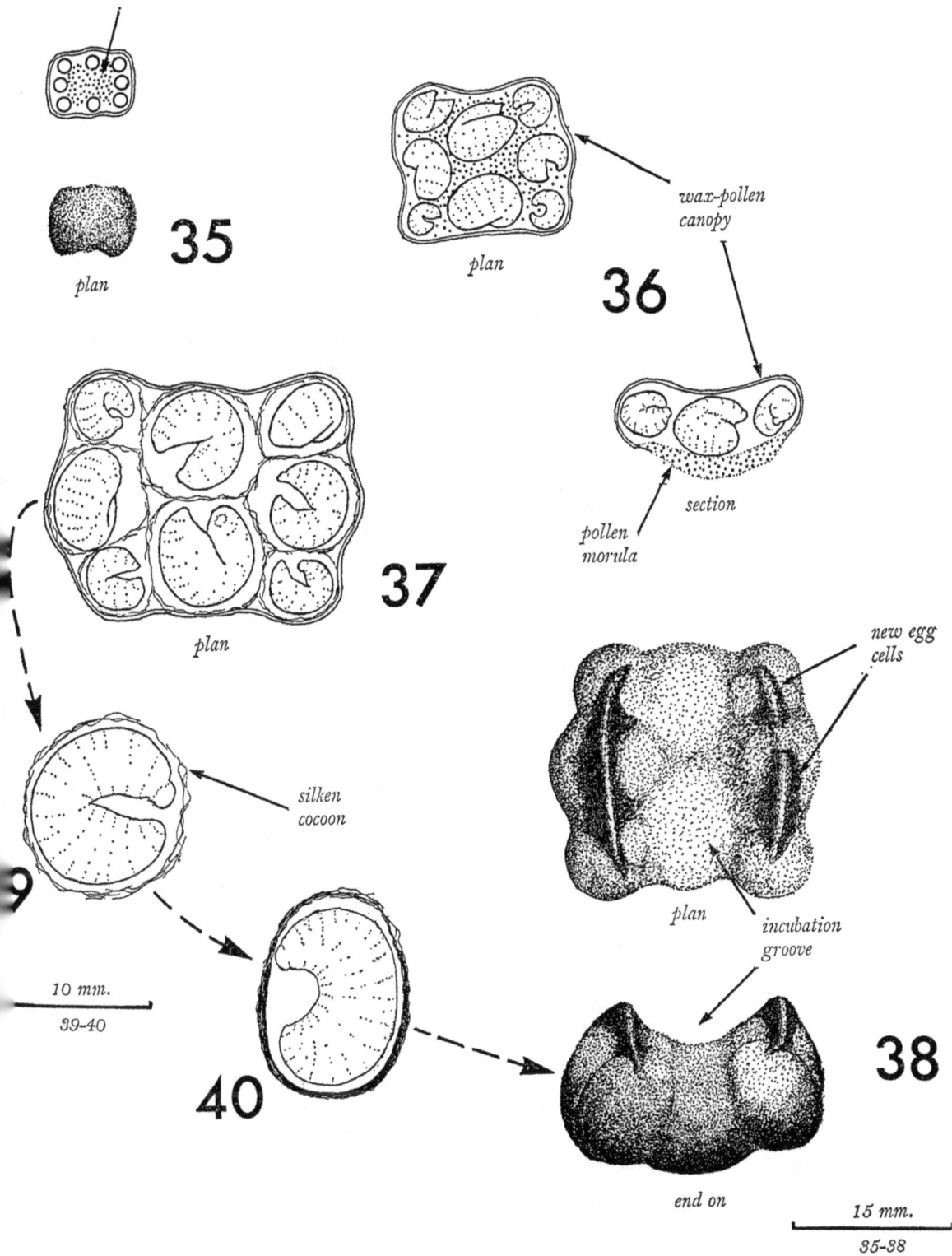

Figs. 35–40. Development of incipient brood clump of *Bombus pascuorum*. 35, egg clump; 36, young larval clump; 37, advanced larval clump; 38, pupal clump; 39, lateral aspect of fully fed larva; 40, larva entering pre-pupal stage, having spun final cocoon.

waxen pot for storing nectar. This structure, traditionally called the honey pot (but perhaps better termed a 'nectar pot' for it rarely, if ever, contains ripe honey), is built at the entrance to the inner nest chamber (Figs. 33, 34). As anticipated by Sladen, following his observations on colony establishment by queens of *B. lapidarius* and *B. hortorum*, most species begin to construct the nectar pot after initiating their egg clump. However, the reverse is true of a few species. Hobbs (1965a) found that ten out of eleven queens of *B. auricomus* and *B. nevadensis* began to build nectar pots before starting their brood clumps. Løken (1961) and Johansen (1967) also record species in which nectar pot construction begins first.

The nectar pot varies in appearance from species to species. Those of *B. pratorum*, for example, are very light in colour, while those of *B. hortorum*, *B. pascuorum*, and many other species, are yellowish or brownish. Pollen is not usually incorporated into the wax forming the walls of the nectar pot (Hoffer, 1882–3; Wagner, 1907), so these colour variations are largely, if not entirely, due to differences in the wax. A typical nectar pot measures approximately 15 mm. at its widest diameter and is 15 to 20 mm. high; they are described by Sladen as being 'capable of holding nearly a thimbleful of honey'. During favourable weather the queen collects sufficient nectar to fill the pot. This food reserve is used, if need be, during the night and day, and is especially useful during bad weather, when the queen is unable to forage. The mouth of the pot is constantly altered by the queen, and is widest when the nectar level is low. Plath (1934) mentioned that a *B. separatus* queen built a double nectar pot.

Once the eggs hatch, the resulting larvae feed on the initial pollen lump, and soon, whether originally in separate parts of the pollen lump or not, they come to share a common cavity below the wax-pollen canopy (Fig. 36). The original food supply is soon exhausted and so the foundress queen must immediately collect more pollen. In pocket-making species, the larvae are supplied with pollen via two 'pockets' which the queen constructs below, and at either side of, the brood clump. The pollen is then forced below the larvae, as and when it is collected, so that they come to lie upon a mushroom-like cushion of pollen (Fig. 36). In the later stages of development, larvae may also be fed on a mixture of pollen and nectar, regurgitated to them through temporary holes made by the queen in the wax-pollen envelope.[1] As pointed out by Hobbs (1967b) the forcing of pollen beneath the clump pushes up the sides in relation to the middle, thus contributing to the presence of a median groove (see below). Although at the earliest stages of development of the initial brood clump, larvae of pollen-storers also feed directly on pollen, most if not all subsequent feeding is by regurgitation. In the case of pollen-storers, pellets of pollen may be placed around the periphery of the young brood clump, to be used later for personal consumption by the queen, or for feeding to the larvae.

When not foraging, or performing other duties, the queen lies over her brood

---

[1] This liquid food, mixed in the crop, is squirted into the cluster of larvae by several rapid contractions of the queen's abdomen.

clump, usually facing towards the nest entrance and nectar pot, with her legs spread out and her abdomen flattened and distended (Figs. 33, 34). The depression over the top of the clump, in which the queen lies, is termed the incubation groove. Almost invariably this is formed in line with the nectar pot and nest entrance. In some instances (for example, clumps of *B. hortorum*) a depression is present over the clump from the outset; in other cases, however, an incubation groove may not become obvious until later. It is usually most in evidence at the pupal stage (Fig. 38). An incubating queen presses her body firmly against the brood clump and performs rapid and rhythmic respiratory movements (obvious as alternate expansions and contractions of the abdomen). Heat, produced in the thorax and transferred to the abdomen in the blood, is then conducted to the clump via the more or less hairless underside of the abdomen. In this way a queen significantly increases the temperature of the brood, which is maintained at or about 30° to 32°C. (Heinrich, 1972d). Heat loss from the upper parts of the queen's body is greatly reduced by the coat or pile, which acts as an insulating layer. Heinrich (1972c) has recently shown that a 'broody' overwintered queen (that is, one physiologically ready to care for a batch of brood), whether or not in the presence of brood, maintains a thoracic temperature of between 37·4° and 38·8°C. more or less continuously, during the day and night. In contrast, the body temperature of a queen which is not broody approaches ambience, except during periods of activity.

The duration of the various developmental stages of bumblebees (egg, larva, pupa) varies according to temperature, and possibly differs from species to species. Larval development is probably also affected by factors such as the quality and quantity of the food supplied. On average, eggs take about five days to hatch, larvae feed for approximately fourteen days, and development within the pupa lasts for a further fourteen days, so that roughly five weeks elapse from the time an egg is laid until an adult bee emerges. The total period of development, however, may be reduced to three weeks or, particularly as a result of delay in the pupal stage, may be extended to seven weeks.

As the larvae grow the incipient brood clump expands, both upwards and outwards, and the foundress queen must add more wax-pollen to the canopy for the cluster of brood to remain covered. The larvae adopt a typical C-shaped posture and the position of each, below the canopy, becomes noticeable externally as a slight swelling; this is particularly so in the later stages of development. The centre-most larvae tend to be larger and more advanced than the others (Fig. 36).

Once larvae enter the fourth and final instar they spin loose, flimsy cocoons of silk (Sladen, 1912; Frison, 1928, 1929, 1930a) (Fig. 39) and so become separated from each other (Fig. 37). During this instar, larvae grow considerably and very rapidly. Throughout the feeding period the gut of the larva has been blocked by cells, but towards the end of the final instar these break down, allowing waste matter to flow into the rectum, finally to be voided through the anus. When full-grown each larva spins a yellowish, paper-like cocoon. Faeces are smeared over the walls, mainly at the sides and base, which in consequence become stained reddish brown. The larva then adopts a more or less upright stance, forcing the cocoon to become oval and elongated (Fig. 40). Finally, the walls of the cocoon, including the deposited faeces, dry and harden to form a tough case within which the larva eventually pupates. When the larvae are forming their pupal cocoons, or just before, the foundress queen removes the wax-pollen covering from the top of each and uses this for constructing egg cells of the second and third brood

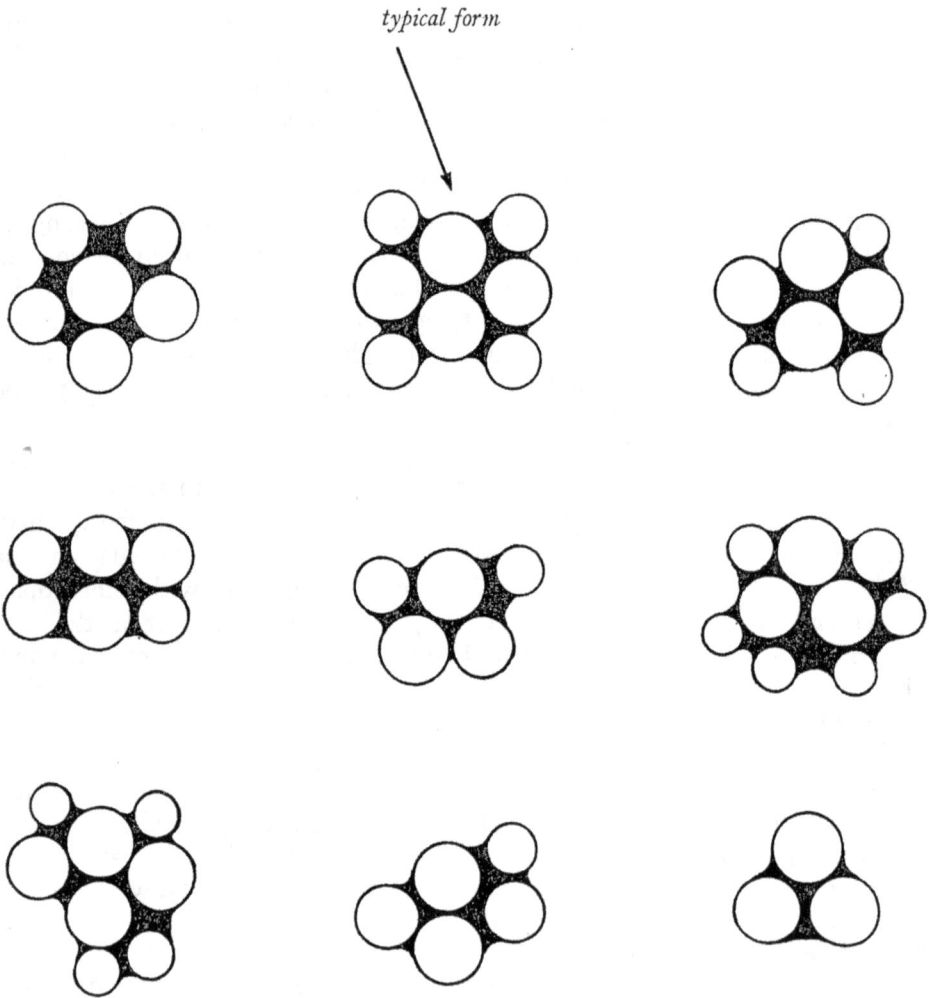

typical form

41

Fig. 41. Arrangement of pupal cocoons in incipient brood clumps of *Bombus pascuorum*.

batches. In most species, these are built in two more or less complete and parallel rows on top of the pupal cocoons, along either side of the incubation groove. The lateral cocoons of an incipient pupal clump are inclined inward, so that the post-incipient egg cells along the lateral crests of the clump do not impede the emergence of adult bees yet to complete their development (Fig. 38).

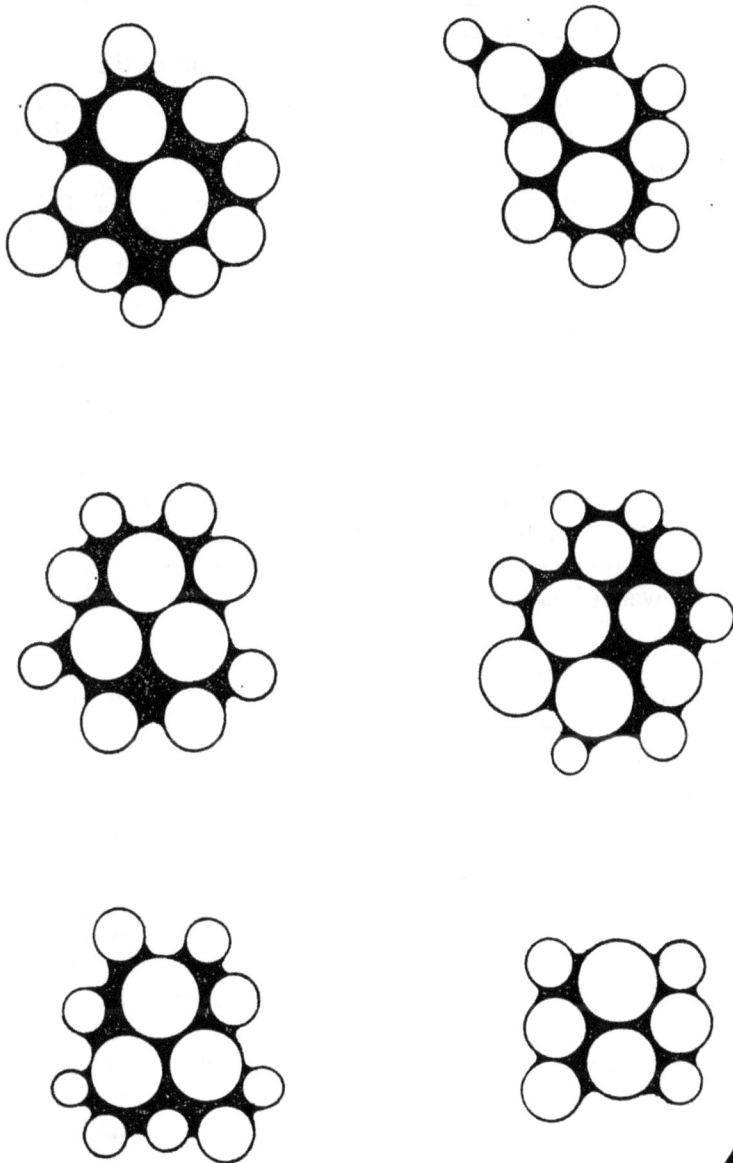

42

Fig. 42. Arrangement of pupal cocoons in incipient brood clumps of *Bombus hortorum.*

The incipient pupal clump is a compact structure, with the cocoons firmly stuck together. It may be handled without breaking, although care must be taken not to crush the less durable, lighter-coloured, paper-like tops of the cocoons, through which the adult bumblebees will eventually make their escape. As previously indicated, the spatial arrangement of individuals in the clump is similar to that found at both the egg and larval stage. In clumps of *B. pascuorum*, *B. ruderarius*, and some other species, there are typically two large cocoons immediately below the incubation groove, two large cocoons on either side of these and four smaller cocoons at each corner (Fig. 41). Comparable symmetry about the axis of the incubation groove also occurs when either fewer or more than eight cocoons are present, and is typical of most species (e.g. Fig. 42).

Approximately four to five weeks after the initial egg clump was formed by the queen, the first adult bumblebees make their appearance. All emerge over a period of two to five days, although if the clump is a large one, with many individuals, the period of emergence may be extended. All adults in the first brood batch are workers; occasionally a male is produced, but this is abnormal. After shedding its pupal skin a young bumblebee must escape from its cocoon by biting through the top, and in this task it is frequently helped by the queen or any workers that have already emerged. A bumblebee generally makes several attempts to force its way out of the cocoon before the hole is finally large enough for it to struggle through. As soon as the bee emerges, she cleans her legs and antennae, removing any remaining pieces of the pupal skin. She then moves unsteadily to the nectar pot and drinks some of the food before returning to the brood clump and nestling down against the warm body of the queen. A newly-emerged adult is silvery grey in colour; the coat is damp and the hairs are matted together and flattened down against the body. The recently expanded wings are soft and curved down over the abdomen, but within a day or so they become hardened and functional. After several hours the pile dries out, and the true adult coat colour patterns are acquired. Except for their much smaller size, the workers are usually identical in appearance to the mother queen.

The first adults produced in an incipient colony emerge from the cocoons immediately below the incubation groove. It is frequently stated that this is because the warmth of the incubating queen's body has enabled the centrally-placed members of the brood batch to develop most rapidly; however, it is also true that, in many cases, the individuals at the centre have resulted from the first eggs laid in the brood clump (Hobbs, 1965a; Alford, 1970a, 1970b). The last adults to appear usually emerge from cocoons at the extreme periphery of the clump. These bees are frequently very small, and many have crippled wings so they are never able to fly. A gradation in the body size of individuals from incipient (and subsequent) brood batches is typical of bumblebee colonies. In the case of *B. pascuorum* (Alford, 1970b), and also other species, it is often possible to distinguish two groups of first-brood adults, the earlier-emerging and larger bees, reared from the central cocoons, and the later-emerging and smaller bees, reared from the peripheral cocoons. It is suggested that this subdivision enables a division of labour to be established within the worker force of the colony from the outset, and this aspect of bumblebee behaviour will be considered more fully later (Chapter 4).

In contrast with post-incipient brood clumps, mortality of individuals in the first brood batch is low, and a queen usually succeeds in rearing adults from all of the eggs in her first batch. If the weather is unfavourable during the period of brood-rearing the resultant first-brood adults may be smaller than normal, but poor conditions do not normally result in brood losses (Hobbs, 1967b); the same is true of incipient colonies headed by debilitated foundress queens (Alford, 1968).

With the appearance of her first workers, the long, solitary existence of the foundress queen (that has lasted since she left her maternal colony in the previous season) is at an end, and a new bumblebee colony, as a true social unit, is at last established.

CHAPTER 4

Life in the Colony

AS already mentioned, the foundress queen of a young colony begins to construct egg cells of her second and third brood batches when the first-brood larvae cease feeding and spin their pupal cocoons. These cells typically form two more or less complete, elevated series along either side of the incubation groove, although when this is ill-defined, as is the case in incipient pupal clumps of *B. subterraneus*, they are arranged towards the periphery of the clump and do not then form distinct ridges. There are usually from two to six eggs in each second or third-brood egg cell, the number varying somewhat from species to species. Further egg cells are built by the queen as and when the larvae of second and subsequent brood batches become full-grown and pupate. These cells are constructed either at the junction of two or more cocoons (as in *B. pascuorum*) or directly on top of individual cocoons (typical of *B. lapidarius*), and are so placed as to avoid blocking the escape of the future adult bees from within the underlying cocoons. Brian (1951a) found that queens of *B. pascuorum* constructed their egg cells on batches of newly formed pupal cocoons or, if these were not present, on the youngest cocoons available.

When forming an egg cell the queen makes an oval-shaped foundation wall of wax-pollen about 4 mm. high, enclosing an area of approximately 4 by 6 mm., the floor of which is formed by the outer layers of the pupal cocoon or cocoons upon which the cell is built. When ready to begin egg-laying the queen lowers the tip of her abdomen into the egg cell, grasping the walls with her hind pair of legs. During the ensuing few minutes she usually deposits several eggs, and each time an egg is laid the queen's sting is protruded through, or thrust just over, the wall of the cell. When egg-laying is completed the queen immediately seals over the cell. Eggs of the second and all subsequent brood batches are deposited more or less horizontally and usually form a cluster lying directly on the floor of the cell.[1] However, queens of some species, notably *B. hortorum* and *B. ruderatus* (subgenus *Megabombus*) place a small quantity of pollen in the bottom of each egg cell before laying their eggs. These two species were classified by Sladen (1912) as 'pollen-primers' (see Chapter 9). Sladen observed that *B. subterraneus* queens would also prime their egg cells with pollen, and Hobbs (1966b) has since found this to be a consistent habit among Canadian species of the subgenus *Subterraneobombus*. Egg cells of species belonging to the subgenus *Pyrobombus* are also, if not always, primed

---

[1] The Nearctic species *B. auricomus* (subgenus *Bombias*) is unusual in that only one egg is laid per cell (Hobbs, 1965a) and the larvae remain isolated from one another throughout their development (Frison, 1917, 1918).

with pollen (Plath, 1934; Hobbs, 1964a, 1967b; Johansen, 1967). Of the British species in this group, *B. pratorum* is known to adopt this method; the pollen-priming habit is probably shared by both *B. jonellus* and *B. lapponicus* but, as far as I am aware, this has never been substantiated. The priming of egg cells with pollen is reminiscent of the brood-rearing method adopted by most non-social bees and is usually regarded as primitive.[1] Hobbs has suggested that the pollen-priming habit in the subgenus *Pyrobombus* may represent a link between the primitive ('pocket-maker') and more advanced ('pollen-storer') bumblebee groups (see Chapter 9).

In advance of the emergence of the first-brood adults the queen will usually have begun feeding the larvae of her second and possibly even the third brood batch, but soon worker bees are available to help in the various household and foraging duties. Workers, however, do not assist queens in constructing egg cells. The queen may continue to forage whilst her first-brood adults are still emerging, but soon she will be relieved of this hazardous occupation. She is then able to remain full-time within the comparative shelter and safety of the nest and can rely on her workers for the collection and maintenance of the colony's food supplies.

The second, and subsequent, brood batches in a bumblebee colony, unlike the first, develop without the presence of incubation grooves. Each larval clump gradually swells, but remains covered by a more or less continuous wax-pollen canopy which is enlarged by the worker bees as the larvae increase in size. Depending upon the species, the common canopy may or may not be retained after the larvae enter the fourth instar and spin their individual, flimsy, silken cocoons.

In pocket-makers (*Odontobombus*, see Chapter 9) the wax-pollen canopy enclosing a group of young larvae is moulded below one side to form a bottomless, cup-like receptacle into which pollen, collected by the foragers, is deposited. This pollen, moistened with nectar or honey, is then forced under the larval clump so that the larvae, as in an incipient brood clump, come to lie above a mushroom-like morula of food (Fig. 36). This food mass is thicker in the centre than at the edges, and consequently larvae towards the middle of the brood cluster will tend to be more favourably placed to obtain food than those at the periphery. There is usually one pollen pocket per larval clump, but there may sometimes be two or even more. When larvae within a brood clump cease feeding the pollen pocket or pockets are broken down.

Pollen-storers (*Anodontobombus*, see Chapter 9) do not construct pollen pockets and, apart from the first brood batch reared by the queen at the commencement of colony development (and excluding any pollen used to prime post-incipient egg cells – subgenus *Pyrobombus*), their larvae are fed on nectar (or honey) and pollen

---

[1] Females of non-social bees provision their brood cells with pollen moistened with nectar and lay one egg in each before finally sealing them. The resulting larvae then complete their development in isolation, and rely entirely upon the original food supply to sustain them. This method of brood-rearing is termed 'mass-provisioning'. Larvae of most allodapine bees, which are primitively social (see Michener, 1971), bumblebees and honey bees, however, continue to receive food after they have hatched from the egg. This more advanced method of brood-rearing is termed 'progressive feeding'.

regurgitated by the nurse bees. This food is usually supplied as a mixture, but honey may be provided separately and daubed, as droplets, on the inner walls of the larval cocoon or wax-pollen canopy (Rau, 1924). Some observers (e.g. Wagner, 1907; Hobbs, 1966a) have seen nurse bees extending their tongues when supplying food to larvae. However, according to Sakagami & Zucchi (1965) and Katayama (1973) food is passed to the larvae between the bees' mandibles, with their tongues remaining folded. It should be emphasized that although the regurgitated food may be placed directly on to the body of a larvae, mouth to mouth food transfer does not take place. During the early larval instars this regurgitated food is received through the common wax-pollen canopy. Later, however, when larvae have spun their individual cocoons, members of the brood batch are fed individually. Each fourth-instar larva is typically surrounded by a loose fabric of silk, which is itself covered over by a thin layer of wax-pollen. This wax-pollen envelope is usually incomplete at the sides, and it is through these gaps, where the silken cocoon is also more or less wanting, that the nurse bees inject food.

The build-up of workers in a bumblebee colony is at first slow, but their numbers increase rapidly during the expansive period of colony development. As the worker population grows the economy of the colony is increased and more food is then available for feeding larvae; also, nest conditions become stabilized and the colony approaches the climax of its development, culminating in the production of males and young queens (Chapter 5). The number of eggs laid in an egg cell tends, at least is some species, to be related to the number of pupae present in the brood clump (Brian & Brian, 1948; Brian, 1951a), and as brood numbers increase there will be a corresponding increase in the number of eggs laid by the queen.

From the work of several investigators it is clear that many more eggs are laid in a bumblebee colony than will attain the adult stage. Data provided by Cumber (1949a) and Brian (1951a), for example, show that only about one third of the queen's eggs will be reared through to adults. Most brood mortality occurs during the egg or very early larval stages. Brian has suggested that cannibalism may sometimes be responsible for early brood losses, but this has not been substantiated. I was never able to induce cannibalism in laboratory *in vitro* cultures of eggs and larvae (starving or otherwise) of *B. lucorum*, *B. terrestris*, *B. pratorum* or *B. pascuorum*, but more evidence is needed. Worker bumblebees are known to eat eggs; this distinctive behaviour is considered later (p. 67).

In large colonies (for example, prolific colonies of *B. lucorum*, *B. magnus*, *B. terrestris* and *B. lapidarius*) several hundred workers may be produced, but they will not all be alive at the same time. Workers can live for about two months, and sometimes even longer, but their longevity varies according to the duties they perform, house-bees tending to live longer than foragers. In a poor season the average life span of a large number of workers in a colony may be reduced to about three weeks (Brian, 1952).

A prolific bumblebee colony may be able to produce two hundred or more males and young queens, but far fewer are reared in colonies of less productive species, where the total worker force may be well below one hundred individuals. Bumblebee colonies in the tropics, by comparison, can contain over 2,000 workers (Michener & Laberge, 1954), and Dias (1958) has reported that in Brazil nests of *B. incarum* may produce as many as 2,500 males and young queens. Associated with this greater productivity, nests are apparently scarce. The production of males and young queens will be considered in the following chapter.

It is generally accepted that workers of pocket-making species tend to be more variable in size than those produced by pollen-storers, and this difference is usually associated with the distinctive methods of larval nutrition adopted by these two groups. Size variation within brood batches of pocket-makers is thought to be due primarily to the uneven distribution of food supplies within a brood clump and also to larval competition (von Buttel-Reepen, 1903; Sladen, 1912; Cumber, 1949a). However, Plowright & Jay (1968) found that, under laboratory conditions, when nurse bees of pocket-makers were forced to feed their worker larvae solely by regurgitation, the resulting adults from any one brood batch still exhibited considerable size variation; this would seem to suggest that there are 'differences in the physiological mechanisms which control larval growth'.

Frison (1927a) believed that the average size of the workers reared in a bumblebee colony increased as the season progressed, but quantitative data on this subject were not produced until Richards (1946) measured the size of workers in three colonies of *B. pascuorum*. He found that specimens with a more worn appearance (considered to be older bees) tended to be smaller than those with fresh coats (considered to be younger bees), which supported Frison's hypothesis. On the other hand, data obtained by Cumber (1949a), for the same species, led him to conclude that there was no seasonal increase in mean body size of the workers. Brian (1951a) also failed to demonstrate an increasing size for *B. pascuorum* workers produced in successive brood batches. The methods adopted by these investigators, however, are subject to certain errors or variations in interpretation (Free & Butler, 1959). It is, therefore, difficult to draw firm conclusions from their results. More recently, Knee & Medler (1965a) concluded that three North American species of bumblebee tended to produce larger workers in consecutive brood batches, but their data only demonstrate significant increases late in the season. More positively, Röseler (1970) found that there was a general seasonal increase in the size of workers produced in a *B. terrestris* colony, although at the start of the season there was a decline in mean body size. Plowright & Jay (1968) obtained information showing that there was a seasonal increase in the mean body size of workers produced by some species but not by others. Cumber has pointed out that (in both pocket-makers and pollen-storers) as the season advances there is a rise in the number of small workers produced in colonies, and although larger workers are produced during the summer months than earlier in the season, the mean size of individuals may not necessarily increase. The phenomenon could also be masked or upset by factors, such as poor weather conditions, affecting the normal pattern of colony development.

In most nests of pocket-makers it is possible to identify individual brood clumps since the larvae from one egg batch keep together throughout their development. Also, at the pupal stage, the cocoons tend to remain firmly attached to one another. In nests of pollen-storers, however, it is frequently impossible to determine which brood members are from the same egg batch, for there may be only partial attachment of adjacent cocoons and larvae from a single brood batch tend to become dissociated. This situation is typical of *B. lucorum* and *B. terrestris* brood combs, where the individual pupal cocoons are readily separated.

Most pupal cocoons are directed more or less upwards. However, in order that adult bees can eventually escape, it may be necessary for cocoons at the periphery or base of a brood clump to lie horizontally. In severely confined nesting spaces, such as a small underground cavity or a bird-box, cocoons within the brood comb may be orientated in all directions (Alford, 1973b).

In general terms a bumblebee comb develops upwards and outwards, becoming roughly hemispherical, but its precise form varies from species to species (e.g. Weyrauch, 1934). For example, that in a nest of *B. pascuorum* is usually composed of a peripheral ring of individual brood clumps at various stages of development, encircling a lower series of vacated cocoons also formed into distinct batches adjacent clumps of brood or old cocoons readily break away from each other, but in themselves they remain well cemented together. The comb in *B. sylvarum* is more compact and the separate brood clumps are firmly attached to one another (Wójtowski, 1963c) while, as first mentioned by Wagner (1907), *B. ruderarius* nests have their brood clumps arranged into several overlapping tiers. The combs of *B. hortorum*, *B. ruderatus* and *B. subterraneus* usually lack a definite structure; those of the latter species are poorly organized. Little or no precise structure is to be found in combs of *B. lucorum* or *B. terrestris*. However, those of *B. lapidarius* are usually well arranged and have a very attractive, clean appearance.

Workers in populous colonies of, for example, *B. lucorum*, *B. terrestris* and *B. lapidarius*, usually construct a thin wax-pollen ceiling over the top of their brood combs. These canopies are formed about a bee's-width above the comb and are supported in places by pillars of wax. In some cases, as in *B. lapidarius* nests (this species is a prolific producer of wax), a more or less complete canopy may be formed over the entire comb. Canopies are protective and help to stabilize humidity and temperature conditions within the nest (see below), but they are only rarely, if ever, found in nests of predominantly surface-nesting species.

Workers of underground nests may form a pseudo-nest of grass or moss at the entrance to the tunnel leading to their colony. Bumblebees may also camouflage nest entrances with soil or grass (Hobbs, 1967b, 1968). I once removed a large colony of *B. lucorum* from below the partly-earthen floor of a garden shed and left the pseudo-nest *in situ* at the original tunnel entrance. Some five or six days later, when this was re-examined, several workers were found in occupation; wax had been secreted and a few eggs laid. The pseudo-nest, in this instance, had been occupied by worker bees not collected when the colony was taken and a secondary, queenless colony had resulted. These workers eventually reared some male bumble-bees. Establishment of nests by workers has also been noted by Hobbs (1965a, 1965b). In normal colonies the ovaries of some workers may develop and these bumblebees may successfully construct egg cells and deposit eggs which, being unfertilized, will develop into males. However, while the queen remains dominant, all male brood in the colony will result from unfertilized eggs that she has laid. Egg-laying by workers will be considered later.

Colonies of *B. pascuorum* are probably the most long-lived of any British species. In southern England they are frequently founded in late April or early May and they continue in existence well into September, and sometimes later. Those of *B. sylvarum* are also among the last to die out, but they are established rather late in the season. *Bombus lucorum* and *B. terrestris* colonies, although often large, are usually at an end by mid- or late August, their development being rapid and covering a maximum period of about eighteen weeks. Some species, *B. pratorum*, *B. jonellus*, *B. hortorum* and *B. ruderarius*, for example, produce relatively small colonies that reach the peak of their development somewhat earlier in the year; this is particularly true of *B. jonellus* and *B. pratorum* (see Wójtowski, 1963a).

Typically, there is one generation of colonies in a season and the new, young queens, instead of attempting to found colonies, enter hibernation. However, at least two of our species, *B. jonellus* and *B. pratorum* (both subgenus *Pyrobombus*) seem to be partially double-brooded. Although these species normally complete their colony life cycle early in the summer, workers, males and young queens of both are often observed in September and even October. Alfken (1913) considered that in Germany *B. jonellus* had two generations in a season, and data provided posthumously by Meidell (1968) indicate that this is also the case in Norway. Hobbs (1967b) has recorded second-generation colony establishment by queens of two Canadian species of *Pyrobombus* (viz. *B. frigidus* and *B. bifarius nearcticus*). During the middle of July, 1971 I captured a fresh-looking fertilized female of *Psithyrus sylvestris* with developing ovaries. This was an exceptionally late date for an overwintered female of this inquiline species to still be flying, and raises the question of whether two generations of *P. sylvestris* (the hosts of which are *B. jonellus* and *B. pratorum*) could also occur. *Bombus hortorum* is another British species suspected of sometimes being double-brooded (Sladen, 1912).

In order that a young queen can initiate a colony, rather than enter hibernation, changes must take place in her physiology. The corpora allata must presumably become active so that hormones, stimulating or enabling the ovaries to develop, will be produced. Normally these physiological changes only occur during or following the period of winter inactivity, although ovaries of worker bumblebees will, of course, develop without this obligatory period of diapause. I have obtained successful ovarian development of fertilized, young *B. pratorum* queens by keeping them confined in nest-boxes with plenty of food, but the reasons for the change remained unexplained. It does not seem to be recorded whether young queens producing second generation colonies under natural conditions remain in their maternal nests or whether they establish completely new ones. I suspect that they stay in their original colonies, and this would seem to be supported by Milliron's (1971) isolated observation of young queens of *B. bimaculatus* (also subgenus *Pyrobombus*) 'provisioning a nearly-inactive parental nest, possibly with intent to start a second generation'.

Cocoons from which adults have emerged are never re-used for brood-rearing, but the bumblebees do store supplies of nectar or honey (and sometimes pollen) in them. Before placing food in an empty cocoon the worker bees will remove the remains of the old pupal skin and may, where necessary, line or repair it with wax. As a group, bumblebees are economical in their use of wax (Gontarski, 1940) and they continually re-use it; the disused comb in a nest is, in fact, mostly composed of the non-waxy remains of the cocoons formed by the larvae prior to pupation.

When vacated cocoons are used for storing food some wax may be added to the rims, thus increasing their capacity. As newer cocoons become available, the older ones may be emptied and, especially in large, subterranean nests where there may be little room for colony expansion, they may be broken down. In addition to using vacated cocoons some species, notably the pollen-storers, construct special waxen nectar pots, usually in groups of two or more, at the periphery of the brood comb. Sometimes the first series is formed over the top of the original nectar pot used during the incipient stages of the colony, but often this pot is abandoned, falls into disrepair and grows mouldy. Alternatively, the old nectar pot may be broken down and the wax re-used for other purposes. As pointed out by Sladen, the nectar in the specially-constructed pots is usually thin, showing that it is freshly gathered, and is used for virtually immediate consumption, while that in the cocoons may become a very thick honey, and would then only be used in an emergency. Cocoons containing thick honey may be sealed over with wax, and are usually found below the centre of the comb. If a colony's food reserves are large some of the nectar pots may also be filled to capacity and sealed.

Although young foundress queens of pollen-storers may accumulate several loads of pollen before the emergence of their first-brood adults, and place these around the periphery of the incipient brood clump, once workers emerge, the pollen may be kept, like nectar, in vacated pupal cocoons. In more advanced colonies, however, the pollen is stored in special waxen cylinders constructed within the brood nest.[1] If the colony is populous and prolific these pollen-storage cylinders may be very large and rise well above the level of the rest of the comb. Pocket-makers normally store their pollen in the pockets associated with the larval clumps, and a few species, including *B. pomorum*, produce pollen cylinders which they develop from modified pollen pockets (see Hobbs, 1966a). Foragers may continue

---

[1] Both Medler (1959) and Hobbs (1967b) have reported that *Bombus huntii* (subgenus *Pyrobombus*) will lay large numbers of eggs in the pollen kept in these storage vessels. Exceptionally, eggs have also been laid by pocket-makers directly into pollen pockets at the base of young larval clumps (Katayama, 1965, 1966).

to deposit pollen in pollen pockets even after the larvae in the brood clump have finished feeding, and this is consumed by adult bees when the pocket is eventually broken down (Katayama, 1966). However, when no suitable larval clumps are available, pollen may be placed in empty cocoons or special cells near the top of the brood mass. These stores are most frequently observed in colonies producing males and young queens, particularly towards the end of a colony's development when, with no more larvae to be fed, pollen will, nevertheless, still be required for the young adult bees.

The digestible part of pollen includes protein, fat and carbohydrate, but it is the protein which is most valuable, and indeed essential, to bumblebees. Nectar, on the other hand, is mainly a watery solution of various sugars (fructose, glucose and sucrose usually predominate), although it also contains small quantities of acids, salts, proteins, enzymes and other substances. The conversion of nectar into honey is accompanied by the inversion of much of the sucrose (a disaccharide sugar) into the two simpler monosaccharides fructose and glucose, and the reduction of its water content to approximately twenty per cent. Thick bumblebee honey may be as little as thirteen per cent water, or even less (Knee & Medler, 1965b). Enzymes, especially invertase (which is important for the breakdown of sucrose), are added to the nectar stores by bees as they feed or by those collecting and replenishing the nectar supplies in the colony. Manipulation of nectar, and evaporation of the water by using the tongue, is not practised by bumblebees; most, if not all, evaporation of water from nectar takes place within the storage vessels. Honey production in the bumblebee colony, therefore, is not the (teleologically-speaking) deliberate process known in the advanced honey bee society.

Maurizio (1964) examined the honey of several bumblebee species and found that, in many cases, it had a high fructose content, and contained considerably less glucose and sucrose than honey produced by honey bees. Pollen from several different plant species may occur in a sample of bumblebee honey but, as noted by Faegri (1961), the dominant species of pollen may not be the same as that predominating in the colony's pollen stores.

In bumblebee colonies there is usually no direct food exchange between the adult bees, although investigations with radio-active tracers have indicated that an indirect trophallaxis occurs via the nectar pots (Lecompte, 1963; Lecompte & Pouvreau, 1968). The foundress queen, and also other bees, may feed on pollen in the corbicula of foragers recently returned from the field; also, foragers will sometimes disgorge nectar if molested by workers guarding the nest entrance, and this will be licked up by the attackers (Brian, 1952; Free, 1955e). Normally, however, food is obtained directly from the colony's food stores. Honey or nectar stores in a colony are usually at their largest at the climax of colony development. Brian (1954) found that in certain colonies food stores may be depleted overnight, and that during a protracted period of bad weather they may prove insufficient to sustain the colony. This is unlikely to happen, however, in successful colonies with a high level of economy.

So long as nectar or honey, which the adult bees can utilize as fuel for heat production, is available temperatures within nests can be regulated. If without food,
bees cease incubating, and nest temperatures, including that of the brood, inevitably
decline (see Heinrich, 1972c). It appears that optimum brood-nest temperatures
range from about 30° to 32°C. Brood development is retarded by low temperatures
(Himmer, 1927, 1932; Plath, 1934; Jordan, 1936b), so that maintenance of an
adequate temperature throughout the day and night is essential; according to
Eugène (1957) 10°C. is the critical level for larva survival. During the early stages
of colony development nest temperatures are unstable and tend to fluctuate according
to ambient conditions, but as the worker population increases a point is reached at
which they become independent of external values. Although during the early part
of colony development nest temperatures may fluctuate widely this may not greatly
affect the brood, as Fye & Medler (1954c) have shown that its temperature can be
controlled effectively by only a few bees. The greatest differences between external
and internal nest temperatures usually occur during the night. However, the greater
number of bees then in the nest (because foraging will have ceased) will aid temperature conservation; at night, workers may even obstruct the nest entrance with
their bodies, thus preventing excessive heat loss (Wójtowski, 1963b).

Cumber (1949a) recorded temperatures of between 20° and 25°C. in young
colonies of both surface- and underground-nesting species, but found values some
10°C. higher at the climax of colony development. Hasselrot (1960) demonstrated
a mean variation of 5°C. in nests during the period of colony development, but
found that during the period of greatest stability, when colonies were at their peak,
variations were reduced to 2·5°C. The duration of the period in which temperatures
fluctuate markedly is dependent upon the rate of build-up of the worker population.
A large proportion of the worker force of a colony is usually present in the nest at
any one time, even allowing for the absence of foragers, and this helps the bees to
maintain a sufficiently high brood-nest temperature (Brian, 1952); nevertheless,
Eugène found that when nest temperatures were low, bees which would normally
be foraging actually remained in the nest in order to prevent the brood from cooling
down. Both male and female bumblebees incubate the brood, spreading and flattening
their bodies against the pupal cocoons or wax-pollen covers of the younger brood
batches. It has been shown recently (Ishay & Ruttner, 1971) that the pupae of
hornets (*Vespa crabro*) produce a pheromone[1] which stimulates the adults to incubate
them; pupal cocoons of bumblebees are especially 'attractive' to incubating bees,
but here pheromone emission has not been demonstrated.

When disturbed, bumblebees in a colony can become very active and, as a result,
nest temperatures may temporarily rise above normal. Wójtowski recorded a
temperature of 35·5°C. in an agitated colony of *B. sylvarum*; this high temperature
was maintained for about two minutes. Under normal conditions, however, there is
little danger of a bumblebee nest overheating (Himmer, 1933), and excessive

---

[1] A pheromone is a chemical secreted by an animal which causes a specific reaction in a receiving individual of the
same species.

temperatures can be avoided by ventilating the colony. This is achieved by fanning and also by opening up temporary holes in the nest covering. Workers, particularly of subterranean nests, may sometimes be seen fanning at the entrance to their nests – Sladen once located a colony of B. *pratorum* by the sound of ventilating workers. Few details are available concerning the temperatures at which bumblebees commence cooling their colonies. It might be expected that some species will tolerate higher temperatures than others; Lindhard (1912), for example, found that B. *terrestris* workers began cooling their nest at temperatures of 32·5 to 33°C., while Jordan noticed that cooling in a B. *muscorum* colony was initiated at 29°C.

Humidity within bumblebee nests is also controlled by the bees. According to Hasselrot and Wójtowski, humidity generally ranges from sixty to seventy per cent, and during the period of nest stability it is, like temperature, independent of external conditions. Both a deficiency and an excess of water vapour in the colony is considered harmful; in the latter case mould forms on the comb (Eugène, 1957), and this may lead to brood mortality.

It has often been reported that fanning of the wings, accompanied by a characteristic buzzing sound, is initiated early each morning by one particular bumblebee in a colony. This has led to a fanciful story regarding the presence in the bumblebee community of a so-called 'trumpeter' or 'drummer' bee. The first reference to this behaviour was made in the late seventeenth century by the Dutch painter, J. Goedart (1700). Goedart described the activity of a bee which allegedly mounted the top of the comb at about seven o'clock each morning and for about fifteen minutes sounded a reveille, calling the other nest inhabitants to begin work. This anthropomorphic statement was upheld by other observers and, apparently, was not questioned until Réaumur (1742), being unable to confirm Goedart's findings, concluded that the existence of the trumpeter was a myth. Réaumur's view became generally accepted, and held sway for many years, until Hoffer (1882–3), on the basis of his observations, reinstated Goedart's account of the trumpeter. Several other authors quickly followed Hoffer in accepting the validity of the trumpeter story. However, in contrast with this then widely-held opinion, Pérez (1889) concluded that trumpeter bumblebees were no more than young bees exercising their wing muscles in training for future flight – Plath (1923a), however, later demonstrated that such fanning was largely conducted by old, and not young bees. Pérez also pointed out that since bumblebees were deaf the sound produced by the so-called trumpeter would not be effective in arousing other bees. Later, von Buttel-Reepen (1903, 1907), Lie-Pettersen (1906), Wagner (1907), Bischoff (1927), and many others, concluded that the behaviour of the trumpeter was merely connected with a need to ventilate the nest, and that the bee either fanned to expel accumulated carbon dioxide or disagreeable odours, or to lower nest temperature or humidity. Most writers have since treated the ventilation theory as a plausible explanation for the actions of the trumpeter, but Haas (1961) has produced a new interpretation. He rejects the ventilation theory since, in his experience with both large and small colonies, the trumpeter phenomenon can occur at low nest temperatures and also when air within the nest is fresh. Further, he has shown that the action of the trumpeter occurs in response to light entering the nest; he believes it to be a 'light-alarm', which is connected with colony defence in that it alerts the guard bees. Acceptance of the 'light-alarm' theory, as the true explanation for the behaviour of the so-called trumpeter bee, does not, however, imply any contradiction of the fact that bumblebees ventilate their nests by fanning.

In populous colonies of *B. lucorum* and *B. terrestris*, guard bees are frequently present just inside the nest (tunnel) entrance. Only a few individuals of a colony ever act as guards; these bees also forage for their colonies and undertake various household duties (Free, 1958). A guard bee may patrol the whole length of the entrance tunnel but, according to Free, individuals tend to show a preference for a particular section. The guards scrutinize with their antennae each bee entering the colony. Strangers or intruders may be attacked or, if of equal or superior strength, may be threatened; several bees may co-operate in attempting to overcome or expel an unwanted guest.

Sometimes foragers may be attacked on returning to their own nest. It is possible that such individuals have either partly lost the characteristic odour of their colony or have gained some strange smell from elsewhere. The members of a bumblebee colony acquire a characteristic odour from their food, nest material and comb, and this is retained in the wax coating of the body hairs. An insect's sense of smell is extremely acute, and bees are readily able to detect intruders entering nests. Free found that when bees were artificially exposed to the odour of a strange colony they were immediately attacked on being returned to their own nest, presumably because they had picked up the smell of the strange colony.

Bumblebees tend to react less aggressively towards strangers of their own species. Although an intruder may be attacked on entering a nest, aggression on the part of the defenders does not persist and if the stranger is able to hide within the nest material, or below the comb, in all probability she will be ignored and soon accepted into the colony. Bumblebees of other species are frequently killed, but if such a bee successfully evades death, injury or expulsion, she too may eventually be accepted as a member of the colony (Free & Butler, 1959; Hasselrot, 1960). Frison (1928) has suggested that the calm and deliberate behaviour often adopted by a *Psithyrus* female when invading a *Bombus* nest may reduce hostility among the bees of the colony (see Chapter 7), and so aid her inception. Similarly, *Bombus* females entering strange nests are less likely to be attacked if they adopt a passive and defensive attitude with their legs and wings held close to their bodies and the segments of the abdomen contracted together (Sladen, 1900; Frison, 1928; Free, 1958).

In addition to more normal methods of colony defence, the American species *B. fervidus* uses honey to combat powerful enemies such as *Psithyrus* females. Several *B. fervidus* workers will in turn approach such an intruder and each then places a small, sticky drop of regurgitated honey on to its body. The invader soon becomes wet and sticky and is forced to retreat from the nest (Plath, 1922a). Plath suggested that the European species *B. distinguendus* and *B. subterraneus* (both subgenus *Subterraneobombus*) might be 'honey-daubers', since they are closely related to *B. fervidus* (subgenus *Fervidobombus*); Hobbs (1966a, 1966b) has observed this behaviour in nests of *B. appositus* (subgenus *Subterraneobombus*), but direct confirmation for the British species is wanting.

Although bumblebees are well able to protect their nests from many intruders, they seem powerless to defend them against the ravages of wax-moth larvae and other deadly enemies such as mutillid wasps and brachicomid flies; enemies of bumblebees are considered in detail later.

When a bumblebee nest is disturbed the bees within become temporarily excited and buzz loudly for a few seconds. Some bees tend to react more violently than others and, at least in young colonies, it is the foundress queen which buzzes loudest and longest. Further disturbance will result in a greater and longer period of agitation, and some of the workers may leave the nest to investigate. Although a vertebrate animal, such as man, may be attacked with both sting and mandibles by bees flying up from the nest, foragers returning home usually wheel away at the sight of an intruder and do not join in the attack.

If their colonies are disturbed some social insects can produce pheromone (chemical) alarm substances but this defensive system has not developed in the case of bumblebees, presumably because their colonies are relatively small and inhabitants will become aware of any disturbance more or less directly (Maschwitz, 1964).

It is well-known that some bumblebee species are more aggressive than others. Of our British species, both *B. terrestris* and *B. muscorum* possess rather pugnacious workers and disturbing their nests can be a painful experience if done indiscreetly. In the case of *B. muscorum*, Johnson (1897) had 'no great difficulty in finding their nests for as soon as one was disturbed they made a most ferocious onslaught on any person at hand'. Sladen noted that whereas *B. muscorum* workers would follow a retreating invader for some distance and launch their attacks at head height, *B. terrestris* workers were inclined to stay closer to their nests and only attacked the lower parts of the body. Most of our species, however, have a comparatively mild disposition and instead of flying up to confront an intruder the bees roll on to their backs and remain ready to sting or grasp, with legs or mandibles, any object that touches them. In this position the abdomen is curved upwards with the sting slightly exposed; frequently a drop of venom is visible at its tip. Often, if disturbed or picked up, such bumblebees will forcibly eject their rectal contents.

Some individuals of the colony are more aggressive towards intruders than others, and in small colonies the more pugnacious bees tend to show a greater degree of ovarian development (Free, 1958). Such individuals also tend to be aggressive towards their fellow bees. In colonies of some species the appearance of egg-laying workers also leads to egg-eating by adult bees. Free, *et al.* (1969) observed that when *B. lapidarius* workers constructed egg cells, the foundress queen ate any eggs they laid and then appropriated the cells for her own use. However, the queen was unable, at this time, to fully dominate the workers, and they retaliated and frequently succeeded in destroying her eggs. Earlier in the life of a colony, however, workers do not attempt to eat eggs and will quickly repair any of the queen's egg cells that become accidentally broken. However, should an egg drop out of a cell this will be eaten; similarly, any larvae falling out of a damaged brood clump will be carried out of the nest and discarded.

As first noted by Huber (1802), and later confirmed by many other observers, aggressive workers usually only attempt to steal eggs that are less than a day old, eggs older than this remaining unmolested. Attacks are frequently launched while the queen is actually engaged in egg-laying. These are furiously repulsed by the queen, and any damage to the egg cell is quickly repaired. However, whilst the queen is in combat with one individual her egg cell may be plundered successfully by other aggressive individuals, and on occasions the complete egg cell may be destroyed.

Neither egg-eating nor mutual hostility between workers is typical within a bumblebee colony until the appearance of egg-laying workers. Ovarian development usually occurs in house-bees rather than in foragers. Free (1955e) found that, in colonies of B. pratorum and B. pascuorum, the frequency of attacks between workers increased at about the time that the first worker laid eggs, but then declined. Sladen wrote as follows: 'The eggs of the workers are as large as those of the queen; even the tiny workers lay full-sized eggs, although they cannot develop more than one or two at a time. Several workers will lay their eggs in the same cell,[1] and while they are ovipositing there is a great deal of rivalry and quarrelling between them. But unless the queen is unprolific, or dies early, the workers produce very few offspring, indeed in many nests they produce none.' Frison (1917), Plath (1934), Brian (1952) and Katayama (1971) also refer to this animosity between egg-laying workers, and Free found that in several species, including B. pratorum and B. pascuorum, a social hierarchy, based on dominance, occurred. In a queenless colony, for example, the most aggressive individual usually assumes the rôle of 'queen' and she maintains her position by dominating the next most aggressive and dominant worker. Pardi (1948) has shown that in colonies of Polistes wasps a linear hierarchy based on dominance frequently exists, and that mutual aggression between the workers occurs continually. However, in bumblebee colonies aggression is usually limited to the period when the social order is established, and only a very few bees (according to Free 'only one or two and never more than three') initiate attacks on their fellow workers. Free noted that the dominant bee generally remained on the top of the brood comb and that she was avoided by the other workers. Free has suggested that the aggressive behaviour exhibited by egg-laying workers reduces the tendency for other workers to lay eggs and so contributes towards 'maintenance of colony stability and of an efficient division of labour'.

Egg-laying aside, a division of labour exists in the worker force of a bumblebee colony, enabling the various needs of the colony to be fulfilled efficiently. It has frequently been observed that foragers tend to be the larger workers (Coville, 1890; Sladen, 1912; Richards, 1946; Cumber, 1949a; and others) and since large bees are able to collect more food per trip than small ones this is an obvious advantage.

[1] Eggs laid by workers are typically orientated irregularly within the egg cell (Wagner, 1907; Katayama, 1971).

Brian (1952), however, although conceding that on a day-to-day basis there is a division of labour based on size, found that, at least in colonies of *B. pascuorum*, very few workers did not forage at some time, and she concluded that 'the age at which a worker will start to forage has no connexion with the needs of the colony but is a constitutional, non-plastic character which varies from individual to individual and is associated with differences in weight . . . The small house-bees, in addition to their nursing duties, may be regarded as a foraging reserve, which, in the normal course of events will come into action about the time that the primary foragers become depleted through premature deaths and no young ones are available to replace them'. This is confirmed by Miyamoto (1963b) who observed that in June and July most foragers of *B. ignitus* were medium or large bees, but that later in the season the size range was more varied; small-sized workers only foraged towards the end of the season. Sakagami & Zucchi (1965) also concluded that all individuals in a colony may carry out any task. However, colony needs may be such that the smallest individuals will never forage (Sladen, 1912; Miyamoto, 1959).

Meidell (1934) observed that some bumblebees were inclined to concentrate their efforts into particular tasks, and Free (1955b) found that most workers were either consistent foragers or house-bees, and that the longer a worker carried out household or foraging duties the less likely it was to change from one occupation to the other. However, when in their nests, foragers will undertake household tasks, but they usually work less eagerly than young bees (Sakagami & Zucchi, 1965). Brian noted that in the case of *B. pascuorum* 'the discovery by one or two workers of an easily obtained source of nest material may, when it is scarce, lead to all workers helping in its collection'. Conversely, if the forager population, which normally makes up about one third of the total worker force, is suddenly depleted, the reserve of small house-bees may take their place; in some instances the foundress queen, who has long since ceased to forage, may even collect food (Free, 1955b; Michener, 1969).

Wax glands in bumblebee workers are functional on the second day of adult life, but the production of wax declines after about a week (Röseler, 1967b). Their activity may be prolonged, as is no doubt the case in consistent house-bees, but normally there is an ontogenetic sequence of behaviour among individuals and wax secretion, and associated tasks, are typically the responsibility of the younger workers of the colony. Nevertheless, wax may still be secreted by foragers and, as pointed out by Meidell, these bees will inevitably mix wax and pollen together when cleaning their bodies. Although workers tend to progress from household to foraging duties as they become older, the rates at which behavioural changes of individuals occur will vary and, as indicated above, may even be reversed according to the needs of the colony. Worker populations in bumblebee colonies are, compared with those of honey bees or vespid wasps, relatively small, so that behavioural plasticity is of some importance and increases the efficiency of the worker force available to the colony at any given time.

The ultimate decline of a bumblebee colony will be hastened by the premature death of the foundress queen, and even in the case of the most prolific and long-lived queen a time will come when egg-laying, and hence brood-rearing, ceases. Decline of the colony is also advanced by the excessive feeding by young adult males and queens on the food reserves of the colony (Hasselrot, 1960), and by the invasion of the nest by parasites. Towards the end of the life of a colony nest temperatures fall (Neilsen, 1938) and also fluctuate greatly. Hasselrot, for example, recorded variations in mean temperatures of 12° to 15°C. in declining nests. When there is no brood in a colony, the body temperature of the bees is allowed to approach ambience during the night, which prevents unnecessary wastage of the colony's food reserves (Heinrich, 1972c). This behaviour is of importance if young queens are still in the nest, because if food stores are depleted before they leave to take up overwintering quarters their chances of surviving to the next season are greatly reduced. As fewer and fewer bees remain alive in the colony, temperatures both during the day and night come to depend upon external conditions. At this stage a few workers, and the old, languid queen (often with tattered wings and, in some species – for example, *B. terrestris* – a shiny, almost hairless body), along with the remains of their brood comb, will be all that is left of the colony. All foraging will now have ceased and, as the food reserves in the nest dwindle and finally run out, the remaining bees become increasingly somnolent and eventually die.

CHAPTER 5

Males and Queens: Production and Mating

IN a bumblebee colony males are usually produced in advance of the young queens. Typically, following successive batches of purely worker brood, males and workers are reared together, followed perhaps by batches of entirely male brood. These may be superseded by mixed batches of male and queen brood, and then by batches giving rise entirely to queens. Mixed brood batches of queen, worker and male larvae may sometimes occur together, for example in *Bombus pascuorum* (see Cumber, 1949a), before the main period of queen production, but these were considered by Sladen (1912) to be exceptional. Although, as in some pocket-makers, a few workers may arise from the same brood batches as the first new queens, once the main production of queens takes place, further worker bees are never reared; Cumber (1949c) also found this to be the case in a long-lived, over-wintering nest of *B. terrestris* in New Zealand. The above suggests that the change-over from worker to male and queen production is a gradual process. However, this is not always so. In some pocket-maker species, for example, the switch to sexual brood is notably abrupt, the worker larvae being fed via pollen pockets while batches of male and queen brood receive regurgitated food, the nurse bees changing their brood-rearing behaviour from that of a typical pocket-maker to that more characteristic of a pollen-storer (see Hobbs, 1964a).

Males, unlike queens and workers, are, of course, reared from unfertilized eggs. However, it is evident that male brood is not initiated by the exhaustion of sperm reserves in the queen's spermatheca, because it typically precedes queen production and hence the laying of further fertilized eggs. It is thought, however, that bee density within the colony will influence when a foundress queen will begin to lay unfertilized eggs and so initiate the production of male brood (Röseler, 1967c).

The factors responsible for initiating queen production in colonies are not fully understood, and those governing caste determination in bumblebees are also imperfectly known. Before considering these two phenomena it is probably neces-sary first to review the differences between worker and queen bumblebees.

Structurally, queen and worker bumblebees are identical and caste cannot, there-fore, be determined on a morphological basis, or by comparing body indices (Krüger, 1920, 1924), other than the often arbitrary division of absolute size. Although, as pointed out previously, specific characters (features of sting membranes, sculpturing, and so on) may be better defined in queens than in workers, these cannot be con-sidered as caste features since they are merely consequences of differences in body size.

Although queen bumblebees are typically larger than workers of the same species, in some cases, particularly in pocket-makers, there may be some degree of overlap between the sizes of large workers and small queens, and determining the caste of a moderate-sized individual may be impossible if body size is taken as the only criterion. A size bimodality, differentiating queens and workers of a species, is most obvious in the case of pollen-storers (see, for example, Plowright & Jay, 1968) and in many species, such as *B. lucorum*, *B. magnus*, *B. terrestris* and *B. lapidarius*, there is usually an upper size-limit for workers which is noticeably below the minimum for queens. Differentiation of castes on the basis of body size in these species, therefore, is not difficult. As far as coat colour patterns are concerned, in most species there are few or no differences between queens and workers. However, there are odd exceptions: for example, in *B. terrestris* and *B. pratorum* (see Chapter 9).

Caste differences in bumblebees are largely physiological. Enormous quantities of fat are stored in the fat bodies of young queens, whereas workers (whether young or old) have very limited powers of accumulating reserves in their fat cells (Alford, 1969a). Both Richards (1946) and Cumber (1949a) found that a size bimodality in female bumblebees is best demonstrated by considering weight; queens, on account of their fat bodies, proving relatively heavier than workers. A useful division is achieved by plotting a regression of wing length (expressed logarithmically) on body weight (Michener, 1962). Longevity is also a feature of caste, queens living very much longer than workers. As described earlier, queens are able to survive the winter but workers cannot, and this may be considered the fundamental difference between castes of bumblebees in temperate and subtemperate regions.

Mature queens are normally fertilized, whereas the spermatheca of a worker will not contain sperm (there are, however, isolated records of workers having mated – body size usually being the criterion for caste identification). It should, perhaps, be repeated here that mating or fertilization is not a necessary precursor to fat body development, the reserves accumulating normally in both fertilized and unfertilized individuals. Typically, ovaries of queens do not develop until after an obligatory period of dispause; ovaries of workers, on the other hand, may become functional at any time if the bees are adequately fed and kept under suitable conditions (Free, 1957). Differences in the activity of the corpora allata are thought to govern the production of a gonadotrophic hormone that is necessary for ovary development in bumblebees; however, hormonal relationships may not be this simple. The corpora allata are largest and most active in healthy overwintered queens at the time of their emergence from hibernation, that is, just prior to the period of normal ovarian development, whereas in young queens before the hibernation period they are small and inactive (Palm, 1948). However, Röseler (1967c) observed that the volume of the corpora allata in newly-emerged females (both queens and workers) was linearly correlated to body size, and he concluded that these bodies were not, therefore, a feature of caste difference. Nevertheless, there would seem to be important physiological distinctions between castes of bumblebees which control both their internal physiology and behaviour.

Queens are usually only reared when colonies have reached a certain stage of prosperity; that is, when adequate food stores are available for feeding the brood, and nest temperatures are particularly stable. However, colonies do not have to be large in order to produce queens, although where a foundress queen's fecundity is high, male and queen production is usually delayed until there is a large worker force. In arctic regions worker bumblebees tend to be scarce (Richards, 1931), and in *B. polaris* colonies, for example, only one generation of workers is produced before the sexual forms are reared. Low fecundity of the foundress queen is of value in such cases, as it enables sexual brood to be produced in short favourable seasons. Richards indicated that in the Arctic, bumblebees foraged on a wide range of different plants, thus ensuring that in spite of the limited season they will collect sufficient food to rear new queens.

By no means all bumblebee colonies successfully survive to produce sexual forms. Cumber (1953) followed the fate of eighty nests of *B. pascuorum* and found that of these nine produced only workers and males, ten produced fewer than eight queens and only thirteen reared more than eight queens. The remaining colonies were either destroyed or died out prematurely before producing sexual forms. Cumber suggested that losses may not be so great in those species which nest below ground.

All fertilized eggs of bumblebees are capable of developing into either queens or workers; whether an egg is laid early or late in the life of a foundress queen has no intrinsic effect upon its caste potential. In support of this, Sladen (1912), Free (1955a), and others, have shown experimentally that so long as larvae are adequately fed, queens may be reared from eggs deposited at the very beginning of colony development.

In order that a bumblebee larva can develop into a queen it must receive sufficient food. In the past it was thought that qualitative differences in the food were responsible for producing queens; Lindhard (1912), for example, suggested that larvae destined to become queens were fed on malaxated (chewed) eggs removed from egg cells by the workers, and in consequence received a more nutritious diet than did worker larvae. However, it is now accepted that caste in bumblebees is typically determined by quantitative not qualitative feeding. There is no addition of a special 'brood food' or 'royal jelly' to the food of presumptive queen larvae; basically, queen, worker and male larvae all receive the same food. However, as previously mentioned, there may be differences in the method of feeding sexual as opposed to worker brood (see p. 71).

Under normal circumstances the ratio of workers to larvae in a colony will, at least in some cases, influence the size of adults reared in a particular brood batch and, following the initial work by Richards (1946), various investigators have found that queens rather than workers may be produced if the worker/larva ratio rises to a sufficiently high level, frequently about one to one. No doubt threshold ratios vary somewhat according to species and also to extrinsic factors such as availability of food. In addition, estimates of worker/larva ratios are subject to considerable error and limitations in interpretation; for example, they do not take into account the varying food requirements of larvae of different ages (Plowright & Jay, 1968).

Cumber (1949a) noted that 'in the normal colony the production of queens does not occur till late in its life, and almost invariably is accompanied by the presence of male brood, so that the advent of this male brood would seem to be a signal for a reduction in the brood/worker ratio to the point where queens are produced.' Röseler (1967c) has since suggested that the presence of male brood in the colony is the switch mechanism that influences the workers, probably as a result of the contact made during feeding of the larvae, to alter the worker/brood ratio in favour of queen rearing. It is interesting to find that in colonies of social wasps the presence of male pupae has been considered the stimulus for the workers to construct queen cells (Spradbery, 1965). As suggested by Cumber, the rearing of male bumblebees just prior to queen production may aid nest economy since larval male food requirements are smaller than those of queen larvae; the reduction in brood numbers at this time will also allow food reserves to be at an optimal level in readiness for feeding the presumptive queen larvae. In the case of *B. pascuorum* Cumber found that 'Up till the time of male production the range in weight of female pupal brood ... is 60–120 mg. After male production, the range of normal female pupal brood is 200–500 mg., which indicates a stabilization in trophic condition.'

It should be remembered that some factors operating upon or within a colony may affect the number of queens reared, but will not directly influence caste determination. Similarly, it has been shown, again by Cumber, that nest temperatures do not bring about the changeover from worker to queen rearing, although stable and optimal temperatures may play a part in ensuring that larvae will successfully develop into queens.

Although it is apparent that the amount of food fed to a female larva has a profound influence on its caste potential, larval physiology is also involved in caste determination. According to Röseler (1967c) larvae of *B. terrestris* only remain caste plastic (capable of developing into either queens or workers) so long as they are no older than three and a half days. Plowright & Jay concluded that in the case of *B. terricola* (like *B. terrestris*, a pollen-storer) caste of female larvae was determined, at least in part, prior to entering the fourth instar, but that in *B. ternarius* (also a pollen-storer) larvae were probably still caste plastic even on entering the fourth larval instar. In brood clumps producing both workers and queens, caste of the larvae is not apparent until those destined to become workers have ceased feeding. Potential queen larvae in such clumps will then, to quote Plowright & Jay, 'experience a sudden increase in food supply which effectively delays the onset of pupation and causes them to continue to grow until they attain queen-size'. It follows, therefore, that queen larvae develop over a longer period than worker larvae; Röseler (1970) found a difference of about three days in the case of *B. terrestris* larvae, with a corresponding extension of about four days for pupae.

It is well-known that death or removal of a foundress queen early in the life of a colony may lead to a few new queens being reared earlier than normal. This occurs because, as a result of the cessation in egg-laying, there will be an increase in the worker/larva ratio so that some larvae may receive sufficient attention (feeding) to develop into queens. In the case of *B. terrestris* Röseler (1970) has demonstrated that the foundress queen inhibits her workers from rearing new queens; it is thought that an inhibitory pheromone may be involved. Presumably the queen influences the extent to which workers will supply food to the larvae, inhibition ceasing as the queen ages. This method of control over queen production in bumblebee colonies is probably restricted to the more advanced pollen-storers.

The cumulative total of eggs laid by a bumblebee queen during her lifetime typically follows an S-shaped curve. Plowright & Jay consider that when the rate of egg-laying is steady, negligible adult mortality will lead to an increase in the worker/larva ratio, and that this increase will become linear at the point where the number of eggs laid begins to decline – the natural decline in the number of eggs laid usually occurs at about the time that unfertilized eggs appear (Cumber, 1949a). Cumber, however, concluded that because of the high rate of brood mortality in colonies the worker/larva ratio was independent of the oviposition rate of the queen and was controlled by the workers which destroyed any surplus eggs. However, although Cumber considered that the rate of egg destruction increased at about the time of male production, as Brian (1951a) – later supported by the work of Plowright & Jay – points out, an increase in brood destruction is not necessary for initiating queen rearing since, in the presence of a stable level of brood loss, a suitable worker/larva ratio will be achieved following the normal decline in the rate of egg-laying by the ageing queen. Nevertheless, increased destruction of brood does occur, at least in some species, at about the time of the production of sexual brood, and this must influence the worker/larva ratio. Egg-eating by workers is particularly common in colonies of *B. lapidarius* (and to a lesser extent *B. terrestris*) at this time; egg destruction has also been observed in a colony of *B. lucorum* (Free, 1955a), but the only pocket-maker known to adopt this habit is the North American species *B. fervidus* (Plath, 1923b). Röseler (1967c) reported that as a result of the presence of male brood in their colony, workers were stimulated to throw out larvae; he also noted that the same thing occurred in queenless colonies where the appearance of male brood from eggs laid by workers brought about the removal of about one third of the larvae, so producing roughly a one to one worker/larva ratio.

Caste determination is a highly involved subject which has received much attention, both with regards to bees and other social insects. Reviews by Brian, M. V. (1957, 1965) and Michener (1962, 1969) will repay study; they also provide a useful guide to further reading. A rather dated, but historically interesting, account of sex and caste determination in bumblebees is given by Frison (1927a).

During the first few days of adult life young bumblebee queens remain in their maternal nests and spend much of their time incubating the brood. They will also assist the workers by performing other household tasks. According to Frison

75

(1928) young queens can secrete wax, but this would seem to be exceptional. It is frequently stated that young queens forage for their colonies before they eventually leave the nest to enter hibernation. However, this cannot be regarded as the normal ontogenetic sequence of behaviour. As pointed out by Schmiedeknecht (1878) young queens are rarely found foraging in the field, a view substantiated by the extensive studies of Sladen. Many of the so-called queens that are reported foraging late in the year will prove on dissection to have reduced fat bodies (Alford, unpublished) and probably they will never enter hibernation; even if they do, they may not survive the winter. Such individuals are frequently diseased (Skou, et al., 1963) and some at least may be considered physiologically workers rather than queens. Where there is an adequate worker force to cater for the food requirements of a bumblebee colony there would seem to be no logical reason why a young queen should waste her energy in the hazardous task of foraging before she enters hibernation. Typically, queens enter hibernation whilst still quite young and their pile normally shows no sign of wear. Indeed, the 'fresh' appearance of overwintered queens in the spring, shortly after their arousal from hibernation (Plate 3), is frequently remarked upon. Nevertheless, it must be conceded that if a colony's food stores and the worker force are depleted, young queens will of necessity collect both nectar and pollen.

Queens become fertilized early in their life, usually making a mating flight when about five days old (Cumber, 1953). At this time they may be ready to take up their winter quarters, but if not, or if unable to find a suitable overwintering site, they return to their nest. Cumber found that about thirty to forty per cent of the young queens present in *B. pascuorum* nests were fertilized and that in nests of *B. hortorum* more than half had already mated. Young queens returning to their nests usually prove to be fertilized, which suggests that few have difficulty in finding a mate.

Young adult males, in common with young queens, also help to incubate the brood, but they do not concern themselves with other domestic duties. During their stay in the maternal nest they feed on both honey and pollen, as do the young queens. Most males leave their nest when they are between two and four days old and normally, once they have flown, they never return. However, it would seem that young males of some species may sometimes do so (Frison, 1917, 1928) (see also Wild, 1924). Males generally live for about three or four weeks and during this time they are able to survive independently in the field, obtaining their day-to-day food requirements from flowers, to which they are frequent visitors. However, their primary task is to find and inseminate a young nubile queen of their own species.

Males of both *Bombus* and *Psithyrus* often spend the night and periods of inclement weather on flowers, and are especially common on the heads of knapweeds (*Centaurea*) and thistles (*Carduus* and *Cirsium*) bees may occur singly or in groups. Sleeping aggregations of aculeate Hymenoptera on flowers are well-known (Evans & Linsley, 1960; Linsley, 1962). Gregarious sleeping by bumblebee males sometimes occurs in sheltered places in or on the ground (Snieżek, 1894), a habit also noted in the case of certain species of *Halictus* (Schremmer, 1955). Early on a July morning in Surrey I once found several males of *B. hortorum* collected together below the shelter of a clump of grass; this was presumed to be a sleeping aggregation, and it is interesting to find that *B. hortorum* was a species which Snieżek accredited with the habit of spending the night collectively in the ground. Lack of reports of this phenomenon in bumblebees suggests that it is not common; however, the habit may only occur among certain species, and could equally well have been largely overlooked.

Methods adopted by male bumblebees for locating young queens vary according to the species. In some, for example *B. confusus* and *B. mendax* (see Saunders, 1909; Krüger, 1951), males possess enormous compound eyes, and they rely, initially at least, upon their visual powers to find a mate. Each male stations himself on, or hovers slowly above, any suitable object such as a rock, a flower, or even a small piece of bare ground, ready to pounce upon any passing bumblebee queen, or dart away if disturbed. The males are apparently unable to distinguish queens at a distance and will chase any likely-looking insect, or even a small bird, that might happen to fly past. Males of a few species congregate around nest entrances where they await the appearance of young queens. Smith (1858) observed several males of *B. subterraneus* hovering about the entrance to a nest and described the event as follows: 'at last we observed the cause of this assemblage of males; a fine fresh example of the female at last showed herself at the entrance to the nest, this was a signal for a more furious buzzing than before; numbers alighted within a few inches of the female, and a fierce combat ensued; about ten or twelve of these males clung together and rolled over and over, struggling in close combat; the female, who had retreated into the burrow, again appeared, and this time took flight; in a moment every male was gone, the whole host, not less than twenty or more, flew off in chase of the female, – we saw them no more. We noticed another day an assemblage of males as before, but we saw no second female take flight.' Sometimes males of *B. subterraneus* may pursue a young queen down the nest entrance tunnel (Tuck, 1897a) and, as in the case of *B. ruderarius*, which behaves similarly (Krüger, 1951), mating may then take place within the nest. In most species, however, location of a mate, and subsequent mating, occurs in the field (see below).

Particularly on fine summer days, male bumblebees are frequently to be seen flying one after another along established routes, each bee pausing at intervals to hover momentarily at a series of predetermined visiting places, such as the base of a tree, a twig, a leaf or a grass clump. This phenomenon was described by Newman (1851), well over a hundred years ago, and was also studied by Charles Darwin (1886). Darwin's work on the flight paths of male bumblebees has been largely overlooked, but a valuable transcript of his original, and previously unpublished, field notes has been produced recently by Freeman (1968). Darwin's observations were mostly confined to males of *B. hortorum*.

Males establish their flight paths immediately after leaving their nests, and as location and characteristics of the flight routes and visiting places chosen vary from species to species, the different species of bumblebees tend to separate and congregate in particular areas. Sometimes flight paths are established at ground level. Thus, *B. hypnorum* males frequently visit the base of shrubs, and *B. hortorum* (perhaps our most frequently observed species) often selects the dark recesses at the foot of trees. Other species course at or about the level of herbage; examples are *B. pomorum* and *B. terrestris* (Haas, 1949a), *B. lucorum* and *B. magnus* (Krüger, 1951). These bumblebees frequently pause at the tips of grasses or visit the base of low-growing plants. Burtt (1923) observed that males of *B. cullumanus* 'flew at a height of about a foot above the ground, pausing at the base of a tuft of clover and pursuing their course across the field'. Awram (1970) followed *B. terrestris* males in a wheat field and found that they flew to the base of a plant and then rose slowly up the stem to the ear before continuing to another plant; the males apparently paid attention to several wheat plants at each visiting place.

Males of *B. sylvarum* favour bushy areas (Haas, 1949a) and visit leaves on low bushes or plants such as thistles (*Carduus* and *Cirsium*), knapweeds (*Centaurea*) and scabious (*Knautia*); they usually fly at a height of about 1·5 to 1·8 or 2·0 m. Haas found that *B. pratorum* males flew up to a height of 3 m., but usually kept between 1 and 2·5 m., while *B. pascuorum* flew at 5 to 6 m. Awram, however, recorded *B. pratorum* at heights of 4 m. and observed *B. pascuorum* males visiting wheat stems much like *B. terrestris* males.

Several species establish very high flight paths. Sladen (1912) noted that, unlike its close relative *B. hortorum*, *B. ruderatus* males flew at tree-top height. *B. lapidarius* also flies at the tops of tall trees, but according to Haas not above 20 m. Awram found males of *B. terrestris* and *B. lucorum* visiting the tops of tall trees, and sometimes males of both species were seen at the same visiting place. However, the peak of flight activity of *B. lucorum* males occurred somewhat earlier in the day than that of *B. terrestris*, so the two species were probably separated temporarily. Another difference was that, unlike *B. terrestris* males, those of *B. lucorum* did not visit isolated trees. As shown by Krüger the height and details of a flight route may be conditioned by circumstances; for example, in tree-less zones *B. lapidarius* will fly at bush height. Similarly, an absence of trees in Krüger's study area probably explains why he found *B. lucorum* males flying at ground level.

Most males fly along a linear circuit and will visit numerous places along the route. A bumblebee following a flight path usually flies in one direction, but sometimes individuals will reverse their course. Frank (1941) found that males of *B. hortorum*[1] followed a flight path approximately 300 m. long and visited twenty-eight points (twenty-seven being the bases of fir trees, and one a tree stump) which were usually 5 to 15 m. apart. The furthest distance between visiting places was 33 m. but some points, when on the same tree, were as close as 30 to 40 cm. Individuals completed over twenty circuits (a distance of 6 km.) in an hour.

[1] Although Frank refers to *B. terrestris*, it would appear that he was actually observing *B. hortorum* males.

Within an area there will usually be several overlapping flight paths belonging to males of the same species, and some individuals may share certain visiting places. However, different males do not usually pause at precisely the same point if sharing a visiting place (see below). Particularly in the case of *B. hortorum*, several males may arrive and leave the same visiting place within a comparatively short time, and an observer might at first assume (as did both Darwin and Frank) that the bees are workers flying in and out of a nest.

Males of certain species sometimes rest for short periods in sunny places along their flight paths. Frank noted that such stops were most frequent during mid-morning. According to Haas, when the two large-eyed species *B. confusus* and *B. mendax* are not lying in wait for young queens to pass their sunning places, they will set up flight paths, but these species fly along irregular rather than linear circuits.

According to Haas (1949b) flight path characteristics of at least some species of *Psithyrus* differ from those of *Bombus* in that visiting places are more diffuse, often covering several leaf laminae rather than more localized points. Males of *P. sylvestris* frequently establish flight paths along hedgerows or in woods, visiting, for example, foliage on trees and bushes about 1 m. above the ground. Haas estimated that this species flew thirty circuits in a day, covering perhaps 9 to 10 km. This is a much shorter distance than that sometimes claimed for *Bombus* males. However, total distances covered by males in any one day are often over-estimated because no allowance is made for time spent foraging on flowers. Males of some *Psithyrus* species will often hover over meadows and grassy slopes. According to Sladen (1912) *P. rupestris* males frequent open, grassy slopes facing north-west where they fly at grass height; *P. barbutellus* males behave similarly, but occur on slopes near trees. Males of *P. campestris* also fly over open, sloping ground, rapidly coursing the area a metre or more above the ground. Krüger observed that, unlike males of *P. rupestris* which were restricted to stretches of short grass, those of *P. bohemicus* flew along the crowns of embankments. Flight paths of *P. vestalis* do not appear to have been observed in the wild; this is rather surprising as this species is common in many areas and, during the summer months, the males are often abundant.

Bumblebees must leave their flight paths periodically to feed at flowers. Krüger found that males generally deserted their flight routes in the early afternoon and were then to be seen foraging. Males are commonly found on flowers in the middle of a hot day, and in some cases the flowers visited may be related to, or be part of, the flight path complex (Haas, 1949b). Foraging and flight path activity are, however, distinct and separate phenomena. With regards to males of *B. hortorum*, Newman (1851) commented as follows: 'Any observer may watch them in their unsteady flight, very near the ground, paying visits to the roots of trees, holes in banks, etc. At first appearance they look as though they intend to alight at these haunts, but they never do, until a round of probably a quarter of a mile is made in this manner, when they require nourishment; they then return to the

79

thistles and flowers, where they frequently remain all night, particularly in cold weather, and may be seen dormant in the morning; when taken in the warm hand they soon recover and fly away.'

Weather greatly influences flight path activity and in very cool or wet conditions males may be discouraged from flying altogether, remaining all day on the flower heads on which they spent the previous night. Towards the end of the season males spend more and more of their time on flowers and, after a peak period of intense activity, flight paths eventually become deserted as, one by one, the males perish.

Although the attraction of the visiting places puzzled early observers, it is now accepted that these are scent-marked by pheromones secreted from the mandibular glands (Stein, 1962). Males mark the visiting places at the beginning of each day, whilst negotiating their first circuit (Haas, 1946, 1952) and will also scent-mark sites after a shower of rain. Several observers have confirmed that males may omit certain visiting places or incorporate new ones into their flight paths, so that the precise routes adopted can vary somewhat from day to day. Nevertheless, there is a considerable degree of uniformity in site selection; Darwin, for example, noted that some visiting places were favoured by different *B. hortorum* males over a period of several years. Awram observed that at visiting places males of various species approached visibly conspicuous objects at each pass (which he termed 'focal points'), but scented other, adjacent objects enclosing a diffuse area (which he called the 'site') immediately surrounding the 'focal point'. Awram found that, with the possible exception of *B. hortorum*, flight paths of individual males were interconnected through 'sites', but not 'focal points', and this he believed to be important in lessening the chances of males encountering one another during flight path activity. Although 'focal points' of *B. hortorum* were usually found to be at or near the bases of trees, Awram noted that males sometimes scented the same trees at heights of 2 or even 3 m. 'Sites' for this species, therefore, were particularly diffuse when compared with those of other species.

When held in the hand males of some bumblebee species are noticeably fragrant. The same scent is detectable at their visiting places, and also at their sunning places (Frank, 1941) but, according to Awram, males do not scent-mark flowers. Each species produces a different odour and, as mentioned by Sladen, males of one species do not visit points to which those of another are attracted. Although the smell of some males is quite pleasant to man, some species, for example, *B. hypnorum* (Frank, 1941), emit a rather unpleasant odour, while others, like *B. pomorum*, produce no distinct smell (Haas, 1946).

Calam (1969) was able to demonstrate that the major volatile substance from heads of *B. lucorum* males was different to that from heads of the closely-related species *B. terrestris* (see Bergstrom, *et. al.*, 1968). It is agreed that male pheromones used for marking flight routes are species specific, and Haas (1946) thought that scents may even vary between varieties of one and the same species. This suggestion is supported by Kullenberg, *et al.* (1970); they found chemical differences in the volatile components of secretions from light and dark colour forms of *B. lucorum* males, although it is possible that their sample was composed of males of *B. lucorum* and *B. magnus* respectively (see p. 175). According to Stein (1963a, 1963b) the pheromone of *B. terrestris* males is farnesol (3,7,11-trimethyldodeca-2,6,10-trien-1-ol) and is derived from fatty oils contained in flowers. However, Bergstrom, *et al.* were unable to detect farnesol in this species; they isolated another substance (2,3-dihydro-trans-6-farnesol); see also Kullenberg, *et al.* (1970).

When scent-marking, a male bumblebee crawls over (or along the edge of) a leaf, twig, or other such object, with the mandibles held agape, while the area between the mandibles is daubed with mandibular gland secretion. Awram has suggested that the beards on the mandibles of male bumblebees (Fig. 3) may be used in scent-marking. Scenting techniques vary somewhat from species to species. Awram found that *B. pratorum* males scent-marked from three to six times at any one site, *B. hortorum*, *B. lucorum* and *B. terrestris* from two to four times, *B. pascuorum* from one to three times, and *B. lapidarius* only once. The last-mentioned species was apparently less precise in its scenting behaviour than were the others. Also, although *B. lapidarius* usually marked several sites in succession, males of other species usually did not.

Sladen suggested that, in scent-marking their visiting places, males not only attracted other males of the same species but also the young queens; and Awram has recently confirmed that this is so. Krüger considered that visual sense played the major part in the attraction of males to the visiting places, and that the scent was mainly or entirely for attracting females of the species. However, both Darwin and Haas found that males were seldom distracted by visual changes in the visiting sites or their immediate surroundings, and it has been shown experimentally that males are attracted by the scent (Kullenberg, 1956). Although a male probably locates an established flight path by the scent, vision is obviously important in selecting focal points and will also be of importance later when, with repeated flights, the position of each visiting place becomes implanted by experience.

As already indicated, male activity on flight routes tends to be at its height during the morning, and Hobbs (1965a, 1965b, 1967b) has noted that in several *Bombus* species the young queens mated during the morning and then entered their hibernation quarters in the afternoon. In most cases, it appears that bumblebee queens mate only once, although multiple mating does occur in some species, for example *B. hypnorum* (Pouvreau, 1963a). Hobbs (1967b) observed that some queens of *B. huntii* 'mated at least three times and many mated at least twice before hibernating'.

Males are attracted to young, nubile queens when these are offered on flight paths (Frison, 1927b; Cumber, 1953; Awram, 1970; Free, 1971) but, although lured by queens near a visiting site, they usually ignore those presented elsewhere. Having perceived a queen the male usually lands upon her thorax, knocking her to the ground. The male then climbs on to her back and attempts to copulate, grasping her body with his legs. If and when coition is achieved the queen's sting is protruded (see Hobbs, 1965a) and the male, presumably to avoid the sting,

81

releases his hold and falls backwards, the pair remaining attached only in the genital region. Bumblebees remain *in copula* for anything from a few minutes to about an hour (or longer, according to some authorities). Pairs are perhaps most frequently observed on the ground or on leaves of trees, although young queens with males clinging to their backs are sometimes seen in flight. Lie-Pettersen (1901) was able to beat numerous pairs of *B. terrestris* and *B. pascuorum* from the foliage of deciduous trees in Norway, apparently in an area where males and young queens were unusually numerous. Several investigators have remarked upon the apparent absence of queens within flight path zones. However, for various reasons, Awram considered that the chances of observing a queen at a visiting site were slight, and, as noted by Free (1971), although a pair may commence mating at a visiting place they will be unlikely to remain there, because of the likelihood of being disturbed by other males.

Males of several species of solitary bee scent-mark flowers and establish flight paths nearby, where they await the arrival of foraging females (Haas, 1949b, 1960; Kullenberg, 1956). However, Awram has suggested that in bumblebees, with the appearance of an industrious, non-reproductive, worker caste, the functions of reproduction and foraging became separated, and that this was particularly neces-sary because of the general inability of males to distinguish queens from workers. In honey bees too, the functions of foraging and mating are spatially separated, the nubile queens being attracted to special areas where large numbers of drones from various colonies congregate (e.g. Zmarlicki & Morse, 1963; Ruttner, 1966; Ruttner & Ruttner, 1969). It is thought likely that a bumblebee flight path complex, as with a drone assembly place, is frequented by males from several colonies, thus encouraging outbreeding. It is also suggested (Wynne-Edwards, 1962) that the flight path phenomenon may in some way serve to regulate population densities.

CHAPTER 6

Foraging

BUMBLEBEES are almost entirely dependent upon plants for food, and through-out the life of their colony they must forage for both nectar and pollen. A foraging bumblebee may collect about half its own body weight of nectar, but individual loads vary considerably. Similarly, pollen-gatherers may bring home more than half their own body weight of pollen, but again, the size of loads is extremely variable (Clements & Long, 1923; Free, 1955c). As is to be expected, larger bees tend to collect more food than do smaller individuals. Small foragers generally collect nectar rather than pollen, so that to some extent a division of labour within the forager force of a colony is established (Brian, 1952; Free, 1955b; Miyamoto, 1957b). In the short term, Free considered many foragers to be either consistent nectar-gatherers or consistent pollen-gatherers, but he found they displayed little constancy over a longer period of time. On any one trip a bumblebee may forage for both nectar and pollen and, in the majority of cases, predominant pollen-gatherers will also collect some nectar (Brian, 1952; Free, 1955c). A nectar-gatherer may inadvertently become dusted with pollen whilst visiting a flower but as she is able to discard unwanted pollen this may not necessarily be carried back to the nest.

The amount and type of food collected is in part related to the current needs of the colony. For example, Free found that *Bombus lucorum* and *B. sylvarum* foragers collected the bulk of their nectar in the early morning, and that at this time of day pollen collection was relatively low. Presumably this followed the need to replenish nectar supplies depleted during the night when the adult population in the nest would be at its peak. Nectar-gatherers may cease to forage if the colony's nectar or honey pots are full. Pollen collection is, to some extent, related to the presence of larvae in the colony (Free, 1955b). However, towards the end of the season, even when brood-rearing has ceased, pollen may still be collected (Sladen, 1912; Brian, 1952) as it is required by the young adult queens for building up their fat body reserves prior to hibernation.

When a forager returns from the field she searches within her colony for a suitable receptacle into which to unload the pollen or nectar she has collected. A bumblebee may examine several nectar pots before finally selecting one and re-gurgitating into it the contents of her crop; it has been suggested (Free & Butler, 1959) that this behaviour may enable a forager to gauge the food requirements of the colony. A degree of selectivity is also shown by foragers depositing their pollen loads. Brian (1951b) found that individual foragers of *B. pascuorum* tended to deposit their pollen loads into the same pollen pocket.

When unloading pollen a bumblebee places both hind legs into the receptacle and the pollen is forced off by the middle pair of legs. The pollen may then be packed down by the forager or by one of the house-bees. If pollen loads are small, or present on one leg only (part of the load having been dislodged by accident) the forager may leave the nest without depositing them. Bumblebees unloading pollen tend to remain in the nest for longer between foraging trips than nectar-gatherers (Taniguchi, 1955; Free, 1955c). This is partly due to the pollen-gatherers having also collected nectar. Taniguchi timed nectar-gatherers as taking 2 to 4 minutes between trips and pollen-gatherers 5 to 7 minutes; Free found that the time interval between trips varied with the species, *B. pratorum* and *B. pascuorum* foragers, for example, taking only half as long to unload nectar or pollen as did *B. lucorum* foragers.

Bumblebees are remarkably proficient at remembering the precise location of their nest. It has been suggested that colony odour may help a returning bumblebee to find her colony (Frison, 1930b), but it seems more likely that the bee relies upon her visual memory and acuity. On leaving her nest for the first time a bumblebee studies the features of the nest entrance, and once familiar with the details she ventures out and flies a short distance into the air. She then circles and zigzags above the ground, the height and extent of the arcs gradually increasing, until, when familiar with the location of the nest and its surroundings, she eventually flies away. Similar orientation flights are carried out subsequently, but to a lesser degree, until finally further orientation becomes unnecessary. Young queens leaving their maternal nests also make orientation flights (but not always efficiently) and so, as previously described, does an overwintered queen when she finally locates a suitable nesting place in the spring. However, male bumblebees do not orientate because they usually leave their colonies for good on their first flight (Frison, 1930b; Free, 1955d; Manning, 1956b).

Although familiar with the layout of the ground in the vicinity of their nest, foragers may experience some difficulty in locating the entrance if the vegetation is disturbed, for example, by wind, a falling tree or a passing animal. Under these circumstances several returning foragers may be seen circling and hovering near the nest unable, at first, to locate it. However, most, if not all, of them will eventually succeed in finding their way home. Bumblebees will readily orientate to a new position if their colonies are moved experimentally (see Free, 1955d) and when, under natural conditions, the nest surroundings have been altered the foragers will reorientate to familiarize themselves with the new conditions. Orientating bumblebees take account of prominent objects in the vicinity and may memorize not only the position of their nest site but also that of certain food sources. Sometimes foragers may even orientate, briefly, to individual food plants (Darwin, 1876; Manning, 1956b). Like honey bees, foraging bumblebees navigate by the sun, taking into account changes in its position throughout the day (Jacobs-Jessen, 1959).

Bumblebees are renowned for foraging under a wide range of weather conditions.

In arctic regions they will fly even when air temperatures are below freezing and they may be active throughout the whole twenty-four hours of continuous summer daylight (Longstaff, 1932; Richards, 1973). Even in England overwintered queens are known to forage in snow (Fox Wilson, 1929) and Heinrich (1972c) reported bumblebees, in America, flying at dawn with a frost on the ground and ambient temperatures at 2° to 3°C.

Bumblebees may forage from sunrise to sunset or even longer, but different species tend to commence and discontinue flying at different times (Løken, 1949). Also, the individual foragers in a colony may begin and end foraging activities at different times, so that early in the morning and late in the evening the proportion of active foragers will be reduced (Free, 1955c; Taniguchi, 1955). A peak in bumblebee activity is often reached by mid-morning, and in hot weather there may be a noticeable decline during the middle of the day (Løken, 1949; Miyamoto, 1960). Miyamoto (1957a) noted that although many workers regularly foraged throughout the day, some nectar-gatherers would only fly during certain limited periods. Such periodicity is probably related to the times at which particular flowers are presenting nectar.

Fog and heavy rain will both reduce foraging activity (Løken, 1949; Miyamoto, 1957b, 1960). Sladen (1912) observed that 'In a sudden shower a *lapidarius* or *terrestris* worker will sometimes take shelter under the eaves of a building or the horizontal bough of a tree'. Similarly, I have seen foragers (and males) of *B. lucorum*, *B. hortorum*, and other species, settle on the lee side of trees when caught in the spray from a garden hose. On the whole, however, bumblebees tend to be relatively tolerant of bad weather, being far less affected than honey bees (e.g. Skovgaard, 1952), and will continue to forage even under very cold, wet and windy conditions (see below). Both Hulkkonen (1928) and Løken have reported that weather has less effect on foraging activity early in the season, the time of year when food reserves in a colony will be small.

Although temperature and humidity both influence foraging activity, light intensity is also an important factor. Løken (1954) observed foraging bumblebees in Norway at the time of a total eclipse of the sun. She found that as totality approached, and the light dimmed, bumblebee activity rapidly dwindled and then virtually ceased when darkness fell. As the eclipse passed, and light intensity increased, foraging bumblebees began to return and soon the pre-eclipse level of activity was restored. Neither humidity nor temperature altered significantly during the ecliptic period, which strongly suggests that foraging activity was influenced by the changes in light values. Foragers often remain away from their nests at night. Free (1955c), for example, found that about a quarter of the foragers from a *B. lucorum* colony did not return home in the evening; he attributed this high proportion to the relatively long duration of foraging trips undertaken by this species. It is believed that individuals remain in the field overnight if light intensity suddenly drops below the requirement for flight activity (Hobbs, *et al.*, 1962).

Nectar-gatherers generally spend less time on a foraging trip than pollen-gatherers

D

(Brian, 1952; Free, 1955c; Taniguchi, 1955; Miyamoto, 1957a) and there is a tendency for foragers of larger species to remain away from their nests for a longer period than those of smaller species. Free, for example, found that *B. lucorum* foragers took, on average, 53·6 and 128·9 minutes to collect nectar and pollen respectively, whereas mean times for three smaller species (*B. pratorum*, *B. pascuorum* and *B. sylvarum*) ranged from 12·4 to 20·3 minutes for nectar-gatherers and 17·5 to 33·3 minutes for pollen-gatherers. As larger bumblebees collect more food than smaller individuals they can visit more flowers per trip and may, therefore, venture further afield. It follows that foragers of small species will tend to make more trips per day than those of larger species. Again, Free recorded up to twenty-seven foraging trips in one day for *B. sylvarum*, compared with a maximum of seventeen for *B. lucorum*.

In order to fly, and hence forage, a bumblebee must be able to maintain a relatively high body (thoracic) temperature. Immediately prior to flight, heat may be produced by shivering, and the thoracic temperature will rise rapidly as a result of the muscular activity (Krogh & Zeuthen, 1941). These movements may be audible as a low-pitched, flutter-like buzz, and have been mentioned previously as occurring when hibernating queens are disturbed (p. 38). A somnolent forager which has remained on a flower overnight will also, if disturbed whilst still drowsy, produce a low buzzing sound and rapidly become more alert. An active or semi-torpid bee may raise a middle leg into the air and if molested further may roll on to its back, threatening to sting. Such bees often fall to the ground and remain temporarily in a defensive attitude; like those in disturbed colonies they may discharge fluid from their anus. A silphid beetle (*Necrophorus investigator*) is said, if disturbed, to mimic bumblebees in both sound and movement, including the forcible ejection of faeces (Lane & Rothschild, 1965).[1]

In addition to raising their body temperature by muscular activity bumblebees (*Bombus*) are also able to produce heat by chemical means (Newsholme, *et al.*, 1972) (see below). During warm-up, which may or may not involve wing muscle movement, the wings are held in repose; abdominal respiratory movements increase, both in amplitude and frequency, until such time as flight is initiated. In flight a bumblebee maintains a thoracic temperature of approximately 35° to 40°C.; the temperature of the abdomen, however, approaches ambience and is not regulated (see Heinrich, 1972b). Although a high abdominal temperature is not necessary for

---

[1] Certain other insects also resemble bumblebees (Plate XXX). The following are examples: the rare beetle *Trichius fasciatus*, with its light brown and unusually hairy thorax; the day-flying bee hawk moths (*Hemaris fuciformis* and *H. tityus*), frequent visitors to Rhododendron and bugle (*Ajuga reptans*) respectively; some solitary bees, especially the relatively large and hairy, black-bodied females of *Anthophora pilipes* and *A. retusa* (which have conspicuous orange hairs on their hind legs but, unlike bumblebees, no corbicula), commonly seen in the spring foraging on low plants such as white dead-nettle (*Lamium album*); and several flies, including the bee-flies (*Bombylius major* and *B. minor*), and the large tachinid *Echinomyia grossa*. Surphid flies, particularly the large narcissus fly (*Merodon equestris*) (Plate 8), *Criorhina ranunculi* and *Volucella bombylans* (see Chapter 8), are often mistaken for bumblebees but, in common with other flies, they can at once be distinguished as, unlike bees, they have only one pair of wings; their mouthparts, antennae, eyes and legs are also noticeably different to those of bumblebees. Some of the above-mentioned insects undoubtedly gain a certain degree of protection from potential enemies, such as birds, by resembling (mimicking) bumblebees; the interesting subject of insect mimicry is reviewed by Rettenmeyer (1970).

flight, should that of the thorax drop below 29° to 30°C. then flight becomes impossible as the bee is unable to support itself in the air (Krogh & Zeuthen, 1941). The body temperature of a foraging bumblebee falls slightly if in shade (Heinrich, 1972b) and, obviously, when ambient temperatures are low more energy must be expended, and fuel utilized, to maintain a sufficiently high thoracic temperature for flight to be possible. Nevertheless, bumblebees are capable of flying even when air temperatures approach or drop below freezing (Bruggemann, 1958; Richards 1973).

It is uneconomical to maintain a high body temperature whilst not in flight and Heinrich (1972a) demonstrated that when foragers of *B. vagans* landed on flowers of fireweed (*Epilobium angustifolium*)[1] their thoracic temperature dropped but was maintained at 32° to 33°C., that is, just above the minimum level necessary for flight. When visiting this plant species a forager will fly from flower to flower so that inter-flight periods are relatively short. However, bumblebees also collect food from more compact inflorescences, where they can crawl, rather than fly, from one flower or floret to the next. Under these conditions maintenance of a high body temperature is unnecessary and the thorax may cool down below the level at which flight is possible, thus saving fuel; warm-up must then occur before the bee can fly away. For foraging to be worthwhile more nectar must be collected than is used as fuel for flight and heat production. At low ambient temperatures and where nectar rewards per flower are small, maintenance of a high body temperature may be prohibitive so that collection of food from spatially isolated flowers could become uneconomical. However, reduction in activity and in body temperature whilst gathering the nectar may overcome this. Under poor weather conditions, for example, bumblebees visiting fruit blossom may crawl, as opposed to fly, from flower to flower (Fox Wilson, 1929). Heinrich points out that at low temperatures other insects will not be foraging, so that competition for the available nectar in flowers will be largely eliminated; at such times, therefore, foraging by bumblebees will be more profitable than it might otherwise be. The ability of bumblebees to forage under adverse weather conditions is thought to be assisted by the high level of fructose diphosphatase activity in their flight muscles; this enzyme is believed 'to provide a substrate-cycle between fructose 6-phosphate and fructose diphosphate for the generation of heat during short periods of rest when food is being collected' (Newsholme, *et al.*, 1972). Apparently little or no activity of this enzyme is present in the flight muscle tissue of *Psithyrus* or honey bees.

When collecting pollen from a flower, a forager may scrabble over the anthers or disturb them by rapid wing vibrations. Unlike more passive methods of pollen collection these are active processes during which body (thoracic) temperatures will inevitably remain at a high level. Consequently, if sufficient nectar is not provided by, or collected from, these flowers the pollen-gatherers must forage elsewhere for nectar which they can use as fuel. Alternatively, they must leave their nests with sufficient nectar or honey in their crops to fulfil their energy requirements during the trip.

[1] Also known as rose-bay (*Chamaenerion angustifolium*).

The hairy coat of a bumblebee is an effective insulator which considerably reduces heat loss by convection. The insulating properties of the pile are dependent upon its density rather than its length and, as might be expected, species of *Bombus* are better able to retain heat than *Psithyrus* (see Church, 1960). Also, heat loss will tend to be greater in small, rather than large, bees. Certain species produce larger, more hairy forms in cold regions; arctic bumblebees, for example, are large and have long, shaggy coats (Downes, 1962). Arctic bumblebees also tend to be dark in colour and are thereby able to retain warmth from solar radiation (see Richards, 1973).

Foragers do not collect food indiscriminately in the area surrounding their nests. Thus, Brian (1952) found that members of a *B. pascuorum* colony established five separate flight paths, radiating out from the nest in different directions, and the individual foragers remained more or less constant to one route. Most bumblebees probably forage within a few hundred metres of their nest, but they may venture further afield. Rau (1924) showed that some workers of *B. pennsylvanicus* were able to return to their nests from distances greater than 2 km. Free (Free & Butler, 1959) found that foragers of *B. lapidarius* and *B. pascuorum* could find their way home when released several hundred metres from their nests; his results also suggested that the former species had a greater foraging range than the latter.

Foraging bumblebees may interact when two individuals arrive at the same flower, either or both of them taking flight (Kikuchi, 1963). This behaviour reduces the possibility of overcrowding, by dispersing the bees, and thus increases foraging efficiency. On large inflorescences, such as sunflowers (*Helianthus annuus*), however, two or more bumblebees may feed at the same time without disturbing one another. The various species of bumblebee tend to differ in both their aggressiveness and sensitivity to attack (Brian, A. D., 1957). Brian writes as follows: '*pratorum* is definitely aggressive towards other species, its attacks having an effect on *agrorum* [*pascuorum*] but little on *lucorum*; *lucorum* is least affected by aggressiveness in other bees (comparable to the position of the top hen in a peck order) and *agrorum* [*pascuorum*] is only moderately aggressive under normal conditions, aggressiveness increasing as a result of attacks by other bees.' Brian suggests that bumblebees are able to recognize members of their own species, possibly by characteristics of coat pattern, although specific odours may also play a part. Foragers of some species may actually be discouraged from visiting particular plants when certain other forager species are present. For example, Brian found that *B. pascuorum* was deterred from foraging on black currant (*Ribes nigrum*) bushes that were already being worked by *B. lucorum* and *B. pratorum*. Similarly, she noted that in the presence of these two species *B. hortorum* will not visit flowers of sycamore (*Acer pseudoplantanus*), although in their absence it does so (Heslop Harrison, 1939). Foraging bumblebees also react to the presence of other insects. It is suggested, for example, that they tend to avoid sites occupied by large numbers of foraging honey bees (Holmes, 1964).

Most species of bumblebee will collect food from several different plant species, although some show a definite preference for certain kinds of flower. A few species are strikingly more discriminating than others. Løken (1961), for example, found that *B. consobrinus* occurred only within the range of *Aconitum septentrionale*, and that the queens, workers and males rarely visited other plants while the aconite (whose flowering period, with only local exceptions, covered the flight season of *B. consobrinus*) was in flower.

Brian, A. D. (1957), Hobbs, *et al.* (1961) and Hobbs (1962), among others, have shown that the flower preference exhibited by different species of *Bombus* is, at least in part, related to the lengths of the tongue and hence to the ease at which nectar can be collected from a flower. Knuth (1906) believed that male bumblebees had much shorter tongues than workers of the same species and were, therefore, restricted to collecting nectar from flowers with shorter corolla tubes. However, Hobbs *et al.* (1961) found that workers and males of a species tended to prefer the same flowers and that in most cases mean tongue lengths of both were similar. Bumblebees with long tongues tend to work faster (visit more flowers per minute) than species with short tongues (see Holm, 1966). Comparative morphometric data on bumblebee mouthparts are given by Medler (1962a, 1962b, 1962c).

Several investigators have studied the floral preferences of bumblebee populations in particular regions; for example, Fye & Medler (1954a) in America, and Leclercq (1960) in France. Details of the favourite flowers of British bumblebees are provided by Sladen (1912), Walton (1922, 1927), Laidlaw (1930) and Yarrow (1945); see also Chapter 9.

To some extent the degree of flower constancy exhibited by a foraging bumblebee will be determined by the number and availability of different flowers growing in a given area (Brittain & Newton, 1933; Spencer-Booth, 1965). It is to be expected, therefore, that bumblebees occurring in habitats with little floral diversity, or where a suitable or favourite floral host is predominant or particularly numerous (a heather-clad moor is an example), will show a greater degree of flower constancy than bumblebees foraging in gardens or in other places with a rich and varied flora.

The degree of flower constancy shown by bumblebees varies from species to species (e.g. Clements & Long, 1923; Brian, 1951b, 1952, 1954; Free, 1970a). Both Brian (1951b) and Free found that foragers from *B. lucorum* colonies collected pollen from fewer plant species than did foragers of *B. pascuorum*. Brian considered it possible that there was some attempt to mobilize the forager force of a *B. lucorum* colony to exploit a particular plant species, and Free lends support to this hypothesis by showing that the forager forces from two contemporaneous *B. lucorum* colonies in the same area exploited the surrounding flora in different ways. It is generally accepted that, unlike honey bees, bumblebee foragers do not communicate information on food sources to fellow workers when returning from a foraging trip[1] (e.g. Jacobs-Jessen, 1959; Esch, 1967). However, Free suggests that the scent of predominant pollens in a bumblebee nest may induce the pollen-gatherers to seek them.

[1] although Blackith (1957) found that when a foraging bee, and particularly a young queen, entered the nest this increased the likelihood of others leaving.

If this is so, then one might expect such 'information' to be disseminated most readily in nests of species, such as *B. lucorum*, which tend to restrict their visits to relatively few plant species.

Pollen-gatherers often collect a single type of pollen on a foraging trip, and individual foragers may remain faithful to specific plants for several successive flights (see Free, 1970b). On the other hand a bumblebee may collect several pollens in one trip, but even when mixed loads are collected the different pollens may be segregated in the corbicula into distinct layers, indicating that different species of plant have not been visited indiscriminately. Free (1970a) showed that bumblebees visiting more than one floral host species will frequently collect the same combination of pollens on successive trips, and that the proportions of these are often similar. Mixed loads may include small quantities of pollen remaining from previous excursions, or pollen grains acquired by accident, either in the field or in the nest, and Free has suggested that, for this reason, flower constancy, as measured from examination of pollen loads, is frequently underestimated.

Constancy in floral visitation is advantageous to the plant in that the chances of cross-pollination occurring are greatly increased; the hairy coat of a bumblebee is ideal for picking up pollen grains and transferring them from flower to flower. Constancy also enables the bee to work more rapidly since she will have learnt from experience the position of the nectaries (Darwin, 1876).

It is well-known that bumblebees of certain short-tongued species bite holes in the corolla tubes of flowers, thus enabling them, and other bees with tongues too short to reach the nectar in the normal way, to work the flowers. *Bombus lucorum*, *B. mastrucatus* and *B. terrestris*, for example, are especially liable to adopt this habit. The holes are made near the nectary of the flower either by piercing with the tongue or biting with the mandibles. A robber bee (those biting the flowers are termed 'primary robbers') does not pollinate the flower when collecting nectar by way of a hole, although it has been suggested that movement caused by a robber bee may be sufficient to transfer pollen from the anthers to the stigma and hence pollinate a self-fertile flower (Soper, 1952). Other bumblebees and honey bees which do not, or cannot, perforate flowers ('secondary robbers') may nevertheless obtain nectar through holes made by primary robbers. The number of robber honey bees working a crop may depend on the number of robber bumblebees present (e.g. Pedersen & Sørensen, 1935; Jany, 1950; Free, 1968). Many wild flowers, for example common comfrey (*Symphytum officinale*), woundworts (*Stachys*) and yellow toadflax (*Linaria vulgaris*), and also important crops, such as runner bean (*Phaseolus multiflorus*), field bean (*Vicia faba*) and red clover (*Trifolium pratense*), are prone to the attention of robber bumblebees. Free estimated that in a single day a robber bumblebee could perforate 2,000, or more, runner bean flowers. Bumblebees robbing pierced flowers work faster than those entering flowers in the normal way (e.g. Darwin, 1876; Brian, A. D., 1957). In Norway, Løken (1949) found that in areas where long-tongued bumblebees were predominant few flowers were perforated, but in places

90

where foraging populations were mostly composed of *B. mastrucatus* nearly all the flowers were mutilated.

Hole-biting is regarded as detrimental to the plant or crop concerned (e.g. Curtis, 1860; Williams, 1925; Stapel, 1934; Eaton & Stewart, 1969), particularly when honey bees act as secondary robbers and no longer collect nectar through the front of the flowers, thereby failing to pollinate them. However, it is possible that the nectar-gatherers working a crop, albeit via perforated corolla tubes, may subsequently attract pollen-gatherers from their colonies and so lead to an overall increase in the level of pollination (Free & Butler, 1959; Hawkins, 1961). Bees collecting pollen will enter perforated flowers just as frequently as unperforated ones (Skovgaard, 1936). Further, hole-biting does not appear to prevent seed or pod formation; nor are pierced flowers shed any earlier than unperforated ones (Free, 1970b).

It has been suggested that hole-biting is instinctive (Lie-Petterson, 1906; Pittioni, 1942), but Kugler (1943) considered this behaviour to be entirely a question of learning. However, Kugler's hypothesis does not explain why long-tongued species such as *B. hortorum* do not bite holes in flowers where even they cannot normally reach the nectaries. Kugler supposed that *B. hortorum* had weak mouthparts, but this is questioned by Brian, A. D. (1957). She alternatively suggests that the difference is innate, *B. hortorum* being 'conservative and stereotyped, always visiting flowers by the obvious and correct entrance' while a hole-biter such as *B. lucorum* 'is an opportunist obtaining nectar by a variety of methods'.

In addition to collecting nectar from flowers, bumblebees will also visit extra-floral nectaries which are to be found on certain plants including field bean (*Vicia faba*) and sunflower (*Helianthus annuus*). Fox Wilson (1926) observed that on sunny days *Bombus* queens and workers were attracted to sap exuding from the trunks of forest trees. Bumblebees also visit aphids to collect honeydew (e.g. Hulkkonen, 1929; Longstaff, 1932; Brian, A. D., 1957); foragers of *B. lucorum* and *B. terrestris* are particularly attracted to this type of food source. Bischoff (1927) reported seeing *B. hypnorum* collecting honeydew from aphids on oak trees, apparently in preference to visiting nearby bramble (*Rubus fruticosus*) flowers, to which *B. hypnorum* foragers are normally much attracted. Finally, *B. pascuorum* has been observed to collect honeydew secreted by the psyllid *Psylla crataegi* (Walton, 1927).

Much has been written concerning the relationship of bees and flowers, but only cursory mention of this subject will be made here. The colour, shape and characteristic scent of flowers are all important in attracting bumblebees and, of course, other pollinating insects (see Kugler, 1943). Bumblebees are able to distinguish between blue, green and yellow, and probably ultra-violet is also visible to them as a distinct colour. Nectar-guides, the markings found on the petals of many flowers, such as foxglove (*Digitalis purpurea*), assist novice foragers to locate the nectaries, but they become less important once a bee gains experience (see Manning, 1956a). Bumblebees may become conditioned to the colour of a flower (Manning, 1956b), although they will also visit flowers of different colours on one and the same foraging trip.

Bumblebees are especially attracted to irregularly-shaped flowers (Leppik, 1953) and are able to distinguish depth so that, as well as taking account of the flower's outline, they also appreciate, and seem particularly attracted to, flowers offering a three-dimensional picture (Kugler, 1943). With experience, bumblebees can also recognize the form of certain plants (Darwin, 1876; Manning, 1956b). The characteristic scent of a flower may help in identification and may also act as a stimulus for alighting, but this may only be important after a forager becomes accustomed to visiting a particular species of flower. Lex (1954) has shown that a scent gradient may exist in some flowers, and that in others various parts of the flower may produce different odours; in either case a scent pattern is produced. This is detectable by a searching bumblebee and may guide the bee to the nectaries. Bumblebees have good olfactory powers and can detect and react to the scent of certain flowers considered odourless by man (Kugler, 1932); two well-known examples are yellow toadflax (*Linaria vulgaris*) and viper's bugloss (*Echium vulgare*).

At one time it was believed that foraging bumblebees were serious competitors of honey bees, and Huish (1817) even went so far as to suggest that, in consequence, they and their nests should be destroyed. However, bumblebees and honey bees do not utilize the available forage in the same way, for example, their flower preferences tend to be different (e.g. Leclercq, 1960, 1961; Free, 1970c), so that although some degree of competition for food may occur, this will be relatively unimportant. Further, it is now realized that bumblebees are useful as pollinators of certain agricultural or horticultural crops (see Free, 1970b), a fact first demonstrated by Darwin (1859). Bumblebees are also valuable as pollinators of various wild plants, particularly of those bearing flowers with long corolla tubes. Some flowers, such as heartsease (*Viola tricolor*), rely almost entirely on bumblebees for effective pollination and in the Arctic where, apart from Diptera (true flies), few other suitable pollinating insects exist, the value of bumblebees as pollinators is considerable (e.g. Panfilov, *et al.*, 1960; Chernov, 1966; Shamurin, 1966; Kevan, 1972).

CHAPTER 7

Social Parasitism

INSTEAD of forming nests of their own, *Bombus* queens of certain species may attempt to take over those already established by other queens. As mentioned previously, some *Bombus* species, and even some queens of one and the same species, may emerge from hibernation considerably later in the spring than others, and it is such individuals, on finding nesting sites already occupied, which are likely to become invaders. In Canada, for example, Hobbs (1965b) recorded a particularly high incidence of supersedure among queens of the late-appearing species *B. rufocinctus*. Usurpation by *Bombus* is liable to be particularly prevalent when suitable nesting sites are in short supply (relative to the number of searching queens), and Sladen (1899, 1912) observed that in seasons when hibernated queens of *B. terrestris* and *B. lapidarius* were abundant several queens in succession would invade a single nest; on one occasion Sladen actually found as many as twenty dead *B. terrestris* queens in the same nest. Multiple cases of successful or attempted queen replacement have also been recorded by Voveikov (1953) and Bohart (1970). Usurpation of nests by a queen of the same or of a different species is referred to as intraspecific and interspecific supersedure respectively.[1] The phenomenon has also been termed temporary or incipient social parasitism.

Usurpation always results in the death of one, if not both, queens (Hobbs, 1967b). Sladen described the conflict as follows: 'The foundress of the nest at first ignores the stranger, who takes care to keep out of her way as much as possible. After a short while, however, the intruder grows bolder, and begins to pay close attention to the brood. Jealousy then arises, and a mortal duel is the result. The two queens seize and endeavour to sting one another in the most ferocious and desperate manner, rolling over, locked in a deadly embrace. One of them succeeds, usually within a few seconds, in piercing the other, the sting in most cases penetrating between two of the segments of the abdomen.' Although Sladen considered that aggression between the queens was delayed, it is also apparent that queens of at least some species will fight as soon as they encounter one another. Sladen was also of the opinion that the foundress queen, unless is some way debilitated, usually defeated the infiltrator, but the opposite view is expressed by other authorities. Species may vary in this respect, but it is not always possible to make a decision either way, since

---

[1] In the case of perennial, tropical bumblebee colonies natural replacement of a mother queen by a mated daughter queen is also known as 'supersedure'; this process follows more closely the pattern of queen replacement occurring in honey bee colonies.

the finding of one dead and one live queen in a nest will often provide no clue as to which had priority.

If an invader successfully overthrows the foundress queen she adopts the original brood and continues to care for it, seemingly with as much attention as the rightful owner, but should multiple supersedures occur in a nest, probably because of the repeated interruptions to brood-rearing, then colonies become weak. However, a single (Hobbs, 1965b) or a two-fold (Voveikov, 1953) replacement of queens will lead to the development of a strong colony. Successful invasion of nests rarely, if ever, occurs once the workers of the second brood batch have emerged.

Bombus terrestris is well-known as an occasional usurper of colonies of *B. lucorum* (both subgenus *Bombus*), and in North America Plath (1924, 1934) found that *B. affinis* frequently invaded incipient colonies of *B. terricola* (both also subgenus *Bombus*). In both cases the victim is an earlier-emerging species and has the more northern distribution. It has been suggested (Richards, 1927) that the habit of usurping nests of a close relative is most likely to occur where the invading species is at the northern edge of its range and so is tending to appear later in the spring than normal. However, in such a relationship the northern species is not necessarily the victim. Thus, *B. distinguendus*, a species which appears particularly late in the spring, is well-known for usurping nests of *B. subterraneus*, its more southerly-distributed relative (e.g. Lindhard, 1912; Fleming, 1926). Although documenting many cases of interspecific supersedures among bumblebees in Canada, Hobbs never found an example involving species from different subgenera. It is generally supposed that characteristics of colony odour and differences in nest site requirements are to some extent involved in separating species or groups of closely related species from one another so, presumably, there will be a tendency for a usurper queen only to invade a nest belonging to her own, or a very similar, species.

In arctic Canada, queens of *B. hyperboreus* are reported to usurp established nests of *B. polaris* (both species subgenus *Megabombus*) (Milliron & Oliver, 1966; Richards, 1973). As mentioned previously, in the short favourable arctic season *B. polaris* colonies usually produce only a single batch of workers before sexual forms appear, and, following invasion by a queen of *B. hyperboreus*, the fertilized eggs she lays are typically reared as queens and not workers. Friese (1923) was unaware of the inquilinous habit of *B. hyperboreus* and, because of the apparent absence of workers, considered it to be a solitary species of *Bombus*. However, workers of *B. hyperboreus* are known to occur in northern Europe so the dependence of this species upon *B. polaris* is not necessarily complete. Nevertheless, the usurper-host relationship between these two species is clearly closer than it is known to be in the case of other *Bombus* species. Future research, however, may show that a similar or even greater degree of dependence upon a *Bombus* host is exhibited by the rare European species *B. inexspectatus*. This little-known species was recently described by Tkalcu (1963), and it is now believed (although not yet proven) that this is a truly worker-less species which is entirely dependent for its survival upon another species of *Bombus* (Yarrow, 1970). It appears likely that *B. inexspectatus* queens have lost the ability to collect pollen loads or to secrete wax, so they have become unable to establish colonies of their own or to rear their brood unaided. *B. inexspectatus* is extremely rare and, so far, is known only from certain mountainous regions in the Alps, Cantabrians and Dolomites. Yarrow has suggested that its close relative *B. ruderarius* may prove to be the host species upon which it is dependent. Details of the biology of this remarkable bumblebee are awaited with considerable interest.

The relationship between a usurper species of *Bombus* and its 'host' is, with one or two possible exceptions, entirely optional. However, bumblebees of the genus *Psithyrus* are wholly dependent upon other bumblebees for their existence. *Psithyrus* females do not have a pollen-collecting apparatus on their hind legs; they are also unable to produce wax. A *Psithyrus* female is, therefore, incapable of founding a colony and in order to survive to produce the next generation, she must invade a nest already established by a *Bombus* queen. Presumably as an aid to the successful usurping of *Bombus* colonies, *Psithyrus* females possess more powerful stings and stronger, more powerful jaws than their hosts. They are also better equipped for defence; their exoskeleton is particularly strong, and the abdomen relatively inflexible and more or less incurved; also, the potentially vulnerable, membranous, intersegmental regions are much reduced in extent. Once successfully installed in a suitable colony the *Psithyrus* female lays eggs and these are eventually reared by the *Bombus* workers. *Psithyrus* lacks an industrious (worker) caste of its own, and all brood-rearing is, therefore, dependent upon the activities of the host bees. Although known as permanent social parasites, *Psithyrus* species are not parasites in the strict sense as they live at the expense of, rather than on, their *Bombus* hosts; the term 'inquiline bumblebees' is, therefore, more appropriate. They are also known as 'cuckoo bumblebees'.

Psithyrus females emerge from their winter quarters somewhat later in the spring than their *Bombus* hosts and, initially, they spend much of their time lazing on flowers, where they feed on both nectar and pollen. In some areas they are particularly attracted to dandelions (*Taraxacum officinalis*,). Although *Psithyrus* females do not collect pollen loads, their bodies are frequently dusted with pollen grains, sometimes so much so that it may be difficult at first glance to recognize the species. *Psithyrus* females are far less alert than *Bombus* queens, their flight is more laboured and, when foraging on flowers, their movements are slow and rather ponderous.

Once their ovaries develop, *Psithyrus* females begin to roam the countryside in search of bumblebee nests. They search diligently in likely-looking areas, and the characteristic colony odour produced by the particular species of *Bombus* upon which perpetuation of their kind depends is said to play a part in helping them find a suitable nest (Frison, 1930b). *Psithyrus* females may sometimes reside temporarily in the nests of non-host species of *Bombus* but, according to Sladen's observations, only in those still with few or no workers. Sometimes, however, they will enter honey bee colonies, only to be thrown out unceremoniously by the bees (e.g.

Plath, 1927c).[1] It has been suggested that bumblebee nests with long entrance tunnels will tend to escape the attention of *Psithyrus*. However, although a superficial nest may be easier to locate, a long tunnel evidently does not safeguard a colony from attack as Plath (1934) has recorded finding *Psithyrus*-ridden colonies with entrance tunnels 1·5 to 3 m. long; Plath has also demonstrated the fallibility of Wagner's (1907) suggestion that bumblebee nests constructed high above ground level would escape attacks by *Psithyrus*.

In most cases a particular species of *Psithyrus* will only victimize a single host species or, alternatively, a small group of closely related host species. However, the extensive studies made by Hobbs show that certain inquilines, for example *P. insularis*, can successfully invade, and have their brood reared in, colonies of host *Bombus* species of different subgenera. Hobbs (1967b, 1968) also reports that, in Canada, species of *Bombus* which appear early in the season are more heavily victimized by *Psithyrus* than are later-appearing species, and he considers that 'early emerging species apparently compensate for this much higher rate of depreda-tion by having much higher biotic potentials'. This would not seem to be applicable to the British fauna where, with local exceptions affecting both early- and late-appearing species (see below), attacks upon *Bombus* hosts do not normally reach serious proportions. Admittedly, however, there are few available data which relate directly to the frequency of *Psithyrus* attacks among the various host *Bombus* species in these islands. In my experience *Psithyrus* is not usually a major problem, although females and particularly males of some species are commonly found in the field in many areas. Recently, however, Awram (1970) noted that more than half of the nests of *B. pratorum* (an early-appearing species) which he obtained in Hertfordshire during the period 1967 to 1969, were victimized by *P. sylvestris*, and Sladen reported over sixty years ago that in East Kent *P. rupestris* invaded 'from 20 to 40 per cent of the colonies of *B. lapidarius*' (a late-appearing species). It should be remembered that *Psithyrus* is not the only enemy of *Bombus*, and many species suffer considerable losses as a result of attacks by a variety of parasites and predators. These destructive agents are considered in detail in the next chapter.

If attacked when entering a bumblebee nest, an invading *Psithyrus* female draws her legs up tightly against her body and then remains almost motionless; Frison (1926a) maintained that 'the calm and deliberate attitude of the female' was impor-tant in ensuring her successful ingratiation into a colony. However, some females may, nevertheless, fail in their bid to establish themselves, and may be killed or driven out by the bees. Perhaps the most suitable time to enter a colony is when the first batch of *Bombus* workers has been produced, as at this stage the bees show little hostility towards an invader and induction of a *Psithyrus* female will in all

---

[1] *Bombus* queens will also enter honey bee hives, as will both bumblebee workers and males, probably after having been attracted by the smell. Bumblebees entering, or attempting to enter, hives may be killed and their bodies thrown on to the ground below the hive entrance. In the struggle, the body hairs of the bumblebee are frequently removed; the shiny, black, more or less hairless carcasses of *Bombus* queens are often mistaken for dead *Psithyrus* females. Often, however, bumblebees will be attacked briefly at the colony entrance, but will then escape unharmed (Morse & Gary, 1961).

probability be successful. On the other hand, should a *Psithyrus* female attempt to enter a populous colony, her reception will be far from peaceful. Several workers may furiously attack the stranger, forming a tight mass of bees around her, each intent upon stinging. Free & Butler (1959) likened this aggregation of workers to the 'ball' formed by worker honey bees around an *Apis* queen recently introduced into a hive. Although well protected by her thick cuticle, the *Psithyrus* female is, nevertheless, vulnerable, principally in the 'neck' region, and eventually she is likely to be fatally stung, but not before several of her attackers have been slain. Death among the workers may not always be due directly to the *Psithyrus* as in their efforts to kill the female, the *Bombus* workers may inadvertently sting some of their colleagues. Sometimes a *Psithyrus* female will enter a *Bombus* nest before any workers have been reared. However, in such cases the *Bombus* queen often abandons her home (Hobbs, 1965a), and the incursion is abortive. It seems improbable that a *Bombus* queen could successfully defend her young colony from attack by a fit *Psithyrus*, although death of an inquiline is sometimes, rightly or wrongly, accredited to the *Bombus* queen (Frison, 1921a). Usually, however, if the *Psithyrus* loses her life, it is a result of concerted attacks mounted by the *Bombus* workers.

Once having successfully entered a *Bombus* colony, the *Psithyrus* at first tries to avoid contact with the host bees. She frequently hides between the cocoons or within the nest material, and presumably, in this way, she quickly acquires the characteristic odour of the colony. In the vast majority of cases where a *Psithyrus* female successfully invades a colony, both the inquiline and the *Bombus* queen live amicably together (e.g. Hoffer, 1882b, 1889; Plath, 1922c; Frison, 1926a; Hobbs, *et al.*, 1962; Hobbs, 1965a). The deposed *Bombus* queen may sometimes approach the invader, but any animosity she displays is usually short-lived. Sladen, however, believed that the *Psithyrus* always killed the host queen, and he wrote: 'I have taken a great many nests of *lapidarius* and *terrestris* in all stages, but have seen no evidence to show that the *Bombus* queen ever succeeds in killing the *Psithyrus*, or that she ever escapes being destroyed by the latter. Here, however, my observations are opposed to those of Hoffer, who found the *Psithyrus* queen and the *Bombus* queen living in the nest on good terms with one another, and both of them producing young males and queens. But Hoffer's observations were made chiefly on two species of *Psithyrus* which I have not been able to study, namely, *Ps. campestris*, which breeds in the nests of *B. agrorum* [*B. pascuorum*] and *B. helferanus* [*B. humilis*], and *Ps. quadricolor* [*P. sylvestris*], which preys on *B. pratorum*. Evidently these species of *Bombus*, which it may be noted, are milder tempered than *B. lapidarius* and *terrestris*, do not object, in Styria at least, to the *Psithyri* laying their eggs in their nests.' Unfortunately, I have never found *P. vestalis* or *P. rupestris* in bumblebee nests; however, I have observed *P. campestris* living in apparent harmony with *B. pascuorum* queens, and Awram (1970) reports similarly on *P. sylvestris* and *B. pratorum*.

Various observers have described how a *Psithyrus* female, having successfully invaded a *Bombus* nest, may catch hold of and maul several worker bees in turn, rolling over and over with them before relaxing her hold and releasing them. Such behaviour is reminiscent of the domineering attitude adopted by a *Bombus* queen towards laying-workers in her nest, and is presumably associated with a need for the *Psithyrus* to assert her dominance in the colony. Later, the *Psithyrus* female may also have to defend her newly-laid eggs against attacks launched by the more belligerent *Bombus* workers; Sladen believed that the callosities and incurvation of the tip of the abdomen, common to all *Psithyrus* females to a greater or lesser degree, were useful for handling such individuals.

Eggs laid by *Psithyrus* are more slender, less curved and blunter than those of *Bombus*; they may also be somewhat longer than those of the host species. As the abdomen of a *Psithyrus* female must usually accommodate many more ovarioles than is the case in *Bombus* – Cumber (1949d) recorded as many as thirty-three ovarioles in a *P. rupestris* female – the development of thinner eggs is presumably related to the need to conserve space as the eggs ripen. The *Psithyrus* female deposits her eggs in rather thick-walled cells placed, as in *Bombus*, on existing pupal cocoons. The inquiline constructs each cell herself, using wax-pollen taken from other parts of the comb. A *Psithyrus* female is capable of laying a large number of eggs at one sitting. The eggs may be laid in rapid succession, and Sladen once watched a *P. rupestris* female deposit twenty-three in six minutes. As in *Bombus* cells, the eggs are placed in horizontal, parallel bundles. Young *Bombus* brood in a colony occupied by *Psithyrus* is often destroyed by the invader, although if the host colony is small such depredations may be delayed. *Psithyrus* females will eagerly open *Bombus* egg cells and eat the contents; the wax-pollen from a broken-down egg cell may then be used by the *Psithyrus* for constructing a cell of her own. Plath observed a *P. laboriosus* female, which had infiltrated a *B. vagans* colony, break down a young larval clump belonging to its host.

Development of *Psithyrus* brood is similar to that of *Bombus* (except, of course, that none of the fertilized eggs is raised as a worker) and it is liable to attacks by the same parasites or predators. Older larvae may be distinguished from those of *Bombus* by their more pointed, falcate mandibles (cf. Figs. 26 and 27). Sladen noted that pupal cocoons of at least most British species of *Psithyrus* 'differ from those of their *Bombus* hosts in that they quickly lose their fresh lemon tint, and become of a dull ochreous colour, and later turn semi-transparent, crackling when they are dented – qualities that are possessed in only a very slight degree by the *Bombus* cocoons'.

The period of development of a colony headed by a *Psithyrus* female is shorter than normal, the male and female progeny of the invader appearing rather earlier than would sexual forms of the host species in healthy, *Psithyrus*-free nests. The number of *Psithyrus* individuals reared in a colony varies according to the species and is also governed by the size of the available *Bombus* worker force. Data provided by various observers suggest that about twice as many males as females are produced. The size of *Psithyrus* adults reared in a colony is to a large extent determined by the amount of food available to them at the larval stage. Females are particularly liable to be affected, and under poor trophic conditions very small individuals, no larger than normal-sized males, may be reared. However, these small specimens are not equivalent to *Bombus* workers, as was once supposed, since in common with full-sized females they are non-industrious and are capable of developing large fat bodies, mating, successfully overwintering and, later, invading *Bombus* colonies.

Although *Psithyrus* males are frequently observed in the field during the summer months (Chapter 5), young females, like young *Bombus* queens, are far less often noticed. They may, however, sometimes be found on flowers and also at hibernation sites where, in common with *Bombus* queens, they will spend the winter.

There is little doubt that *Psithyrus* has evolved from *Bombus*, but there are conflicting opinions as regards the nature of their descent. Some authorities maintain that all members of *Psithyrus* have a common ancestry and are of monophyletic origin; others, however, consider that the genus has two or more ancestral lines and is of polyphyletic origin.

It is probable that in some way the usurpation of nests by *Bombus* has led to the permanent and obligatory inquilinism exhibited by *Psithyrus*. In most cases usurpation by *Bombus* will not be habitual and so, as pointed out by Richards, it will not develop further. However, a more permanent relationship can occur, as is seen today in the case of *B. hyperboreus* (and possibly to an even greater degree in *B. inexspectatus*). Richards's suggestion that the usurper-host relationship is likely to become more permanent where an invading species is at the northern limits of its range is given support by the findings of Reinig (1935) who has noted that in most instances a *Psithyrus* does not occur as far north as the host species. The fact that usurping *Bombus* queens only invade nests of the same or closely related species suggests that the origin of *Psithyrus* may be polyphyletic, with members of each group typically restricting their attacks to particular host species. However, it is also possible that limitation in host selection by particular *Psithyrus* species followed establishment of the permanent and obligatory 'parasitic' way of life.

Although some species of *Psithyrus* resemble the colour patterns of their hosts, the significance of this is obscure. Sladen believed that there was 'no evidence to show that any species of *Psithyrus* has sprung from the particular species of *Bombus* on which it preys, such resemblances as it may show to it in coat-colour, etc., being pretty clearly attributable to mimicry or exposure to the same conditions of life, and not to ancestry'. Plath, on the other hand, maintained that similarities in coat coloration probably were indicative of common origin, a view also expressed by Reinig. Geographical variation of a *Psithyrus* may closely match that of its *Bombus* host, and Reinig considered that such similarities were probably due to a common orthogenetic process which was influenced in the same direction by external conditions such as climate and food. Reinig dismissed mimicry as a factor; and, certainly, the suggestions sometimes expressed that resemblance between a *Psithyrus* and its main host confers some benefit on the former are not at all convincing. As far as coloration of the European species is concerned, Richards concluded: 'The resemblance between *Psithyrus* species and their hosts is scarcely greater than might be expected on the laws of chance in such polymorphic genera. Nevertheless, it is, perhaps, significant that *Ps. sylvestris*, Lep., and *Ps. rupestris*, F., the only species in which red appears in the tail, parasitise subgenera of *Bombus* in which also red often appears. Similarly, the hosts of *Ps. campestris*, Pz., a species in which white is always absent from the tail, also lack the white. The other species of *Psithyrus* normally have white tails and so have their hosts. Thus, although the details of the colour-patterns of host and parasite do not resemble one another in a significant way, yet these patterns appear to be governed in part by the same fundamental laws. This is further evidence in favour of the polyphyletic origin of *Psithyrus*.'

Morphological evidence, however, tends on the whole to point to a monophyletic origin for *Psithyrus*, and Milliron (1971) has recently stated that to consider *Psithyrus* as being of other than monophyletic origin is 'unthinkable'. However, although it is true that *Psithyrus* species share many structural features not found in *Bombus* (see Richards's paper for details), and that this is indicative of a common ancestry, several such characters (for example, absence of the pollen-collecting apparatus, reduced pilosity, and presence of a strong exoskeleton) are shared by many 'parasitic' bees. It must, therefore, be considered possible that the morphological similarities of the various species of *Psithyrus* are, at least in part, a result of convergence in response to their inquilinous way of life.

CHAPTER 8

Enemies and Nest Commensals

A LARGE and varied assemblage of insects, mites and other creatures are closely associated with bumblebees. Many occur in their nests as accidental visitors or harmless scavengers, and some may be useful denizens, but several are parasites of adult bees, or are harmful to the brood or comb. Bumblebees and their nests are also victimized by various predatory animals. In the following account of parasites, predators and commensals, for ease of reference each taxonomic group is considered separately. To avoid unnecessary interruption in the text, formal references to family names and other such details are omitted, but they may be found in the Appendix lists.

Insects

LEPIDOPTERA (BUTTERFLIES AND MOTHS)

Several species of moth are known to breed in bumblebee nests, and although most are relatively harmless one species, the pyralid *Aphomia sociella*, whose caterpillars feed on bumblebee comb and are often responsible for the premature destruction of colonies, must be regarded as an important enemy. Hoffer (1882–3), in fact, considered this insect to be the worst enemy of bumblebees. *A. sociella* occurs commonly throughout the British Isles, particularly in the south, and is also regarded as a pest in other parts of Europe, including France (Pouvreau, 1967), Germany (Hoffer, 1882–3; Hase, 1926) and Scandinavia (Kivirikko, 1941; Valle, 1955; Hasselrot, 1960). It has also been introduced into America (Forbes, 1923). Although *A. sociella* sometimes invades subterranean nests, the caterpillars are more frequently found in surface nests; *Bombus ruderarius*, for example, is a heavily victimized species.

Adults of *A. sociella* have a wingspan of approximately 30 to 35 mm. and are whitish yellow in colour, with dark brown markings. In fresh specimens the fore wings are suffused with green, but when worn they are almost, if not entirely, straw-coloured. Moths appear from June to August, and as they fly in the late evening and at night, host bumblebee nests are probably located by smell; this would, at least in part, explain the tendency for this insect to invade colonies of surface-nesting bumblebees.

The eggs, which are globular and shiny white, are laid in irregular masses (Fig. 43). They hatch in about a week, depending on the temperature, and the young larvae then live gregariously, each spinning a loose silken web into which they retreat rapidly when disturbed. At first the caterpillars feed mainly on nest debris and empty cocoons, but later all parts of the comb, including the food stores and even the brood, may be attacked. Within a matter of days a bumblebee comb can be completely destroyed and riddled with silken tunnels; to use Sladen's (1912) apt description, the comb then becomes 'an impenetrable, sponge-like mass of web and debris'. With their brood and food stores destroyed, the adult bumblebees remaining in the nest become increasingly listless and eventually they die of starvation.

Within any one infested bumblebee colony there are usually at least one hundred *Aphomia* larvae. A full-grown caterpillar is approximately 25 to 32 mm. long (Fig. 44) and is dull yellowish in colour, with the back pale greyish green; the head, and the prothoracic and anal plates, are reddish brown. When the caterpillars have finished feeding, usually in September but sometimes earlier, they crawl out

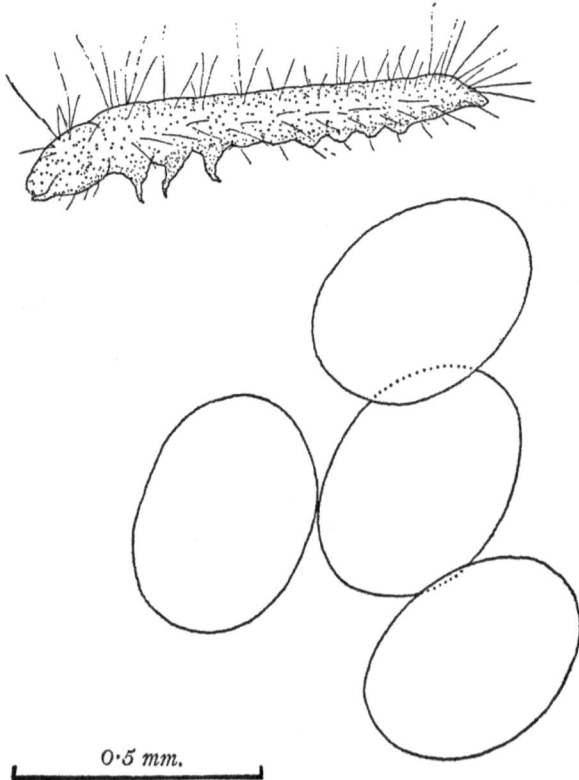

0·5 mm.

43

Fig. 43. Eggs and first-instar larva of *Aphomia sociella*.

102

of the nest *en masse*. If in an underground nest, the larvae may spin a web of silk along the tunnel leading to the nest entrance, thereby aiding their escape. Each then spins a tough, whitish, elongate cocoon . The cocoons are constructed alongside one another, often forming a ball-like mass under some protective cover, such as a large stone or a piece of wood. Larvae remain in their cocoons throughout the winter, pupating in the spring. Overwintering larvae lose their green coloration and become bright lemon-yellow; this probably accounts for the description given by Buckler (1899) for *A. sociella* larvae reared in wasp (*Vespula*) nests.

In contrast with *A. sociella*, the typical American wax-moth (*Vitula edmandsii*) is a comparatively harmless species, the larvae feeding on wax, pollen and nest debris in bumblebee colonies, but apparently not on the brood; nor does it bring about the destruction of the host colony, although once a comb is neglected by the bumblebees, after the natural decline of the colony, it is soon degraded by the wax-moth larvae (Frison, 1926a). This species of wax-moth does not occur in Europe.

Davidson (1894) reported the moth *Ephestia kühniella* as a pest of *Bombus fervidus* in America, the larvae presumably feeding on the colony food stores or nest debris, and Milum (1940) suggested that the closely related species *E. cautella*, which sometimes occurs in honey bee hives, might also attack bumblebee nests; he also considered that the honey bee wax-moths *Achroia grisella* and *Galleria mellonella* could similarly invade their nests. The latter species has since been recorded in *Bombus* nests in Japan (Miyamoto, 1957c), and successfully reared on bumblebee comb by Oertel (1963). Frison (1926a) found that in Illinois his laboratory-based bumblebee colonies were victimized by yet another pyralid, the Indian meal moth (*Plodia interpunctella*). As far as I am aware none of these species has yet been reared from wild bumblebee nests in the British Isles, although all commonly occur here either as warehouse or apiary pests (see Beirne, 1952).

A warehouse moth which does sometimes breed in bumblebee nests in Britain

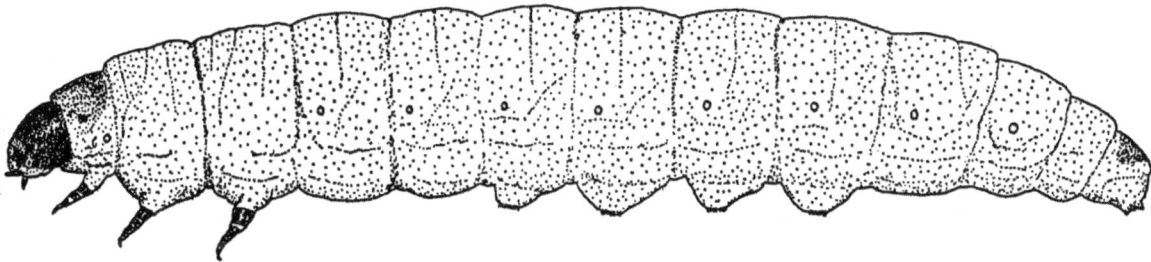

3 mm.

44

Fig. 44. Final-instar larva of *Aphomia sociella*.

is *Endrosis sarcitrella*. This species, unlike *A. sociella*, is harmless, the larvae feeding mainly on nest debris. Further, in contrast with *A. sociella*, the eggs are pear-shaped and generally laid singly (Fig. 45); the caterpillars are not gregarious, are much smaller (approximately 10 to 14 mm. long when full-grown), whitish yellow in colour, far less active and do not inhabit silken webs. *Endrosis* was apparently first recorded from a bumblebee nest by Smith (1851) and is probably the 'small lepidopterous caterpillar that much resembles the young larva of the wax-moth' mentioned by Sladen. *E. sarcitrella* frequently lives in dwelling houses, although it is normally considered a warehouse pest (Richards & Waloff, 1947; O'Farrell & Butler, 1948); it has also been recorded breeding in birds' nests

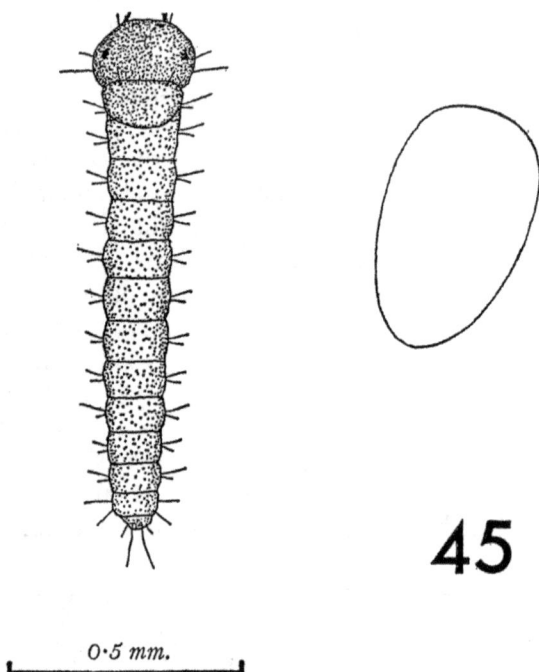

Fig. 45. Eggs and first-instar larva of *Endrosis sarcitrella*.

(Curtis, 1860; Waters, 1929) and on insects occurring in or near spiders' webs (Hinton, 1943). It can, therefore, survive under a variety of environmental conditions. *E. sarcitrella* occurs commonly in honey bee hives, and I have reared it from nests of *Bombus hortorum*, *B. pascuorum*, *B. ruderarius* and *B. subterraneus*.

Although the temperature and humidity conditions suitable for completion of the life cycle of *Endrosis* exist in bumblebee nests, they are usually unsuitable for the development of *Hofmannophila pseudospretella*, an abundant moth which, elsewhere, frequently occurs in association with *E. sarcitrella* (see Woodroffe, 1951a, 1951b). However, one autumn I found three larvae of *H. pseudospretella* feeding on dead adult bumblebees in the remains of a *B. pascuorum* colony, previously established in a bird-box. In this case the moth larvae, artificially reared indoors, pupated in the following July and adults eventually emerged during the middle of August.

Surprisingly few other tineid species have been recorded in association with bumblebee nests. Miyamoto (1963a) attributed destruction of a nest of *B. ignitus* to larvae of *Tinea simplicella*, but it is not known whether this common species of clothes-moth is ever harmful to bumblebees in Britain.

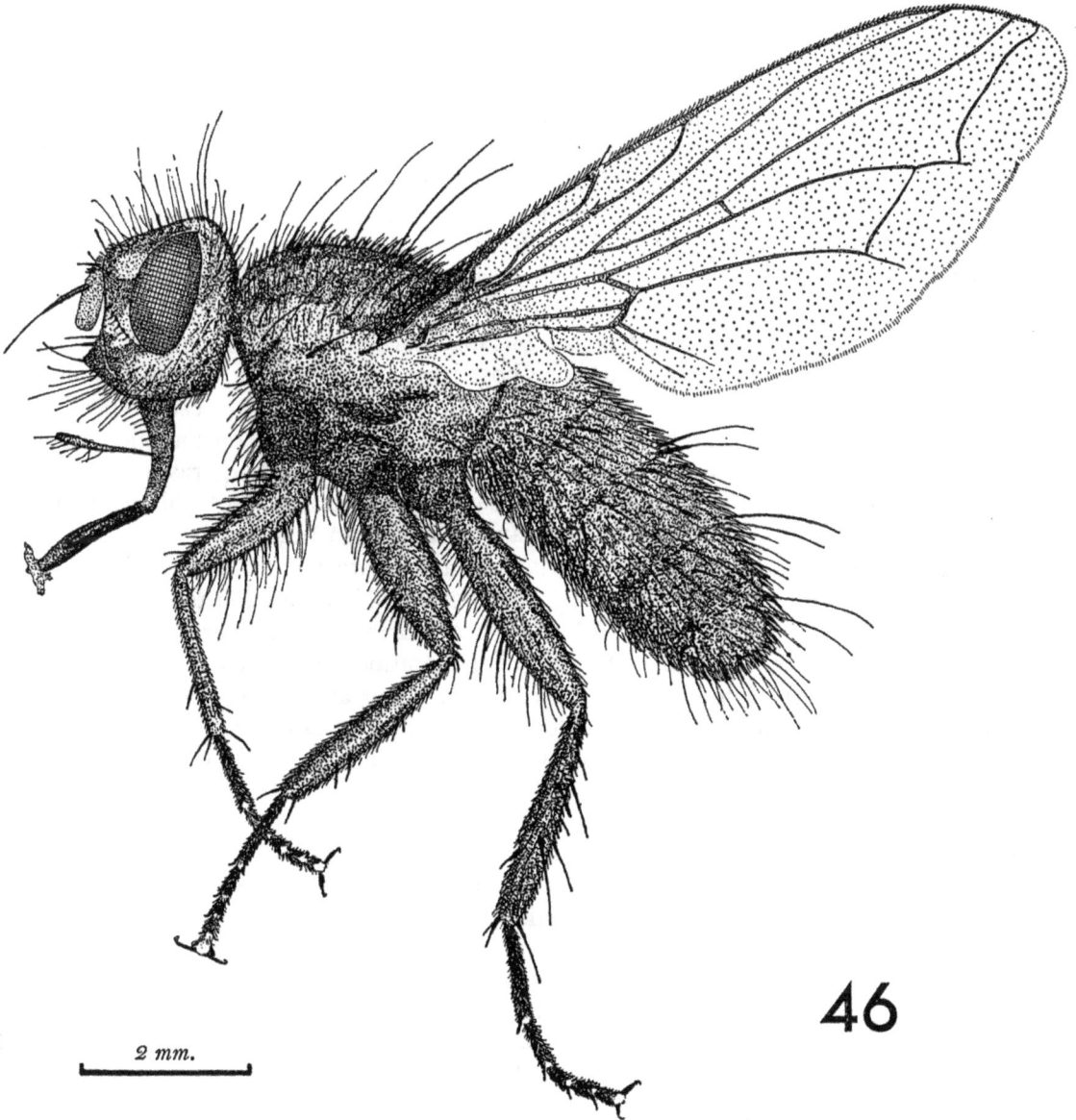

2 mm.

46

Fig. 46. *Brachicoma devia*.

DIPTERA (TRUE FLIES)

The brood of British bumblebees is often attacked by a parasitic fly known as *Brachicoma devia*. Abroad these flies or their close relatives (for example, in America, *B. sarcophagina*) are similarly destructive. The latter species has been recorded as most frequently attacking brood in nests of *Bombus bimaculatus* and *B. fervidus* (Townsend, 1936); Cumber (1949d) considered that *Brachicoma devia* would be most liable to attack bumblebee nests formed near the surface or those with exposed entrances.

Adults of *Brachicoma* (Fig. 46) are superficially similar to house flies and they invade bumblebee nests in the spring. The female fly is viviparous, depositing small, young larvae instead of eggs. These are placed in cells or brood clumps containing bumblebee larvae, but they do not attack their hosts until the latter spin individual cocoons in preparation for pupation (Fig. 40). *Brachicoma* larvae are typical dipterous maggots; they are legless, pointed anteriorly and truncated behind, white and translucent, clearly segmented and devoid of spines (Fig. 47). A full-grown larva varies somewhat in size but may exceed 15 mm. in length.

Several of the parasites can attack one host larva. Normally, however, no more than four, and frequently only one will be found in each cocoon. The maggots do not devour the entire body of the host but feed on the body contents, leaving the skin more or less intact. Cocoons containing the parasites have a soft, watery appearance, and if a colony is heavily attacked a disagreeable odour is detectable. *Brachicoma* maggots develop rapidly and when full-grown escape from the host cocoon and move quickly down into the nest material at the sides or below the comb to pupate. The puparium (Fig. 48), within which pupation takes place, is formed from the cast skin of the final-instar larva. During the summer, flies emerge in one or two weeks; there may be several generations in a season. *Brachicoma* overwinters in the puparium as a pupa (Fig. 49), either among the remains of the bumblebee nest in which development took place or, more usually, in debris somewhere nearby. The puparia are light brown in colour, but those of the overwintering generation are dark reddish brown.

Several members of a completely different dipterous group, the conopid or 'big-headed' flies, are also important parasites of bumblebees. It has been stated erroneously (Hoffer, 1882–3; Sladen, 1912; Friese, 1923) that conopids develop in the larvae and pupae of bumblebees, and later emerge from dead adults. However, it is now known that these flies are direct parasites of adults. Foraging worker bumblebees are most frequently attacked, but my own observations in parts of southern England show that *Bombus* males, especially those of *B. lucorum* and *B. terrestris*, are also victimized; Postner (1952) has similarly reported parasitization of both workers and males of *Bombus*. Bumblebee queens usually fly about too early in the season to be affected by conopids, although in Canada late-appearing *Bombus* queens are often attacked by *Physocephala texana*, a common North American species

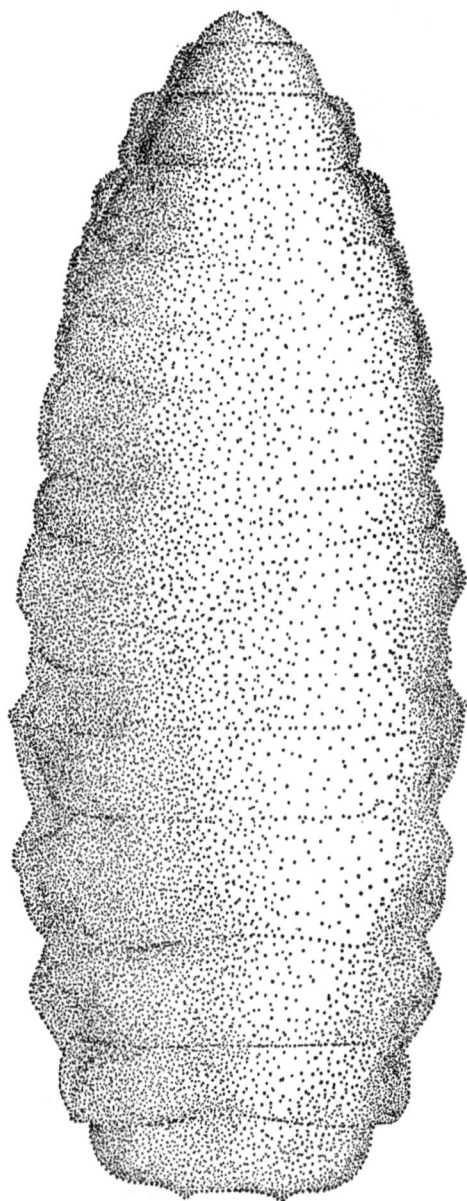

2 mm.

Fig. 47. Larva of *Brachicoma devia*.

of conopid fly (Hobbs, 1965b, 1966a, 1966b). In spite of having examined many *Psithyrus* males and females I have never found conopid larvae in bees of this genus, even in areas where contemporaneous attacks on *Bombus* were relatively high.

Eggs of conopid flies may be found in adult bumblebees from June to August. They are laid by the adult flies directly into the host through an intersegmental membrane of the abdomen. A conopid fly spends much of its time on or near flowers, where it awaits the arrival of a suitable host, but bumblebees are not attacked within their nests. The conopid egg (Fig. 50) is sausage-shaped with a pointed anterior (head) end and a filamentous or anchor-like process at the posterior end which may, at least in some species, help to attach the egg to the host's viscera (Clausen, 1940).

2 mm.

48

Fig. 48. Puparium of *Brachicoma devia*.

108

Normally, a parasitized host contains a single egg or larva but occasionally more than one may be present. When such superinfection occurs it is doubtful whether more than one parasite would successfully complete its development. The presence of two different parasite species in one and the same host, termed multiparasitism, sometimes occurs; I have, for example, found a conopid larva in a bumblebee also parasitized by wasp larvae of the genus *Syntretus* (Alford, 1968). Again, presumably, one of the parasite species would fail to survive.

After emerging from the egg a conopid larva attaches itself to an air sac in the abdomen of its host. A conopid larva is more or less pear-shaped (Figs. 51 and 52). There is an obvious, black, internal cephalopharyngeal skeleton anteriorly, bearing a pair of mandibles; there are also paired, black spiracles which in most conopid

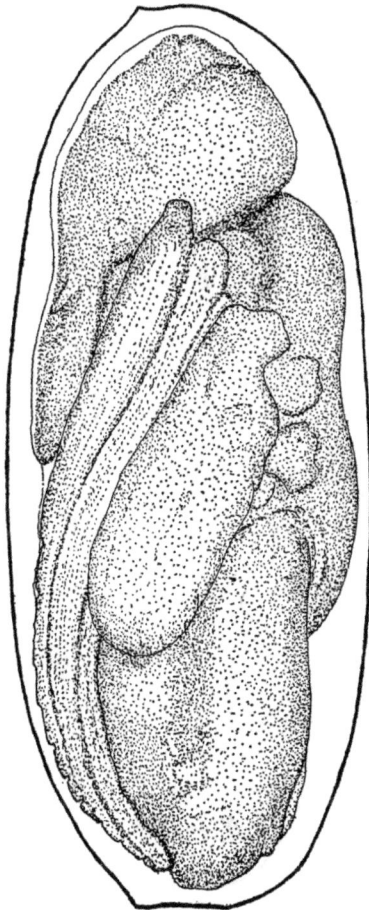

2 mm.

49

Fig. 49. Pupa of *Brachicoma devia*.

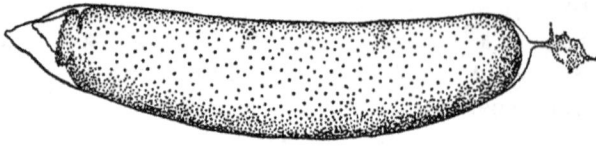

50

0·5 mm.

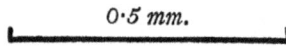

Fig. 50. Egg of *Physocephala rufipes*.

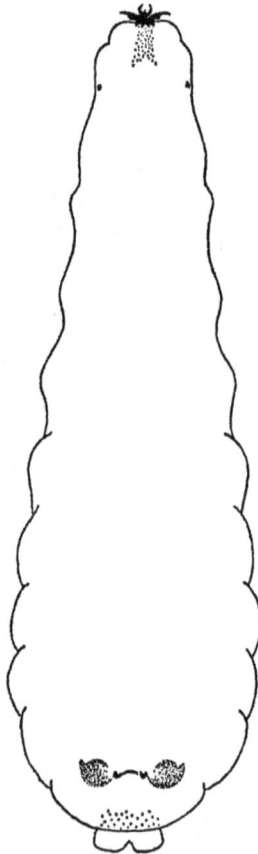

51

1 mm.

Fig. 51. Second-instar larva of *Physocephala rufipes*.

genera lie posteriorly. The larvae develop through three instars, and it is often possible to find within a host's body the cast skin or skins of any previous instars.

The anterior body segments of third-instar conopid larvae are attenuated and this has been shown to be, at least in the genus *Thecophora*, an adaptation for feeding on the thoracic contents of the host (Smith, 1966); first- and second-instar larvae of *Thecophora* feed entirely within the abdomen of their hosts, but shortly before pupation the final-instar larva thrusts the anterior part of its body through the

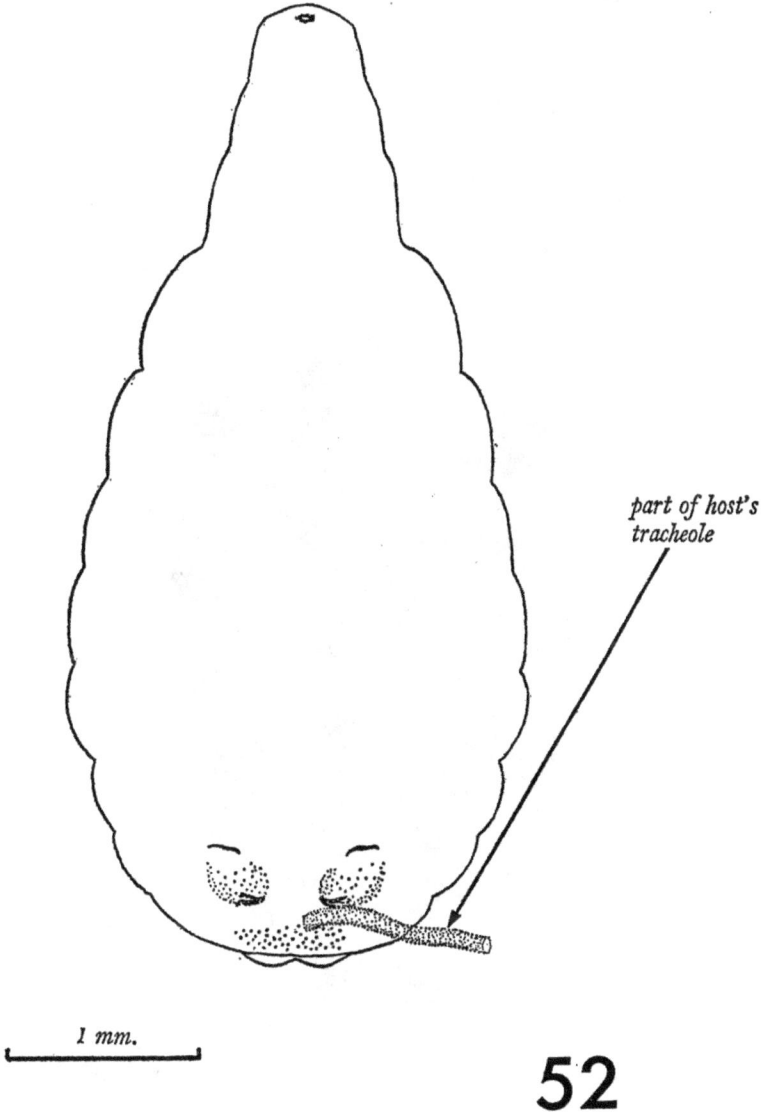

part of host's tracheole

1 *mm.*

52

Fig. 52. Third-instar larva of *Physocephala rufipes*.

petiole into the thorax of its host, which then dies. After feeding on the contents of the thorax the anterior segments of the parasite are withdrawn and the full-grown larva then pupates within the protective shell of the host's abdomen. It is probable that this method of feeding is also adopted by conopid larvae of other genera. The puparium is a robust-looking, barrel-shaped object (Fig. 53) which frequently will completely fill the husk-like remains of the host's abdomen. Dead, parasitized bumblebees are often found within the nest material of their colonies, and they are instantly recognizable because of their bloated abdomens. If handled, the head, thorax and abdomen (the latter containing the parasite puparium) readily separate from one another. In contrast, a non-parasitized corpse is shrunken and the head, thorax and abdomen usually remain more firmly attached after death. Conopids overwinter within their puparia, the adult flies emerging in the following summer. According to Smith & van Someren (1970) adult emergence is linked with ambient temperature conditions and rainfall.

The incidence of conopid attack among foraging populations of bumblebees is sometimes relatively high. For example, de Meijere (1904) and Postner (1952) recorded infestation levels of up to or in excess of thirty per cent among certain

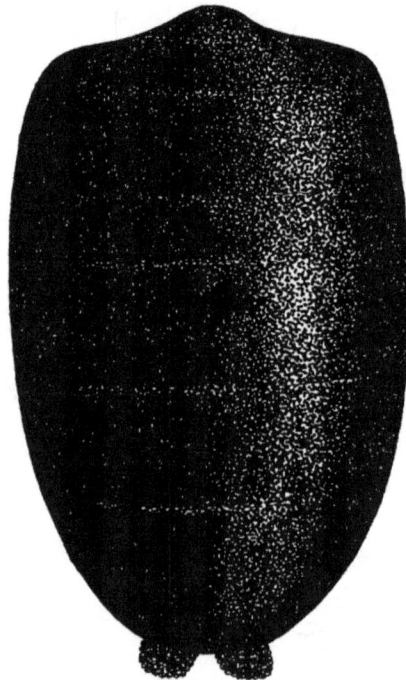

2 mm.

53

Fig. 53. Puparium of *Physocephala rufipes*.

Bombus hosts on the Continent. Cumber (1949d) found that about twelve per cent of foraging workers sampled near London in June and July 1946 were victimized; this included a thirty-eight per cent infestation level for *Bombus pascuorum*. However, the importance of conopid flies is less than might be supposed as parasitized bumblebees are still able to forage for their colonies until the final stages of attack.

The most frequently observed conopid parasite of British bumblebees would appear to be *Physocephala rufipes* (Figs. 54 and 55), but at least some bumblebees in Britain are hosts to species of *Conops* and *Sicus ferrugineus* (Fig. 56). For a comprehensive bibliography of conopid biology, and host lists, reference should be made to the papers by Smith (1959, 1966, 1969).

There are several references to the finding of single or many non-conopid, dipterous larvae in adult bumblebees, and in some instances adult flies have been reared and identified. *Macronichia polyodon* (literature spelling varies) and *Gonia*

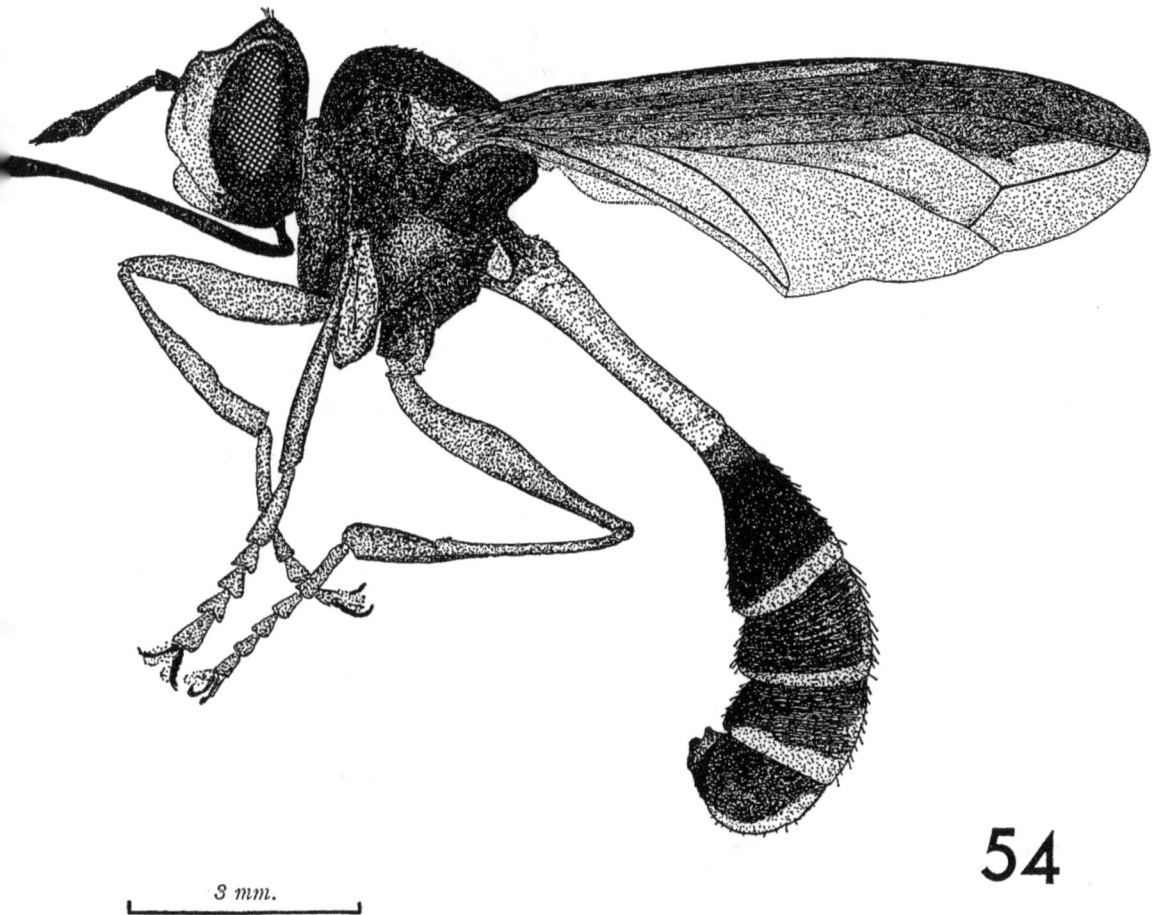

54

Fig. 54. *Physocephala rufipes* male.

3 mm.

113

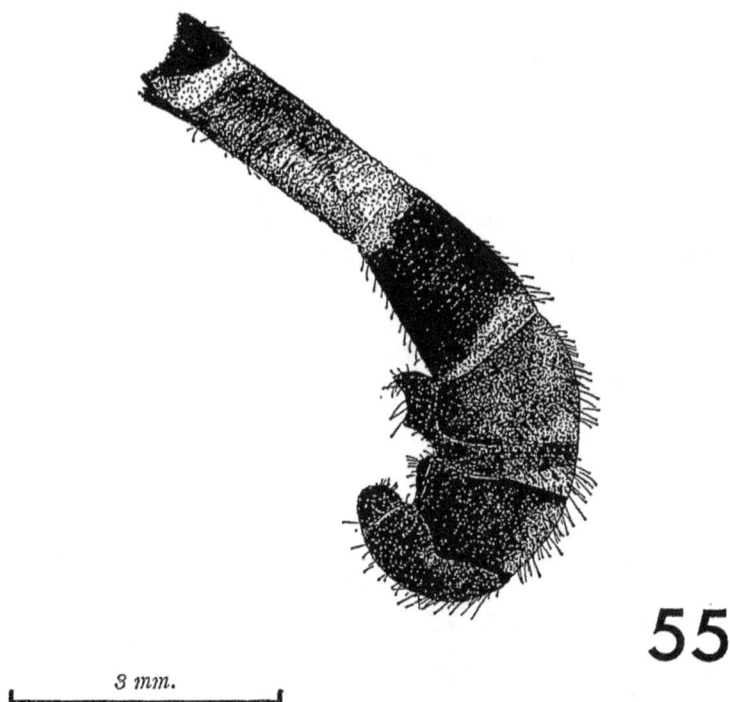

55

3 mm.

Fig. 55. Abdomen of *Physocephala rufipes* female.

fasciata (syn. *Salmacia sicula*), for example, are both reported as parasites of *Bombus terrestris* (Baer, 1921), although the latter dipterous species is more commonly a parasite of agrotid moths, especially *Agrotis segetum* (Colyer & Hammond, 1951). Boiko (1949) found *Senotainia tricuspis* parasitizing adults of both *Bombus terrestris* and *B. lapidarius* in the Ukraine, and I have reared adults of a species of *Megaselia* (Fig. 57) from gregarious larvae found parasitizing a *Bombus terrestris* queen. At least in some of the above cases bumblebees were probably acting merely as fortuitous hosts; it is also possible that some of the flies only victimize bumblebees which for some reason have become debilitated and hence more or less moribund.

Few predacious insects attack bumblebees, but in many parts of the world robber-flies are known to prey upon them. Records of asilid attacks on bumblebees are particularly numerous in American literature (e.g. Brown, 1929; Fattig, 1933; Bromley, 1936, 1949). *Bombus* species are the usual victims but *Proctacanthus hinei* is known to attack *Psithyrus* (Bromley, 1934). In Britain our largest species of robber-fly is *Asilus crabroniformis* (Fig. 58) and this probably includes bumblebees among its victims. Robber-flies are robust, active fliers which catch their prey on the wing with the aid of their strong legs. The asilid predator inserts its proboscis into the body of its victim, which immediately becomes motionless, probably as a result of the injection of some toxic substance. The robber-fly sucks out the blood of the

114

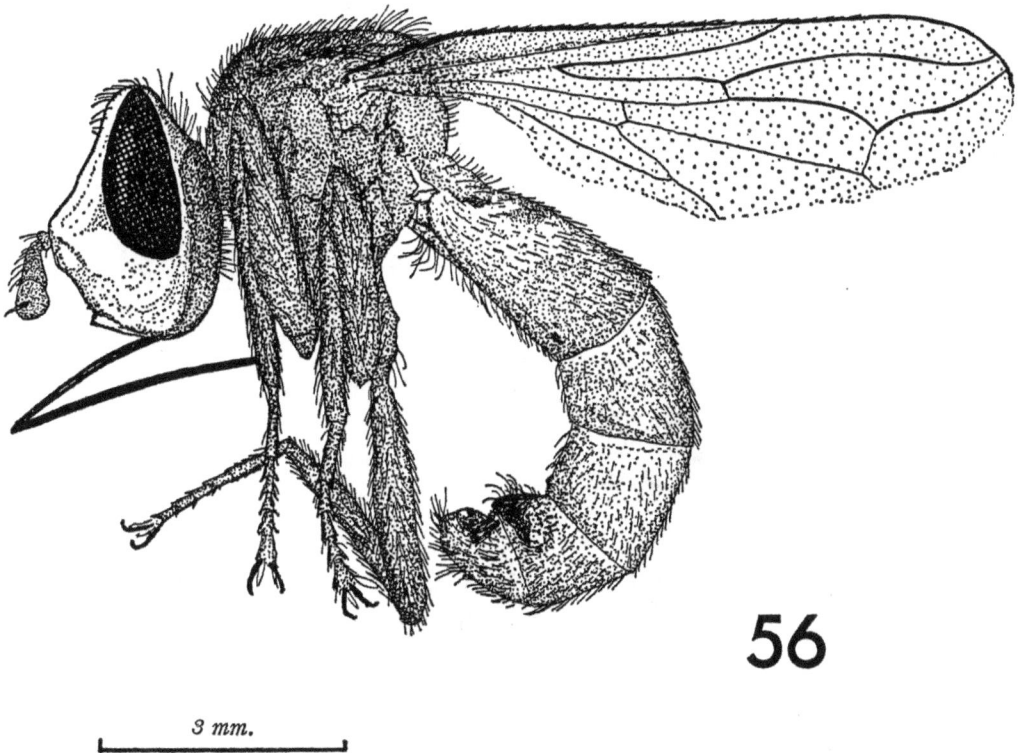

3 mm.

Fig. 56. *Sicus ferrugineus* male.

captured insect, the lifeless body of which is then discarded. Some robber-flies mimic particular species of bumblebee, and Brower, *et al.* (1960) observed that the asilid *Mallophora bomboides* preyed extensively on its model, *Bombus americanorum*. Apparently, *Mallophora orcina* attacks *B. impatiens* in preference to larger species such as *B. separatus* (Fattig, 1933).

Mention must be made of another species of fly which mimics bumblebees, namely *Volucella   bombylans*. Adults   of this hover-fly resemble certain species of bumblebee in their general body size and colour patterns. There are two main colour forms, both of which occur commonly in most parts of the country. One form is black and yellow, and has a white tail; this is similar in appearance to *Bombus hortorum* and *B. jonellus*. The other is black with a red tail, thus mimicking females of *B. lapidarius* and *B. ruderarius*. When held, *Volucella* will emit a bee-like buzz and if disturbed it will raise one of its middle legs in a similar manner to a bumblebee (Gabritschevsky, 1924). Its flight is also similar to that of a bumblebee, and when on the wing *Volucella* may very easily be mistaken for one or other of its models. Females of *V. bombylans* lay their eggs in bumblebee nests. However, as the larvae commonly occur both in nests of model and non-model *Bombus* species, the mimicry displayed by the adults is probably not an adaptation for assisting the fly's

115

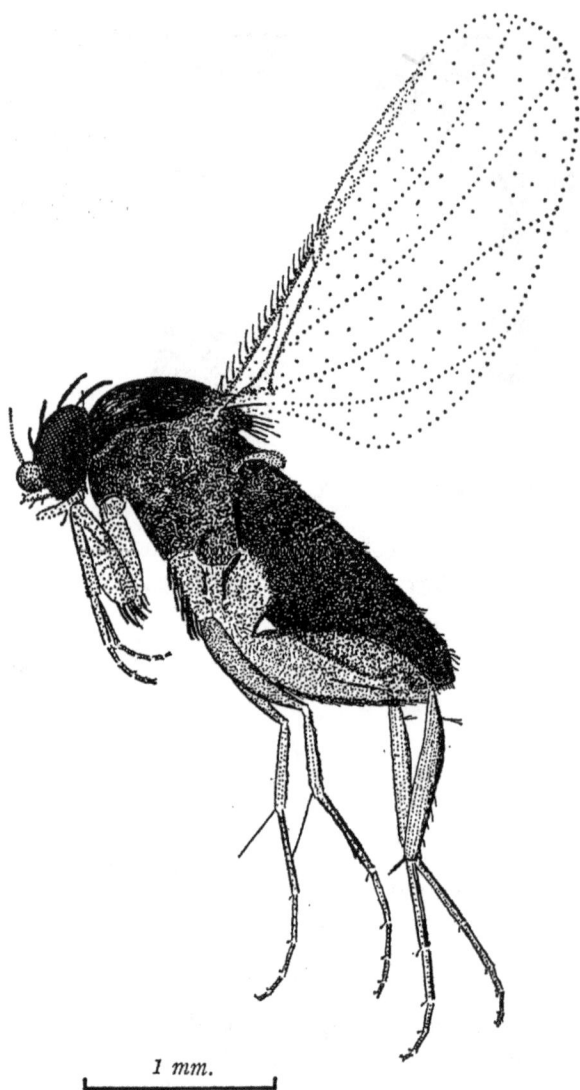

1 mm.

57

Fig. 57. *Megaselia.*

peaceful entry into a bumblebee colony, as was suggested by Gabritschevsky, but merely a protection against potential predators in the field.

A *Volucella* female immediately lays eggs if she is killed, so even if stung to death by a bumblebee when entering, or having recently entered, a nest, at least some eggs will be deposited. This phenomenon is a reflex action of the fly's egg-laying apparatus which increases the chances of survival of the species in the, at least initially, hostile environment of a bumblebee colony. *Volucella* eggs (Fig. 59) are relatively large, elongate, white in colour and rather hard. Newly-laid eggs are covered with a sticky coating which hardens on contact with the air. This helps to attach the eggs to the nest material, bumblebee comb or other surface and probably prevents their being eaten by the bumblebees.

Volucella larvae (Fig. 60) are dirty whitish yellow, and when full-grown they attain a length of about 22 to 26 mm. Their skin is hard and wrinkled; the body tapers anteriorly and at the broader posterior end there are, characteristically, six long spines. There are also two rows of small spines running along either side of the body. Posteriorly, on the upper surface, there is a prominent, reddish brown respiratory siphon; this is often mistaken for the ventrally placed anus, which is far

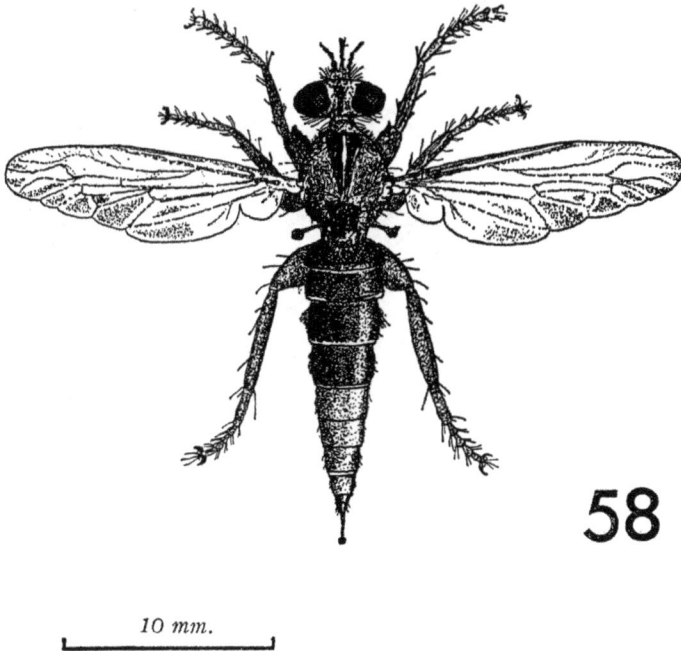

10 mm.

Fig. 58. *Asilus crabroniformis* female.

less obvious. The larvae are mainly scavengers and are most usually to be found below the comb, feeding on nest debris. Sometimes, as a result of their activities, the comb becomes loosened at its base (Hasselrot, 1960). Neither Sladen (1912) nor Frison (1926a) considered *Volucella* to be harmful, although attacks on bumblebee brood have sometimes been observed (e.g. Schmiedeknecht, 1878; Hoffer, 1882–3; Robson, cited by Wingate, 1906; Postner, 1952; Miyamoto, 1957a; Hobbs, 1967b). However, such interference is usually limited to the final stages of nest development and probably only occurs in the case of heavy nest infestations. *Volucella bombylans* overwinters in its puparium, adult flies emerging in the following spring. There may be two generations in a season.

E

Fannia canicularis (Fig. 61) is an ordinary-looking fly which commonly breeds in bumblebee nests. The adults are similar in appearance to *Brachicoma devia*, but are somewhat smaller and greyer; their immature stages, however, are unmistakable. *Fannia* larvae are even more bizarre than those of *Volucella bombylans*, as in addition to six long posterior spines there are also series of long, segmentally arranged, spines along the sides and down the back (Fig. 62). The larvae are dirty greyish brown, and about 10 to 15 mm. long when fully grown. They are usually considered to be harmless scavengers, feeding mainly on excrement. *Fannia* larvae thrive in nest-boxes where the floors have been allowed to become wet and fouled with bumblebee faeces. The puparia (Fig. 63), which usually lack the characteristic spines of the larvae, may be found singly, or clumped together in masses, below the comb or in adjacent debris.

Several other species of fly have been recorded from bumblebee nests, but most

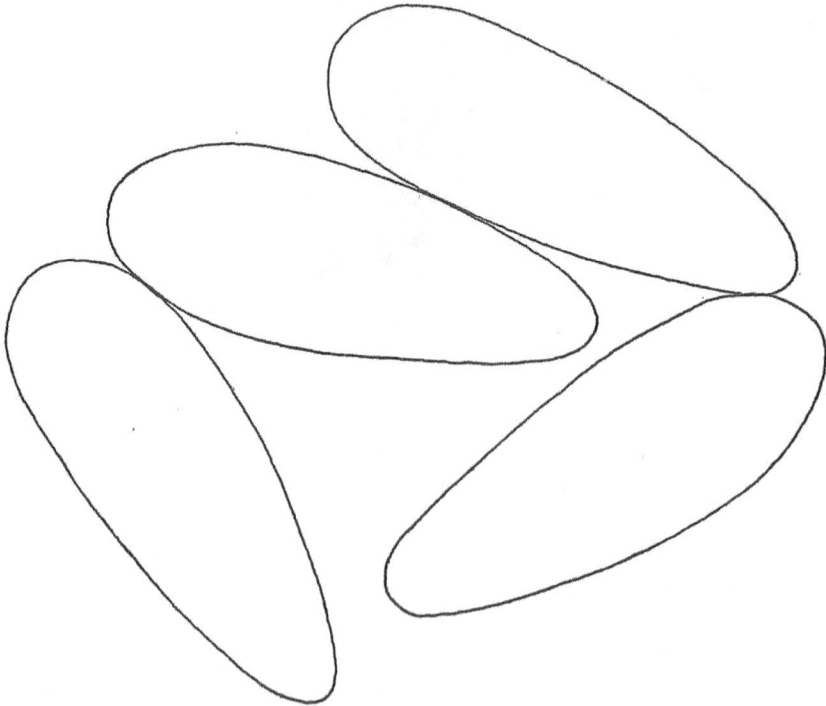

59

|_____ 0·5 mm. _____|

Fig. 59. Eggs of *Volucella bombylans.*

118

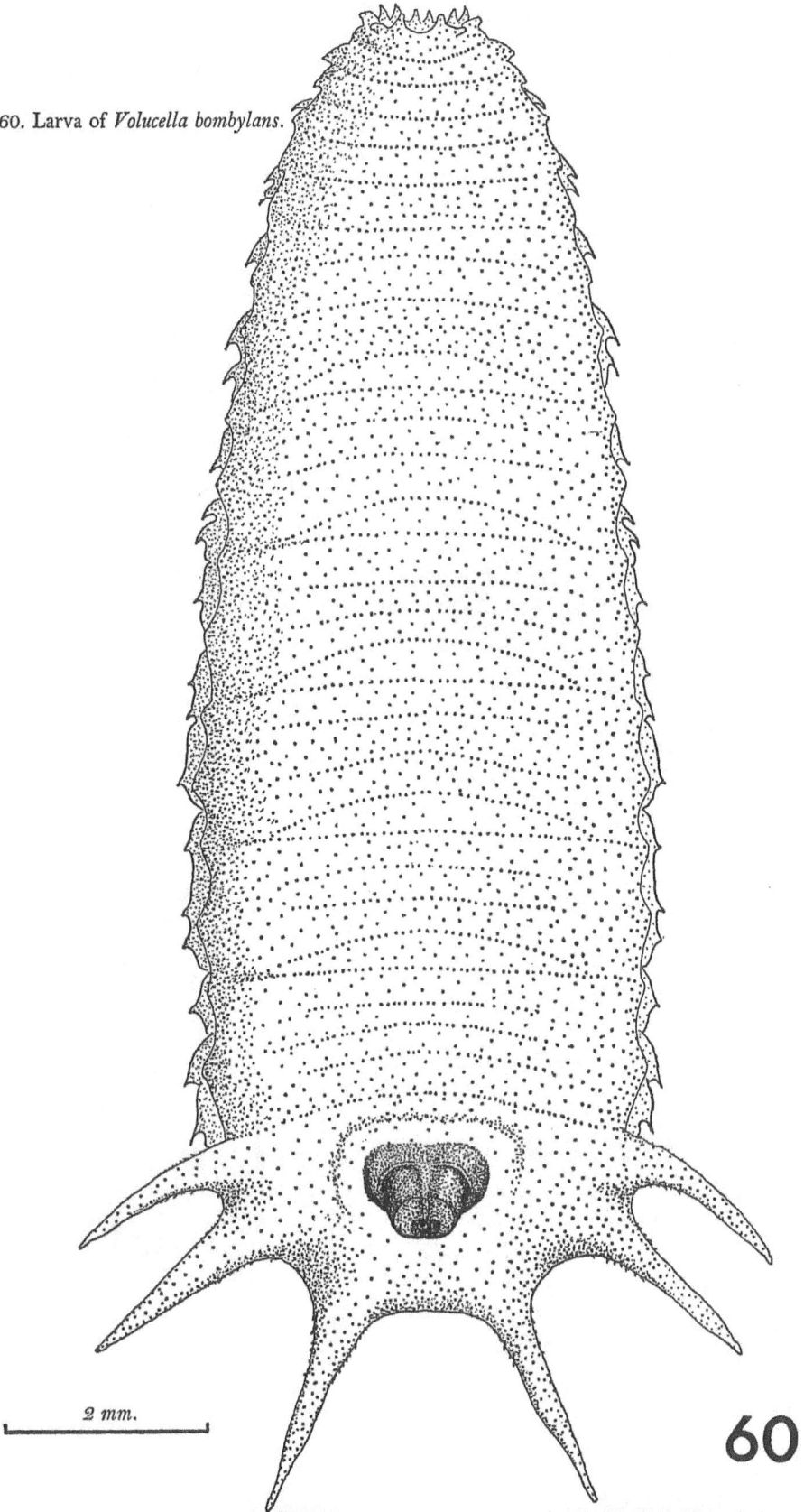

Fig. 60. Larva of *Volucella bombylans*.

2 mm.

60

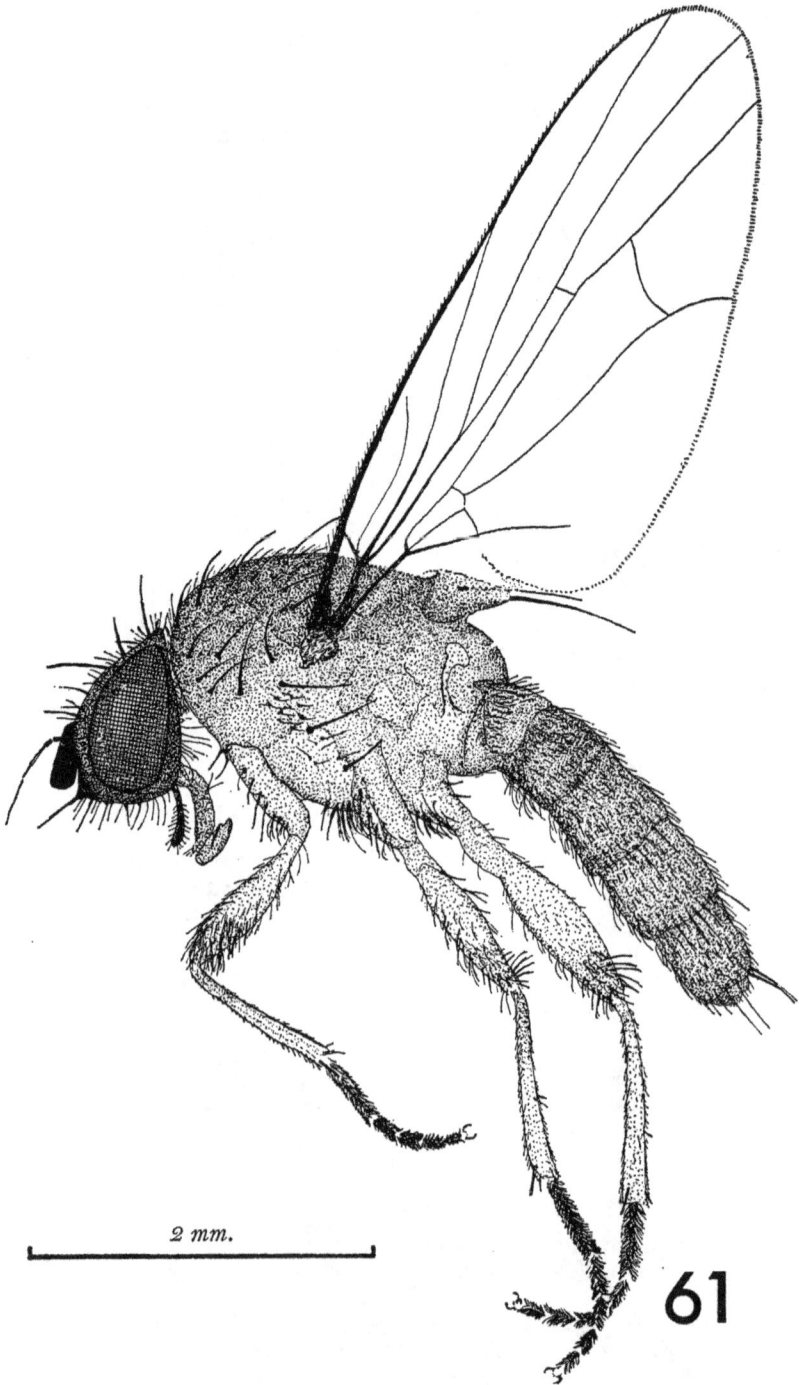

2 mm.

Fig. 61. *Fannia canicularis* male.

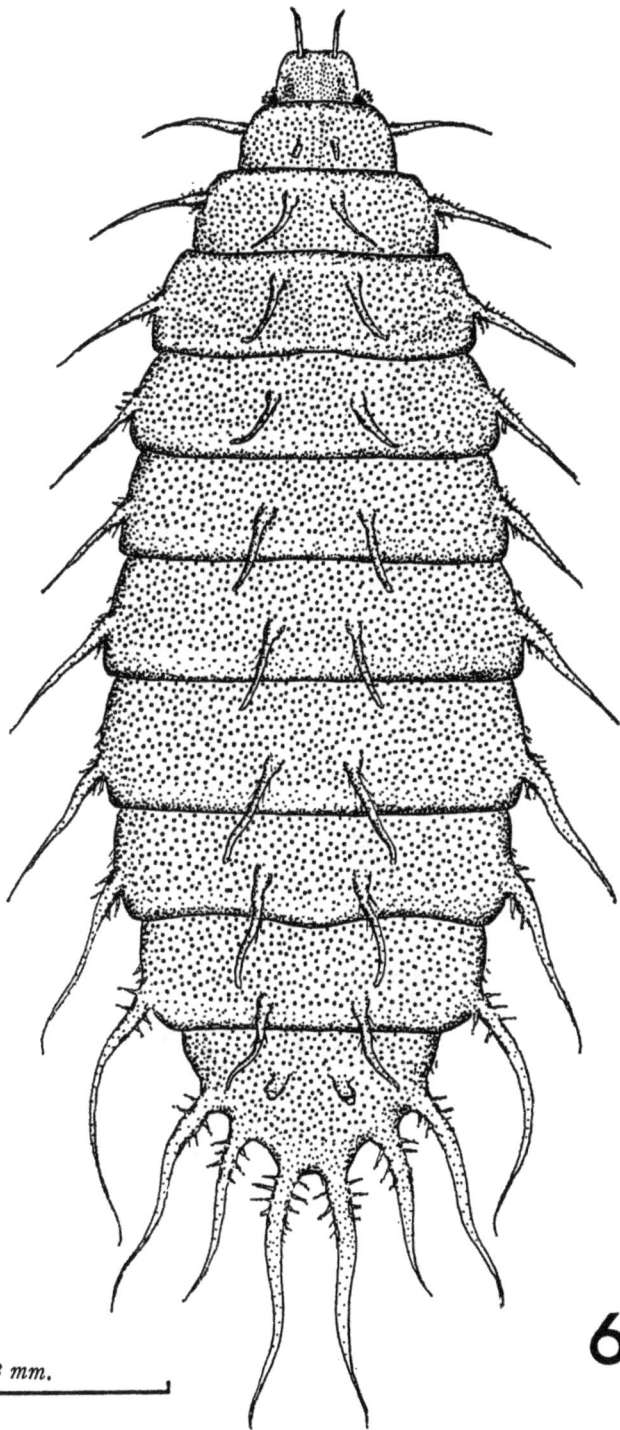

3 mm.

62

Fig. 62. Larva of *Fannia canicularis.*

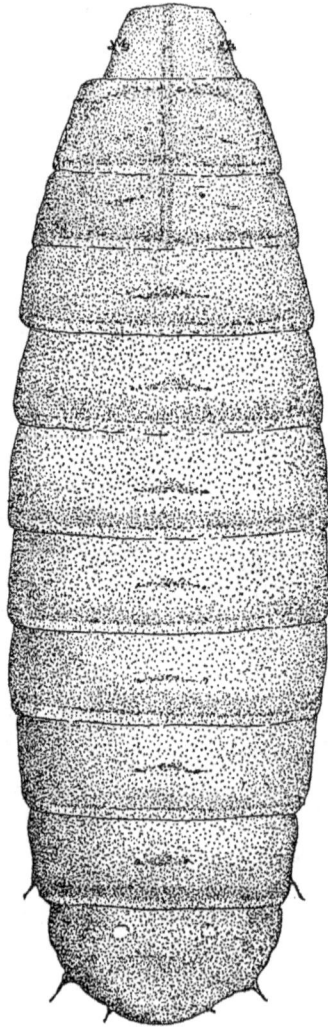

2 mm.

63

Fig. 63. Puparium of *Fannia canicularis*.

are probably casual denizens. Sciarid flies (Fig. 64) or 'fungus gnats', for example, are sometimes found among the nest material, the larvae presumably feeding on moulds within the nest. However, the small, black phorid fly *Gymnoptera vitripennis* (Fig. 65), with its noticeably iridescent wings, is a more frequent visitor to bumblebee nests, the adults darting rapidly over the comb or nest material in the typical phorid manner. The larvae of this particular species were thought by Sladen to feed on bumblebee eggs, but it seems more likely that they live on dead animal matter; two specimens of this fly, now in the collection of the British Museum, were actually reared from the hair of a corpse exhumed nearly a year after burial!

I have sometimes found fruit-flies (*Drosophila*) to be an unmitigated nuisance in bumblebee nest-boxes; the adults and larvae will often invade and drown in the syrup feeders if hygiene is neglected, but they are not normally a problem.

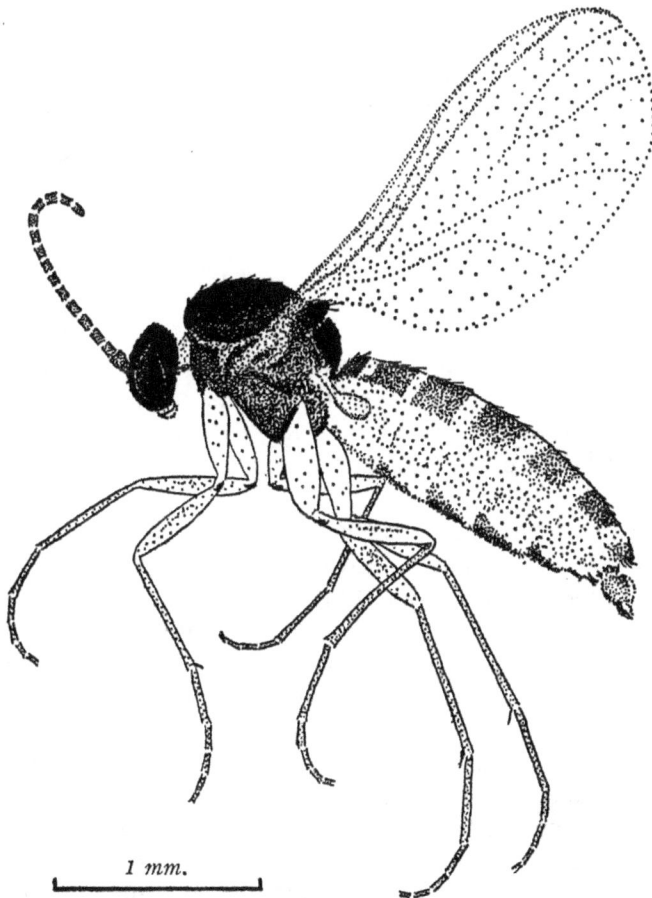

1 mm.

64

Fig. 64. *Lycoriella* male.

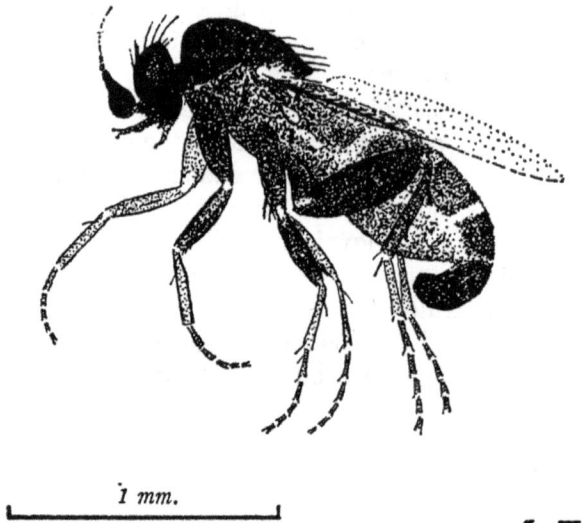

1 mm.

65

Fig. 65. *Gymnoptera vitripennis* male.

COLEOPTERA (BEETLES)

There are few close associations between bumblebees and Coleoptera. However, a considerable number of beetles have been recorded in the nests of bumblebees; over fifty different species are listed by Tuck (1896, 1897b). The vast majority are probably accidental visitors and hence only temporary lodgers, but a few are more permanent residents.

Without doubt, the beetle most frequently inhabiting bumblebee nests in Britain is *Antherophagus nigricornis*. This species (Fig. 66) is yellowish brown, approximately 5 mm. long and 1·5 mm. wide. Other species of this genus, e.g. *A. pallens* in Europe and *A. ochraceus* in America, are also closely associated with bumblebees (Wheeler, 1919; Donisthorpe, 1920). *Emphylus glaber*, *Epuraea depressa* and various species of *Cryptophagus* are examples of other beetles found frequently in bumblebee nests.

Young *Antherophagus* adults occur on flowers, and each gains entry to a bumblebee nest by clinging to the tongue, leg or antenna of a foraging bumblebee which, being unable to discard its passenger, will then carry the beetle back to its colony (von Frisch, 1952). Once inside a bumblebee nest the beetle releases its grip and drops down or crawls below the comb where, in due course, a generation of beetle larvae will develop. Phoresy, forcible hitch-hiking, is characteristic of several denizens of bumblebee nests (particularly in the case of mites); both bumblebees and other nest inhabitants may act as the carriers.

124

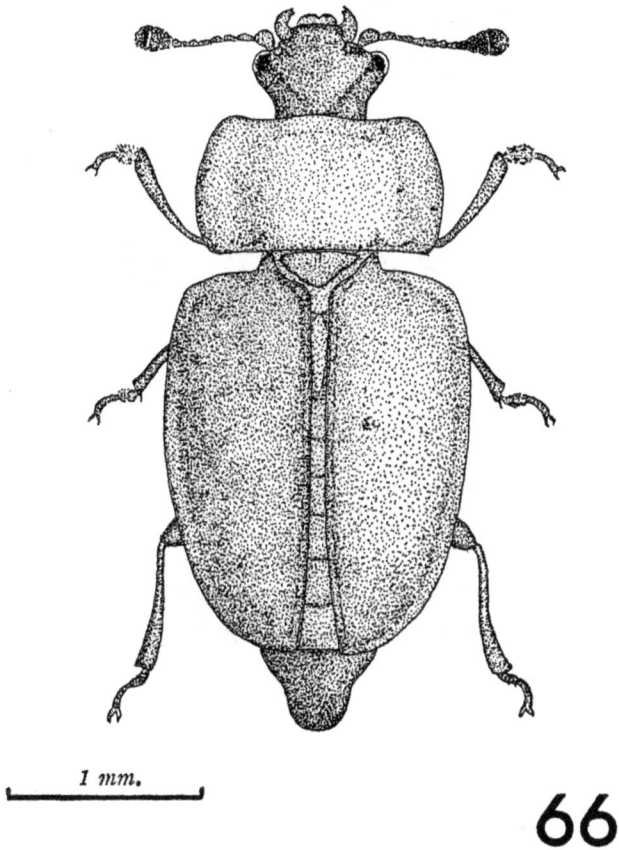

1 mm.

66

Fig. 66. *Antherophagus nigricornis.*

Antherophagus larvae are active creatures; they are yellowish in colour, about 8 mm. long when full-grown, and have distinct horns at both their anterior and posterior ends (Figs. 67 and 68). Wagner (1907) believed that *Antherophagus* caused considerable destruction in bumblebee colonies, but later observations have shown that the larvae are scavengers (Wheeler, 1919; Frison, 1921b). Masses of *Antherophagus* larvae may often be found feeding on nest debris, particularly in late summer; they probably aid in the destruction of the comb, once this becomes abandoned by the bumblebees (Frison, 1926a). *Antherophagus* overwinters as a larva (Scott, 1920); adults first appear in May or June, and those of a second generation may be found on flowers during the summer.

The beetle *Trichodes ornatus* (which does not occur in Britain) is known to eat bumblebee larvae and pupae (Hobbs, *et al.*, 1962) but most beetles in bumblebee nests are merely innocuous detritus feeders or vagrants.

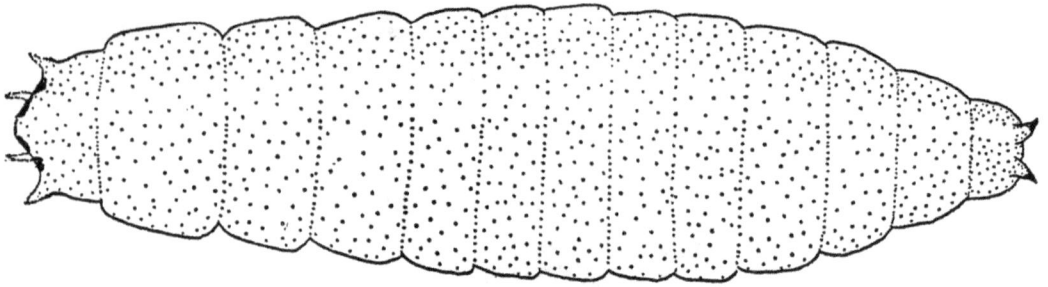

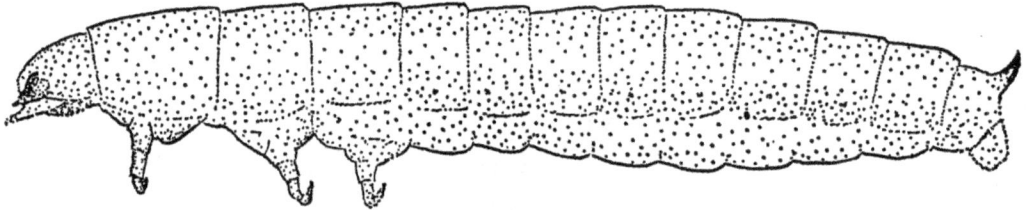

1 mm.

Figs. 67–68. Larva of *Antherophagus nigricornis*. 67, dorsal aspect; 68, lateral aspect.

HYMENOPTERA (ANTS, BEES, WASPS, ETC.)

In America, during the 1920s, Plath found several unidentified insect larvae developing in the bodies of adult bumblebees. Some of these larvae, and their cocoons, were later illustrated in his book on bumblebees (Plath, 1934). Some years after Plath's discovery, similar larvae were observed by Legge (1937) parasitizing a *Bombus terrestris* queen in this country; subsequently, Cumber (1949d) obtained several similarly-parasitized bumblebees near London, and Hasselrot (1960) found infested queens of *B. lucorum*, *B. terrestris* and *B. pascuorum* in Sweden. In all cases, however, adults were never reared and so the identity and systematic position of this parasite remained in doubt. However, in 1965 I had the good fortune to find several bumblebees parasitized by larvae whose general description matched those given by the above authors; the biology of this insect was subsequently studied, and adults were eventually reared (Alford, 1968). The parasite proved to be *Syntretus splendidus* (Fig. 69), a small braconid wasp originally described by Marshall (1887) from adults captured in Wiltshire. Similar parasitic larvae have recently been found attacking bumblebees in Denmark (Holm, personal communication) and Holland (Poinar & van der Laan, 1972), but it remains to be seen whether British, Continental and American examples are one and the same species.

Syntretus splendidus is a gregarious endoparasite of adult bumblebee queens, workers and males; both *Bombus* and *Psithyrus* are victimized. Egg-laying has not yet been observed but, as in cases of conopid fly attack, it probably occurs in the field during flower visitation by the hosts, since only bumblebees which must have foraged during the infective period (May and June) have ever been found to be parasitized by *S. splendidus*. Overwintered queens of later-nesting species, for example *B. pascuorum*, are more liable to be attacked than overwintered queens of earlier-nesting species, such as *B. lucorum* and *B. terrestris* (in the latter two species

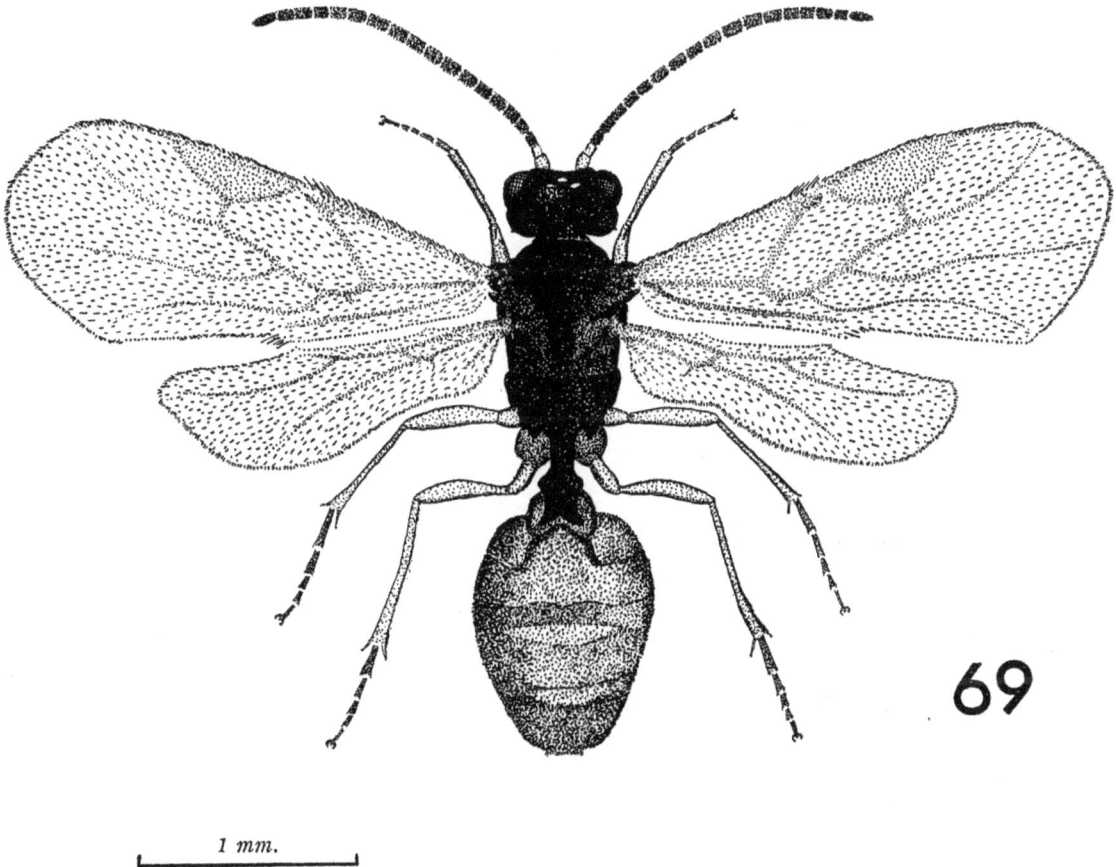

1 mm.

Fig. 69. *Syntretus splendidus* male.

foraging workers are the main victims), and this clearly relates directly to host availability in the field during the infective period. To date no cases of parasitization of the abundant species *B. hortorum* have been reported. This may indicate that the faster working-speed of this species, when foraging, reduces its chances of being attacked (see Alford, 1968).

Eggs of *S. splendidus* (Fig. 70) enlarge considerably once they are laid, and they commonly occur in the thorax of the host. Development of the larvae, however, normally takes place in the haemocoel of the abdomen. The eggs are probably deposited into the thorax of the host through the membranous tissue of the neck. Parasitized queens usually contain more than thirty parasite eggs or larvae and sometimes more than seventy (Alford, 1968; 1973c) but in workers there are usually fewer than twenty per host. This suggests that, to some extent at least, the

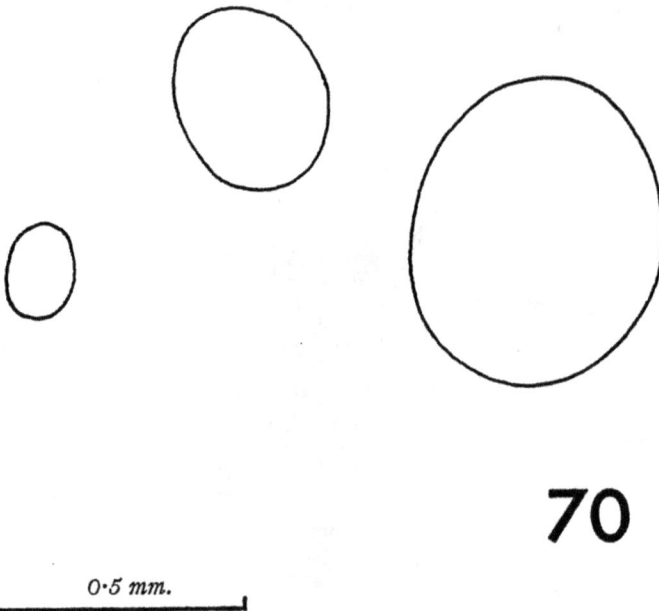

0·5 mm.

Fig. 70. Developing eggs of *Syntretus splendidus*.

number of eggs laid in any one host is regulated according to the body size of the victim.

In common with development of other parasitic Hymenoptera (see Jackson, 1924, 1928, 1935) the cells of the embryonic membrane (the membrane below the egg-shell or chorion and surrounding the embryo) persist individually after the larva escapes from the egg. They absorb fat from the body fluid of the host, while themselves increasing considerably in size. These hypertrophied cells are the major food source of the *Syntretus* larvae (Figs 71 to 73); the larvae do not feed directly on the viscera of the host. There are five larval instars, the last of which

(Fig. 74) is a non-feeding migratory stage. Full-grown larvae are approximately 5 mm. long.

Once larvae moult to the final instar they break out of the host, usually to one side of the body, through the intersegmental membrane linking the first and second abdominal segments. The active larvae then burrow individually below the surface of the ground, and each spins a white, silken cocoon in which pupation eventually takes place. Unlike many braconid parasites closely related to *Syntretus*, which overwinter as first-instar larvae within their hosts (Clausen, 1940), *S. splendidus* spends the winter in the cocoon, either as a pupa (Fig. 75) or as an adult, the adult wasps emerging in the late spring or early summer.

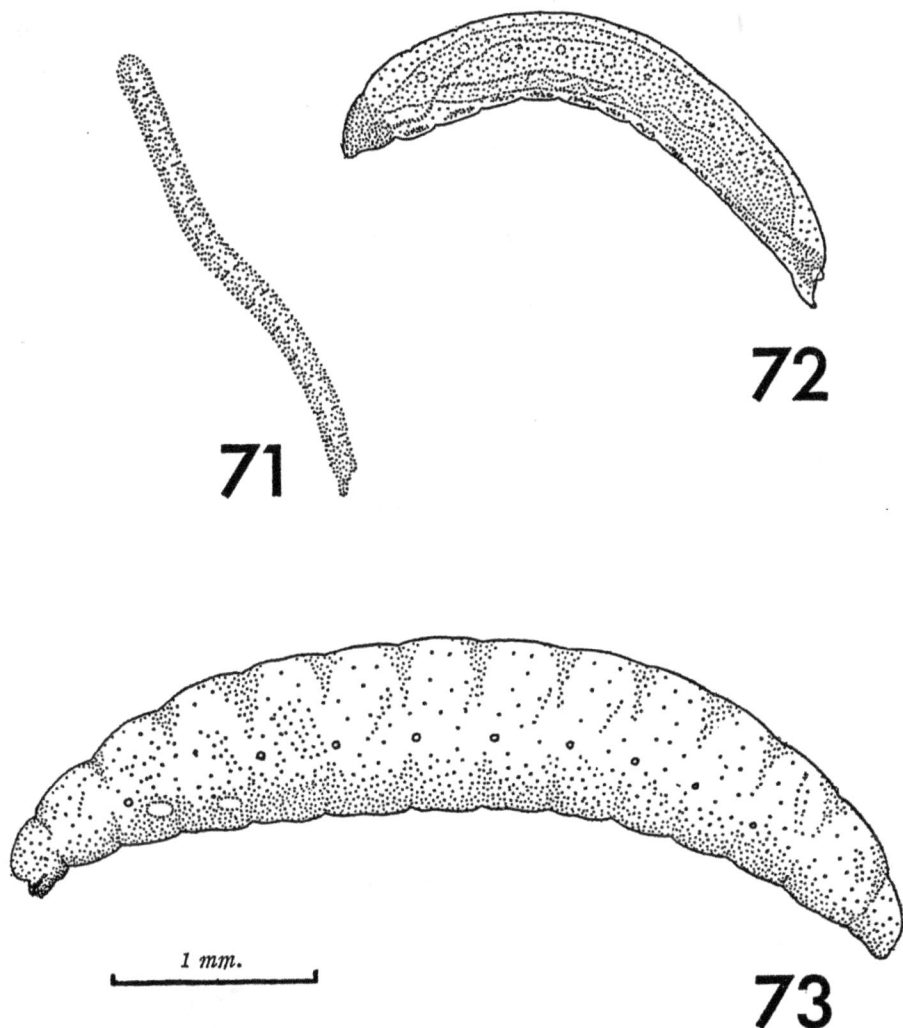

1 mm.

Figs. 71–73. Larvae of *Syntretus splendidus*. 71, first-instar; 72, second-instar; 73, fourth-instar.

129

Syntretus-parasitized bumblebees behave more or less normally, but the ovaries of attacked queens degenerate so that egg-laying ceases. Presumably, this is simply a case of nutritional castration. The brood-rearing ability of young foundress queens is also impaired, probably as a result of a reduction in their foraging efficiency; it has been shown that the first-brood adults reared by parasitized queens of *B. pascuorum* are significantly smaller than those produced by healthy queens (Alford, 1968). Parasitized bumblebees become noticeably weak and sluggish shortly before fifth-instar *Syntretus* larvae emerge from their bodies. At this stage they abandon their brood, and shortly after the appearance of the parasites they die; the host bumblebee is not killed as a direct result of the damage caused by the escaping parasites but, being too weak to feed, probably dies of starvation. *S. splendidus* is relatively unimportant as a parasite of foraging bumblebees. However, this insect must be considered a potentially serious enemy of certain host species,

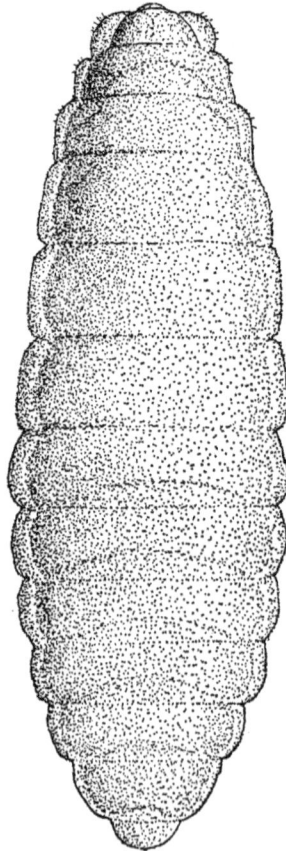

1 mm.

74

Fig. 74. Fifth-instar larva of *Syntretus splendidus*.

as it can lead to the premature death of many bumblebee colonies by victimizing young foundress queens at or just before the early stages of colony initiation.

One hymenopterous parasite of bumblebees which has been known for many years is *Mutilla europaea*, a devastating, aculeate parasite of bumblebee brood. This mutillid wasp sometimes enters honey bee hives, and will then attack the brood in the same way as in a bumblebee colony. *M. europaea* is an unusual and intriguing insect, but it is by no means common in the British Isles; most British records of this species stem from the southern or eastern counties of England.

The ant-like adult of *M. europaea* is about 14 mm. long and has an orange-red thorax which is lightly clothed with black hairs; the rest of the body (including the legs) is black, although on the abdomen, which is thickly covered with long hairs, there are (three in the female and two in the male) silvery white bands. The female

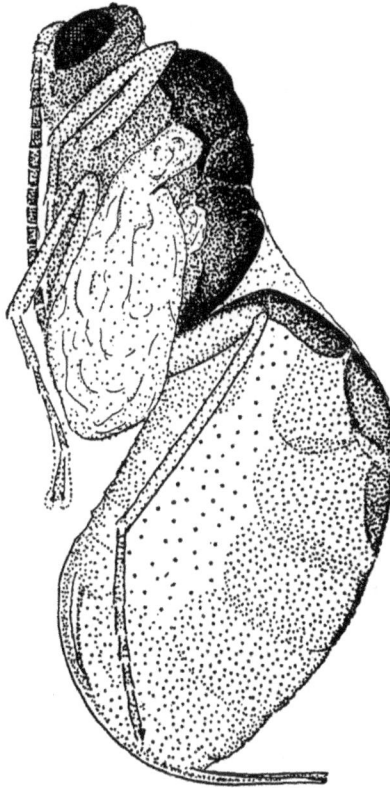

75

1 mm.

Fig. 75. Pupa of *Syntretus splendidus* female.

is completely wingless. The general appearance of *Mutilla* has led to it being called the 'ant-like fosser' or 'velvet-ant'. Males are sometimes to be found feeding on flowers such as bramble (*Rubus fruticosus*), and at night they are attracted to light; females are less often seen away from bumblebee nests.

The female of *M. europaea* invades a bumblebee colony some time during the early summer, and deposits her eggs inside bumblebee cocoons containing young pupae or prepupae. Mutillid wasps, in general, place their eggs on the inner walls of cocoons or directly against the body of their hosts (Mickel, 1928), and Jordan (1935) considered that *M. europaea* bit open the bumblebee cocoon and then placed an egg against its victim. However, according to Meyerhoff (1954) the egg is actually laid within a host larva. Although the ovipositor of *Mutilla* is capable of jabbing an adversary the female has no need to sting its host, as these are attacked at a quiescent stage.

0·2 mm.

Fig. 76. Right mandible of larva of *Mutilla europaea*.

The larva of *M. europaea* is similar to that of a bumblebee, but the mandibles are quadridentate (Fig. 76). If the parasite develops within a worker cocoon then eventually most, if not all, of the host will be devoured. However, if the host is large, as would be a queen pupa, then it is only partially consumed. When full-fed the larva spins a tough, white cocoon within that originally spun by its host. The parasite then pupates and rapidly develops into an adult. Typically, more females than males are produced (Friese, 1926). Hoffer (1886) considered the well-known size variation among adults of *M. europaea* to be related to the food supply at the larval stage, and this was later confirmed by Mickel; mutillid adults reared in honey bee colonies are considerably smaller than normal (Meyerhoff, 1954). Following their emergence, adult mutillids feed on the honey stores of the host colony. Adults of *M. europaea* can strigilate by moving certain of the dorsal tergites relative to one another. The sound is a hiss-like chirp, and as well as being produced by fully mature adults it can also be made by those yet to break out of their cocoons. An interesting summary of the earliest observations on sound production by *Mutilla* is given by Lubbock (1882); further details are provided by Mickel (1928). Although males of *M. europaea* leave the bumblebee colony shortly after they emerge from their cocoons, the departure of females is delayed. At least in some cases the females must stay in the remains of the host nest until the following spring, for they have been found in old bumblebee nests during the winter (Shuckard, 1866).

In some countries, chalcid wasps of the genus *Melittobia* parasitize the brood of bumblebees.[1] *Melittobia* may also victimize other nest denizens (Johansen, 1967). The presence of this parasite can adversely affect the size of bumblebee adults produced from any healthy brood remaining in the colony, and prevent the rearing of new queens (Knee & Medler, 1965a). *Melittobia* is known to attack both *Psithyrus* and *Bombus* larvae (Plath, 1922c). A species of *Melittobia* (*M. acasta*) occurs in the British Isles but, although this is capable of successfully attacking the brood of bumblebees (*Bombus terrestris*) (Holm & Skou, 1972), I know of no instance where this has parasitized the brood of bumblebees in the wild state; it would appear that its natural hosts are mainly solitary bees and wasps. For an extensive account of the biology of *Melittobia* reference should be made to the paper by Balfour-Browne (1922).

The solitary wasp *Philanthus bicinctus* is a predator of bumblebees in America (Armitage, 1965). This species apparently selects bumblebees of particular sizes, and Mason (1965) demonstrated that there was 'a definite lower size limit of acceptability of a bee as prey'. *Philanthus triangulum*, the only member of this genus to occur in Britain, is known to catch honey bees (Clausen, 1940), but it is not recorded as an enemy of bumblebees.

Ants frequently invade *Bombus* nests. They are usually only harmful at the early stages of bumblebee colony development, but can be a considerable problem to more advanced colonies housed in nest-boxes or artificial domiciles. The ants do not attack adult bees, but enter the colonies in order to feed on the brood and honey or nectar stored in the comb. Sladen (1912) observed that *Lasius niger* and *Myrmica rubra* were troublesome in this respect, but the equally common species *Lasius flavus* was not. Without detriment to the bumblebees, ants frequently eat dead adults, including those discarded by birds. Roadside casualties are often plundered by ants, the nectar in the crop taken and the softer parts of the victim's body carried home and fed to their brood.

Vespid wasps also utilize dead bumblebees as a source of food; these insects are often particularly interested in the muscle content of the thoraces of freshly killed bees. A wasp will quickly bite off the abdomen, legs, wings and head from a dead bumblebee and carry the thorax away. Wasps, like ants, sometimes enter bumblebee nest-boxes, both in the field and in the laboratory, to feed on the nectar or honey stores; it is probable that on occasions wild colonies are also robbed. Wasps

---

[1] The North American torymid *Monodontomerus montivagus* has also been reported as an enemy of bumblebee brood (Krombein, 1958).

have been observed to kill inebriate bumblebees foraging on lime (*Tilia*) trees.[1] According to Stacey (1955) wasps 'attack the heavier bumble-bee on the tree. The contestants fall to the ground and the fight is soon over. The wasp sucks its victim dry and flies off, soon to return. I have seen scores of carcases lying alongside the grass verges, the light wind piling them in heaps'. Foragers of *Bombus lucorum* and *B. terrestris* usually form the bulk of such casualties.

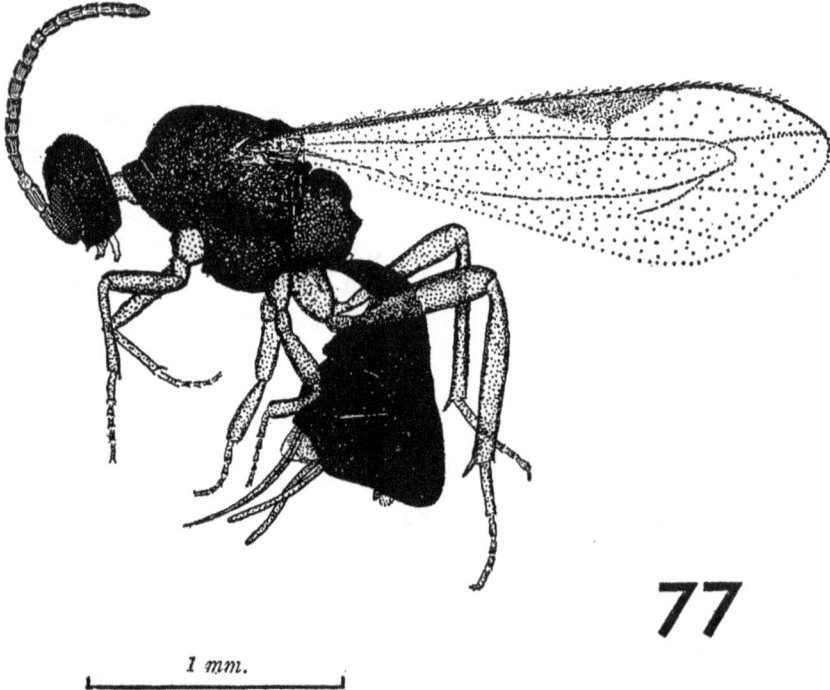

Fig. 77. *Blacus paganus* female.

If the contents of a bumblebee nest are carefully examined it is often possible to find adults of various braconid and ichneumonid wasps. These insects are parasites, but in the vast majority of cases their hosts are not bumblebees, or the bumblebee brood, but other nest denizens. The beetle *Antherophagus*, for example, is frequently parasitized; Sladen recorded the braconid *Hysteromerus mystacinus* as a likely enemy, and Postner (1952) listed *Stenocryptus* as one of its parasites. I have found *Blacus paganus* (Fig. 77) parasitizing larvae of *Antherophagus* in underground colonies; this frequently-recorded braconid parasite has also been captured in surface nests, such as those of *Bombus pascuorum* (Richards, 1946). Species of *Apanteles* are often found in bumblebee nests in Britain, but are not, to my knowledge, positively designated to particular hosts; in Japan, however, *Apanteles* is known to parasitize the moth

---

[1] It is thought that the intoxicating and often lethal effects of lime and certain other nectars is due to the presence of toxic monosaccharide sugars such as galactose and mannose (Geissler & Steche, 1962).

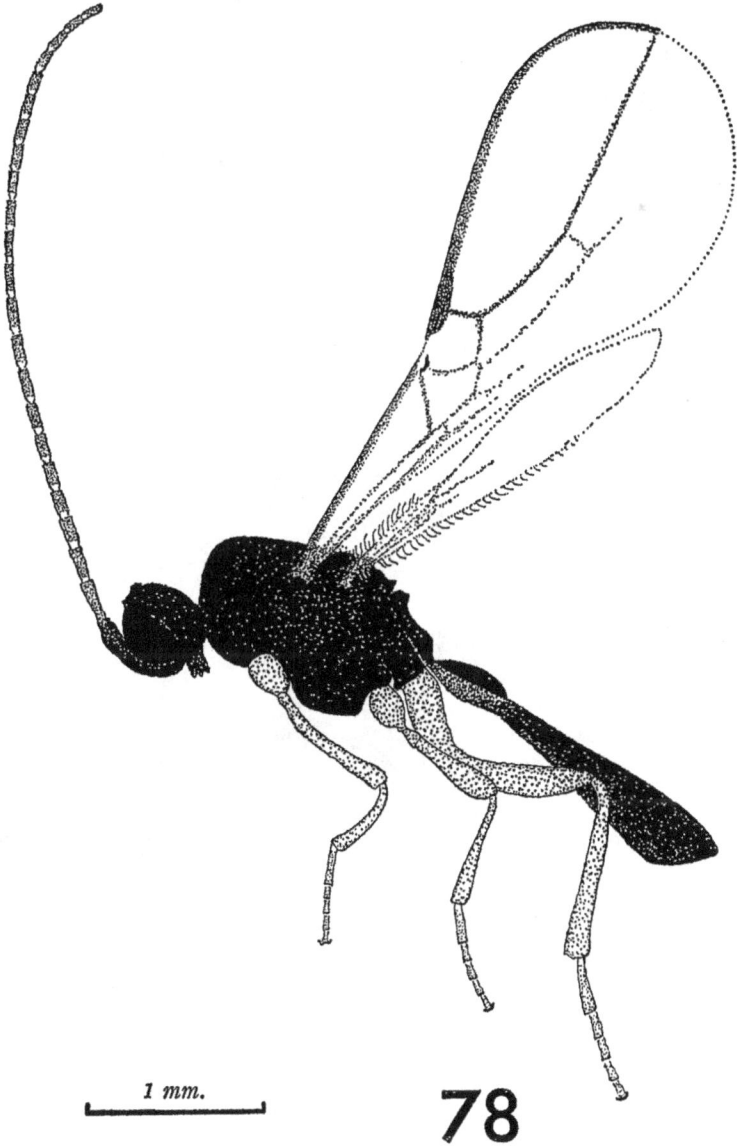

1 mm.

78

Fig. 78. *Aspilota.*

denizen *Tinea simpliciella*. The wax-moth *Aphomia sociella* seems to be without a major insect parasite, although two braconids (*Meteorus pulchricornis* and *M. salicorniae*) are listed among its enemies (Fahringer, 1922). Sometimes the Diptera in bumblebee nests are parasitized. Scott (1920), for example, reared specimens of *Orthostigma pumilum* from phorid flies (*Aphiochaeta rata*) found in a nest of *Bombus ruderarius*, and Postner found *Aspilota* (Fig. 78) parasitizing the fly *Megaselia rufipes*. Members of the genus *Aspilota* are usually regarded as parasites of phorid flies (Fischer, 1972). The ichneumonid *Stilpnus gagates* (Fig. 79) is, likewise, a parasite of *Fannia canicularis*; the parasitized puparia of *Fannia* are at once distin-

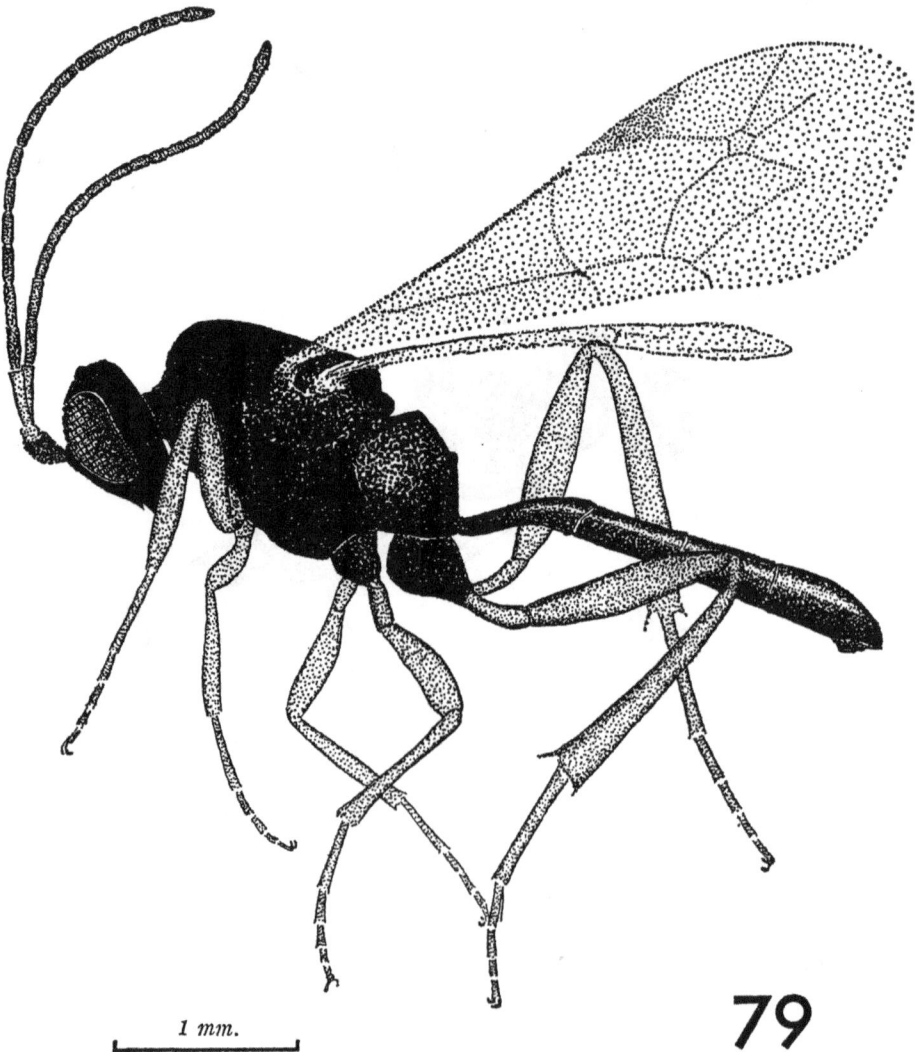

1 mm.

79

Fig. 79. *Stilpnus gagates*.

guished from those of healthy individuals (Fig. 63) as, unlike the latter, they tend to retain the conspicuous spines of the original larval skin.

MISCELLANEOUS

Representatives of several other insect orders may also occur within bumblebee nests. Some, notably bird-fleas (e.g. *Ceratophyllus gallinae*), may have been formerly associated with the original occupant of the nest or accumulator of the nest material, but few are anything more than casual or accidental visitors.

Occasionally, the common earwig (*Forficula auricularia*) will enter bumblebee colonies and feed on the young brood. Earwigs may also cause the foundress queen of a small colony to desert her nest (Holm, 1960). Pouvreau (1966) cites a case where a confined *Bombus pratorum* colony was completely devastated by these predatory insects. Earwigs may sometimes disturb hibernating queens in the soil (Bols, 1939), but under natural conditions they cannot be considered as important enemies of bumblebees.

The ambush bug *Phymata pennsylvanica americana* is known to capture foraging bumblebees in North America (Balduf, 1939; 1941), but there are no equivalent hemipterous predators of bumblebees in Britain. *Phymata* inhabits flowers and feeds upon various insects which visit them.

Arachnids

MITES

Bumblebees are frequently found with large, light brown mites crawling over or clinging to their bodies, mainly on the hinder part of the thorax. As many as a hundred, or even more, may be clustered on a single bumblebee. These mites, of which there are several different species, belong to the genus *Parasitus*. In Britain, and probably elsewhere in Europe, *Parasitus fucorum* is the most frequently encountered species; under this name are included many other 'species', such as *Parasitus bomborum*, now considered in synonymy (see Vitzthum, 1930; Colombo, 1961; Micherdziński, 1969).

Parasitus mites (Figs. 80 and 81) are not parasites, but are more or less harmless commensals within bumblebee colonies (some species live elsewhere); they occur, often in considerable numbers, in most, if not all, bumblebee nests. Although often considered as predators of other mites in the nest fauna, they will feed on pollen, and possibly also on faeces or nest debris. The mites roam actively throughout the nest material, and their early stages (along with mites of other groups) even occur inside the wax-pollen envelopes covering developing bumblebee eggs or larvae.

There are several generations of *Parasitus* in a season. *Parasitus* develops from egg to adult through a larval (Fig. 82), protonymphal and deutonymphal (Fig. 83) stage, but it is only the pre-adult deutonymphs which attach themselves to adult bumblebees. The deutonymphs, although sometimes present on worker and male bumblebees, are most frequently found on young queens and on recently hibernated individuals, to which they were attached throughout the winter. In spring, the mites leave their bumblebee carrier as soon as a suitable nest has been founded, in this way completing their transfer from the bumblebee nests of one season to those of the next. *Parasitus* will also survive the winter on hibernating females of *Psithyrus*.

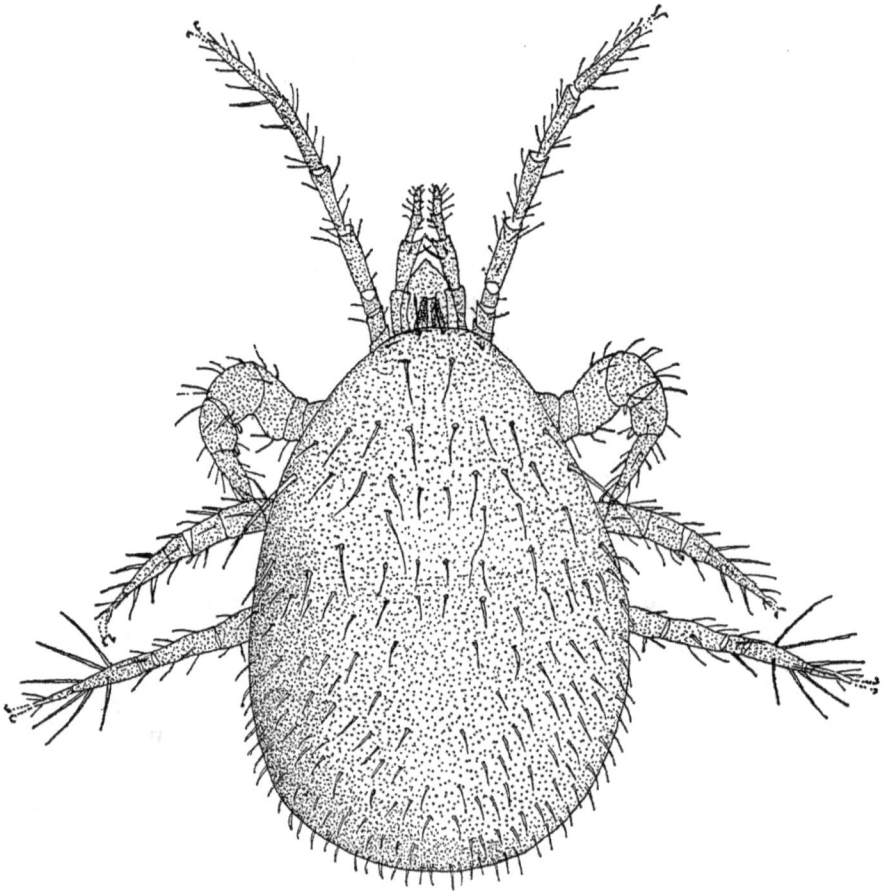

80

1 mm.

Fig. 80. *Parasitus* male.

Under normal circumstances the deutonymphs do not inconvenience or harm the bumblebees upon which they are phoretic, and it is obviously not in their own interests to do so. Excessive numbers (most likely to occur on weak, young queens) may, however, restrict the movements of the bumblebee, but this is unusual. It has been suggested that *Parasitus* deutonymphs may act as vectors of disease (Skou, *et al.*, 1963).

Parasitus, and possibly other mites (of which there are many) within the fauna of bumblebee nests, are often parasitized by a small, scale-like mite known as

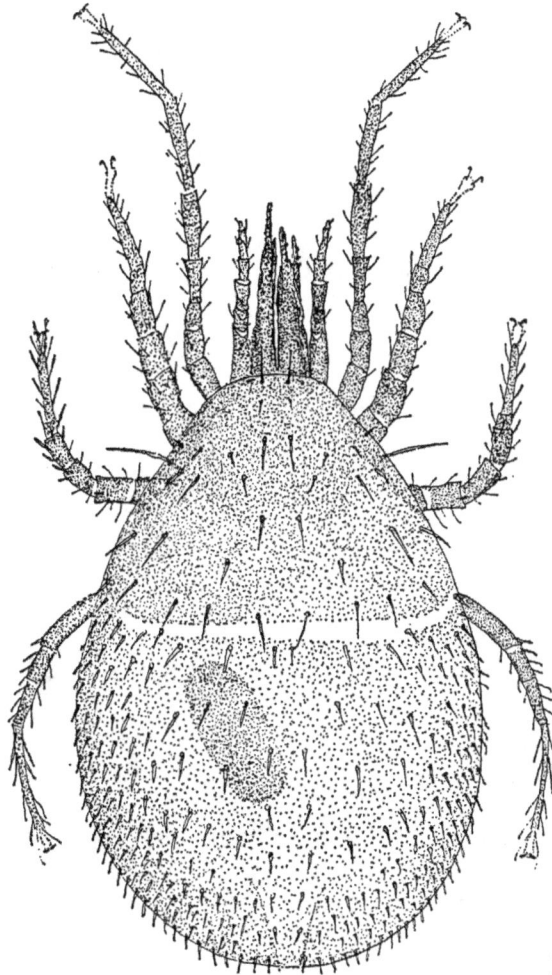

1 mm.

Fig. 81. *Parasitus fucorum* female.

Scutacarus acarorum (syn. *S. femoris*) (Fig. 84) (Karafiat, 1959). This species is sometimes found on adult bumblebees, attached to the legs of phoretic mites.

Kutzinia (=*Tyrophagus*) *laevis* is another mite which, like *Parasitus*, occurs
abundantly in bumblebee nests and is transported in large numbers on the bodies
of adult bees. However, compared with *Parasitus*, it is far less often noticed, mainly
because of its much smaller size. Within bumblebee nests *Kutzinia* probably feeds
on moulds and nest detritus. Development is as follows: egg, larva, protonymph,

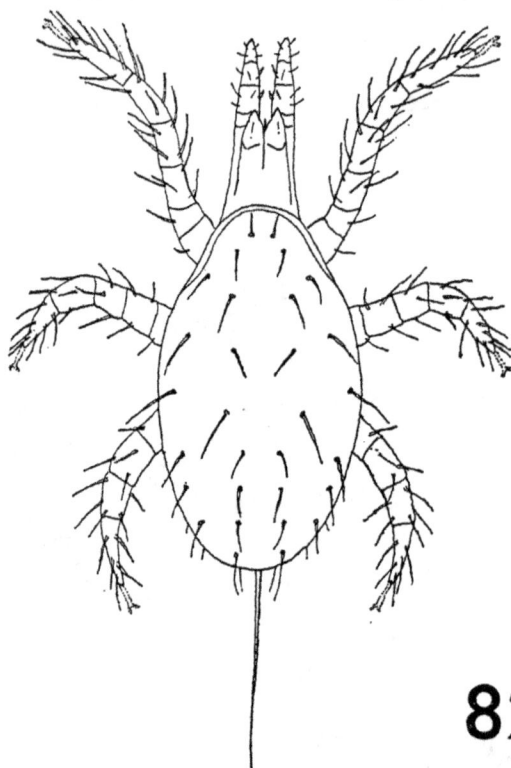

0·3 mm.

82

Fig. 82. Larva of *Parasitus*.

(deutonymph), tritonymph, adult; the deutonymph (Fig. 85) is an optional, non-
feeding, hypopial stage. These hypopi, each approximately 0·2 mm. long, and
brownish in colour, attach themselves to adult bumblebees, and are most often
found crowded together on the hind part of the thorax (for example, on the propodeum) and towards the base of the abdomen; they may also occur in large numbers between the hairs on the more apical abdominal tergites. *Kutzinia laevis* is
abundant on both *Bombus* and *Psithyrus*. Although at first active, the hypopi soon
attach themselves to the bumblebee's cuticle by means of a sucker located on their
ventral surface. Unlike deutonymphs of *Parasitus*, hypopi of *Kutzinia* remain

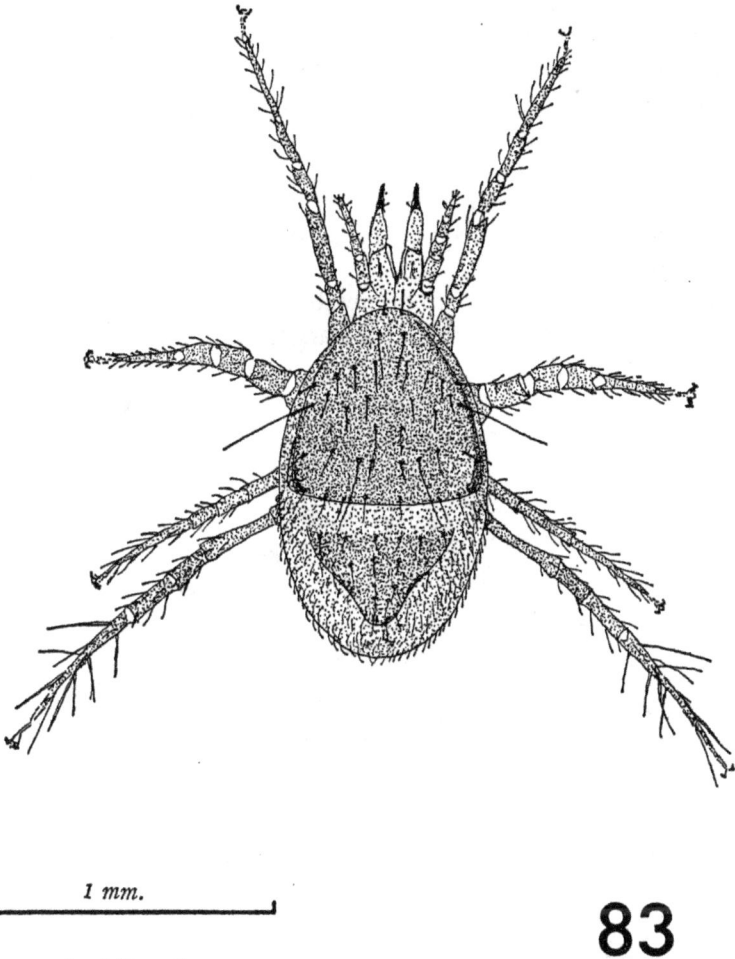

1 mm.

83

Fig. 83. Deutonymph of *Parasitus*.

attached to dead bumblebees and will, themselves, die *in situ*. The dead hypopi may be found on old bumblebee specimens stored away in museum collections, but because of their small size they usually go unnoticed. The hypopi of *K. laevis* are more common on some species of bumblebee than on others; young queens of *Bombus terrestris*, for example, often being particularly heavily infested (Colombo, 1961; Skou, *et al.*, 1963). The latter authors have suggested that the level of infestation for a species may be related to specific differences in individual hygiene.

Within the mite genus *Hypoaspis* (*sensu lato*) (Fig. 86) there are numerous species primarily associated with bumblebees (Evans & Till, 1966).[1] They occur in bumblebee nests as eggs, larvae, protonymphs, deutonymphs and adults. It is the

[1] Some authorities follow Berlese (1921) and Willman (1953) in using *Pneumolaelaps* for members of *Hypoaspis* which have large stigmata and are associated with bees.

141

adult females which attach themselves to bumblebees, each clinging with its legs to a body hair on the bee's thorax, usually near the wing bases. The mites remain attached with their gnathosoma near, but not quite touching, the body of the bee (Hunter, 1966). Species of *Hypoaspis* may be saprophagous, or possibly predacious on other members of the bumblebee nest fauna.

Members of the genus *Proctolaelaps*, also treated as *Garmania* or *Garmaniella* (see Westerboer, 1963; Linquist & Evans, 1965), are also denizens of bumblebee nests where, like hypoaspids, they may be predators; the adults are also recorded as phoretic on bumblebees.

Numerous other mites occur in bumblebee nests, gaining entry by phoresy. These include *Fuscuropoda marginata*, a large, opaque, chestnut-brown species, commonly found on mouldy organic matter (Evans, *et al.*, 1961). It is the deuto-nymphs of *Fuscuropoda* (Fig. 87) which are phoretic; they attach themselves to bumblebees (I have also found them attached to larvae of *Volucella bombylans*) by

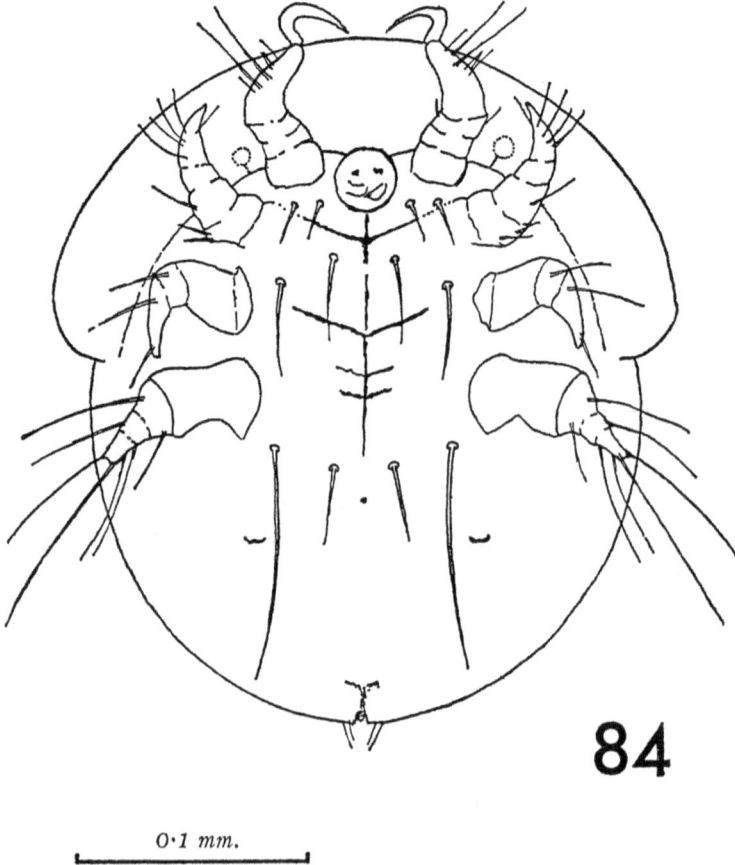

0·1 *mm.*

Fig. 84. *Scutacarus acarorum.*

means of a whitish stalk or pedicel which is secreted from special glands situated in the region of the anus.

Two whitish, long-haired mites (*Glycyphagus ornatus* and *G. domesticus*) (Fig. 88) are common inhabitants of bumblebee nests where they feed on pollen and probably other organic matter. Adults of *Glycyphagus*, and various other tyroglyphid mites, are, again, phoretic on bumblebees (see Türk & Türk, 1957). *Acarus siro* is yet another pollen-feeding, phoretic mite often found in bumblebee nests.

One species of mite, *Bombacarus* (=*Locustacarus*) *buchneri*, is an internal parasite of adult bumblebees and, like *Acarapis woodi*, the well-known endoparasitic mite affecting honey bees, it lives in the tracheal system of its host. The parasite was

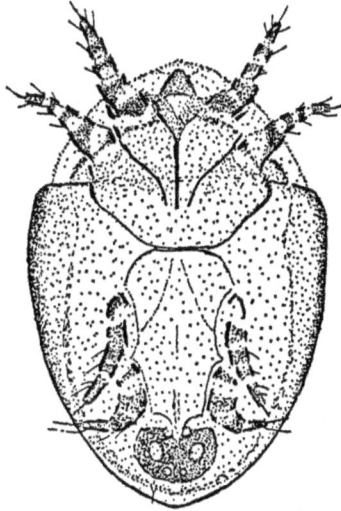

85

0·1 *mm.*

Fig. 85. Deutonymph of *Kutzinia laevis.*

reported in bumblebees by Toumanoff (1930), and the first account of its life history was given by Cumber (1949d). The mite is widely distributed in Europe (e.g. Stammer, 1951; Postner, 1952; Hasselrot, 1960), and is also found in North America (Husband, 1968) and New Zealand (Macfarlane, 1973). Both *Bombus* and *Psithyrus* are attacked.

Bombacarus buchneri occurs in the large tracheal air sacs located in the first abdominal segment of bumblebees. The developmental pattern is simple, eggs giving rise directly to adults. Gravid females overwinter inside hibernating bumblebees, and once hosts become active in the spring the parasites, several of which may

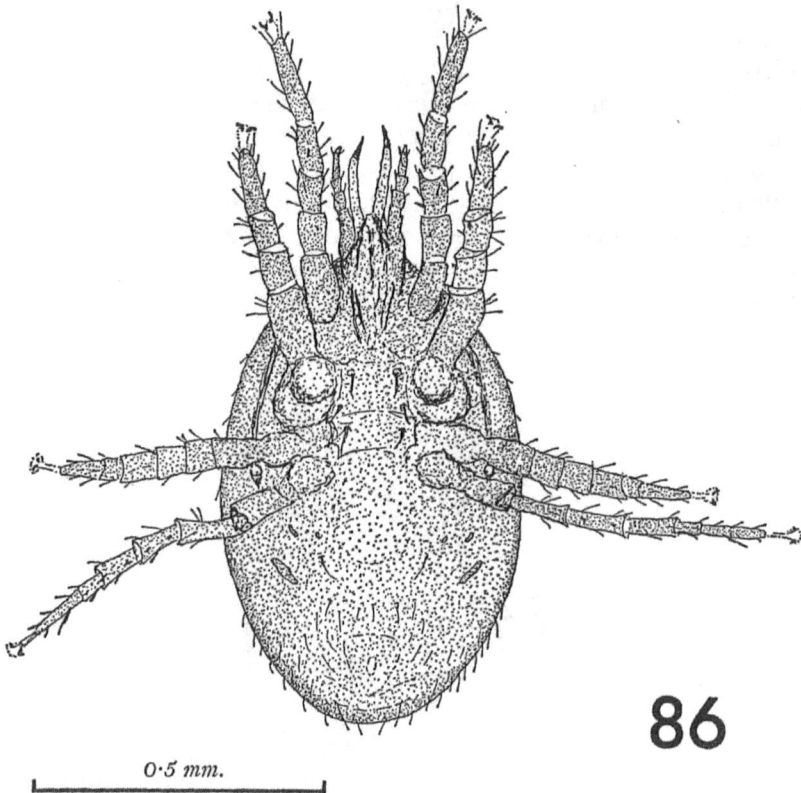

0·5 mm.

Fig. 86. *Hypoaspis* female.

infest a single host, feed on haemolymph after piercing the trachael wall with their mouthparts. Each female then enlarges considerably, becoming round and sac-like (Fig. 89), and eggs (Fig. 90) are eventually laid. A single parasite may deposit up to fifty eggs, which may be found clustered together in sticky masses within the air sacs of the host. Nest establishment by the host is not impaired and by the time that the first bumblebee workers have been reared the *Bombacarus* eggs will have hatched into six-legged larviform males (Fig. 91) or females (Fig. 92). After mating, the female parasites migrate via the host's spiracles, and infest worker bees within the nest; some females, however, may remain within the original host, and produce another generation of parasites. Once enlarged, the *Bombacarus* female does not migrate. Although wandering larviform females usually enter the abdominal spiracles of adult bumblebees, they have been found in a pupa (Husband, 1969). Several generations of *B. buchneri* occur during the season, but survival of the parasite is dependent upon it being able, eventually, to infest young bumblebee queens before these leave their maternal colonies to take up winter quarters.

In nature, attacks by *Bombacarus buchneri* are relatively benign. However, some-

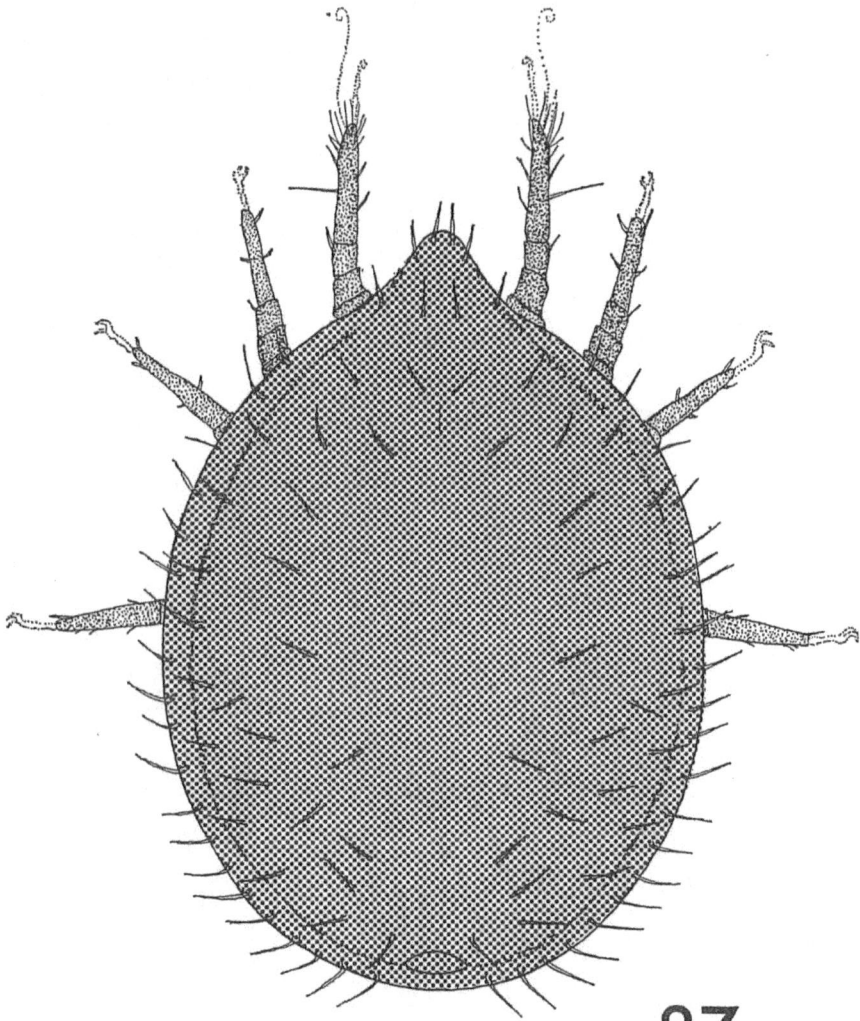

87

0·3 mm.

Fig. 87. Deutonymph of *Fuscuropoda marginata*.

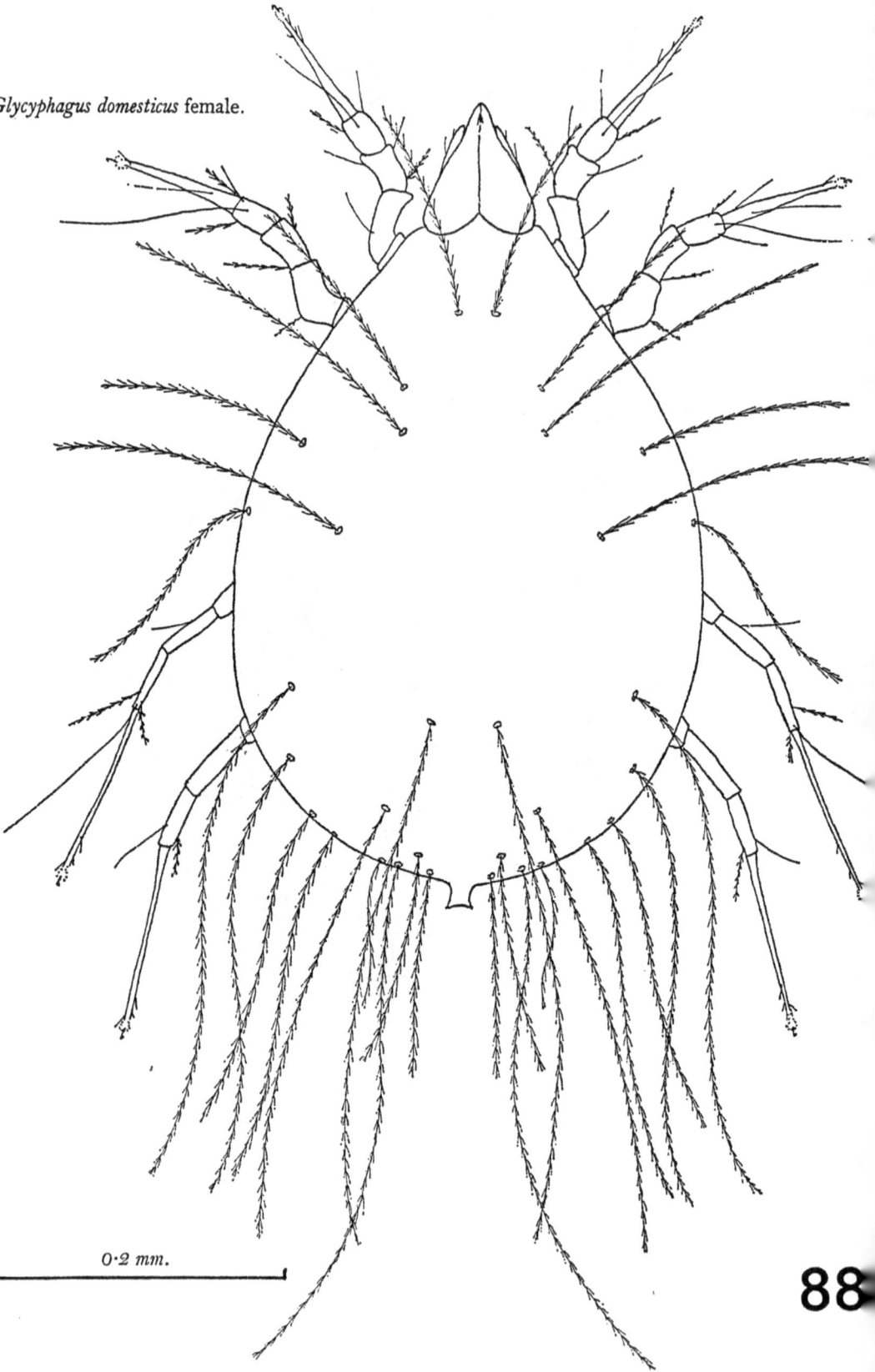

Fig. 88. *Glycyphagus domesticus* female.

0·2 mm.

88

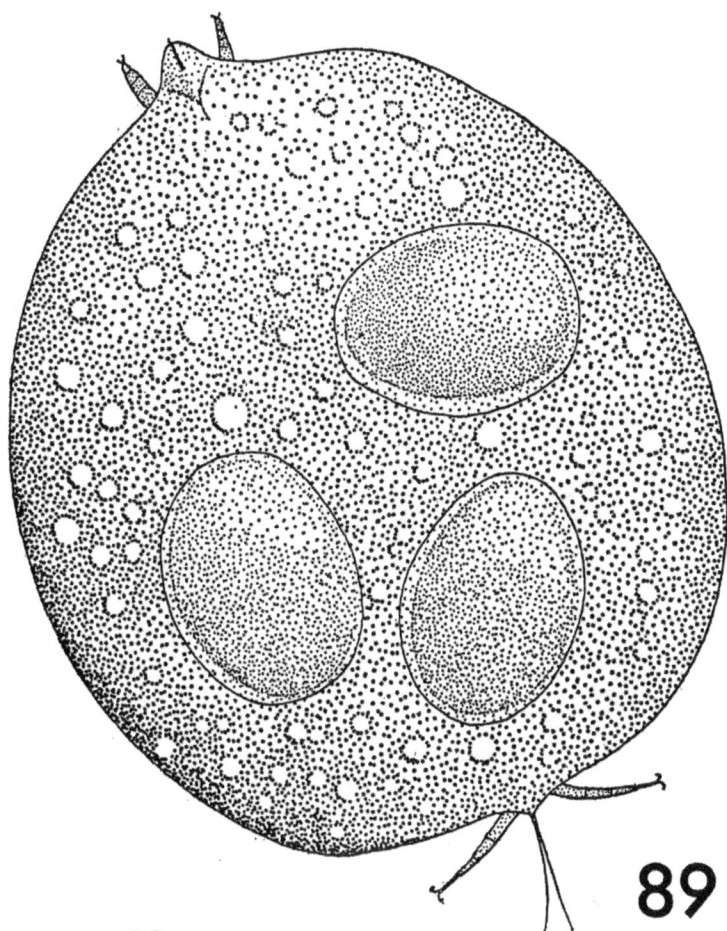

0·2 mm.

Fig. 89. Gravid female of *Bombacarus buchneri*.

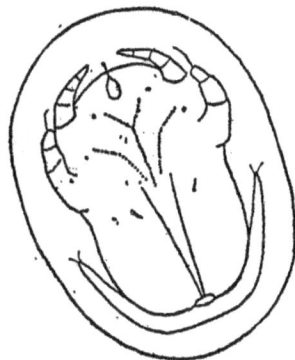

0·1 mm.

Fig. 90. Egg of *Bombacarus buchneri*.

times hosts become very weak as a result of an infestation; particularly towards the end of the season, bumblebees may be noticeably affected, as the number of mites in their bodies increases (Husband & Sinha, 1970). Skou, *et al.* (1963) have reported that *B. buchneri* is likely to be a particularly important enemy of bumblebees kept in confinement.

·0·05 mm.

91

Fig. 91. Larviform male of *Bombacarus buchneri*.

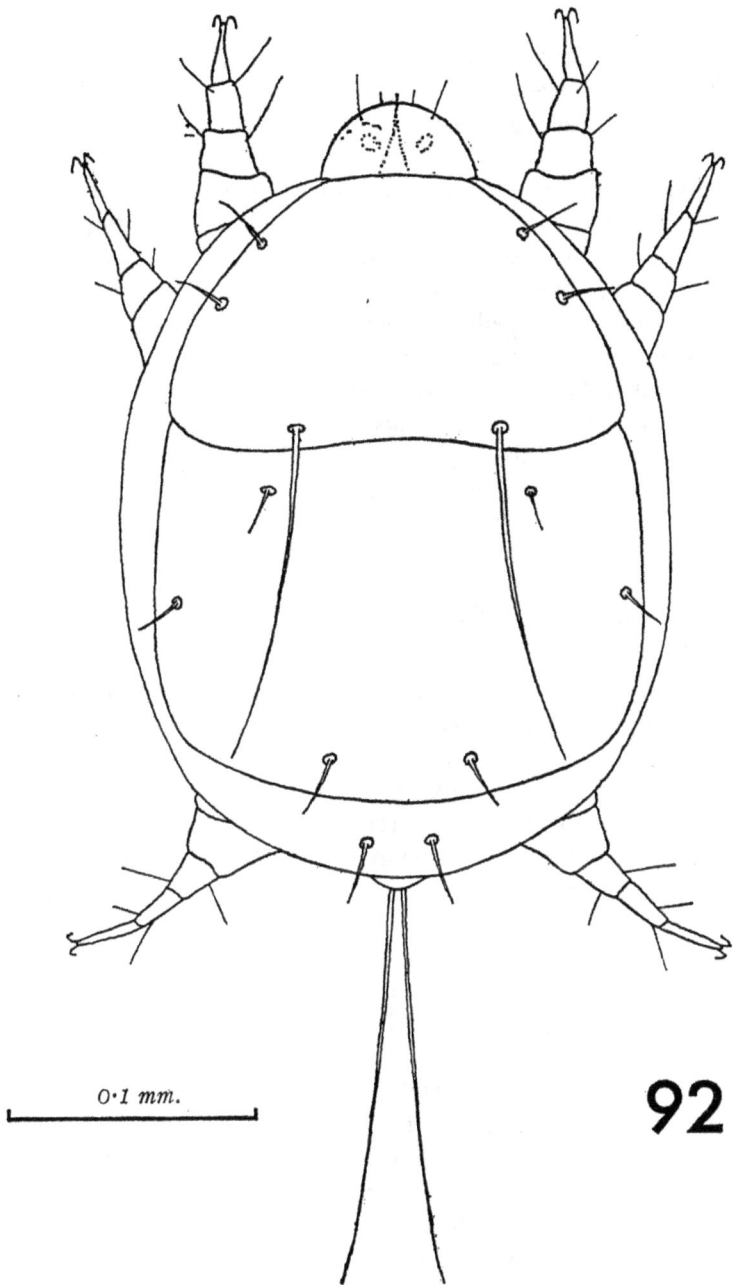

Fig. 92. Larviform female of *Bombacarus buchneri*.

MISCELLANEOUS

Spiders and pseudoscorpions occasionally appear in bumblebee nests where they may reside as temporary predators. The latter usually arrive by phoresy, being carried into the nests by foraging bumblebees in much the same way as *Antherophagus* beetles.

Plath (1934) mentioned two species of spider (*Argiope aurantia* and *Misumena vatia*) which he frequently observed in America feeding on foraging bumblebees. The latter species, which also occurs in southern England, does not spin a web, but awaits the arrival on flowers of unsuspecting foraging insects. The female is frequently found on white or yellow flowers, where it is often remarkably well camouflaged; to some extent the spider is able to change colour to suit its background (Bristow, 1958). Although bumblebees are sometimes caught up in spiders' webs, I know of no British web-spinning species that habitually includes bumblebees in its diet; however, the large species *Argiope bruennichi*, a relatively recent addition to our fauna, would seem better equipped to do so than most.

Nematodes

Many insects are parasitized by small worm-like creatures known as nematodes, and one such parasite, *Sphaerularia bombi*, is a formidable enemy of adult bumblebees. *Sphaerularia bombi* occurs in North America and is particularly common in parts of Europe. However, with the exception of a recent record from New Zealand (Macfarlane, 1973), it is not known to occur in the southern hemisphere or in the tropics. This parasite was known to Réaumur (1742) and although originally described by Léon Dufour in 1837, von Siebold (1838) was the first to recognize it as a nematode.

Parasitization of bumblebees takes place in the soil during the summer or autumn, when free-living, fertilized female nemotodes (Fig. 98) enter the bodies of young *Bombus* queens or *Psithyrus* females which have dug into the ground to hibernate. A bumblebee may be infested by one or many nematodes. During subsequent development within the host, the uterus of each parasite everts and enlarges considerably; eventually, some weeks after the host has emerged from hibernation, eggs are released into the haemocoel. These later give rise to larvae which live for a while within the host's haemocoel before finally escaping to the outside world. During the summer or early autumn the now free-living nematodes become adult, mating takes place and the fertilized female parasites then seek new hosts. The presence of *S. bombi* (whether one or many) prevents development of the ovaries of the host bumblebee and also affects its post-hibernation behaviour. Parasitized bumblebees do not initiate or invade colonies but instead, before they die, they

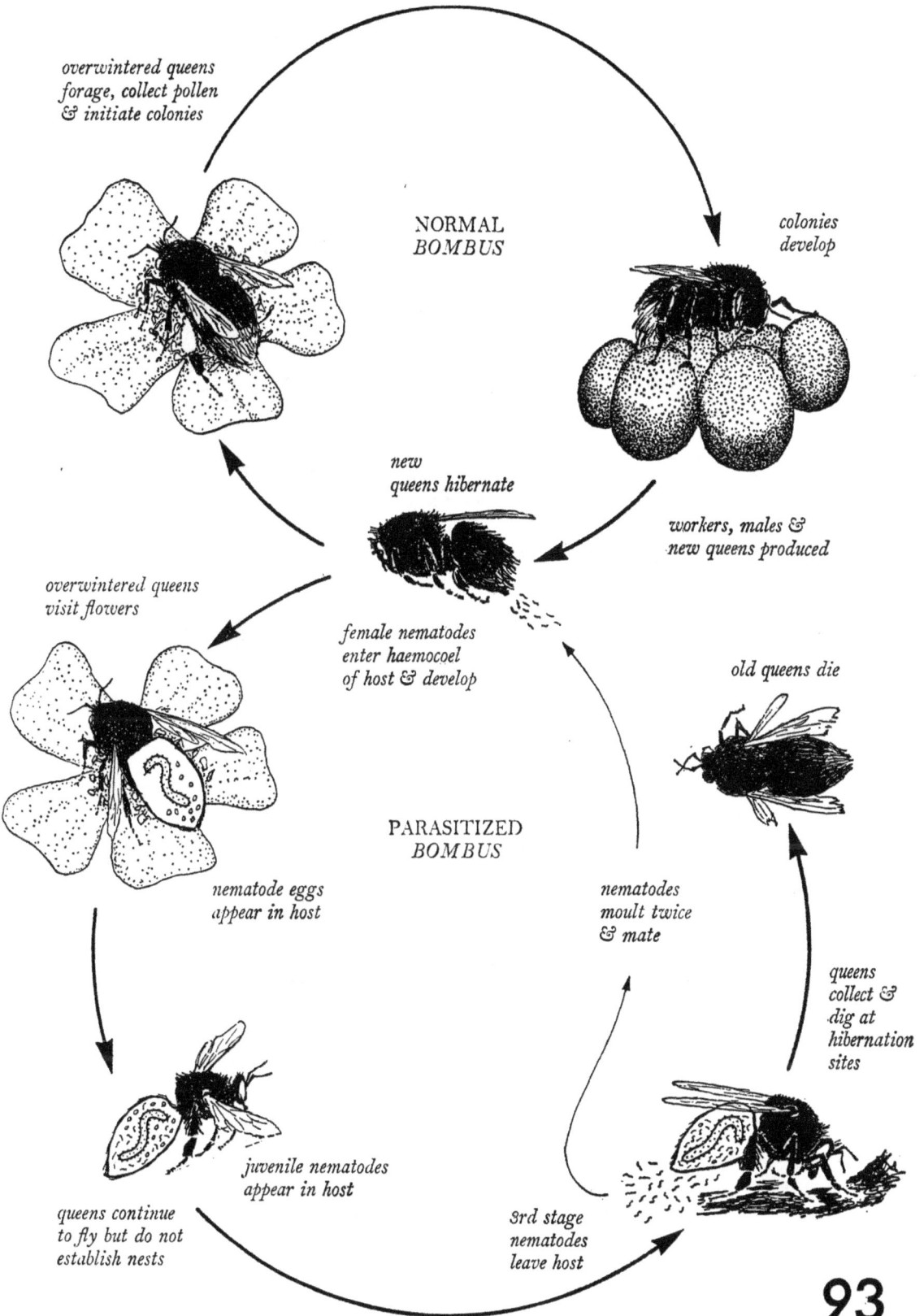

overwintered queens forage, collect pollen & initiate colonies

NORMAL
BOMBUS

colonies develop

new queens hibernate

workers, males & new queens produced

overwintered queens visit flowers

female nematodes enter haemocoel of host & develop

old queens die

PARASITIZED
BOMBUS

nematode eggs appear in host

nematodes moult twice & mate

queens collect & dig at hibernation sites

juvenile nematodes appear in host

queens continue to fly but do not establish nests

3rd stage nematodes leave host

93

Fig. 93. Life cycle of *Sphaerularia bombi* and *Bombus* host (based on Poinar & van der Laan, 1972).

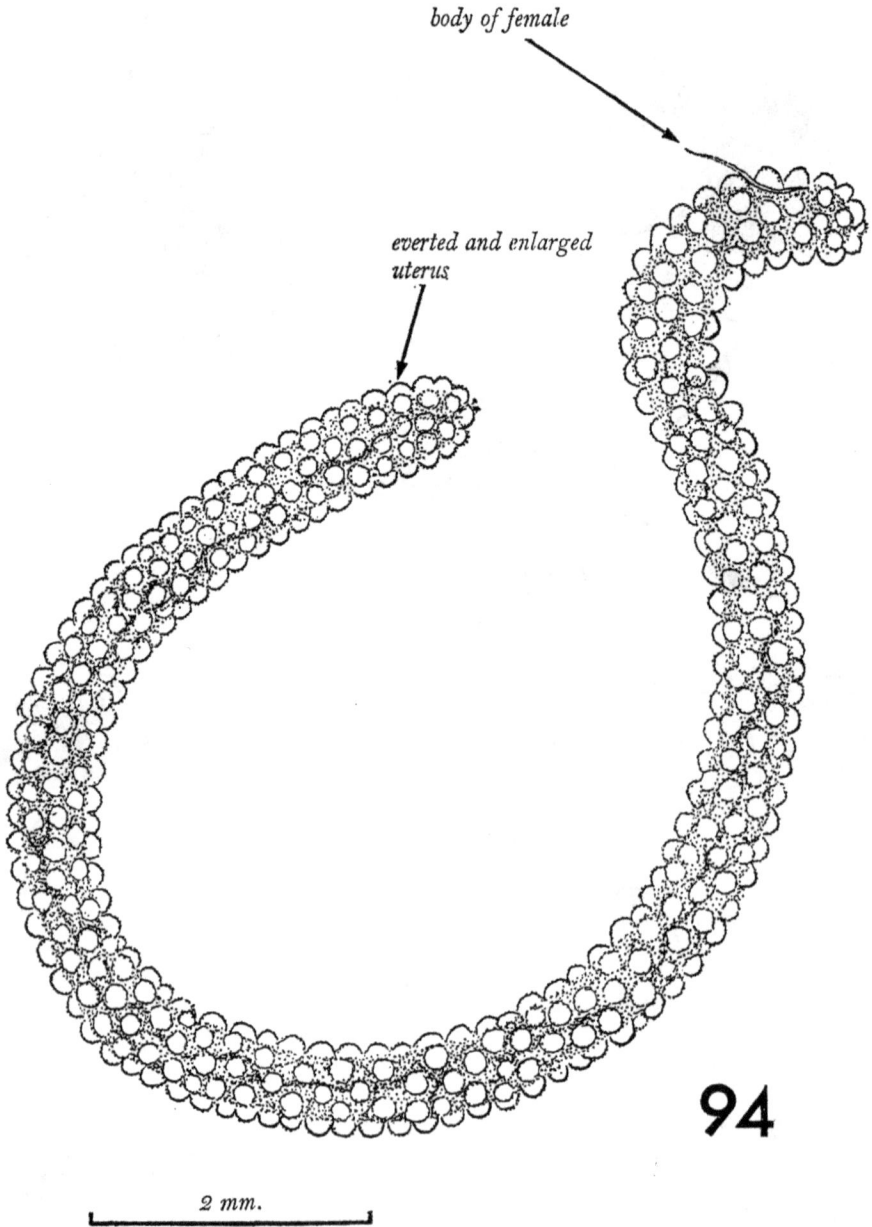

body of female

everted and enlarged
uterus

2 mm.

Fig. 94. *Sphaerularia bombi* female with everted and hypertrophied uterus.

return to hibernation sites where dissemination into the soil of juvenile nematodes occurs (see Fig. 93).

Some authors have suggested that parasitization of bumblebees by *Sphaerularia bombi* actually occurs in the nest. Schneider (1883), for example, thought that the nematodes were in some way carried into colonies by foraging workers and then fed to larvae in the food; Stein (1956b) considered it possible that bumblebee larvae might become infested following invasion of healthy nests by parasitized queens, and Pouvreau (1963b) suggested that infested *Psithyrus* females could similarly act as vectors. More recently, Nickle (1967) illustrated the life cycle of *S. bombi*, assuming bumblebee larvae to be attacked in the soil. However, under natural conditions live *S. bombi* parasites have never been found in bumblebee nests, either in adult or larval bumblebees; nor have worker or male bumblebees ever been shown to harbour the parasite. If bumblebee larvae were in fact the vulnerable stage, then the absence of the parasite in workers and males would need explaining. Furthermore, none of the above authors' views takes into account the important posthibernation changes in host behaviour brought about by the presence of the parasite (see below); nor does involvement of bumblebee larvae in the life cycle of *S. bombi* accord with known features of the biology of either the parasite or its host.

Infective adult females of *Sphaerularia bombi* (Fig. 98) are approximately 1 to 2 mm. long, and they probably enter the host via the gut. However, the precise method of penetration into bumblebees is not known, although it has been suggested that the parasites may invade via the reproductive tract, through intersegmental membranes, or even by way of the tracheal system (Pouvreau, 1962).

Eversion and enlargement of the parasite uterus and associated reproductive structures occurs once the nematode enters the body cavity of the host. When fully developed (Fig. 94), the uterus may measure up to 20 mm. in length and be about 1 to 2 mm. wide; this has been estimated as being 15,000 to 20,000 times greater in volume than the original female body, which remains attached as a minute appendage. Where many parasites are present in a single host the uteri tend to be somewhat smaller than normal, but there is considerable variation in the size of individuals (e.g. Leuckart, 1885; Stein, 1956b). Early investigators, including Dufour, von Siebold, and also Lubbock (1861, 1864) believed the everted uterus to be the entire female parasite, and the small attachment (the female body) was assumed to be the male in a permanent state of copulation. However, the true nature of the parasite was eventually discovered by Schneider (1883).

Well-developed parasite uteri have sometimes been found in young *Bombus* queens during the late summer or early autumn, and although the parasite is usually single-brooded, it is possible that, under favourable conditions, there might be at least a partial second generation (Pouvreau, 1964; Poinar & van der Laan, 1972).

Large numbers of eggs are produced from each parasite uterus, and following their release into the haemocoel of the host, first- and second-instar parasites may be seen developing within them (Fig. 95). Soon, third-instar larvae break through

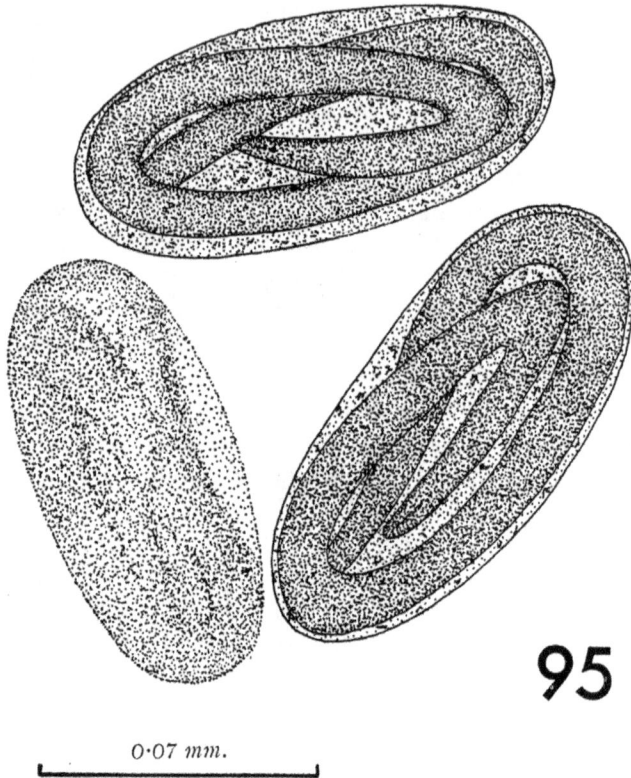

95

0·07 mm.

Fig. 95. Eggs of *Sphaerularia bombi* containing first- or second-instar larvae.

the egg membranes and may then be found swimming actively in the host's haemolymph (Fig. 96). Within any one parasitized bumblebee there may be upwards of 100,000 eel-like, juvenile parasites, each about 1 mm. long. Although most numerous in the abdomen, *Sphaerularia* eggs and larvae may also occur in the head and thorax of their host.

Palm (1948) found that in parasitized, overwintered bumblebees the corpora allata remained small and apparently inactive (like those of healthy, young queens about to enter hibernation in summer or autumn), whereas those of unparasitized (normal) specimens were enlarged and active. It would appear that in parasitized specimens gonadotrophic hormones are not secreted so that their ovaries do not develop. The post-hibernation behaviour of parasitized individuals (as already indicated) also differs from normal, since they are not induced to establish nests or invade colonies. Instead, they remain on the wing long after healthy individuals have formed colonies and are to be found, often in large numbers, at or adjacent to hibernation sites. In such areas the parasitized bees fly low over the ground, often appearing rather weak and clumsy, stopping at intervals to dig shallow holes in the soil or to force their way under leaves, moss or other ground cover, as described by

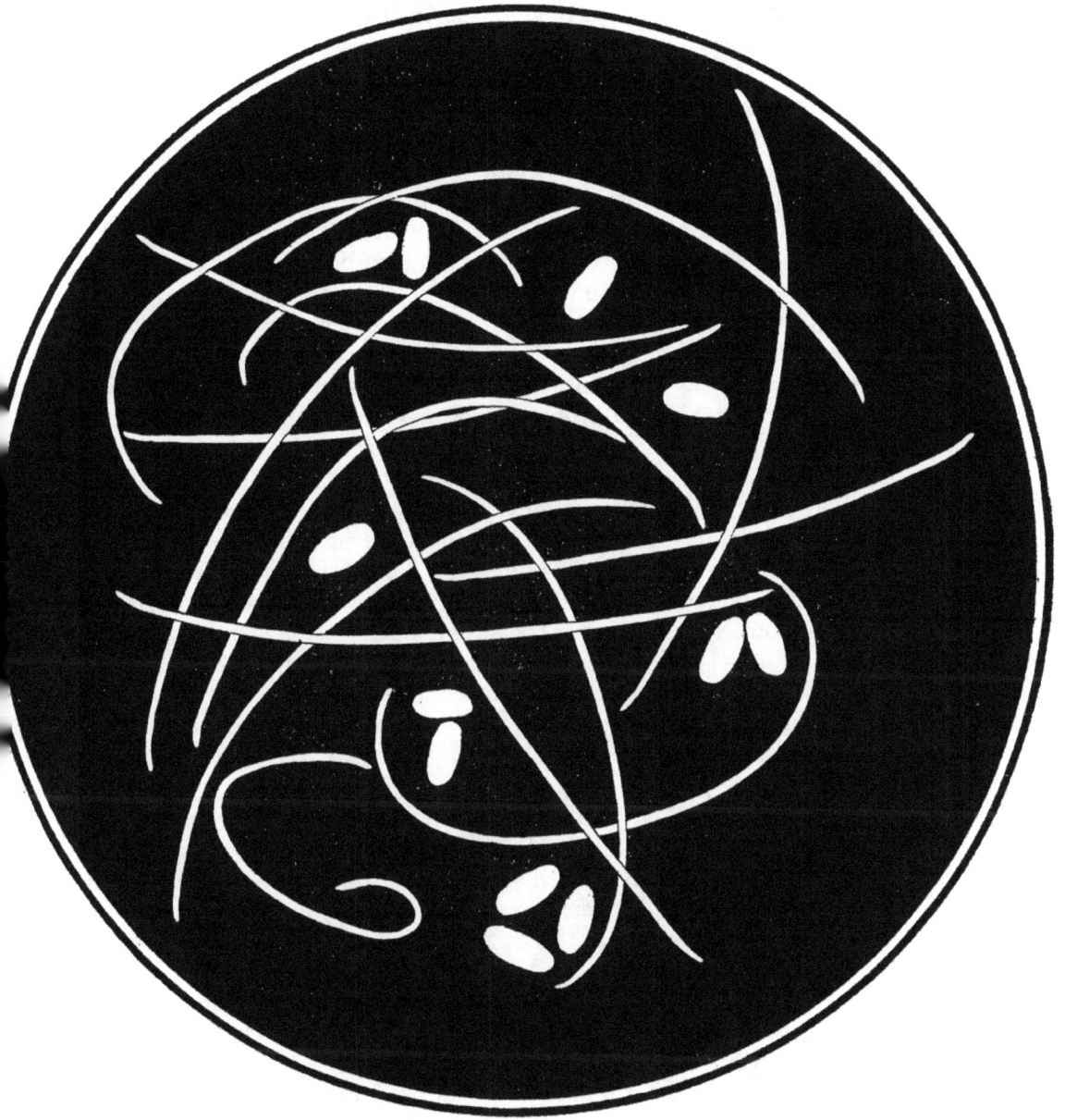

0·5 mm.

Fig. 96. Developing eggs and third-instar larvae of *Sphaerularia bombi*.

Bols (1939) and many other observers. Parasitized bumblebees are most numerous at such sites in the late spring and early summer. In the early part of the spring parasitized queens are relatively active and at first sight are indistinguishable from healthy specimens. (Parasitized individuals do not, of course, collect corbicular pollen-loads, as they do not establish colonies; a queen with pollen-loads, therefore, will be healthy[1]). Later in the season, however, as they become more laboured in their flight, they are easy to distinguish. Parasitized bumblebees tend to occur in the same or similar types of hibernation site as those in which their species normally overwinters. For instance, *Sphaerularia*-infested individuals of *Bombus lapidarius*, *B. hortorum* and various *Psithyrus* species, mainly frequent banks with a north-west exposure, while infested *B. lucorum* and *B. terrestris* queens tend to congregate on tree-covered, north-west slopes (Alford, 1969c). Poinar & van der Laan concluded from their studies that the special gathering sites of parasitized bumblebees and preferred hibernation sites did not coincide exactly, but simply overlapped in certain areas, thus ensuring that only a proportion of new potential hosts frequenting a *Sphaerularia*-infested overwintering site would become parasitized.

Third-instar *Sphaerularia* larvae remain in the haemocoel of their host for several days, but eventually they enter the alimentary and reproductive tracts, and also other tissues, and then finally escape to the outside. The parasites are frequently expelled in the host's faeces and, undoubtedly, large numbers are released into the soil at the special gathering sites, as the infested bumblebees move over, or dig into, the soil. Some two months later, after a transitory fourth-instar larval stage, the nematodes become adult (Figs. 97 and 98). In artificial cultures Madel (1966) found a sex ratio of two to one in favour of females. Eventually, mating occurs and the impregnated females then seek new hosts. The return of infested bumblebees to areas where new hosts will be available, later in the year, is the essential link in the life cycle of this unique parasite (Fig. 93).

Sphaerularia bombi normally only attacks bumblebees, although it may occur rarely in *Vespula* queens (Cobbold, 1888). Wasps will sometimes overwinter in the same habitats chosen by bumblebees – when searching for hibernating bumblebees I have occasionally unearthed *Vespula* queens from shaded banks and from soil around the base of trees – and no doubt at such times they could be liable to chance attack by the parasite.

In some localized regions infestation levels among bumblebee populations may be high, whereas in others few parasitized individuals will occur (e.g. Schneider, 1883; Leuckart, 1885). However, as pointed out by Hattingen (1956) there are various difficulties associated with obtaining reliable estimates of infestation levels. A major problem is that as the season advances, parasitized individuals will form larger and larger proportions of samples, since healthy individuals will have established or invaded colonies, thereby being found less and less frequently flying in the field.

---

[1] Occasionally, however, a bumblebee overcomes an attack and may then successfully establish a colony; Alford (1969b), for example, found two apparently successful, young, foundress queens of *Bombus hortorum*, each containing in their abdomens several dead female *S. bombi* parasites with everted uteri.

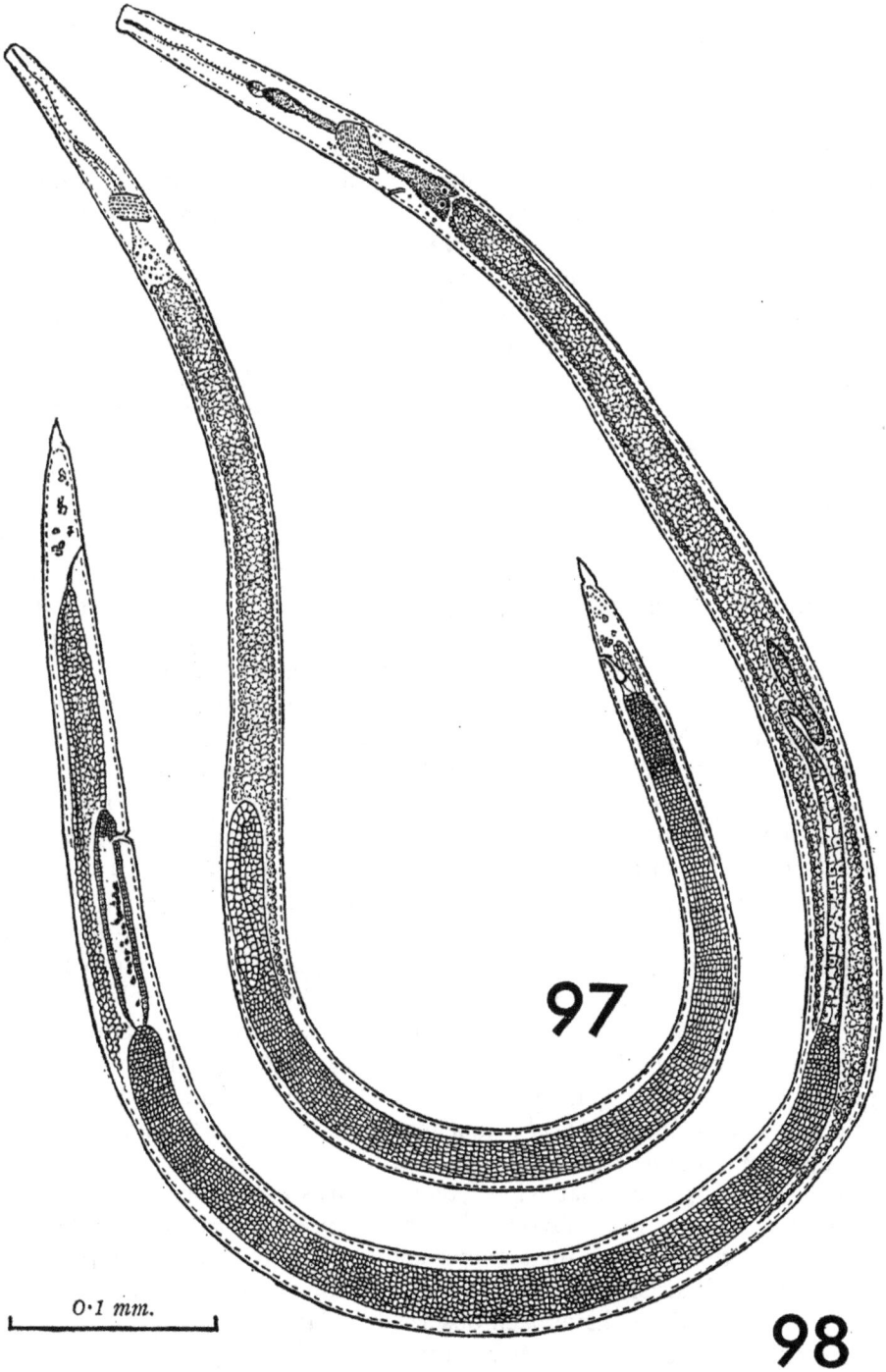

0·1 mm.

Figs. 97–98. *Sphaerularia bombi* adults. 97, male; 98, female (after Poinar & van der Laan, 1972).

This effect is demonstrated by data accumulated by many investigators, including Cumber (1949d), Hattingen (1956) and Pouvreau (1962). Also, different species tend to emerge from hibernation and establish colonies at different times in the spring, thus complicating the seasonal trend. A further complication is that, particularly later in the spring, parasitized individuals tend to accumulate at their special gathering sites; as a result, in such places most, if not all, queens sampled will prove to be infested (e.g. Minderhoud, 1951), whereas elsewhere, for example at foraging sites, infestation levels will be very much lower.

Evidence accumulated by many authorities has shown that in any one area certain species of bumblebee may be more heavily victimized by *Sphaerularia* than others, and it would appear that abundant host species are particularly liable to attack (e.g. Cumber, 1949d; Hattingen, 1956; Alford, 1969b). Various estimates suggest that in some areas up to seventy per cent of overwintered *Bombus* queens of common species may be affected by *S. bombi*. It is probable that the parasite will spread more effectively when hosts are numerous, so that abundant species should tend to be more seriously affected. Undoubtedly, as first suggested by Leuckart (1887), choice of hibernation site is a major factor in determining infestation levels. However, although the various bumblebee species tend to select particular types of site for overwintering, and in the following year parasitized individuals exhibit similar preferences, specific requirements are not always sufficiently distinct to explain fully the variations in infestation levels noted between host species. It is known, for example, that in at least some areas a wide range of different bumblebee species may inhabit a single *Sphaerularia*-infested site (Bols, 1939).

Although in many instances a bumblebee is only attacked by one nematode, frequently several females will invade a single host, and it would appear from published data that there may be a correlation, or at least an association, between the level of infestation in an area (and possibly also between the degree of infestation in any particular host species) and the number of adult parasites present in individual bumblebees. Thus, in Canada, where infestation levels appear to be lower than in many parts of Europe, no more than six adults of *S. bombi* have been reported in any one host (Medler, 1957; Fye, 1966). However, in Europe, much larger numbers per host have often been observed: e.g. thirty-four by both Hattingen and Stein (in Germany); forty-two by Alford (in England); sixty-eight by Cumber (in England); seventy-two by Poinar & van der Laan (in Holland); Palm (1948) stated that unparasitized, overwintered *Bombus* queens were rare near Lund, Sweden, and recorded up to one hundred parasites per host.

Hattingen has suggested that winter temperatures may affect infestation levels, with mild winters being more favourable for the parasite than cold ones. Both soil and weather conditions during the summer and autumn may also be important since higher incidences of parasitism of certain entomophilic nematodes, probably related to soil moisture conditions, have been observed in damper areas (Welch, 1965). In addition to climatic and soil conditions, the distribution of bumblebee hibernation sites in an area, and the relative concentrations of potential hosts in different sites and areas, are also likely to influence infestation levels, both interspecifically and between host populations as a whole.

Micro-organisms

Bumblebees are often parasitized by the protozoan *Nosema bombi* (Fig. 99), a species essentially similar to *Nosema apis*, the well-known parasite of honey bees. Fantham & Porter (1914) believed that both species of *Nosema* could attack either

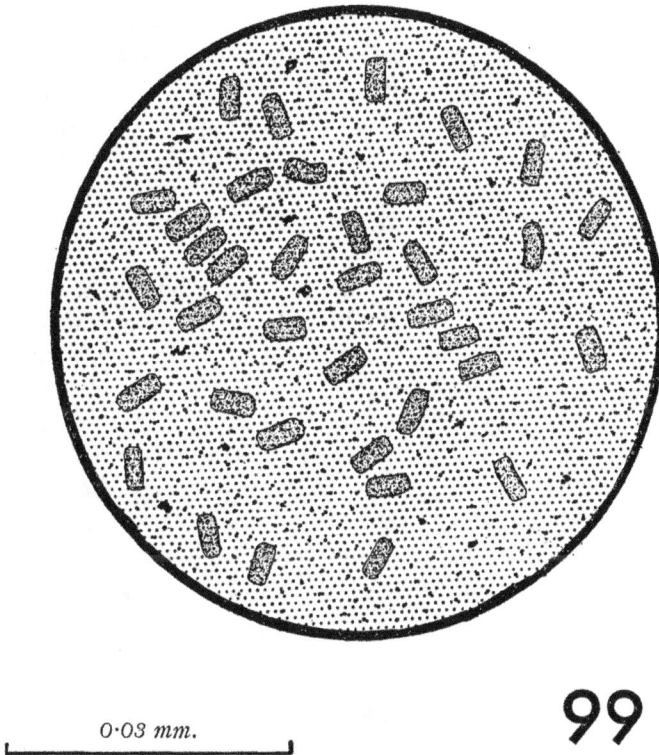

0·03 mm.

99

Fig. 99. Spores of *Nosema bombi*.

Bombus or *Apis* hosts and that cross inoculation occurred when bumblebees invaded honey bee colonies; similarly, Jordan (1962) considered it possible that honey bees robbing bumblebee colonies might become infected with spores of *N. bombi*. Showers, *et al.* (1967) once claimed that *N. apis* could infect bumblebees under laboratory conditions. However, even if this were so the disease would not develop since in bumblebees *N. apis* spores fail to generate (Bailey, personal communication).

Nosema bombi invades the tissue of the gut and Malpighian tubules; an infected bumblebee can become weak, incapable of flying, and will often die. The disease is apparently widespread in bumblebees, and Betts (1920) found that all the over-wintered queens of *Bombus pascuorum* she examined in the spring were infected. Skou, *et al.* (1963) were most readily able to detect *Nosema* in bumblebees during the late autumn, when they found severe attacks in *Bombus terrestris* queens which had not entered hibernation, suggesting that the seasonal severity of nosematosis in bumblebees is different to that in honey bees. Presumably, *N. bombi* will only survive from one season to the next when present in young queens as a mild infection. Although *Nosema* is apparently responsible for much bumblebee mortality, details of the epidemiology of the parasite among British bumblebee populations have not been studied fully.

Other protozoans, and various bacteria and fungi, have also been recorded from bumblebees but most, including species of *Penicillium* and *Aspergillus* which are probably only present as *post mortem* growths (Skou, 1967), and yeasts in the gut[1] (Mooser, 1958; Skou, *et al.*, 1963) are of no significance as parasites or pathogens. However, some micro-fungi are considered to be pathogenic; these include common entomogenous fungi such as *Beauveria bassiana*, a species listed as a parasite of *Bombus pratorum* in this country (Leatherdale, 1970). Little or nothing is known of the diseases of bumblebee brood.

Bailey & Gibbs (1964) have shown that in nature bumblebees may be infected with acute bee-paralysis virus but, unlike honey bees, they are not apparently hosts of chronic bee-paralysis virus. Acute bee-paralysis virus has also been found in pollen loads accumulated by bumblebees (from flowers of red clover [*Trifolium pratense*] not being visited by honey bees); it is seemingly added, in the fluid secreted from the salivary glands, as the pollen is collected (Bailey, 1971).

Rarely, bumblebees may be vectors of micro-organisms. For example, bumble-bees visiting secondary pear blossom are implicated in the spread of the bacterium *Erwinia amylovora*, the causative organism of fireblight, a serious disease of apple and pear trees (Emmett & Baker, 1971).

Vertebrates

FISH, AMPHIBIANS AND REPTILES

Bumblebees are very occasionally eaten by amphibians and reptiles (Knowlton, *et al.*, 1946; Norris, 1953; Korschgen & Moyle, 1955) but they do not form more than a small fraction of the total diet of these animals. In Ireland, brown trout have been reported to take bumblebees which inadvertently land on the water (Hinchliffe, 1914); apparently the fish will swallow bees, including honey bees, live.

---

[1] Yeasts also occur in the honey stored in bumblebee colonies (Spencer, *et al.*, 1970).

BIRDS

Shrikes are well-known predators of bumblebees, and in Britain the red-backed shrike, *Lanius collurio*, often attacks adults of both *Bombus* and *Psithyrus* (Witherby, *et al.*, 1958). Shrikes commonly impale their prey on thorns or spikes (forming their so-called larders); on Fair Isle (in the Shetlands) Williamson (1949) found *Bombus muscorum smithianus* impaled on barbed wire. Owen (1948) reported that bumblebee queens figured prominently in larders of *Lanius collurio*, but observed that small bumblebees (workers, males and carder bees) and honey bees were usually eaten as soon as they were caught. In a recent study of the food and feeding habits of the great grey shrike, *Lanius excubitor*, in Finland (this species is a winter visitor to Britain), Grönlund, *et al.* (1970) found that insects formed fifty-five per cent of the shrike's food in summer, with bumblebees representing a quarter of this, and ninety-four per cent in the autumn, when bumblebees then made up as much as forty-one per cent of the total diet. It is thought that the high proportion of insects eaten in the autumn (in favour of vertebrate prey) is related to an increased need for sugar; bumblebees with their large, sugary crop contents would thus be particularly suitable as food at this time.

Apart from shrikes, insectivorous birds generally avoid or learn to avoid bumblebees (Carrick, 1936). However, the great tit, *Parus major*, is known to attack bumblebees in their overwintering sites, and included in the list of victims are ailing queens parasitized by *Sphaerularia bombi* (Bols, 1939). The great tit is also known to catch drowsy bumblebees foraging on lime (*Tilia*) trees (Saunders, 1907); the bird pecks open the abdomen of the bumblebee and feeds upon the nectar contained in the crop. Large numbers of bumblebees mutilated by birds may be found under some lime trees and, as in the case of wasp predation, foragers of *Bombus lucorum* and *B. terrestris* are especially common victims. Birds are known to eat bumblebees in Greenland (Longstaff, 1932), but reports of other such cases are rare.

MAMMALS

Some mammals must be listed as enemies of bumblebees. In North America, skunks (*Mephitis mephitis*) frequently destroy colonies, eating the brood, comb and adult bees (see Plath, 1923d, 1934). In parts of the British Isles the badger (*Meles meles*) is similarly harmful. Bumblebees also form a small part of the summer diet of foxes (Southern & Watson, 1941). Sladen (1912) mentioned that moles (*Talpa europaea*) and weasels (*Mustela nivalis*) destroy bumblebee colonies. Mice (*Apodemus*), shrews (*Sorex*) and voles (*Clethrionomys* and *Microtus*) frequently enter incipient colonies before the emergence of the first bumblebee workers and devour the brood; presumably, such attacks are made when the foundress queen is away foraging. Col. Newman's (1851) estimation that two-thirds of the bumblebee colonies in England are destroyed by field-mice (*Apodemus sylvaticus*) is often quoted. It should be added, however, that field-mice are also beneficial, since their deserted nests, in common with those of other small mammals, are frequently utilized by bumblebees for nesting. Indeed, in the spring, the availability of disused mammal nests has a considerable bearing on the number of bumblebee colonies likely to be established in any one area.

Man, of course, has a considerable influence on bumblebee populations and is today a formidable enemy. Many bumblebees are killed by motor vehicles, and many undoubtedly die as a result of poisoning by pesticides or other chemicals. Sadly, nests are sometimes destroyed in ignorance or, unavoidably, by accident. However, to a large extent the above depredations are ephemeral losses. Far more important are the long-term effects wrought by the wholesale, and often permanent, destruction of suitable habitats where bumblebees can hibernate, establish nests and forage for food on a succession of floral hosts throughout the season (Alford, 1973a).

The modern activities of man are not always detrimental to bumblebee survival, and several species will readily colonize man-made habitats such as urban parks and gardens. *Bombus hypnorum*, for example, shows a particularly strong preference for areas inhabited by man (Haeseler, 1972; Løken, 1973).

THE BRITISH SPECIES

CHAPTER 9

Classification and Descriptions

BUMBLEBEES have long been known to comprise two distinct types, the truly industrious species (genus *Bombus* Latreille 1802), and the non-industrious, inquiline species (genus *Psithyrus* Lepeletier 1832) which lack a worker caste and depend for their existence on the 'true' bumblebees in whose nests they are reared. Since both *Bombus* and *Psithyrus* contain a heterogenous assemblage of species, many authors have found it necessary to subdivide each genus into several groups or subgenera. Such divisions are not merely of academic or taxonomic interest, but are also of considerable value when considering the behaviour and biology of bumblebees; this is particularly so in the case of the genus *Bombus*.

Von Dalla Torre (1882) attempted to group species of *Bombus* according to their coat colour, and Plath (1922c) once used characteristics of coloration for subdividing the American species of *Psithyrus*. However, although a grouping on account of colour may at times be useful (see Alford, 1970–72), such a division has little or no taxonomic status and is entirely artificial, since similarly-coloured species may in fact be far from closely allied (for example, in the British fauna, *Bombus lapidarius* and *B. ruderarius*). Valid and reliable subdivisions may, however, be made on the basis of certain structural or behavioural characteristics.

Radoszkowski (1884) first subdivided species of *Bombus* into various groups according to the form of the male genitalia, and later Vogt (1911) produced a classification, also based on genital features, in which he divided *Bombus* into several subgenera; similar systems have since been put forward by Ball (1914), Krüger (1920) and Skorikov (1922). Diagnostic features of the various subgenera of *Bombus* are included in a recent paper by Richards (1968) and this work should be consulted for more detailed information.

Various authors have proposed the elevation of certain subgenera to generic rank, or intended group names to be applied on a generic level, but with the exception of Milliron's system this need not concern a discussion of the British fauna. Milliron (1961) divided *Bombus* into three genera, two of which he subdivided into subgenera, as follows:

Genus	Subgenus
1. *Bombus* Latreille	
2. *Megabombus* von Dalla Torre	*Bombias* Robertson *Megabombus* von Dalla Torre

165

Genus	Subgenus
3. *Pyrobombus* von Dalla Torre	$\left\{ \begin{array}{l} \textit{Cullumanobombus} \text{ Vogt} \\ \textit{Pyrobombus} \text{ von Dalla Torre} \end{array} \right.$

If this classification were employed here, then British species would be included in all three genera. However, Milliron's system has not been generally accepted and seems unsatisfactory in various respects. Richards (1968) has commented, for example, that Milliron's key to genera 'depends largely on venational characters, which prove to be quite unworkable in a number of species on which they have been tested. Moreover, two of his genera, *Pyrobombus* von Dalla Torre and *Megabombus* von Dalla Torre, each fall in two halves of his key, so that their reintegration is essentially arbitrary. A number of exceptions have to be made for particular species suggesting that perhaps his genera would really be better split.'

Returning to more generally accepted classifications, it is evident that certain subgenera of *Bombus* are more closely allied to one another than to others, and consequently some may be grouped conveniently together. Krüger (1920), for example, divided *Bombus* into two major sections – *Odontobombus* and *Anodontobombus* – basically according to the presence or absence of a spinose projection at the hind apex of the mid basitarsus, and this division will be seen to be important when considering the British fauna.

Behaviour was first used as a basis for subdividing the genus *Bombus* when Smith (1876) split the British species into either *Surface-builders* or *Underground-builders* according to their nesting habits. However, although many species characteristically establish their nests below ground, whilst others typically nest on the surface, several species (including *Bombus pratorum*, *B. lapidarius*, *B. hortorum* and *B. sylvarum*) may nest either above or below ground level. Smith's classification is, therefore, of limited value.

Important groupings of *Bombus* reflecting differences in behavioural characteristics were, however, established by F. W. L. Sladen following his extensive and painstaking observations on the biology of many of our British species. Sladen (1896) first drew attention to differences in the brood-rearing and pollen-storing methods adopted by bumblebees. He later (1899) wrote of *Bombus*: 'It appears that each species has habits and proclivities more or less peculiar to itself, and these, if they could be accurately observed and recorded, would help very much in the systematic arrangement of the species, which in this interesting genus is unusually difficult, owing to the lack of easily recognisable structural differences, and to the little reliance that can be placed on colouring.'

'. . . most of the *Bombi* found in this country may be separated into two groups, on what seems to be a rather important difference in the manner of raising their young. These groups may be conveniently named (1) the "*pouch-makers*" and (2) the "*pollen-storers*". The *pouch-makers* form little pockets or pouches of wax at the side of a wax-covered mass of growing larvae, into which the workers drop the pellets of pollen direct from their hind tibiae on their return to the nest from the fields. The *pollen-storers*, on the contrary, store the newly gathered pollen in waxen cells specially made for the purpose, or in old cocoons specially set apart to receive it, from which it is taken and given to the larvae through the mouths of the nurse-bees as required'. Sladen (1912) later substituted the term *'pocket-makers'* for *'pouch-makers'*. It is significant that Sladen's behavioural classification is consistent with one based on structure, the *pollen-storers* being *Anodontobombus* and the *pocket-makers* *Odontobombus*.

Plath (1927a) has pointed out that since certain American and, as noted by Sladen (1912), some British *pocket-makers*, will under certain circumstances store pollen away from their brood in special cells or vacated cocoons, the term *pollen-storers* was unsuitable in any comprehensive classification of *Bombus*. Also, Plath noted that in some American *pocket-makers* (e.g. *Bombus americanorum* and *B. fervidus*) the pocket-making habit was employed only for worker brood, queen and male larvae being reared on regurgitated food in the manner of *pollen-storers*. However, Plath conceded that the method of rearing worker larvae was characteristic and distinctive, and this, he felt, justified retention of the term *pocket-makers*. He did, however, advocate the use of new names for both – *Marsipoea* for *pocket-makers* and *Amarsipoea* for *pollen-storers*, later (Plath, 1934) altered to *Marsipopoea* and *Amarsipopoea*, respectively. Plath's terminology, however, is rarely applied, whereas Sladen's far more convenient names have survived and are still usefully employed, even within the present system of dividing *Bombus* into subgenera.

In addition to his major biological groupings of *Bombus* Sladen (1912) also 'subdivided the Pocket-makers into the **Pollen primers,** comprising four large long-tongued species [*B. hortorum, B. ruderatus, B. distinguendus, B. subterraneus*] that lay their eggs in cells primed with pollen and dwell under the ground, and the **Carder-bees,**[1] comprising five small species [*B. humilis, B. muscorum, B. pascuorum, B. ruderarius, B. sylvarum*] that dwell, as a rule, on the surface of the ground, lay shorter and rounder eggs than the other species, and, in the male, have the joints of the antennae swollen behind'. Observations made in 1912, however, after the main text of his book was written, suggested to Sladen that *B. subterraneus* may not be in fact a regular pollen-primer, and he therefore proposed (his Additional Notes, p. 275) substituting the term *'Long-faced Humble-bees'* for *pollen-primers*, the latter term then being retained only for *B. hortorum* and *B. ruderatus* (it being assumed that *B. distinguendus* behaved in the same way as its close ally *B. subterraneus*).

Although Sladen had then categorized the above species into acceptable groups (cf. list of species and subgenera on p. 169), as pointed out by Plath, the names themselves had certain disadvantages. Firstly, the pollen-priming habit is not restricted to members of the *hortorum-ruderatus* group since some non-pocket-making species (subgenus *Pyrobombus*) also prime egg cells with pollen. Secondly,

---

[1] So called 'because they collect material from around the nest and add it to the nest, combing it together with their mandibles and legs.'

the term 'long-faced humble-bees' cannot be used in any wide context because species of many not closely allied *Bombus* groups have long faces. Thirdly, the term 'carder-bees', although heading a valid *Bombus* group (subgenus *Thoracobombus*) was also considered unsuitable since, according to Plath (1927a), most if not all species of *Bombus* will collect nesting material from around their nests. The collecting method adopted by carder-bees, however, is more or less characteristic.

Finally, having rejected Sladen's terminology, Plath suggested a new subdivision of the pollen-storers (then his *Amarsipoea*) into the *Phaneroschadoneta* and the *Cryptoschadoneta* – later (Plath, 1934) altered to *Phaneroschadonia* and *Cryptoschadonia* – based upon the method of rearing larvae, keeping them either partially enclosed or fully enclosed by wax. Plath used this subdivision tentatively since Sladen had reported that *B. subterraneus* (*Marsipoea*) kept their larvae uncovered. Plath commented: 'This seems strange, since the other *Marsipoea* studied are very solicitous to keep their larvae completely covered with wax, and this fact suggests the possibility that Sladen's observations . . . may have been made during extremely hot weather, when, due to the softening of the wax, all bumblebee larvae are likely to become exposed.' However, Sladen's observations have since been upheld and it is now known that *B. subterraneus* and its close allies (subgenus *Subterraneobombus*) secrete comparatively little wax (Hobbs, 1966b) and so in fact they do keep their larvae poorly covered.

Following present-day terminology, and the use of subgenera, the British species may be tabulated as follows. To maintain a degree of uniformity the order in which subgenera of *Bombus* are arranged is that used by Richards (1968), while that for *Psithyrus* agrees with Pittioni (1939). Authors vary in their arrangement of species within subgenera; here, for convenience and as no untoward ambiguities are thereby introduced, species are dealt with alphabetically.

Genus *Bombus* Latreille

SECTION *ANODONTOBOMBUS* KRÜGER

Species	Subgenus
1. *B. soroeensis* (Fabricius)	*Kallobombus* von Dalla Torre
2. *B. lucorum* (Linnaeus)	
3. *B. magnus* Krüger	*Bombus* Latreille
4. *B. terrestris* (Linnaeus)	
5. *B. cullumanus* (Kirby)	*Cullumanobombus* Vogt
6. *B. jonellus* (Kirby)	
7. *B. lapponicus* (Fabricius)	*Pyrobombus* von Dalla Torre
8. *B. pratorum* (Linnaeus)	
9. *B. lapidarius* (Linnaeus)	*Melanobombus* von Dalla Torre

SECTION *ODONTOBOMBUS* KRÜGER

10. *B. hortorum* (Linnaeus)	*Megabombus* von Dalla Torre
11. *B. ruderatus* (Fabricius)	
12. *B. humilis* Illiger	
13. *B. muscorum* (Linnaeus)	
14. *B. pascuorum* (Scopoli)	*Thoracobombus* von Dalla Torre
15. *B. ruderarius* (Müller)	
16. *B. sylvarum* (Linnaeus)	
17. *B. distinguendus* Morawitz	*Subterraneobombus* Vogt
18. *B. subterraneus* (Linnaeus)	
19. *B. pomorum* (Panzer)	*Rhodobombus* von Dalla Torre

Genus *Psithyrus* Lepeletier

20. *P. bohemicus* (Seidl)	*Ashtonipsithyrus* Frison
21. *P. vestalis* (Geoffroy in Fourcroy)	
22. *P. rupestris* (Fabricius)	*Psithyrus* Lepeletier
23. *P. barbutellus* (Kirby)	*Allopsithyrus* Popov
24. *P. campestris* (Panzer)	*Metapsithyrus* Popov
25. *P. sylvestris* Lepeletier	*Fernaldaepsithyrus* Frison

Species 1 to 9 are regarded as 'pollen-storers' and 10 to 19 as 'pocket-makers'. Brief details of synonymy are given with the descriptions of individual species; additional information is available in Chapter 11.

All of the British species of bumblebee occur elsewhere in Europe, but in some cases our native forms are sufficiently distinct that they have been given racial or subspecific names. The British race of *Bombus terrestris*, for example, differs from the typical white-tailed Continental form in having a more or less tawny tail, and for systematic purposes is distinguished by the trinomial name *Bombus terrestris audax*.

Differences in climate and other environmental pressures, even within the limited British range of a species, may over a period of time bring about the development of distinct forms. For example, in response to such pressures *B. jonellus* and *B. muscorum* have both produced races on certain off-shore islands which are very different from those occurring in mainland areas. In essence, subspecies represent more or less arbitrary subdivisions within the geographic range of a species and although two or more forms may be spatially isolated, in many instances they may grade imperceptibly into one another, hybridizing freely over adjoining areas, so that they become distinct only at the extreme ends of their range. In the latter case, as in the northern and southern British forms of *B. pascuorum*, the point at which a subdivision is made cannot be defined in precise terms and becomes very much a matter of opinion.

Some of our species, for example *B. soroeensis* and *B. humilis*, are more or less constant in appearance throughout their British range (although both vary considerably on the Continent), but others, *B. pascuorum* and *Psithyrus campestris* for example, are liable to great variation; both of these species produce dark and light colour forms as well as many intermediate types. Subspecific status, however, is only accorded when distinct forms breed true from parent to offspring and have geographical significance; although both *B. pascuorum* and *P. campestris* are considered to have produced valid subspecies within their British range (see below), many of the colour forms of these species are merely varieties.

As previously mentioned the body surface or 'skin' of a bumblebee is typically black (although parts of the limbs may be more or less testaceous); descriptions of body colour patterns, therefore, relate to the overall appearance of the body hairs forming the pile or coat. Unless otherwise stated, colour patterns referred to here are those on the upper surface of the body. In descriptions the following terms are applied frequently (see Fig. 100): *collar*=the pale anterior thoracic band of hairs, present in several species; *scutellum*=the hind-most dorsal part of the thorax, often bearing pale hairs; *interalar band*=a black band of hairs across the thorax between the wing bases; *tail*=a term of convenience to describe the more distal (apical), dorsal part of the abdomen – often excludes the extreme tip of the abdomen since the hairs on the last visible tergite may be differently coloured to the rest of the tail, although not altering its general appearance.

The coat of a bumblebee may be dense or, as found in *Psithyrus*, thin. The hairs themselves may be long or short, or may vary in length to produce an uneven, shaggy appearance; also, they may be decumbent (lying more or less flat over the body surface) or erect. Occasionally, bumblebees are found with irregular patches of white hairs on their bodies; these abnormalities are questionably said to result from injuries sustained as larvae or pupae. Similarly, adults with abnormally brownish-tinged coats were probably chilled during the pupal stage. Melanization, or darkening of specimens by the increase of black hairs, occurs in some species and may lead to difficulties in recognizing the species concerned. However, among the British fauna only a few species are significantly affected in this way and, with the exception of *B. ruderatus* and *P. campestris*, the occurrence of entirely black specimens is extremely rare. Lighter-than-normal specimens will result from a reduction of dark in favour of paler hairs, and again such variations may cause confusion. Coats may also become dusted with pollen grains and this too may be misleading.

Because coat colour patterns of bumblebees are subject to much variation, wear and also fading, they are notoriously unreliable for identifying species, although they are useful guides and, in detail, often specific. For accurate determination of species, therefore, reference should be made to structural features. Illustrated keys to sexes, genera and species, based largely on structural characteristics, are included in Chapter 10 and these are intended to supplement the following descriptions of individual species. Maps showing the distribution of the various species and subspecies in the British Isles (including Ireland) are presented in Appendix I.

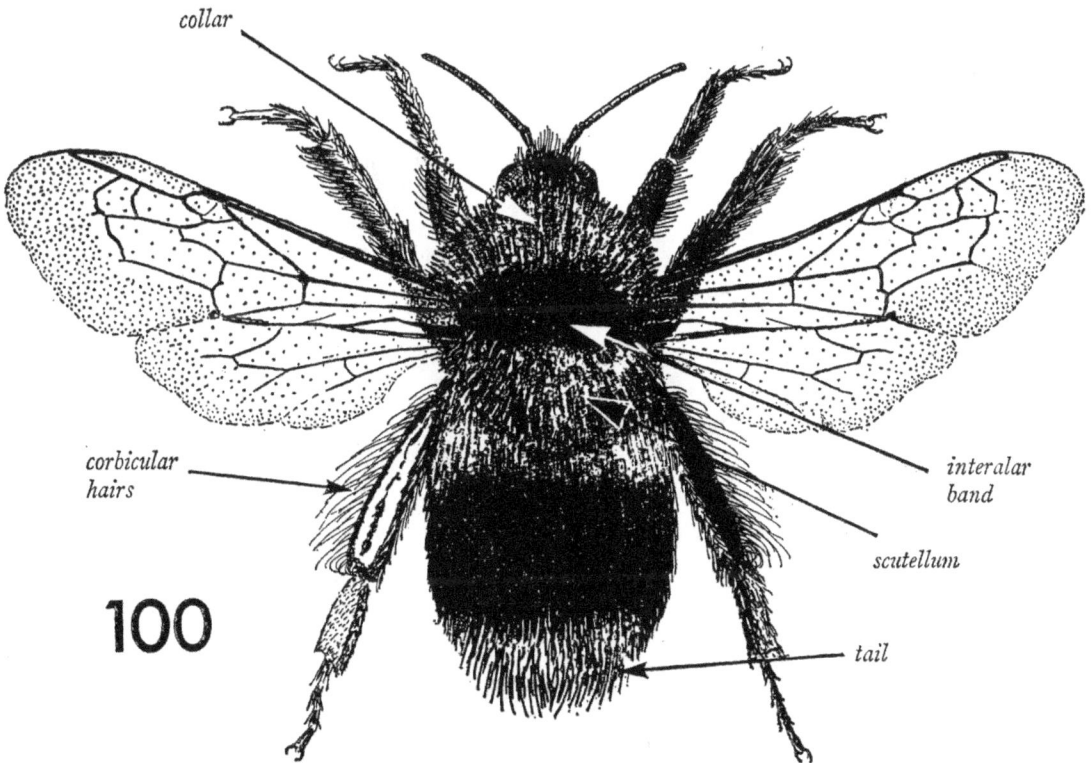

Fig. 100. Dorsal aspect of generalized *Bombus* female.

Genus *Bombus* Latreille

synonym: *Bremus* Jurine

Industrious species with females divided into queen and worker castes. The hind tibiae of females are adapted for carrying pollen. The hind tibiae of males are more or less flattened and, compared with those of *Psithyrus* males, are relatively shiny with noticeably less hair on the outer-surface, particularly centrally (see Key A in next Chapter).

Section *Anodontobombus* Krüger

SUBGENUS *KALLOBOMBUS* VON DALLA TORRE

1. *Bombus soroeensis* (Fabricius)

Distribution map 2.

QUEEN: small, length 15–17 mm., wingspan 28–33 mm.[1] Head black. Thorax black with a yellow collar. Abdomen black with a yellow band on T2, and a white tail. Liable to be confused with *lucorum* but the yellow band on T2 is interrupted or much reduced in the middle (N.B. yellow band of *lucorum* may frequently appear broken due to accidental depilation), and is composed of longer, more ragged and decumbent hairs; yellow often extends on to sides of T1. Tail usually a dingy white, and frequently marked with red at the base (T4) and sides. At once known from *lucorum* by reference to the mandibles (Fig. 123) and clypeus (Fig. 128) (see Key B, couplet 8). Sting (Fig. 126) also distinct.

WORKER: length 10–14 mm., wingspan c. 23 mm. Resembles the queen except in size.

MALE: length 12–14 mm., wingspan 25–28 mm. Head black with few or no yellow hairs. Thorax black with a yellow collar. Abdomen black with T1 and T2 yellow, although base of T1 may be black; tail white or pinkish white, but often red towards base (on T4). At once known from males of similarly-coloured species by the slender base of the hind basitarsus and the longer hairs on the hind margin (Fig. 155). Antennae of medium length, flagellum c. 5·5 mm. Genitalia (Fig. 157) distinct.

Although widely distributed in England, Scotland and Wales, *B. soroeensis* is local and must be regarded as one of our rarer species. It is apparently absent from Ireland.

---

[1] These figures are intended as a guide to the relative size of individuals of the various species, sexes and castes; they should not be considered as size limits. Variation within a species, particularly in the case of workers, can be considerable.

Overwintered queens appear later in the spring than those of many other species. Colonies are established below ground level but, unlike those of several underground-nesting species, they are small and never populous. Favourite flowers of *B. soroeensis* include raspberry (*Rubus idaeus*), bramble (*Rubus fruticosus*), greater knapweed (*Centaurea scabiosa*), hardhead (*Centaurea nigra*) and hogweed (*Heracleum sphondylium*).

SUBGENUS *BOMBUS* LATREILLE

2. *Bombus lucorum* (Linnaeus)

Distribution map 3.

QUEEN: large, length 18–21 mm., wingspan 36–39 mm. Body black, with a lemon-yellow band on the collar and on abdominal T2, and a white tail. Sting (Fig. 127) similar to that of *terrestris* but less strongly chitinized; the outer projections of the sting sheath are wider (Fig. 131).

WORKER: 9–16 mm., wingspan 20–33 mm. Similar to the queen but smaller. Usually distinguishable from workers of *terrestris* by the brighter yellow bands and pure white tail; however, it is by no means certain that all white-tailed specimens are *lucorum*. Small workers of these two closely allied species may be impossible to separate with certainty, even after critical examination of structural features.

MALE: 14–16 mm., wingspan 29–33 mm. Hairs on face and top of head mainly or entirely yellow. Thorax with collar, and often also scutellum, lemon-yellow; the yellow often very extensive and in extreme cases the black is reduced to a narrow interalar band which may also be encroached upon by pale hairs. When present, the yellow on the scutellum merges more or less imperceptibly into the black anteriorly so that a distinct yellow band is not formed. Abdomen in dark examples is black, with T2 lemon-yellow and the tail white. Pale hairs on T3 and T4 may form narrow bands, and in lighter specimens both T1 and T2, and sometimes also T3 and T4, are entirely lemon-yellow. Coat longer and more ragged than that of *terrestris*. Antennae short, flagellum c. 5 mm. Genitalia similar to *terrestris* (Fig. 159) but apex of volsella narrower (Fig. 162).

B. *lucorum* is an abundant species throughout most of the British Isles, including Ireland; in the north of Scotland it entirely replaces *terrestris*, while in the Orkney Islands it is itself replaced by *magnus*.

It is one of our earliest-appearing species, overwintered queens becoming active from March onwards – occasional specimens are even seen in February if the weather is unusually warm. Queens are partial to willow or sallow (*Salix*) catkins. Colonies are formed below ground, usually at the end of a short tunnel; they are established earlier in the season than those of *terrestris* and reach maturity sooner. Nests are often formed in disused mouse nests under the floors of garden sheds. In large colonies, several hundred bees may be reared, but the workers are far less aggressive than those of *terrestris*. *B. lucorum* visits the same flowers as *terrestris* (see p. 176) but is renowned for its liking of Ericaceous species.

3. *Bombus magnus* Krüger

subspecies *magnus* Krüger

Distribution map 4.

QUEEN: large or very large, length 19–22 mm., wingspan 38–42 mm. Coloured like *lucorum* but the yellow band on the collar is wider, extending down below the level of the tegulae and often continued backwards below the wings (Fig. 132). Scutellum usually fringed with some yellowish or brownish hairs. Yellow band on abdominal T2 wide and extending to tergite base. Sometimes there are also yellow hairs on the apex of T1. Tail pinkish or yellowish white. Corbicular hairs mostly golden brown rather than black, except in Irish specimens. Unfortunately, the sting appears to be identical to that of *lucorum*.

WORKER: 11–17 mm., wingspan 22–34 mm. Similar to the queen except in size.

MALE: at present males cannot be separated with certainty from those of *lucorum*. As far as coat colour is concerned then, at least where *magnus* females are known to occur, it is possible that '*lucorum*' males with black faces suffused with yellow hairs will prove to be this species (Yarrow, *in litt.*). The genitalia appear to be indistinguishable from those of *lucorum*.

Although *magnus* was formerly considered by Vogt to be a large variety of *lucorum*, Krüger (1954) has since treated it as a distinct species. The situation is clearly in need of further investigation and critical studies of the offspring of undoubted *magnus* females should prove rewarding.

B. magnus occurs commonly in the north of Scotland, although it is also found further south, extending into Wales and the western half of England, where it appears to be associated with heath or moorland areas. It is not uncommon in Ireland.

B. magnus queens may appear later in the spring than those of *lucorum* (Krüger, 1954; Løken, 1973), but the biology of both species is probably very similar. Foraging *magnus* females (and no doubt males) are particularly fond of bramble (*Rubus fruticosus*) and members of the Ericaceae.

4. *Bombus terrestris* (Linnaeus)[1]

subspecies *audax* (Harris)

Distribution map 5.

QUEEN: large or very large, length 20–23 mm., wingspan 38–43 mm. Body black with a brownish or golden-yellow band on the collar and on abdominal T2, the tail tawny or buff; the yellow, especially on the collar, sometimes much reduced and darkened. Sting similar to that of *lucorum* (Fig. 127) but stronger; the outer projections of the sting sheath are narrower (Fig. 130).

WORKER: length 11–17 mm., wingspan 22–34 mm. Some specimens, especially larger ones, are coloured like the queen, but in most cases the tail is white or gingery-white. Usually the white of the tail grades into buff basally, the buff colour often forming a more or less distinct band separating the white from the black.

MALE: length 14–16 mm., wingspan 30–33 mm. Coloured like the queen, but the tail usually white or gingery-white. As in workers the white usually grades into buff basally. Antennae short, flagellum c. 5 mm. Genitalia (Fig. 159) very similar to those of *lucorum*, but apex of volsella broader (Fig. 161).

This species is subject to melanization in both sexes, although even in the darkest specimens traces of paler hairs usually remain on both the collar and abdomen. On the Continent, and in the Channel Islands, the typical form (subspecies *B. terrestris terrestris*) has the tail white, not buff.

B. terrestris is common in the British Isles, particularly in the southern half of England. It is less abundant in the north, its range not extending to the extreme north of Scotland.

Queens appear early in the season and are frequent visitors to willow or sallow (*Salix*) catkins, and other spring flowers. Nests are formed below ground, usually in cavities approached by a long, downward-sloping tunnel. Colonies are often very populous and, if disturbed, are tenaciously defended by the inhabitants. The dark brown comb is rather untidy in appearance, as individual cocoons are only loosely attached to their neighbours. A wax-pollen canopy is frequently constructed over the comb. Large quantities of pollen are collected by the workers and stored in tall waxen cylinders. Foundress queens characteristically lose much of their hair as they age . *B. terrestris* visits a wide variety of flowers including bramble (*Rubus fruticosus*), black currant (*Ribes nigrum*), flowering currant (*Ribes sanguineum*), lavender (*Lavandula*), Himalayan balsam (*Impatiens glandulifera*), poppies (*Papaver*), charlock (*Sinapis arvensis*), white clover (*Trifolium repens*), rose-bay willow-herb (*Chamaenerion angustifolium*), apple (*Malus*), cherry (*Prunus*) and limes (*Tilia*).

[1] synonym: *virginalis* (Kirby).

SUBGENUS *CULLUMANOBOMBUS* VOGT

5. *Bombus cullumanus* (Kirby)

Distribution map 6.

QUEEN: black with a red tail; very similar to *lapidarius*,[1] but some yellow hairs are present among the black on both the collar and scutellum. The wings are darker than in *lapidarius*, and the hind basitarsi are distinctly shiny and black, being clothed with only a few branched hairs – in *lapidarius* the hind basitarsi appear yellowish white and powdery, being densely covered with short branched hairs (cf. Figs. 138 and 139). Further differences are listed by Richards (1927) and Yarrow (1954). Sting (Fig. 137) distinct.

WORKER: coloured like the queen but some yellow hairs are present on the abdomen basally. Otherwise, resembles the queen but smaller.

MALE: length 13–15 mm., wingspan 26–28 mm. Hairs on top of head and on face yellowish grey. Thorax black with collar and scutellum greyish yellow. Abdomen with T1 and T2 yellowish grey, T3 black, T4–6 red, soon fading to orange. Although similarly coloured to males of *pratorum*, *ruderarius* and *sylvarum*, those of *cullumanus* are at once known by the genitalia (Fig. 164). Antennae of medium length, flagellum c. 5.5 mm.

B. *cullumanus* is exceedingly rare in Britain, and is known from only a few chalk-land localities in the south of England.[2] After a gap of thirty years in the British records of this species, Sladen rediscovered it in 1911, and although since that time specimens were subsequently recorded from several localities (see Yarrow, 1954), none has been captured now for many years. With the drastic reduction in the extent and number of suitable chalkland habitats that has taken place over the past few decades, the continued existence of *cullumanus* in England must be open to serious doubt.

Little is known of the biology of *cullumanus* in Britain, although it is apparently a late-appearing species, queens probably emerging from hibernation in May. Most British records refer to males captured in late August or September. Imms (1922), however, obtained a fresh male at the end of July, 1921. This species has been recorded visiting marjoram (*Origanum vulgare*), thistles (*Carduus nutans*, *Cirsium acaulon*), white clover (*Trifolium repens*) and hardhead (*Centaurea nigra*).

---

[1] Statements that British females of *cullumanus* are coloured like *pratorum*, are erroneous (see p. 247).

[2] The single Irish record is erroneous (Orr, 1911), and that published for Barton Mills, Suffolk (Morley, 1936) no doubt relates to the single specimen from Barton Hills, Bedfordshire (Palmer, 1923), the locality having been cited incorrectly in Nevinson (1923).

SUBGENUS *PYROBOMBUS* VON DALLA TORRE

6. *Bombus jonellus* (Kirby)[1]

subspecies *jonellus* (Kirby)

Distribution map 7.

QUEEN: small, length 15–18 mm., wingspan 27–32 mm. Top of head usually with yellow hairs, face black. Thorax black with collar and scutellum yellow. Abdomen black with T1 and usually base of T2 yellow; the tail white or yellowish white, the tail colour normally commencing on T4 but sometimes extending on to T3. Corbicular hairs usually reddish. Sting (Fig. 125) like that of *lapponicus* and *pratorum*. Although superficially coloured like *hortorum*, *jonellus* is readily distinguished by the short head (cf. Figs. 109 and 111); the abdomen is also noticeably more bulbous. WORKER: length 9–14 mm., wingspan 17–26 mm. Similar to the queen except in size.

MALE: length 11–14 mm., wingspan 23–27 mm. Face and top of head yellow. Thorax black with yellow collar and scutellum. Abdomen black with T1 and base of T2 yellow, and a white tail. Antennae of medium length, flagellum c. 5 mm. Genitalia similar to those of *lapponicus* and *pratorum*, but nevertheless distinct (see Key C and cf. Figs. 168 to 174). As with females, the male is at once known from *hortorum* by its short head and less elongate body. Males of *jonellus* often more closely resemble small, light coloured males of *lucorum*. However, in *jonellus* the yellow of the abdomen is restricted to T1 and to the base of T2, while T3 and T4 remain black; the hind tibiae are also more hairy (cf. Figs. 104 and 105). Doubtful specimens are easily known by reference to their genitalia.

Specimens from the Orkney Islands are somewhat larger than the typical mainland form, the coat is longer and the corbicular hairs tend to be black rather than reddish. More extreme colour forms occur on the Isle of Man, in the Shetland Islands and in the Outer Hebrides, and these are generally considered distinct subspecies – *monapiae* Kruseman, *vogtii* Richards and *hebridensis* Wild, respectively; the last two forms have also been treated as the variety *nivalis* Smith.

subspecies *monapiae* Kruseman

Similar to *jonellus jonellus*, but according to Kruseman (1953) the yellow tends to be more greenish in tint. The corbicular hairs are black or at best black with red tips. Abdominal T4–6 are white, but somewhat buffish.

[1] synonym: *scrimshiranus* (Kirby).

subspecies *vogtii* Richards

Differs from mainland form in that the yellow collar is as broad or almost as broad as the black interalar band; abdominal T2 is mostly yellow, and the tail buffish or yellowish white. The corbicular hairs are black. Coat hardly longer than in normal form.

subspecies *hebridensis* Wild

Yellow collar broader than in normal form, about half to threequarters that of the black interalar band; basal half of abdominal T2 yellow; the tail yellowish orange-white. The corbicular hairs are black, tipped with red. Coat slightly longer than in mainland form.

Bombus jonellus is widely distributed in England, Ireland, Scotland and Wales, but is local, occurring mainly on, or in the close vicinity of, heaths and heather moorlands.

The queens appear relatively early in the spring and may be seen feeding at willow or sallow (*Salix*) catkins. Wild (1931) found the Hebridean race nesting on and just below the surface of the ground, and described the wax as bright orange. *B. jonellus* has also been found nesting in a fallen bird's nest (Fraser, 1947) and high above ground in a squirrel's drey (Sladen, 1912). Its general biology is probably similar to that of *pratorum*. Foraging bees are partial to broom (*Sarothamnus scoparius*), bilberry (*Vaccinium myrtillus*), bramble (*Rubus fruticosus*), and members of the Ericaceae.

7. *Bombus lapponicus* (Fabricius)

subspecies *scoticus* Pittioni

Distribution map 8.

QUEEN: medium, length 16–18 mm., wingspan 33–35 mm. Head black with yellow hairs on top and sometimes also some on the face. Thorax black with collar, and to a lesser extent the scutellum, pale yellow. In dark specimens the scutellum may be entirely black. Abdominal T1 black, T2–6 yellowish red, although T2 may be black basally. Coat even and, on the abdomen, very long. Sting like that of *jonellus* (Fig. 125). Corbicular hairs black. Abdomen rather broad in relation to its length.
WORKER: length 9–15 mm., wingspan 25–28 mm. Similar to the queen but smaller.

MALE: length 13–15 mm., wingspan 25–28 mm. Coloured like the female although pale hairs on the head may be more evident, and abdominal T1 may also be partly yellowish. Antennae of medium length, flagellum c. 5 mm. Genitalia similar to those of *jonellus* and *pratorum* (Fig. 168), but distinguishable by reference to the sagitta (Figs. 169 and 170) and volsella (Figs. 171 and 172).

B. *lapponicus* is a local species being confined mainly to the *Vaccinium* zone of mountains and moorlands; errant specimens are, however, occasionally found elsewhere. Although common in many suitable localities in Scotland and Wales, and also present in several of the higher parts of England, it is not found in Ireland.[1]

Queens begin to appear early in the season and often visit willow or sallow (*Salix*) catkins. Nests are usually established on or just below the surface of the ground. This species forages on various flowers, including bilberry (*Vaccinium myrtillus*), heaths or heathers (*Erica*), ling (*Calluna vulgaris*), bramble (*Rubus fruticosus*), cinquefoil (*Potentilla*) and self-heal (*Prunella vulgaris*).

8. *Bombus pratorum* (Linnaeus)

Distribution map 9.

QUEEN: small, length 15–17 mm., wingspan 28–32 mm. Body black with a yellow band on the collar and another on abdominal T2; tail (T5 and T6, and sometimes also T4) orange-red. Yellow band on the collar may be more or less interrupted in the middle; that on T2 may also be broken or reduced and is sometimes absent. Coat rather uneven and, particularly on the abdomen, long and ragged in appearance. Unlike those of *terrestris* the yellow hairs on T2 are decumbent and of different lengths; the yellow is also brighter. Sting (Fig. 136) like that of *jonellus* and *lapponicus*. Structurally, may be distinguished from *terrestris* by reference to the sting, mandibles and clypeus (see Key B).

WORKER: length 9–14 mm., wingspan 18–26 mm. In workers the yellow band on abdominal T2 is frequently absent, and black hairs on the body may be pale at their tips; otherwise similar to the queen except in size.

MALE: length 11–13 mm., wingspan 23–26 mm. Face and top of head usually yellow. Thorax black, usually with a very wide yellow band on the collar; some yellow hairs may also be present on the scutellum. Abdomen with T1 and T2 yellow, T3 and T4 black, T5–7 red or orange; the tail colour may spread on to T4. In dark specimens the yellow on T1 and T2 may be much reduced or even absent,

---

[1] On 23 April, 1974 a fresh-looking queen of *lapponicus* was captured in Ireland, near Dublin, by Dr M. C. D. Speight. The specimen was foraging on bilberry (*Vaccinium myrtillus*) in what appeared to be a suitable montane habitat (Speight, *in litt.*). Major headquarters of *lapponicus* lie about 140 km. to the east (in Snowdonia, North Wales) and north-east (Isle of Man) of Dublin, and chance migration of this errant species to Ireland from one or other of these areas is by no means inconceivable. The true status of *lapponicus* in Ireland remains to be established.

and only T6 and T7 may be red or orange. Antennae of medium length, flagellum c. 5 mm. Genitalia (Fig. 168), although variable and similar to the previous two species, are nevertheless distinct (Figs. 169 to 174).

B. pratorum is widespread and generally abundant throughout the British Isles, although until very recently (Faris, 1949) there were no Irish records. It has since become well established in Ireland (see O'Rourke, 1955, 1956; Stelfox, 1955).

Queens appear and establish nests early in the spring, and colonies are often at an end by the middle or end of July. Nevertheless, workers are sometimes found in the late summer and autumn, which suggests that under certain conditions this species, as with other members of the same subgenus, may be partially double brooded (see p. 61). *B. pratorum* is very cosmopolitan in its choice of nesting site, nests occurring both above and below ground level. Colonies are frequently established in birds' nests, heaps of rubbish, and other similar places. They are generally small and the occupants are very mild tempered. The comb is dark brown, but the initial nectar pot constructed by the queen in the spring, at the incipient stages of colony development, is very pale.

B. pratorum queens are abundant on spring flowers, especially white dead-nettle (*Lamium album*), red dead-nettle (*Lamium purpureum*), willow or sallow (*Salix*) catkins, and garden flowers such as flowering currant (*Ribes sanguineum*) and *Aubretia*. The workers and males occur in great profusion on raspberry (*Rubus idaeus*). They are also partial to *Cotoneaster*, woody nightshade (*Solanum dulcamara*), bramble (*Rubus fruticosus*) and various other Rosaceous species.

SUBGENUS *MELANOBOMBUS* VON DALLA TORRE

9. *Bombus lapidarius* (Linnaeus)

Distribution map 10.

QUEEN: large, length 20–22 mm., wingspan 37–40 mm. Body black with tail (T4–6) red; corbicular hairs black; wings hyaline. Abdomen relatively long in relation to its width. This species is subject to little colour variation but rarely the collar may be marked with pale, yellowish grey hairs.[1] Coat short, even and dense. Sting, Fig. 134.

WORKER: length 12–16 mm., wingspan 24–30 mm. Similar to the queen but smaller.

MALE: length 14–16 mm., wingspan 27–30 mm. Hairs on face and top of head yellow. Thorax with a broad yellow band on the collar; scutellum often with some yellow hairs posteriorly but may be entirely black. Abdomen black, sometimes with

---

[1] There seems to be a greater tendency for pale hairs to occur on the collar of workers rather than queens; Sladen has suggested that their presence may be the result of unfavourable conditions pertaining during larval development.

yellow on T1; T4–7 red. Fresh specimens are brightly coloured, but the colours soon fade. Abdomen relatively long. Antennae short, flagellum c. 4·5 mm. Genitalia (Fig. 163) distinct.

Females of *lapidarius* are at once known from *ruderarius*, our only other common red and black species of *Bombus*, by the black corbicular hairs.

B. lapidarius is a common species over much of the country, but absence of suitable forage plants can limit its distribution. It is often abundant in chalk downland areas, and is said to be the most numerous species of bumblebee on the Isles of Scilly. It is often common on or near sand-dunes; and in the north of Britain it is mainly a coastal species (Laidlaw, 1930).

Queens tend to emerge from hibernation somewhat later in the spring than those of many other species. They establish their nests in all manner of sheltered places, both above and below ground level; *lapidarius* is so named for its habit of nesting below stones. As concisely noted by Sladen 'A large number of workers are produced. The comb has a particularly neat and clean appearance. The cocoons are pale yellow. The wax is of a lighter brown than that of any other species, in fact it is almost yellow; it is produced in great quantity, and the bees work it skilfully into thin sheets and cells'. The comb is usually roofed over by a wax-pollen canopy.

B. lapidarius is a frequent visitor to flower species favoured by honey bees, and is particularly fond of clovers (*Trifolium*), thistles (*Carduus* and *Cirsium*), knapweed (*Centaurea scabiosa*), hardhead (*Centaurea nigra*), common birdsfoot trefoil (*Lotus corniculatus*), sycamore (*Acer pseudoplantanus*) and blackthorn (*Prunus spinosa*). Males are often abundant on *Centaurea* from July onwards.

Section *Odontobombus* Krüger

SUBGENUS *MEGABOMBUS* VON DALLA TORRE

10. *Bombus hortorum* (Linnaeus)

subspecies *hortorum* (Linnaeus)

Distribution map 11.

QUEEN: medium, although rather variable, in size, length 17–22 mm., wingspan 35–40 mm. Head black. Thorax black with a broad yellow band on the collar and a narrower yellow band on the scutellum. Abdomen black with T1 and base of T2 yellow; T4 and T5 white with the white extending on to the apex of T3. Corbicular hairs black. Occasionally, dark specimens occur in which the yellow is much reduced in extent and is far less bright; the white of the tail may also be darkened. Coat relatively long and shaggy. Head very long, at once distinguishing this species from the similarly coloured *jonellus* (cf. Figs. 109 and 111). Sting like that of *ruderatus* (Fig. 117).

WORKER: length 11–16 mm., wingspan 28–32 mm. Coloured like the queen but smaller.

MALE: length 13–15 mm., wingspan 28–32 mm. Face black, but some yellow hairs on top of head. Thorax black with yellow collar and scutellum. Abdomen with T1 and base of T2 yellow, the rest of T2, T3 and T7 black, T4 and T5 white, T6 black in the middle but white laterally. As with queens dark specimens sometimes occur. Rarely the white of the tail may be more or less replaced by yellow. The coat is noticeably shaggy and rather long. Head very long. Beard on the mandibles more or less black. Abdomen relatively long and narrow. Antennae long, flagellum c. 6–6·5 mm. Genitalia (Fig. 147) similar to those of *ruderatus*, but otherwise distinct.

subspecies *ivernicus* Sladen

Irish specimens of *hortorum* may be treated as a distinct race (*hortorum ivernicus*).

183

They are larger than the normal English form, and the yellow on the thorax is more extensive; also, the coat is of a rougher appearance. As in *Bombus magnus* (q.v.) the yellow of the collar extends down the sides of the thorax.

B. hortorum is an abundant and widely distributed species throughout the British Isles, including Ireland.

Queens generally appear in April, and during the period of nest establishment they are frequent visitors to white dead-nettle (*Lamium album*). Nests may be found on or just below the surface of the ground, and they sometimes occur in unexpected situations well above ground level. Colonies are usually small; the comb is yellowish in colour. The size of workers produced from a single brood batch tends to vary considerably in this species. Males of *hortorum* are particularly common in July and are frequently observed during their characteristic flight path activity (see Chapter 5).

B. hortorum has a very long tongue and tends to visit flowers with long corolla tubes. It is especially attracted to foxglove (*Digitalis purpurea*), woundworts (*Stachys*), red clover (*Trifolium pratense*), black horehound (*Ballota nigra*), honeysuckle (*Lonicera periclymenum*), common snapdragon (*Antirrhinum majus*), *Nasturtium*, and many other garden flowers.

11. *Bombus ruderatus* (Fabricius)[1]

Distribution map 12.

QUEEN: large or very large, length 21–24 mm., wingspan 40–43 mm. The lightest specimens are coloured like *hortorum* with the thoracic collar and scutellum, and base of the abdomen, yellow, and the tail white. Unlike *hortorum*, however, the yellow is far less bright and of a deeper tint; also, the yellow bands on the collar and scutellum are of similar widths, at least in the middle, and the yellow on the abdomen is usually restricted to T1, and even there is more or less replaced by black in the middle; the white of the tail is more restricted in extent and is usually dingy. Abdominal T5 is frequently entirely black and traces of the yellow bands on both thorax and abdomen may be visible only as brown hairs scattered among the black. The darkest specimens – var. *harrisellus* (Kirby) – are entirely black. The coat of *ruderatus* is shorter and more even than that of *hortorum*. The head is long, although proportionately less so than in *hortorum*. The sting (Fig. 117) is like that of *hortorum*. Structurally, *ruderatus* is very similar to *hortorum* but T6 is more deeply sculptured (cf. Figs. 120 and 121).

[1] synonyms: *harrisellus* (Kirby), *tunstallanus* (Kirby).

WORKER: length 11–18 mm., wingspan 21–35 mm. Banded or entirely black specimens occur, but usually intermediate forms do not, except in the case of very large individuals. Small or worn specimens may be difficult or even impossible to distinguish from those of *hortorum*.

MALE: length 15–17 mm., wingspan 30–33 mm. Usually entirely black or banded specimens occur. The latter are coloured like males of *hortorum* but the yellow is of a duller, more golden tint. In some cases the white of the tail may be more or less yellow, especially at the sides. In banded specimens the yellow scutellum is very distinctive, being prominent and clearly demarcated from the black anteriorly. In *hortorum* males the long yellow hairs on the scutellum merge gradually into the black anteriorly so that the scutellum is of a far less striking appearance. Overall, the coat of *ruderatus* is noticeably shorter and more even than that of *hortorum*. Intermediately-coloured specimens are black with the tail greyish brown. These and the entirely black form, may be confused with dark males of *Psithyrus campestris*, but specimens of *ruderatus* are at once known by their elongate heads. As in *hortorum* the abdomen is relatively long; the antennae are also long, flagellum c. 6·5 mm. In *ruderatus* the beard on the mandible is orange-red. Also in contrast with those of *hortorum*, the long hairs on the hind edge of the hind basitarsus do not continue round the apex; the long hairs on this segment are also less elongate than in *hortorum*, particularly basally (cf. Figs. 151 and 152). Genitalia like those of *hortorum* (Fig. 147), but otherwise distinct.

Var. *harrisellus* has no geographical significance, both light and dark forms of *ruderatus* being produced by the same parent, although it is apparently unknown outside the British Isles.

B. ruderatus is widespread but does not occur in Scotland (see p. 304) or in Ireland.[1] Although formerly considered to be a very common species in England, at least in the southern counties, this certainly does not apply at the present time, and *ruderatus*, although not necessarily rare, must be regarded as one of our less common species. It has a more southerly distribution than its near relative *hortorum*, and in this and several other respects there is a similar situation to that existing between *lucorum* and *terrestris*. For example, the larger, more southern species (here *ruderatus*) also emerging from hibernation later in the year, and producing larger colonies which die out later in the season.

Nests of *ruderatus* are typically established below ground. The comb is somewhat darker than that of *hortorum*. Like *hortorum*, *ruderatus* visits flowers with long corolla tubes, including white dead-nettle (*Lamium album*), woundworts (*Stachys*) and red clover (*Trifolium pratense*).

---

[1] Sladen records a single queen from Borris, Co. Carlow. The Irish record published by Johnson (1918) subsequently proved to be *hortorum* (Stelfox, 1927).

SUBGENUS *THORACOBOMBUS* VON DALLA TORRE

12. *Bombus humilis* Illiger[1]

Distribution map 13.

QUEEN: small, length 16–18 mm., wingspan 30–32 mm. Head with pale yellowish or brownish hairs but also some black, mostly around the eyes and on top. Thorax orange-brown, but soon fades, and usually with at least a few black hairs above the tegulae; sometimes black hairs may be intermixed evenly within the brown over much of the thorax apart from the middle. Abdomen pale yellow with a distinct brownish band on T2; a similar but narrower and less obvious band on T3, and sometimes an even narrower band on T4. T6 black, but black hairs never present on T1–5, even in dark examples. Long corbicular hairs mostly pale. Coat rather short and relatively even, with the abdomen appearing distinctly pointed apically. Hairs at sides of T3 arise from coalescing punctures (Fig. 115). Sting (Fig. 113) distinct, although liable to confusion with that of *muscorum* (Fig. 114).

WORKER: length 9–15 mm., wingspan 20–28 mm. Similar to the queen but smaller and often darker in appearance.

MALE: length 12–14 mm., wingspan 23–27 mm. Coloured like the queen. Coat relatively short and even. Antennae long, flagellum c. 5·5 mm. Genitalia (Fig. 145) distinct.

Although not an abundant species, *humilis* is widely distributed in the south, south-east and south-west of England, and it is common in parts of Wales. In the north it is rare and it is apparently absent from both Ireland and Scotland. *B. humilis* occurs most frequently in coastal areas and on or near chalk downland.

Queens tend to appear rather late in the season. Nests, in common with those of other species of the subgenus *Thoracobombus*, are typically formed on the surface of the ground. The comb has a neat appearance and is yellowish in colour. The bees are mild tempered. Foraging bees visit various flowers including dead-nettles (*Lamium*), clovers (*Trifolium*), greater knapweed (*Centaurea scabiosa*), hardhead (*Centaurea nigra*) and scabious (*Knautia*).

---

[1] synonyms: *helferanus* (Seidl), *solstitialis* (Panzer), *variabilis* Schmiedeknecht, *venustus* Saunders, *venustus* Smith (in part).

13. *Bombus muscorum* (Linnaeus)[1]

Plate 14.   Distribution maps 14 and 15.

Within the British Isles, *muscorum* produces a complex array of subspecies and these will be considered separately following a general description of the typical English form.

subspecies *sladeni* Vogt

QUEEN: medium in size, length 17–19 mm., wingspan 32–35 mm. Coloured very much like *humilis*, but there are no black hairs on the thorax above or near the tegulae. The orange-brown of the thorax grades into pale yellow on the collar and scutellum. Abdomen yellowish with a diffuse pale brown band on T2 and a similar, but narrower, band on T3. The band on T2 appears darker than it actually is, because on the erectness of the hairs. T6 black but, as in *humilis*, black hairs are never present on T1–5. Long corbicular hairs mostly pale. Coat longer and denser than that of *humilis*, and the abdomen appears less obviously pointed apically. Hairs at sides of T3 arise from pustules (Fig. 116). Sting (Fig. 114) distinct.
WORKER: length 10–16 mm., wingspan 22–30 mm. Resembles the queen except in size.
MALE: length 13–15 mm., wingspan 26–29 mm. Coloured like the queen but abdomen lacks the brown bands. Coat longer and somewhat denser than that of *humilis*. Antennae long, flagellum c. 5·5 mm. Genitalia (Fig. 146) distinct.

subspecies *pallidus* Evans[2]

This is the typical Irish and Scottish mainland form, although it is also present on some offshore islands. Queens differ from ssp. *sladeni* in having a darker, redder tint to the thorax, there being few or no pale hairs on the collar or scutellum. The coat is also somewhat longer. Intermediate forms between the English and Scottish races occur, probably as hybrids.

subspecies *smithianus* auctt. nec White
(s.l.)

Forms of *muscorum* with more or less black, rather than pale, legs and undersides occur on certain offshore islands around the British Isles, and for many years these

---

[1] synonyms: *cognatus* Stephens, *smithianus* auctt. nec White (s.l.), *venustus* Smith (in part).
[2] Differences between *sladeni* and *pallidus* are so slight that both might more simply be treated as the ssp. *pallidus*, this name having priority.

were treated as the subspecies *smithianus* White; some authorities, in fact, have accorded *smithianus* specific status. *B. muscorum smithianus* (sensu lato) actually embraces several distinct subspecies, so that here *B. m. smithianus* (sensu stricta) is used and applied only to the subspecies of *muscorum* found in the Shetlands and on certain of the Hebridean islands. The true designation of the name *B. smithianus* is explained on p. 249.

subspecies *smithianus* auctt. nec White
(s.s.)

This subspecies is larger and has a longer coat than the typical mainland form of *muscorum*. The thorax is a rich chestnut colour and the abdomen is of a more distinct lemon yellow tint. In females, the legs, the head (with the exception of the top), and the underside of the body are black. Males are similar in colour but some pale hairs occur on the face, on top of the head, and on the underside of the body. This subspecies occurs in the Shetland Islands and is also found on certain islands in the Inner and Outer Hebrides. Richards (1935) has recorded this subspecies from West Inverness-shire, but it does not seem to be established in such areas and its presence may be due entirely to 'occasional chance dispersal from the islands which constitute its headquarters' (Spooner, 1937). The temporary appearance in the nineteen thirties of '*smithianus*' on the mainland and on islands such as Raasay, Rona and Scalpay has been explained by Heslop Harrison (1943) as follows: 'I believe that, in 1933 or 1934, a movement of *B. smithianus* from the Outer Isles took place which reached as its maximum limits the shores of Wester Ross. In the area thus occupied it flourished for some time; then, for some reason, possibly wholly or in part due to hybridity with *B. muscorum*, it failed to maintain itself and died out.'

subspecies *orcadensis* Richards

This form, found in the Orkney Islands, is similar in size and colour to mainland specimens of *muscorum* but the coat is longer. Compared with *pallidus* there is a slight increase in the extent of black hairs on the face, and there are traces of black on the legs and underside of the body.

subspecies *allenellus* Stelfox

Perhaps the most striking of all the subspecies. It is similar in colour to '*smithianus*' (s.s.) but black extends on to the upper surface of the abdomen, T1 being entirely black; the sides and base of T2 are also black. This subspecies occurs only in the Aran Islands (Eire), where it may be found flying alongside *pallidus* (Yarrow, 1967).

188

subspecies *scyllonius* Richards

Similarly coloured to '*smithianus*' (s.s.) but pale hairs are intermixed with the black on the face, legs and underside of the body. Body size and length of coat is similar to that of mainland examples of *muscorum*. This subspecies occurs in the Isles of Scilly and also on Alderney in the Channel Islands.[1] It has been said that the worker of '*smithianus*' found at Dover, Kent (Perkins, 1890) was a stray from Alderney, but this seems unlikely. Perhaps as Perkins himself suggested many years later (Perkins, 1945), the specimen was merely a dark '*smithianus*'-like aberration from a 'normal' *muscorum* nest. This record is not included in Distribution map 15.

B. muscorum is a local species although it occurs more or less generally in Ireland and Scotland. In the south and south-east of England it is decidedly uncommon and restricted mainly to marshy, coastal areas. As detailed above this species occurs on many islands off the coasts of England, Ireland and Scotland.

Queens make their appearance rather late in the season. Nests are formed on the surface of the ground, often in deep moss. The comb is similar to that of *humilis* but the colour is darker. Unlike its close allies, *muscorum* is aggressive towards intruders and colonies are defended pugnaciously. This species tends to occur in damp or exposed situations and apparently flourishes best in cold, damp summers. Flowers visited include white dead-nettle (*Lamium album*), hardhead (*Centaurea nigra*), woundworts (*Stachys*), sea holly (*Eryngium maritimum*), thistles (*Carduus* and *Cirsium*), heaths or heathers (*Erica*) and ling (*Calluna vulgaris*). Laidlaw (1931) recorded large numbers of overwintered queens on red dead-nettle (*Lamium purpureum*).

14. *Bombus pascuorum* (Scopoli)[2]

Distribution map 16.

QUEEN: small, length 15–18 mm., wingspan 28–32 mm. Head with black, and yellowish or brownish hairs intermixed. Thorax dorsally yellowish or reddish brown, often more or less darkened by the admixture of black hairs, but in some forms black may be absent; when scarce, black hairs are restricted to the front of the collar but if numerous they may constitute a darkened area shaped like an inverted triangle, with its base towards the front of the collar and the extended apex terminating near the mid point of the scutellum. Abdomen yellowish or reddish brown, with black hairs intermixed. In very dark examples the abdomen may be

---

[1] Pale specimens of *muscorum* also occur in the Channel Islands. These have been said to resemble specimens from the English mainland but they may be closer to the Continental form, *Bombus muscorum muscorum*.

[2] synonym: *agrorum* (Fabricius).

G*

entirely black, except for some pale hairs on T1 and at the apical fringes of T2–5. More usually, however, T1 remains pale yellow, while T2–6 are largely pale brownish, although somewhat more tawny on T4 and T5, with black being restricted to the sides of the segments. Frequently, T3 and much of T4 are black, but fringed with pale hairs apically. In the lightest specimens black hairs are nearly always to be found at the sides of T2, and in most cases at the sides of T3 and T4 also. Light specimens may have a brownish band on T2 and so resemble *humilis* in general appearance. Coat relatively thin, long and shaggy. Sting (Fig. 112) easily distinguished from that of *humilis* or *muscorum*.

WORKER: length 9–15 mm., wingspan 20–28 mm. Resembles the queen but is usually smaller. Faded specimens may be almost entirely grey in colour.

MALE: length 12–14 mm., wingspan 24–27 mm. Coloured like the queen. Antennae long, flagellum c. 5·5 mm. Genitalia (Fig. 144) distinct.

B. pascuorum is an extremely variable species, and frequently many different colour forms may be found in one and the same locality. Four subspecies are recognized in these islands.

subspecies *septentrionalis* Vogt

Specimens from Scotland and parts of the north of England tend to be very light in colour, black hairs being absent from the thorax and restricted on the abdomen to the sides of T2–4. Such specimens are referrable to this subspecies.

subspecies *vulgo* (Harris)

This subspecies occurs in central and southern England and Wales, where specimens of *pascuorum* are often extremely variable but usually more or less darkened; black hairs are typically present on the thorax, often noticeably so, and they are widespread on the abdomen, particularly on the basal tergites. Both *septentrionalis* and *vulgo* interbreed freely over a wide area in the north of England and Wales.

subspecies *floralis* (Gmelin)

This subspecific name is applied to Irish specimens. These are coloured like *vulgo* but, although the abdomen may be very black, especially in males, black hairs on the thorax are normally scarce. This subspecies shows little variation, and the lower parts of the sides of the thorax are greyish rather than yellowish (Kruseman, 1950).

subspecies *flavidus* Krüger

This subspecies occurs in the Channel Islands and is extremely constant in colour

(Yarrow, *in litt.*). There are usually no black hairs on the thorax and few or none on the abdomen.

B. pascuorum is an abundant species over much of the British Isles including Ireland. It occurs in many types of habitat, but tends to prefer sheltered rather than exposed situations. It is absent from most offshore islands inhabited by *muscorum*, but recently it appears to have become established on Lundy Island.

Queens usually emerge from hibernation in April and nests are soon initiated. Development of colonies is prolonged, and in spite of their comparatively early start they continue in existence well into September, and sometimes later, being among the last to break up at the end of the season. *B. pascuorum* frequently nests above ground level in birds' nests or other unconventional situations, but normally nests are formed on the surface in the shelter of long or tussocky grass, and on rough banks. This species is very mild tempered. The comb is yellowish brown, often with a reddish tint. The bees visit white dead-nettle (*Lamium album*), red dead-nettle (*Lamium purpureum*), broom (*Sarothamnus scoparius*), horse–chestnut (*Aesculus hippocastanum*), clovers (*Trifolium*), wood-sage (*Teucrium scorodonia*), thistles (*Carduus* and *Cirsium*), knapweeds (*Centaurea*), scabious (*Knautia*), raspberry (*Rubus idaeus*), common snapdragon (*Antirrhinum majus*), lavender (*Lavandula*) and many other garden flowers.

15. *Bombus ruderarius* (Müller)[1]

Distribution map 17.

QUEEN: small, length 16–18 mm., wingspan 29–32 mm. Body black with tail (abdominal T4–6) red, fading to yellowish red. Corbicular hairs red. Coat relatively thin and shaggy. Sting (Fig. 135) similar to that of *sylvarum*.

WORKER: length 9–16 mm., wingspan 20–28 mm. Coloured like the queen but corbicular hairs sometimes only red at their tips.

MALE: length 12–14 mm., wingspan 24–26 mm. Head black, usually with admixture of greyish or yellowish grey hairs. Thorax black, with collar and scutellum more or less suffused with grey or yellowish grey. Abdomen black with T4–7 red, fading to yellowish orange. T1 and T2 usually marked with grey or yellowish hairs, in light examples these forming a distinct yellow or brownish yellow band on T2. Occasionally red hairs may extend on to T3. Coat relatively thin and shaggy. Antennae long, flagellum c. 6 mm. Genitalia (Fig. 165) distinct.

B. ruderarius is a widespread species. It is often common in the south and southeast of England, but is usually most frequent in lower-lying habitats. It is scarce or absent in many parts of the country.

[1] synonym: *derhamellus* (Kirby).

Although not among the first of the British species to appear in the spring, colonies are initiated with little delay, often in April, and usually ahead of those of other members of *Thoracobombus*. Nests are formed on the surface of the ground, frequently in moss or in garden compost heaps. This species is mild tempered. The comb is dark brown and the cocoons rather deep yellow in appearance. In spring, overwintered queens forage on flowers of white dead-nettle (*Lamium album*) and ground ivy (*Glechoma hederacea*); workers frequently visit bramble (*Rubus fruticosus*) and males are partial to knapweeds (*Centaurea*).

16. *Bombus sylvarum* (Linnaeus)

subspecies *distinctus* Vogt

Distribution map 18.

QUEEN: small, length 16–18 mm., wingspan 29–32 mm. Head and face largely pale greenish or yellowish grey, becoming black on top. Thorax with black centrally and more or less forming an interalar band, but shading into pale greenish or greyish yellow on the collar and scutellum, and often also at the sides; the pale scutellum is particularly distinct. Abdominal T1 and T2 pale greenish or yellowish grey, with a partial band of black hairs on T2; T2 often with a brownish orange tinge; T3 black, but with a pale greenish band apically; T4–6 mostly orange, each tergite fringed with pale greenish hairs. Coat relatively short and uneven. Abdomen distinctly pointed apically. Sting resembles that of *ruderarius* (Fig. 135).
WORKER: length 10–15 mm., wingspan 21–27 mm. Similar to the queen but smaller.
MALE: length 12–14 mm., wingspan 23–26 mm. Coloured like the queen, but the orange on abdominal T4 may be replaced by black. Coat relatively short and uneven. Antennae long, flagellum c. 6 mm. Genitalia (Fig. 166) distinct.

On the Continent a variety which is coloured like *ruderarius*, and known as var. *nigrescens* Pérez, frequently occurs. This variety has been found in England at Seaford, Sussex (Mortimer, 1922), but in these islands it is evidently exceedingly rare. Males may be distinguished from those of *ruderarius* by their genitalia and by differences in their antennae (see Key C, couplet 15); in females, the areas between the punctures on the apical tergites should be examined – these are shiny in *sylvarum* but dull in *ruderarius*.

B. sylvarum is a widespread species, particularly in the south, but is by no means generally common. It is absent from Scotland (see p. 304), and is very rare in Ireland (Stelfox, 1922, 1927, 1933a).
Queens emerge from hibernation later in the season than most other species.

Nests are established either on or just below ground level, often in the shelter of a small bush. Colonies are relatively small, but remain in existence well into September. The comb is light yellow and has a neat appearance. Little wax is secreted by this species. *B. sylvarum* has a very characteristic, nimble flight and is well-known for its shrill hum which, with experience, is instantly recognizable. This species visits flowers of white dead-nettle (*Lamium album*), woundworts (*Stachys*), red bartsia (*Odontites verna*), scabious (*Knautia*), knapweeds (*Centaurea*), and many others.

SUBGENUS *SUBTERRANEOBOMBUS* VOGT

17. *Bombus distinguendus* Morawitz

Distribution map 19.

QUEEN: large or very large, length 19–22 mm., wingspan 38–42 mm. Body mostly yellow or brownish yellow, with a distinct black interalar band. Some black hairs are intermixed with the yellow on the face. In pale specimens the black interalar band may merge into pale hairs at the sides. The yellow on abdominal T2 is somewhat browner than the rest. Coat relatively long and dense, particularly towards the base of the abdomen. A distinct median keel is present on the last visible sternite (St6) (Fig. 119). The sting (Fig. 118) is similar to that of *subterraneus*.

WORKER: large, length 11–18 mm., wingspan 23–35 mm. Similar to the queen but smaller.

MALE: length 14–16 mm., wingspan 28–31 mm. Coloured like the queen. Unlike the lightest specimens of *subterraneus* there are no black hairs on the sides of abdominal T2. Coat relatively long and dense. Abdomen rather elongate. Antennae long, flagellum c. 6 mm. Genitalia (Fig. 148) similar to those of *subterraneus* but known by the shape of the preapical process of the sagitta (Fig. 149) (see Key C, couplet 6).

 B. distinguendus is rare and of sporadic occurrence in the south of England, but more frequent in the north and west, although it is nowhere particularly common. Its range extends to the extreme north of Scotland, and includes the Hebrides and Orkney Islands. It also occurs in Ireland.

 This species nests below ground[1] but is not very prolific, producing only a few queens (O'Rourke, 1957). Its general biology is probably similar to that of *subterraneus* to which it is closely allied. The working-speed (Dennis & Haas, 1967; Poulsen, 1973) and flight of this species is rapid and the bees are easily disturbed when foraging. They are attracted to various flowers, including hardhead (*Centaurea nigra*), kidney vetch (*Anthyllis vulneraria*) and bramble (*Rubus fruticosus*).

---

[1] Duncan (1935), however, found many nests in the Orkneys, all on the surface of the ground.

18. *Bombus subterraneus* (Linnaeus)[1]

subspecies *latreillellus* (Kirby)

Distribution map 20.

QUEEN: large or very large, length 19–22 mm., wingspan 38–42 mm. Head black. Thorax black with a dusky, dull yellow band on the collar and a similar but much narrower band on the scutellum. The yellow on the collar is often much reduced, especially centrally, while the yellow on the scutellum may be reduced to a few brownish hairs. Abdomen black with T4 and T5 white or dingy white, and often with brownish or whitish hairs at the posterior fringes of T1–3. Coat very short, particularly on the basal segments of the abdomen. Head long, although less so than in *ruderatus*, dull-coloured specimens of which it much resembles. Unlike *ruderatus*, however, there is a distinct keel on St6 (see Fig. 119). Sting, although similar to that of *distinguendus* (Fig. 118), quite different to that of *ruderatus*.

WORKER: large, 11–18 mm., wingspan 23–35 mm. Similar in appearance to the queen, but the scutellum (and, particularly in small individuals, T1) may be entirely black.

MALE: length 14–16 mm., wingspan 28–31 mm. Head black, with face and top partly pale greenish or brownish yellow. Thorax mostly pale greenish yellow with a black interalar band. Much of the abdomen is pale greenish or brownish yellow, but T2 and T3 usually have a black or brown band basally; T6 and T7 are black in the middle. In very light specimens black hairs may be confined to the sides of T2, whereas in dark specimens additional black hairs may be apparent on both T4 and T5. Coat short. Abdomen rather elongate. Antennae long, flagellum c. 6 mm. Genitalia similar to those of *distinguendus* (Fig. 148) but known by the shape of the preapical process of the sagitta (Fig. 150) (see Key C, couplet 6).

B. *subterraneus* is one of our less common species, and although widely distributed in the south of England it is generally scarce. It is absent from both Ireland and Scotland.

This is a late-appearing species. Nests are formed below ground, and although they may be relatively populous the number of workers produced is far less than in colonies of, for example, *terrestris*. Queens rear a large number of workers in their first brood batch, and males and young queens are produced relatively early in the life of the colony. According to Sladen, *subterraneus* does best in a short season. Individual workers of *subterraneus* are often surprisingly large. Little wax is produced by members of the subgenus *Subterraneobombus*, and as a result the larvae, as they grow, are poorly covered. The comb in a *subterraneus* colony is very

---

[1] synonym: *latreillellus* (Kirby).

194

untidy in appearance. Foraging bees mostly visit flowers with long corolla tubes; they are, for example, frequently attracted to various members of the Labiatae.

SUBGENUS *RHODOBOMBUS* VON DALLA TORRE

19. *Bombus pomorum* (Panzer)

Distribution map 21.

QUEEN: medium in size, length c. 18 mm., wingspan c. 35 mm. Body usually black with a red tail, the red shading gradually into black on abdominal T3. Corbicular hairs black. Structurally, this species is distinguished from *lapidarius* (and *cullumanus*) by the elongate head and the presence of a spine on the mid basitarsus (Fig. 108), and from *ruderarius* by the longer head (and the black corbicular hairs).
WORKER: probably similar to the queen except in size.
MALE: length 14–16 mm., wingspan 26–27 mm. Rather *Psithyrus*-like in form, and has been mistaken for a colourful variety of *Psithyrus rupestris*. Head black, thorax black with both the collar and scutellum yellowish grey. Abdomen mostly red, but T1 yellowish grey. Head elongate, the mandibles without a beard. Hind tibiae covered with short hairs. Antennae of medium length, flagellum c. 5 mm. Genitalia (Fig. 160) distinct.

All the known British examples of *pomorum* were captured near Deal in Kent during the nineteenth century, but none has been reported since 1864 (see Chapter 11 for details). On the Continent *pomorum* is said to occur near sand-dunes and marshy areas. The Deal area was, therefore, a suitable habitat. Apparently, *pomorum* is characterized by its wild flight. The females are reported to be partial to flowers of red clover (*Trifolium pratense*) and males to scabious (*Knautia*).

As pointed out by Perkins (1921) this species might easily be overlooked in Britain. However, although accidental immigration from the Continent could occur from time to time, and it is conceivable that the species might then survive for a while, it must be optimistic to still regard *pomorum* as a breeding British species.

Bombus elegans (Seidl)

Perkins (1921) recorded a specimen of *B. elegans* (syn. *mesomelas* Gerstäcker), a mountain species allied to *pomorum* (but similar in appearance to *distinguendus*), among the Bignell collection of British bees in Plymouth Museum, Devonshire. The bee, placed under *lapponicus*, was unlabelled but is most probably of foreign origin.

Genus *Psithyrus* Lepeletier

synonym: *Apathus* Newman

Inquiline species which lack a worker caste. The hind tibiae of females are not adapted for carrying pollen. The flight of *Psithyrus* females is weaker than that of *Bombus* and the hum is of a distinctly lower pitch. The wings are generally more opaque than in *Bombus* and in both sexes the coat, particularly on the abdomen, is relatively thin and the basal tergites are often clearly visible. The last visible sternite of the female (St6) bears characteristic elevations or callosities, not found in *Bombus*. *Psithyrus* males are rather similar in appearance to those of *Bombus*, but the head (often elongate in *Bombus*) is particularly rounded in outline, and the hind tibiae are noticeably hairy all over. Further differences between these two genera are given in Key A (Chapter 10); see also information in Chapter 7.

SUBGENUS *ASHTONIPSITHYRUS* FRISON

20. *Psithyrus bohemicus* (Seidl)[1]

Distribution map 22.

FEMALE: large, length 18–20 mm., wingspan 36–39 mm.; may be much smaller (see below). Head black. Thorax black with a broad, pale yellow band on the collar, and often with pale or pale-tipped hairs on the scutellum. Abdominal T1 and T2 black; T3 pale yellow at the sides (soon fading to white), black in the middle; T4 more or less white; T5 black, but white at the sides. Black hairs on the thorax and basal tergites of the abdomen may be tinged with grey or brown. Coat rather dense, long and uneven. Callosities on St6 ridge-like, terminating near apex of segment (Fig. 180). T6 brilliantly shiny. Very small specimens, no larger than normal-sized males,

---

[1] synonym: *distinctus* Pérez.

sometimes occur. Such specimens that bear red-haired, rather than black-haired, hind tibiae and basitarsi are the variety *subrufipes* of Perkins.

MALE: length 15–17 mm., wingspan 29–33 mm. Head black, sometimes with pale yellow hairs on top. Thorax black with a broad yellow band on the collar; usually the scutellum is also marked with yellow. Abdominal T1 usually yellow; T2 black; T3 black in the middle and towards the base, but pale yellow at the sides; T4, T5, and sides of T6, white; remainder of T6 and T7, more or less black. As in females the yellow soon fades. A variety occurring in Scotland has the white of the tail replaced by yellow. Coat rather dense, long and uneven. Antennae short, flagellum c. 5 mm. Genitalia (Fig. 193) similar to those of *vestalis*, but inner edges of the volsella and squama less hairy (Fig. 195).

P. bohemicus is an inquiline of *Bombus lucorum* and, although sometimes occurring in the southern counties of England, it is more frequent in the west and from the Midlands northwards. It is widespread in Ireland, Scotland and Wales.

It was suggested by Perkins (1921) that var. *subrufipes* might be an inquiline of *B. soroeensis*, but this has never been substantiated.

P. bohemicus females appear in April and May, and like other species of the genus *Psithyrus* they often feed on flowers of dandelion (*Taraxacum officinale*).

In the summer males may be found on thistles (*Carduus* and *Cirsium*), and on various other flowers.

21. *Psithyrus vestalis* (Geoffroy in Fourcroy)

Distribution map 23.

FEMALE: large, length 20–22 mm., wingspan 40–43 mm. Head black. Thorax black with a yellow or brownish yellow collar. Abdominal T1 and T2 black; T3 black in the middle, lemon yellow at the sides; T4 white; T5 black but white at the sides. The yellow thoracic band is often darkened and narrowed. Coat somewhat shorter and less dense than that of *bohemicus*. Callosities on St6 ridge-like, terminating short of apex of segment (Fig. 179). T6 shiny, but less so than in *bohemicus*.

MALE: length 15–17 mm., wingspan 30–35 mm. Head black, sometimes with yellow on top. Thorax black, with a yellow collar and, occasionally, with a few pale hairs on the scutellum. Abdominal T1 yellow; T2 black; T3 yellow, but black centrally at the base; T4 and T5 white; T6 black, with white at the sides; T7 more or less black. Coat even and relatively short. Antennae long, flagellum c. 6 mm. Genitalia (Fig. 192) similar to those of *bohemicus*, but inner edges of the volsella and squama more hairy (Fig. 194).

P. vestalis victimizes colonies of *B. terrestris*. It is relatively common and widespread in the south of England, but is less common further north. It is absent from, or at best is exceedingly rare in, Scotland and Ireland.

As is the case with other species of *Psithyrus*, males are more often seen than females, and like those of the previous species, they are partial to flowers of thistles (*Carduus* and *Cirsium*); they are also commonly found on knapweeds (*Centaurea*) from July onwards.

SUBGENUS *PSITHYRUS* LEPELETIER

22. *Psithyrus rupestris* (Fabricius)

Distribution map 24.

FEMALE: large, length 20–23 mm., wingspan 39–45 mm. Head and thorax black. Abdominal T1–3 black; T4 and T5 orange-red, T6 dull and clothed with very short, inconspicuous, red hairs. Rarely, pale hairs may occur on the collar. Coat very short and thin. St6 with large flange-like callosities (Fig. 175), clearly visible from above. Wings dark brown.

MALE: length 15–17 mm., wingspan 30–33 mm. Head and thorax black, but collar and scutellum usually suffused with yellowish grey hairs, which may form indistinct bands. Abdominal T1 and T2 black, often with yellowish grey hairs intermixed, especially at the sides and along the posterior fringes of each segment; T3 black, but sometimes with red hairs; T4–7 dull red, fading to orange. Very dark specimens sometimes occur; Sladen refers to an entirely black specimen. Coat rather long and shaggy. Antennae relatively stout and short, flagellum c. 5 mm. Genitalia (Fig. 188) distinct.

This species is an inquiline of *B. lapidarius* and, like its host, is widely distributed. At present, however, it appears to be our rarest *Psithyrus*, but this has not always been so. In 1857 Frederick Smith remarked 'I captured about twenty specimens of the female of this bee on the heads of thistles, at Sandwich in Kent. Twenty years ago I met a similar number in a gravel-pit at the top of Coomb Wood; these are unusual occurrences, the insect being rather scarce, at least the female, and only captured at intervals'. Sladen (1912), on the other hand, described *rupestris* as 'plentiful in East Kent' and 'particularly common in many parts of Suffolk and Norfolk', statements that certainly do not hold true today. Possibly, populations of this species are subject to periodic fluctuations in abundance.

Females of *rupestris* emerge later in the season than any other species, usually entering nests of the *Bombus* host in June. As indicated above, males of *rupestris* are more frequently found than females.

SUBGENUS *ALLOPSITHYRUS* POPOV

23. *Psithyrus barbutellus* (Kirby)

Distribution map 25.

FEMALE: medium in size, length 17–19 mm., wingspan 36–39 mm. Head black, with brownish yellow hairs on top. Thorax black with a brownish yellow band on the collar, and a narrower, somewhat lighter band on the scutellum. Abdominal T1 mostly black, but often with yellow hairs intermixed; T2 and T3 black, but T3 may be yellow apically; T4 and T5 white. Callosities on St6 prominent, forming a semi-circle (Fig. 178). T6 dull, with a distinct median keel (Fig. 182).

MALE: length 15–17 mm., wingspan 29–33 mm. Head black with some yellow hairs on top. Thorax black with a broad yellow band on the collar; the scutellum also yellow, but there the pale hairs may be much reduced in extent. Abdominal T1 more or less yellow; T2 black; T3 black, often white at the sides; T4 and T5 white; T6 black in the middle, white at the sides; T7 black. St6 with two rounded apical callosities (Fig. 197). Antennae relatively short, flagellum c. 5·5 mm. Genitalia (Fig. 191) distinct.

P. barbutellus breeds in nests of *B. hortorum* and, like its host, is widely distributed. Again, in common with other *Psithyrus* species, males are more often found than females.

SUBGENUS *METAPSITHYRUS* POPOV

24. *Psithyrus campestris* (Panzer)

Distribution map 26.

FEMALE: medium in size, length 17–19 mm., wingspan 35–38 mm. Head black with a few yellow hairs on top, but these may be more or less absent in dark specimens. Thorax black with a wide yellow or brownish yellow band on the collar and a wide, often much darkened band on the scutellum. Abdomen black with the sides of T3–5 yellow; yellow on sides of T3 usually confined to the apex of the segment. Dark specimens often occur and, rarely, entirely black females are found. Callosities on St6 large and rounded, but pointed towards the apex (Fig. 177). T6 shiny and without a median keel (Fig. 181).

MALE: length 15–16 mm., wingspan 28–31 mm. Extremely variable in colour. Head black, but in light specimens there are yellow hairs on top. Thorax black, or black with yellow collar and scutellum. Abdomen largely yellow, but T2 and T7 are black, and the yellow on T1, T3, T4 and T5 is more or less interrupted in the middle by black; yellow on T1 often reduced. Dark specimens may be black apart from the sides of T4 and T5 which remain brownish; entirely black males often occur. St6 with a slight median groove and prominent lateral tufts of black hair (Figs. 196). Antennae long, flagellum c. 6·5 mm. Genitalia (Fig. 190) distinct.

subspecies *swynnertoni* Richards

FEMALE: head black with some yellow hairs on top. Thorax entirely yellow except for black hairs on the disc. Abdominal T1 yellow at the sides, black in the middle; T2 black at the sides, black and yellow intermixed in the middle; T3–5 mostly yellow, although with some black hairs in the middle.

MALE: head black but yellow on top. Thorax entirely yellow except for a few black hairs on the disc. Abdomen entirely yellow except for the black apices of T6 and T7; erectness of the hairs on T2 gives the impression of a brownish band.

This striking colour form of *campestris* occurs in parts of Scotland where it presumably victimizes nests of *B. pascuorum septentrionalis* (Richards, 1936).

P. campestris is a relatively common and widespread species. It is an inquiline of *B. pascuorum* and possibly also of *B. humilis*. Both Sladen (1912) and Stelfox (1927) considered *campestris* to be the commonest species of *Psithyrus* in Ireland.

SUBGENUS *FERNALDAEPSITHYRUS* FRISON

25. *Psithyrus sylvestris* Lepeletier[1]

Distribution map 27.

FEMALE: small, length 14–16 mm., wingspan 32–35 mm. Head black, sometimes with yellowish hairs on top. Thorax black with a broad yellow band on the collar; sometimes the hairs on the scutellum are tinged with yellow or brownish yellow. Abdominal T1 black or, especially at the sides, more or less yellow; T2 black; T3 white or yellowish white; T4 white; T5 and T6 dark golden brown. Callosities on St6 small and inconspicuous (Fig. 176). Tip of abdomen more strongly incurved than in other species (Fig. 183).

MALE: length 13–15 mm., wingspan 27–30 mm. Head black, usually with yellow on top. Thorax black with a yellow collar, and often with yellow hairs on the scutellum. Abdominal T1 more or less yellow, but may be entirely black in dark

---

[1] synonym: *quadricolor* Lepeletier, a name also applied to *globosus* Eversmann (see Richards, 1928).

specimens; T2 black; T3 and T4 more or less white or yellow; T5 black, but often white or yellow at the sides; T6 more or less black, sometimes reddish, particularly apically; T7 red or orange. Antennae short, flagellum c. 5 mm. Genitalia (Fig. 189) distinct.

P. sylvestris is widely distributed and is common in many areas. It preys upon *B. pratorum* and possibly, at least in Ireland, also on *B. jonellus*. It is usually the first *Psithyrus* species to emerge from hibernation. Males are reared relatively early in the season. They are often common from June to July on raspberry (*Rubus idaeus*) and various other flowers.

CHAPTER 10

Keys

Perhaps no genus presents more difficulties in determining the species than Bombus; there are males, females, and neuters of two sizes, and the hairs with which they are clothed vary in colour with age; it is therefore only by examining their nests that the species can be ascertained, and perhaps not then with constant or unerring success.

JOHN CURTIS (1835)

The species of *Bombus* are exceedingly difficult to distinguish apart, the colour of the pubescence varies so greatly in different specimens of some species that it is wise to rely only on structure as a character in the discrimination of the species; these characters are often very obscure, and difficult to appreciate. There are several species which, as a rule, are quite easy to recognize, but of which rare varieties occur quite unlike the typical form. The most reliable character is the form of the ♂ genital armature; this will always guide one rightly, but in the absence of the ♂ it is sometimes impossible to say for certain what a ♀ or ☿ is.

EDWARD SAUNDERS (1896)

The following keys are intended to help in the correct identification of British specimens. The species keys are not designed to show relationships; they are, therefore, largely artificial. Their usefulness will be greatly facilitated if a good hand lens or a low-power binocular microscope is available. Illustrations of important features are given at the end of each key;[1] see also, various figures in Chapter 1 and Fig. 100 (p. 171).

Structural characteristics of the sting, especially of the inner projections of the sting sheath, are often useful for distinguishing between certain species of *Bombus*. These projections may be examined by opening the sting chamber (parting T6 and St6) and withdrawing the sting, which may be left attached to the specimen or removed for closer examination (see Fig. 205, p. 259). The sting should be viewed 'end on' with the main shaft directed away from the observer. In this position the sting sheath forms an inverted stirrup-shaped 'V' with the inner projections clearly visible. A similar procedure may be followed for examining the male genitalia (Fig. 204), nomenclature of which is given in Fig. 20 (p. 22). Apart from the possible need to expose the sting or the male genitalia, dissection of specimens is not required for appreciation of the characters mentioned in these keys.

Specific characters of females are usually better expressed in large rather than in small specimens, and it may prove impossible to distinguish with certainty small workers of closely allied species, such as *lucorum* and *terrestris*, *hortorum* and *ruderatus*.

A. Key to Sexes and Genera

1. Antennae 12-segmented (Fig. 4); abdomen with 6 visible segments (i.e. 6 tergites and 6 sternites); sting present; apex of abdomen pointed (=FEMALE)
.. .. 2
— Antennae 13-segmented (Fig. 3); abdomen with 7 visible tergites and 6 visible sternites; sting absent; apex of abdomen blunt (=MALE) 3

2. Hind tibia with outer-side flat, shiny and hairless, with long lateral hairs forming corbiculum (Fig. 12); mandibles with apical edges more or less at right angles to long axes (Fig. 103), and capable of overlapping when in repose; coat, particularly on abdomen, more dense, usually hiding tergites; industrious species with a worker caste .. .. *Bombus* (Key B)
— Hind tibia with outer-side convex, dull and very hairy, but hairs not forming corbiculum (Fig. 101); mandibles with apical edges aligned obliquely to long axes (Fig. 102), and not capable of overlapping when in repose; coat, particularly on abdomen, thin, with tergites clearly visible; inquilinous species, without a worker caste .. .. *Psithyrus* (Key D)

[1] Figs. 101–107 follow Key A   Figs. 175–185 follow Key D
Figs. 108–141 follow Key B   Figs. 186–201 follow Key E
Figs. 142–174 follow Key C

3. Genitalia with squama and apical part of volsella strongly sclerotized (Fig. 20); hind tibia more or less flattened and shiny on outer-side (Fig. 104), with hairs if present on disc (Fig. 105) not feathery .. .. .. *Bombus* (Key C)
— Genitalia with squama and apical part of volsella membranous; hind tibia convex, dull and hairy all over (Fig. 106), with hairs on outer-side much branched (Fig. 107) .. .. *Psithyrus* (Key E)

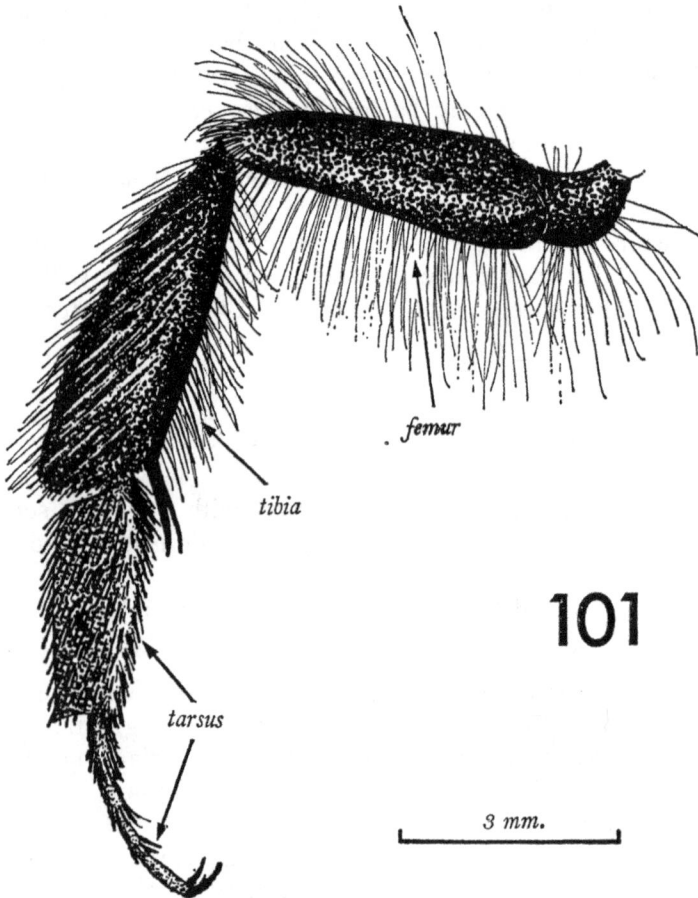

Fig. 101. Right hind leg of *Psithyrus sylvestris* female.

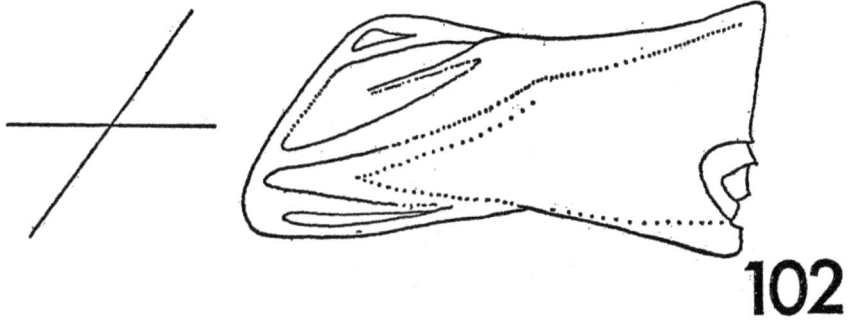

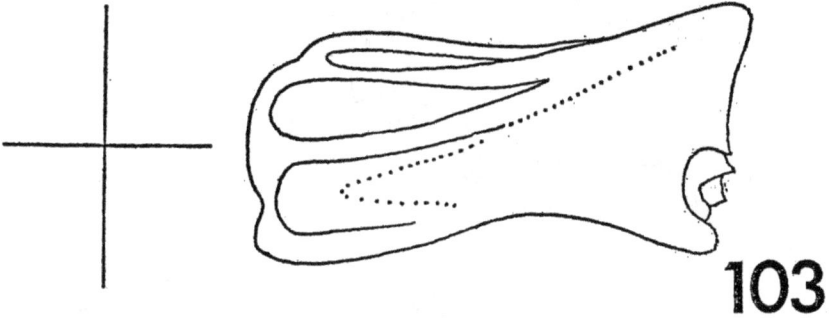

Figs. 102–103. Left mandible of female. 102, *Psithyrus bohemicus*; 103, *Bombus terrestris*.

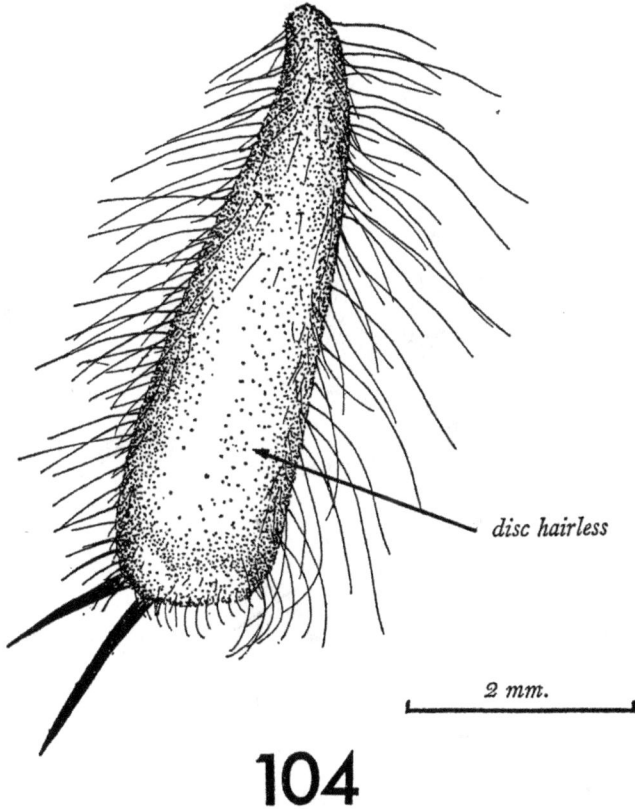

disc hairless

2 mm.

104

Fig. 104. Left hind tibia of *Bombus lucorum* male.

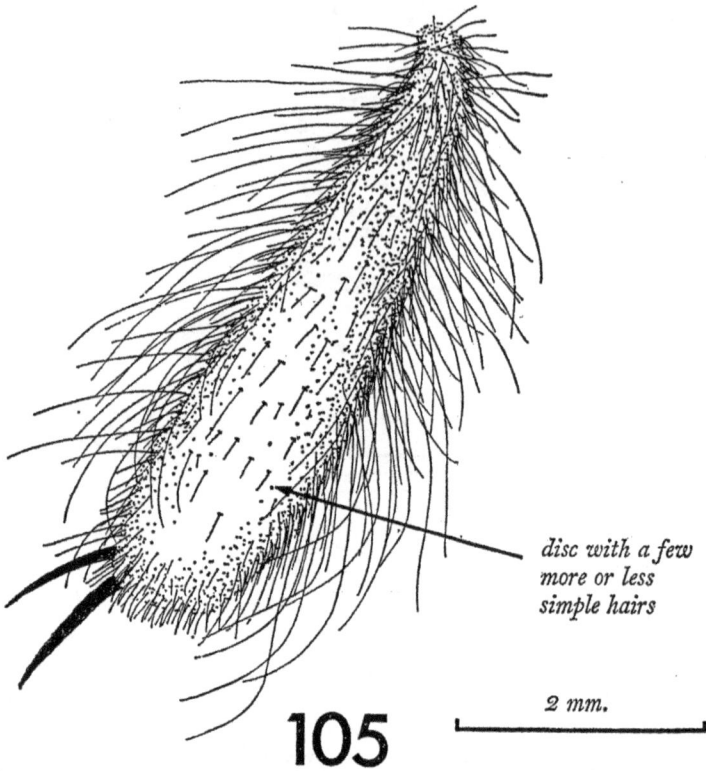

disc with a few more or less simple hairs

2 mm.

105

Fig. 105. Left hind tibia of *Bombus jonellus* male.

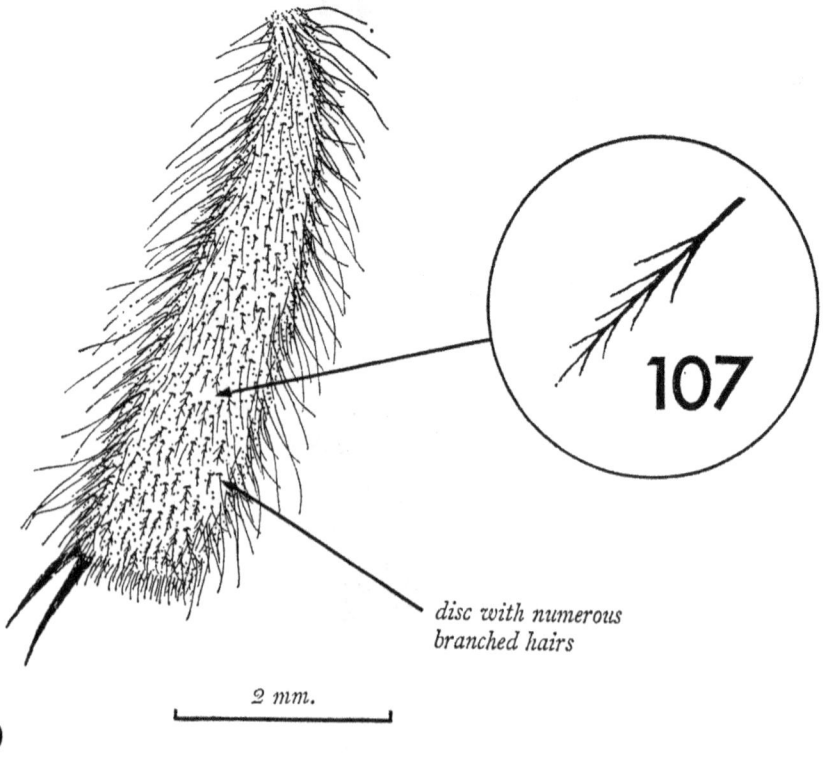

107

disc with numerous branched hairs

2 mm.

106

Fig. 106. Left hind tibia of *Psithyrus vestalis* male.
Fig. 107. Branched hairs from disc of hind tibia of *Psithyrus vestalis* male.

B. Key to *Bombus* Females

1. Body more or less yellowish, reddish brown or blackish brown above; black hairs, when numerous on the thorax, never forming an interalar band. Head slightly elongate. Mandibles with sulcus obliquus but without incisura (see Fig. 124). Mid basitarsus with spine (Fig. 108). Queens small to medium-sized
.. .. 2
 — Thorax black, and usually with at least part of both collar and scutellum yellow or brownish; tail yellowish, brown, white or black, but not pink, orange or red. Body may be entirely black. Head more or less elongate (Figs. 109 and 110). Mandibles with sulcus obliquus but without incisura (see Fig. 124). Mid basitarsus with spine. Queens medium to large or very large 4
 — Thorax black, and usually with collar, collar and scutellum, or scutellum only, yellow or brownish yellow; tail white, pinkish or tawny, but not red (although some red hairs may occur at the sides and base); abdominal T1 and/or T2 usually yellow or brownish yellow. Head short (Fig. 111). Mandibles with or without sulcus obliquus; if with, then also with incisura (see Fig. 124). Mid basitarsus without spine. Queens small to large or very large 7
 — Thorax entirely black, or black with collar, or collar and scutellum, yellow or greyish; tail red or orange, but not white, black or brown. Mandibles with incisura or with sulcus obliquus, but not both (see Fig. 124). Includes species with and species without spinose mid basitarsi. Queens small to large .. 11

2. Black hairs frequently present on thorax and abdomen, particularly on basal tergites, and at least present at sides of T2;[1] brown band only occasionally apparent on T2. Inner projections of sting sheath narrower (Fig. 112)
.. .. *pascuorum*
 — No black hairs on upperside of abdomen,[2] apart from on T6 (last visible tergite) which is black, and few or none on thorax; abdomen usually with at least suggestion of brown band on T2. Inner projections of sting sheath broader (Figs. 113 and 114) 3

3. T2 with characteristic brown band; thorax with at least a few black hairs above tegulae; coat slightly shorter and less dense; slightly smaller species with more pointed abdomen; hairs at sides of T3 arise from coalescing punctures (Fig. 115). Inner projections of sting sheath bifid at ventral end (Fig. 113). .. *humilis*
 — Brown band on T2 less distinct; no black hairs on upperside of thorax; coat slightly or much longer and more dense; slightly larger species; hairs at sides of T3 arise from pustules (Fig. 116). Inner projections of sting sheath simple at ventral end (Fig. 114). .. .. *muscorum*

[1] Black hairs often absent in Channel Island form (*pascuorum flavidus*).
[2] T1 and much of T2 are black in *muscorum allenellus* which, like some other races of *muscorum*, has an entirely black underside to both thorax and abdomen; underside of body not black in *pascuorum*.

4. Head, malar space and tongue exceptionally long (Fig. 109); no keel on St6; inner projections of sting sheath with characteristic indentations (Fig. 117) .. 5

— Head, malar space and tongue less elongate (Fig. 110); distinct keel on St6 (Fig. 119); inner projections of sting sheath simple (Fig. 118). 6

5. Coat long and uneven; smaller species; yellow on thorax and abdomen usually bright. Sculpturing on T6 usually far less marked and less extensive (Fig. 120). .. .. *hortorum*

— Coat shorter and more even; larger species; yellow on thorax and abdomen usually somewhat darkened, and often much reduced or even absent. Sculpturing on T6 very rough and more extensive (Fig. 121). .. .. .. *ruderatus*

6. Thorax brownish yellow, with a distinct black interalar band; abdomen brownish yellow, with deeper brownish band on T2; coat long. .. .. *distinguendus*

— Thorax black with dingy yellow or brown collar and narrow band of dingy yellow hairs on scutellum; abdomen with T4 and T5 white, often with brownish or whitish hairs at posterior fringes of T1 and T3; coat very short .. .. *subterraneus*

7. Thorax usually with collar and scutellum yellow; T1 and base of T2 yellow. Mandible without sulcus obliquus but with incisura (Fig. 122); sting sheath membrane with dark patches (not present in virgins), inner projections of sting sheath simple (Fig. 125) .. .. *jonellus*[1]

— Scutellum black, collar yellow or brownish; T1 black, T2 mostly or entirely yellow. Mandible with sulcus obliquus, but if without then also lacking incisura; sting sheath without dark patches 8

8. Yellow abdominal band reduced or broken centrally. Mandible with no sulcus obliquus or incisura[2] (Fig. 123); depressions at apex of clypeus well separated from each other (Fig. 128); inner projections of sting sheath simple (Fig. 126) .. .. *soroeensis*

— Yellow abdominal band normally continuous, but often broken due to accidental depilation. Mandible with both sulcus obliquus and incisura (Fig. 124); clypeal depressions almost meeting in mid-line (Fig. 129); inner projections of sting sheath emarginate (Fig. 127) 9

9. Yellow darker and often less extensive; tail tawny, brownish white, white, or white with buff hairs at base. Outer projections of sting sheath ventrally narrower (Fig. 130); surface of T2 very shiny below hairs, due to shallow sculpturing .. .. *terrestris*

— Yellow brighter; tail usually white or pinkish white. Outer projections of sting sheath ventrally wider (Fig. 131); surface of T2 dull below hairs, due to deeper sculpturing 10

[1] Tail normally white, but some subspecies (see p. 179) have a yellowish or tawny tail; at once known from *pratorum* by the yellow scutellum.
[2] An inconspicuous incisura may be present.

10. Yellow of collar wide, extending down sides below level of tegulae and often projecting backwards below wings (Fig. 132); yellow band on T2 wide and reaching tergite base; larger species .. .. *magnus*

— Yellow of collar narrower and usually ending about level with tegulae (Fig. 133); yellow abdominal band narrower, with black hairs at base; smaller species .. .. *lucorum*

11. Thorax black with at best only trace of greyish or yellowish hairs; abdomen black with tail red or orange-red 12

— Thorax with collar, or collar and scutellum, yellow or grey; abdomen often at least partly grey or yellow, with tail red or orange 14

12. Corbicular hairs red; tail orange-red. Mid basitarsus spinose (Fig. 108); inner projections of sting sheath very broad and almost meeting in mid line (Fig. 135); [areas between punctures on apical tergites dull] .. .. *ruderarius*

[— As above, but areas between punctures on apical tergites shiny ..]
[.. .. .. ..*sylvarum* var. *nigrescens* (very rare in Britain)]
[— Corbicular hairs black; tail red, grading into black on T3. Head very]
[long; mid basitarsus spinose .. .. *pomorum* (doubtfully British)]

— Corbicular hairs black; tail red. Mid basitarsus without spine; inner projections of sting sheath narrow, especially ventrally 13

13. Outer surface of hind basitarsus densely covered with short yellowish white hairs (Fig. 138); inner projections of sting sheath simple (Fig. 134) .. *lapidarius*

— Outer surface of hind basitarsus with few hairs (Fig. 139), and appearing shiny black; inner projections of sting sheath inwardly swollen dorsally (Fig. 137) .. .. *cullumanus* (very rare)

14. Abdomen with greenish grey and black bands; tail orange; tip of abdomen sharply pointed; thorax grey or greenish grey with black interalar band. Sting like that of *ruderarius* (Fig. 135); mid basitarsus spinose (Fig. 108) .. *sylvarum*

— Abdomen black with red or orange-red tail, the red sometimes extensive; T1 or T2 frequently yellow; thorax black, with collar, or collar and scutellum, yellow. Inner projections of sting sheath narrower, especially ventrally (Fig. 136); mid basitarsus without spine 15

15. Thorax with collar, and frequently also scutellum, yellow; T1 sometimes yellow; red on abdomen very extensive and bright. Disc of clypeus strongly punctured (Fig. 141) .. .. *lapponicus*

— Scutellum black; much of abdomen black, but T2 usually with yellow band (often absent in workers); red on tail far less bright and at best only present on last three tergites. Disc of clypeus weakly punctured (Fig. 140) .. .. *pratorum*

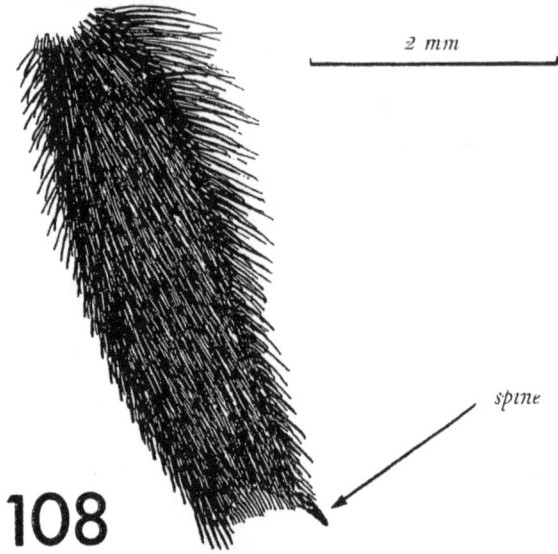

Fig. 108. Left mid basitarsus of *Bombus hortorum* (ODONTOBOMBUS) female.

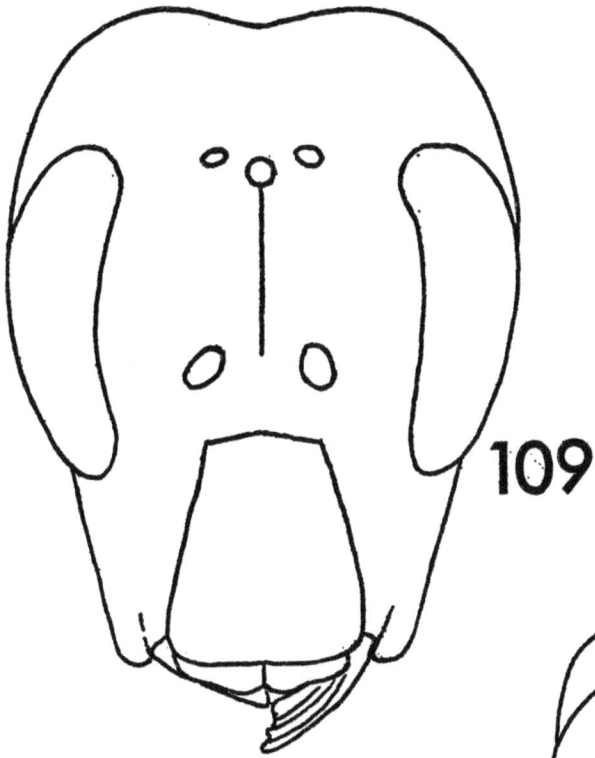

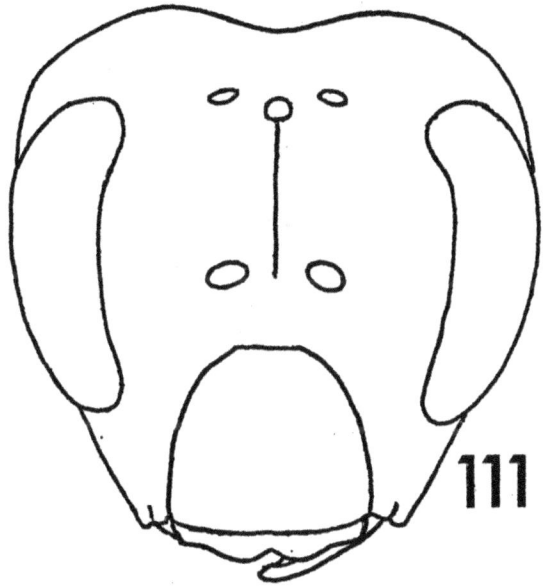

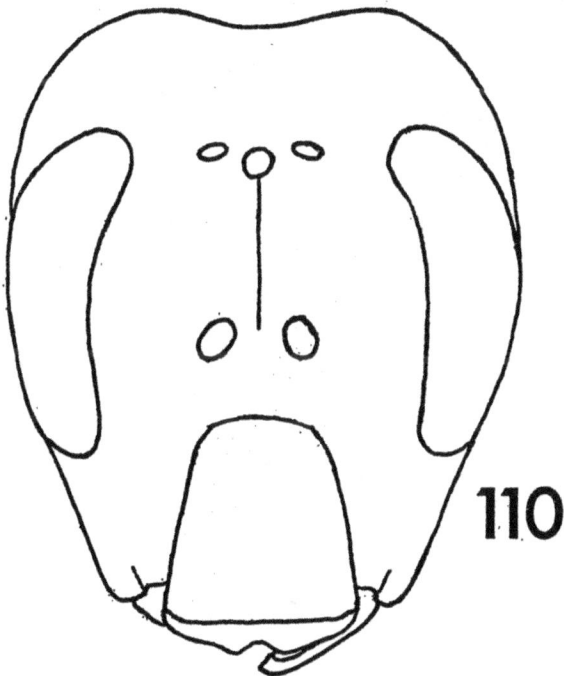

Figs. 109–111. Head of female. 109, *Bombus hortorum*; 110, *Bombus subterraneus*; 111, *Bombus jonellus*.

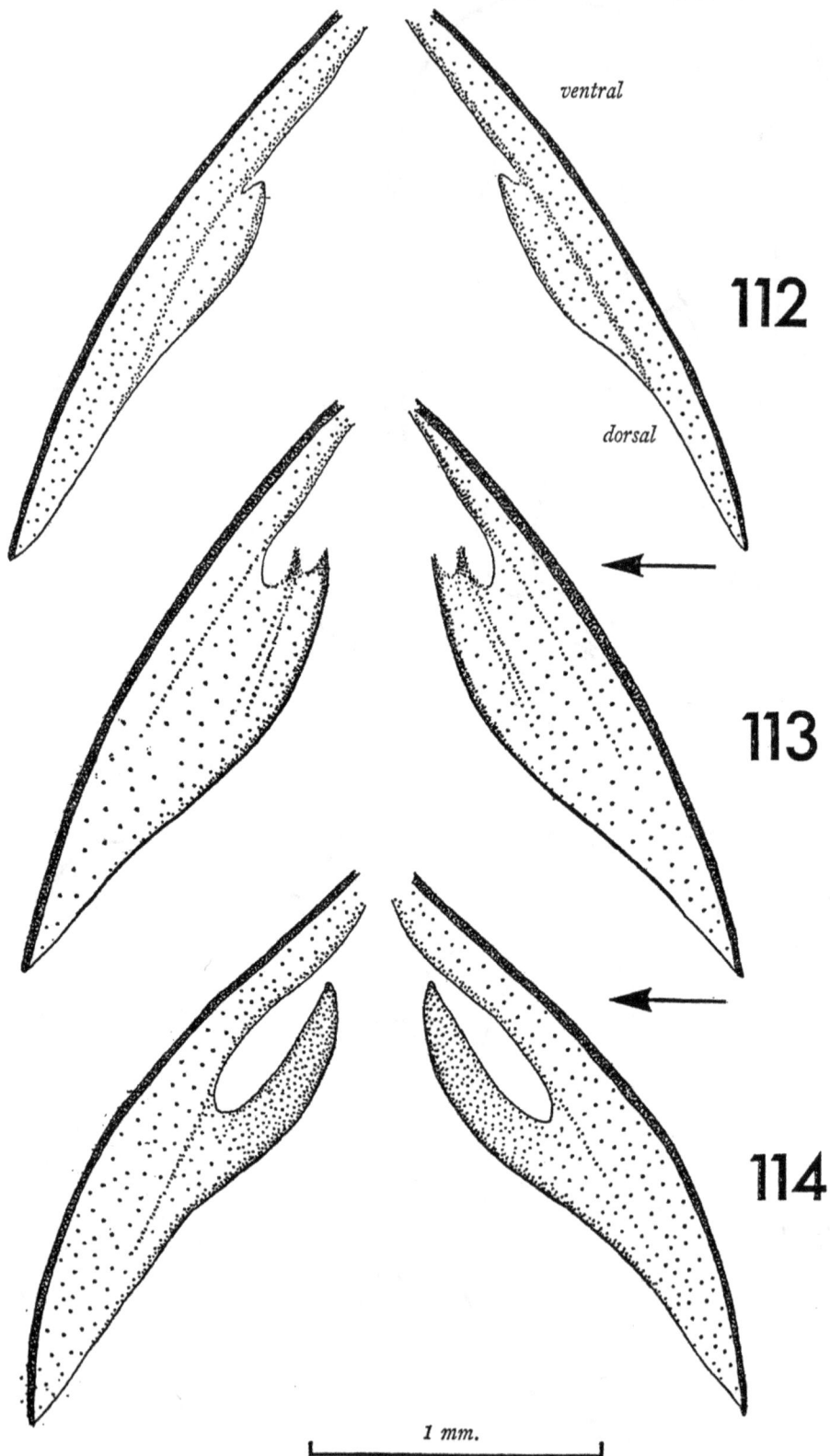

ventral

112

dorsal

113

114

1 mm.

Figs. 112–114. Inner projections of sting sheath. 112, *Bombus pascuorum*; 113, *Bombus humilis*; 114, *Bombus muscorum*.

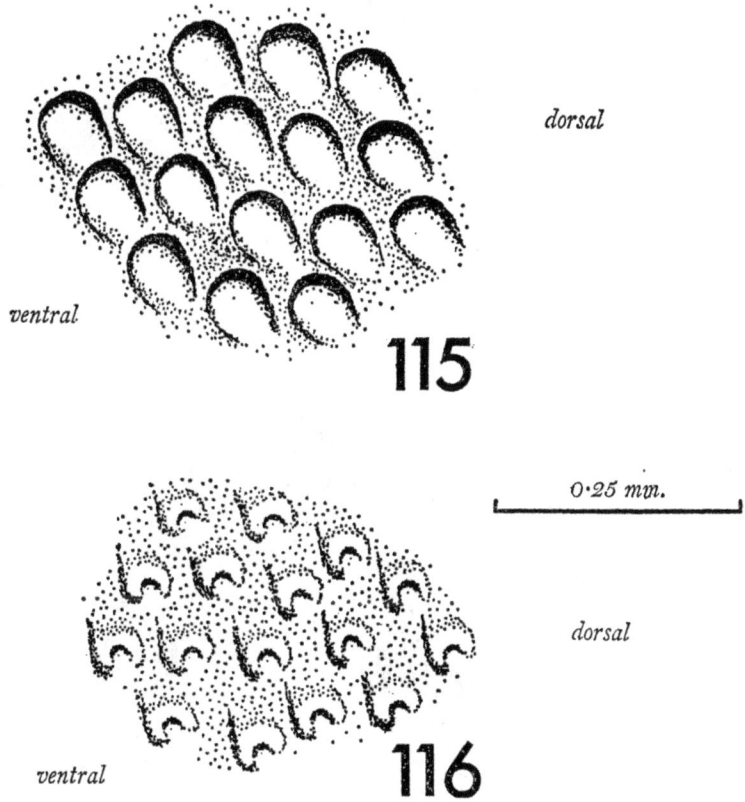

Figs. 115–116. Sculpturing at left side of third tergite (T3) of female (hairs not shown). 115, *Bombus humilis*; 116, *Bombus muscorum*.

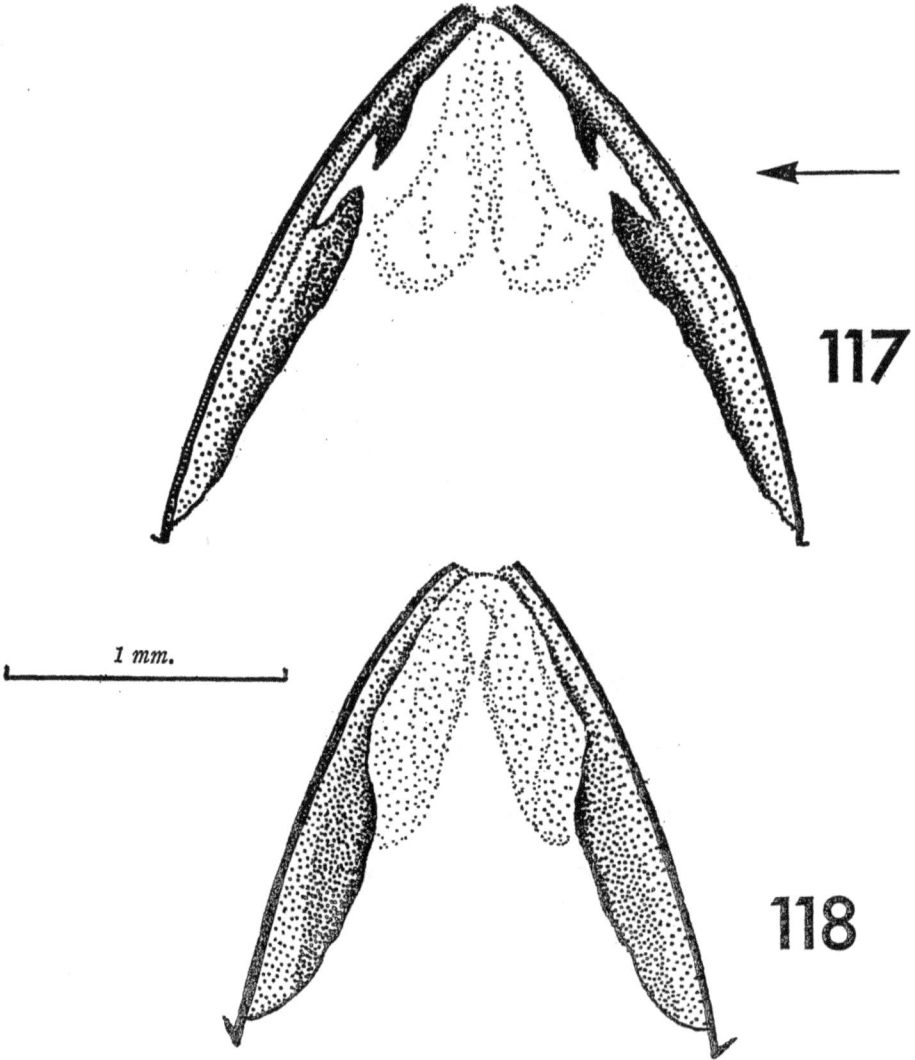

1 mm.

Figs. 117–118. Inner projections of sting sheath. 117, *Bombus ruderatus*; 118, *Bombus distinguendus*.

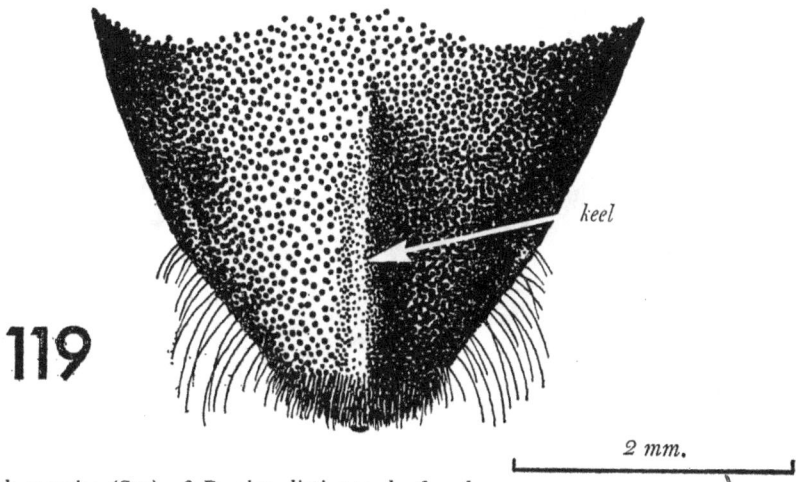

Fig. 119. Sixth sternite (St6) of *Bombus distinguendus* female.

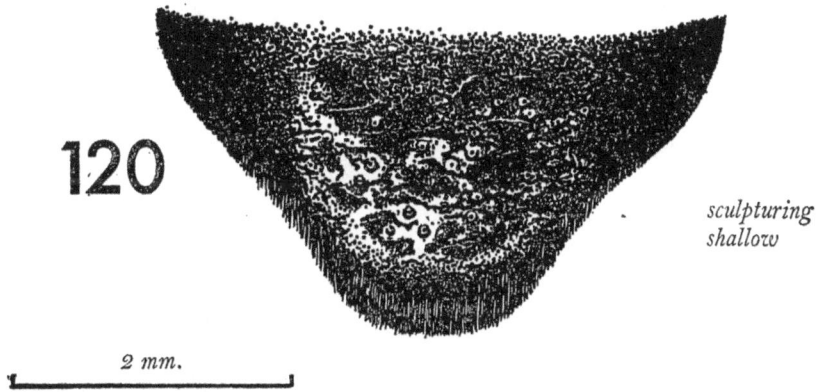

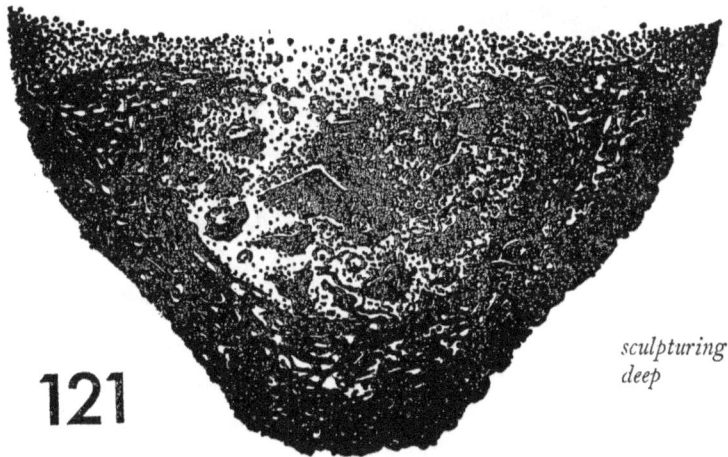

Figs. 120–121. Sixth tergite (T6) of queen. 120, *Bombus hortorum*; 121, *Bombus ruderatus*.

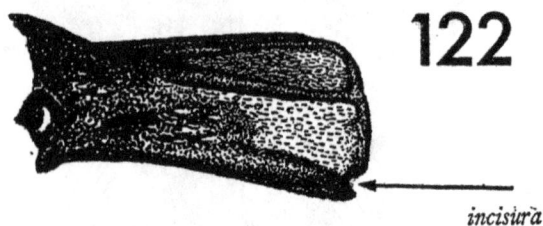

incisura

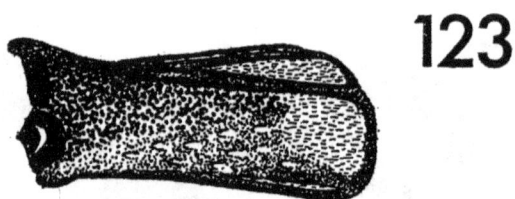

1 mm.

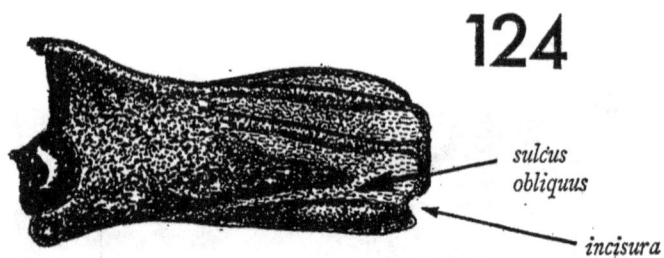

*sulcus
obliquus*

incisura

Figs. 122–124. Right mandible of female. 122, *Bombus jonellus*; 123, *Bombus soroeensis*; 124, *Bombus lucorum.*

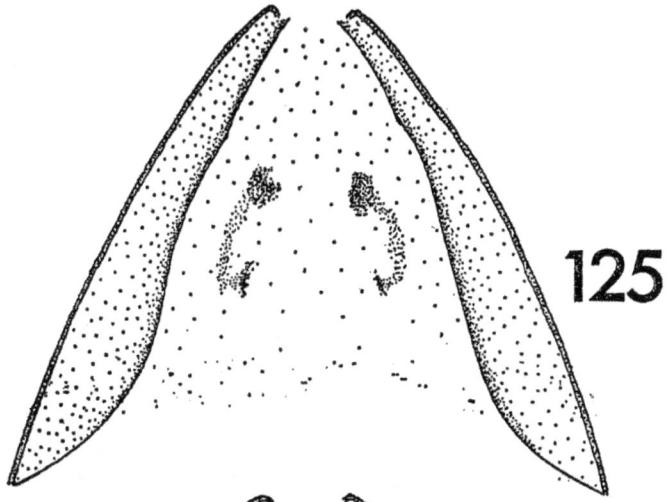

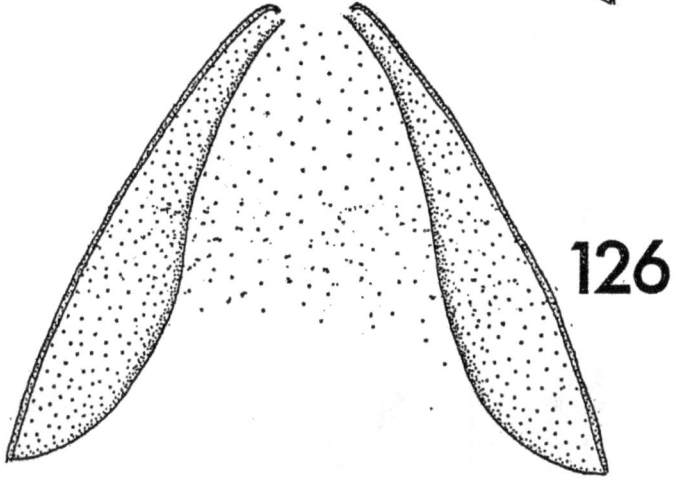

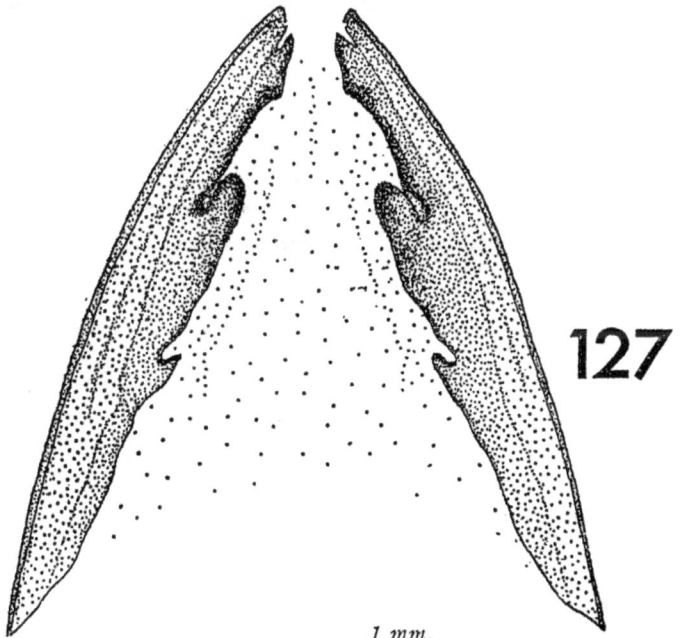

1 mm.

Figs. 125–127. Inner projections of sting sheath. 125, *Bombus jonellus*; 126, *Bombus soroeensis*; 127, *Bombus lucorum*.

128

129

1 mm.

Figs. 128–129. Apex of clypeus of female. 128, *Bombus soroeensis*; 129, *Bombus lucorum*.

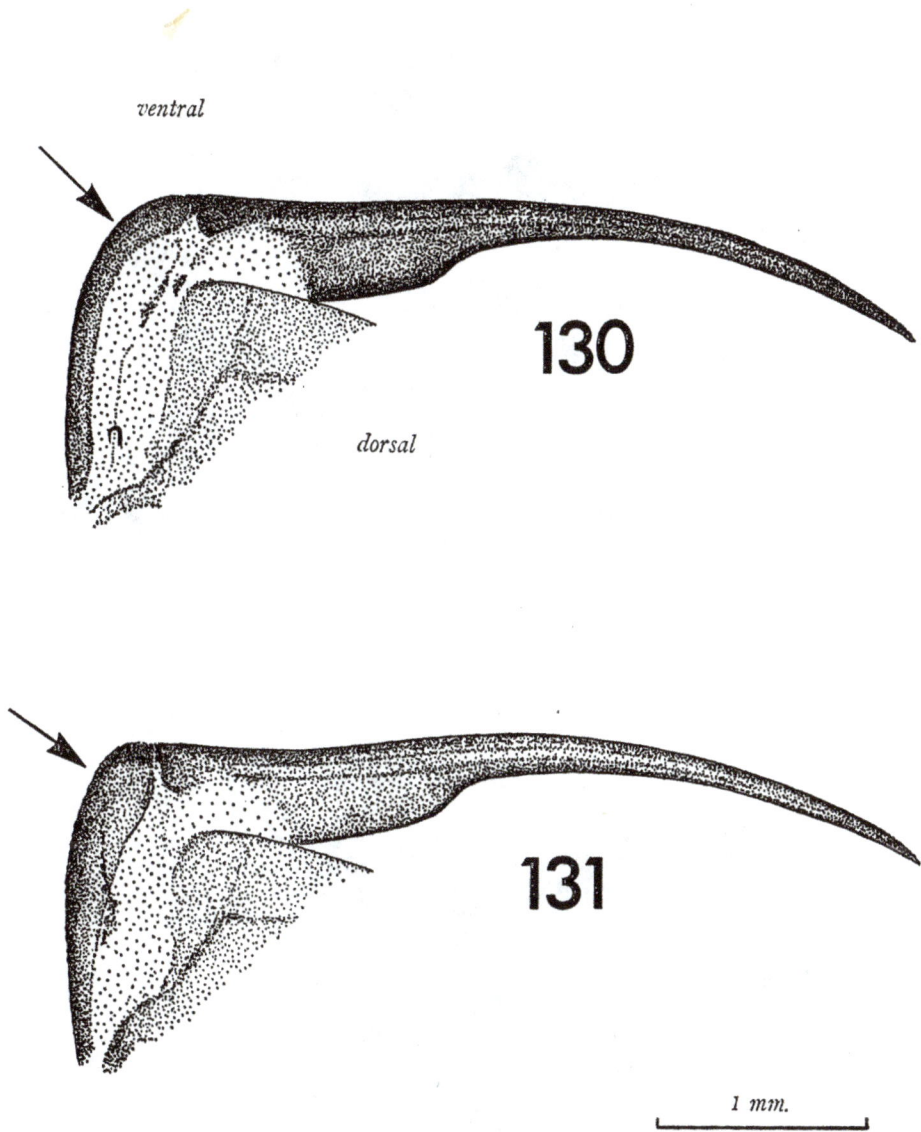

Figs. 130–131. Outer projection (arrowed) of sting sheath. 130, *Bombus terrestris*; 131, *Bombus lucorum*.

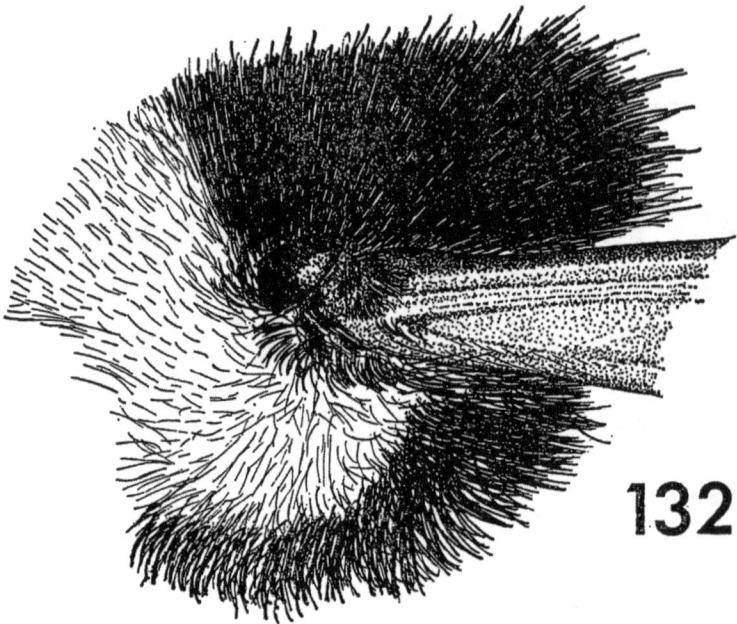

5 mm.

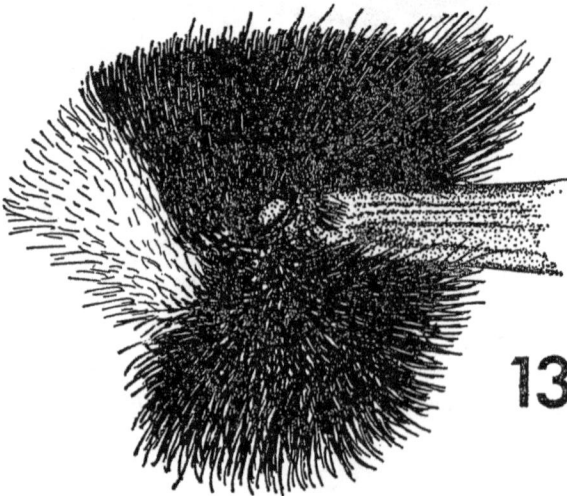

Figs. 132–133. Left lateral aspect of thorax of female. 132, *Bombus magnus*; 133, *Bombus lucorum*.

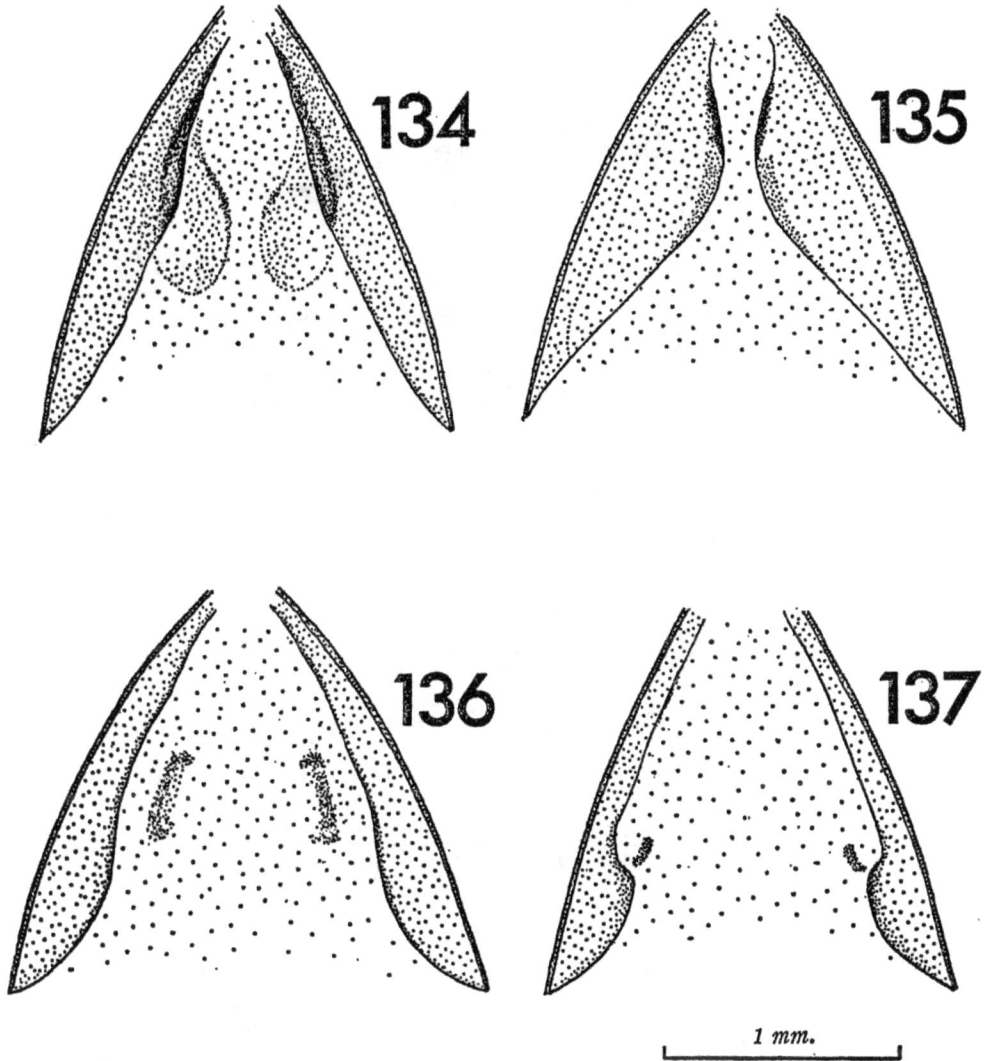

Figs. 134–137. Inner projections of sting sheath. 134, *Bombus lapidarius*; 135, *Bombus ruderarius*; 136, *Bombus pratorum*; 137, *Bombus cullumanus* (after Richards, 1927).

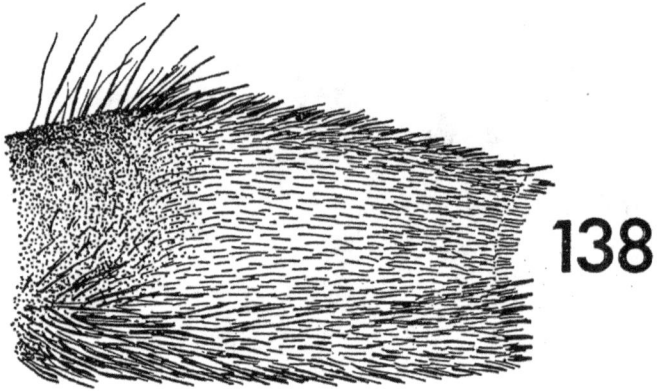

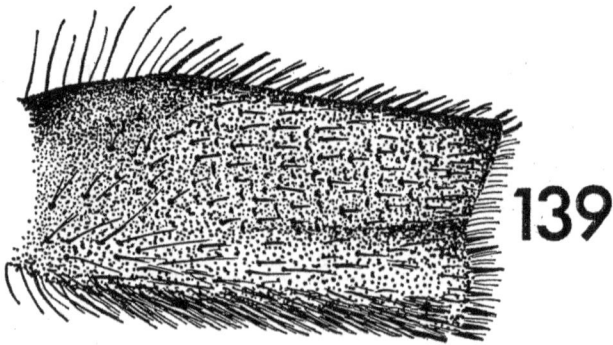

2 mm.

Figs. 138–139. Left hind basitarsus of female. 138, *Bombus lapidarius*; 139, *Bombus cullumanus* (drawn from Spanish specimen, but reference made to British examples).

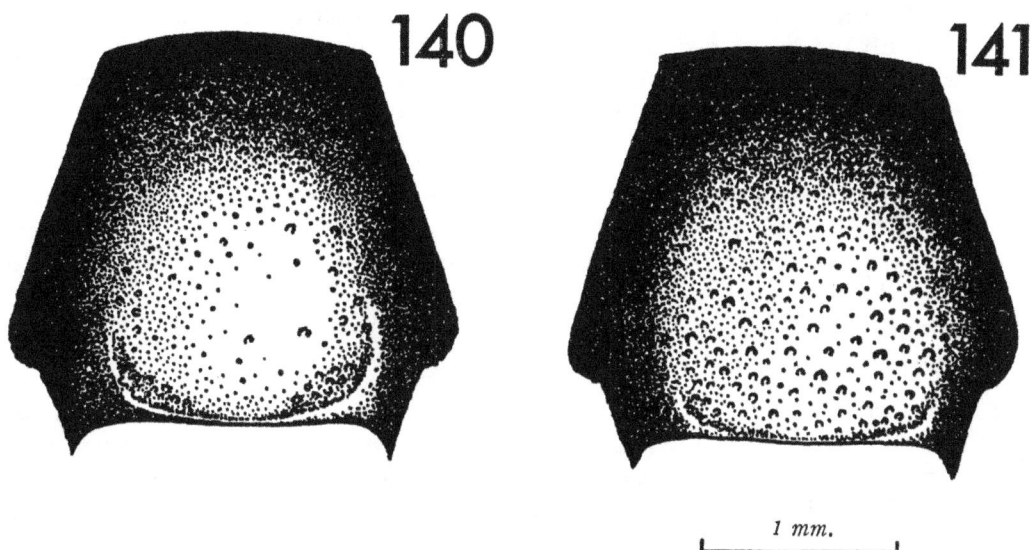

Figs. 140–141. Clypeus of female. 140, *Bombus pratorum*; 141, *Bombus lapponicus*.

C. Key to *Bombus* Males

1. Thorax more or less yellowish, reddish brown or blackish brown above; black hairs, when numerous, never forming an interalar band. Third segment of antenna shorter than fifth. Volsella with apical and preapical tooth, and a rounded process, but the latter not strongly produced (cf. Fig. 167); squama with large inwardly directed spine or lamella; tip of sagitta not inwardly directed 2

— Thorax black, and usually with at least part of both collar and scutellum yellow, greenish yellow or brownish; tail yellowish, brown, white or black, but not pink, orange or red; body may be entirely black. Head more or less elongate; antennae relatively long; abdomen more or less elongate. Volsella simple, apart from hook-like tip; squama with large, curved, inwardly directed and apically toothed lamella, but if not, then sagitta very long and toothed at apex and in mid region, the latter projection tridentate; tip of sagitta not inwardly directed 4

— Thorax black, and usually with collar, or collar and scutellum, yellow or brownish yellow; yellow may be extensive but black hairs always at least present on disc of thorax; tail white, pinkish, yellowish or tawny, but not red (although some red hairs may occur at the sides and base). Head short; antennae relatively short. Squama with at best only small inwardly directed basal spine; tip of sagitta inwardly directed in one species only 7

— Thorax more or less black, or black with collar, or collar and scutellum, yellow

223

or greyish; tail red or orange, but not white, black or brown. Tip of sagitta inwardly directed (several species), but if not then either (two species) volsella with apical and preapical tooth, and a distinct, very strongly produced, rounded process (Fig. 167), or (one species) genitalia as in Fig. 160 10

2. Abdomen, and often thorax, with some black on upperside. Flagellar segments of antennae strongly swollen ventrally, especially at apical end of a segment (Fig. 142). Sagittae serrated, but simple apically (Fig. 144) ..   *pascuorum*
— Abdomen without black on upperside, apart from on last visible tergite (T7).[1] Flagellar segments of antennae less strongly swollen ventrally, swellings symmetrical (Fig. 143). Sagittae hooked apically and not serrated (Figs. 145 and 146)   3

3. Distinct brown band on T2; coat slightly shorter and less dense. Teeth on volsella more elongate, with subapical tooth pointed and bifid; squama with broad lamella; stipes noticeably inwardly directed at apex (Fig. 145) .. *humilis*
— No distinct brown band on T2; coat slight longer and more dense. Teeth on volsella blunt, simple, and less elongate; squama with elongate, pointed lamella; stipes less noticeably inwardly directed at apex (Fig. 146) .. *muscorum*

4. Face very long. Sagitta rod-like (Fig. 147) 5
— Face less elongate. Sagitta toothed apically and in mid region (Fig. 148) .. 6

5. Coat long and uneven; yellow bands on thorax poorly defined, particularly on scutellum; beard on mandible more or less black. Hairs on hind margin of hind tibia longer, and usually continued round apex (Fig. 151)· ..   .. *hortorum*
— Coat shorter and more even; yellow bands on thorax better defined (entirely black specimens occur frequently); beard on mandible orange-red. Hairs on hind margin of hind tibia shorter and not continued round apex (Fig. 152) ..   .. *ruderatus*

6. Abdomen brownish yellow; facial hairs pale; thorax with well defined black interalar band, the collar and scutellum yellowish. Preapical process of sagitta indistinctly tridentate, with projection nearest to apex of sagitta short and blunt (Fig. 149)   ..   .. *distinguendus*
— Abdomen greenish yellow and with at least some black hairs; facial hairs mainly dark; black on thorax more extensive and less well defined, the pale areas greenish yellow. Preapical process of sagitta clearly tridentate, with projection nearest to apex of sagitta long and pointed (Fig. 150) .. *subterraneus*

7. Third segment of antenna shorter than fifth, antennae longer (Fig. 153); hind basitarsus narrowed basally, hairs of hind margin long (Fig. 155). Sagittae terminating in outwardly directed hooks (Fig. 157) ..   ..   .. *soroeensis*
— Third and fifth segments of antenna about equal in length, antennae shorter

[1] T1 and much of T2 are black in *muscorum allenellus* which, like some other races of *muscorum*, has an entirely black underside to both thorax and abdomen; underside of body not black in *pascuorum*.

(Fig. 154); hind basitarsus not so narrowed basally, hairs of hind margin short (Fig. 156). Apices of sagittae not outwardly hooked 8

8. Abdominal T1 and base of T2 yellow; smaller species. Hind tibia with several short hairs on disc (Fig. 105). No inwardly directed spine on squama; sagittae terminating in scythe-like, inwardly directed, hooks (Fig. 158) .. *jonellus*[1]
— Abdominal T1 yellow or black, T2 mostly or entirely yellow; larger species. Hind tibia without hairs on disc (as in Fig. 104). Squama with inwardly directed spine; sagittae not hooked apically (Fig. 159) 9

9. Facial hairs usually black; yellow on thorax and abdomen darker; tail sometimes white, but usually brownish or yellowish, especially basally. Apical hook of volsella broader (Fig. 161) .. .. *terrestris*
— Facial hairs mainly or entirely yellow; yellow on thorax and abdomen paler and often far more widespread; tail white. Apical hook of volsella narrower (Fig. 162) .. .. *lucorum* (includes *magnus*)

10. Abdomen mainly red. Mandibles without a beard; hind tibia convex and hairy, rather *Psithyrus*-like. Genitalia distinct (Fig. 160) *pomorum* (doubtfully British)
— Red on abdomen usually far less extensive. Mandibles with a beard (Fig. 3); hind tibia more or less flat, but if convex then noticeably less hairy on disc than in above species 11

11. Third segment of antenna about equal to or longer than fifth. Apex of volsella emarginate (Figs. 163, 168, 171 and 172) .. .. · .. 12
— Third segment of antenna shorter than fifth. Apex of volsella sharply pointed (Fig. 165 and 166) or blunt (Fig. 164) but not emarginate 14

12. Apex of sagitta sharply pointed inwardly; sagitta without ventral projection; volsella projecting well beyond squama; squama with small, rounded, inwardly directed, basal projection (Fig. 163) .. .. *lapidarius*
— Apex of sagitta hook-like and not so sharply pointed; sagitta with or without ventral projection; volsella hardly projecting beyond squama; squama without basal projection (Fig. 168) 13

13. Red on abdomen restricted to last three or four tergites; T2 usually yellow. Ventral side of sagitta less emarginate basally and usually lacking ventral projection; projection, when present, situated near mid region of sagitta (Fig. 169); apex of volsella less strongly emarginate (Fig. 172) .... .. *pratorum*[2]
— Red on abdomen brighter and extending over last four or five tergites, usually no yellow on anterior tergites. Ventral side of sagitta basally emarginate and with obvious projection near base (Fig. 170); apex of volsella more strongly emarginate (Fig. 171) .. .. *lapponicus*

---

[1] Tail normally white, but some subspecies have a yellowish or tawny tail (see footnote relating to couplet 13).
[2] Parapenial process of stipes shorter and wider than in *jonellus* (cf. Figs. 173 and 174), some subspecies of which have a reddish or tawny, rather than white, tail (see p. 179), and hence resemble *pratorum*.

14. Apex of volsella sharply pointed; apex of sagitta with slightly outwardly directed hook; squama with elongate, inwardly directed projections (Figs. 165 and 166)   15
— Apex of volsella blunter; apical projection of sagitta scythe-like and inwardly directed; inwardly directed projections of squama short (Fig. 164) ..   ..
..   ..   *cullumanus* (very rare)

15. Body greenish grey with black interalar band; T3 and sometimes T4 more or less black, tail orange [the rare var. *nigrescens* is coloured like the following species]. Third segment of antenna slightly longer than fourth. Subapical tooth of volsella broad; squama with long, narrow projection (Fig. 166) .. *sylvarum*
— Body black with orange tail, but frequently the collar, scutellum, and abdominal T1 and T2, are suffused with brownish yellow, or greyish, hairs. Third segment of antenna distinctly longer than fourth. Subapical tooth of volsella narrower; squama with projection broader (Fig. 165) ..   .. *ruderarius*

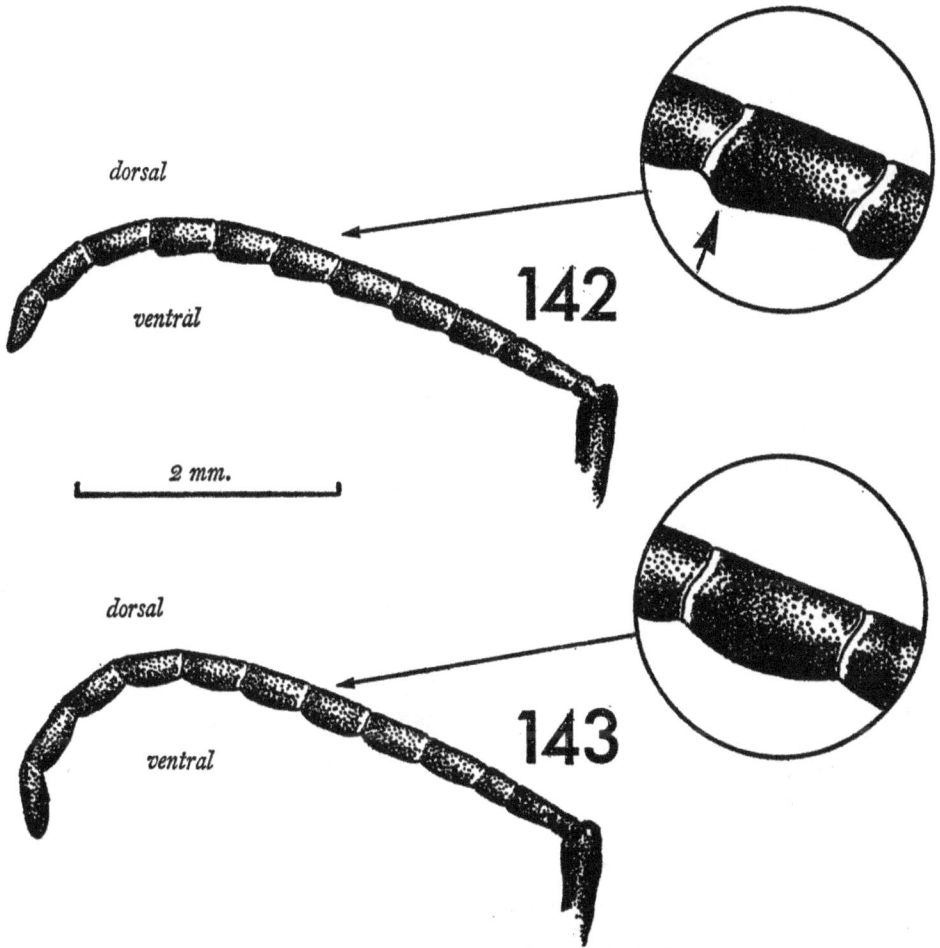

Figs. 142–143. Antenna of male, showing ventral swelling on flagellar segments. 142, *Bombus pascuorum*; 143, *Bombus muscorum*.

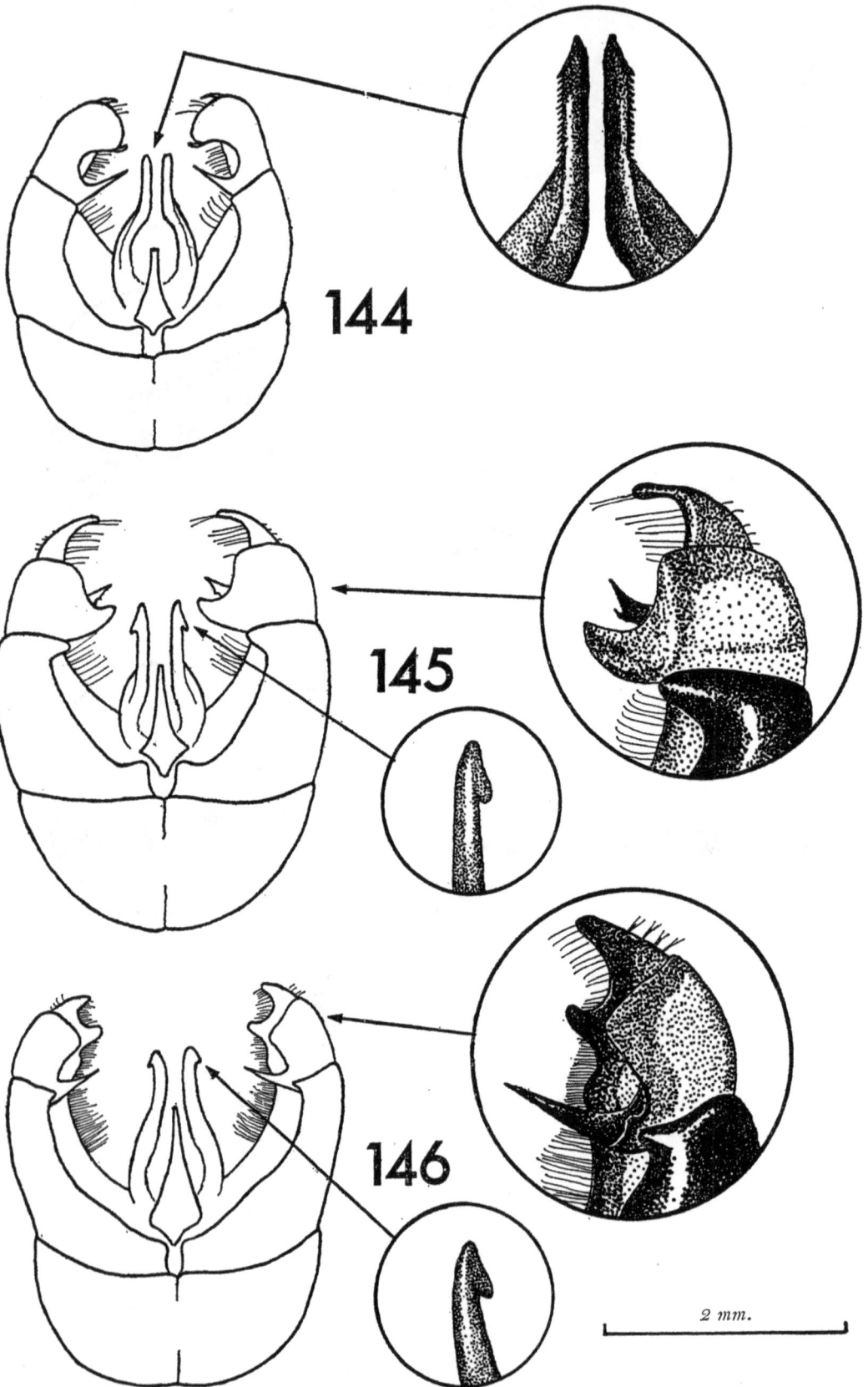

Figs. 144–146. Male genitalia. 144, *Bombus pascuorum*; 145, *Bombus humilis*; 146, *Bombus muscorum*.

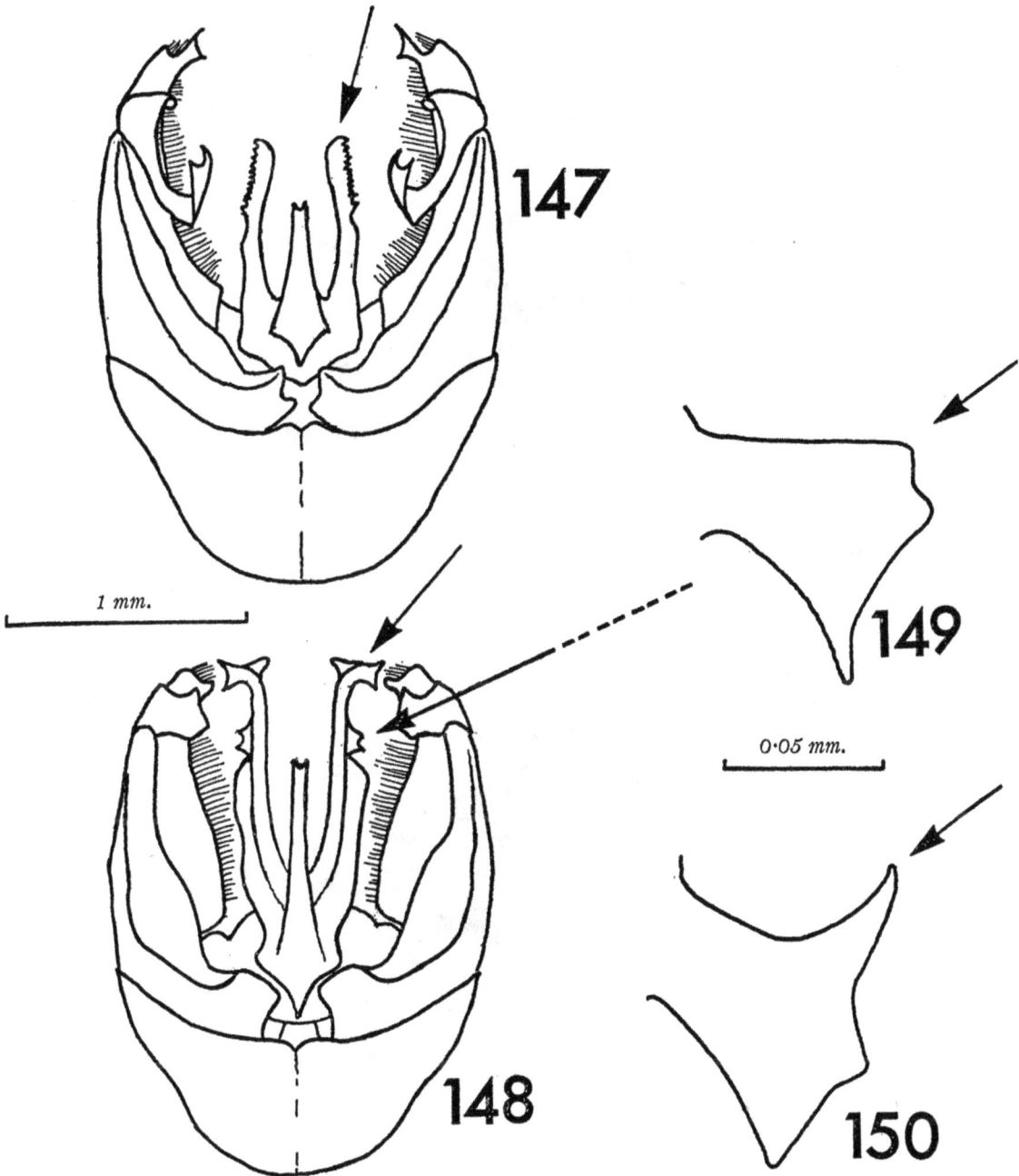

Figs. 147–150. Male genitalia. 147, *Bombus hortorum*; 148, *Bombus distinguendus*; 149, preapical process of sagitta of *Bombus distinguendus*; 150, preapical process of sagitta of *Bombus subterraneus*.

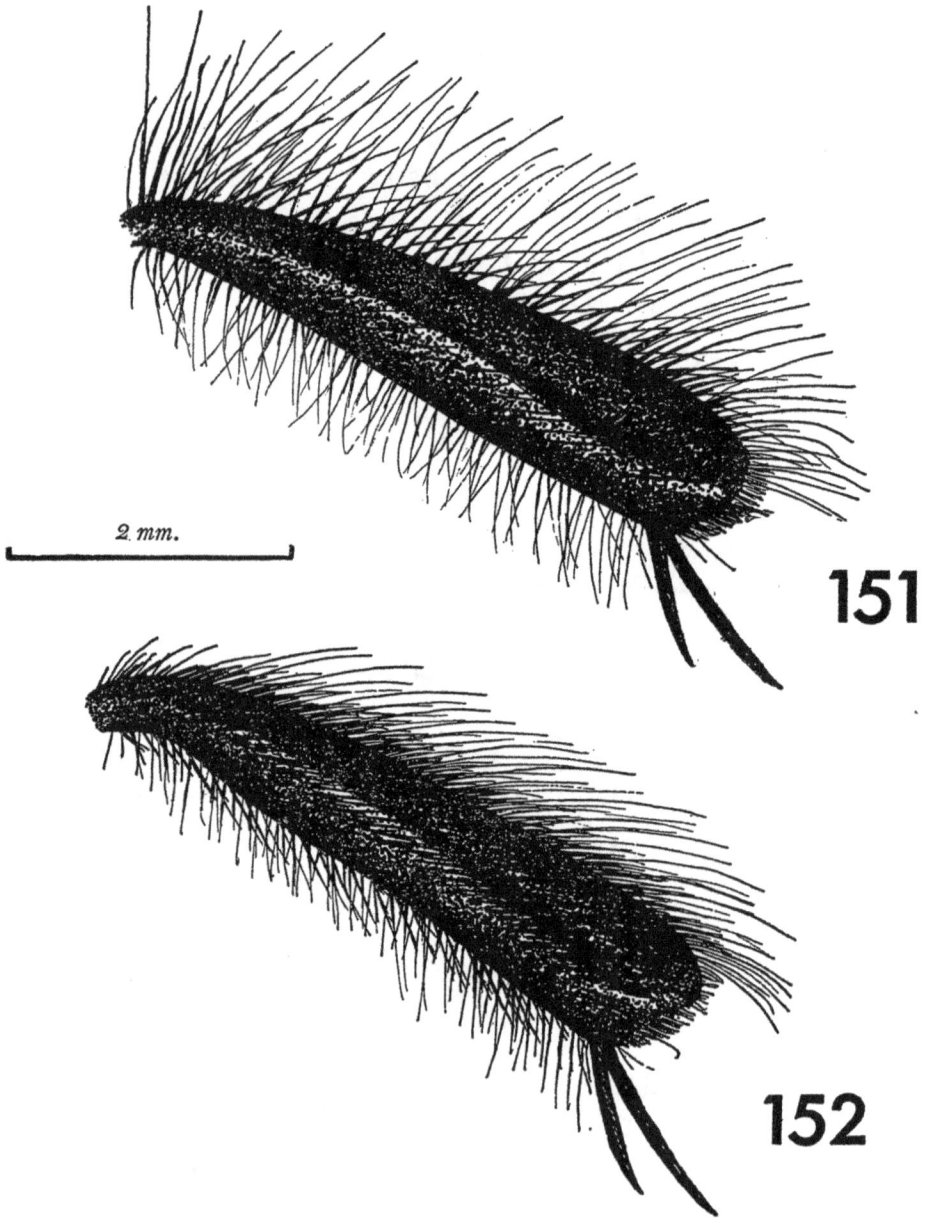

2. mm.

151

152

Figs. 151–152. Anterio-lateral aspect of right hind tibia of male. 151, *Bombus hortorum*; 152, *Bombus ruderatus*.

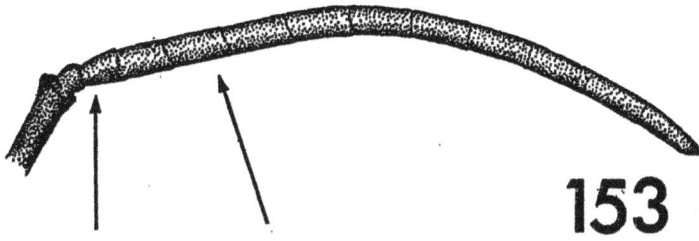

153

3rd   *5th*

2 mm.

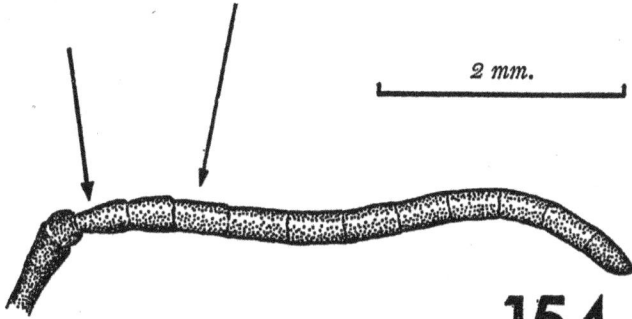

154

Figs. 153–154. Antenna of male. 153, *Bombus soroeensis*; 154, *Bombus lucorum*.

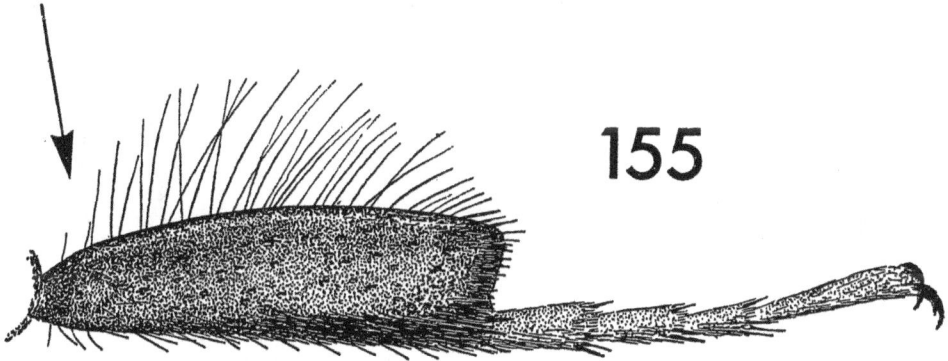

155

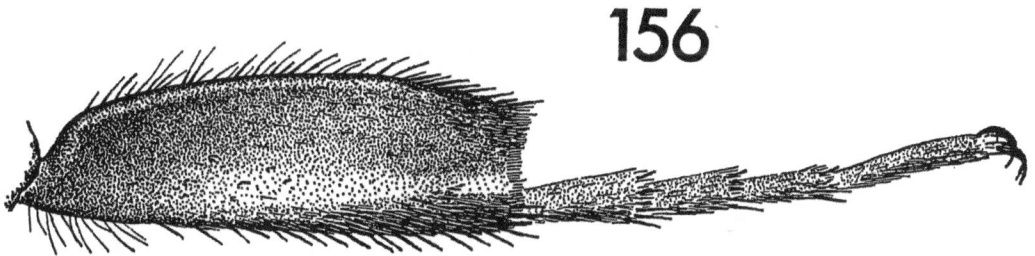

156

2 mm.

Figs. 155–156. Tarsal region of mid leg of male. 155, *Bombus soroeensis*; 156, *Bombus lucorum*.

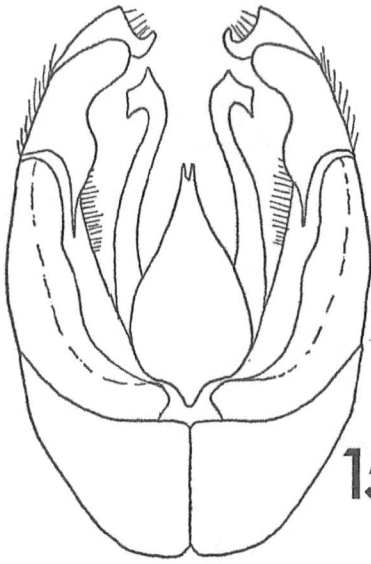
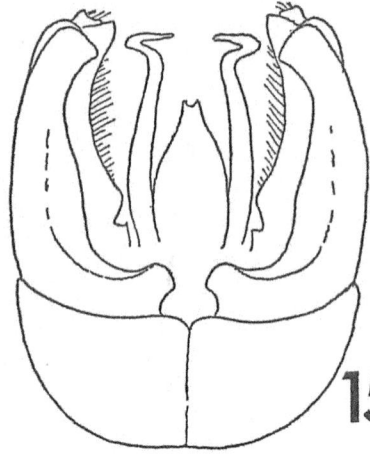
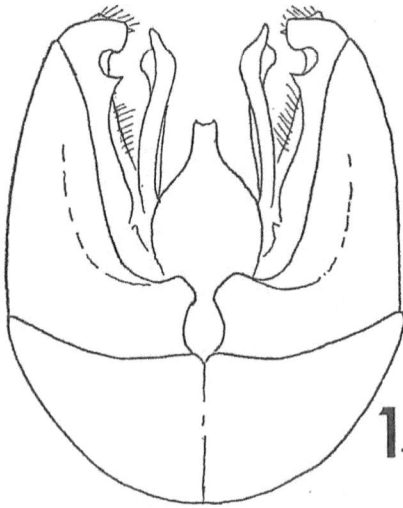
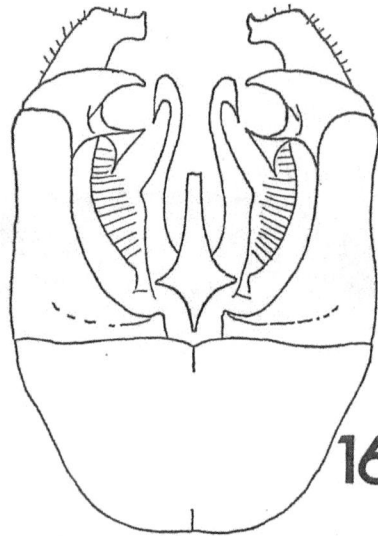

Figs. 157–160. Male genitalia. 157, *Bombus soroeensis*; 158, *Bombus jonellus*; 159, *Bombus terrestris*; 160, *Bombus pomorum* (drawn from Austrian specimen).

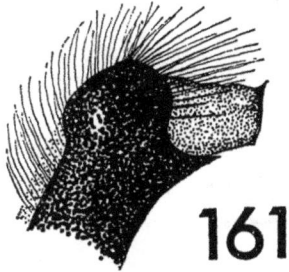

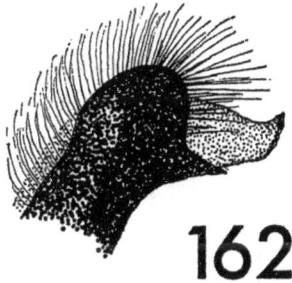

0·5 mm.

Figs. 161–162. Male genitalia; ventral aspect of apex of volsella. 161, *Bombus terrestris*; 162, *Bombus lucorum*.

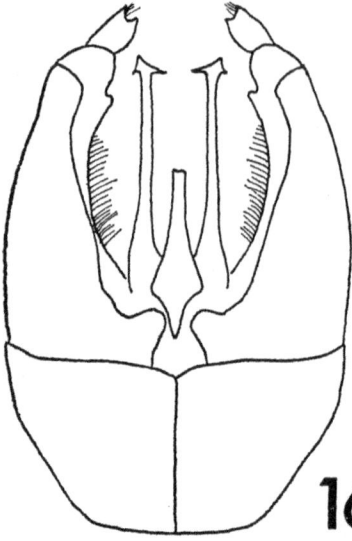

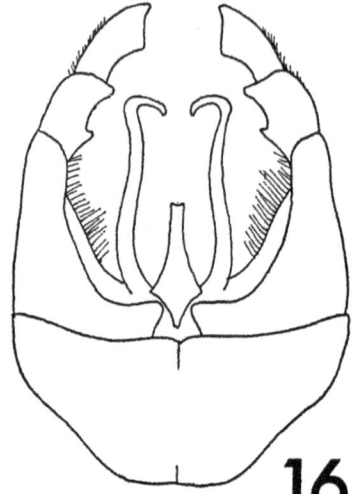

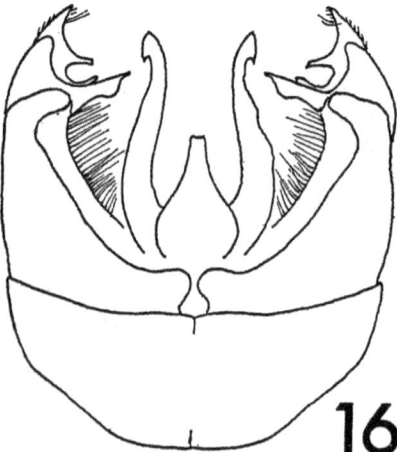

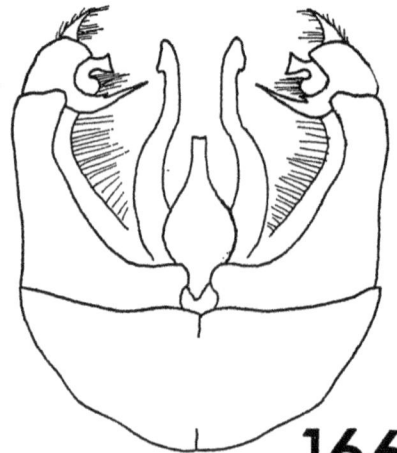

2 mm.

Figs. 163–166. Male genitalia. 163, *Bombus lapidarius*; 164, *Bombus cullumanus*; 165, *Bombus ruderarius*; 166, *Bombus sylvarum*.

Fig. 167. Male genitalia; ventral aspect of volsella of *Bombus sylvarum*.

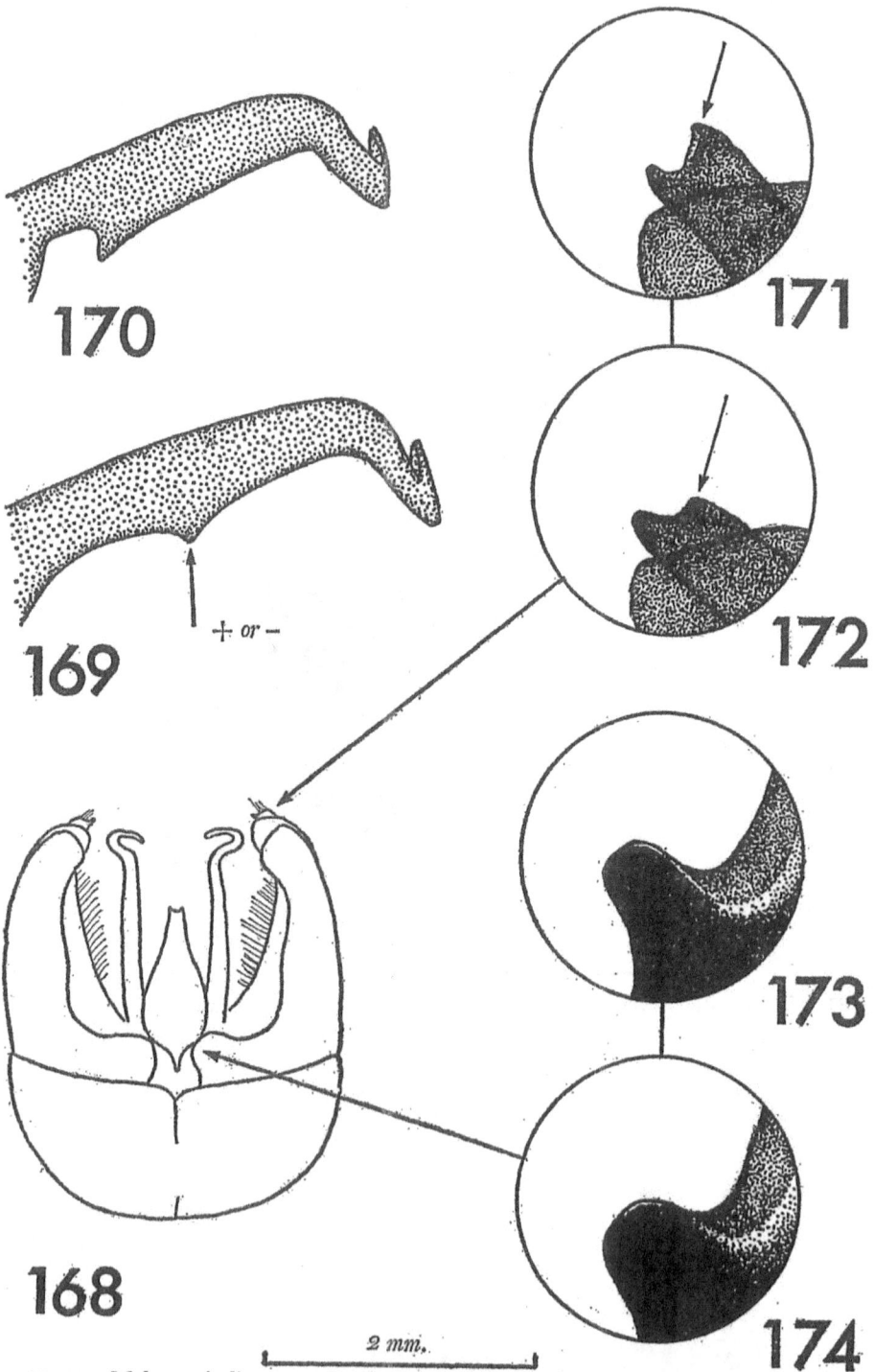

170

169 + or –

171

172

168

173

174

2 mm.

Figs. 168–174. Male genitalia. 168, *Bombus pratorum*; 169, lateral aspect of sagitta of *Bombus pratorum*; 170, lateral aspect of sagitta of *Bombus lapponicus*; 171, apex of volsella of *Bombus lapponicus* (hairs not shown); 172, apex of volsella of *Bombus pratorum* (hairs not shown); 173, parapenial process of stipes of *Bombus jonellus*; 174, parapenial process of stipes of *Bombus pratorum*.

D. Key to *Psithyrus* Females

1. Coat usually black with red tail; wings very dark. Callosities on last visible sternite (St6) large and flange-like (Fig. 175), clearly visible from above .. .. *rupestris*
— Coat differently coloured; wings more hyaline. Callosities not clearly visible from above 2

2. Thorax usually black with yellow collar and scutellum, but rarely may be entirely black, or alternatively, yellow with black hairs limited to disc. Callosities large 3
— Thorax black with yellow collar, scutellum black or brownish. Callosities small 4

3. No white on abdomen; sides of T4 and T5 usually yellow, but may be brownish or black. T6 very shiny with few, but large, punctures (Fig. 181); callosities pointed at apex (Fig. 177) .. .. *campestris*
— Abdominal T4 and T5 usually white. T6 dull, punctate, and with median keel (Fig. 182); callosities forming semi-circle (Fig. 178) .. .. *barbutellus*

4. Abdominal T3 and T4 mainly white; small species. Tip of abdomen pointed and strongly incurved (Fig. 183); callosities poorly developed (Fig 176) .. .. *sylvestris*
— Middle of abdominal T3 black, the sides yellow or yellowish white; usually larger species. Tip of abdomen less pointed and less incurved; callosities ridge-like (Figs. 179 and 180) 5

5. Yellow of thorax and abdomen darker; coat shorter; larger species. T6 more strongly punctured (Fig. 184) and less shiny; callosities end short of apex of segment (Fig. 179) .. .. *vestalis*
— Yellow of thorax and abdomen paler and rapidly fading; coat longer and more uneven; smaller species. T6 shallowly punctured, almost impunctate on disc (Fig. 185), and more shiny; callosities end nearer apex of segment (Fig. 180) .. .. *bohemicus*

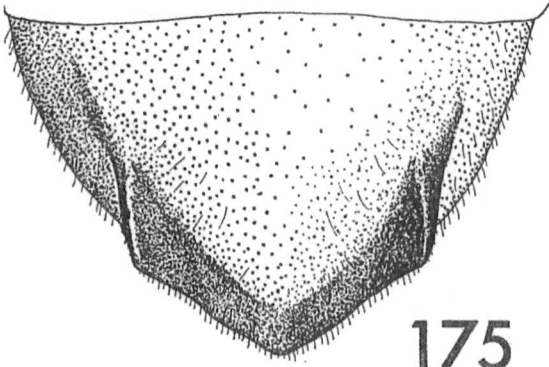 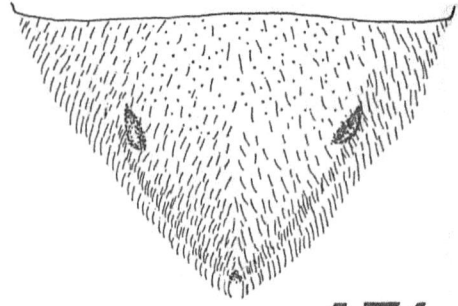

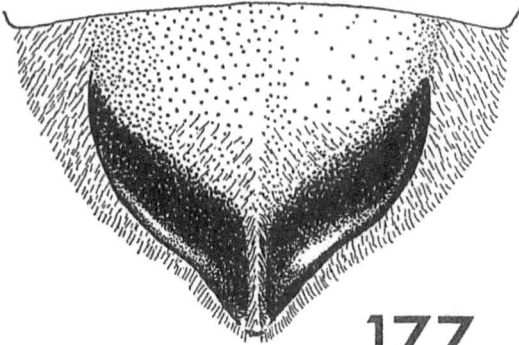 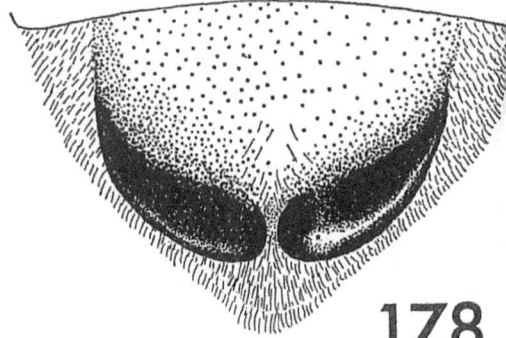

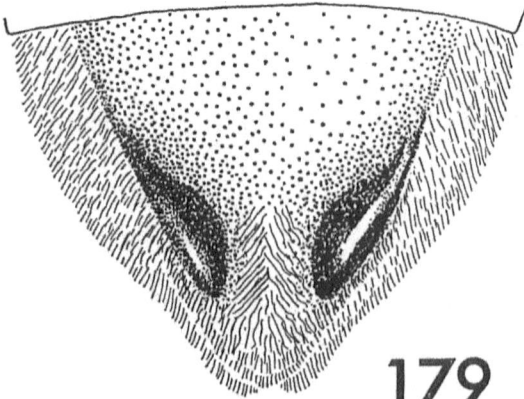 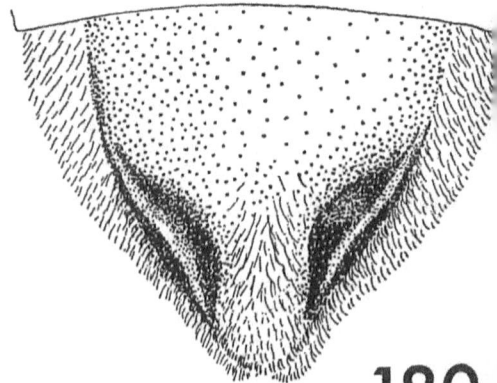

2 mm.

Figs. 175–180. Callosities on sixth sternite (St6) of female. 175, *Psithyrus rupestris*; 176, *Psithyrus sylvestris*; 177, *Psithyrus campestris*; 178, *Psithyrus barbutellus*; 179, *Psithyrus vestalis*; 180, *Psithyrus bohemicus*.

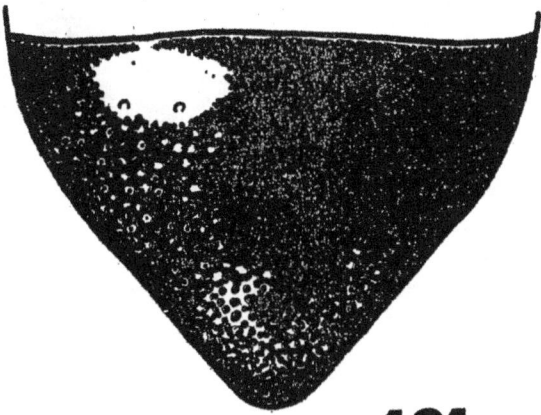
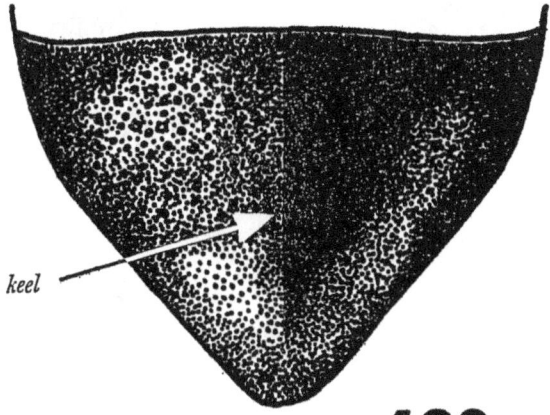

keel

Figs. 181–182. Sixth tergite (T6) of female. 181, *Psithyrus campestris*; 182, *Psithyrus barbutellus*.

Fig. 183. *Psithyrus sylvestris* female; legs not shown.

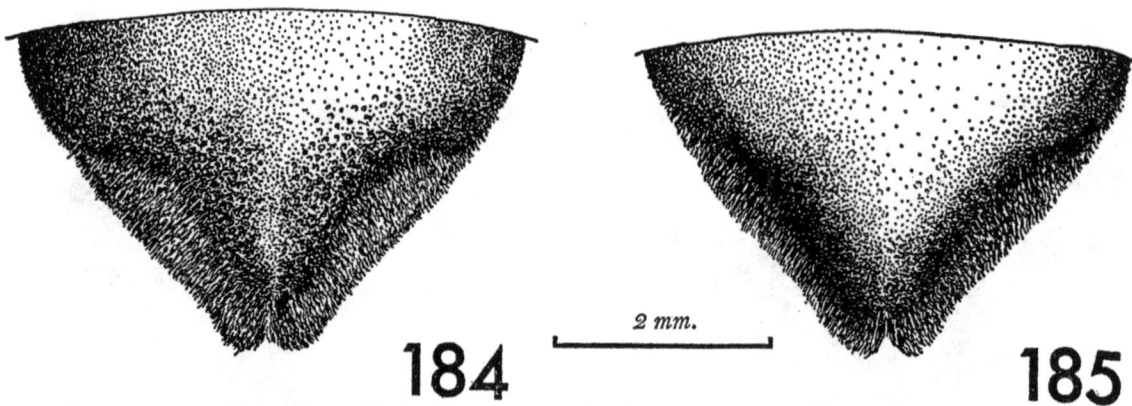

Figs. 184–185. Sixth tergite (T6) of female. 184, *Psithyrus vestalis*; 185, *Psithyrus bohemicus*.

E. Key to *Psithyrus* Males

1. Third segment of antenna shorter than fifth (Fig. 186)   2
— Third and fifth segments of antenna about equal in length (Fig. 187) 4

2. Thorax black, usually with only the collar yellow; T3 with yellow lateral patches, sometimes meeting in mid-line; coat short and even. Inner border of volsella and squama covered in short stiff hairs (Figs. 192 and 194); sagitta not toothed beneath ..   .. *vestalis*
— Thorax black with both collar and scutellum yellow, but may be entirely black or rarely yellow with black hairs limited to disc; T3 black, white or yellowish but lacking lateral patches; coat longer and uneven. Inner border of volsella and squama less hairy; sagitta toothed beneath 3

3. Tail yellow or black. Antennae longer; St6 flat with slight median groove and tuft of black hairs on either side (Fig. 196). Volsella broadly triangular (Fig. 190) ..   .. *campestris*
— Tail white. Antennae shorter; St6 callose towards apex (Fig. 197). Volsella elongate distally (Fig. 191) ..   .. *barbutellus*

4. Abdomen usually with at least the tip red or reddish. Sagitta toothed beneath 5
— No red on abdomen; tail white or yellow. Sagitta not toothed beneath ..   .. *bohemicus*[1]

5. Tail red; coat rather long. Squama strongly produced inwards and bearing a tuft of curled hairs (Fig. 188) ..   .. *rupestris*[2]
— Tail grading from white or yellow, through black, to red at tip. Squama lacking hair tuft and not inwardly pointed (Fig. 189) ..   .. *sylvestris*

[1] Genitalia (Fig. 193) similar to *vestalis* but inner border of volsella and squama less hairy (cf. Figs. 194 and 195). The two species at once distinguished by reference to the antennae (cf. Figs. 186 and 187).
[2] Coat pattern similar to that of males of *Bombus ruderarius*. If genitalia are not visible, the two species are at once distinguished by reference to the antennae (cf. Figs. 198 and 199) and hind basitarsi (cf. Figs. 200 and 201).

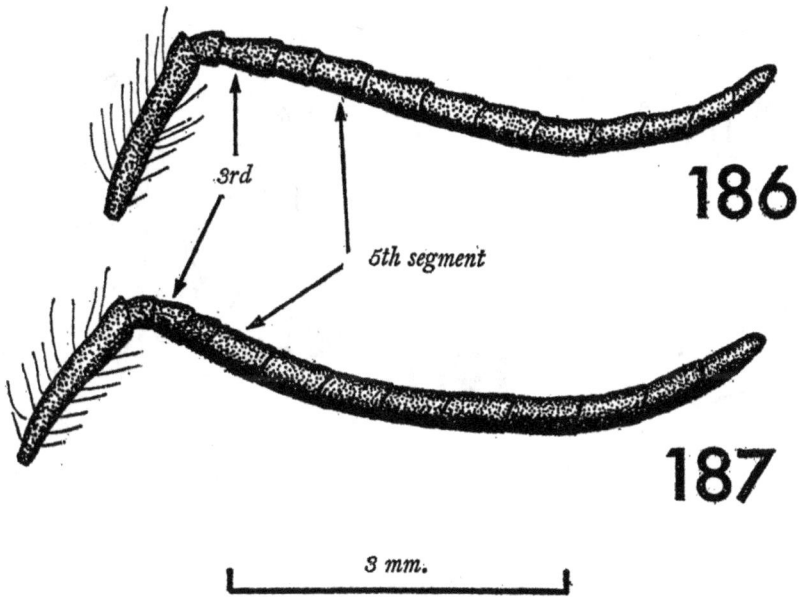

3rd

5th segment

186

187

3 mm.

Figs. 186–187. Antenna of male. 186, *Psithyrus bohemicus*; 187, *Psithyrus vestalis*.

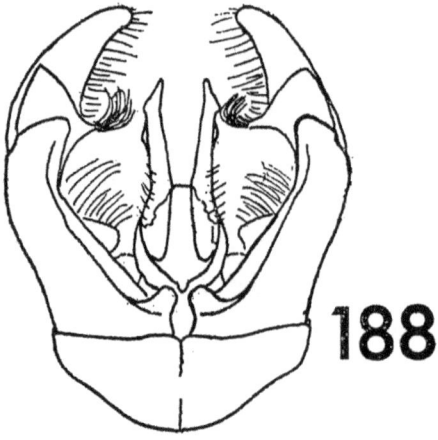

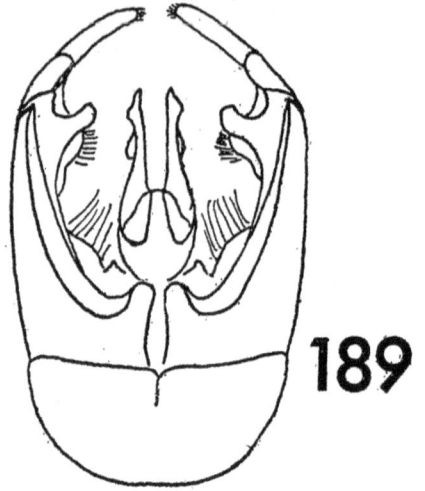

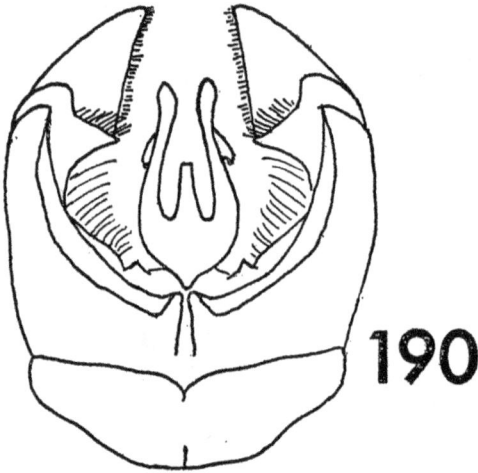

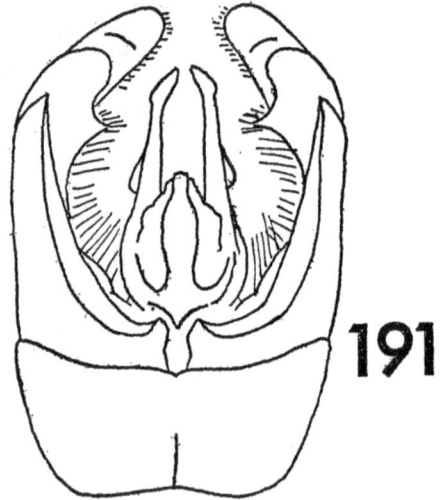

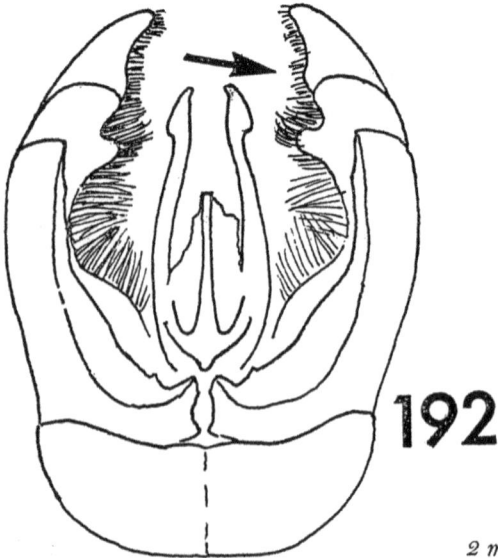

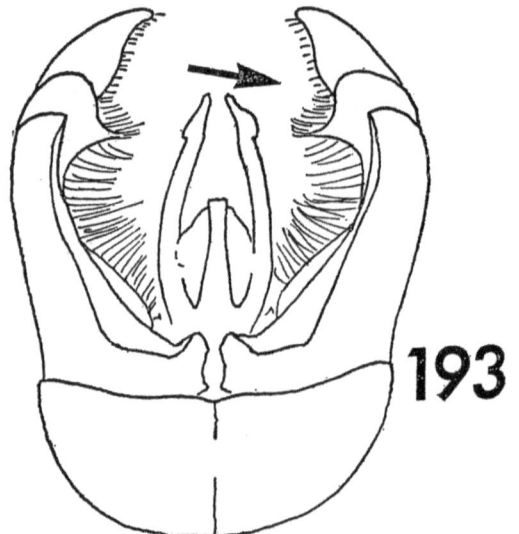

Figs. 188–193. Male genitalia. 188, *Psithyrus rupestris*; 189, *Psithyrus sylvestris*; 190, *Psithyrus campestris*; 191, *Psithyrus barbutellus*; 192, *Psithyrus vestalis*; 193, *Psithyrus bohemicus*.

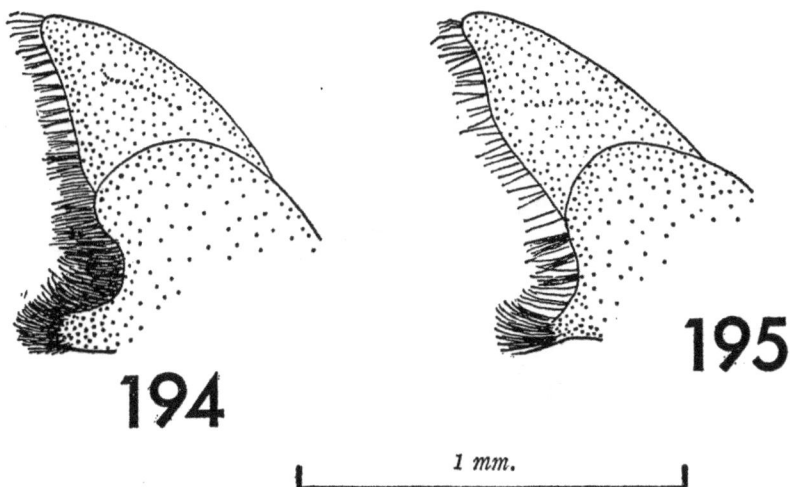

Figs. 194–195. Male genitalia; apex of volsella and squama. 194, *Psithyrus vestalis*; 195, *Psithyrus bohemicus*.

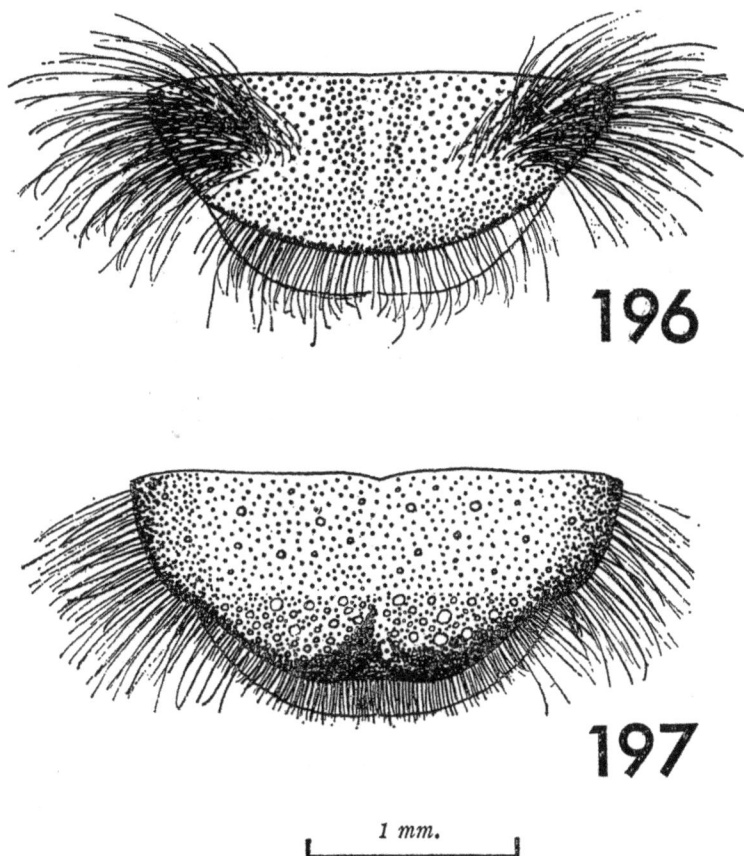

Figs. 196–197. Sixth sternite (St6) of male. 196, *Psithyrus campestris*; 197, *Psithyrus barbutellus*.

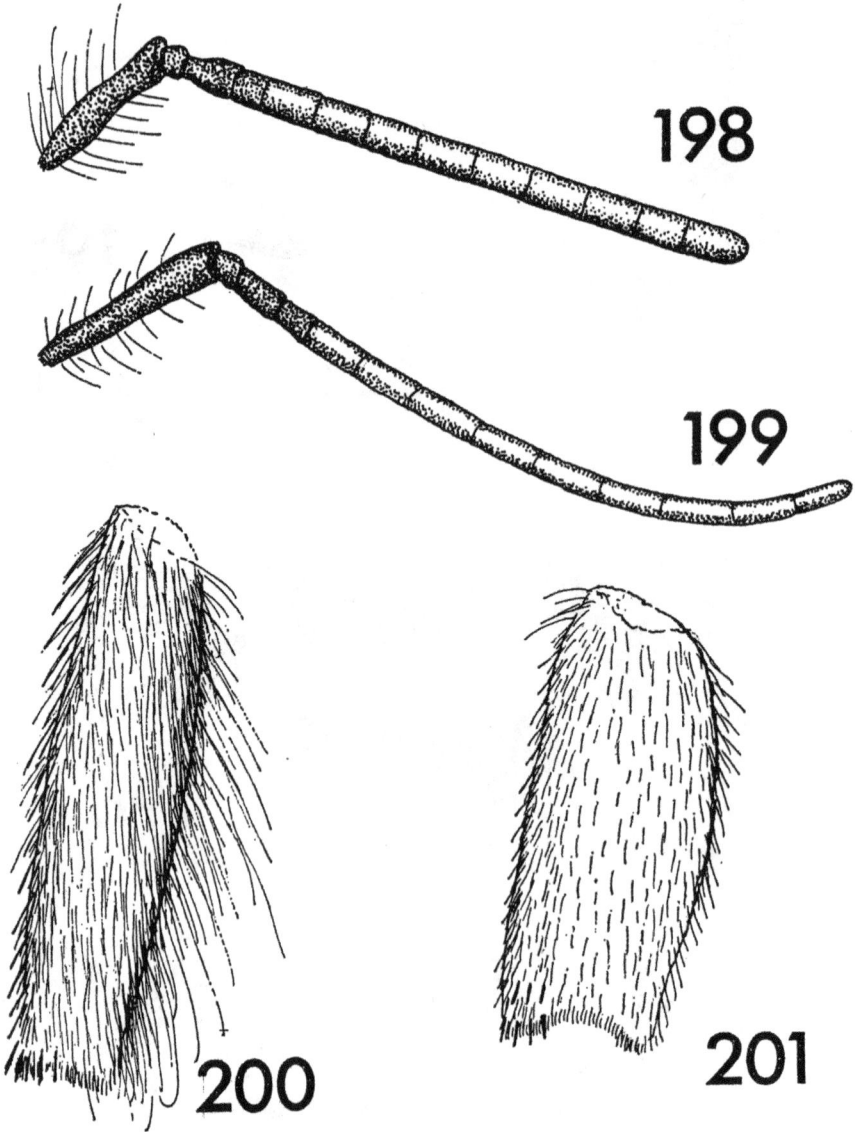

2 mm.

Figs. 198–199. Antenna of male. 198, *Psithyrus rupestris*; 199, *Bombus ruderarius*.

Figs. 200–201. Left hind basitarsus of male. 200, *Psithyrus rupestris*; 201, *Bombus ruderarius*.

CHAPTER 11

History

THE earliest entomological work known to have been published in Great Britain was Thomas Mouffet's *Theatrum Insectorum*. This treatise, written in Latin, was published in 1634, and in 1658 Edward Topsel produced an English translation. This work contained information on bees (including the domesticated honey bee) but although from the descriptions given it is possible to identify some of the wild insects mentioned, species of bumblebee cannot be recognized. In 1710 the classic *Historia Insectorum* by John Ray was published. Ray brought together much information on British bees and his treatment is especially interesting since he arranged them into two generic-like groups, *Apis* and *Bombylius*. In the former Ray included honey bees and solitary bees, while bumblebees were placed under the latter. Solitary bees of the 'modern' genus *Anthophora* were thought by the earliest entomologists to be identical to bumblebees; *Anthophora* species were therefore included by Ray in the *Bombylius* group. It is not possible to positively identify all the species of bumblebee described by Ray, but it is thought that the following were represented: *Bombus hortorum, B. humilis, B. lapidarius, B. pascuorum, B. ruderarius, B. sylvarum, B. terrestris* and *Psithyrus barbutellus*.

The first scientist to adopt a logical system for the naming of animal (and plant) species was the Swedish botanist and zoologist Carl Linné, better known as Linnaeus. His system was standardized in the 10th edition of his book *Systema Naturae* published in 1758 and all true zoological nomenclature dates from that time. Under the Linnean system each species was given a generic name, each genus being a group of species with similar characters and thought to be more closely related to one another than to species included in other genera. This name was followed by a scientific trivial name, the name of the describing author and finally, to establish priority, the date of publication of the original description. To avoid international misunderstanding both generic and scientific trivial names were derived from Greek or Latin. Linnaeus included bumblebees, along with other bees, under the genus *Apis*, and in most early publications our British bumblebees were similarly treated; Ray's *Historia Insectorum* was a notable exception.

During the eighteenth century Linnaeus, and also the Danish entomologist Fabricius, named and described hundreds of different insects, including many bumblebees. Both Linnaeus and Fabricius are recognized today as the original authors for about one half of all the British species of bumblebee.

The first British entomologist to produce readily identifiable colour illustrations of insects was Moses Harris, and in his *Exposition of English Insects* published in

I

1782 he figured a small number of bumblebees. Of these the worker and male of *Bombus lapidarius* are most life-like. In passing, it is worth noting that in his book Harris also included coloured illustrations of *Mutilla europaea* the rare, but well-known, parasite of bumblebees; both the male and female are beautifully portrayed. Another early British entomologist to illustrate bumblebees was Edward Donovan. Three species, *Bombus lapidarius*, *B. muscorum* and *Psithyrus barbutellus*, were included in his *Natural History of British Insects* published between 1792 and 1813. In Vol. 6 (1797) Donovan also included *Mutilla europaea*, having found the parasite 'on a sandy pathway near the entrance of Coombe Wood, Surrey'.

In 1802 the Rev. William Kirby produced his classic *Monographia Apum Angliae*. Kirby recognized sixteen British species of bumblebee and added descriptions of another twenty-one. However, as he anticipated, many of the 'species' are now in synonymy. At present, Kirby is considered as the valid author of three British species of bumblebee, namely, *Bombus cullumanus*, *B. jonellus* and *Psithyrus barbutellus*. Brief details of synonymy for Kirby's species are given below. This information is based on that published by F. Smith and I. H. H. Yarrow, both of whom have examined Kirby's type material. Annotations to the list are mostly based on the findings published by Yarrow.

Synonymy of the Bumblebees described in
Monographia Apum Angliae

Kirby (1802)	Smith (1866)	Yarrow (1968)
74. *Apis muscorum* Linnaeus	= *Bombus senilis* (Fabricius)	= *Bombus muscorum* (auctt. nec Linnaeus)[1]
75. *Apis francillonella* Kirby	= *Bombus muscorum* (Linnaeus)	= *Bombus agrorum* (Fabricius)[2]
76. *Apis floralis* Gmelin	,,	,,
77. *Apis sowerbiana* Kirby	,,	,,
78. *Apis beckwithella* Kirby	,,	,,
79. *Apis curtisella* Kirby	,,	,,
80. *Apis forsterella* Kirby	,,	,,
81. *Apis agrorum* Fabricius[3]	,,	,,
82. *Apis sylvarum* Linnaeus	= *Bombus sylvarum* (Linnaeus)	= *Bombus sylvarum* (Linnaeus)
83. *Apis fragrans* Pallas	= *Bombus fragrans* (Pallas)	= *Bombus distinguendus* Morawitz
84. *Apis latreillella* Kirby	= *Bombus latreillellus* (Kirby)	= *Bombus subterraneus* (Linnaeus)
85. *Apis rossiella* Kirby	= *Apathus campestris* (Panzer)	= *Psithyrus campestris* (Panzer)
86. *Apis leeana* Kirby	,,	,,
87. *Apis francisana* Kirby	,,	,,
88. *Apis campestris* Panzer	,,	,,
89. *Apis lucorum* Linnaeus	= *Bombus lucorum* (Linnaeus)	= *Bombus lucorum* (Linnaeus)
90. *Apis jonella* Kirby	= *Bombus scrimshiranus* (Kirby)	= *Bombus jonellus* (Kirby)
91. *Apis hortorum* Linnaeus	= *Bombus hortorum* (Linnaeus)	= *Bombus hortorum* (Linnaeus)[4]

Kirby (1802)	Smith (1866)	Yarrow (1968)
92. *Apis scrimshirana* Kirby	=*Bombus scrimshiranus* (Kirby)	=*Bombus jonellus* (Kirby)[5]
93. *Apis barbutella* Kirby	=*Apathus barbutellus* (Kirby)	=*Psithyrus barbutellus* (Kirby)
94. *Apis tunstallana* Kirby	=*Bombus subterraneus* (Linnaeus)[6]	=*Bombus ruderatus* (Fabricius)
	[=*Bombus latreillellus* (Linnaeus)	=*Bombus subterraneus* (Linnaeus)][7]
95. *Apis vestalis* Geoffroy	♀[=*Apathus vestalis* (Geoffroy)	=*Psithyrus bohemicus* (Seidl)][8]
	♂ =*Apathus barbutellus* (Kirby)	=*Psithyrus* male[9]
96. *Apis virginalis* Geoffroy	♀ =*Bombus lucorum* (Linnaeus)	Note [10]
	♂ =*Bombus terrestris* (Linnaeus)	=*Bombus terrestris* (Linnaeus)
97. *Apis terrestris* Linnaeus	=*Bombus terrestris* (Linnaeus)	Note [11]
98. *Apis soroensis* Fabricius	=*Bombus subterraneus* (Linnaeus)[6]	=*Bombus ruderatus* (Fabricius)
99. *Apis subinterrupta* Kirby	♀ =*Bombus pratorum* (Linnaeus)	=*Bombus pratorum* (Linnaeus)
	♂ =*Apathus rupestris* (Fabricius)	=*Psithyrus rupestris* (Fabricius)
100. *Apis donovanella* Kirby	♀[=*Bombus cullumanus* (Kirby)	=*Bombus pratorum* (Linnaeus)][12]
	♂ =*Bombus derhamellus* (Kirby)	=*Bombus ruderarius* (Müller)
101. *Apis burrellana* Kirby	=*Bombus pratorum* (Linnaeus)	=*Bombus pratorum* (Linnaeus)
102. *Apis cullumana* Kirby	=*Bombus cullumanus* (Kirby)	=*Bombus cullumanus* (Kirby)
103. *Apis pratorum* Linnaeus	=*Bombus pratorum* (Linnaeus)	=*Bombus pratorum* (Linnaeus)
104. *Apis albinella* Kirby	=*Apathus rupestris* (Fabricius)	=*Psithyrus rupestris* (Fabricius)
105. *Apis derhamella* Kirby	=*Bombus derhamellus* (Kirby)	=*Bombus ruderarius* (Müller)
106. *Apis lapidaria* Linnaeus	=*Bombus lapidarius* (Linnaeus)	=*Bombus lapidarius* (Linnaeus)
107. *Apis raiella* Kirby	[=*Bombus pratorum* (Linnaeus)	=*Bombus ruderarius* (Müller)][13]
108. *Apis rupestris* Fabricius	=*Apathus rupestris* (Fabricius)	=*Psithyrus rupestris* (Fabricius)
109. *Apis subterranea* Linnaeus	=*Apathus campestris* (Panzer)	=*Psithyrus campestris* (Panzer)
110. *Apis harrisella* Kirby	=*Bombus subterraneus* (Linnaeus)[6]	=*Bombus ruderatus* (Fabricius)[14]

Note 1. Kirby's series also includes males of *Bombus pascuorum* (Scopoli) and *B. humilis* Illiger.
    2. Now treated as *B. pascuorum* (Scopoli).
    3. Yarrow questions the British origin of Kirby's single specimen.
    4. Kirby's series also includes *B. ruderatus* (♀ ♂) and *B. jonellus* (☿).
    5. Kirby's series also includes *B. hortorum* (♂) and *B. subterraneus* (♂).
    6. In using *B. subterraneus* for this species Smith was at variance with other authorities.
    7. Kirby's series also includes *B. subterraneus* (♀ ☿ ♂).
    8. In Britain *P. bohemicus* and *P. vestalis* were not generally treated as distinct until 1912 (see p. 252).
    9. Specimen too badly damaged for specific determination, but thought most likely to be *P. sylvestris* (Yarrow, *in litt.*).
  10. Although the male is *B. terrestris*, Kirby's series also includes workers of *B. soroeensis* (Fabricius) and two small workers of either *B. lucorum* or *B. terrestris*.
  11. Kirby's series is a mixture of *B. lucorum*, *B. terrestris* and *B. soroeensis*.
  12. Smith incorrectly assumed that the female of *B. cullumanus* would look like that of *B. pratorum*. This has led to numerous erroneous determinations; the female '*cullumanus*' illustrated in Step (1932), for example, is merely *pratorum*.
  13. Kirby's series also includes a worker of *B. lapidarius*, but no examples of *B. pratorum*.
  14. All are melanic specimens, var. *harrisellus*.

Also in 1802, the Frenchman Latreille separated bumblebees from other bees and placed them in the genus *Bombus* (Greek, βόμβος; Latin, *bombus*; referring to their buzz or hum). The name *Bombus* was adopted by most hymenopterists, but later it was pointed out by Morice and Durrant (1914) that in 1801 the generic name *Bremus* had been proposed for bumblebees by Jurine.[1] American authors (e.g. Frison, 1919; Plath, 1922a, 1922b, 1922c) then rejected *Bombus* in favour of *Bremus*.

[1] *In:* Panzer (1801).

However, the name *Bremus* received little or no support in Britain. Confusion was inevitable, from an international standpoint, and in 1937 the Committee on Generic Nomenclature of the Royal Entomological Society of London concluded that 'In view of the extensive literature associated with the name *Bombus*, we are of the opinion that the adoption of the name *Bremus* would cause more confusion than uniformity'. They recommended its rejection and eventually, following a ruling by the International Commission on Zoological Nomenclature (Hemming, 1939) the name *Bremus* Jurine, 1801 was set aside and *Bombus* Latreille, 1802 was universally adopted.

Kirby was the first entomologist to notice that females of some bumblebees lacked a pollen collecting apparatus on their hind legs, but he did not realize the significance of this important discovery. However, later, following the discovery of the 'parasitic' way of life of these bumblebees, Newman (1834b) separated them from the 'true bumblebees' and placed them in the genus *Apathus* (ά=without; πάθος=sympathy or affection). At about the same time the genus *Psithyrus* (Greek, ψίθυρος; referring to the soft, whispering hum) was erected for these inquilinous species by the French entomologist Lepeletier (1832). For some while there was confusion as to which name had priority, and although *Apathus* was retained by British entomologists for many years it was eventually dropped in favour of *Psithyrus*.

In the first half of the nineteenth century many now classic books on British entomology were published, but apart from Kirby's monograph few devoted much space to bumblebees. However, the works of two entomologists deserve attention. From 1824 to 1839 John Curtis published his superbly illustrated *British Entomology*. Curtis incorporated little information on bumblebees, although he did figure the queen of *Psithyrus rupestris* in Vol. 10 (1833), and in Vol. 12 (1835) he illustrated the yellow (pale) form of a male *Bombus lucorum*, believing this to be *B. ericetorum* (Panzer) and a species new to Britain. This particular specimen had been mentioned previously by Curtis in 1829 when he produced his systematic catalogue entitled *A Guide to the Arrangement of British Insects*. In Vol. 12 of *British Entomology* Curtis also mentioned *Bombus pomorum* and stated that he 'took this handsome species near Dover the middle of August'. No year of capture was given. This is probably the specimen mentioned by Smith (1858), but I have found no reference to this specimen in subsequent catalogues. The *Bombus regelationis* of Curtis presumably related to the male of *B. lapidarius*. A second eminent entomologist claiming an addition to the British list of bumblebees was J. F. Stephens. In a supplement to his *Illustrations of British Entomology* (1827–1835) Stephens described and illustrated a male of *Bombus cognatus* captured on Leigh Down, Bristol; however, as anticipated by Stephens this later proved to be merely an immature example of a previously known species. Concerning this bumblebee, Saunders (1896) later stated 'I have re-examined the type of *cognatus* Steph., which is in the British Museum. The specimen is very immature, the pubescence being exceedingly pale, and the legs testaceous, the nature of the pubescence is uneven and ragged like that of *agrorum*, of which I believe it to be an immature example. F. Smith placed it in the British Museum collection under *muscorum* "immature". It is certainly not the species known on the Continent as *cognatus*.'

The first British examples of *Bombus lapponicus* were captured on the Black Mountain, Brecknockshire (Breconshire) by Edward Newman (1834a). At first it was believed that these specimens represented the female of *Bombus regelationis* (Panzer) (a name at that time applied on the Continent to males of *B. lapidarius*). Newman described his discovery as follows: 'I found fine females of this beautiful bee, which, I believe, has not hitherto been recorded as British, feeding on the blossoms of the whortleberry, on the marshy summit of the Black Mountain. They were in great abundance, but exceedingly difficult to capture owing to the high wind and the rapidity of their flight.'

Another addition to the British list followed shortly after the discovery of *B. lapponicus*, when Mr. A. W. Griesbach took the first known British example of *B. soroeensis* at Westow, Yorkshire (Smith, 1844); this specimen, a male, was described at that time as a new species and named *B. collinus*. Later, at Yarm in Yorkshire, Mr. G. T. Rudd captured the first known British female of *soroeensis* (Smith, 1855).[1] This was considered to be an additional British species, and only later was the synonymy of *collinus* and *soroeensis* appreciated. Incidentally, Yarrow (1968), on examining Kirby's 1802 type material found several previously overlooked females of *soroeensis* mixed in with series of *B. lucorum* and *B. terrestris* (see p. 247).

In the Shetlands, White (1851) discovered 'a Lapland species of Humble-bee, new to the British fauna, which occurs not uncommonly . . . at Lerwick, is still more frequent in . . . Sandlodge opposite Mousa, and seems even more abundant in Unst.' For many years this Shetland bee has been known as *Bombus smithianus* White. *B. smithianus* has sometimes been regarded by authors as a distinct species, but most frequently the name '*smithianus*' has been applied loosely to several dark forms of *muscorum* (see p. 188). It has also been used for 'normal' pale forms of *muscorum*, for example, by Perkins (1890), Sladen (1898) and Evans (1901). Correctly, however, *B. smithianus* White refers to a subspecies of *B. pascuorum* (*B. pascuorum smithianus* White=*B. arcticus* Dahlbom), and this designation has been recently re-established by Løken (1973). For the present, however, *B. muscorum smithianus* must remain in use (as *B. m. smithianus* auctt. nec White) until some of our *muscorum* subspecies, which comprise the '*smithianus*' complex, are re-named.

In 1852 *Bombus nivalis*, already known from abroad, was discovered in the Shetlands, near Lerwick; *nivalis* is now regarded as the subspecies *vogtii* of *B. jonellus* (Richards, 1933).

In 1855 Frederick Smith compiled a *Catalogue of British Hymenoptera in the Collection of the British Museum*.[2] The following bumblebees were included (present nomenclature or status given in parentheses):

---

[1] Earlier use of the name *soroeensis* referred to the species now known as *B. ruderatus*.

[2] '. . . it is not a Catalogue but a Monograph, and as such probably the most useful work which has yet been "printed by order of the Trustees" of the British Museum' (Stainton, 1856).

249

Genus *Bombus*
           muscorum[1] (=*pascuorum*)
           senilis[1] (=*humilis*)
           smithianus (=subspecies of *muscorum*)
           fragrans (=*distinguendus*)
           sylvarum
           lapponicus
           derhamellus (=*ruderarius*)
           pratorum
           nivalis (=subspecies of *jonellus*)
           scrimshiranus (=*jonellus*)
           collinus (=*soroeensis*)
           terrestris
           lucorum
           soroensis (=*soroeensis*)
           lapidarius
           hortorum
           latreillellus (=*subterraneus*)
           subterraneus (=*ruderatus*)
Genus *Apathus* (=*Psithyrus*)
           rupestris
           campestris
           barbutellus
           vestalis

Eleven years later, Smith (1866) published a revision of the British bumblebee species. The species list was identical to that given in the 1855 catalogue, except for the inclusion of *Bombus pomorum* and *B. cullumanus*, and the recognition of his *collinus* and *soroensis* as one and the same species. Shortly before Smith's work, Shuckard (1866) had listed the British species, but he included neither *pomorum* nor *cullumanus*. The omission of *pomorum* is understandable since records of its capture in Britain were confused (see below), but *cullumanus* had then been known as British for many years. The exclusion of *cullumanus* from Smith's 1855 list presumably meant nothing more than its absence at that time from the British Museum collection. Neither author treated Stephens's *cognatus* as a separate species, it being included by Smith under *senilis*.

The details surrounding the capture by Frederick Smith of *Bombus pomorum* in these islands are confused. In June 1864 his son apparently obtained a female on the sand hills at Deal, Kent (Smith, 1865). Smith also mentioned in his 1865 note the capture of three males from the same locality in 1837. Similar details concerning the capture of these specimens are given in his 1866 revision of the British species, but in a later work (Smith, 1876) the date of capture of the males is given as 1863;

---

[1] Both probably included the true *muscorum*.

according to yet another note (Smith, 1858) the year of capture would seem to be 1857![1] Originally the three males were thought by Smith to be 'very highly-coloured examples of the male of *Apathus rupestris*' and in his 1855 catalogue *pomorum* is given (with a mark of doubt) as a variety of *A. rupestris*. That males of *pomorum* bear a superficial resemblance to those of *Psithyrus* (*Apathus*) has been mentioned previously (Chapter 9).

Smith's 1876 *Catalogue of the British bees in the Collection of the British Museum*, a facsimile edition of which appeared in 1891, included twenty British species of *Bombus* and four of *Psithyrus*. All the species mentioned in his 1866 exposition were included plus what is now the true *muscorum* (but given by Smith as *agrorum*). There were a few changes in nomenclature; thus, *fragrans* was replaced by *elegans*, *scrimshiranus* by *jonellus*, *senilis* by *venustus*, and *terrestris* by *virginalis*.

Following the publication of the first edition of Smith's catalogue, the next major work on the British species was produced by Edward Saunders (1884). This paper is particularly interesting as it contains drawings of the male genitalia. Saunders adopted *Psithyrus* Lepeletier as the correct genus for the inquilinous bumblebees, and he established *P. quadricolor* (now *P. sylvestris*) as a British species. In Britain this species had previously been confused with *P. barbutellus*. Saunders only recognized sixteen British species of *Bombus*, his 1884 list differing from Smith's in that *cognatus* was used to include *venustus* and, presumably, what is now *muscorum*. In addition, Saunders used *hortorum* to include both the *hortorum* and *subterraneus* of Smith, *terrestris* for *lucorum* and *virginalis*, and *latreillellus* for *latreillellus* and *elegans*. Saunders was doubtful of the validity of retaining *nivalis* as a distinct species, but did not make any alteration. Later, however, in his book on aculeate Hymenoptera (Saunders, 1896), he referred to *nivalis* as a variety of *jonellus*. In other respects bumblebee species in this work were as given in the 1884 paper, except that the name *agrorum* was used in place of his earlier *muscorum*, and *venustus* replaced *cognatus*. Synonymy for this grouping, according to Saunders (1896), is given below:

venustus, Smith (*cognatus*, Saund. nec Steph., *variabilis*, Schmied., *muscorum*, Kirb., *senilis*, Smith)

agrorum, Fab. (*muscorum*, Smith, Saund., *cognatus*, Steph., *floralis*, Kirb., *Beckwithellus*, Kirb., *Francillonellus*, Kirb., *Forsterellus*, Kirb., *Sowerbianus*, Kirb., *Curtisellus*, Kirb., *agrorum*, Kirb., *agrorum*, Smith)

Saunders included two distinct species (now known as *humilis* and *muscorum*) in his *venustus*.

The next to consider the taxonomy and systematics of bumblebees in this country was F. W. L. Sladen and in his much sought after book *The Humble-bee*, published in 1912, he included taxonomic details of each species and supplemented these with super bphotographic colour plates. Sladen recognized seventeen species of *Bombus* [*lapidarius*, *terrestris*, *lucorum*, *soroensis*, *pratorum*, *jonellus*, *lapponicus*, *cullumanus*,

---

[1] Perkins (1917) found Smith's female *pomorum* unlabelled but a male clearly marked 'July 1857'; he also concluded, 'That the males were not caught in 1837 is certain as the pins used are of much later date.'

ruderatus, hortorum, latreillellus (now *subterraneus*), *distinguendus, derhamellus* (now *ruderarius*), *sylvarum, agrorum* (now *pascuorum*), *helferanus* (now *humilis*) and *muscorum*]. He excluded both *smithianus*, which he treated as a subspecies of *muscorum*, and *pomorum*, which he considered of doubtful British status. Sladen separated *Psithyrus distinctus* (now *P. bohemicus*) from *P. vestalis*, thus establishing a new British species and increasing the number of known British *Psithyri* to six. In addition, Sladen gave each species of *Bombus* a 'common' English name. However, English names for bumblebees, although appearing in one form or another in several works, both before and after 1912, have never had a common usage; since their adoption can only lead to confusion and would have only a limited, parochial value I neither perpetuate not advocate their use here.

Apart from minor nomenclatorial changes little alteration to the British list of bumblebees has taken place on the species level since Sladen's book was published.[1] The only addition concerns the recognition of *Bombus magnus* as separate from *B. lucorum*. Originally, Vogt (1911) used the name *magnus* for large specimens of *lucorum* occurring in the Orkney Islands and north of Scotland, but as previously mentioned, Krüger (1954) has since treated *magnus* as a distinct species. The true status of *magnus*, however, has yet to be established.

This century, several previously unrecorded races of British bumblebee have been found and described. A striking example was the discovery by C. W. Allen of a remarkable black and brown form of *Bombus muscorum* on the Aran Islands; this race was subsequently named *allenellus* (Stelfox, 1933b). Mention must also be made of the yellow race of *Psithyrus campestris* discovered in Scotland and named *swynnertoni* by Richards (1936).

One final event worthy of note was the capture by Richards (1926) of the first British females of *Bombus cullumanus*. Richards found a worker in 1924 and two years later obtained a queen. Prior to this, all British records of *cullumanus* had related entirely to males, although a small number of females were subsequently found in existing collections (see Yarrow, 1954). *B. pomorum* aside, *cullumanus* is by far our rarest species, and although a relative spate of males was noted by Mr. Holland in Berkshire during 1916 (Burtt, 1923), and some forty males were obtained by Messrs Nevinson at Seaford, Sussex in 1923 (Nevinson, 1923), no British specimens have been taken now for almost half a century.

As indicated above, nomenclature for several of our species of bumblebee is extremely confused, although with care it is generally (but by no means always!) possible to recognize the species to which a particular author refers; Saunders's 1884 description of *muscorum*, for example, clearly relates to the species now known as *pascuorum*. Unfortunately, however, for one reason or another some of the names at present in use are considered unsuitable and further changes at both the specific and subspecific level will have to be made (Yarrow, *in litt.*).

[1] The recent discoveries of *Bombus lapponicus* and *B. pratorum* in Ireland have already been mentioned (Chapter 9).

TECHNIQUES

CHAPTER 12

Collection and Domestication

Collecting Bumblebees

FOR any serious study of bumblebees it is usually necessary to identify the various species encountered, and for such purposes a small 'type' collection is often invaluable. Zoogeographical and taxonomic studies, for example, may well call for larger scale collecting, but the mere accumulation of specimens should never be considered an end in itself.

Bumblebees of one species or another are generally active from March to September, but they are most numerous during the summer months. They are easily collected from flowers, and may also be found at their nests and elsewhere.[1] Many entomologists capture bees with the aid of a net, but my own preference is for small, wide-mouthed, polystyrene tubes, 60 by 40 mm. With practice these may be placed over a feeding bumblebee and then sealed with the lid. A large muslin-covered hole (or several small uncovered holes) in the lid will reduce the likelihood of condensation but it is not necessary if specimens are only kept in the tubes for short periods. Except for the largest specimens, I have also used 75 by 25 mm. (3 by 1 inch) glass tubes with almost unerring success, but their disadvantage is one of reduced safety (and longevity) as they tend to break. Larger containers, such as honey jars, sometimes reduce the chances of error, but they are cumbersome and bulky in the rucksack or pocket. Tubed specimens should be kept cool and preferably placed in the dark; they must never be exposed to direct sunlight. Bumblebees may also be collected in, or transferred to, glass-bottomed entomological pillboxes; these have the advantage of preventing condensation. Flowers or other plant material should not be included in collecting boxes or tubes as these are a potential source of unwanted moisture.

Active bumblebees can be immobilized by placing them for a short period in a refrigerator at a temperature of about 4°C. (the normal main compartment working temperature of a domestic refrigerator); they usually recover fully when returned to room temperature, but although queens are relatively tolerant of low temperatures males and workers will often be killed, particularly if treatment is prolonged for more than a few hours. Bees are particularly susceptible to cold if their food reserves are low; in such cases death can result within an hour or so. With care, it is

---

[1] Bumblebees are sometimes caught in pit-fall, suction or scented traps (e.g. Fye, 1966; Hamilton, *et al.*, 1970) and they are occasionally attracted to insect light traps (e.g. Frost, 1973). However, such traps are of little or no practical use for collecting bumblebees.

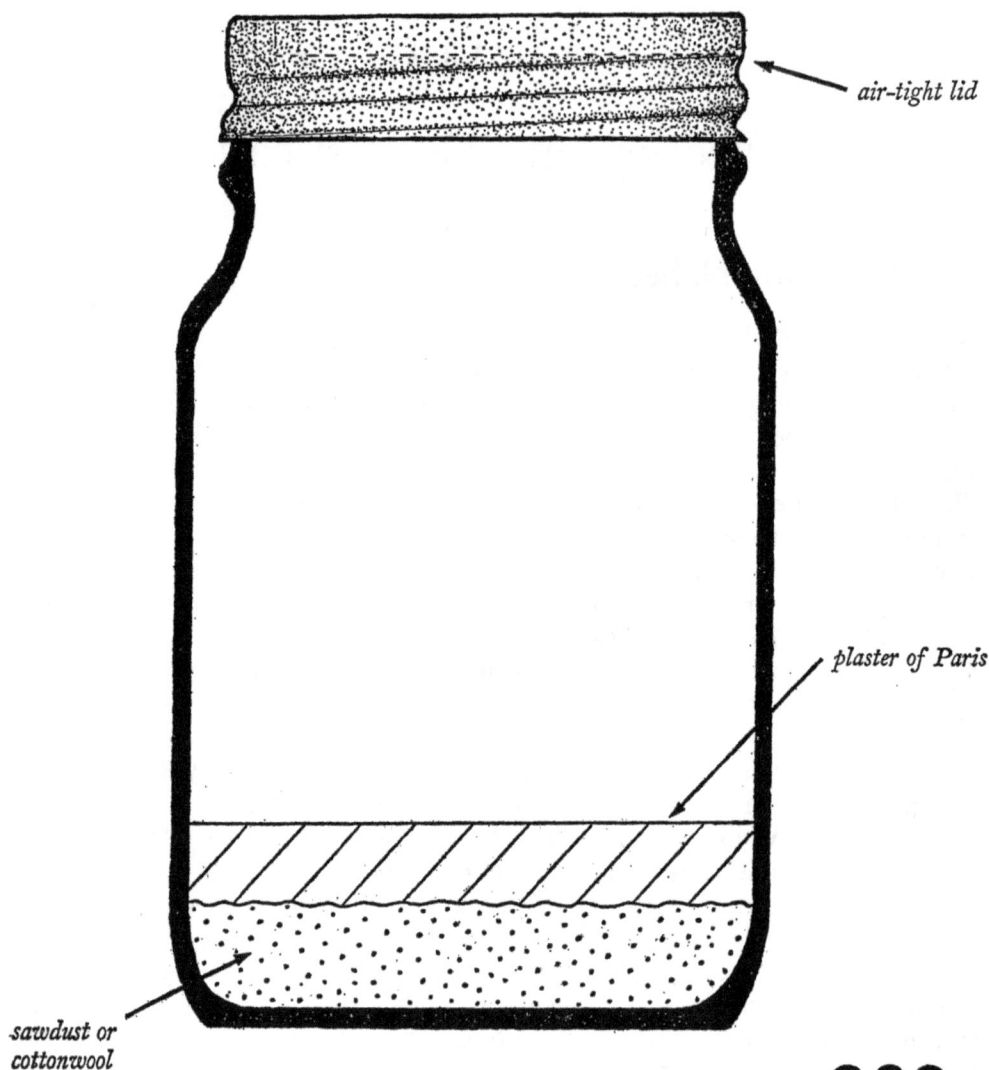

air-tight lid

plaster of Paris

sawdust or
cottonwool

202

Fig. 202. Killing bottle.

possible to immobilize bumblebees temporarily with carbon dioxide or nitrous oxide gas, and by exposing them to sublethal doses of chloroform or other anaesthetics.[1]

Bumblebees may be killed with small quantities of ethyl acetate, using a glass-stoppered or corked jar as a killing bottle, the killing fluid being placed on a small

---

[1] Kendall & Wiltshire (1973) have recently described how small CO_2 cork removers (bottle openers) can be used for anaesthetizing or killing insects in the field. These CO_2 'Sparklets' are ideal for temporarily immobilizing bumblebees in small specimen tubes, and may be used many times before the gas from one bulb is exhausted.

wad of cotton wool held at the top of the bottle by the lid. Specimens in glass collecting tubes may be killed in the same way, but it should be remembered that ethyl acetate dissolves polystyrene. Alternatively, a more permanent killing bottle can be made up, using a wide-necked glass jar (capacity about 500 cc.) fitted with an airtight lid. Fill the bottle with clean sawdust or cotton-wool to a depth of about 20 mm. and pour on a 10 to 15 mm.-thick layer of plaster of Paris (Fig. 202). Poke a few small holes through the plaster before this hardens, and when the bottle has completely dried out it may be charged by adding a quantity of killing fluid. Whether specimens are being killed in small containers or a killing bottle they must on all accounts be kept dry. Ethyl acetate has the considerable advantage of keeping specimens soft and flexible for many hours after death, enabling various parts of the body such as mouthparts, legs and genitalia to be manipulated or set in the required

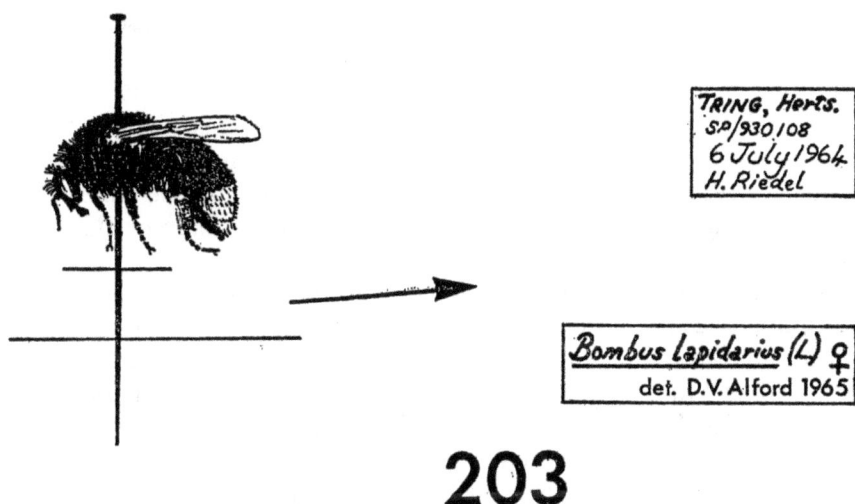

Fig. 203. Method of pinning and labelling bumblebee.

position before storage. Several killing agents (including chloroform and carbon tetrachloride) will rapidly harden specimens and are, therefore, far less suitable.

Bumblebees should be pinned through the mesothorax as soon as they are removed from the killing bottle. Black entomological pins are most suitable for bumblebees but the size used is largely a matter of personal choice. However, they should be neither too short nor too fine. Suitable grades are the Continental style No. 5 (38 mm.) and the thicker and shorter English style No. 12 (30 mm.); several others are no longer available. Bumblebees should be placed well up the pin, allowing about 8 mm. of shaft exposed at the top for adequate handling of the specimen (Fig. 203). It is preferable to use curved entomological forceps for moving pinned specimens.

Apart from the general neatness of appearance, and for display purposes (e.g. Plates 9 to 16), there are few advantages in setting bumblebees with their wings spread and legs symmetrically arranged, in the way that the lepidopterist arranges his butterflies and moths. It is far more important to ensure that essential structural features (e.g. mandibles, antennae, genitalia and, where necessary, sting) are adequately exposed to view, thus enabling each specimen to be properly examined under the lens or low-power microscope. The genital capsule or armature of recently killed males may be extruded from the tip of the abdomen with fine forceps or a needle and drooped downwards so that on drying its essential features will be clearly visible (Fig. 204). Similarly, the sting of a *Bombus* female (unnecessary in the case of *Psithyrus*) may be withdrawn fully from the sting chamber with a pair of forceps and should then be pitched over the dorsal side of the abdomen so that the sting sheath forms an inverted 'V', visible when the specimen is viewed more or less end on (Fig. 205). Care should be taken to ensure that a displayed armature or sting does not hide essential features of the last visible body segment. Older, hardened specimens must be relaxed before their genitalia or stings can be exposed, by placing them overnight (longer, if necessary) in a moist atmosphere. A tin or rigid plastic sandwich-box makes a suitable relaxing box. This should contain a thin layer of firm absorbent material, such as plastic foam, capable of firmly gripping a pin and to which specimens to be relaxed may be pinned. The relaxing tin is charged by moistening the foam with water to which a few drops of phenol have been added to prevent the formation of mould. Care must be taken to prevent insects from coming into direct contact with water in the foam or that condensing out on the sides or lid of the relaxing box.

All specimens collected should be adequately labelled (Fig. 203). One label should state the date and place of capture and, optionally, the name of the collector. Details of locality are essential but very often they are insufficient or too parochial to enable specimens to be reliably placed by anyone other than the original captor. A specimen labelled 'Newport', for example, could have been taken in England, Ireland or somewhere in Wales! This difficulty may be overcome if a recognizable map grid reference, county or vice-county name is also given. Some collectors use reference numbers for their specimens which relate to capture and other details filed in a card index or notebook. In such expanded systems useful data of flowers visited, associated parasites, phoretic insects or mites, nest commensals, and so on, may be given. A second label attached lower down the pin should give the name of the species and, where appropriate, the name of the person who made the determination. A data label should be placed so that it can be read easily from above without disturbing the specimen, but this requirement does not apply to the determination label which may be attached to the pin either face upwards or face downwards.

Bumblebees may be stored in double-sided insect storeboxes or in cabinets with sliding, glass-topped drawers, and so long as the collection is protected by napthalene or paradichlorobenzene from the ravages of museum beetles (*Anthrenus museorum*), and other potential invaders, it will remain in good condition more or less indefinitely.

Collections of the early stages of bumblebees may be stored in tubes containing 70 per cent ethyl alcohol, but material preserved for future dissection of soft,

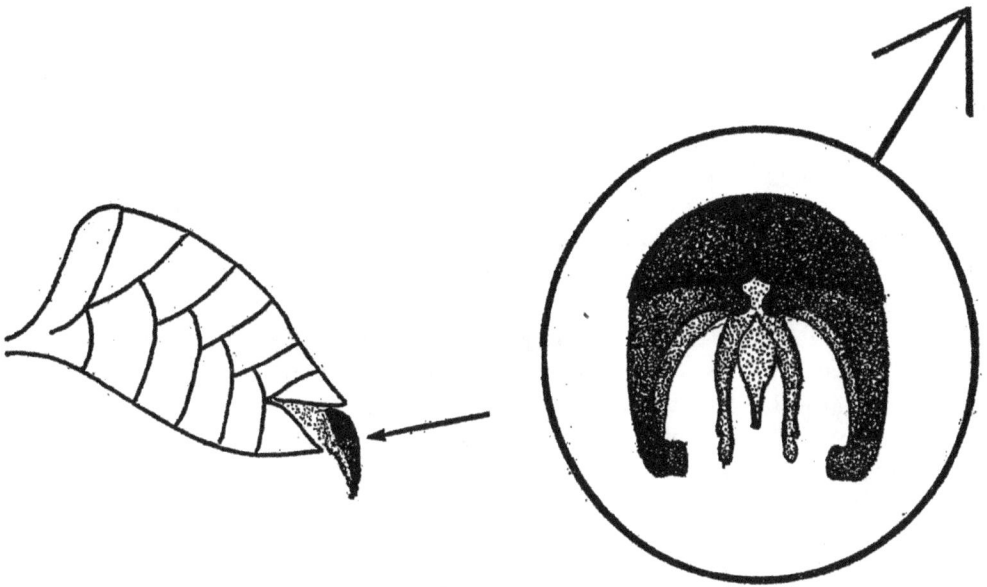

204

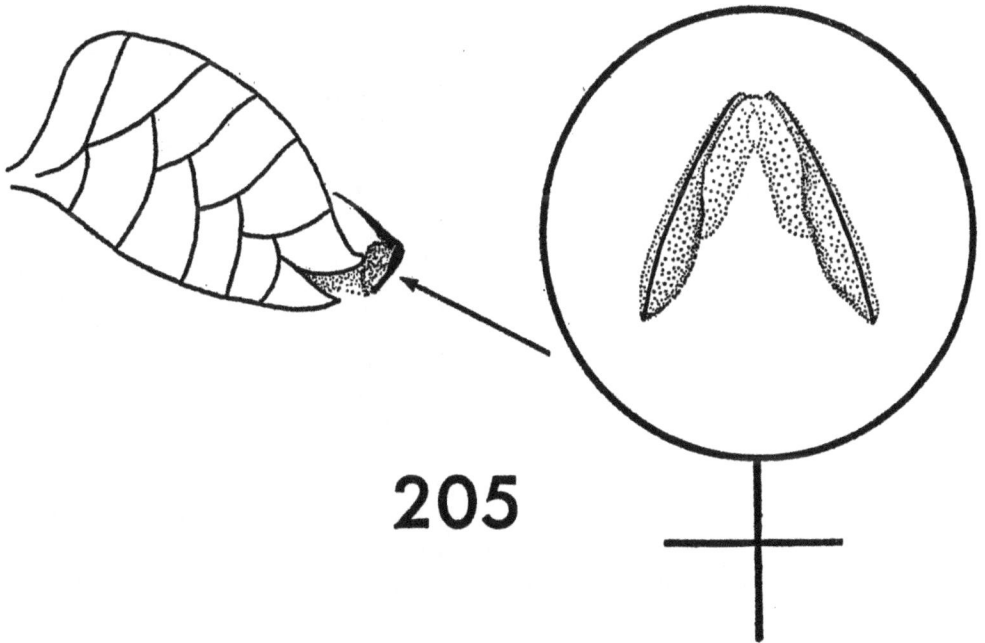

205

Figs. 204–205. 204, method of displaying male genitalia; 205, method of displaying female sting.

internal structures (whether immature or adult) should be kept in Pampel's fluid (30 parts by volume of distilled water; 15 of 95 per cent alcohol; 6 of 40 per cent formaldehyde; 4 of glacial acetic acid) as alcohol alone tends to cause brittleness. Alcoholic Bouin (2 g. of picric acid; 15 ml. of glacial acetic acid; 60 ml. of 40 per cent formaldehyde; 150 ml. of 80 per cent alcohol) is a suitable fixative and storage medium for both adult and immature material. Methods adopted for preserving parasites or nest commensals will depend upon the kind of material. For example, parasite larvae might be best stored in alcohol but the adults would probably be better kept dry and either glued on to card points or pinned directly, according to their size; mites are best placed on microscope slides and mounted in gum chloral. For detailed techniques on handling such material reference should be made to appropriate literature on the group concerned. The British Museum (Natural History) booklet *Instructions for Collectors No. 4A INSECTS* (5th Edn, 1973) is a useful source of information; see also the 1969 facsimile reprint of the *Hymenopterist's Handbook*, originally published in 1945 by the Amateur Entomologists' Society.

Locating Bumblebee Nests

The kinds of site chosen for nesting often vary considerably from species to species (for example, some are essentially surface-nesters and others underground-nesters). There may also be considerable variation within one and the same species. Basically a bumblebee requires a readily available source of suitable nesting material in a sufficiently protected place, where its future comb and colony may develop. Deserted nests of mammals, and sometimes of birds, are favourite sites, both above and below ground level, but bumblebee colonies can also be established in piles of rubbish, compost heaps, haystacks, old mattresses, deep moss, and in various other places where suitable conditions exist. Undisturbed tussocky grassland, and grassy banks, dykes and verges, are particularly suitable as nesting sites for surface-nesting species (e.g. *Bombus pascuorum* and *B. ruderarius*). However, it is generally more difficult to assess the potential of an area for subterranean nests; places with a high water table will be unsuitable, but banks and other places where there might be underground cavities affording shelter for nests of small mammals are likely to be occupied by subterranean-nesting species such as *B. lucorum*, *B. terrestris* and *B. lapidarius*.

The earnest student of bumblebees will doubtless develop his own methods and skills for finding their nests, but the following hints might prove helpful. Although bumblebee nests are most easily found in the summer when they have large forager populations and bee traffic in and out of the nest entrance is likely to attract attention, with patience it is also possible to find small colonies, even before the first workers emerge. This is possible by observing overwintered queens with large pollen loads and following them back to their nests (Alford, 1970b). Early in the season, when suitable forage is often localized and the distraction of competitive insect activity is minimal, it may also be possible to plot the flight path taken by foraging bumblebees and subsequently trace their nest. Coville (1890) considered this 'lining' method to be impracticable for tracking bumblebees, but although this is generally true in the summer I have successfully located young colonies of bumblebees by 'lining' on workers or on individual foraging foundress queens earlier in the season.

Disturbing vegetation in a likely-looking nesting site, so that any returning foragers are at first unable to find the entrance to their nest, is sometimes a helpful technique for locating bumblebee nests, as this causes bees to accumulate in the air near the colony. Hoffer (1882b, 1889) actually traced *Bombus* colonies by following searching *Psithyrus* females.

Transferring Nests

For removing nests from the field to the laboratory or a new site where they might be studied more conveniently, containers are needed to house the comb and adult bees. Surface nests are easily collected as they are usually readily accessible, but it may require considerable physical effort before colonies below ground can be exposed. The best time to remove a nest is early in the morning or in the evening, when most of the bumblebees will be at home. In the case of surface nests it is often possible to scoop the complete colony into a collecting box within a matter of minutes, without losing a single bee. More often, however, before obtaining the comb it is necessary to gradually open up the nest, and capture the adults individually as they appear. Particularly in populous colonies of subterranean-nesting species it is essential to capture the first workers to leave a disturbed nest as these are likely to be guard bees and hence the most aggressive. With care, however, it is usually possible to collect a bumblebee nest without receiving a single sting, but a bee veil might prove a worthwhile investment when dealing with difficult colonies of *B. terrestris* or *B. muscorum*. Some authorities advocate collecting the adult bees in jars, retaining many individuals per container. This is perfectly feasible, but I find it easier and very much quicker to capture the bees singly or in small numbers with collecting tubes (see p. 255). Admittedly more containers are required but this is obviously a matter of personal choice. Bees may be tubed directly or first picked up by the hind legs with forceps. Many bumblebees, instead of becoming active when disturbed, will roll on to their backs, and as such individuals attempt to grasp any object touching them they may be transferred easily to tubes or jars by using forceps, a small twig, or even a blade of grass. It is essential to capture the foundress queen (I always keep her separate and in a distinctive container when collecting a colony) and if necessary a special search must be made for her. It is also worthwhile to obtain as many of the workers as possible. During the day a large proportion of the forager force of a colony will probably be foraging. Therefore, once the bulk of the workers in the colony has been taken, the collector should move a short distance away from the colony, thereby giving returning foragers a chance to settle on their nest material or comb, so that they too may be captured. Subterranean nests will have to be dug up, and to locate the comb it is usually best to follow the entrance tunnel. A flexible tube pushed down the hole will help trace its course, while the whereabouts and proximity of the actual comb may be judged periodically by listening for the buzzing of the associated bees. If available, a carbon dioxide gas cylinder is a useful, although luxury, aid for collecting the bees in large colonies, but care must be taken not to asphyxiate the inhabitants.

The bumblebee comb must be treated gently to prevent damage to the clumps of brood. It must always be kept upright, otherwise nectar or honey might spill out of the storage vessels. The comb should be transferred to a box large enough to accommodate it in its original form; it should be protected below and on all sides by the nest material, supplemented where necessary by pieces of dry grass. The top of the comb may also be covered with a layer of fine nest material which will act as an insulating layer during the homeward journey. The comb, like the adult bees already captured, must not be exposed to direct sunlight. Colonies may be collected from the field in wooden nest-boxes (see below) or in special collecting boxes. In the latter case, as an example, robust metal insect boxes 180 mm. in diameter and 100 mm. deep are ideal for all but the smallest and largest colonies.

Having successfully collected the comb and the majority of the bees, the rest of the nest material and the immediate surroundings should be scrutinized carefully for further bees and for evidence of parasites and nest commensals. If it is possible to return to the site at the end of the day or early the following morning it may be worthwhile leaving some nest material on the original site as an assembly point for foragers still away in the field. Capture of these individuals will be simplified if the nest material is contained in a small open box which may be rapidly sealed with cork or lid when the site is revisited.

Housing Colonies

Having collected a bumblebee colony the comb and the bees must be reunited as soon as possible. The colony may be re-sited in a convenient, protected position out of doors, but plenty of nest material must be provided so the bees can adequately cover their comb. A hole in the ground, covered with a small paving slab, can be used to house a subterranean colony, a lateral entrance tunnel being made with a crowbar or similar tool (Fig. 206). A surface nest may be put in a similar but more superficial situation with direct access to the outside world. A colony may also be housed in a small purpose-built hive (see later) or put in a nest-box which itself is protected from the elements by a larger weather-proof container; an empty honey bee brood chamber plus floor board and lid is ideal for this purpose.

Observation of colonies is more simple and rewarding, however, if they are kept

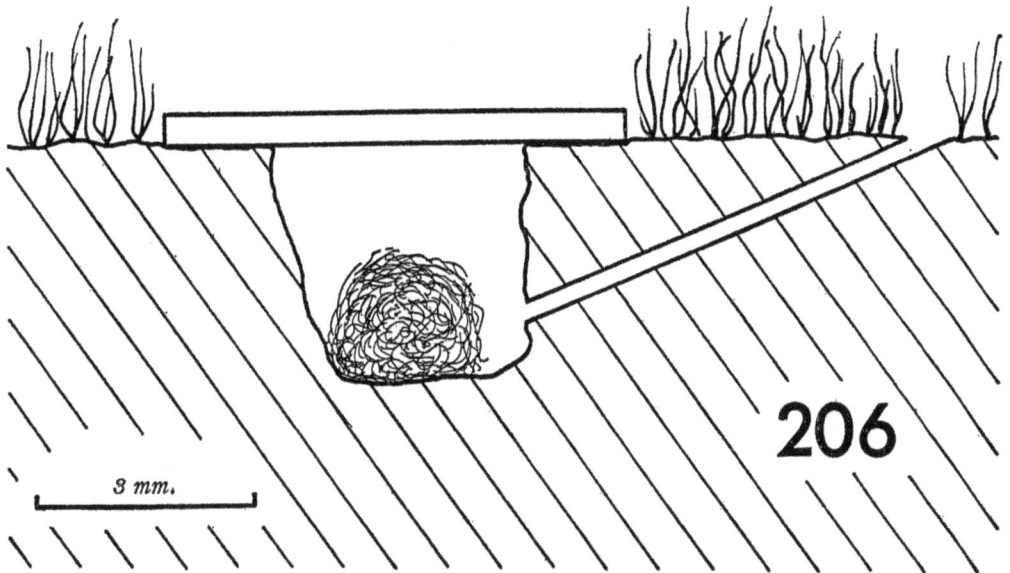

Fig. 206. Underground domicile for bumblebees.

indoors in observation boxes. Circumstances will largely govern the techniques and types of box used; the details given here are intended merely as guidelines. My own nest-boxes were constructed of deal (approximately 10 mm. thick) and were designed around an available source of half-plate size (120 by 163 mm.) photographic glass which was used for covering the tops. Because of the safety angle perspex might be a better material than glass in certain situations. The box illustrated in Fig. 207 has a main nest compartment with a sliding half-plate cover and a small, optional vestibule covered with a cut-down piece of glass. Grooving the wood to accommodate the glass or perspex covers is well worth while but not essential.[1] The base of the box is made of hardboard, with the smooth surface uppermost. Ventilation, feeding and access holes bored in the sides, ends and middle partition are all 28 mm. in diameter so that each can be closed, if and when necessary, with the same size of cork and one large enough to hold a feeding tube (Fig. 207). Side holes may be blocked with zinc gauze as required. Placing gauze on the *inner* walls of the boxes has two advantages: it readily allows any hole to be blocked temporarily with a cork, for example when anaesthetizing the bees, and it reduces the number of hiding places inside the compartment. The zinc gauze is easily attached with wire staples. The floor of a nest-box should be lined with corrugated cardboard and if required this may be sealed around the edges of the box with melted wax. This prevents the bees chewing at the loose ends of the cardboard. One of the access holes to the vestibule may be connected to the outside world by a length of tubing thus allowing the bees to forage. If this is done then the exit point

[1] Some temporary means of anchoring the glass, whether accommodated in grooves or not, is a useful precaution (see Fig. 207); bumblebees are themselves capable of moving insecure lids and escaping.

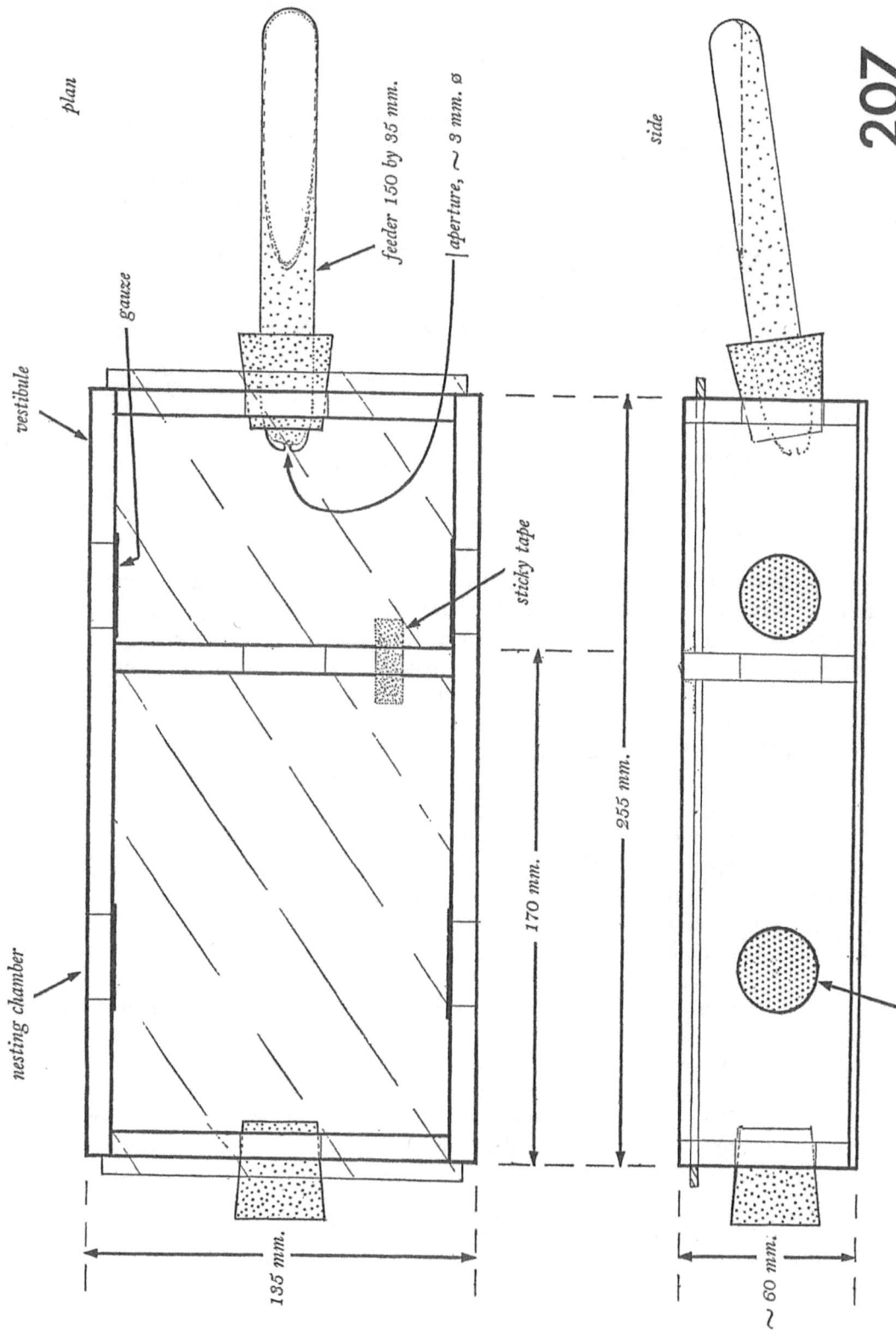

plan

vestibule

gauze

feeder 150 by 35 mm.

aperture, ~ 3 mm. ø

sticky tape

nesting chamber

side

207

hole 28 mm. ø

135 mm.

170 mm.

255 mm.

~ 60 mm.

Fig. 207. Small nest-box for bumblebees.

must be clearly marked (for example, with a coloured disc) so returning bees will have no difficulty in finding it. If necessary a small alighting platform can be fixed below the flight hole. The tunnel must be of sufficient width to allow incoming and outgoing bees to pass one another! The bees will probably collect sufficient pollen for their colony's needs, but if necessary reserves may be supplemented by pollen taken from honey bee colonies. Liquid food can be provided as either diluted honey or a 50:50 mixture by weight of water and sucrose. Artificial feeding is, of course, essential to sustain colonies unable to collect their own food, but excessive feeding of colonies with access to the outside will discourage bees from foraging. Syrup may be dispensed from a gravity feeder made from a glass test tube with the aperture restricted (by heating the tube in a Bunsen flame) to a diameter of 2 to 3 mm. A hole just large enough to accommodate the feeder should be made through a cork, using a cork-borer. The feeder may then be filled and attached to the nest-box as shown in Fig. 207. Feeders must be kept clean, and fresh food should be made up at least twice a week; feeders should not be refilled without first being thoroughly rinsed out.

The kind of nest-box described above can also be made without the vestibule section. The small single-chambered nest-box makes a very convenient container for small colonies or for experiments with individual or small numbers of adult bees. Large colonies, however, will require a more substantial home, such as that illustrated in Fig. 208. In this case two half-plate sized pieces of glass fitted crossways adequately cover the box and provide the observer with three direct access points, one across the middle (very useful for picking bees off the comb) and one at either end. A nest-box of this size (230 by 175 by 120 mm.) will take large bumblebee colonies with ease. Even larger boxes can be made up, but bumblebee colonies are rarely of sufficient size to justify this.

When placing a colony in a nest-box as little of the nesting material as possible should be used, otherwise the comb will be covered over by the bees and observations of their subsequent activity will be impaired. However, the comb must be held firmly since if it is insecure batches of brood might be damaged. Movement of the comb will also disturb the adult bees. Small combs can be anchored to the floor of the box with melted wax; this is an excellent method for attaching incipient brood clumps. Large pieces of debris should be picked off the top of the comb before introducing the adult bees, but smaller fragments and soil particles are best removed by gentle blowing. However, absolute cleanliness is not required as the adult bees will tidy up the comb themselves. Before putting the adult bees into the nest-box they may be calmed down if necessary by a mild anaesthetic or by brief exposure to cold, but it is best not to chance this treatment in the case of the foundress queen.

Occupied nest-boxes must be kept out of direct sunlight and away from draughts. They should also be placed on a firm base as vibration or jarring seriously disturbs the bees. Immediate commotion will also ensue if the observer breathes into a nest-box; for this reason Sladen advocated developing the practice of exhaling through the sides of the mouth when closely studying bumblebees kept in a nest-box. Bumblebees usually defaecate in the corners of their nest-boxes, but an accumulation of damp faeces may be overcome by the addition from time to time of dry soil. However, if the nest-box has a vestibule then it is likely that much of the waste matter will be deposited there rather than in the main chamber, particularly if available floor space in the latter is limited. It is a simple matter to replace periodically the corrugated cardboard floor covering of the vestibule and clear out the debris.

Establishing Artificial Colonies

Bumblebee queens may be induced to establish their colonies in field domiciles (e.g. Sladen, 1912; Frison, 1926b; Fye & Medler, 1954b; Hobbs, et al., 1960, 1962; Hobbs, 1967a) or in laboratory nest-boxes (e.g. Frison, 1927b; Plath, 1923c; Hasselrot, 1952; Valle, 1955; Holm, 1960; Zapletal, 1961; Plowright & Jay, 1966). A useful review of the subject is given by Holm (1966a).

In the field bumblebees will sometimes occupy suitably protected accumulations of dry moss or fine grass set out at ground level or below ground according to the arrangement shown in Fig. 206. The degree of success achieved, however, is often disappointing and may not justify the time and effort involved. Hobbs and his co-workers in Canada have developed techniques for providing acceptable, purpose-built hives for bumblebees, setting them in the field during the spring for subsequent occupation by bumblebee queens (see Hobbs, 1967a). A simple, roughly cuboid (150 mm.) hive can be constructed of strong (18 mm.) plywood (Fig. 209). The single entrance hole should be no larger than 15 mm. in diameter, otherwise small mammals might raid the box. Hives must be lined with nesting material; uphol-sterers' cotton is a suitable artificial medium, but bumblebees have difficulty in manipulating cotton-wool which must not be used. Hive lids can be hinged and, for security, provided with hook and eye catches. It was once thought that previous occupation by mice was necessary before domiciles or nesting material would be acceptable to bumblebees, but this is now known to be untrue. This means that hives or other domiciles may be positioned in the early spring rather than in the previous autumn, thus avoiding exposure to the rigorous winter weather. Hives should be set out along the edges of fields and woods, and in other sites, where over-wintered bumblebee queens are likely to search for suitable abodes. Hives can either be placed on the surface or sunk into the ground and the box connected to the out-side via an entrance tunnel of suitable length. Bumblebee colonies established in field domiciles are subject to attack by many enemies including some, such as ants, not normally harmful to natural colonies. Attaching hives to trees or poles will help safeguard them from invasion by ants and certain mammals, and is also a protection against flooding; however, this technique does not prevent colonies being located by *Psithyrus* females (see Hobbs, 1967a).

Hives can also be used to house naturally-formed colonies collected from the field. For such purposes a larger size of box might be more suitable. To observe bees in

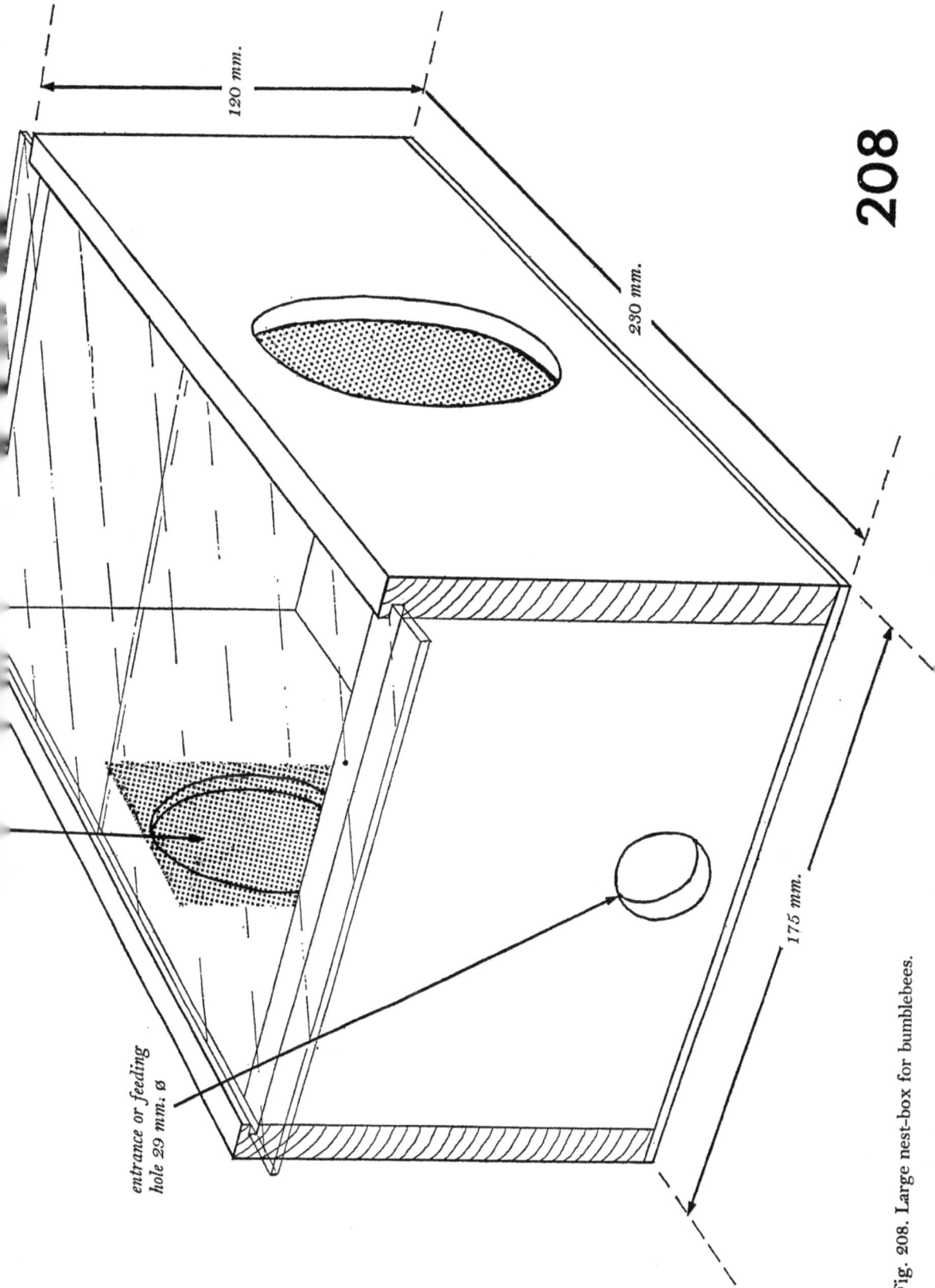

120 mm.

230 mm.

175 mm.

entrance or feeding
hole 29 mm. ø

208

Fig. 208. Large nest-box for bumblebees.

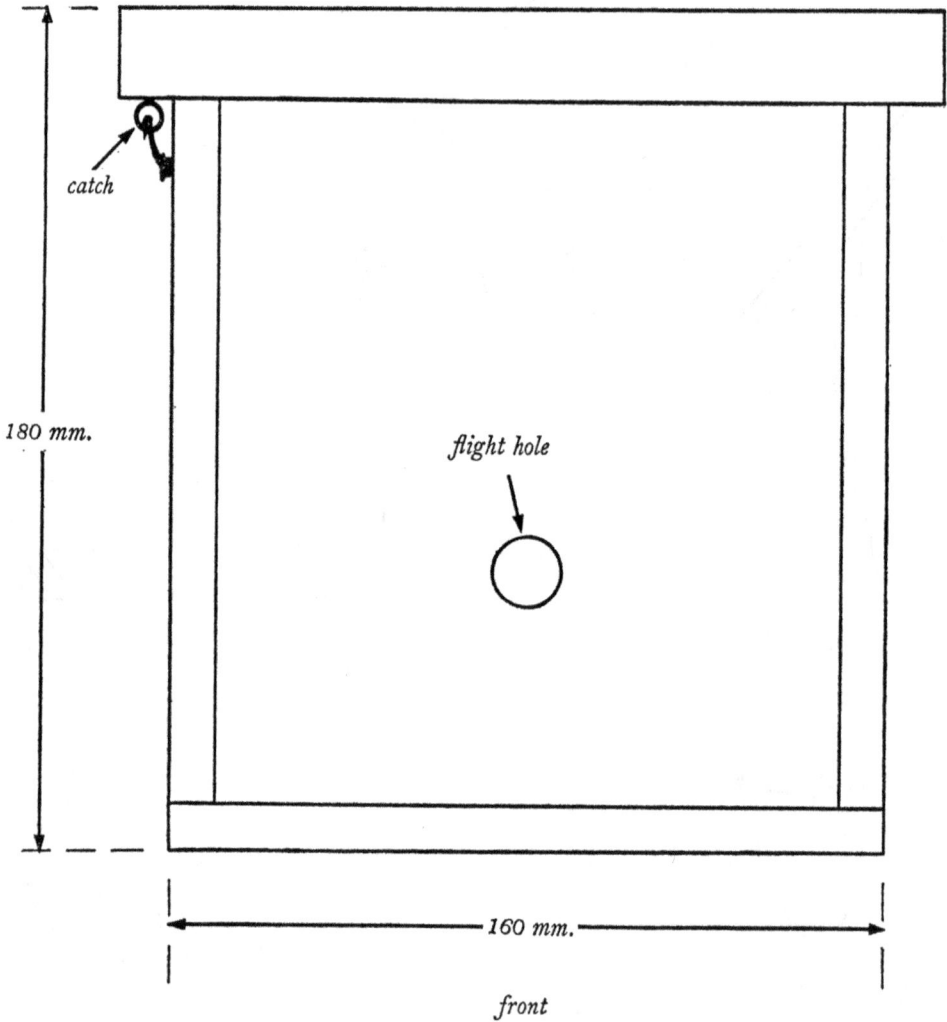

Fig. 209. Hive for bumblebees.

the hive it is essential that the lid can be removed easily, without causing a disturbance. If required, a transparent glass or perspex cover can be fitted below the lid, but it is as well to have some simple arrangement for quietly lifting this out (Fig. 210).

Many different techniques have been used to induce bumblebee queens to establish colonies in confinement (see Holm, 1966). Some species are more difficult subjects than others, and of the common British species best results are most likely to

nged or removable lid

nesting material

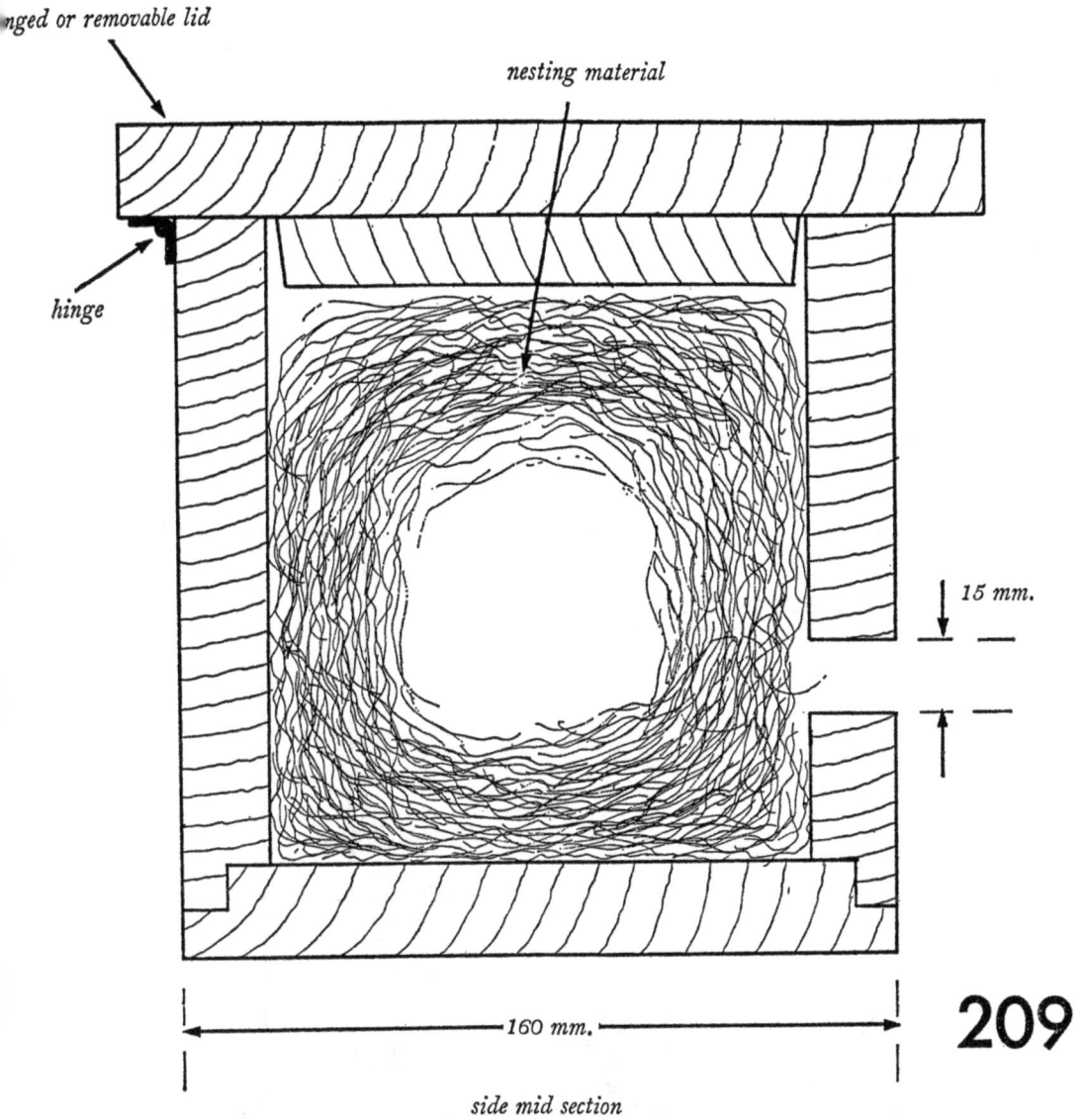

hinge

15 mm.

160 mm.

209

side mid section

be achieved with *Bombus lucorum*, *B. terrestris* and *B. pratorum*. I have found the following simple method suitable for establishing colonies of these and other species. However, success cannot be guaranteed.

Individual queens should be confined in small nest-boxes and provided with fresh syrup (preferably diluted honey) and pollen. A lump of fresh pollen about the size of a pea should be anchored with melted wax to the centre of the nest chamber, and the boxes kept at a reasonable room temperature (20°C.) or above; lower temperatures should be avoided. Provision of nest material is unnecessary (but see below). Queens selected for breeding should be those actively searching for nest-sites in the spring; that is to say, those physiologically ready to establish colonies. A suitable queen soon shows interest in the pollen lump and will be noticeably 'broody'. If the pollen lump becomes fragmented, or if much of it is consumed by the queen, then a fresh supply must be introduced. Before egg-laying a queen usually moulds the pollen lump and although the initial egg cell is normally built on it this is not always so. A cell might be built on the wall of the nest-box or, exceptionally, even on a feeder cork. Plowright & Jay have suggested that provision of suitable nest material may reduce the tendency of queens to build their egg cells

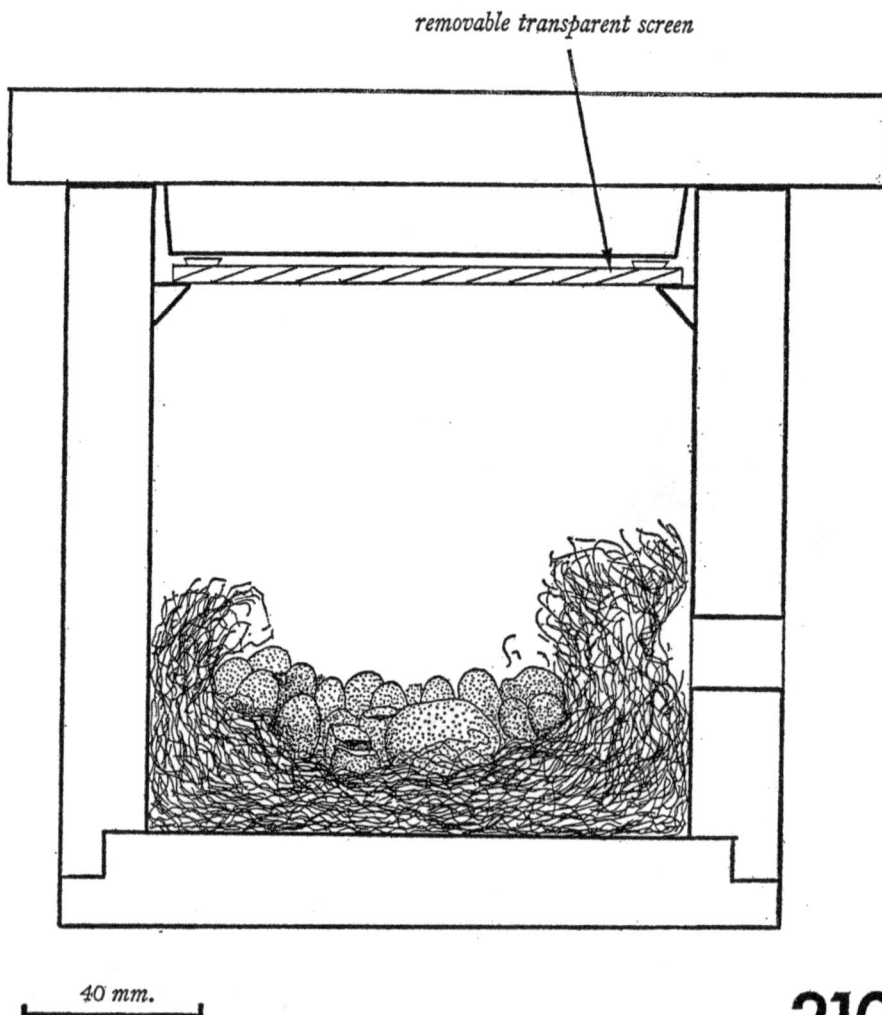

removable transparent screen

40 mm.

210

Fig. 210. Outdoor observation hive for bumblebees.

away from the pollen lump. Queens that fail to show an interest in the pollen lump and give no indication of being broody after a week or two in confinement, should be discarded. Failure of queens is sometimes due to the presence of parasites; for example, queens infested with *Sphaerularia bombi* might have been collected in mistake for healthy individuals. However, confinement itself can upset the physiology of queens, causing their ovaries to abort (Medler, 1962d; Fridén, 1966) and their fat bodies once again to accumulate large reserves of fat (Alford, 1969a). Confined queens should be disturbed as little as possible, but nest-boxes and feeders must be kept clean; food supplies must always be fresh. The queen's requirement for food will increase once brood-rearing is initiated and there are larvae to be fed. Once the first workers appear it is worthwhile to allow them to forage. However, it is advisable to make the exit hole from the nest-box too small for the queen to pass through as confined queens, if released, have a tendency to get lost. Once a box is opened to the outside it may be more difficult for the bees to maintain an adequate brood-nest temperature. Steps must, therefore, be taken to exclude draughts; the entrance tunnel should not be too short and, if necessary, the entrance can be kept closed at night and in cool weather.

It is also possible to establish colonies by confining more than one queen together in the same box. In such cases they will co-operate in brood-rearing, although there will usually come a time when one queen will kill the other (or others). Co-operation can exist between two queens of different species. Another method likely to increase the chances of success is to confine a queen with a small number of workers. However, the latter are usually in short supply at the time that suitable queens are available. A further method is to confine the queen with a small pupal clump obtained from another colony. The queen may accept this and commence brood-rearing on her own account, soon to be assisted by the workers emerging from the adopted clump.

Rather than allow bees from nest-boxes to forage in the field, colonies can be placed in unheated greenhouses (provided there is sufficient protection from excessive heating during sunny weather), insectaries or special flight rooms, and the bees allowed to collect food from potted plants, bouquets of flowers, or other sources.

Mating and Overwintering Bumblebees

True domestication of bumblebees involves not only the establishment of nests under artificial conditions but also the controlled fertilization and overwintering of queens. Mating bumblebees in captivity is usually no problem and can be achieved either in nest-boxes or by allowing males and females to contact one another more naturally in larger enclosures. Overwintering the queens, however, can prove more difficult. It is possible to confine queens individually in small containers and keep them undisturbed in cool, humid conditions throughout the winter period, but unless a queen has sufficient honey in her crop and adequate reserves of glycogen and fat in her fat body she will not survive (e.g. Holm, 1972). A second method is to allow previously fertilized and suitably fed queens to dig themselves into artificial mounds of sterilized peat specially provided for them in insectaries or unheated glasshouses. Unfortunately, however, it seems particularly difficult to induce artificially overwintered queens to start colonies in confinement (Holm, 1966b).

Marking Bumblebees

Bumblebees, preferably anaesthetized, can be marked with quick-drying, acetone-based paints. Only a small amount should be used, and this should be placed on the middle of the thorax whilst steadying the bee gently by hand. Holding bees in the required position with the aid of a pair of forceps is less positive and liable to cause injury. Members of one colony may all be marked with the same colour paint and with the same symbol, but if it is necessary to identify bees individually or to categorize them into identifiable groups then a combination of colour and symbol codes should be used. After a time, some of the paint may tend to flake off, and this must be borne in mind when designing a series of symbols. Abdominal and wing markings are not recommended for bumblebees.

Maps showing the Distribution of Bumblebees in the British Isles

MAP 1 shows the distribution of the various British and Irish vice-counties, and also indicates the position of certain off-shore islands.[1] Unlike the species distribution maps the Shetland, Orkney and Channel Islands are shown in their correct position relative to mainland Britain.

Maps 2–27 show the recorded distribution of each British species of bumblebee, records being based on 10 by 10 km. squares of the British or Irish National Grids. Where appropriate, the distribution of subspecies is also indicated. Following the system presently adopted by the Biological Records Centre records are divided into two date classes, 'pre 1960' and '1960 onwards'.

The distribution maps are followed by lists of vice-county records for England and Wales (Table I), Scotland (Table II) and Ireland (Table III).

---

[1] Details of vice-county boundaries are provided by Dandy (1969).

Key to Map 1

ENGLAND, WALES & SCOTLAND

1. W. Cornwall (+Scilly Isles)
2. E. Cornwall
3. S. Devon
4. N. Devon (+Lundy Island)
5. S. Somerset
6. N. Somerset
7. N. Wiltshire
8. S. Wiltshire
9. Dorset
10. Isle of Wight
11. S. Hampshire
12. N. Hampshire
13. W. Sussex
14. E. Sussex
15. E. Kent
16. W. Kent
17. Surrey
18. S. Essex
19. N. Essex
20. Hertfordshire
21. Middlesex
22. Berkshire
23. Oxfordshire
24. Buckinghamshire
25. E. Suffolk
26. W. Suffolk
27. E. Norfolk
28. W. Norfolk
29. Cambridgeshire
30. Bedfordshire
31. Huntingdonshire
32. Northamptonshire
33. E. Gloucestershire
34. W. Gloucestershire
35. Monmouthshire
36. Herefordshire
37. Worcestershire
38. Warwickshire

39. Staffordshire
40. Shropshire
41. Glamorgan
42. Breconshire
43. Radnorshire
44. Camarthenshire
45. Pembrokeshire
46. Cardiganshire
47. Montgomeryshire
48. Merionethshire
49. Caernarvonshire
50. Denbyshire
51. Flintshire
52. Anglesey
53. S. Lincolnshire
54. N. Lincolnshire
55. Leicestershire (and Rutland)
56. Nottinghamshire
57. Derbyshire
58. Cheshire
59. S. Lancashire
60. W. Lancashire
61. S.E. Yorkshire
62. N.E. Yorkshire
63. S.W. Yorkshire
64. Mid-west Yorkshire
65. N.W. Yorkshire
66. Durham
67. S. Northumberland
68. N. Northumberland
69. Westmorland (and N. Lancashire)
70. Cumberland
71. Isle of Man
72. Dumfriesshire
73. Kirkcudbrightshire
74. Wigtownshire
75. Ayrshire
76. Renfrewshire

77. Lanarkshire
78. Peeblesshire
79. Selkirkshire
80. Roxburghshire
81. Berwickshire
82. E. Lothian
83. Midlothian
84. W. Lothian
85. Fifeshire (and Kinross)
86. Stirlingshire
87. W. Perthshire
   (and Clackmannan)
88. Mid Perthshire
89. E. Perthshire
90. Angus
91. Kincardineshire
92. S. Aberdeenshire
93. N. Aberdeenshire
94. Banffshire
95. Moray
96. E. Inverness-shire (and Nairn)
97. W. Inverness-shire
98. Argyll Main
99. Dunbartonshire
100. Clyde Isles
101. Kintyre
102. S. Ebudes
103. Mid Ebudes
104. N. Ebudes
105. W. Ross
106. E. Ross
107. E. Sutherland
108. W. Sutherland
109. Caithness
110. Outer Hebrides
111. Orkney Islands
112. Shetland Islands
113. Channel Islands

IRELAND

1. S. Kerry
2. N. Kerry
3. W. Cork
4. Mid Cork
5. E. Cork
6. Waterford
7. S. Tipperary
8. Limerick
9. Clare (+Aran Islands)
10. N. Tipperary
11. Kilkenny
12. Wexford
13. Carlow
14. Leix

15. S.E. Galway
16. W. Galway
17. N.E. Galway
18. Offaly
19. Kildare
20. Wicklow
21. Dublin
22. Meath
23. W. Meath
24. Longford
25. Roscommon
26. E. Mayo
27. W. Mayo

28. Sligo
29. Leitrim
30. Cavan
31. Louth
32. Monaghan
33. Fermanagh
34. E. Donegal
35. W. Donegal
36. Tyrone
37. Armagh
38. Down
39. Antrim
40. Londonderry

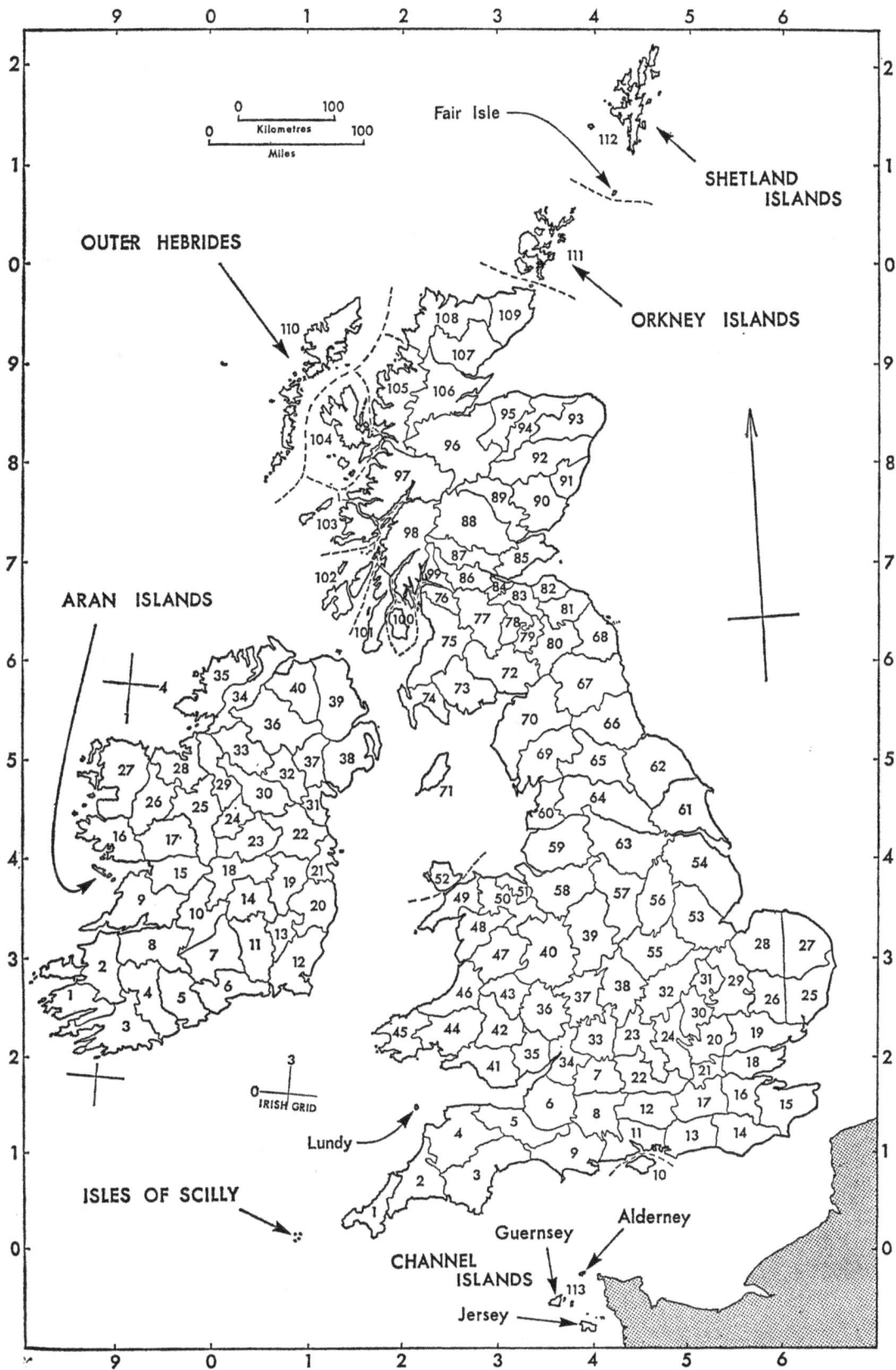

Map 1. Vice-counties and various off-shore islands.

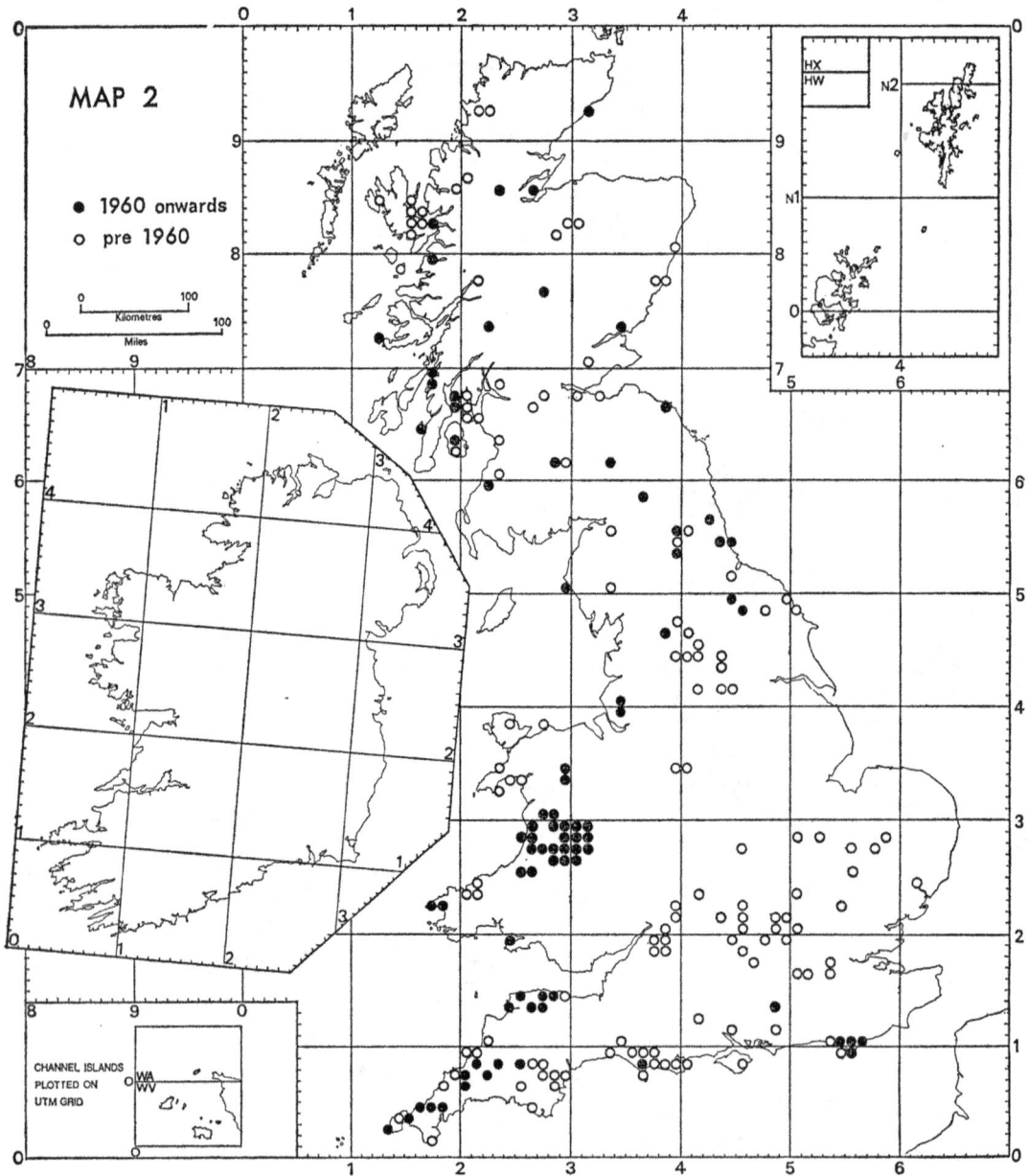

Map 2. *Bombus soroeensis* (Fabricius).

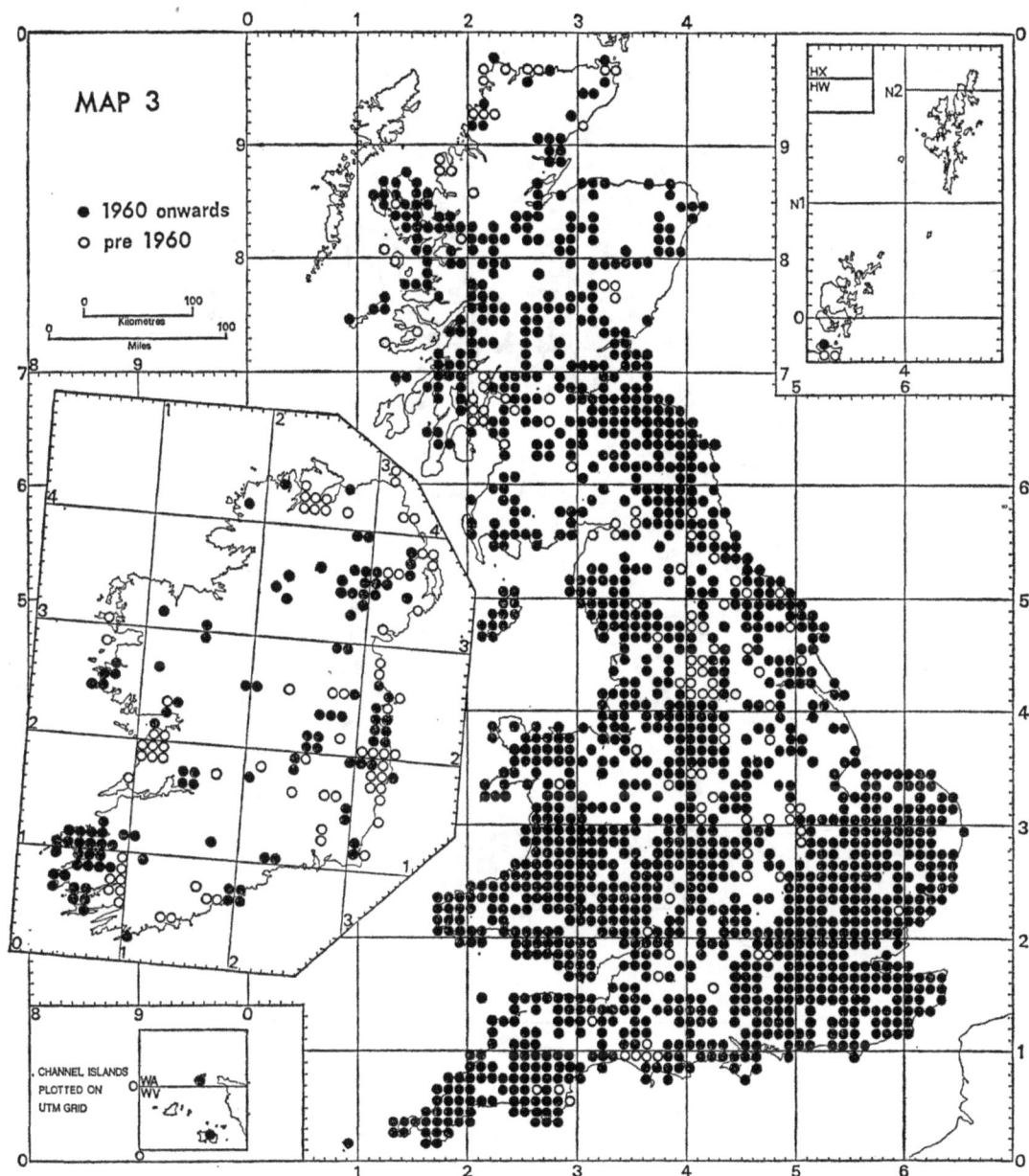

MAP 3

● 1960 onwards
○ pre 1960

Kilometres
Miles

CHANNEL ISLANDS
PLOTTED ON
UTM GRID

Map 3. *Bombus lucorum* (Linnaeus).

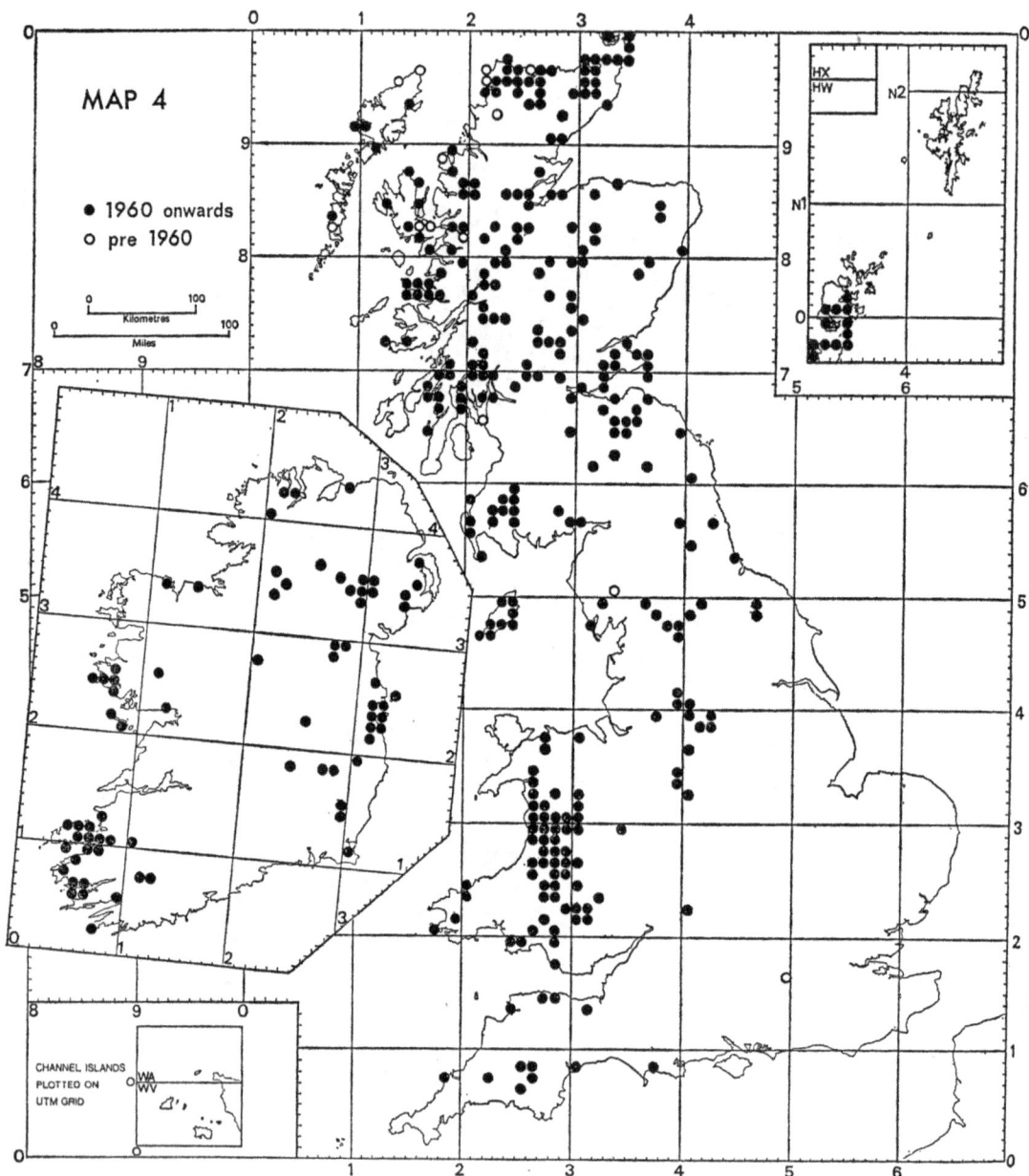

MAP 4

- 1960 onwards
- ○ pre 1960

Kilometres

Miles

CHANNEL ISLANDS
PLOTTED ON
UTM GRID

Map 4. *Bombus magnus* Krüger. Only records confirmed as belonging to *magnus* are included here; doubtful records have been placed under *B. lucorum* (Map 3).

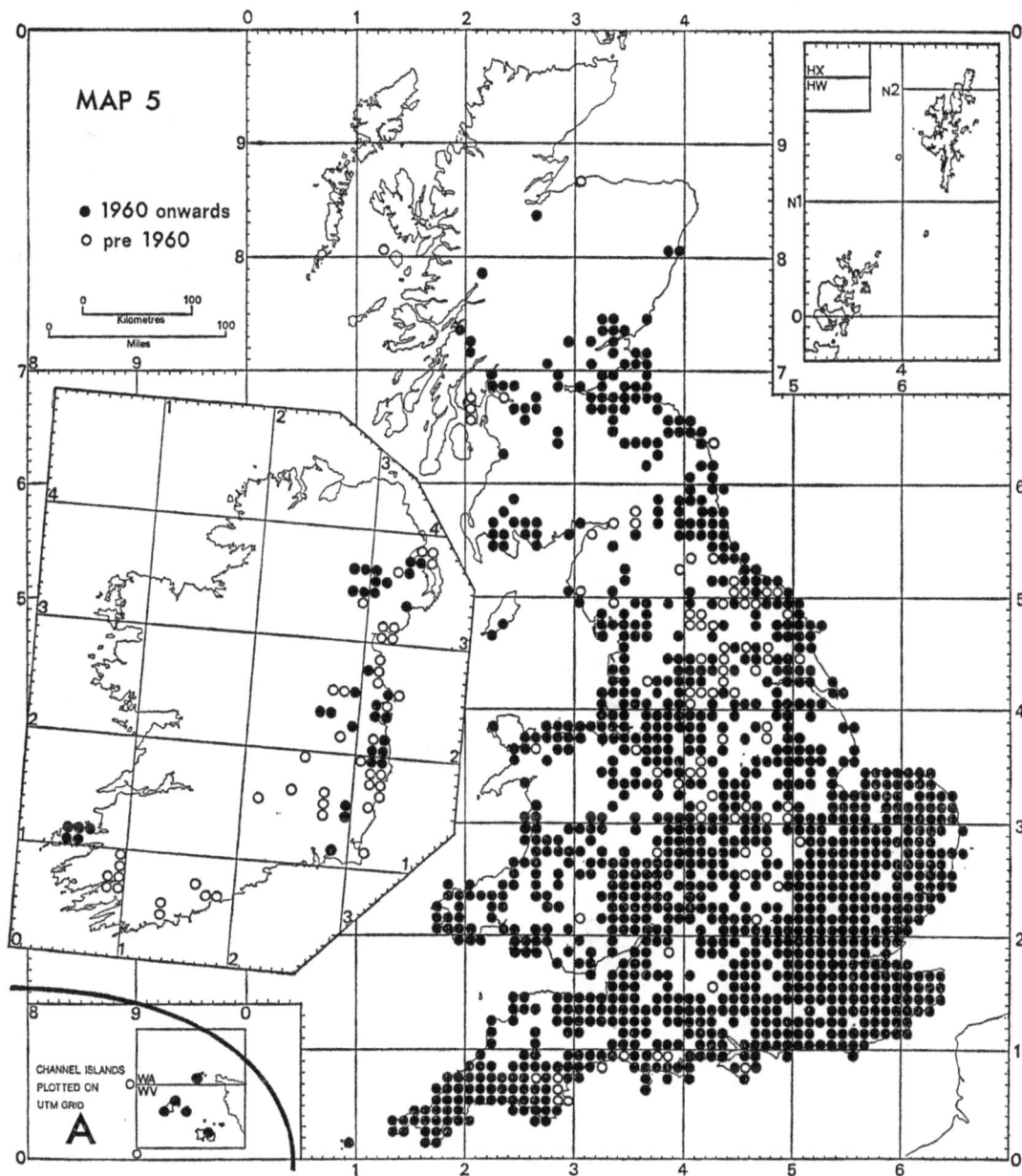

Map 5. *Bombus terrestris* (Linnaeus). Subspecies: *Bombus terrestris audax* (Harris);
A—*Bombus terrestris terrestris* (Linnaeus).

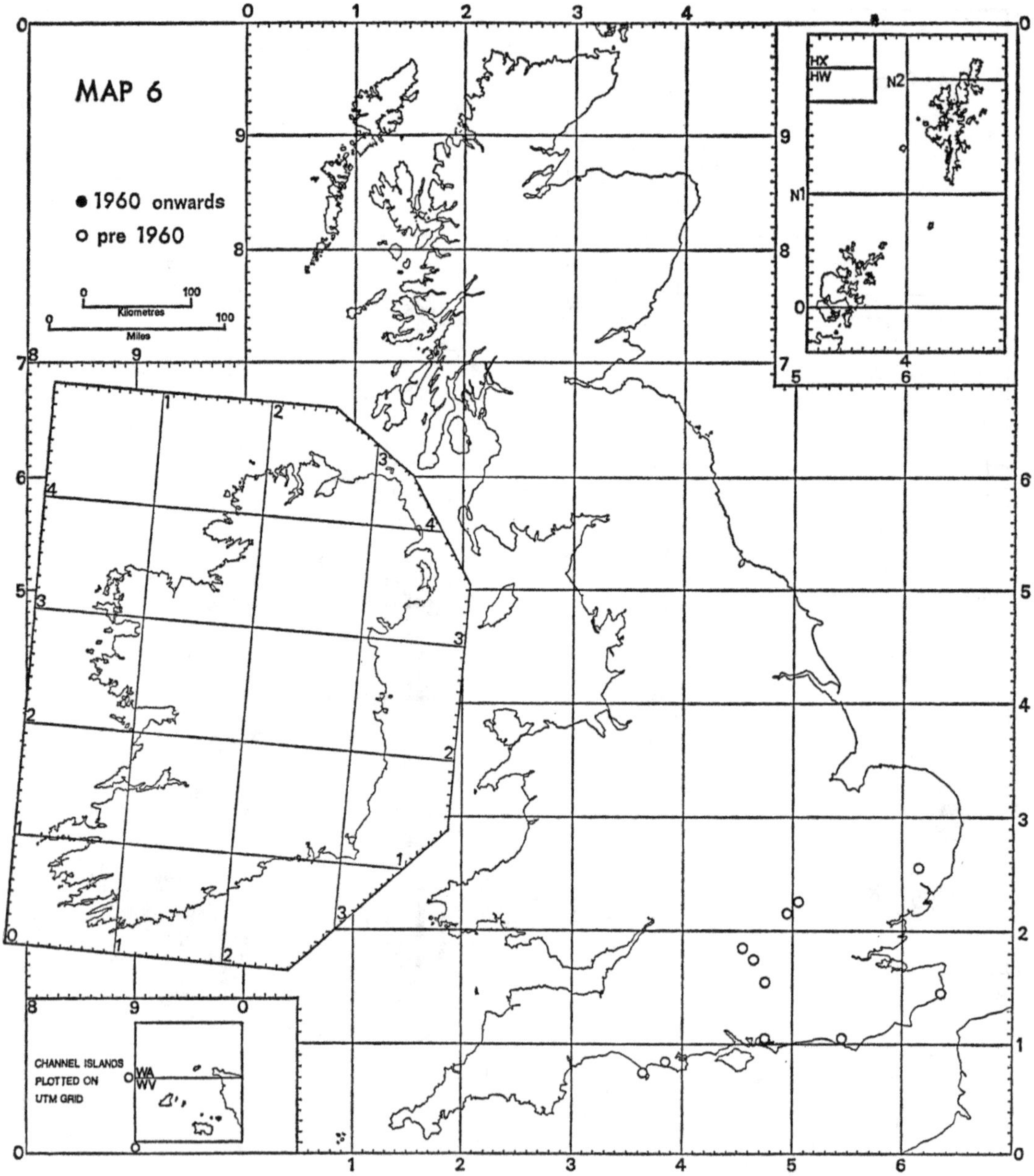

MAP 6

● 1960 onwards
○ pre 1960

Map 6. *Bombus cullumanus* (Kirby). All are pre-1930 records.

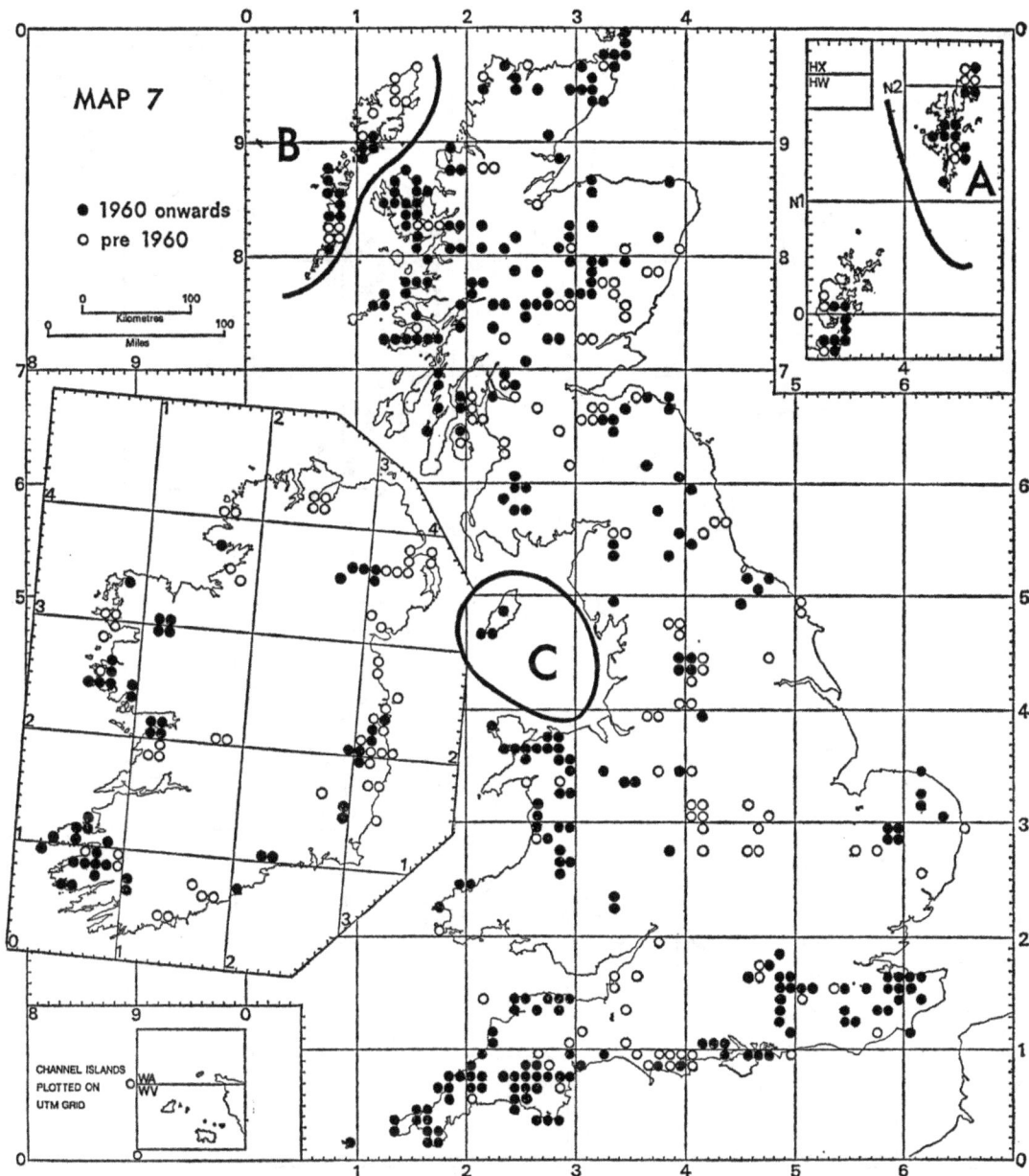

Map 7. *Bombus jonellus* (Kirby). Subspecies: *Bombus jonellus jonellus* (Kirby); A—*Bombus jonellus vogtii* Richards; B—*Bombus jonellus hebridensis* Wild; C—*Bombus jonellus monapiae* Kruseman.

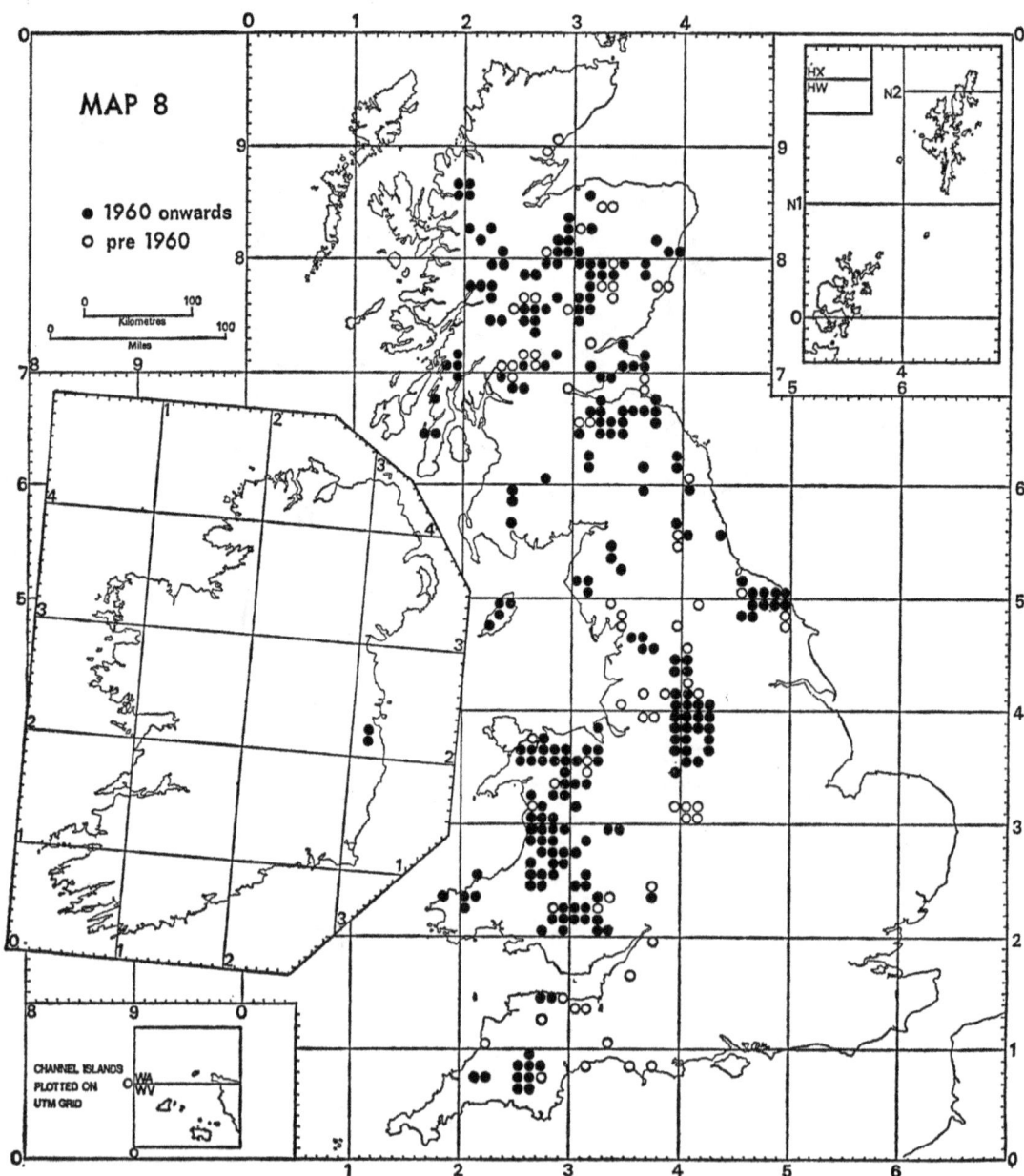

Map 8. *Bombus lapponicus* (Fabricius). NOTE ADDED IN PROOF: In July 1974 a second Irish specimen
a (worker) was captured in Co. Wicklow (cf. footnote on p. 180). This record is plotted on the map·

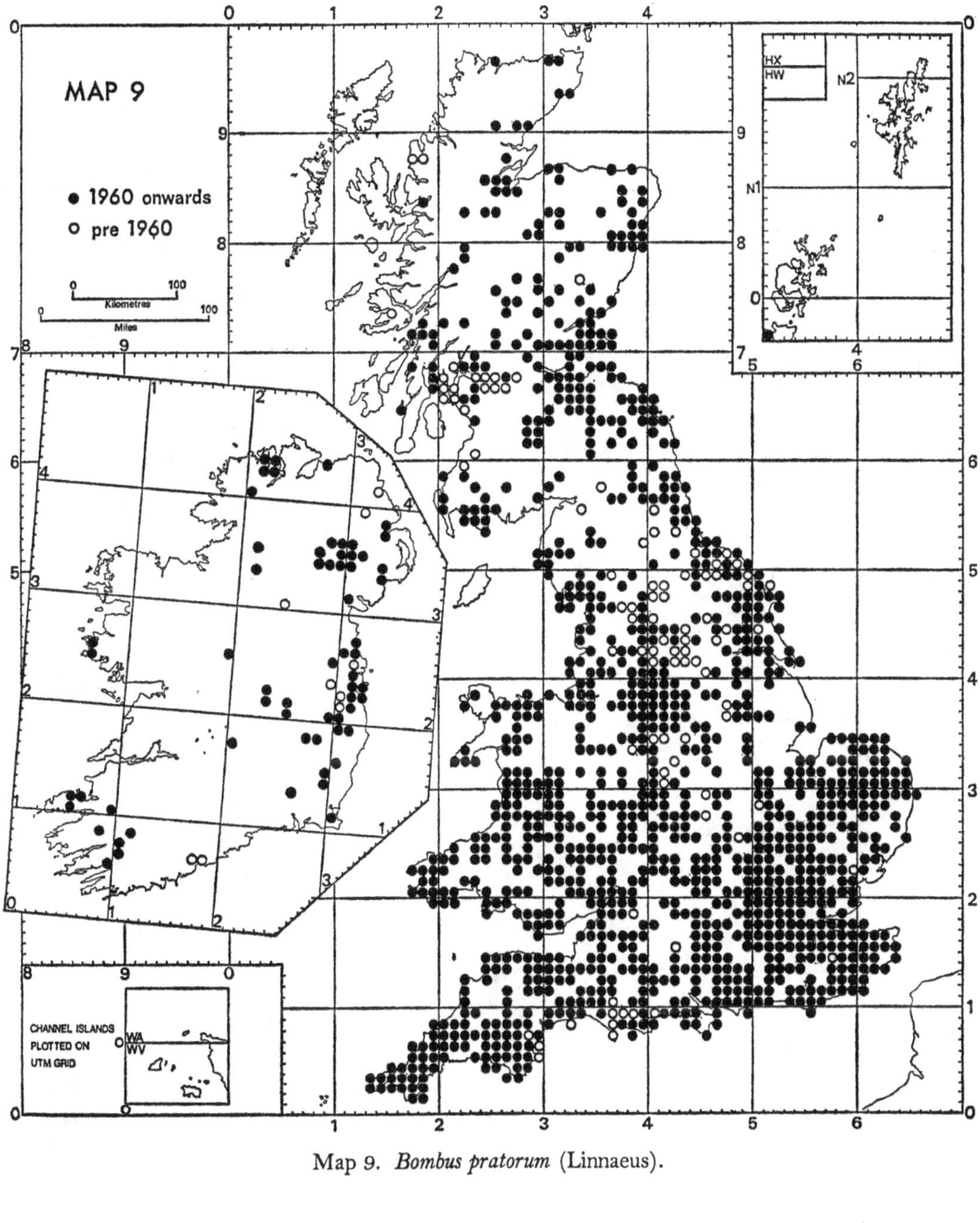

MAP 9

● 1960 onwards
○ pre 1960

Map 9. *Bombus pratorum* (Linnaeus).

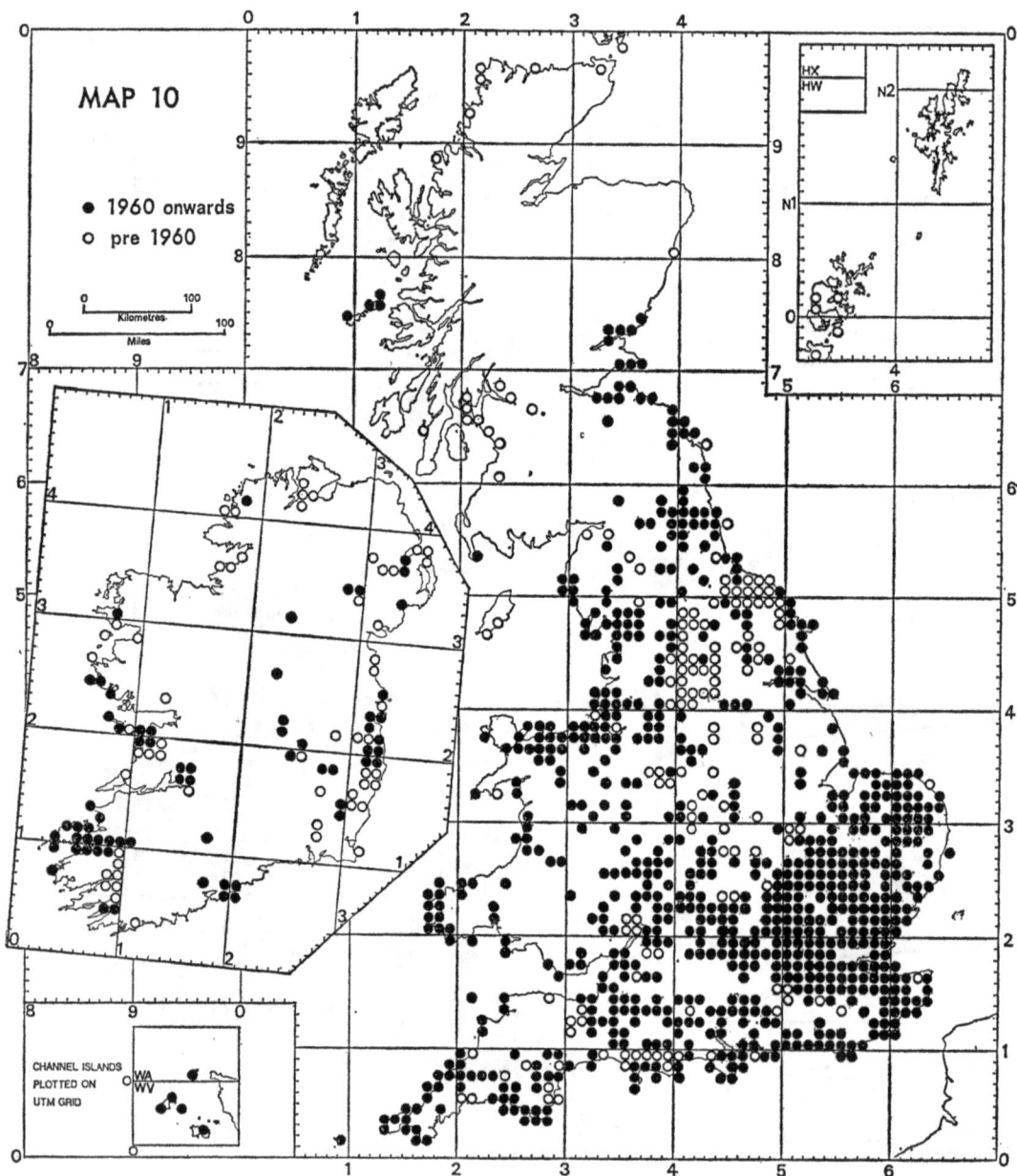

MAP 10

- 1960 onwards
○ pre 1960

Map 10. *Bombus lapidarius* (Linnaeus).

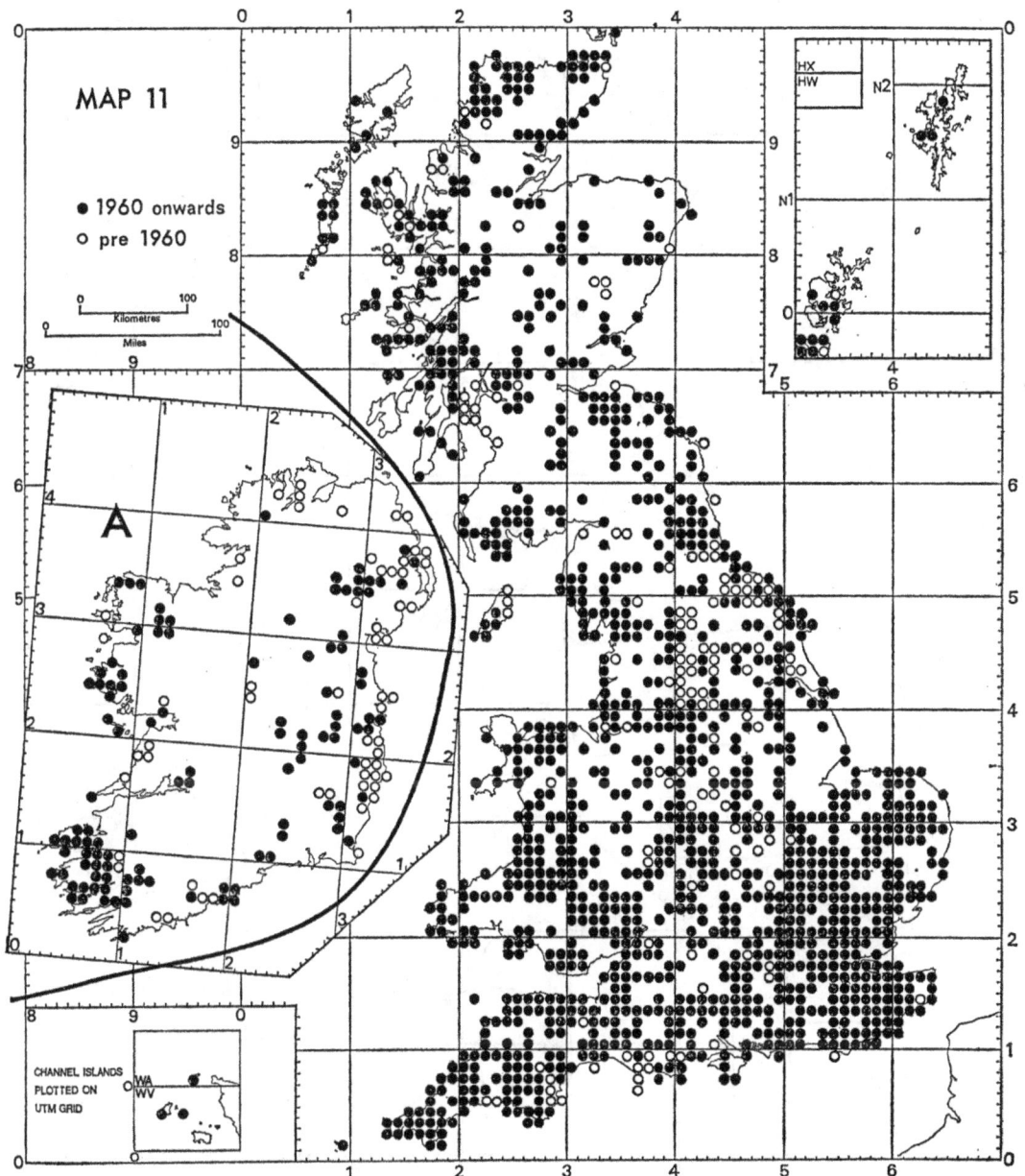

Map 11. *Bombus hortorum* (Linnaeus). Subspecies: *Bombus hortorum hortorum* (Linnaeus);
A—*Bombus hortorum ivernicus* Sladen.

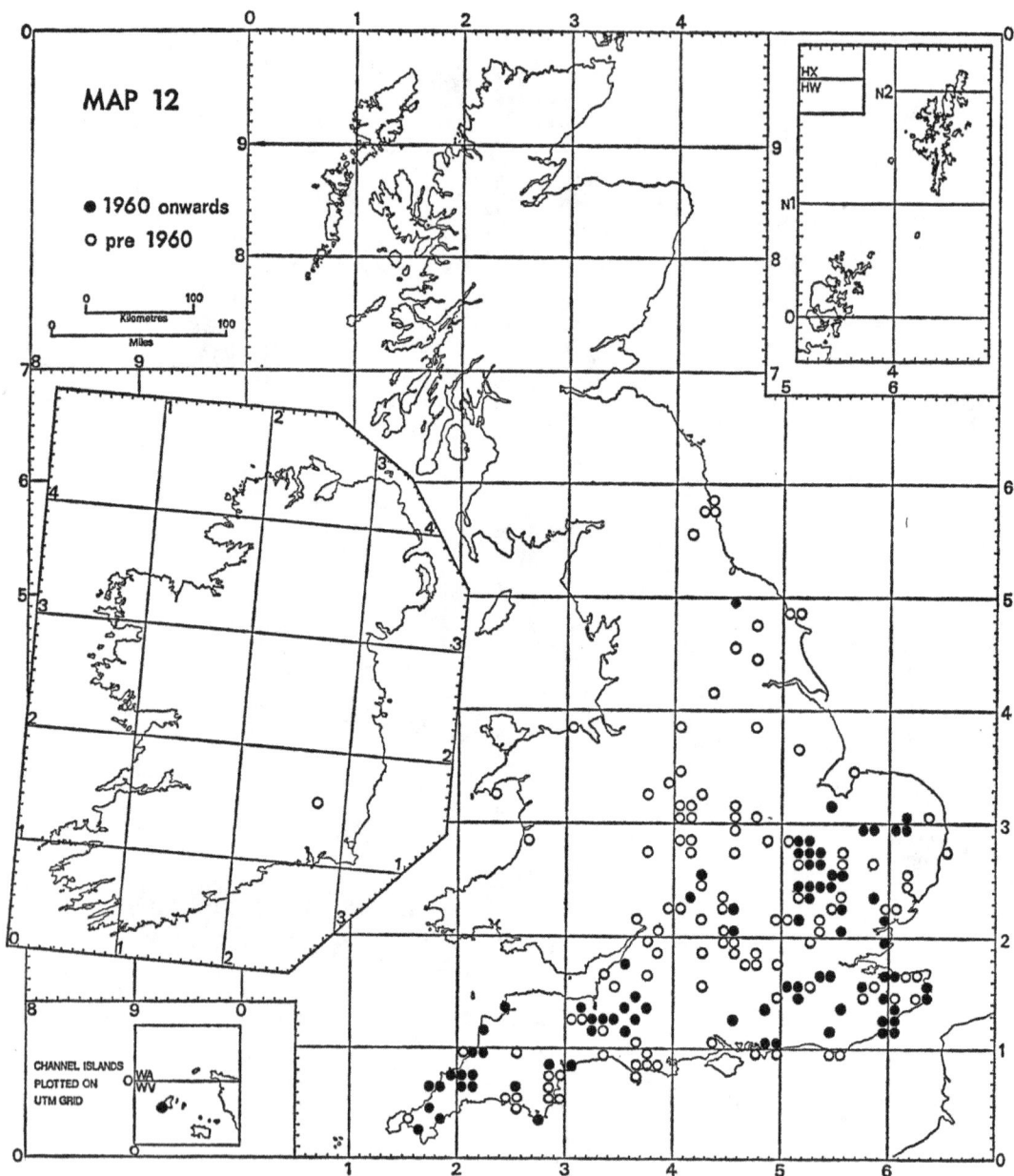

Map 12. *Bombus ruderatus* (Fabricius).

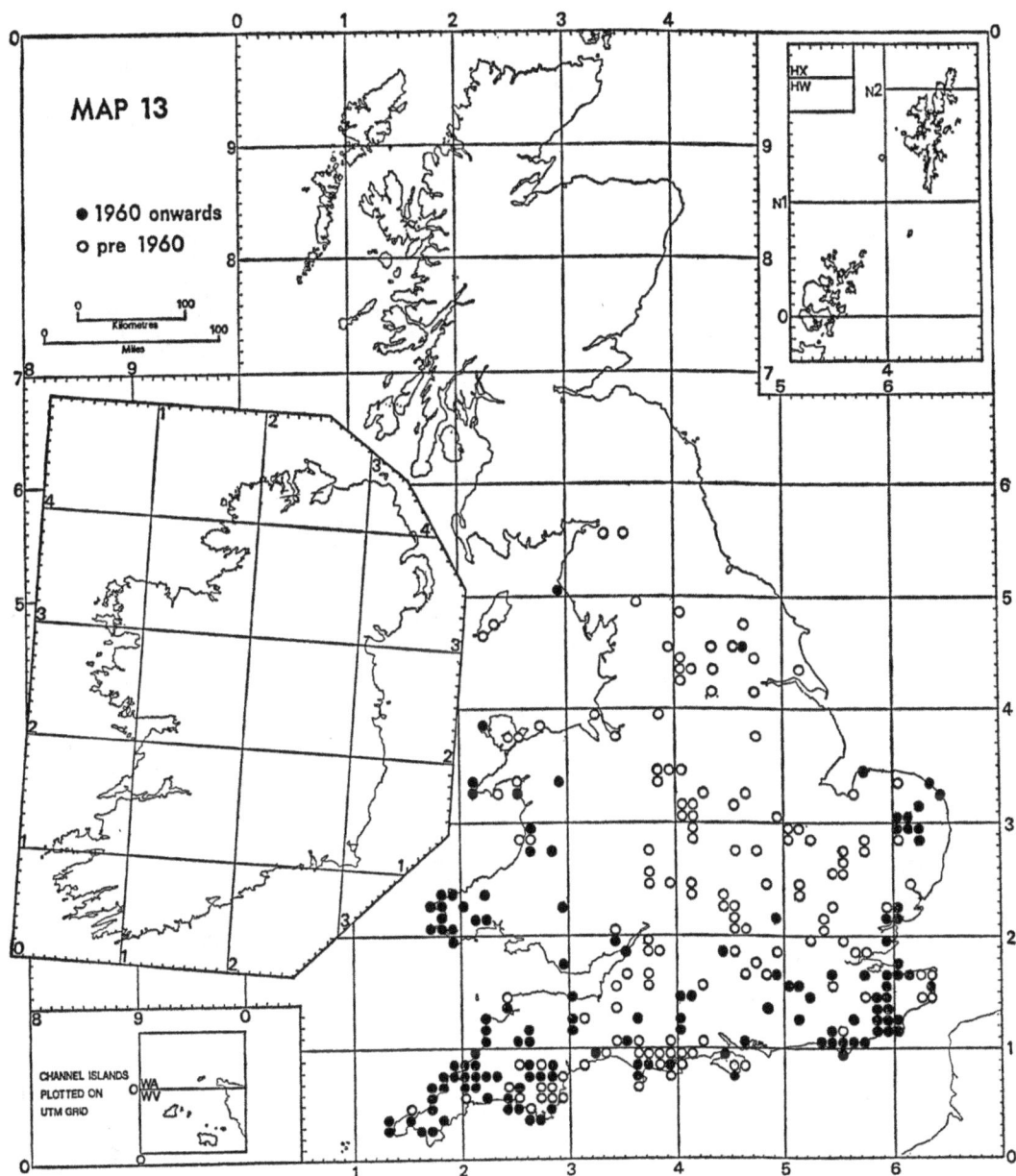

MAP 13

● 1960 onwards
○ pre 1960

Kilometres
Miles

CHANNEL ISLANDS
PLOTTED ON
UTM GRID

Map 13. *Bombus humilis* Illiger.

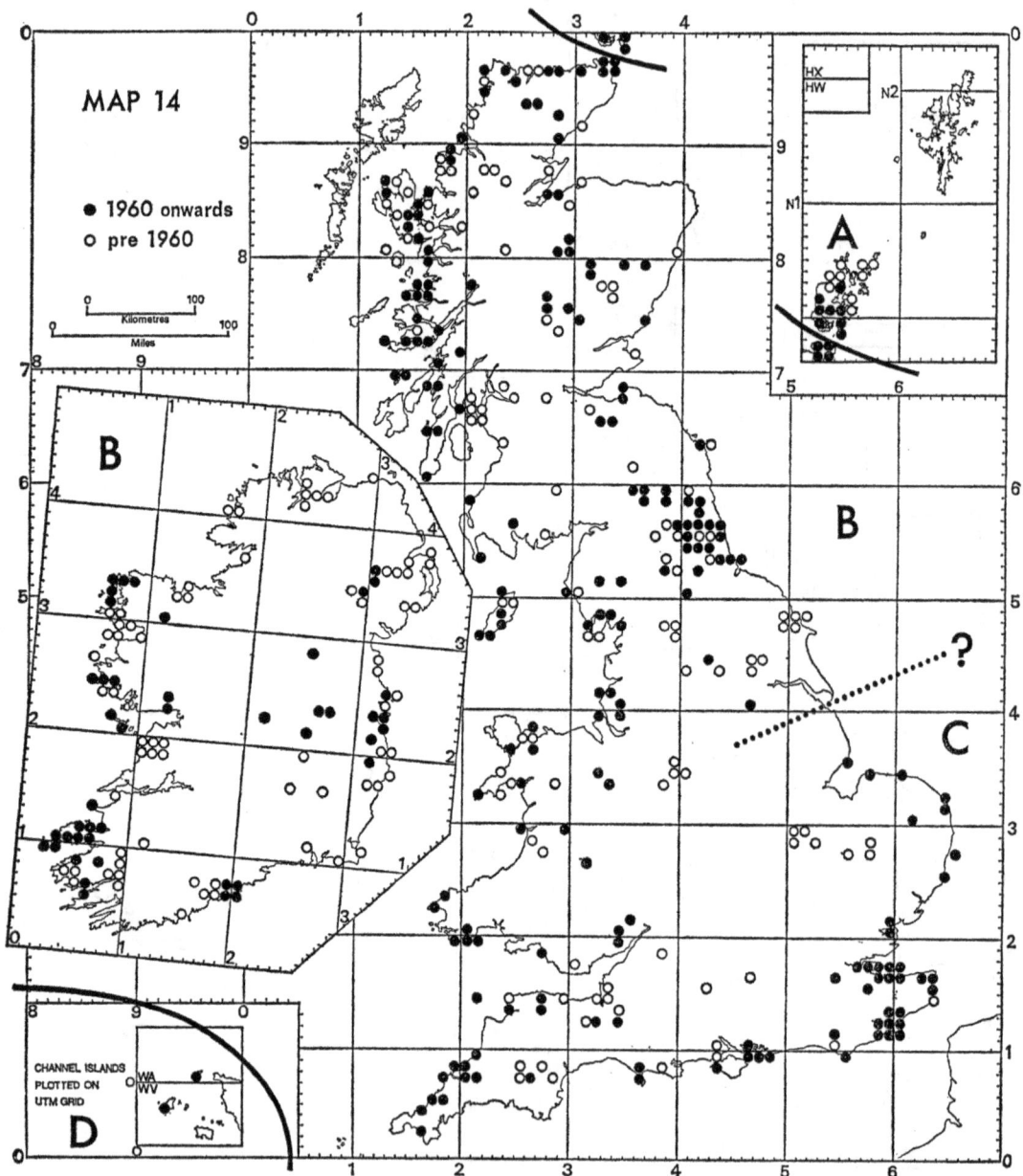

Map 14. *Bombus muscorum* (Linnaeus). Subspecies: A—*Bombus muscorum orcadensis* Richards; B—*Bombus muscorum pallidus* Evans; C—*Bombus muscorum sladeni* Vogt; D—*Bombus muscorum muscorum* (Linnaeus) (?).

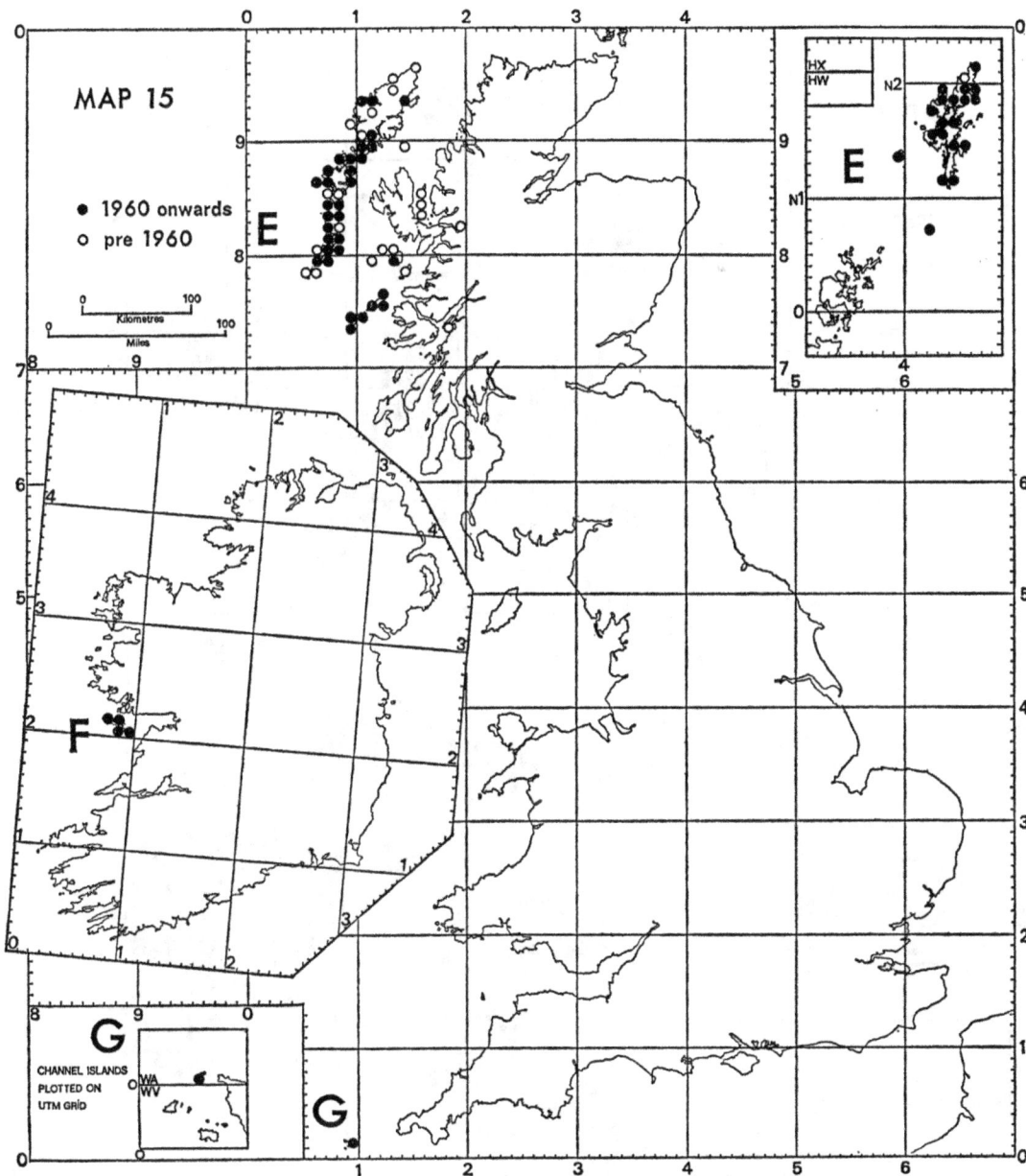

Map 15. *Bombus muscorum smithianus* auctt. nec White (s.l.). Subspecies: E—*Bombus muscorum smithianus* auctt. nec White (s.s.); F—*Bombus muscorum allenellus* Stelfox; G—*Bombus muscorum scyllonius* Richards.

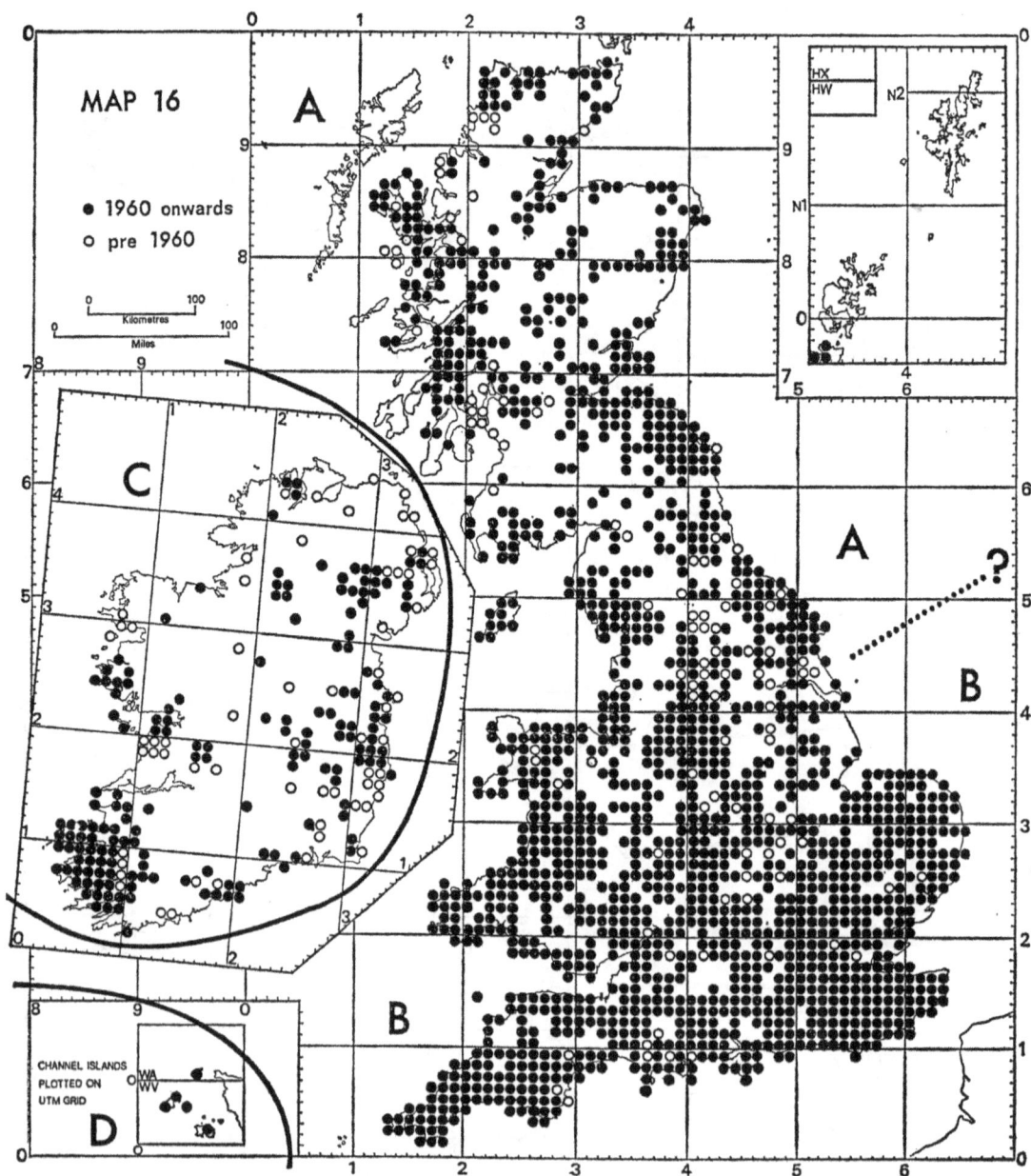

MAP 16

● 1960 onwards
○ pre 1960

Map 16. *Bombus pascuorum* (Scopoli). Subspecies: A—*Bombus pascuorum septentrionalis* Vogt; B—*Bombus pascuorum vulgo* Vogt; C—*Bombus pascuorum floralis* (Gmelin); D—*Bombus pascuorum flavidus* Kruger.

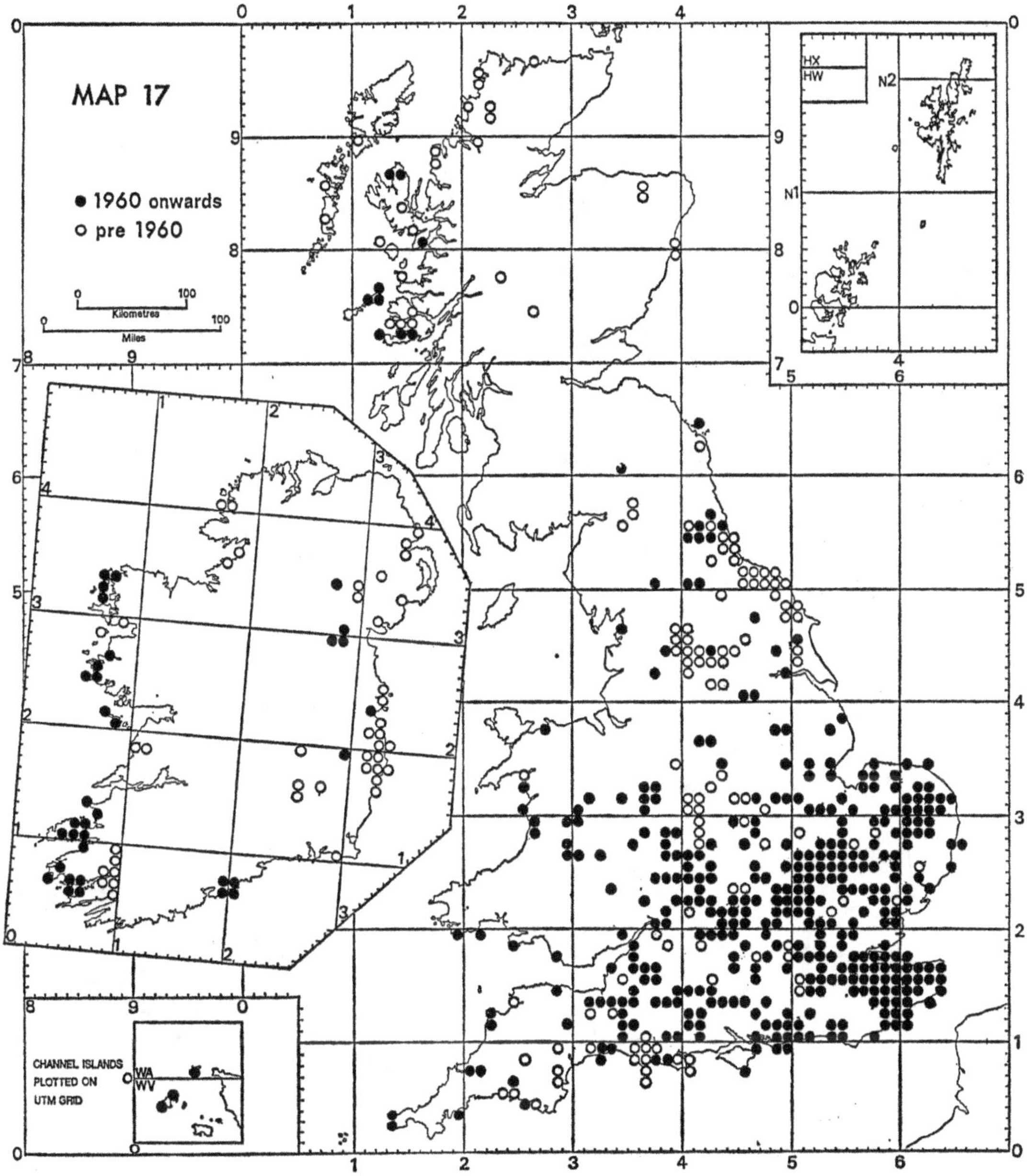

Map 17. *Bombus ruderarius* (Müller).

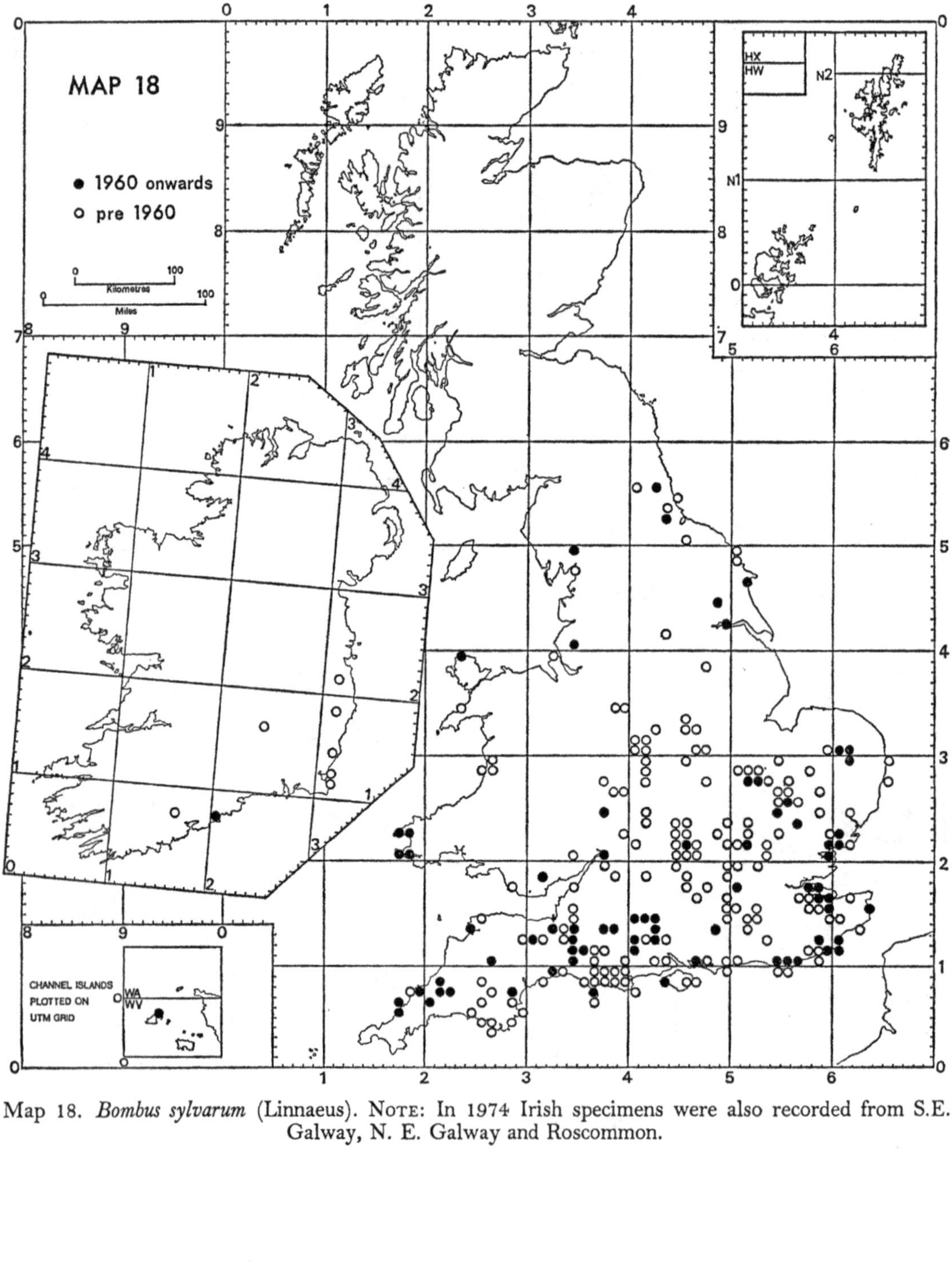

Map 18. *Bombus sylvarum* (Linnaeus). NOTE: In 1974 Irish specimens were also recorded from S.E. Galway, N. E. Galway and Roscommon.

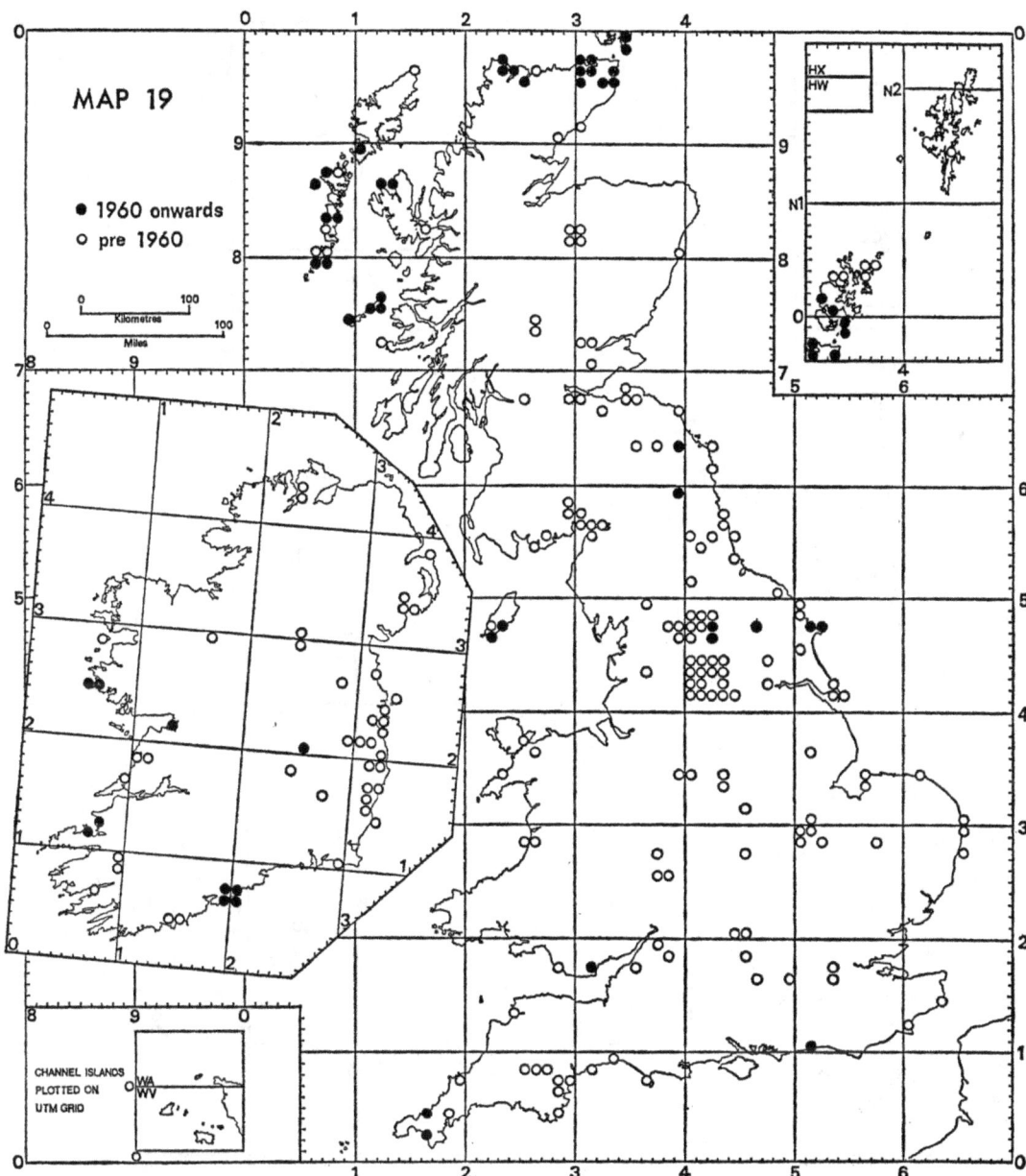

MAP 19

● 1960 onwards
○ pre 1960

Map 19. *Bombus distinguendus* Morawitz.

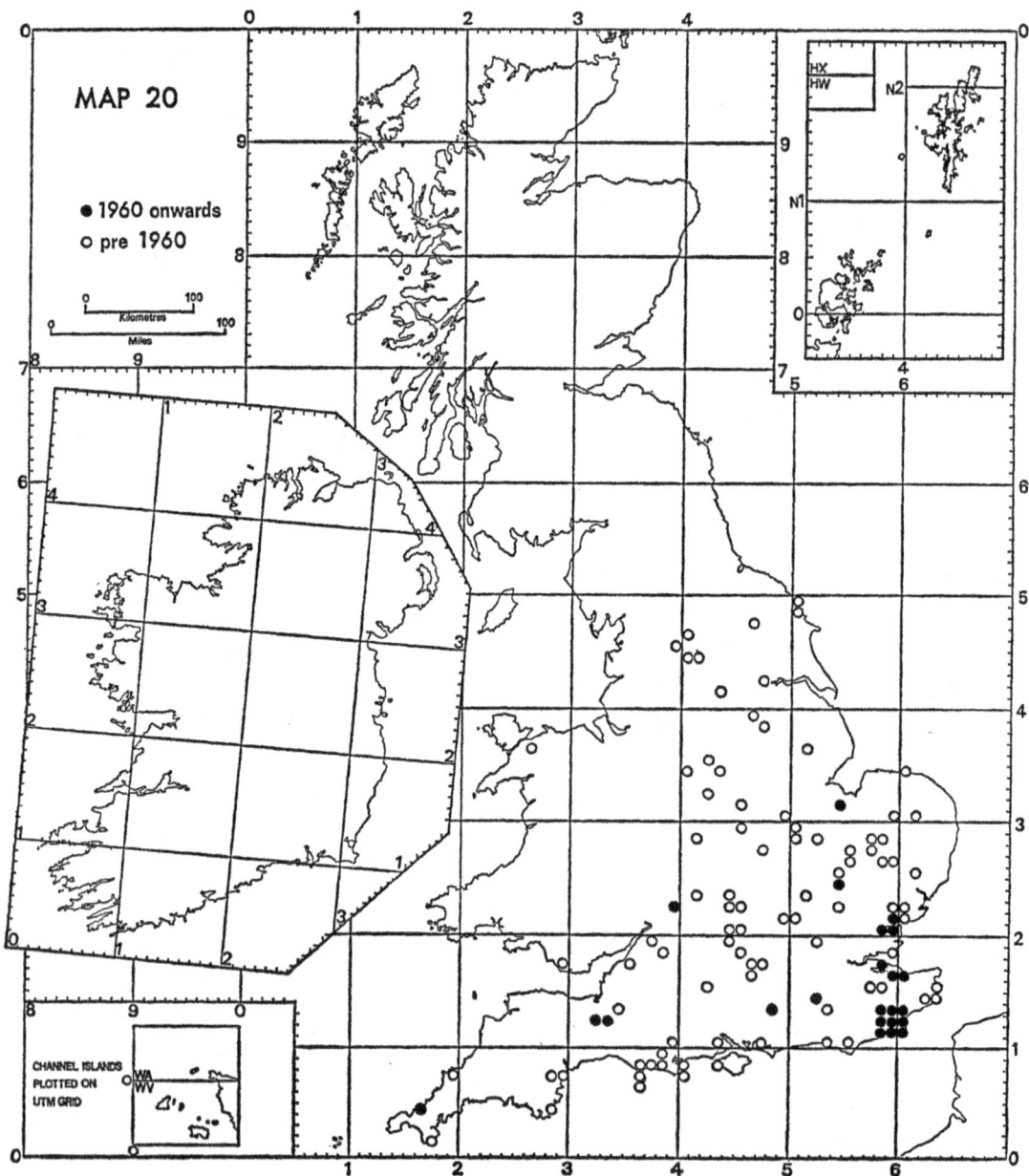

MAP 20

● 1960 onwards
○ pre 1960

CHANNEL ISLANDS
PLOTTED ON
UTM GRID

Map 20. *Bombus subterraneus* (Linnaeus).

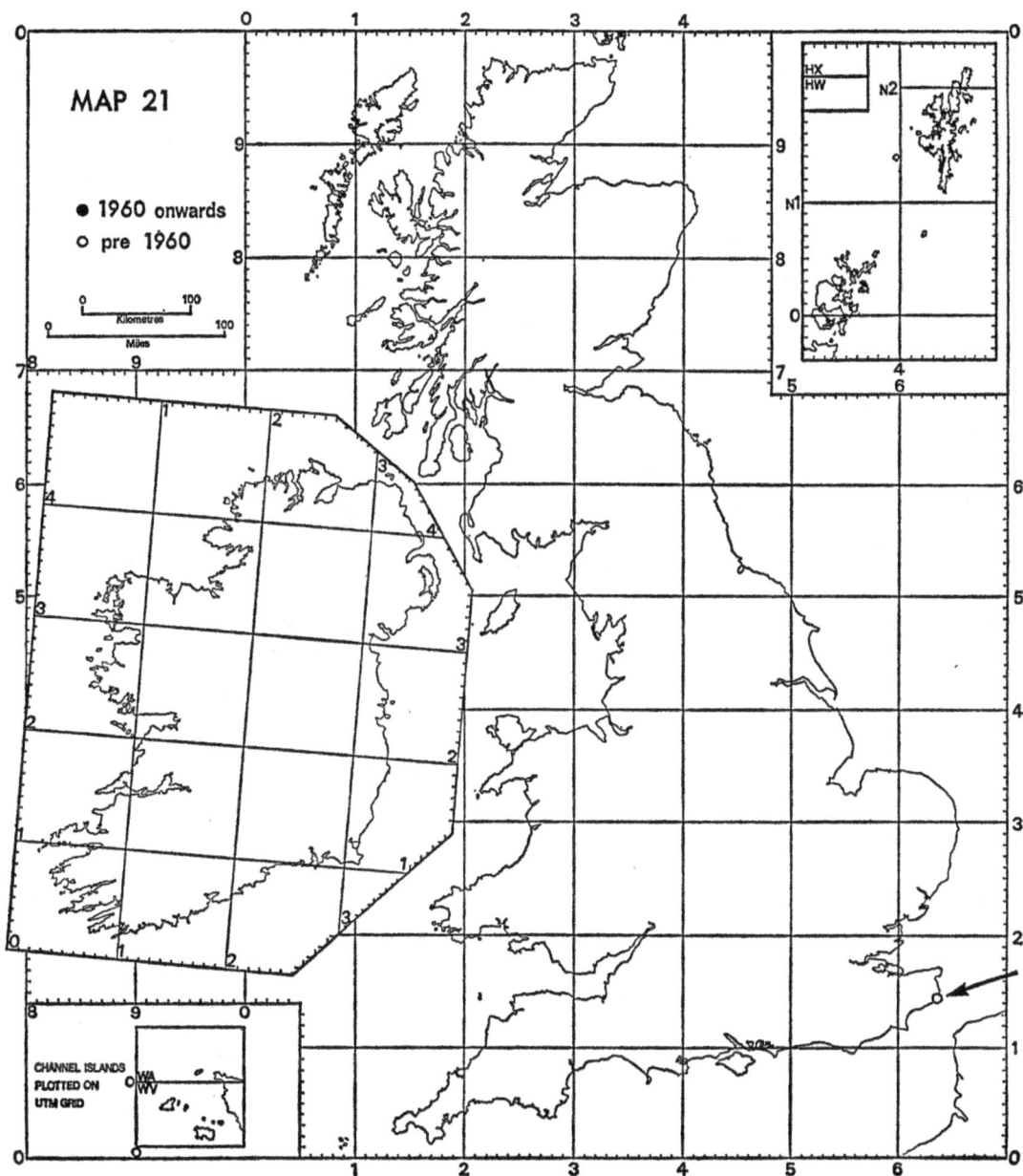

MAP 21

● 1960 onwards
○ pre 1960

Kilometres
100
Miles
100

CHANNEL ISLANDS
PLOTTED ON
UTM GRID

Map 21. *Bombus pomorum* (Panzer). All are pre-1865 records.

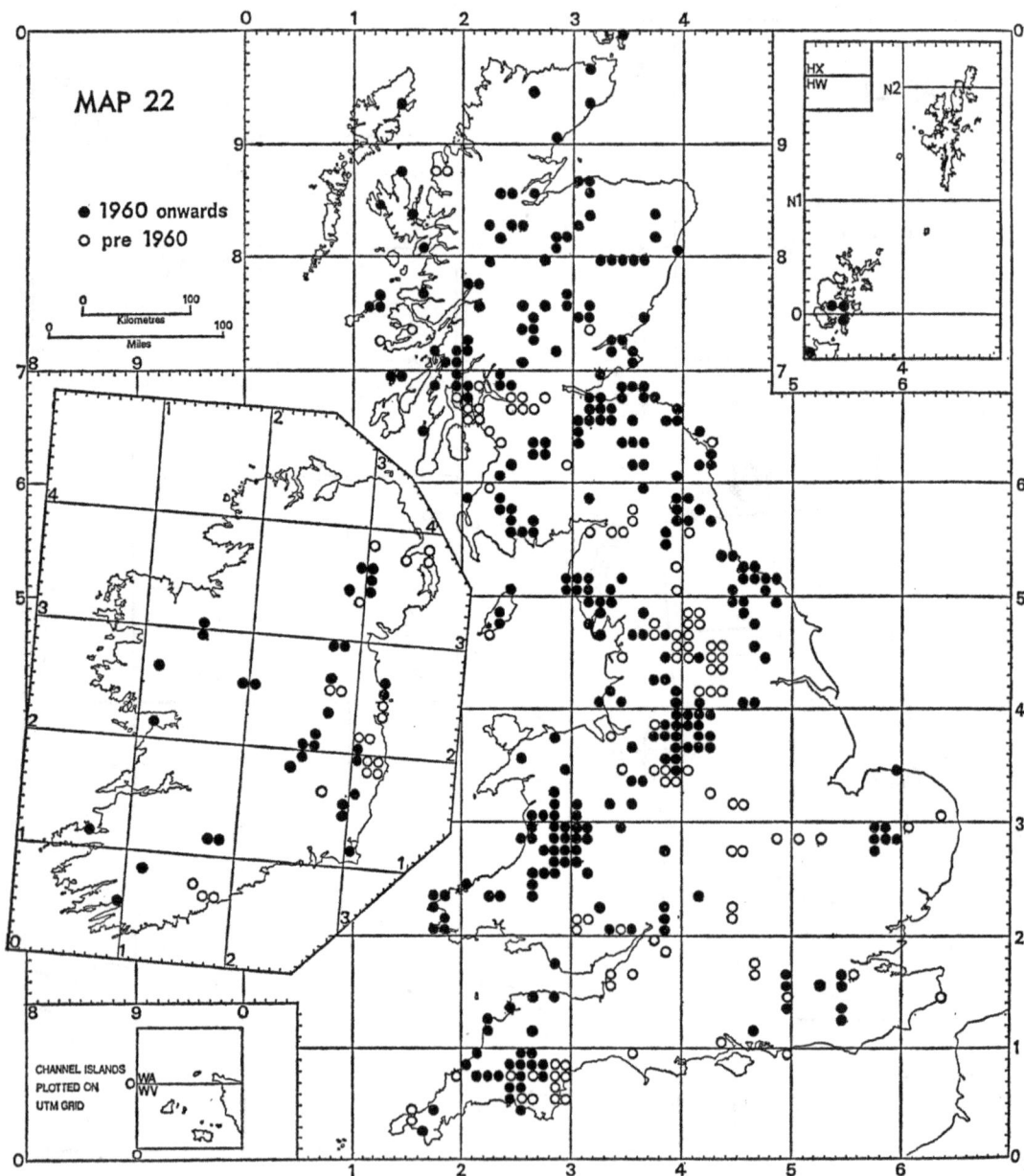

MAP 22

● 1960 onwards
○ pre 1960

Kilometres

Miles

CHANNEL ISLANDS
PLOTTED ON
UTM GRID

Map 22. *Psithyrus bohemicus* (Seidl).

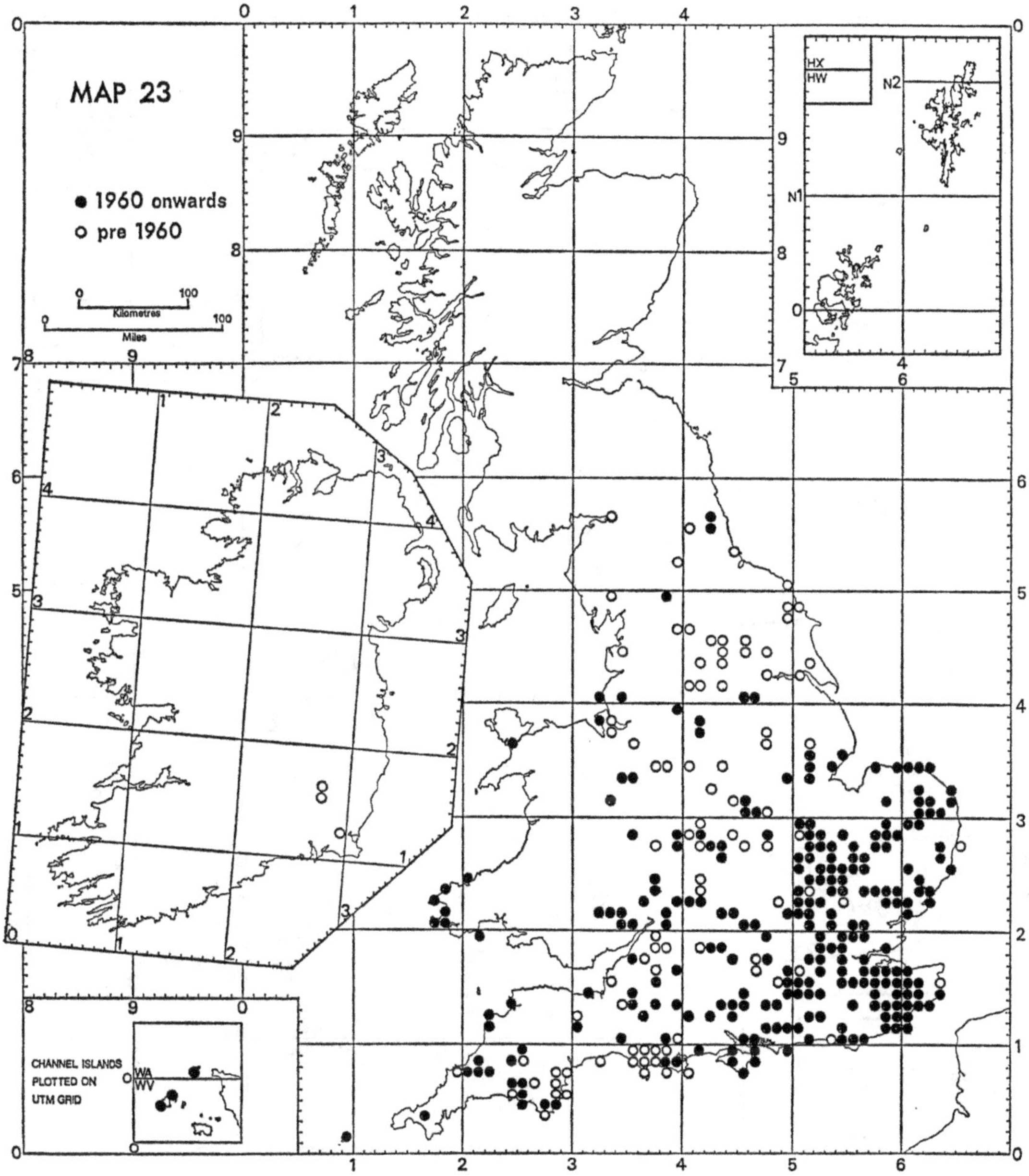
MAP 23
● 1960 onwards
○ pre 1960
Kilometres
Miles
CHANNEL ISLANDS PLOTTED ON UTM GRID
WA
WV
HX
HW
N2
N1

Map 23. *Psithyrus vestalis* (Geoffroy in Fourcroy).

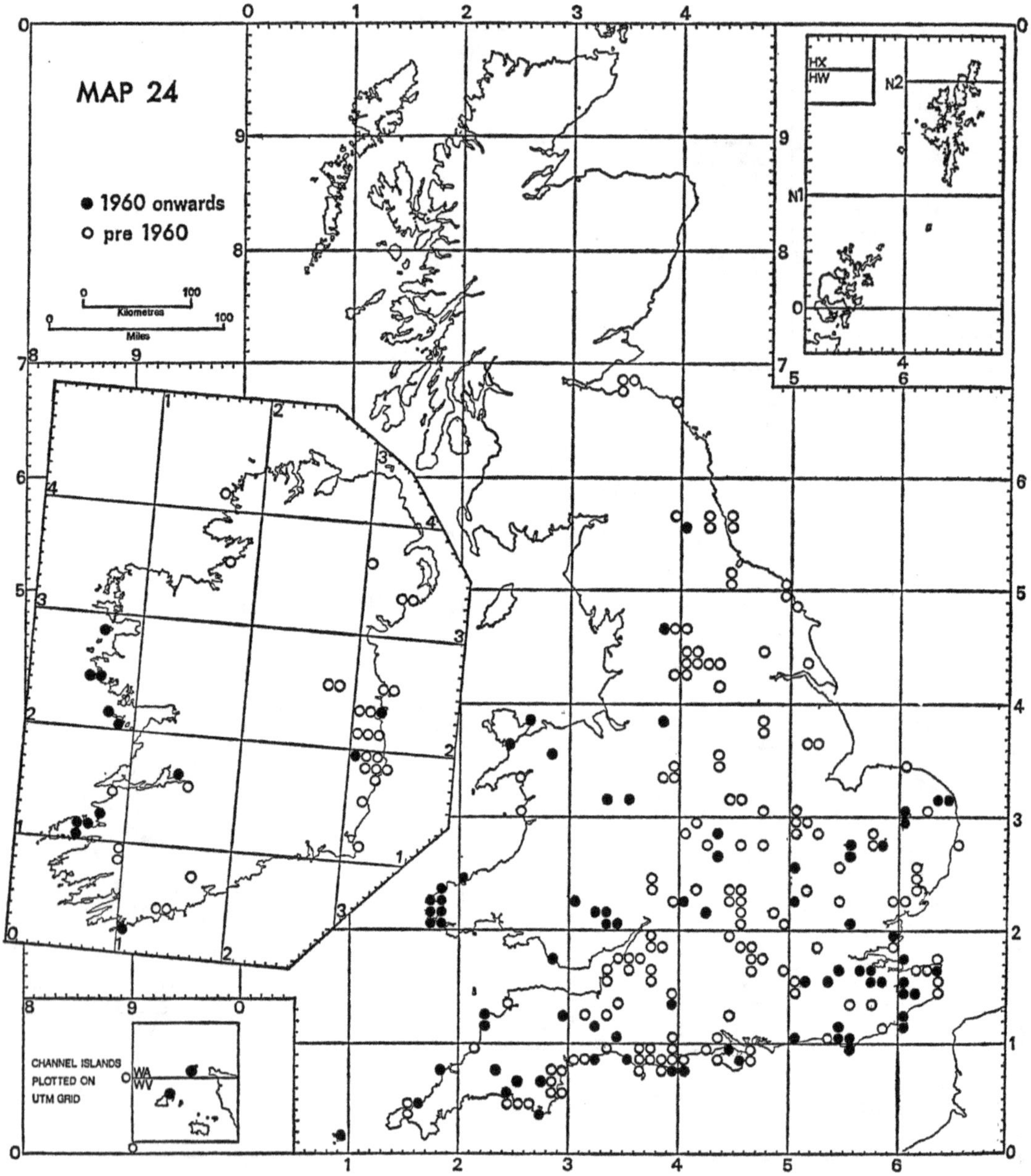

MAP 24

● 1960 onwards
○ pre 1960

Map 24. *Psithyrus rupestris* (Fabricius).

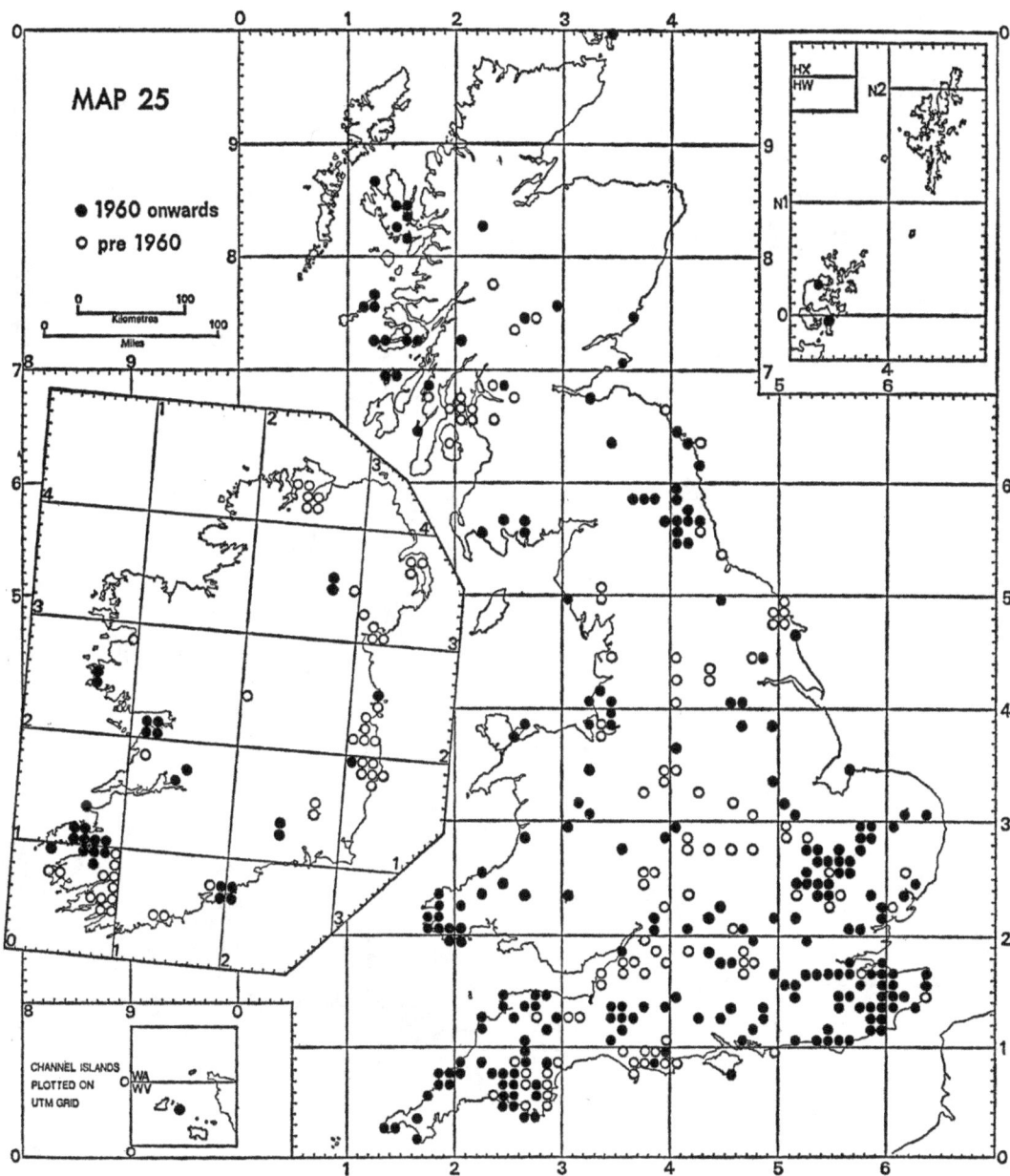

Map 25. *Psithyrus barbutellus* (Kirby).

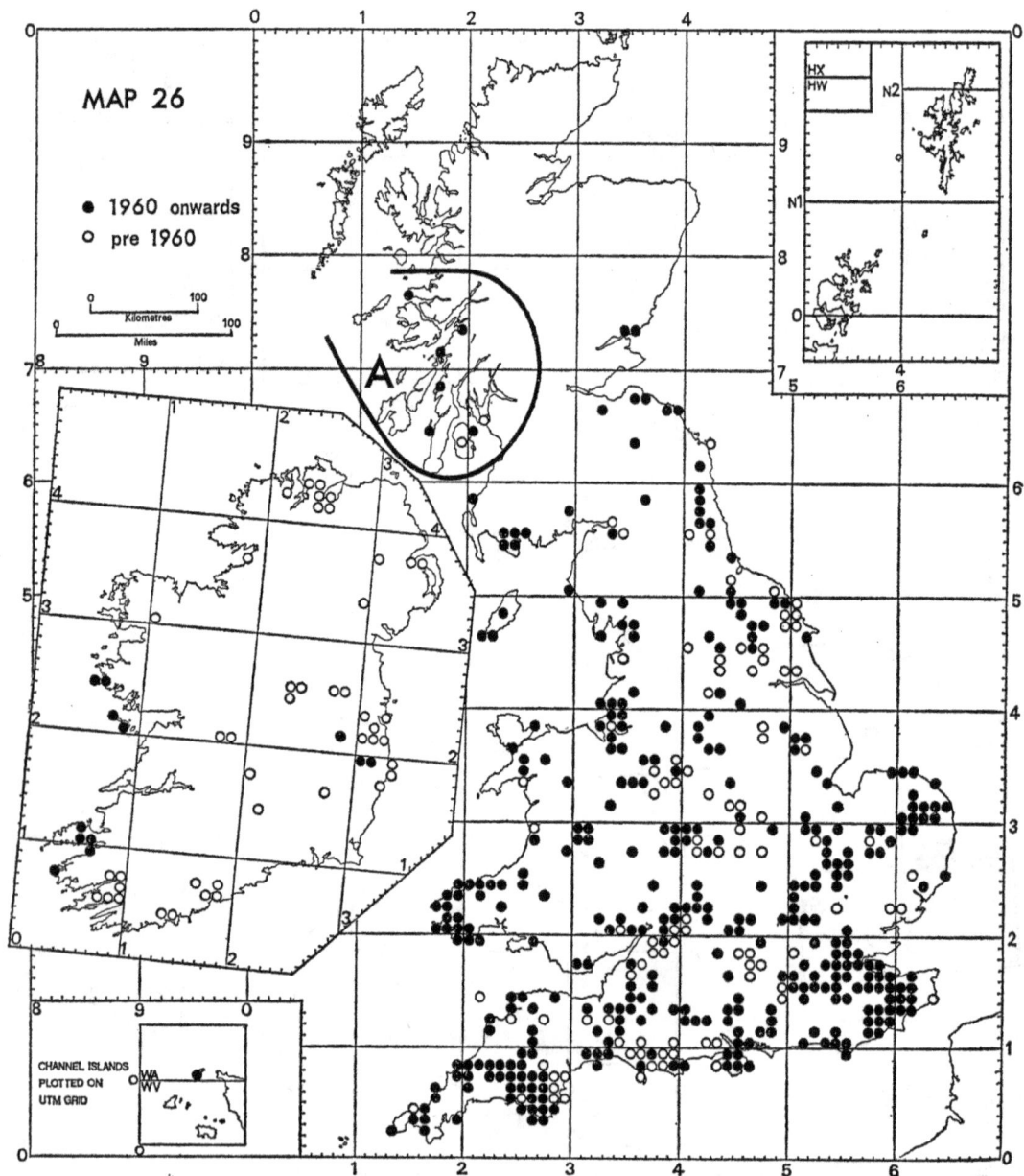

Map 26. *Psithyrus campestris* (Panzer). Subspecies: *Psithyrus campestris campestris* (Panzer);
A—*Psithyrus campestris swynnertoni* Richards.
NOTE: In the Royal Scottish Museum, Edinburgh, there is a very old male *swynnertoni* labelled
'Dumfries (Service) 4/64', but I know of no other specimens captured so far away from the Loch
Sween area. To prevent confusion this old record is not plotted on the map.

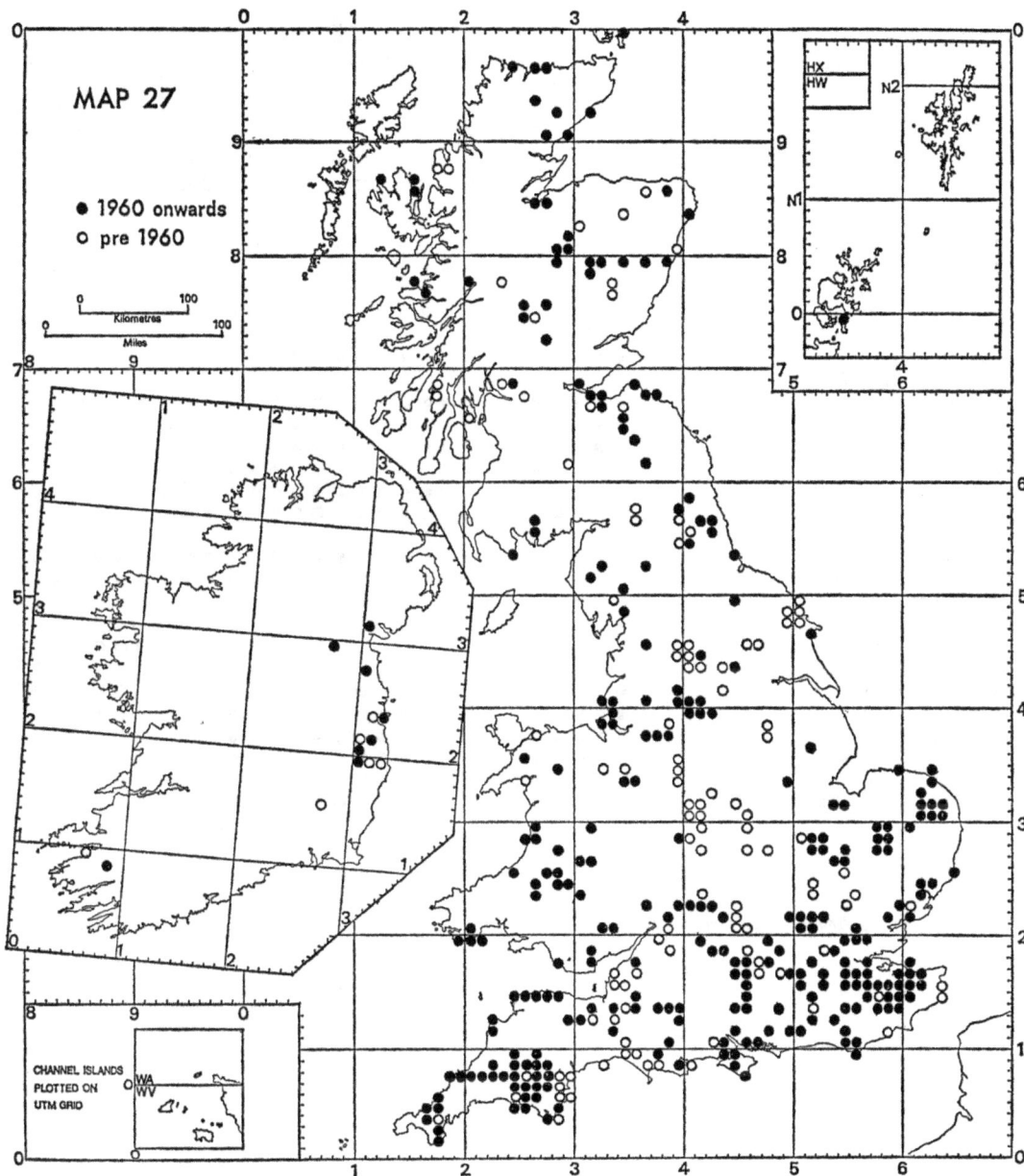

MAP 27

● 1960 onwards
○ pre 1960

CHANNEL ISLANDS
PLOTTED ON
UTM GRID

Map 27. *Psithyrus sylvestris* Lepeletier.

TABLE I

VICE-COUNTY RECORDS FOR ENGLAND AND WALES

VICE-COUNTY columns:

1 W. Cornwall (—Scilly Is.) · (Scilly Isles) · 2 East Cornwall · 3 South Devon · 4 North Devon · (Lundy Island) · 5 South Somerset · 6 North Somerset · 7 North Wiltshire · 8 South Wiltshire · 9 Dorset · 10 Isle of Wight · 11 South Hampshire · 12 North Hampshire · 13 West Sussex · 14 East Sussex · 15 East Kent · 16 West Kent · 17 Surrey · 18 South Essex · 19 North Essex · 20 Hertfordshire · 21 Middlesex · 22 Berkshire · 23 Oxfordshire · 24 Buckinghamshire · 25 East Suffolk · 26 West Suffolk

MAP	SPECIES	1	Sc	2	3	4	Lu	5	6	7	8	9	10	11	12	13	14	15	16	17	18	19	20	21	22	23	24	25	26
2	*Bombus soroeensis*	●		●	●	●		●		○	○	●	○	○	●	●	○		○	○		○	○		○	○	○	○	○
3	*Bombus lucorum*	●	●	●	●	●		●	●	●	●	●	●	●	●	●	●	●	●	●	●	●	●	●	●	●	●	●	●
4	*Bombus magnus*	●		●	●	●		●			●			●								○							
5	*Bombus terrestris*	●	●	●	●	●		●	●	●	●	●	●	●	●	●	●	●	●	●	●	●	●	●	●	●	●	●	●
6	*Bombus cullumanus*							○		○	○		○	○									○		○		○		
7	*Bombus jonellus*	●	●	●	●	●	●	●	●	○		●		●	●	●	●	●	●	●					●			○	●
8	*Bombus lapponicus*	●	●	●				●	○		○			●															
9	*Bombus pratorum*	●		●	●	●		●	●	●	●	●	●	●	●	●	●	●	●	●	●	●	●	●	●	●	●	●	●
10	*Bombus lapidarius*	●	●	●	●	●		●	●	●	●	●	●	●	●	●	●	●	●	●	●	●	●	●	●	●	●	●	●
11	*Bombus hortorum*	●	●	●	●	●		●	●	●	●	●	●	●	●	●	●	●	●	●	●	●	●	●	●	●	●	●	●
12	*Bombus ruderatus*	●		●	●			●	○	○	○	●	●	●	●	●	●	●	●	●	●	●	○	○	●	○	○	○	○
13	*Bombus humilis*	●		●	●	●		●	●	○		●	●	●	●	●	●	●	●	●	●	●	○	●	●	○	○	○	○
14	*Bombus muscorum**	●		●	●	●	●	●	○	○	●	●	●		○	○	●	●						○				●	○
15	*B. m. smithianus* (s.l.)	●																											
16	*Bombus pascuorum*	●		●	●	●		●	●	●	●	●	●	●	●	●	●	●	●	●	●	●	●	●	●	●	●	●	●
17	*Bombus ruderarius*	●		●	●	●		●	●	●	●	●	●	●	●	●	●	●	●	●	●	●	●	●	●	●	●	●	●
18	*Bombus sylvarum*	●		●	●	●		●	●	○	●	●	●	●	●	●	●	○	●	●	●	●	●	●	○	●	○	○	○
19	*Bombus distinguendus*	●		○	○	○		○	○		○			●		○		●		○					○	○		○	○
20	*Bombus subterraneus*	●		○	○			●	○	○	○	○	○	○	●	○	●	○	●	●	●	○	○	○	○	○	○	○	○
21	*Bombus pomorum*																			○									
22	*Psithyrus bohemicus*	●		●	●	●		●	○	○		○		●		○	●	○	●	●				○	○				●
23	*Psithyrus vestalis*	●	●	●	●	●		●	●	○	●	●	●	●	●	●	●	●	●	●	●	●	●	●	●	●	●	●	●
24	*Psithyrus rupestris*	●		●	●	●		●	○	○	○	●	●	○	○	●	●	●	●	●	●	●	●	○	○	○	●	○	○
25	*Psithyrus barbutellus*	●		●	●	●		●	●	●	●	●	●	●	●	●	●	●	●	●	●	●	●	●	●	●	●	●	●
26	*Psithyrus campestris*	●		●	●	●	○	●	●	○	●	●	●	●	●	●	●	●	●	●	●	●	●	●	●	●	●	●	●
27	*Psithyrus sylvestris*	●		●	●	●		●	●	●	●	●	●	●	●	●	●	●	●	●	●	●	●	●	●	●	●	●	●

● 1960 onwards
○ pre 1960
* excluding *Bombus muscorum smithianus* (s.l.)

27 East Norfolk
28 West Norfolk
29 Cambridgeshire
30 Bedfordshire
31 Huntingdonshire
32 Northamptonshire
33 East Gloucestershire
34 West Gloucestershire
35 Monmouthshire
36 Herefordshire
37 Worcestershire
38 Warwickshire
39 Staffordshire
40 Shropshire
41 Glamorgan
42 Breconshire
43 Radnorshire
44 Carmarthenshire
45 Pembrokeshire
46 Cardiganshire
47 Montgomeryshire
48 Merionethshire
49 Caernavonshire
50 Denbyshire
51 Flintshire
52 Anglesey
53 South Lincolnshire
54 North Lincolnshire
55 Leicestershire (+Rutland)
56 Nottinghamshire
57 Derbyshire
58 Cheshire
59 South Lancashire
60 West Lancashire
61 South-east Yorkshire
62 North-east Yorkshire
63 South-west Yorkshire
64 Mid-west Yorkshire
65 North-west Yorkshire
66 Durham
67 South Northumberland
68 North Northumberland
69 Westmorland (+N. Lancashire)
70 Cumberland
71 Isle of Man
113 Channel Isles

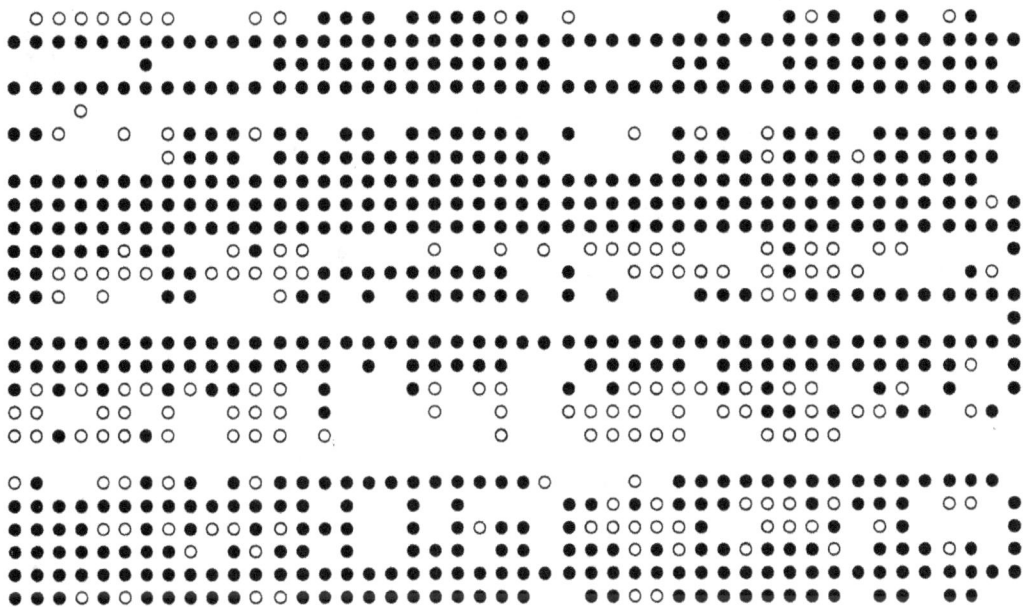

TABLE II

VICE-COUNTY RECORDS FOR SCOTLAND

The table lists bumblebee species (by MAP number) against Scottish vice-counties:

Vice-counties (columns):

72 Dumfriesshire · 73 Kirkcudbrightshire · 74 Wigtownshire · 75 Ayrshire · 76 Renfrewshire · 77 Lanarkshire · 78 Peeblesshire · 79 Selkirkshire · 80 Roxburghshire · 81 Berwickshire · 82 East Lothian · 83 Midlothian · 84 West Lothian · 85 Fifeshire (+Kinross) · 86 Stirlingshire · 87 W. Perthshire (+Clackmannan) · 88 Mid Perthshire · 89 East Perthshire · 90 Angus · 91 Kincardineshire · 92 South Aberdeenshire · 93 North Aberdeenshire · 94 Banffshire · 95 Moray · 96 E. Inverness-shire (+Nairn) · 97 West Inverness-shire · 98 Argyll Main · 99 Dunbartonshire · 100 Clyde Isles · 101 Kintyre · 102 South Ebudes · 103 Mid Ebudes · 104 North Ebudes · 105 West Ross · 106 East Ross · 107 East Sutherland · 108 West Sutherland · 109 Caithness · 110 Outer Hebrides · 111 Orkney Islands · 112 Shetland Islands

Species (rows, with MAP number):

MAP	SPECIES
2	*Bombus soroeensis*
3	*Bombus lucorum*
4	*Bombus magnus*
5	*Bombus terrestris*
7	*Bombus jonellus*
8	*Bombus lapponicus*
9	*Bombus pratorum*
10	*Bombus lapidarius*
11	*Bombus hortorum*
14	*Bombus muscorum**
15	*B. m. smithianus* (s.l.)
16	*Bombus pascuorum*
17	*Bombus ruderarius*
19	*Bombus distinguendus*
22	*Psithyrus bohemicus*
24	*Psithyrus rupestris*
25	*Psithyrus barbutellus*
26	*Psithyrus campestris*
27	*Psithyrus sylvestris*

VICE-COUNTY

● 1960 onwards
○ pre 1960
* excluding *Bombus muscorum smithianus* (s.l.)

[1] *B. m. orcadensis*   [2] see p. 188.

NOTE: Although *Bombus ruderatus* and *B. sylvarum* have been said to occur in Scotland (e.g. by Sladen, 1912) there are no specimens of Scottish origin in the collections of either the Royal Scottish Museum, Edinburgh (Smith, E. M., *in litt.*) or, as far as I am aware, the British Museum (Natural History), London, and neither species seems to appear in Scottish locality lists or literature records. The confirmed distribution patterns for both species (Maps 12 and 18) suggest that the northern limits of their ranges fall short of the Scottish border.

TABLE III

VICE-COUNTY RECORDS FOR IRELAND

VICE-COUNTY (column headings, left to right):

40 Londonderry
39 Antrim
38 Down
37 Armagh
36 Tyrone
35 West Donegal
34 East Donegal
33 Fermanagh
32 Monaghan
31 Louth
30 Cavan
29 Leitrim
28 Sligo
27 West Mayo
26 East Mayo
25 Roscommon
24 Longford
23 West Meath
22 Meath
21 Dublin
20 Wicklow
19 Kildare
18 Offaly
17 North-east Galway
16 West Galway
15 South-east Galway
14 Leix
13 Carlow
12 Wexford
11 Kilkenny
10 North Tipperary
(Aran Islands)
9 Clare (—Aran Is.)
8 Limerick
7 South Tipperary
6 Waterford
5 East Cork
4 Mid Cork
3 West Cork
2 North Kerry
1 South Kerry

MAP	SPECIES
3	*Bombus lucorum*
4	*Bombus magnus*
5	*Bombus terrestris*
7	*Bombus jonellus*
8	*Bombus lapponicus*
9	*Bombus pratorum*
10	*Bombus lapidarius*
11	*Bombus hortorum*
12	*Bombus ruderatus*
14	*Bombus muscorum* *
15	*B. m. smithianus* (s.l.)
16	*Bombus pascuorum*
17	*Bombus ruderarius*
18	*Bombus sylvarum*
19	*Bombus distinguendus*
22	*Psithyrus bohemicus*
23	*Psithyrus vestalis*
24	*Psithyrus rupestris*
25	*Psithyrus barbutellus*
26	*Psithyrus campestris*
27	*Psithyrus sylvestris*

● 1960 onwards
○ pre 1960
* excluding *Bombus muscorum smithianus* (s.l.)

[1] a single queen from Borris, Co. Carlow, is the only confirmed Irish record

APPENDIX II

List of plants mentioned in the text

Plants marked * are non-British

Flowering Plants

Family RANUNCULACEAE
  Aconitum L.
    *Aconitum septentrionale Koelle
Family PAPAVERACEAE
  Papaver L. — Poppies
Family CRUCIFERAE
  Sinapis L.
    Sinapis arvensis L. — Charlock
  Nasturtium Brown — Nasturtium
Family CRASSULACEAE
  Sedum L.
    Sedum album L. — White stonecrop
Family VIOLACEAE
  Viola L.
    Viola tricolor L. — Heartsease
Family TILIACEAE
  Tilia L. — Limes
Family BALSAMINACEAE
  Impatiens L.
    Impatiens glandulifera Royle — Himalayan balsam
Family ACERACEAE
  Acer L.
    Acer pseudoplantanus L. — Sycamore
Family HIPPOCASTANACEAE
  Aesculus L.
    Aesculus hippocastanum L. — Horse-chestnut
Family PAPILIONACEAE
  Sarothamnus Wimmer
    Sarothamnus scorparius (L.) Koch — Broom
  Trifolium L.
    Trifolium pratense L. — Red clover
    Trifolium repens L. — White clover
  Anthyllis L.
    Anthyllis vulneraria L. — Kidney vetch
  Lotus L.
    Lotus corniculatus L. — Common birdsfoot trefoil
  Vicia L.
    Vicia faba L. — Field bean
  Phaseolus L.
    Phaseolus multiflorus Willdenon — Runner bean
Family ROSACEAE
  Rubus L.
    Rubus idaeus L. — Raspberry
    Rubus fruticosus L. — Bramble (blackberry)

Potentilla L. — Cinquefoil
Prunus L. — Cherry, etc.
  Prunus spinosa L. — Blackthorn (sloe)
Malus L. — Apple
Cotoneaster Ehrhart — Cotoneaster
Family GROSSULARIACEAE
  Ribes L.
    Ribes nigrum L. — Black currant
    Ribes sanguineum L. — Flowering currant
Family ONAGRACEAE
  Chamaenerion Adanson
    Chamaenerion angustifolium (L.) Scopoli — Rose-bay willowherb
    (syn. Epilobium angustifolium L.) — Fireweed
Family ARALIACEAE
  Hedera L.
    Hedera helix L. — Ivy
Family UMBELLIFERAE
  Eryngium L.
    Eryngium maritimum L. — Sea Holly
  Heracleum L.
    Heracleum sphondylium L. — Hogweed
Family SALICACEAE
  Salix L. — Willows and sallows
    Salix caprea L. — Pussy willow
    Salix atrocinerea Brotero — Common sallow
Family ERICACEAE
  Calluna Salisbury
    Calluna vulgaris (L.) Hull — Ling
  Erica L. — Heaths or heathers
  Vaccinium L.
    Vaccinium myrtillus L. — Bilberry
Family RHODODENDROIDEAE
  Rhododendron L. — Rhododendron
Family LOGANIACEAE
  Buddleja L.
    Buddleja davidii Franchet — Buddleia
Family BORAGINACEAE
  Symphytum L.
    Symphytum officinale L. — Common comfrey
  Echium L.
    Echium vulgare L. — Viper's bugloss

Family SOLANACEAE
  Solanum L.
    Solanum dulcamara L.   Woody nightshade
Family SCROPHULARIACEAE
  Antirrhinum L.
    Antirrhinum majus L.   Common snapdragon
  Linaria Miller
    Linaria vulgaris Miller   Yellow toadflax
  Scrophularia L.   Figworts
  Digitalis L.
    Digitalis purpurea L.   Foxglove
  Odontites Gilibert
    Odontites verna (Bellardi) Dumortier   Red bartsia
Family LABIATAE
  Lavandula L.   Lavender
  Origanum L.
    Origanum vulgare L.   Marjoram
  Prunella L.
    Prunella vulgaris L.   Self-heal
  Stachys L.   Woundworts
  Ballota L.
    Ballota nigra L.   Black horehound
  Lamium L.
    Lamium purpureum L.   Red dead-nettle
    Lamium album L.   White dead-nettle

Glechoma L.
  Glechoma hederacea L.   Ground ivy
Teucrium L.
  Teucrium scorodonia L.   Wood-sage
Ajuga L.
  Ajuga reptans L.   Bugle
Family CAPRIFOLIACEAE
  Lonicera L.
    Lonicera periclymenum L.   Honeysuckle
Family DIPSACACEAE
  Knautia L.   Scabious
Family COMPOSITAE
  Helianthus L.
    Helianthus annuus L.   Sunflower
  Carduus L.
    Carduus nutans L.   Musk thistle
  Cirsium Miller
    Cirsium arvense (L.) Scopoli   Creeping thistle
    Cirsium acaulon (L.) Scopoli   Dwarf thistle
  Centaurea L.
    Centaurea scabiosa L.   Greater knapweed
    Centaurea nigra L.   Hardhead
  Taraxacum Weber
    Taraxacum officinale Weber   Dandelion

Micro-organisms

Fungi

Order ASCOMYCETES
Family EUROTIALES
  Aspergillus Micheli ex Fries
  Penicillium Link ex Fries

Order DEUTEROMYCETES
Family MONILIALES
  Beauveria Vuillemin
    Beauveria bassiana (Balsamo) Vuillemin

Bacteria

Order EUBACTERIALES
Family ENTEROBACTERIACEAE
  Erwinia Winslow, *et al.*
    Erwinia amylovora (Burrill)

List of animals mentioned in the text

Animals marked * are non-British

(A) Protozoa

Order MICROSPORIDIA
Family NOSEMATIDAE
Nosema Naegeli
Nosema apis Zander
Nosema bombi Fantham & Porter

(B) Metazoa

Invertebrates

Nematodes

Order TYLENCHIDA
Family ALLANTONEMATIDAE
Sphaerularia Dufour
Sphaerularia bombi Dufour

Insects

Order DERMAPTERA
Family FORFICULIDAE
Forficula L.
Forficula auricularia L.   Common earwig
Order HEMIPTERA
Family *PHYMATIDAE
**Phymata* Latreille   Ambush bugs
**Phymata pennsylvanica americana* Melin
Family PSYLLIDAE   Suckers
Psylla Geoffroy
Psylla crataegi (Schrank)
Family APHIDIDAE   Aphids
Order LEPIDOPTERA
Family SPHINGIDAE
Hemaris Dalman
Hemaris tityus (L.)   Narrow-bordered bee hawk moth
Hemaris fuciformis (L.)   Broad-bordered bee hawk moth

Family NOCTUIDAE
Agrotis Ochsenheimer
Agrotis segetum (Schiffermüller)   Turnip moth
Family PYRALIDAE
Plodia Guenée
Plodia interpunctella (Hübner)   Indian meal moth
Ephestia Guenée
Ephestia kühniella Zeller   Mediterranean flour moth
Ephestia cautella (Walker)   Dried currant moth
Galleria Fabricius
Galleria mellonella (L.)   Honeycomb moth
Achroia Hübner
Achroia grisella (Fabricius)   Honey bee wax-moth
Aphomia Hübner
Aphomia sociella (L.)   Bumblebee wax-moth
**Vitula* Ragonot
**Vitula edmandsii* (Packard)   Dried fruit moth

Family OECOPHORIDAE
    Endrosis Hübner
        Endrosis sarcitrella (L.)   White-shouldered house
                                 moth
    Hofmannophila Spuler
        Hofmannophila pseudospretella   (Stainton) Large
                              brown house moth
Family TINEIDAE
    Tinea L.
        Tinea simplicella Herrich-Schäffer   Simple clothes
                                 moth
Order COLEOPTERA
Family SILPHIDAE
    Necrophorus Fabricius
        Necrophorus investigator Zetterstedt
Family CLERIDAE
    *Trichodes Herbst
        *Trichodes ornatus Say
Family DERMESTIDAE
    Anthrenus Geoffroy in Müller
        Anthrenus museorum (L.)   Museum beetle
Family NITIDULIDAE
    Epuraea Erichson
        Epuraea depressa (Illiger)
Family CRYPTOPHAGIDAE
    Cryptophagus (Herbst) Paykull
    Antherophagus Latreille
        Antherophagus nigricornis (Fabricius)
        (syn. *A. silaceus* (Herbst))
        *Antherophagus ochraceus Mels
        Antherophagus pallens Oliver
    *Emphylus Erichson
        *Emphylus glaber (Gyllenhal)
        *(syn. Antherophagus glaber Gyllenhal)
Family SCARABAEIDAE
    Trichius Fabricius
        Trichius fasciatus (L.)
Order HYMENOPTERA
Family BRACONIDAE
    Hysteromerus Westmael
        Hysteromerus mystacinus Westmael
    Apanteles Foerster
    Blacus Nees
        Blacus paganus Haliday
    Meteorus Haliday
        Meteorus pulchricornis (Westmael)
        *Meteorus salicorniae Schmiedeknecht
    Syntretus Foerster
        Syntretus splendidus (Marshall)
    Aspilota Foerster
    Orthostigma Ratzeburg
        Orthostigma pumilum (Nees)
Family ICHNEUMONIDAE
    Stenocryptus Thompson
    (syn. *Cubocephalus* Ratzeburg)
    Stilpnus Gravenhorst
        Stilpnus gagates Gravenhorst
Family TORYMYIDAE
    Monodontomerus Westwood

        *Monodontomerus montivagus Ashmead
Family EULOPHIDAE
    Melittobia Westwood
        Melittobia acasta (Walker)
Family FORMICIDAE   Ants
    Lasius Fabricius
        Lasius flavus (Fabricius)
        Lasius niger (L.)
    Myrmica Latreille
        Myrmica rubra (L.)
Family MUTILLIDAE   Velvet ants
    Mutilla L.
        Mutilla europaea L.
Family VESPIDAE   Social wasps
    Vespula Thomson
    Vespa L.
        Vespa crabro L.   Hornet
    *Polistes Latreille
Family SPHECIDAE
    Philanthus Fabricius
        *Philanthus bicinctus (Mickel)
        Philanthus triangulum (Fabricius)
Family APIDAE   Bees
    Halictus Latreille
        Halictus malachurus (Kirby)
    Anthophora Latreille
        Anthophora retusa (L.)
        Anthophora pilipes (Fabricius)
    Bombus Latreille[1]   'True' bumblebees
    Section ANODONTOBOMBUS Krüger
    Subgenus **ALPIGENOBOMBUS* Skorikov
        *Bombus mastrucatus Gerstäcker
    Subgenus *KALLOBOMBUS* von Dalla Torre
        Bombus soroeensis (Fabricius)
    Subgenus *BOMBUS* Latreille
        *Bombus affinis Cresson
        Bombus lucorum (L.)
        Bombus magnus Krüger
        Bombus terrestris (L.)
        *Bombus terricola Kirby
    Subgenus **CONFUSIBOMBUS* Ball
        *Bombus confusus Schenck
    Subgenus **MENDACIBOMBUS* Skorikov
        *Bombus mendax Gerstäcker
    Subgenus **BOMBIAS* Robertson
        *Bombus auricomus Robertson
        *Bombus nevadensis Cresson
    Subgenus **SEPARATOBOMBUS* Frison
        *Bombus separatus Cresson
    Subgenus *CULLUMANOBOMBUS* Vogt
        Bombus cullumanus (Kirby)
        *Bombus rufocinctus Cresson
    Subgenus *PYROBOMBUS* von Dalla Torre
        *Bombus bifarius nearcticus Handlirsch
        *Bombus bimaculatus Cresson
        *Bombus frigidus Smith
        *Bombus huntii Greene
        *Bombus hypnorum (L.)
        *(syn. B. ericetorum (Panzer))

---

[1] Synonyms for British species are given in Chapters 9 and 11.

Bombus ignitus Smith
Bombus impatiens Cresson
Bombus jonellus (Kirby)
Bombus lapponicus (Fabricius)
Bombus pratorum (L.)
Bombus ternarius Say
Bombus vagans Smith
Subgenus *MELANOBOMBUS* von Dalla Torre
Bombus lapidarius (L.)
Subgenus *ALPINOBOMBUS* Skorikov
Bombus balteatus Dahlbom
Bombus hyperboreus Schönherr
Bombus polaris Curtis
Section ODONTOBOMBUS Krüger
Subgenus *MEGABOMBUS* von Dalla Torre
Bombus hortorum (L.)
Bombus ruderatus (Fabricius)
Subgenus *THORACOBOMBUS* von Dalla Torre
Bombus humilis Illiger
Bombus inexspectatus (Tkalcu)
Bombus muscorum (L.)
Bombus pascuorum (Scopoli)
Bombus ruderarius (Müller)
Bombus sylvarum (L.)
Subgenus *SUBTERRANEOBOMBUS* Vogt
Bombus appositus Cresson
Bombus distinguendus Morawitz
Bombus subterraneus (L.)
Subgenus *RHODOBOMBUS* von Dalla Torre
Bombus mesomelas Gerstäcker
*(syn. *Bombus elegans* (Seidl))
Bombus pomorum (Panzer)
Subgenus *FERVIDOBOMBUS* Skorikov
Bombus americanorum (Fabricius)
Bombus fervidus (Fabricius)
Bombus incarum Franklin
Bombus pennsylvanicus De Geer
Psithyrus Lepeletier[1]   'Inquiline' bumblebees
Subgenus *ASHTONIPSITHYRUS* Frison
Psithyrus bohemicus (Seidl)
Psithyrus vestalis (Geoffroy in Fourcroy)
Subgenus *PSITHYRUS* Lepeletier
Psithyrus rupestris (Fabricius)
Subgenus *ALLOPSITHYRUS* Popov
Psithyrus barbutellus (Kirby)
Subgenus *METAPSITHYRUS* Popov
Psithyrus campestris (Panzer)
Subgenus *FERNALDAEPSITHYRUS* Frison
Psithyrus globosus Eversmann
Psithyrus sylvestris Lepeletier
Subgenus *LABORIOPSITHYRUS* Frison
Psithyrus insularis (Smith)
Psithyrus laboriosus (Fabricius)
Apis L.
Apis mellifera L.   Honey bee
Order DIPTERA
Family SCIARIDAE   Fungus gnats
Lycoriella Frey

Family CYRTIDAE   Bee-flies
Bombylius L.
Bombylius major L.
Bombylius minor L.
Family ASILIDAE   Robber-flies
Asilus L.
Asilus crabroniformis L.
Mallophora Macquart
Mallophora bomboides (Wiedemann)
Mallophora orcina (Wiedemann)
Proctacanthus Macquart
Proctacanthus hinei Bromley
Family PHORIDAE
Megaselia Rondani
Subgenus *MEGASELIA* Rondani
Megaselia rufipes (Meigen)
Subgenus *APHIOCHAETA* Brues
Megaselia rata (Wood)
Gymnoptera Lioy
Gymnoptera vitripennis (Meigen)
Family SURPHIDAE
Merodon Meigen
Merodon equestris (Fabricius)   Large narcissus fly
Criorhina Meigen
Criorhina ranunculi (Panzer)
Volucella Geoffroy
Volucella bombylans (L.)
Family CONOPIDAE   Big-headed flies
Thecophora Rondani
Physocephala Schiner
Physocephala rufipes (Fabricius)
Physocephala texana (Williston)
Conops L.
Sicus Scopoli
Sicus ferrugineus (L.)
Family DROSOPHILIDAE   Fruit-flies
Drosophila Fallén
Family LARVAEVORIDAE (=TACHINIDAE)
Salmacia Meigen
(syn. *Gonia* Meigen)
Salmacia sicula (Robineau-Desvoidy)
(syn. *Gonia faciata* Meigen)
Echinomyia Latreille
Echinomyia grossa (L.)
Family CALLIPHORIDAE
Brachicoma Rondani
Brachicoma devia (Fallén)
Brachicoma sarcophagina Townsend
Macronichia Rondani
Macronichia polyodon (Meigen)
Family SARCOPHAGIDAE
Senotainia Macquart
Senotainia tricuspis (Meigen)
Family MUSCIDAE
Fannia Robineau-Desvoidy
Fannia canicularis (L.)
Order SIPHONAPTERA
Family CERATOPHYLLIDAE
Ceratophyllus Curtis
Ceratophyllus gallinae (Schrank)   'Bird-flea'

---

[1] Synonyms for British species are given in Chapters 9 and 11.

Arachnids

ACARINA — Mites
Order MESOSTIGMATA
Family PARASITIDAE
  Parasitus Latreille
    Parasitus fucorum (De Geer)
    (syn. *P. bomborum* Oudemans)
Family DERMANYSSIDAE
  Hypoaspis Canestrini
  (includes *Pneumolaelaps* Berlese)
Family ASCIDAE
  Proctolaelaps Berlese
  (includes *Garmania* Nesbitt and *Garmaniella*
                Westerboer)
Family UROPODIDAE
  Fuscuropoda Vitzthum
    Fuscuropoda marginata Koch
Order ASTIGMATA
Family ACARIDAE
  Acarus L.
    Acarus siro L.
  Kutzinia Zachvatkin
    Kutzinia laevis (Dujardin)
    (syn. *Tyrophagus laevis* Dujardin)

Family GLYCYPHAGIDAE
  Glycyphagus Hering
    Glycyphagus domesticus (De Geer)
    Glycyphagus ornatus (Kramer)
Order PROSTIGMATA
Family PODAPOLIPODIDAE
  Bombacarus Stammer
  (sometimes included in *Locustacarus* Ewing)
    Bombacarus buchneri Stammer
Family SCUTACARIDAE
  Scutacarus Gros
    Scutacarus acarorum (Goeze)
    (syn. *Scutacarus femoris* Gros)
  Acarapis Hirst
    Acarapis woodi (Rennie)
ARANEIDA — Spiders
Family THOMISIDAE
  Misumena Latreille
    Misumena vatia (Clerck)
Family ARGIOPIDAE
  Argiope Savigny
    *Argiope aurantia Lucas
    Argiope bruennichi (Scopoli)
PSEUDOSCORPIONES — Pseudoscorpions

Vertebrates

Fish

Order TELEOSTEI
Family SALMONIDAE
  Salmo L.
    Salmo trutta L. — Trout

Birds

Order PASSERIFORMES
Family PARIDAE
  Parus L.
    Parus major L. — Great tit

Family LANIDAE
  Lanius L.
    Lanius collurio L. — Red-backed shrike
    Lanius excubitor L. — Great grey shrike

311

Mammals

Order INSECTIVORA
Family ERINACIDAE
  Erinaceus L.
    Erinaceus europaeus L. — Hedgehog
Family SORICIDAE
  Sorex L. — Shrews
Family TALPIDAE
  Talpa L.
    Talpa europaea L. — Common mole
Order RODENTIA
Family SCIURIDAE
  Sciurus L. — Squirrels
Family CRICETIDAE
  Clethrionomys Tilesius — Voles
  Microtus Schrenk — Voles

Family MURIDAE
  Apodemus Kaup
    Apodemus sylvaticus (L.) — Long-tailed field mouse
Order CARNIVORA
Family CANIDAE
  Vulpes Oken
    Vulpes vulpes (L.) — Fox
Family MUSTELIDAE
  Meles Brisson
    Meles meles (L.) — Badger
  Mustela L.
    Mustela nivalis L. — Weasel
  Mephitis Saint-Hilaire & Cuvier
    Mephitis mephitis Schreber — Skunk

REFERENCES

Alfken, J. D. (1913). Die Bienenfauna von Bremen. *Abh. naturw. Ver. Bremen 22*: 1–220.

Alford, D. V. (1968). The biology and immature stages of *Syntretus splendidus* (Marshall) (Hymenoptera: Braconidae, Euphorinae), a parasite of adult bumblebees. *Trans. R. ent. Soc. Lond. 120*: 375–393.

— (1969a). Studies on the fat-body of adult bumble bees. *J. Apic. Res. 8*: 37–48.

— (1969b). *Sphaerularia bombi* as a parasite of bumble bees in England. *J. Apic. Res. 8*: 49–54.

— (1969c). A study of the hibernation of bumblebees (Hymenoptera: Bombidae) in southern England. *J. Anim. Ecol. 38*: 149–170.

— (1970a). The incipient stages of development of bumblebee colonies. *Insectes soc. 17*: 1–10.

— (1970b). The production of adults in incipient colonies of *Bombus agrorum* (F.) (Hymenoptera: Bombidae). *Proc. R. ent. Soc. Lond. (A) 45*: 6–13.

— (1970–2). Bumblebee Distribution Maps Scheme. Guide to the British species. Part I. *Entomologist's Gaz. 21*: 109–116. Part II. *Ibid. 22*: 29–36. Part III. *Ibid. 22*: 97–102. Part IV. *Ibid. 22*: 229–234. Part V. *Ibid. 23*: 17–24. Part VI. *Ibid. 23*: 227–236.

— (1971). Egg laying by bumble bee queens at the beginning of colony development. *Bee Wld 52*: 11–18.

— (1973a). Bumblebees in Britain. *Cent. assn Beekeepers*, 12 pp.

— (1973b). Cohabitation of a birdbox by two species of bumblebee. *Entomologist's mon. Mag. 109*: 114–116.

— (1973c). *Syntretus splendidus* attacking *Bombus pascuorum* in Hampshire. *Bee Wld 54*: 176.

Armitage, K. B. (1965). Notes on the biology of *Philanthus bicinctus* (Hymenoptera: Sphecidae) (Mickel), *J. Kansas ent. Soc. 38*: 89–100.

Awram, W. J. (1970). *Flight route behaviour of bumblebees*. Ph.D. thesis, University of London.

Baer, W. (1921). Die Tachinen als Schmarotzer der schädlichen Insekten. Ihre Lebensweise, wirtschaftliche Bedeutung und systematische Kennzeichnung. *Z. angew. Ent. 7*: 349–423.

Bailey, L. (1954). The respiratory currents in the tracheal system of the adult honey-bee. *J. exp. Biol. 29*: 310–327.

— (1971). *Rep. Rothamsted exp. Stn for 1970, Part 1*: 207.

Bailey, L. and Gibbs, A. J. (1964). Infection of bees with acute paralysis virus. *J. Insect Pathol. 6*: 395–407.

Balduf, W. V. (1939). Food habits of *Phymata pennsylvanica americana* Melin (Hemip.). *Can. Ent. 71*: 66–74.

— (1941). Life history of *Phymata pennsylvanica americana* Melin (Phymatidae, Hemiptera). *Ann. ent. Soc. Amer. 34*: 204–214.

Balfour-Browne, F. (1922). On the life-history of *Melittobia acasta* Walker, a chalcid parasite of bees and wasps. *Parasitology 14*: 349–370.

Ball, P. J. (1914). Les bourdons de la Belgique. *Ann. Soc. ent. Belg. 58*: 77–108.

Beirne, B. P. (1952). *British pyralid and plume moths*. London.

Bergstrom, G., Kullenberg, B., Stallberg-Stenhagen, S. and Stenhagen, E. (1968). Studies on natural odouriferous compounds. II. Identification of a 2,3-dihydrofarnesol as the main component of the marking perfume of male bumblebees of the species *Bombus terrestris* L. *Ark. Kemi 28*: 453–469.

Berlese, A. (1921). Centuria quinta di nuovi. *Redia 14*: 143–195.

Betts, A. D. (1920). *Nosema* in humble bees. *Bee Wld 1*: 171.

Bischoff, H. (1927). *Biologie der Hymenopteren*. Berlin.

Blackith, R. E. (1957). Social facilitation at the nest entrance of some Hymenoptera. *Physiol. comp. Oecol. 4*: 388–402.

Bohart, G. E. (1970). The evolution of parasitism among bees. *Utah State University*, 30 pp.

Bohart, G. E. and Knowlton, G. F. (1953). Yearly population fluctuation of *Bombus morrisoni* at Fredonia, Arizona. *J. econ. Ent. 46*: 890.

Boiko, A. K. (1949). [Apimyiasis in bees]. *In Russian. Works vet. Sect. Lenin Acad. agric. Sci. Session 27* [On bee diseases]: 115–135. (*Apic. Abstr. 8*: 387/57).

Bols, J. H. (1937). Observations on *Bombus* and *Psithyrus*, especially on their hibernation. *Proc. R. ent. Soc. Lond. (A) 12*: 47–50.

— (1939). Un remarquable terrain d'hivernation de *Bombus* et de *Psithyrus* près Louvain, à Lubbeek, en Belgique. *Verh. VII int. Congr. Ent.* 1048–1060.

Brian, A. D. (1951a). Brood development in *Bombus agrorum* (Hym., Bombidae). *Entomologist's mon. Mag. 87*: 207–212.

— (1951b). The pollen collected by bumble-bees. *J. Anim. Ecol. 20*: 191–194.

— (1952). Division of labour and foraging in *Bombus agrorum* Fabricius. *J. Anim. Ecol. 21*: 223–240.

— (1954). The foraging of bumble bees. *Bee Wld 35*: 61–67, 81–91.

— (1957). Differences in the flowers visited by four species of bumble-bees and their causes. *J. Anim. Ecol. 26*: 71–98.

Brian, M. V. (1957). Caste determination in social insects. *Ann. Rev. Ent. 2*: 107–120.
— (1965). Caste differentiation in social insects. *Symp. Zool. Soc. Lond. 14*: 13–38.
Brian, M. V. and Brian, A. D. (1948). Regulation of oviposition in social Hymenoptera. *Nature, Lond. 161*: 854–856.
Bristowe, W. S. (1958). *The world of spiders.* London.
Brittain, W. H. and Newton, D. E. (1933). A study in the relative constancy of hive bees and wild bees in pollen gathering. *Can. J. Res. 9*: 334–349.
Bromley, S. W. (1934). The robber flies of Texas (Diptera, Asilidae). *Ann. ent. Soc. Amer. 27*: 74–113.
— (1936). Asilids feeding on bumblebees in New England. *Psyche 43*: 14.
— (1949). The Missouri bee-killer, *Proctacanthus milbertii* Macq. (Asilidae: Diptera). *Bull. Brooklyn ent. Soc. 44*: 21–28.
Brower, J. P., Brower, J. V. Z. and Westcott, P. W. (1960). Experimental studies of mimicry. 5. The reactions of toads (*Bufo terrestris*) to bumblebees (*Bombus americanorum*) and their robberfly mimics (*Mallophora bomboides*), with a discussion of aggressive mimicry. *Amer. Nat. 94*: 343–355.
Brown, C. J. D. (1929). A morphological and systematical study of Utah Asilidae (Diptera). *Trans. Amer. ent. Soc. 54*: 295–320.
Bruggemann, P. F. (1958). Insect environment of the high arctic. *Proc. 10th Int. Congr. Ent. (1956) 1*: 695–702.
Buckler, W. (1899). *Larvae of British butterflies and moths, Vol. 9.* London.
Burtt, B. D. (1923). The occurrence of *Bombus cullumanus* ♂♂ near Reading. *Entomologist's mon. Mag. 59*: 91–92.
Buttel-Reepen, H. von (1903). *Die stammesgeschichtliche Entstehung des Bienenstaates, sowie Beiträge zur Lebensweise der solitären und sozialen Bienen (Hummeln, Melipònen, etc.).* Leipzig.
— (1907). Zur Psychobiologie der Hummeln I. *Biol. Centralbl. 27*: 579–613.
Calam, D. H. (1969). Species and sex-specific compounds from the heads of male bumblebees (*Bombus* spp.). *Nature, Lond. 221*: 856–857.
Carrick, R. (1936). Experiments to test the efficiency of protective adaptations in insects. *Trans. R. ent. Soc. Lond. 85*: 131–139.
Chernov, Yu. I. (1966). [Complex of pollinating insects in the tundra zone]. In: [*Organisms and natural environments. (Problems of geography 69)*]. pp. 76–97. (Voronov, A. G., Dokhman, G. I. and Sobolev, L. N., eds). *In Russian.* Moscow.
Church, N. S. (1960). Heat loss and the body temperatures of flying insects. II. Heat conduction within the body and its loss by radiation and convection. *J. exp. Biol. 37*: 186–212.
Clausen, C. P. (1940). *Entomophagus insects.* New York.
Clements, F. E. and Long, F. L. (1923). Experimental pollination: an outline of the ecology of flowers and insects. *Publs Carnegie Instn, No. 336*: 274 pp.
Cobbold, T. S. (1888). On *Simondsia paradoxa* and on its probable affinity with *Sphaerularia bombi. Trans. Linn. Soc. Lond. 2*: 357–361.
Colombo, K. F. (1961). *The biology of mites associated with bees.* Thesis: University of London.
Colyer, C. N. and Hammond, C. O. (1951). *Flies of the British Isles.* London.
Coville, F. V. (1890). Notes on bumblebees. *Proc. ent. Soc. Wash. 1*: 197–203.
Cumber, R. A. (1949a). The biology of humble-bees with special reference to the production of the worker caste. *Trans. R. ent. Soc. Lond. 100*: 1–45.
— (1949b). Larval specific characters and instars of English Bombidae. *Proc. R. ent. Soc. Lond. (A) 24*: 14–19.
— (1949c). An overwintering nest of the humble-bee *Bombus terrestris. N. Z. Sci. Rev. 7*: 76–77.
— (1949d). Humble-bee parasites and commensals found within a thirty mile radius of London. *Proc. R. ent. Soc. Lond. (A) 24*: 119–127.
— (1953). Some aspects of the biology and ecology of humble-bees bearing upon the yields of red-clover seed in New Zealand. *N. Z. Jl Sci. Technol. B 34*: 227–240.
— (1954). The life-cycle of humble-bees in New Zealand. *N. Z. Jl Sci. Technol. B 36*: 95–107.
Curtis, J. (1835). *British Entomology.* Vol. 12. London.
— (1860). *Farm insects.* Glasgow.
Dalla Torre, K. W. von (1882). Bemerkungen zur Gattung *Bombus* Latr. *Ber. naturw.-med. Ver. Innsbruck 12*: 14–31.
Dandy, J. E. (1969). *Watsonian vice-counties of Great Britain.* London.
Darwin, C. (1859). *The origin of species by means of natural selection.* London.
— (1876). *The effects of cross and self fertilisation in the vegetable kingdom.* London.
— (1886). Über die Wege der Hummelmännchen. In: Krause, E. *Gesammelte kleinere Schriften von Charles Darwin. Ein Supplement zu seinen grösseren Werken.* Vol. 2. Leipzig.
Davidson, A. (1894). On the parasites of wild bees in California. *Ent. News 5*: 170–172.
Dennis, B. A. & Haas, H. (1967). Pollination and seed-setting in diploid and tetraploid red clover (*Trifolium pratense* L.) under Danish conditions. II. Studies of floret morphology in relation to the working speed of honey- and bumble-bees (Hymenoptera: Apoidae). *Kgl. Vet.- og Landbohøjsk. Aarsskr. 1967*: 118–133.
Dias, D. (1958). Contribuição para o conhecimento da bionomia de *Bombus incarum* Franklin da Amazônia (Hymenòptera: Bombidae). *Rev. bras. Ent. 8*: 1–20.
Donisthorpe, H. (1920). The phoresy of *Antherophagus. Entomologist's Rec. J. Var. 32*: 181–187.

REFERENCES

Downes, J. A. (1962). What is an arctic insect. *Can. Ent.* 94: 143–162.

Dufour, L. (1837). Recherches sur quelques Entozoaires et larves parasites des insectes Orthoptères et Hyménoptères. *Ann. Sci. Nat. Zool.* 7: 5–20.

Duncan, C. D. (1939). *A contribution to the biology of North American Vespine wasps.* Stanford.

Duncan, W. (1935). Humble-bees of S. Ronaldshay, Orkney. *Scot. Nat.* (1935): 65–66.

Dylewska, M. (1962). The Apoidea of the Pieniny National Park. Part I. *Megachilidae* and *Apidae* (partim). *Acta zool. cracov.* 7: 423–481.

Eaton, G. W. and Stewart, M. G. (1969). Blueberry blossom damage caused by bumblebees. *Can. Ent.* 101: 149–150.

El-Hariri, G. (1966). Studies of the physiology of hibernating Coccinellidae (Coleoptera): changes in the metabolic reserves and gonads. *Proc. R. ent. Soc. Lond.* (*A*) 41: 133–144.

Emmett, B. J. and Baker, L. A. E. (1971). Insect transmission of fireblight. *Pl. Path.* 20: 41–45.

Esch, H. (1967). Die Bedeutung der Lauterzeugung für die Verständigung der stachellosen Bienen. *Z. vergl. Physiol.* 56: 199–220.

Eugène, G. (1957). Une méthode d'élèvage des bourdons (Hym. Apidae). *Bull. Soc. ent. Fr.* 62: 71–75.

Evans, G. O., Sheals, J. G. and Macfarlane, D. (1961). *The terrestrial Acari of the British Isles.* London.

Evans, G. O. and Till, W. M. (1966). Studies on the British Dermanyssidae (Acari: Mesostigmata) Part II Classification. *Bull. Br. Mus. nat. Hist.* (*Zool.*) 14: 109–370.

Evans, H. E. and Linsley, E. G. (1960). Notes on a sleeping aggregation of solitary bees and wasps. *Bull. S. Calif. Acad. Sci.* 59: 30–37.

Evans, W. (1901). The pale variety of *Bombus smithianus*, White in Scotland. *Entomologist's mon. Mag.* 37: 47.

Faegri, K. (1961). Palynology of a bumble-bee nest. *Veröff. geobot. Inst. Rübel* (*1961*): 60–67.

Fahringer, J. (1922). Beiträge zur Kenntnis der Lebensweise einiger Schmarotzerwespen unter besonderer Berücksichtigung ihrer Bedeutung für biologische Bekämpfung von Schädlingen. *Z. angew. Ent.* 8: 325–388.

Fantham, H. B. and Porter, A. (1914). The morphology, biology and economic importance of *Nosema bombi* n. sp., parasitic in various humble-bees (*Bombus* spp.). *Ann. trop. Med. Parasit.* 8: 623–638.

Faris, R. C. (1949). *Bombus pratorum* L. in Ireland. *I. Nat. J.* 9: 245–246.

Fattig, P. W. (1933). Food of the robber fly, *Mallophora orcina* (Wied.) (Diptera). *Can. Ent.* 65: 119–120.

Fischer, M. (1972). Erste Gliederung der paläarktischen *Aspilota*-Arten (*Hymenoptera, Braconidae, Alysiinae*). *Bull. ent. Pol.* 42: 323–459.

Fleming, S. (1926). Ein auffallender Nestbefund bei Hummeln. *Zool. Jb. Syst.* 52: 395–406.

Forbes, W. T. M. (1923). *The Lepidoptera of New York and neighboring states.* New York.

Fox Wilson, G. (*See under* Wilson, G. Fox).

Frank, A. (1941). Eigenartige Flugbahnen bei Hummelmännchen. *Z. vergl. Physiol.* 28: 467–484.

Fraser, F. C. (1947). *Bombus jonellus* (Kby.) (Hym.) nesting in a discarded bird's nest. *Entomologist's mon. Mag.* 83: 280.

Free, J. B. (1955a). Queen production in colonies of bumblebees. *Proc. R. ent. Soc. Lond.* (*A*) 30: 19–25.

— (1955b). The division of labour within bumblebee colonies. *Insectes soc.* 2: 195–212.

— (1955c). The collection of food by bumblebees. *Insectes soc.* 2: 303–311.

— (1955d). The adaptability of bumblebees to a change in the location of their nest. *Brit. J. anim. Behav.* 3: 61–65.

— (1955e). The behaviour of egg-laying workers of bumblebee colonies. *Brit. J. Anim. Behav.* 3: 147–153.

— (1957). The effect of social facilitation on the ovary development of bumblebee workers. *Proc. R. ent. Soc. Lond.* (*A*) 32: 182–184.

— (1958). The defence of bumblebee colonies. *Behaviour* 12: 233–242.

— (1968). The behaviour of bees visiting runner beans (*Phaseolus multiflorus*). *J. appl. Ecol.* 5: 631–638.

— (1970a). The flower constancy of bumblebees. *J. Anim. Ecol.* 39: 395–402.

— (1970b). *Insect pollination of crops.* London.

— (1970c). The effect of flower shape and nectar guides on the behaviour of foraging honeybees. *Behaviour* 37: 269–285.

— (1971). Stimuli eliciting mating behaviour of bumblebee (*Bombus pratorum* L.) males. *Behaviour* 40: 55–61.

Free, J. B. and Butler, C. G. (1959). *Bumblebees.* London.

Free, J. B., Weinberg, I. and Whiten, A. (1969). The egg-eating behaviour of *Bombus lapidarius* L. *Behaviour* 35: 313–317.

Free, J. B. & Williams, I. H. (1972). The transport of pollen on the body hairs of honeybees (*Apis mellifera* L.) and bumblebees (*Bombus* spp. L.). *J. appl. Ecol.* 9: 609–615.

Freeman, R. B. (1968). Charles Darwin on the routes of male humble bees. *Bull. Br. Mus. nat. Hist.* (*Hist. ser.*) 3: 177–189.

Fridén, F. (1966). Some studies on bumble bees in captivity. *Bee Wld* 47 (Suppl.): 151–166.

Friese, H. (1923). *Die europäischen Bienen.* Berlin.

— (1926). *Die Bienen, Wespen, Grab-u. Goldwespen.* Stuttgart.

Frisch, K. von (1952). Hummeln als unfreiwillige Transportflieger. *Natur u. Volk* 82: 171–174.

Frison, T. H. (1917). Notes on Bombidae, and on the life history of *Bombus auricomus* Robt. *Ann. ent. Soc. Amer.* 10: 277–286.

Frison, T. H. (1918). Additional notes on the life history of *Bombus auricomus* Robt. *Ann. ent. Soc. Amer.* 11: 43–48.

— (1919). Keys for the separation of the Bremidae, or bumblebees of Illinois, and other notes. *Trans. Ill. State Acad. Sci.* 12: 157–166.

— (1921a). *Psithyrus laboriosus* Fabr. in the nests of bumblebees (Hym.). *Can. Ent.* 53: 100–101.

— (1921b). *Antherophagus ochraceus* Mels. in the nests of bumblebees. *Amer. Nat.* 55: 188–192.

— (1926a). Contribution to the knowledge of the inter-relations of the bumblebees of Illinois with their animate environment. *Ann. ent. Soc. Amer.* 19: 203–235.

— (1926b). Experiments in attracting queen bumblebees to artificial domiciles. *J. econ. Ent.* 19: 149–155.

— (1927a). The development of the castes of bumblebees (Bremidae: Hym.). *Ann. ent. Soc. Amer.* 20: 156–180.

— (1927b). Experiments in rearing colonies of bumblebees (Bremidae) in artificial nests. *Biol. Bull. Woods Hole* 52: 51–67.

— (1928). A contribution to the knowledge of the life history of *Bremus bimaculatus* (Cresson) (Hym.). *Ent. Amer.* (N. S.) 8: 159–223.

— (1929). A contribution to the knowledge of the bionomics of *Bremus impatiens* (Cresson) (Hym.). *Bull. Brooklyn ent. Soc.* 24: 261–285.

— (1930a). A contribution to the knowledge of the bionomics of *Bremus americanorum* (Fabr.). (Hymenoptera). *Ann. ent. Soc. Amer.* 23: 644–665.

— (1930b). Observations on the behavior of bumblebees (*Bremus*). The orientation flight. *Can. Ent.* 62: 49–54.

Frost, S. W. (1973). Honeybees and bumblebees taken in light traps. *Ent. News* 84: 235–236.

Fye, R. E. (1966). *Sphaerularia bombi* Duford parasitizing *Bombus* queens in Northwestern Ontario. *Can. Ent.* 98: 88–89.

Fye, R. E. and Medler, J. T. (1954a). Spring emergence and floral hosts of Wisconsin bumblebees. *Trans. Wis. Acad. Sci. Arts Lett.* 43: 75–82.

— (1954b). Field domiciles for bumblebees. *J. econ. Ent.* 47: 672–676.

— (1954c). Temperature studies in bumblebee domiciles. *J. econ. Ent.* 47: 847–852.

Gabritschevsky, E. (1924). Farbenpolymorphismus und Vererbung mimetischer Varietäten der Fliege *Volucella bombylans* und anderer 'hummelähnlicher' Zweiflügler. *Z. Indukt. Abstammungs-u. Vererbungslehre* 32: 321–353.

Geissler, G. and Steche, W. (1962). Natürliche Trachten als Ursache für Vergiftungserscheinungen bei Bienen und Hummeln. *Z. Bienenforsch.* 6: 77–92.

Goedart, J. (1700). *Metamorphosis Naturalis sive Insectorum Historia.* Amsterdam.

Gontarski, H. (1940). Über den Nestbau-Instinkt bei der Honigbiene und bei den Hummeln. *Nat. u. Volk* 70: 532–539.

Grönlund, S., Itämies, J. and Mikkola, H. (1970). On the food and feeding habits of the great grey shrike *Lanius excubitor* in Finland. *Ornis Fenn.* 47: 167–171.

Haas, A. (1946). Neue Beobachtungen zum Problem der Flugbahnen bei Hummelmännchen. *Z. Naturf.* 1: 596–600.

— (1949a). Arttypische Flugbahnen von Hummelmännchen. *Z. vergl. Physiol.* 31: 281–307.

— (1949b). Gesetzmässiges Flugverhalten der Männchen von *Psithyrus silvestris* Lep. und einiger solitärer Apiden. *Z. vergl. Physiol.* 31: 671–683.

— (1952). Die Mandibeldrüse als Duftorgan bei einiger Hymenopteren. *Naturwissenschaften* 39: 484.

— (1960). Vergleichende Verhaltensstudien zum Paarungsschwarm solitärer Apiden. *Z. Tierpsychol.* 17: 402–416.

— (1961). Das Rätsel des Hummeltrompeters: Lichtalarm. 1. Bericht über Verhaltensstudien an einem kleinen Nest von *Bombus hypnorum* mit Arbeiter-Königin. *Z. Tierpsychol.* 18: 129–138.

Haeseler, V. (1972). Anthropogene Biotope (Kahlschlag, Kiesgrube, Stadtgärten) als Refugien für Insekten, untersucht am Beispiel der Hymenoptera Aculeata. *Zool. Jb. Syst.* 99: 133–212.

Hamilton, D. W., Schwartz, P. H. and Townshend, B. G. (1970). Capture of bumblebees and honey bees in traps baited with lures to attract Japanese beetles. *J. econ. Ent.* 63: 1442–1445.

Harrison, J. W. Heslop (1939). *Bombus hortorum* L., at sycamore flowers on the Isle of Coll. *Entomologist's mon. Mag.* 75: 252.

— (1943). The status of *Bombus smithianus* White (Hym., Apidae) on the Isles of Raasay, South Rona, Scalpay and Longay. *Entomologist's mon. Mag.* 79: 62.

Hase, A. (1926). Ueber die Nester der Wachsmottenraupen und der Aphomiaraupen. *Arb. Biolog. Reichsanstalt Land- und Forstwirtschaft* 14: 555–565.

Hasselrot, T. B. (1952). A new method for starting bumblebee colonies. *Agron. J.* 44: 218–219.

— (1960). Studies on Swedish bumblebees (genus *Bombus* Latr.): their domestication and biology. *Opusc. ent. Suppl.* 17: 1–192.

Hattingen, R. (1956). Beiträge zur Biologie von *Sphaerularia bombi* Léon Dufour (1837). *Zentbl. Bakt. ParasitKde Abt. II* 109: 236–249.

Hawkins, R. P. (1961). Observations on the pollination of red clover by bees. I. The yield of seed in relation to the number and kinds of pollinators. *Ann. appl. Biol.* 49: 55–65.

Heinrich, B. (1972a). Temperature regulation in the bumblebee *Bombus vagans*: a field study. *Science* 175: 185–187.

— (1972b). Energetics of temperature regulation and foraging in a bumblebee, *Bombus terricola* Kirby. *J. comp. Physiol.* 77: 49–64.

— (1972c). Patterns of endothermy in bumblebee queens, drones and workers. *J. comp. Physiol.* 77: 65–79.

— (1972d). Physiology of brood incubation in the bumblebee queen, *Bombus vosnesenskii*. *Nature, Lond.* 239: 223–225.

Hemming, F. (1939) Ed. Opinion 135. The suppression of the so-called 'Erlangen List' of 1801. *Opin. Decl. int. Commn Zool. Nom.* 2: 9–12.

Himmer, A. (1927). Ein Beitrag zur Kenntnis des Wärmehaushaltes im Nestbau sozialer Hautflügler. *Z. vergl. Physiol.* 5: 375–389.

— (1932). Die Temperaturverhältnisse bei den sozialen Hymenopteren. *Biol. Rev.* 7: 224–253.

— (1933). Die Nestwärme bei *Bombus agrorum* (Fabr.). *Biol. Zbl.* 53: 270–276.

Hinchliff, F. B. (1914). Trout taking bumble bees. *I. Nat.* 23: 103–104.

Hinton, H. E. (1943). House moths (*Endrosis sarcitrella* and *Borkhausenia pseudospretella*) feeding on dead insects in or near spiders' webs. *Entomologist* 76: 4–5.

Hobbs, G. A. (1962). Further studies on the food-gathering behaviour of bumble bees (Hymenoptera: Apidae). *Can. Ent.* 94: 538–541.

— (1964a). Phylogeny of bumble bees based on brood-rearing behaviour. *Can. Ent.* 96: 115–116.

— (1964b). Ecology of species of *Bombus* Latr. (Hymenoptera: Apidae) in southern Alberta. I. Subgenus *Alpinobombus* Skor. *Can. Ent.* 96: 1465–1470.

— (1965a). Ecology of species of *Bombus* Latr. (Hymenoptera: Apidae) in southern Alberta. II. Subgenus *Bombias* Robt. *Can. Ent.* 97: 120–128.

— (1965b). Ecology of species of *Bombus* Latr. (Hymenoptera: Apidae) in southern Alberta. III. Subgenus *Cullumanobombus* Vogt. *Can. Ent.* 97: 1293–1302.

— (1966a). Ecology of species of *Bombus* Latr. (Hymenoptera: Apidae) in southern Alberta. IV. Subgenus *Fervidobombus* Skorikov. *Can. Ent.* 98: 33–39.

— (1966b). Ecology of species of *Bombus* Latr. (Hymenoptera: Apidae) in southern Alberta. V. Subgenus *Subterraneobombus* Vogt. *Can. Ent.* 98: 288–294.

— (1967a). Obtaining and protecting red-clover pollinating species of *Bombus* (Hymenoptera: Apidae). *Can. Ent.* 99: 943–951.

— (1967b). Ecology of species of *Bombus* (Hymenoptera: Apidae) in southern Alberta. VI. Subgenus *Pyrobombus*. *Can. Ent.* 99: 1272–1292.

— (1968). Ecology of species of *Bombus* (Hymenoptera: Apidae) in southern Alberta. VII. Subgenus *Bombus*. *Can. Ent.* 100: 156–164.

Hobbs, G. A., Nummi, W. O. and Virostek, J. F. (1961). Food-gathering behaviour of honey, bumble, and leaf-cutter bees (Hymenoptera: Apoidea) in Alberta. *Can. Ent.* 93: 409–419.

— (1962). Managing colonies of bumble bees (Hymonoptera: Apidae) for pollination purposes. *Can. Ent.* 94: 1121–1132.

Hobbs, G. A., Virostek, J. F. and Nummi, W. O. (1960). Establishment of *Bombus* spp. (Hymenoptera: Apidae) in artificial domiciles in southern Alberta. *Can. Ent.* 92: 868–872.

Hoffer, E. (1882). Biologische Beobachtungen an Hummeln und Schmarotzerhummeln. *Mitt. naturw. Ver. Steiermark* 18: 68–92.

— (1882-3). *Die Hummeln Steiermarks. Lebensgeschichte und Beschreibung derselben.* Graz.

— (1886). Zur Biologie der *Mutilla europaea* L. *Zool. Jb.* 1: 679–686.

— (1889). Die Schmarotzerhummeln Steiermarks. Lebensgeschichte und Beschreibung derselben. *Mitt. naturw. Ver. Steiermark* 25: 82–158.

Holm, S. N. (1960). Experiments on the domestication of bumblebees (*Bombus* Latr.) in particular *B. lapidarius* L. and *B. terrestris* L. *K. VetHøjsk. Aarsskr* (1960): 1–19.

— (1965). The emergence of bumble bee queens (*Bombus* Latr.) under controlled conditions. *Věd. Práce. výzkum. Ústav včelař. ČSAZV* 4: 79–83.

— (1966a). The utilization and management of bumble bees for red clover and alfalfa seed production. *Ann. Rev. Ent.* 11: 155–182.

— (1966b). Problems of the domestication of bumble bees. *Bee Wld* 47 (Suppl.): 179–186.

— (1972). Weight and life length of hibernating bumble bee queens (Hymenoptera: Bombidae) under controlled conditions. *Ent. scand.* 3: 313–320.

Holm, S. N. and Haas, H. (1961). Erfahrungen und Resultate dreijähriger Domestikationsversuche mit Hummeln (*Bombus* Latr.). *Albrecht-Thaer-Arch.* 5: 282–304.

Holm, S. N. and Skou, J. P. (1972). Studies on trapping, nesting and rearing of some *Megachile* species (Hymenoptera, Megachilidae) and on their parasites in Denmark. *Ent. scand.* 3: 169–180.

Holmes, F. O. (1964). The distribution of honey bees and bumblebees on nectar-secreting plants. *Amer. Bee J.* 104: 12–13.

Huber, P. (1802). Observations on several species of the genus *Apis*, known by the name of humble-bees, and called Bombinatrices by Linnaeus. *Trans. Linn. Soc. Lond.* 6: 214–298.

Huish, R. (1817). *Bees: their natural history and general management.* London.

Hulkkonen, O. (1928). Zur Biologie der südfinnischen Hummeln. *Ann. Univ. Aabo.* (A) 3: 1–81.

— (1929). Die Hummeln als Gäste der Blattläuse. *Ann. Soc. zool. bot. Fenn. Vanamo.* 8: 51–54.

Hunter, P. E. (1966). The genus *Pneumolaelaps* with descriptions of three new species (Acarina: Laelaptidae). *J. Kans. ent. Soc.* 39: 357–369.

L*

Husband, R. W. (1968). Acarina associated with Michigan Bombinae. *Pap. Mich. Acad. Sci. 53*: 109–112.

— (1969). *Bombacarus buchneri* (Acarina: Podapolipodidae) in North America. *Proc. 2nd Int. Cong. Acarology* (1967): 287–288.

Husband, R. W. and Sinha, R. N. (1970). A revision of the genus *Locustacarus* with a key to genera of the family Podapolipidae (Acarina). *Ann. ent. Soc. Amer. 63*: 1152–1162.

Ihering, R. von (1903). Zur Frage nach dem Ursprung der Staatenbildung bei den sozialen Hymenopteren. *Zool. Anz. 27*: 113-118.

Imms, A. D. (1922). On the occurrence of *Bombus cullumanus* (Kirby) Ill. in Britain. *Entomologist's mon. Mag. 58*: 26–27.

— (1947). *Insect natural history*. London.

Ishay, J. and Ruttner, F. (1971). Thermoregulation im Hornissennest. *Z. vergl. Physiol. 72*: 423–434.

Jackson, D. J. (1924). Insect parasite of the Pea-Weevil. *Nature, Lond. 113*: 353–354.

— (1928). The biology of *Dinocampus* (*Perilitus*) *rutilus* Nees, a Braconid parasite of *Sitona lineata* L. Part I. *Proc. Zool. Soc. Lond.* (1928): 597–630.

— (1935). Giant cells in insects parasitised by hymenopterous larvae. *Nature, Lond. 135*: 1040–1041.

Jacobs-Jessen, U. F. (1959). Zur Orientierung der Hummeln und einiger anderer Hymenopteren. *Z. vergl. Physiol. 41*: 597–641.

Jany, E. (1950). Der 'Einbruch' von Erdhummeln (*Bombus terrestris* L.) in die Blüten der Feuerbohne (*Phaseolus multiflorus* Willd.). *Z. angew. Ent. 32*: 172–183.

Johansen, C. (1967). Ecology of three species of bumble bees in southwestern Washington. *Wash. State Univ., Tech. Bull.* No. 57, 12 pp.

Johnson, W. F. (1897). Entomological notes from Poyntzpass. *I. Nat. 6*: 303–304.

— (1918). Aculeate Hymenoptera from the counties Armagh and Donegal. *I. Nat. 27*: 2–3.

Jordan, R. (1935). Die Spinnenameise, *Mutilla europaea*, ein Bienenschädling! *Deutsche Imker* 48: 421–427.

— (1936a). Ein Weg zur zwangsläufigen Nestgründung überwinterter Bombusweibchen an einem bestimmten Platze. *Arch. Bienenk. 17*: 39–44.

— (1936b). Beobachtungen der Arbeitsteilung im Hummelstaate (*B. muscorum*). *Arch. Bienenk. 17*: 81–91.

— (1962). Befällt der Parasit *Nosema apis* Zander ausser dem Mitteldarm auch noch andere Organe der Biene? *Bienenvater* 83: 68–74.

Jurine, L. (1801). (*See under* Panzer, G. W. F.).

Karafiat. H. (1959). Systematik und Ökologie der Scutacariden. In: Stammer, H.-J. *Beitrage zur Systematik und Ökologie Mitteleuropäischer Acarina II. Tyroglyphidae und Tarsonemini I.* pp. 627–712. Leipzig.

Katayama, E. (1965). Studies on the development of the broods of *Bombus diversus* Smith (Hymenoptera, Apidae). I. On the egg-laying habits. *Kontyû* 33: 291–298.

— (1966). Studies on the development of the broods of *Bombus diversus* Smith (Hymenoptera, Apidae). II. Brood development and feeding habits. *Kontyû* 34: 8–17.

— (1971). Observations on the brood development in *Bombus ignitus* (Hymenoptera, Apidae). I. Egg-laying habits of queens and workers. *Kontyû* 39: 189–204.

— (1973). Observations on the brood development in *Bombus ignitus* (Hymenoptera, Apidae). II. Brood development and feeding habits. *Kontyû* 41: 203–216

Kendall, D. A. & Solomon, M. E. (1973). Quantities of pollen on the bodies of insects visiting apple blossom. *J. appl. Ecol. 10*: 627–634.

Kendall, D. A. and Wiltshire, C. W. (1973). A method for anaesthetizing or killing insects in the field. *Entomologist's mon. Mag. 108*: 129.

Kevan, P. G. (1972). Insect pollination of high arctic flowers. *J. Ecol. 60*: 831–847.

Kikuchi, T. (1963). Studies on the coaction among insects visiting flowers. III. Dominance relationship among flower-visiting flies, bees and butterflies. *Sci. Rep. Tôhoku Univ. Ser. 4*, 29: 1–8.

Kilby, B. A. (1963). The biochemistry of the insect fat body. In: *Advances in insect physiology, I.* (Beament, J. W. L., Treherne, J. E. and Wigglesworth, V. B., eds). London.

Kirby, W. (1802). *Monographia Apum Angliae*. Ipswich.

Kivirikko, E. (1941). *Aphomia sociella* L. (Lep., Pyralidae) linnunpönttöjen a sukkaana. *Ann. ent. Fenn. 7*: 206–207.

Knee, W. J. and Medler, J. T. (1965a). The seasonal size increase of bumblebee workers (Hymenoptera: *Bombus*). *Can. Ent. 97*: 1149–1155.

— (1965b). Sugar concentration of bumble bee honey. *Amer. Bee J. 105*: 174–175.

Knowlton, G. F., Maddock, D. R. and Wood, S. L. (1946). Insect food of the sagebrush swift. *J. econ. Ent. 39*: 382–383.

Knuth, P. (1906). *Handbook of flower pollination* (*Trans. by J. R. Ainsworth-Davis*). Oxford.

Korschgen, L. J. and Moyle, D. L. (1955). Food habits of the bull frog in central Missouri farm ponds. *Amer. Midl. Nat. 54*: 332–341.

Krogh, A. and Zeuthen, E. (1941). The mechanism of flight preparation in some insects. *J. exp. Biol. 18*: 1–10.

Krombein, K. V. (1958). Hymenoptera of America north of Mexico-synoptic catalog. *Agric. Monogr.* (*Suppl. 1*) *2*: 1–305.

REFERENCES

Krüger, E. (1920). Beiträge zur Systematik und Morphologie der mitteleuropäischen Hummeln. *Zool. Jb. Abt. Syst.* 42: 289–464.
— (1924). Analytische Studien zur Morphologie der Hummeln. *Zool. Jb. Abt. Syst.* 48: 1–128.
— (1951). Über die Bahnflüge der Männchen der Gattungen *Bombus* und *Psithyrus*. *Z. Tierpsychol.* 8: 61–75.
— (1954). Phänoanolytische Studien an einigen Arten der Untergattung *Terrestribombus* O. Vogt (Hymenoptera, Bombidae) II. *Tijdschr. Ent.* 97: 263–298.
Kruseman, G. (1950). Note sur quelques races de *Bombus agrorum* (F.) *nec* Gmel. *Ent. Ber. Amst.* 13: 43–47.
— (1953). Note on *Bombus jonellus* (Kirby). *Ent. Ber. Amst.* 14: 382.
Kugler, H. (1932). Blütenökologische Untersuchungen mit Hummeln, IV. *Planta* 16: 534–553.
— (1943). Hummeln als Blütenbesucher. *Ergebn. Biol.* 19: 143–323.
Kullenberg, B. (1956). Field experiments with chemical sexual attractants on Aculeate Hymenoptera males I. *Zool. Bidr. Uppsala* 31: 253–354.
Kullenberg, B., Bergström, G. and Ställberg-Stenhagen, S. (1970). Volatile components of the cephalic marking secretion of male bumble bees. *Acta chem. scand.* 24: 1481–1483.
Laidlaw, W. B. R. (1930). Notes on some humble bees and wasps in Scotland. *Scot. Nat.* (1930): 121–125.
— (1931). Notes and observations on humble bees in Aberdeen. *Scot. Nat.* (1931): 181–183.
Landim, C. da Cruz (1963). Evolution of the wax and scent glands in the Apinae (Hymenoptera: Apidae). *J. N. Y. ent. Soc.* 71: 2–13.
Lane, C. and Rothschild, M. (1965). A case of Müllerian mimicry of sound. *Proc. R. ent. Soc. Lond.* (A) 40: 156–158.
Latreille, P. A. (1802). *Histoire naturelle des Fourmis*. Paris.
Leatherdale, D. (1970). The arthropod hosts of entomogenous fungi in Britain. *Entomophaga* 15: 419–435.
Leclercq, J. (1960). Fleurs butinées par les bourdons (Hym. Apidae Bombinae) dans la région liégeoise (1945–1959). *Bull. Inst. agron. Gembloux* 28: 180–198.
— (1961). Fleurs butinées par l'abeille des ruches (*Apis mellifica* L.) dans la région liégeoise (1945–1959). *Bull. Inst. agron. Gembloux* 29: 79–90.
Lecompte, J. (1963). Étude des échanges de nourriture de la colonie de bourdons au moyen de radioisotopes. *C. R. Acad. Sci., Paris* 257: 3664–3665.
Lecompte, J. and Pouvreau, A. (1968). Étude au moyen de l'or radioactif [198] Au, du rayon d'action de colonies de bourdons (*Bombus* sp.) en vue de la pollinisation des plantes cultivées. In: *Isotopes and radiation in entomology*. (International Atomic Energy Agency). Vienna.
Lees, A. D. (1955). *The physiology of diapause in Arthropods*. Cambridge.
Legge, M. M. (1937). Parasitic larvae in *Bombus terrestris* (L.). *Parasitology* 29: 524–525.
Lepeletier [de St Fargeau], A. L. M. (1832). Observations sur l'ouvrage intitulé: 'Bombi Scandinaviae Monographicè Tractati, *etc.*, a Gustav. Dahlbom. Londini Gothorum, 1832'; auxquelles on à joint les caractères des genres *Bombus* et *Psithyrus*, et la description des espèces qui appartiennent au dernier. *Ann. Soc. ent. Fr.* 1: 366–382.
Leppik, E. E. (1953). The ability of insects to distinguish number. *Amer. Nat.* 87: 228–236.
Leuckart, R. (1885). Über die Entwicklung der *Sphaerularia bombi*. *Zool. Anz.* 8: 273–277.
— (1887). Neue Beiträge zur Kenntnis des Baus und der Lebensgeschichte der Nematoden. *Abh. sächs. Akad. Wiss.* 22: 565–704.
Lex, T. (1954). Duftmale an Blüten. *Z. vergl. Physiol.* 36: 212–234.
Lie-Pettersen, O. J. (1901). Biologische Beobachtungen an norwegischen Hummeln. *Bergens Mus. Aarb.* 6: 3–10.
— (1906). Neue Beiträge zur Biologie der norwegischen Hummeln. *Bergens Mus. Aarb.* 9: 1–42.
Lindhard, E. (1912). Humlebien som Husdyr. Spredte Traek af nogle danske Humlebiarters Biologi. *Tidsskr. PlAvl* 19: 335–352.
Linquist, E. E. and Evans, G. O. (1965). Taxonomic concepts in the Ascidae, with modified setal nomenclature for the idiosoma of the Gamasina (Acarina: Mesostigmata). *Mem. ent. Soc. Can.* 47: 3–64.
Linsley, E. G. (1962). Sleeping aggregations of aculeate Hymenoptera II. *Ann. ent. Soc. Amer.* 55: 148–164.
Løken, A. (1949). Bumble bees in relation to *Aconitum septentrionale* in Central Norway (Oeyer). *Nytt. Mag. Naturv.* 87: 1–60.
— (1954). Observations of bumble bee activity during the solar eclipse June 30, 1954. *Univ. Bergen Arb. naturv. rekke* 13: 3–6.
— (1961). *Bombus consobrinus* Dahlb., an oligolectic bumble bee (Hymenoptera, Apidae). *XI Int. Congr. Ent.* (1960) 1: 598–603.
— (1973). Studies on Scandinavian bumble bees (Hymenoptera, Apidae). *Norsk ent. Tidsskr.* 20: 1–218.
Longstaff, T. G. (1932). An ecological reconnaisance in West Greenland. *J. Anim. Ecol.* 1: 119–142.
Lubbock, J. (1861). On *Sphaerularia bombi*. *Nat. Hist. Rev.* 1: 44–57.
— (1864). Notes on *Sphaerularia bombi*. *Nat. Hist. Rev.* 4: 265–270.
— (1882). *Ants Bees and Wasps*. London.
McClintock, D. and Fitter, R. S. R. (1956). *The pocket guide to wild flowers*. London.
Macfarlane, R. P. (1973). *A review of the natural control factors affecting* Bombus *and alfalfa pollinating* Megachile *species in North America, Europe and New Zealand*. Dep. Sci. ind. Res., unpublished report: University of Guelph.
Madel, G. (1966). Beiträge zur Biologie von *Sphaerularia bombi* Leon Dufour 1837. *Z. Parasitenk.* 28: 99–107.

Manning, A. (1956a). The effect of honey-guides. *Behaviour* 9: 114–139.

— (1956b). Some aspects of the foraging behaviour of bumble-bees. *Behaviour* 9: 164–201.

Marshall, T. A. (1887). Monograph of British Braconidae. Part II. *Trans. ent. Soc. Lond.* (*1887*): 51–131.

Maschwitz, U. W. (1964). Alarm substances and alarm behaviour in social Hymenoptera. *Nature, Lond.* 204: 324–327.

Mason, L. G. (1965). Prey selection by a non-specific predator. *Evolution* 19: 259–260.

Maurizio, A. (1964). Mikroskopische und papierchromatographische Untersuchungen an Honig von Hummeln, Meliponen und anderen, zuckerhaltige Säfte sammelnden Insekten. *Z. Bienenforsch.* 7: 98–110.

Medler, J. T. (1957). Bumblebee ecology in relation to pollination of alfalfa and red clover. *Insectes soc.* 4: 245–252.

— (1959). A nest of *Bombus huntii* Greene (Hymenoptera: Apidae). *Ent. News* 70: 179–182.

— (1962a). Morphometric studies on bumble bees. *Ann. ent. Soc. Amer.* 55: 212–218.

— (1962b). Morphometric analyses of bumblebee mouthparts. XI. *Int. Congr. Ent.* (*1960*) 2: 517–522.

— (1962c). Measurements of the labium and radial cell of *Psithyrus* (Hymenoptera: Apidae). *Can. Ent.* 94: 444–447.

— (1962d). Development and absorption of eggs in bumblebees (Hymenoptera: Apidae). *Can. Ent.* 94: 825–833.

Meidell, O. (1934). Dagliglivet i et homlebol. *Naturen* (*1934*): 85–95, 108–116.

— (1968). *Bombus jonellus* (Kirby) (Hym., Apidae) has two generations in a season. *Norsk ent. Tidsskr.* 14: 31–32.

Meijere, J. C. H. de (1904). Beiträge zur Kenntnis der Biologie und der systematischen Verwandtschaft der Conopiden. *Tijdschr. Ent.* 46: 144–224.

Mello, M. L. S. (1970). A qualitative analysis of the proteins in venoms from *Apis mellifera* (including *A. m. adansonii*) and *Bombus atratus*. *J. apic. Res.* 9: 113–120.

Meyerhoff, G. (1954). Beobachtungen zur Eiablage von *Mutilla europaea* L. *Arch. Geflügelz. Kleintierk.* 3: 136–141.

Michener, C. D. (1962). Social polymorphism in Hymenoptera. In: *Insect polymorphism.* (Kennedy, J. S., ed.). pp. 43–56. London.

— (1969). Comparative social behavior of bees. *Ann. Rev. Ent.* 14: 299–342.

— (1971). Biologies of African allodapine bees (Hymenoptera, Xylocopinae). *Bull. Amer. Mus. Nat. Hist.* 145: 219–301.

Michener, C. D. and Laberge, W. E. (1954). A large *Bombus* nest from Mexico. *Psyche* 61: 63–67.

Micherdziński, W. (1969). *Die Familie* Parasitidae Oudemans 1901 (*Acarina, Mesostigmata*). Polskiej Akademii Nauk.

Mickel, C. E. (1928). Biological and taxonomic investigations on the mutillid wasps. *U. S. Nat. Mus. Bull.* 143: 1–351.

Milliron, H. E. (1960). A gynandromorphic specimen of *Psithyrus fernaldae* Fkln (Hymenoptera: Apidae). *Bull. Brooklyn ent. Soc.* 55: 109–113.

— (1961). Revised classification of the bumblebees – a synopsis (Hymenoptera: Apidae). *J. Kans. ent. Soc.* 34: 49–61.

— (1967). A successful method for artificially hibernating *Megabombus f. fervidus*, and notes on a related species (Hymenoptera: Apidae; Bombinae). *Can. Ent.* 99: 1321–1332.

— (1971). A monograph of the Western Hemisphere bumblebees (Hymenoptera: Apidae; Bombinae). I. The genera *Bombus* and *Megabombus* subgenus *Bombias*. *Mem. ent. Soc. Can. No.* 82, 80 pp.

Milliron, H. E. and Oliver, D. R. (1966). Bumblebees from northern Ellesmere Island, with observations on usurpation by *Megabombus hyperboreus* (Schöhn.). *Can. Ent.* 98: 207–213.

Milum, V. G. (1940). Larval pests common to the nests of bumblebees and combs of the honeybee. *J. econ. Ent.* 33: 81–83.

Minderhoud, A. (1951). Het telen van hommels in verband met *Sphaerularia bombi*. *Med. Dir. Landb.* (*1951*): 477–482.

Miyamoto, S. (1957a). Biological studies on Japanese bees. IV. Behavior study on *Bombus ardens* Smith in early stage of nesting. *Sci. Rep. Hyogo Univ. Agric. Ser. agric. Biol.* 3: 1–5.

— (1957b). Biological studies on Japanese bees. V. Behavior study on *Bombus ardens* Smith in developing stage of nest. *Sci. Rep. hyogo Univ. Agric. Ser. agric. Biol.* 3: 6–11.

— (1957c). Biological studies on Japanese bees. VI. Observations on the nest of *Bombus ardens* Smith. *Sci. Rep. Hyogo Univ. Agric. Ser. agric. Biol.* 3: 12–14.

— (1959). On the nest of *Bombus diversus* Smith which collapsed before completion (Biological studies on Japanese bees XI). *Akitu* 8: 85–90.

— (1960). Observations on the behavior of *Bombus diversus* Smith (Biological studies on Japanese bees, XIII). *Insectes soc.* 7: 39–56.

— (1963a). On the nest of *Bombus ignitus* Smith. *Kontyû* 31: 27–32.

— (1963b). Biology of *Bombus ignitus* Smith. *Kontyû* 31: 91–98.

Mooser, J. (1958). Das Vorkommen von Hefen bei Bienen, Hummeln und Wespen. *Zbl. Bakt. Abt. II* 111: 101–115.

Morice, F. D. and Durrant, J. H. (1914). The authorship and first publication of the 'Jurinean' Genera of Hymenoptera. *Trans. ent. Soc. Lond.* (*1914*): 339–436.

Morley, C. (1936). The Hymenoptera of Suffolk. Part II. *Trans. Suffolk Nat. Soc.* 3: 132–162.

Morse, R. A. and Gary, N. E. (1961). Insect invaders of the honeybee colony. *Bee Wld* 42: 179–181

Mortimer, C. H. (1922). A new British Bombus, *nigrescens* (Pérez), from Sussex. *Entomologist's mon. Mag.* 58: 16.

Nevinson, E. B. (1923). The survival of *Bombus cullumanus* Kirby. *Entomologist's mon. Mag.* 59: 277–278.

Newman, E. (1834a). Entomological notes. *Ent. Mag.* 2: 313–328.

— (1834b). Attempted division of British insects into natural orders. *Ent. Mag.* 2: 379–431.

REFERENCES

Newman, H. W. (1851). Habits of the Bombinatrices. *Proc. ent. Soc. Lond.* (*1851*): 86–92.

Newsholme, E. A., Crabtree, B., Higgins, S. J., Thornton, S. D. and Start, C. (1972). The activities of fructose diphospatase in flight muscles from the bumble-bee and the role of this enzyme in heat generation. *Biochem. J.* *128*: 89–97.

Nickle, W. R. (1967). On the classification of the insect parasitic nematodes of the Sphaerulariidae Lubbock, 1861 (Tylenchoidea, Nematoda). *Proc. Hel. Soc. Wash.* *34*: 72–94.

Nielsen, E. T. (1938). Temperatures in a nest of *Bombus hypnorum* L. *Vidensk. Medd. naturh. Foren. Kbh.* *102*: 1–6.

Norris, K. S. (1953). The ecology of the desert iguana *Dipsosaurus dorsalis*. *Ecology* *34*: 265–287.

Oertel, E. (1963). Greater wax moth develops on bumble bee cells. *J. econ. Ent.* *56*: 543–544.

O'Farrell, A. F. and Butler, P. M. (1948). Insects and mites associated with the storage and manufacture of foodstuffs in Northern Ireland. *Econ. Proc. R. Dublin Soc.* *3*: 343–407.

O'Rourke, F. J. (1955). *Bombus pratorum* L. in County Cork. *I. Nat. J.* *11*: 337–338.

— (1956). The *Bombidae* of County Cork. *I. Nat. J.* *12*: 17–19.

— (1957). *Bombus distinguendus* Mor. one of the rarer Irish bumblebees. *I. Nat. J.* *12*: 187–189.

Orr, H. L. (1911). Hymenoptera from Ulster. *I. Nat.* *20*: 76.

Owen, J. H. (1948). The larder of the red-backed shrike. *Brit. Birds* *41*: 200–203.

Palm, N.-B. (1948). Normal and pathological histology of the ovaries in *Bombus* Latr. (Hymenopt.). *Opusc. Ent. Suppl.* *7*: 1–101.

— (1949). The pharyngeal gland in *Bombus* Latr. and *Psithyrus* Lep. *Opusc. Ent.* *14*: 27–47.

Palmer, R. (1923). Occurrence of *Bombus cullumanus* (Kirby) in Bedfordshire. *Entomologist's mon. Mag.* *59*: 237.

Panfilov, D. V., Shamurin, V. F. and Yurtsev, B. A. (1960). [The relative distributions of bumblebees (*Bombus*) and legumes in the Arctic]. In Russian. *Byull. mosk. Obshch. Isp. Prirody* *65*: 53–62.

Panzer, G. W. F. (1801). Nachricht von einem neuen entomologischen Werke, des Hrn. Prof. Jurine in Geneve. *Intelligenzblatt der Litteratur-Zeitung, Erlangen* *1*: 160–165.

Pardi, L. (1948). Dominance order in *Polistes* wasps. *Physiol. Zool.* *21*: 1–13.

Pedersen, A. and Sørensen, N. A. (1935). Undersøgelser over rødkløverens bestøvning og angreb af snudebiller pa rødkløver. *Tidsskr. Frøavl* *12*: 288–300.

Pérez, J. (1889). *Les Abeilles.* Paris.

Perkins, R. C. L. (1890). The distribution of *Bombus smithianus*, White. *Entomologist's mon. Mag.* *26*: 111.

— (1917). Notes on the collection of British Hymenoptera (*Aculeata*) formed by F. Smith (II). *Entomologist's mon. Mag.* *53*: 159–162.

— (1921). Variations in British *Psithyrus* and remarks on *Bombus pomorum*. *Entomologist's mon. Mag.* *57*: 82–87.

— (1945). The Aculeate Hymenoptera of a small area of Dartmoor near Lydford, Devon. *Entomologist's mon. Mag.* *81*: 145–153.

Pittioni, B. (1939). Die Hummeln und Schmarotzerhummeln der Balkan-Halbinsel. *Mitt. Koenigl nat. Inst. Sof.* *12*: 49–115.

— (1942). Hummeln als Blütenbesucher. *Mitt. bulg. ent. Ges.* *12*: 63–126.

Plath, O. E. (1922a). A unique method of defense of *Bremus* (*Bombus*) *fervidus* Fabricius. *Psyche* *29*: 180–187.

— (1922b). Notes on the nesting habits of several North American bumblebees. *Psyche* *29*: 189–202.

— (1922c). Notes on *Psithyrus*, with records of two new American hosts. *Biol. Bull. Wood's Hole* *43*: 23–44.

— (1923a). Observations on the so-called trumpeter in bumblebee colonies. *Psyche* *30*: 146–154.

— (1923b). Notes on the egg-eating habits of bumblebees. *Psyche* *30*: 193–202.

— (1923c). Breeding experiments with confined *Bremus* (*Bombus*) queens. *Biol. Bull. Wood's Hole* *45*: 325–341.

— (1923d). The bee-eating proclivity of the skunk. *Amer. Nat.* *57*: 571–574.

— (1924). Miscellaneous biological observations on bumblebees. *Biol. Bull. Wood's Hole* *47*: 65–78.

— (1927a). Natural grouping of Bremidae (Bombidae) with special reference to biological characters. *Biol. Bull. Wood's Hole* *52*: 394–410.

— (1927b). Notes on the hibernation of several North American bumblebees. *Ann. ent. Soc. Amer.* *20*: 181–192.

— (1927c). *Psithyrus laboriosus*, an unwelcome guest in the hives of *Apis mellifica*. *Bull. Brooklyn ent. Soc.* *22*: 121–125.

— (1934). *Bumblebees and their ways.* New York.

Plowright, R. C. and Jay, S. C. (1966). Rearing bumble bee colonies in captivity. *J. Apic. Res.* *5*: 155–165.

— (1968). Caste differentiation in bumblebees (*Bombus* Latr.: Hym.) 1. The determination of female size. *Insectes soc.* *15*: 171–192.

Poinar, Jr., G. O. and van der Laan, P. A. (1972). Morphology and life history of *Sphaerularia bombi* (Dufour) (Nematodea). *Nematologica* *18*: 239–252.

Postner, M. (1952). Biologische-ökologische Untersuchungen an Hummeln und ihren Nestern. *Veröf. Übersee-Museum Bremen (A)* *2*: 45–86.

Poulsen, M. H. (1973). The frequency and foraging behaviour of honeybees and bumble bees on field beans in Denmark. *J. apic. Res.* *12*: 75–80.

Pouvreau, A. (1962). Contribution à l'étude de *Sphaerularia bombi* (Nematoda, Tylenchida), parasite des reines de bourdons. *Annls Abeille* *5*: 181–199.

Pouvreau, A. (1963a). Observations sur l'accouplement de *Bombus hypnorum* L. (Hyménoptère, Apidae) en serre. *Insectes soc. 10*: 111–118.

— (1963b). Sur la présence de *Sphaerularia bombi* (Nematoda, Tylenchida, Allantonematidae) dans le genre *Psithyrus* (Hymenoptera, Apidae, Psithyrinae). *C. r. hebd. séanc. Acad. Sci. (Paris) 256*: 282–283.

— (1964). Observations d'une infestation précoce des reines de bourdons (Hymenoptera, Apoidea, *Bombus*), par *Sphaerularia bombi* (Nematoda, Tylenchida, Allantonematidae). *Bull. Soc. zool. Fr. 89*: 717–719.

— (1966). Sur quelques ennemis des bourdons. *Bee Wld 47* (Suppl.) : 173–177.

— (1967). Contribution à l'étude morphologique et biologique d'*Aphomia sociella* L. (Lepidoptera, Heteroneura, Pyralidoidea, Pyralididae), parasite des nids de bourdons (Hymenoptera, Apoidea, *Bombus* Latr.). *Insectes soc. 14*: 57–72.

— (1970). Données écologiques sur l'hibernation contrôlée des reines de Bourdons (*Hymenoptera, Apoidea, Bombinae, Bombus* Latr.). *Apidologie 1*: 73–95.

Putnam, F. W. (1864). Notes on the habits of some species of humble bees. *Proc. Essex Inst., Salem. Mass. 4*: 98–104.

Radoszkowski, O. (1884). Révision des armures copulatrices des mâles du genre *Bombus*. *Byull. mosk. Obshch Ispyt. Prir. 59*: 51–92.

Rau, P. (1924). Notes on captive colonies and homing of *Bombus pennsylvanicus* de Geer. *Ann. ent. Soc. Amer. 17*: 368–381.

— (1930). The behavior of hibernating *Polistes* wasps. *Ann. ent. Soc. Amer. 23*: 461–466.

— (1941). A note on the oviposition by the queen bumblebee *Bombus americanorum*. *Can. Ent. 73*: 55–56.

Réaumur, [R. A. F.] de (1742). Histoire des Bourdons velus, dont les nids sont de mousse. In: *Memoires pour servir a l'Histoire des Insectes 6*: 1–38.

Reinig, W. F. (1935). On the variation of *Bombus lapidarius* L. and its cuckoo, *Psithyrus rupestris* Fabr., with notes on mimetic similarity. *J. Genet. 30*: 321–356.

Rettenmeyer, C. W. (1970). Insect mimicry. *Ann. Rev. Ent. 15*: 43–74.

Richards, K. W. (1973). Biology of *Bombus polaris* Curtis and *B. hyperboreus* Schönherr at Lake Hazen, Northwest Territories (Hymenoptera: Bombini). *Quaestiones ent. 9*: 115–157.

Richards, O. W. (1926). Capture in England of female and worker of *Bombus cullumanus* K. (Hym.). *Entomologist's mon. Mag. 62*: 267–268.

— (1927). The specific characters of the British humblebees (Hymenoptera). *Trans. ent. Soc. Lond. 75*: 233–268.

— (1928). A revision of the European bees allied to *Psithyrus quadricolor*, Lepeletier (Hymenoptera, Bombidae). *Trans. ent. Soc. Lond. 76*: 345–364.

— (1931). Some notes on the humblebees allied to *Bombus alpinus* L. *Tromsø Mus. Aarsh. 50* (1927): 1–32.

— (1933). Variation in *Bombus jonellus* Kirby (Hymenoptera, Bombidae). *Ann. Mag. Nat. Hist. 12*: 59–66.

— (1935). *Bombus muscorum* (Linnaeus) and *B. smithianus* White (Hym.). *Trans. Soc. Brit. Ent. 2*: 73–85.

— (1936). On a collection of humble-bees (*Bombus* and *Psithyrus*, Hymenoptera) from Cara Island, Argyllshire. *Entomologist's mon. Mag. 72*: 109–111.

— (1946). Observations on *Bombus agrorum* (Fabricius) (Hymen., Bombidae). *Proc. R. ent. Soc. Lond. (A) 21*: 66–71.

— (1949). The significance of the number of wing-hooks in bees and wasps. *Proc. R. ent. Soc. Lond. (A) 24*: 75–78.

— (1968). The subgeneric divisions of the genus *Bombus* Latreille (Hymenoptera: Apidae). *Bull. Br. Mus. nat. Hist. (Ent.) 22*: 210–276.

Richards, O. W. and Waloff, N. (1947). Seasonal variations in the numbers of some warehouse insects. *Proc. R. ent. Soc. Lond. (A) 22*: 30–33.

Ritcher, P. O. (1933). The external morphology of larval Bremidae and key to certain species (Hym.). *Ann. ent. Soc. Amer. 26*: 53–63.

Röseler, P.-F. (1962). Über einen Fall von Gynandromorphismus bei der Hummel *Bombus agrorum* Fabr. *Mitt. bad. Landesv. Naturk. Natursch. 8*: 289–303.

— (1967a). Lage und Funktionsleistung der Wachsdrüsen bei einigen Hummelarten im Vergleich zu anderen Apiden. *Zool. Anz. (1967)*: 773–783.

— (1967b). Arbeitsteilung und Drüsenzustände in Hummelvölkern. *Naturwissenschaften 54*: 146–147.

— (1967c). Untersuchungen über das Auftreten der 3 Formen im Hummelstaat. *Zool. Jb. Physiol. 74*: 178–197.

— (1970). Unterschiede in der Kastendetermination zwischen den Hummelarten *Bombus hypnorum* und *Bombus terrestris*. *Z. Naturf. 25*: 543–548.

Roubaud, E. (1929). Caractère obligatoire de l'hibernation chez les reines de Vespides annuels. Conséquences biologiques. *Bull. Soc. ent. Fr. (1929)*: 83–84.

Ruttner, F. (1966). The life and flight activity of drones. *Bee Wld 47*: 93–100.

Ruttner, F. and Ruttner, H. (1966). Untersuchungen über die Flugaktivität und das Paarungsverhalten der Drohnen. 3. Flugweite und Flugrichtung der Drohnen. *Z. Bienenforsch. 8*: 332–354.

Sakagami, S. F. and Zucchi, R. (1965). Winterverhalten einer neotropischen Hummel, *Bombus atratus*, innerhalb des Beobachtungskastens. Ein Beitrag zur Biologie der Hummeln. *J. Fac. Sci. Hokkaido Univ. Ser. 6 Zool. 15*: 712–762.

Salt, R. W. (1956). Influence of moisture content and temperature on the cold hardiness of hibernating insects. *Can. J. Zool. 34*: 283–294.

Saunders, E. (1884). Synopsis of British Hymenoptera. Anthophila; part II., Apidae. *Trans. ent. Soc. Lond.* (*1884*): 159–250.

— (1896). *The Hymenoptera Aculeata of the British Isles.* London.

— (1907). *Wild Bees, Wasps, and Ants.* London.

— (1909). Bombi and other aculeates collected in 1908 in the Berner Oberland by the Rev. A. E. Easton, M.A. *Entomologist's mon. Mag. 45:* 83–84.

Schmiedeknecht, O. (1878). Monographie der in Thüringen vorkommenden Arten der Hymenopteren – Gattung *Bombus. Jenaische Zeitschr. Naturw. 12:* 303–430.

Schneider, A. (1883). Ueber die Entwickelung der *Sphärularia bombi. Zool. Beiträge A. Schneider 1:* 1–9.

Schremmer, F. (1955). Beobachtungen über die Nachtruhe bei Hymenopteren, insbesondere die Männchenschlaf-gesellschaften von *Halictus. Öst. zool. Z. 6:* 70–89.

Scott, H. (1920). Notes on the biology of some inquilines and parasites in a nest of *Bombus derhamellus* Kirby; with a description of the larva and pupa of *Epuraea depressa* Illig. (=*aestiva* Auctt: Coleoptera, Nitidulidae). *Trans. ent. Soc. Lond. 68:* 99–127.

Shamurin, V. F. (1966). [Role of pollinating insects in tundra communities]. In: [*Organisms and natural environments.* (*Problems of geography 69*)]. pp. 98–117. (Voronov, A. G., Dokhman, G. I. and Sobolev, L. N., eds). *In Russian.* Moscow.

Showers, R. E., Jones, A. and Moeller, F. E. (1967). Cross-inoculation of the bumble bee *Bombus fervidus* with the microsporidian *Nosema apis* from the honey bee. *J. econ. Ent. 60:* 774–777.

Shuckard, W. E. (1866). *British Bees.* London.

Siebold, C. T. von (1838). Ueber geschlechtslose Nematoideen. *Helminthologische Beiträge 4, Arch. Naturgesch. 4:* 302–314.

Siivonen, L. (1942). Zur Phänologie des Frühjahrsauftretens der Hummel (*Bombus*, Hym., Apidae). *Suom. hyönt. Aikak. 8:* 83–102.

Skorikov, A. S. (1922). Les Bourdons de la faune paléarctique. Partie I. Biologie générale. *Bull. Sta. rég. Prot. Plantes, Petrograd 4:* 102–160.

Skou, J. P. (1967). Diseases in bumble-bees (*Bombus* Latr.). The occurrence, description and pathogenicity of five hyphomycetes. *Kgl. Vet.-og Landbohøsk. Aarsskr.* (*1967*): 134–153.

Skou, J. P., Holm, S. N. and Haas, H. (1963). Preliminary investigations on diseases in bumble-bees (*Bombus* Latr.). *Kgl. Vet.-og Landbohøjsk. Aarsskr.* (*1963*): 27–41.

Skovgaard, O. S. (1936). Rødkløverens bestøvning, humlebier og humleboer. *Kgl. danske Vidensk. Selsk. Skr. Naturvid. Math. 6:* 1–140.

— (1952). Humlebiers og honnigbiers arbejdshastighed ved bestøvningen af rødkløver. *Tidsskr. Planteavl 55:* 449–475.

Sladen, F. W. L. (1896). Humble-bees. *Br. Bee J. 24:* 37, 47–48.

— (1898). *Bombus smithianus* near Rye. *Entomologist's mon. Mag. 34:* 254–255.

— (1899). Bombi in captivity, and notes on *Psithyrus. Entomologist's mon. Mag. 35:* 230–234.

— (1900). Humblebees in winter. *Br. Bee J. 28:* 72–74.

— (1912). *The Humble-bee, its life history and how to domesticate it.* London.

Smith, F. (1844). Notes on the British Humble-Bees (*Bombus* of authors). *Zoologist 2:* 541–550.

— (1851). Notes on the nest of *Bombus derhamellus. Trans. ent. Soc. Lond. 1:* Proc. 111–112.

— (1855). *Catalogue of British Hymenoptera in the Collection of the British Museum.* London.

— (1857). Notes and observations on the Aculeate Hymenoptera. *Ent. Annual* (*1857*): 27–38.

— (1858). Notes on Aculeate Hymenoptera, with some observations on their economy. *Ent. Annual* (*1858*): 34–46.

— (1865). Notes on Hymenoptera. *Ent. Annual* (*1865*): 81–96.

— (1866). A revision of the British species of the genus *Bombus. Entomol. 3:* 240–243, 255–260, 267–269, 281–288, 293–296.

— (1876) [Facsimile edn 1891]. *Catalogue of the British bees in the Collection of the British Museum.* London.

Smith, K. G. V. (1959). The distribution and habits of the British Conopidae (Dipt.). *Trans. Soc. Br. Ent. 13:* 113–136.

— (1966). The larva of *Thecophora occidensis*, with comments upon the biology of Conopidae (Diptera). *J. Zool., Lond. 149:* 263–276.

— (1969). Diptera: Conopidae. *Handbk Ident. Br. Insects 10* (3a): 1–18.

Smith, K. G. V. and van Someren, G. R. C. (1970). The identity of *Physocephala bimarginipennis* Karsch (Diptera, Conopidae) with notes on the immature stages and biology. *J. nat. Hist. 4:* 439–446.

Snieżek, J. (1894). O krajowych gatunkach trzmieli. *Sprawozdanie Kom. Fizyograf. 29:* 1–22.

Snodgrass, R. E. (1956). *Anatomy of the honey bee.* New York.

Soper, M. H. R. (1952). A study of the principal factors affecting the establishment and development of the field bean (*Vicia faba*). *J. agric. Sci. 42:* 335–346.

Soulié, J. (1957). Quelques notes sur l'hibernation chez la fourmi *Cremastogaster scutellaris* Ol. et chez une espèce voisine *Cremastogaster auberti* Em. (Hymenoptera – Formicoidea). *Insectes soc. 4:* 365–373.

Southern, H. N. and Watson, J. S. (1941). Summer food of the red fox in Great Britain: a preliminary report. *J. Anim. Ecol. 10:* 1–11.

Spencer, J. F. T., Gorin, P. A. J., Hobbs, G. A. and Cooke, D. A. (1970). Yeasts isolated from bumblebee honey from Western Canada: identification with the aid of proton magnetic resonance spectra of their mannose-containing polysaccharides. *Can. J. Microbiol.* 16: 117–119.

Spencer-Booth, Y. (1965). The collections of pollen by bumble bees, and its transport in the corbiculae and the proboscidial fossa. *J. Apic. Res.* 4: 185–190.

Spooner, G. M. (1937). *Hymenoptera Aculeata* from the north-west highlands. *Scot. Nat.* (1937): 15–23.

Spradbery, J. P. (1965). The social organization of wasp communities. *Symp. zool. Soc. Lond.* 14: 61–96.

Stacey, G. W. (1955). Bees and *Tilia petiolaris*. *J. R. hort. Soc.* 80: 328–329.

Stainton, H. T. (1856). New works on entomology. Review of 'Catalogue of British Hymenoptera in the Collection of the British Museum. By Frederick Smith, M. E. S.'. *Ent. Annual* (1856): 139–145.

Stammer, H. J. (1951). Eine neue Tracheenmilbe, *Bombacarus buchneri* n. g., n. sp. (Acar., Podapolipodidae). *Zool. Anz.* 146: 137–150.

Stapel, C. (1934). Om rødkløverens bestøvning i Czechoslovakiet. *Tidsskr. Planteavl* 40: 148–159.

Stein, G. (1956a). Beiträge zur Biologie der Hummel (*B. terrestris* L., *B. lapidarius* L. u. a.). *Zool. Jb.* 84: 439–462.

— (1956b). Weitere Beiträge zur Biologie von *Sphaerularia bombi* Leon Dufour 1837. *Z. ParasitKde* 17: 383–393.

— (1957). Über das Verhalten von Hummelköniginnen bei experimentell verhindertem Winterschlaf. *Verh. dt. zool. Ges.* (1957): 106–111.

— (1962). Ueber den Feinbau der Mandibeldrüse von Hummelmännchen. *Z. Zellforsch.* 57: 719–736.

— (1963a). Untersuchungen über den Sexuallockstoff der Hummelmännchen. *Biol. Zbl.* 82: 343–349.

— (1963b). Ueber den Sexuallockstoff von Hummelmännchen. *Naturwissenschaften* 50: 305.

Stelfox, A. W. (1922). *Bombus sylvarum* in Ireland. *I. Nat.* 31: 10–11.

— (1927). A list of the Hymenoptera Aculeata (sensu lato) of Ireland. *Proc. R. Irish Acad.* (B) 37: 201–355.

— (1933a). Some recent records for Irish Aculeata Hymenoptera. *Entomologist's mon. Mag.* 69: 47–53.

— (1933b). On the occurrence of a peculiar race of the humblebee, *Bombus smithianus* White, on the Aran Islands, in western Ireland. *I. Nat. J.* 4: 1–4.

— (1955). The apparent spread of the bumble bee, *Bombus pratorum* L., in Ireland in recent years. *I. Nat. J.* 11: 338–339.

Step, E. (1932). *Bees, wasps, ants and allied insects of the British Isles.* London.

Taniguchi (=Miyamoto), S. (1955). Biological studies on the Japanese bees. II. Study on the nesting behaviour of *Bombus ardens* Smith. *Sci. Rep. Hyogo Univ. Ser. agric.* 2: 89–96.

Thomsen, M. (1954). Neurosecretion in some Hymenoptera. *Kgl. danske Vidensk. Selsk. Skr. Biol.* 7: 1–24.

Tkalcu, B. (1960). Sur l'hibernation des bourdons. *Bull. Soc. ent. Mulhouse* (1960): 96–97.

— (1961). Deuxième contribution sur l'hibernation des Bourdons. *Bull. Soc. ent. Mulhouse* (1961): 105–106.

— (1963). Eine Neue Hummel-Art der Gattung *Agrobombus* Vogt aus dem Alpengebiet (Hymenoptera, Apoidea). *Acta ent. bohemoslovaca* 60: 183–196.

Toumanoff, C. (1930). *Les maladies des abeilles.* Paris.

Townsend, C. H. T. (1936). The mature larva and puparium of *Brachycoma sarcophagina* (Townsend) (Diptera: Metopiidae). *Proc. ent. Soc. Wash.* 38: 92–98.

Townsend, L. H. (1951). The hibernation of *Bombus impatiens* Cresson (Hymenoptera: Bombidae). *Ent. News* 62: 115–116.

Tuck, W. H. (1896). Inquiline and other inhabitants in nests of Aculeate Hymenoptera. *Entomologist's mon. Mag.* 32: 153–155.

— (1897a). Note on the habits of *Bombus latreillellus*. *Entomologist's mon. Mag.* 33: 234–235.

— (1897b). Coleoptera etc., in the nests of Aculeate Hymenoptera. *Entomologist's mon. Mag.* 33: 58–60.

Tulloch, A. P. (1970). The composition of beeswax and other waxes secreted by insects. *Lipids* 5: 247–258.

Türk, E. and Türk, F. (1959). Systematik und Ökologie der Tyroglyphiden Mitteleuropas. In: Stammer, H.-J. *Beiträge zur Systematik und Ökologie mitteleuropäischer Acarina I.* pp. 1–231. Leipzig.

Valle, O. (1955). Untersuchungen zur Sicherung der Bestäubung von Rotklee. *Suom. maataloust. Seur. Julk.* 83: 205–220.

Vitzthum, H. G. (1930). Die Bombus-Parasitiden. Der 'Acarologischen Beobachtungen' 15 Reihe. *Zool. Jb. Syst.* 60: 1–45.

Vogt, O. (1911). Studien über das Artproblem. Mitt. 2. Über das Variieren der Hummeln. Teil 2. *Sber. Ges. naturf. Freunde Berl.* (1911): 31–74.

Voveikov, G. S. (1953). [Natural requeening in bumblebee colonies]. In Russian. *Rev. Ent. U. R. S. S.* 33: 174–181. (*Apic. Abstr.* 8: 2/57).

Wagner, W. (1907). Psycho-biologische Untersuchungen an Hummeln mit Bezugnahme auf die Frage der Gesellligkeit im Tierreiche. *Zoologica, Stuttg.* 19: 1–239.

Walton, C. L. (1922). Some observations on the genus *Bombus*, etc., in Wales. *Entomologist's mon. Mag.* 58: 271–275.

— (1927). Note on the activities of humble bees (*Bombus*) in North Wales. *Ann. appl. Biol.* 14: 465–469.

Waters, E. G. R. (1929). A list of the Microlepidoptera of the Oxford district. *Proc. Ashmol. nat. Hist. Soc.* (1928): 1–72.

Welch, H. E. (1965). Entomophilic nematodes. *Ann. Rev. Ent.* 10: 275–302.

REFERENCES

Westerboer, I. (1963). Die Familie Podocinidae Berlese 1916. In: Stammer, H.-J. *Beiträge zur Systematik und Ökologie Mitteleuropäischer Acarina II. Mesostigmata I.* pp. 179–450. Leipzig.

Weyrauch, W. (1934). Über einige Baupläne der Wabenmasse in Hummelnestern. *Z. Morph. Ökol. Tierre* 28: 497–552.

Wheeler, W. M. (1919). The phoresy of *Antherophagus*. *Psyche* 26: 145–152.

White, A. (1851). Note on the natural history of Shetland. *Proc. Linn. Soc. Lond.* 2: 157–158.

Wigglesworth, V. B. (1942). The storage of protein, fat, glycogen and uric acid in the fat body and other tissues of mosquito larvae. *J. exp. Biol.* 19: 56–77.

— (1972). *The principles of insect physiology.* London.

Wild, O. H. (1924). Observations on the humble-bees of Bute. *Scot. Nat.* (1924): 53–60.

— (1931). Notes on the peculiarities of some Lepidoptera and Hymenoptera from the Inner and Outer Hebrides. *Scot. Nat.* 190: 113–119.

Wilde, J. de (1953). Provisional analysis of the imaginal diapause in an insect (*Leptinotarsa decemlineata* Say). *Acta physiol. pharm. néerl.* 3: 141–143.

Williams, R. D. (1925). Studies concerning the pollination, fertilisation and breeding of red clover. *Bull. Welsh Pl. Breed. Sta. Ser. H,* 4: 1–58.

Williamson, K. (1949). Fair Isle Bird Observatory: First Report, 1948, Part 1. *Scot. Nat.* 61: 19–31.

Willmann, C. (1953). Neue Milben aus den östlichen Alpen. *Öster. Akad. Wiss. Stizber.* 162: 449–519.

Wilson, G. Fox (1926). Insect visitors to sap-exudations of trees. *Trans. ent. Soc. Lond.* 74: 243–254.

— (1929). Pollination of hardy fruits: insect visitors to fruit blossoms. *Ann. appl. Biol.* 16: 602–629.

— (1946). Factors affecting populations of social wasps, *Vespula* species, in England (Hymenoptera). *Proc. R. ent. Soc. Lond. (A)* 21: 17–27.

Wingate, W. J. (1906). A preliminary list of Durham Diptera, with analytical tables. *Trans. Nat. Hist. Soc. North. Durham, Newcastle* 2: 1–416.

Witherby, H. F., Jourdain, F. C. R., Ticehurst, N. F. and Tucker, B. W. (1958). *The handbook of British birds.* London.

Wójtowski, F. (1963a). Observations on the biology and reproduction of bumble-bees (*Bombinae*). *Zoologica Pol.* 13: 3–18.

— (1963b). Studies on heat and water economy in bumble-bee nests (*Bombinae*). *Zoologica Pol.* 13: 19–36.

— (1963c). Observations on the construction and arrangement of bumble-bee nests (*Bombinae*). *Zoologica Pol.* 13: 137–152.

Woodroffe, G. E. (1951a). A life-history study of the Brown House Moth, *Hofmannophila pseudospretella* (Staint.) (Lep. Oecophoridae). *Bull. ent. Res.* 41: 529–553.

— (1951b). A life-history study of *Endrosis lactella* (Schiff.) (Lep. Oecophoridae). *Bull. ent. Res.* 41: 749–760.

Wynne-Edwards, V. C. (1962). *Animal dispersion in relation to animal behaviour.* London.

Yarrow, I. H. H. (1945). Collecting bees and wasps. *Amat. Ent.* 7: 55–81.

— (1954). Some observations on the genus *Bombus*, with special reference to *Bombus cullumanus* (Kirby) (Hym. Apidae). *J. Soc. Brit. Ent.* 5: 34–39.

— (1967). The aculeate Hymenoptera of the Isles of Scilly. *Entomologist's mon. Mag.* 103: 63–65.

— (1968). Kirby's species of British bees: designation of holotypes and selection of lectotypes. Part 1. Introduction and the species of *Apis* Linnaeus now included in the genera *Bombus* Latreille and *Psithyrus* Lepeletier. *Proc. R. ent. Soc. Lond. (B)* 37: 9–15.

— (1970). Is *Bombus inexspectatus* (Tkalcu) a workerless obligate parasite? (Hym. Apidae). *Insectes soc.* 17: 95–112.

Zapletal, F. (1961). Ueber die Domestikation der Hummeln. *Arch. Geflügelz. Kleintierk.* 10: 256–262.

Zmarlicki, C. and Morse, R. A. (1963). Drone congregation areas. *J. Apic. Res.* 2: 64–66.

Author Index

Plant and Animal Index

(A) Plants

White dead-nettle, *Lamium album*, 86, 181, 184, 185, 189, 191, 192, 193

White stonecrop, *Sedum album*, Pl. 7B

Willows or sallows, *Salix*, 44, 174, 176, 179, 180, 181

Wood-sage, *Teucrium scorodonia*, 191

Woody nightshade, *Solanum dulcamara*, 181

Woundworts, *Stachys*, 90, 184, 185, 189, 193

Yellow toadflax, *Linaria vulgaris*, 90, 92

(B) Animals

Numbers in bold type refer to pages with line drawings

Acarapis woodi, 143

Acarina, *see under* mites

Acarus siro, 143

Achroia grisella, honey bee wax-moth, 103

Aculeate Hymenoptera, 22, 76, 131, 251

Agrotid moths, Noctuidae, 114

Agrotis segetum, turnip moth, 114

Allodapine bees, 57

Allopsithyrus, 169, 199

Alpinobombus, 48

Amarsipoea, 167, 168

Amarsipopoea, 167

Ambush bugs, Phymatidae, 137

American wax-moth, *Vitula edmandsii*, 103

Amphibians, 160

Anodontobombus, 57, 166, 167, 169, 173 *et seq.*

Antherophagus, 124, 125, 134, 150

Antherophagus glaber, see under *Emphylus glaber*

Antherophagus nigricornis, 124, **125**, **126**

Antherophagus ochraceus, 124

Antherophagus pallens, 124

Antherophagus silaceus, see under *A. nigricornis*

Anthophora, 245

Anthophora pilipes, 86

Anthophora retusa, 86, Pl. XXX

Anthrenus museorum, museum beetle, 258

Ant-like fossa, 132

Ants, Formicidae, 3, 42, 126, 133, 266

Apanteles, 134

Apathus, 196, 248, 250, 251

Apathus barbutellus, 247, 250

Apathus campestris, 246, 247, 250

Apathus rupestris, 247, 250, 251

Apathus vestalis, 247, 250

Aphids, Aphididae, 91

Aphiochaeta rata, 136

Aphomia, 102

Aphomia sociella, bumblebee wax-moth, 101, **102**, **103**, 104, 136, Pl. 8A, 8B, XXXIIIA

Apis, 97, 159, 245

Apis agrorum, 246

Apis albinella, 247

Apis barbutella, 247

Apis beckwithella, 246

Apis burrellana, 247

Apis campestris, 246

Apis cullumana, 247

Apis curtisella, 246

Apis derhamella, 247

Apis donovanella, 247

Apis floralis, 246

Apis forsterella, 246

Apis fragrans, 246

Apis francillonella, 246

Apis francisana, 246

Apis harrisella, 247

Apis hortorum, 246

Apis jonella, 246

Apis lapidaria, 247

Apis latreillella, 246

Apis leeana, 246

Apis lucorum, 246

Apis mellifera, honey bee, 3, 10, 13, 24, 57, 63, 69, 82, 84, 85, 87, 88, 89, 90, 91, 92, 93, 95, 96, 97, 103, 104, 131, 132, 133, 143, 159, 160, 161, 182, 245, 262, 265

Apis muscorum, 246

Apis pratorum, 247

Apis raiella, 247

Apis rossiella, 246

Apis rupestris, 247

Apis scrimshirana, 247

Apis soroensis, 247

Apis sowerbiana, 246

M

General Index

Numbers in bold type refer to pages with line drawings

www.ingramcontent.com/pod-product-compliance
Lightning Source LLC
Chambersburg PA
CBHW080604270326
41928CB00016B/2923

* 9 781904 846802 *